MEMOIRS OF
PRINCE
VON BÜLOW

· I ·

From Secretary of State to
Imperial Chancellor

1897–1903

Translated from the German by
F. A. VOIGT

ILLUSTRATED

BOSTON   1931
LITTLE, BROWN, AND COMPANY

MEMOIRS as they are understood by other nations are rare in Germany. Goethe's "Dichtung und Wahrheit", Bismarck's "Gedanken und Erinnerungen" have become part of world literature. But they are not memoirs. The "Memoirs of Prince Bülow", which are now published after the death of the author, were conceived by him, who knew so well the memoirs of France and England, as memoirs in the true sense of the word. They contain only what he himself experienced and what he himself did. They describe only those events and persons with whom his long and successful career brought him into contact. Philosophical and historical reflections are included only in so far as they are related to his inner life. The author himself, his actions and his recollections, are the essence of the work.

The subjectivity that pervades the memoirs of Prince von Bülow is a subjectivity that strives, in spite of all obstacles, for absolute precision in the representation of facts, and for justice and objectivity in estimating people and events. In consonance with his true inner nature he endeavoured to write no line, to express no judgment, to evaluate no action, without being convinced of its accuracy. So much did Prince Bülow wish to impress his "Memoirs" with the seal of truth and justice that, despite the urgent appeals of his political friends and admirers, he steadfastly kept to the resolution he had made, to have his Memoirs published only after his death. Thus, foregoing immediate success, and putting his material interests into the background, he considered this the only sure guarantee of that independence of judgment which he endeavoured to achieve. He wished to write exactly as he thought, to evaluate people as he saw them, no matter whether they were sovereigns or his colleagues in diplomacy. He did not wish to be bound by personal considerations, no matter for whom. The world into which life had placed him, the field of activity that God had entrusted to him, he resolved to present to later generations precisely in accordance with the final conclusions that he himself had arrived at, from his high watch tower.   Clear in his conscience and independent in his convictions, he wished to leave judgment on himself to later generations, being too proud to take up his own defence.   The Prince had grown too old and too enlightened to consider every one of his verdicts, every one of his opinions, incontestable.   He would therefore have anticipated, with complete calm, all the contradiction which his work, had it been published during his lifetime, would have encountered.   But what he did wish with all his heart was that the world should believe in the sincerity and the fidelity of what he had written.   And for this, posthumous publication seemed to him the surest guarantee.

The Prince spared no pains to secure in his Memoirs the utmost precision and absolute truth.   He had been used to dictating all his life.   As he walked up and down his study, his sentences were formed just as easily and surely as Bülow, the orator, was wont to unroll his brilliant periods in three parliaments.   In spite of this easy dexterity that was natural to him whenever he did intellectually creative work, Prince Bülow devoted five years to dictating his Memoirs, and three further years to the careful, laborious revision of the text.   The Bismarckian school in which the young attaché, the Secretary of the Berlin Congress, had grown up, revealed itself tenaciously and effectively in his old age.   There was not a name, not a date, not a quotation, that was not verified repeatedly by the use of reference books.   There was not a sentence that was not carefully weighed and pondered again and again.   The growth of the work was considerably facilitated by the Prince's unusually powerful memory; a memory that belonged to him through his public life and lasted to extreme old age; a memory that hoarded not only historical persons and events, but significant quotations that are part of the spiritual life of all civilised countries.   Of documents in the strict sense of the word there were very few; there were in particular few letters.   There was hardly a single letter of the Kaiser's, for Prince Bülow spontaneously, on his own initiative, handed over all the Kaiser's letters — and they numbered hundreds — after his resignation, so that they might be preserved in the archives of the Civil Cabinet. But so precise and sure was his memory that passages quoted from letters and notes were found to correspond not only with the sense, but almost completely with the actual wording of the originals, when these became available later on.

The Memoirs embrace a period from about 1850 to 1919, that is to say, they close with the collapse of Germany. Two sections are devoted to the brilliant and progressive career that in 1897 made him Secretary of State in the Foreign Office in Berlin; three sections to the independent politician who at first guided Germany's foreign policy, under the aged Prince Hohenlohe, and then from 1900 to 1909, the whole policy of the Empire, and so gradually becomes more and more the centre of European politics. In the realm of foreign affairs the Bosnian crisis of 1908–1909 is a culminating point. This crisis ends in a brilliant diplomatic victory for Germany. The culminating point in home affairs is the general election of 1907 that leads to an annihilating defeat of the Socialists and is to clear the way for a far-seeing and wise policy of evolution in which the Prince contemplated carefully improving and modernising the political life of the German people through the medium of parliament. This far-reaching programme, so grandiosely conceived that it was not understood by the small people submerged in the topical politics of the day, came to an abrupt end when Bülow resigned in 1909. It was part of the tragedy that lies over the destinies of the German people that the Prince's successor, Bethmann Hollweg, could announce as his programme that he would not permit Germany and Prussia to be transported into the camp of the parliamentary system. In the last volume it is Bülow the onlooker who speaks as he watches the threatening clouds rise from Bethmann's hesitating policy. An absolute opponent of fatalistic theories and, in the Bismarckian spirit, an equally determined opponent of prophylactic wars, he examines the genesis of the World War with the superior wisdom of a mind sharpened in the school of four decades of political and diplomatic activity. His thesis was that neither Kaiser Wilhelm II, nor the German Government, nor the German people wanted the war, but that inefficient German political leadership in the year 1914 involved the nation in the most disastrous of all wars, at Austria's leading strings. In this thesis there resounds that undertone of deep patriotic sorrow that is peculiar to the third volume and shows what a bitter grief it was for the Prince to see all this disaster happen while he himself was forced to remain inactive.

The intimate relationships between Prince Bülow and Kaiser Wilhelm II brought it about that their views and opinions were more often in conflict than is usual between a sovereign and his Minister. If the "Memoirs of Prince Bülow" are occupied with the Kaiser again and again, it is precisely because of the intimacy of their very long and amicable relationship. But in spite of the difficulties which Kaiser Wilhelm II put in Prince Bülow's way by his thoughtlessness and his lack of tact in foreign and home affairs; in spite of the excited opposition which many a haughty gesture of the Kaiser's called forth amongst the whole German people; in spite of the many things that the Prince, with skilled hand and unknown to the public at large, smoothed out and made innocuous in favour of his imperial master — Bülow's verdict on the Kaiser is never bitter or unfair. Even when he censures or blames his sovereign, he remains just to the Kaiser's significant personality and his fine human characteristics. Even when his judgment is most grave and anxious, it is dictated by amicable, indeed almost paternal sentiments, rather than by the spirit of criticism. This attitude does not change even when the catastrophe of 1918 and the events that prepared the way for it approach. The anxiety for the Kaiser and for the dynasty that had prevailed until then are replaced by the even greater anxiety over the fate of the German people, over the future for the nation.

But nothing could damp the youthful optimism with which the wise old man looked into Germany's future, not even all the things that Germany had to suffer amid collapse, and after the shameful peace of Versailles. Just as his verdict on the breakdown of the old system and the defects that had caused this breakdown was just and objective, so his verdict on the new Germany was dominated by the sincere hope of a greater and happier future, — and this in spite of all the severity with which he castigates the weaknesses of this new Germany. All he suffered inwardly in those years resounds, concise and lucid, in the final sentences of the third volume of the Memoirs, — in those years when he saw the destiny of the nation entrusted to the weak hands of Bethmann, and the hesitating hands of Michaelis, the feeble hands of Hertling, and lastly the neurasthenic hands of Prince Max von Baden; whereas amongst the allied enemies he saw statesmen with the unusual energy and strength of Clemenceau and Lloyd George, who kept the spirit of resistance awake in their own nations and with sure tenacity led the way to final success. A passage in Herodotus is mentioned in this connection. The Prince was fond of measuring the events of his time with the measure of history, that great teacher of mankind. He was particularly fond of going back to the Greeks, with whom he was familiar from his earliest years. A few days before the Battle of Plataea, an eminent Persian, asked why he did not warn the Commander Mardonius against the great danger which he clearly recognised, replied to his eager questioner: "There is no greater sorrow on earth than the possession of insight without power. This great sorrow was conferred upon me." With these sadly tragic words, the Prince sums up his great political career.

FRANZ VON STOCKHAMMERN

GERMAN PUBLISHER'S PREFACE

In the year 1920 Prince Bülow informed us through an intermediary that he intended writing his Memoirs and that he wished to entrust them to the firm of Ullstein for the purpose of future publication. The agreement was drawn up on the 15th of January, 1921.

The essence of the agreement is the clause that the work may only be published when some time has passed after the death of the author.

The manuscript was dictated by the Prince in the years 1921–1926. In the years that followed, the author made continual corrections and emendations in his own hand. He had these changes registered by means of numbers written on separate sheets and confirmed the authenticity of these sheets by signing them with his own hand.

The manuscript existed in three copies. It was preserved in the safe of a bank under a sextuple seal. When the Prince died on October 28, 1929, it was taken out of the safe, the location of which was known to only a few of the initiated, and handed over to the publishers. The work of editing and publishing began at once. It was superintended by the literary executor and editor, Ministerial Director Franz von Stockhammern. His preface to the work was written while the Prince was still alive.

The work is now being published in the precise sequence in which it was written down. Prince Bülow wrote his political memoirs first, that is to say, from the time he was appointed Secretary of State until the War and the collapse of Germany. Later on he augmented the work by including the memoirs of his early years. These will make the final volume of the publication.

The Prince's attitude towards persons and events changed from time to time in accordance with the periods at which he composed the several volumes. This is particularly true of the author's attitude towards the revolution of November, 1918. The Prince expressed himself with hostility towards politicians like Ebert and Erzberger in numerous passages of his Memoirs, but it was characteristic that later on he tried to be objectively just to those men and events that he at first harshly repudiated. The present volume contains several adverse criticisms of Ebert, the first President of the German Republic. But a few years after these criticisms were written down, the Prince, in the third volume of his Memoirs, calls Ebert "a man of natural decency and common sense" and says he has the impression "that he is talking to a straightforward and able man." In this later volume, the Prince goes on to say that Ebert did not convert him to Socialism and to the Republic, and, as before, he condemns the revolution of 1918 in sharp words. Nevertheless he continues literally, "but after a series of four Imperial Chancellors, beginning with Bethmann Hollweg, failed completely in the World War, after Wilhelm II fled abroad, and after the German Empire, created by the genius of Bismarck and the wisdom of the old Emperor Wilhelm I, collapsed, I considered it a piece of good fortune in misfortune that the wave of revolution carried just this man to presidential eminence. He at least gave proof that in our, alas, so unpolitical Germany, the working class can produce considerable political talents as well as characterful personalities and eminent party leaders who deserve all respect."

The editor of the work, Herr von Stockhammern, who, in his daily conversation with the Prince, could follow his gradual inward change of view, therefore reflected whether it would not be possible to tone down or to extirpate some of these attacks on Ebert and other politicians associated with him. But on February 27, 1930, that is to say, before the actual printing began, Herr von Stockhammern died.

In view of the agreements concluded and the assurances given to Prince Bülow in addition to these agreements, the publishers do not see any possibility of making any alterations of this kind.

From the very beginning Prince Bülow attached the greatest importance to writing his Memoirs and having them published in complete independence of all external influences.

When the publishers concluded their agreement, they felt it their obligation to allow a personality of such universal importance as Prince Bülow complete and unrestricted freedom of expression.

And so this work will appear just as the Prince created it. In many parts of it he criticises political events and characterises individual persons in a manner that does not correspond with the views of the publishers, and indeed, is directly opposed to their general views.

BERLIN,
Autumn, 1930

CONTENTS

CHAPTER XIII

CHAPTER XIV

CHAPTER XV

CHAPTER XVI

Contents

CHAPTER XXXIII

CHAPTER XXXIV

CHAPTER XXXV

CHAPTER XXXVI

CHAPTER XXXVII

CHAPTER XXXVIII

CHAPTER XXXIX

Contents

ILLUSTRATIONS

MEMOIRS OF PRINCE VON BÜLOW
From Secretary of State to Imperial Chancellor
1897–1903

CHAPTER I

I am summoned to Berlin (June 21, 1897) — Leave Rome after Bidding Visconti-Venosta and Rudini Farewell — On the Promenade in the Park at Frankfort — In the Barber's Shop of the Kaiserhof at Berlin — In the Wilhelmstrasse: Holstein, Marschall, Hohenlohe — I arrive on Board the Hohenzollern *at Kiel — Conversation with the Adjutant General von Loewenfeld — Kaiser William II's Welcome: "The Badener Has Betrayed Me! You Must Go to the Front!" — Imperial Summons to Take Part in the Journey to St. Petersburg in the Month of August — King Leopold of Belgium — Prince Albrecht of Prussia.*

ON the 21st of June, 1897, there lay on my desk in the Palazzo Caffarelli, which was then the German Embassy in Rome, a deciphered telegram from the Foreign Office, instructing me to report as soon as possible to His Majesty the Kaiser on board the yacht *Hohenzollern*. I felt rather like a traveller who, having long watched the clouds gathering in the heavens, and then flashes of lightning, suddenly finds himself caught in the bursting storm. I went to see the Foreign Minister in order to tell him that I had been summoned to Kiel for a few days. In the phlegmatic manner that was natural to him and harmonised with his reserve that at times was intensified to an almost ludicrous extent, the Marquis Visconti-Venosta only enquired whether I would be travelling via Milan and Switzerland or via Verona and the Tyrol and asked me to remember him to my wife. My parting with the Marquis Rudini, with whom I had closer ties and who was several degrees more friendly to Germany, was of a more cordial character. He assumed it to be rather unlikely that I would return to Rome: *"Ils voudront vous garder à Berlin."* He regretted my departure, especially because of our personal relations, but he thought that I might probably be more useful in promoting the cause of mutual understanding and thereby friendship between Germany and Italy in Berlin than on the banks of the Tiber.

When I reached Milan the next day I read a Berlin despatch in the *Secolo* according to which my appointment as Foreign Secretary could be taken for granted.　On the 23d of June Philipp Eulenburg, who was spending his leave at Hertefeld, a property he owned in the Rhineland, came to meet me at the station in Frankfort.　As I had an hour and a half to wait in Frankfort for the Berlin train, we sat down on a seat by a fountain in the Bockenheimer Promenade, not far from the bust of a vine-crowned Bacchus.　I had often passed by there when I was a child, first in the charge of English nurses and French governesses and, later, under the sterner eye of a German tutor.　Eulenburg urgently wished me not to decline the Kaiser's summons : in the first place he attached importance to having a personal friend as his chief, then too he saw himself playing the rôle towards the Kaiser, of the gift-bringing maiden from foreign parts [1] from whose hand his Imperial friend was to receive all good, all desirable, and all longed-for things.　He explained with all the intensity of which his gentle nature was capable that a refusal on my part would not only disturb the Kaiser very deeply, but he would also look upon it as insubordination if not as desertion.　I also owed it to the country, he argued, not to refuse my service in a situation like the present that was so difficult both at home and abroad. Eulenburg's statements on this matter came sincerely from the heart.　He was rather indifferent towards the German point of view, but, through his education and his family relationships, he had more Prussian sentiment than was generally attributed to him.

As we sat talking in this way a tall, strong-featured and still youthful-looking general, his carriage so taut and erect that he might have been cast in bronze, came riding by on a noble chestnut gelding, keenly intent on training the fine animal.　I recognised my brother Adolf, who had been appointed Commander of the Frankfort Cavalry Brigade not long before.　Who would have predicted that a few months hence this splendid horseman would be lying under the weight of his ponderous charger, with his chest crushed, and in the agony of death?　Who could have prophesied that my companion on the bench would be hiding in his castle at Liebenburg, a shunned and ostracised man, not shattered physically like my brother, but morally wrecked?

[1] An allusion to Schiller's poem " Das Mädchen aus der Fremde."

Wohl, vielerlei mag anschauend der Mensch
Ausspähn; doch weissagt, eh' er geschaut,
Kein Seher die Lose der Zukunft.[1]

When we separated, Eulenburg slipped a note into my hand and said: "This is my last word, my last request to you. It comes from the heart of a true friend and patriot. Only if you take the Kaiser in the right way psychologically, can you be of use to your country. You are Kaiser Wilhelm II's last card." In the note was written:

"Wilhelm II takes everything personally. Only personal arguments make an impression upon him. He wants to teach others, but learns unwillingly himself. He endures nothing that is boring; slow, stiff, or too serious people get on his nerves and have no success with him. Wilhelm II wants to shine and to do and decide everything for himself. What he wants to do unfortunately often goes awry. He loves glory and is ambitious and jealous. In order to get him to accept an idea you must act as though the idea were his. You must make everything easy for him. He readily encourages others to take bold steps but throws them overboard if they fail. Never forget that His Majesty needs praise every now and again. He is one of those people who grow bad tempered if they do not, from time to time, hear words of appreciation from the lips of some important person or other. You will always obtain his consent to all your wishes as long as you do not neglect to express appreciation of His Majesty whenever he deserves it. He is as grateful for it as a good and clever child. If instead of appreciation he gets nothing but unbroken silence, he concludes that there is ill will somewhere. We two will always respect the border line between praise and flattery, we will respect it scrupulously."

Such was the last exhortation Phil addressed to me before I entered the arena — a warning which was as characteristic of him as it was of his exalted friend.

When I arrived in Berlin I took rooms at the Kaiserhof. I at once went to the hotel hairdresser to remove the dust of the journey

[1] Man can look out and much can he scan, but no seer will foretell the future before he has gazed.

by a shampoo and hair cut and was surprised to find that the man sitting in the next chair was my old friend Franz Arenberg. He threw me a wrathful glance from above the white smock with which his shoulders were covered and exclaimed in French, a language into which he lapsed very easily (having spoken it in his childhood) whenever he was excited, "*Que diable viens-tu faire ici?*" — "What the devil are you doing here in Berlin? I hope you won't fall into the trap. You know my party's feelings are deeply ruffled by the resignation of Marschall. We were satisfied with him and he understood us very well too. Besides, his mother's a Catholic. They say you are a Bismarckian and you haven't any parliamentary experience. Do you think you will be able to speak in Parliament at all? It's true I heard you defend a murderer at Metz when you were a barrister — you did it quite well. But, in the first place, that was twenty-four years ago, and in the second, it is easier to defend a murderer than hold your own in debate with Eugen Richter and August Bebel."

The barber's assistants attending us were open-mouthed with interest. I comforted my old true friend as best I could. I pointed out that, although my mother was not a Catholic, my wife was, and that, in any case, I understood the feelings of the Catholics as well as the importance and the just claims of the Catholic Church, and, above all, the necessity of complete parity and broad, generous justice towards both Christian Churches. Besides, I continued, I would be grateful to my dear François if he could show me a way of leaving this place and going back to Rome — a way compatible with my duty to the Kaiser and to my country. Still growling, but a little calmer than before and giving me friendly assurances that he would try to mollify his party, or at least not to stir it up still more, Arenberg went with me to the Foreign Office, where I called on Holstein from whom I had already received an excited letter beseeching me to look up no one in Berlin and to commit myself to nothing before he had spoken to me.

I found Holstein in a rather complicated mood in his famous room next to the Foreign Secretary's into which he dashed every now and again without being announced, thus putting the Foreign

Secretary's nerves and peace of mind to a very hard test. Holstein would have preferred keeping Marschall as Foreign Secretary, for he very well knew how great was his influence upon him. The fact that Marschall's position was badly shaken only increased his liking for the Foreign Secretary, who thereby would become all the more dependent. Nevertheless he would rather have me than many of the other possible successors. He began by going through a list of those who might have realised my hopes by sparing me the bitter draught and sitting down in Marschall's chair. He made the witty and apt observation that Kiderlen was impossible for "the Foreign Office can stand Holstein, and at a pinch, Kiderlen, but Kiderlen and Holstein together are more than it can stand." " Monts," he said, " is out of the question. His gifts are purely neg- ative. He can only criticise. He is incompetent in any positive sense. He is a good economist but no politician and cannot pursue a single political idea to its logical conclusion. And above all, he is perilously tactless. Hitherto he has failed in all his posts." I soon observed that Holstein did not so much fear Monts as suc- cessor (for he regarded him as rather out of the question) nor did he fear Kiderlen (for he knew that he was in disfavour with the Kaiser) but he did fear that Von Berchem might be brought back or even that Herbert Bismarck might return. Ever since his apostasy from the house of Bismarck, Holstein, in sleepless nights, had terrifying visions of Herbert, with his father, like a wrathful Titan, standing behind him. While Holstein begged and besought me again and again not to give the Kaiser a point-blank refusal, he also described the Foreign Office, the relations between the dif- ferent ministers, and indeed the Berlin life in general as a down- right Inferno. In this way he tried to make me timid and uncertain from the start, thus increasing my dependence upon him, the great privy councillor, who, under Hohenlohe, under Caprivi, and through his old and powerful influence on Herbert, had been the dominat- ing personality in the Foreign Office ever since the last years of the Bismarckian era.

While Holstein was urging me in every way not to burn my bridges here in Berlin and particularly when I reached Kiel, a commission-

aire entered, or rather came jumping in, and requested me to see
the Foreign Secretary. Herbert Bismarck had trained the messen-
gers to act in this way. He had kept them in such a permanent
state of tension and fear that when he rang his bell they would dash
into his room like a trout when it leaps over an obstruction. During the twelve years I was in office they were able to revert to more
placid movements. I have rarely known better and more excellent
human beings than the commissionaires in the Foreign Office.
Merely to gaze into their good, trustful faces is to feel that in this
respect no country can compete with us, and just as there is nothing
like a Prussian lieutenant, so is there nothing like a Prussian petty
official in any country in the world. I shall always preserve a
grateful and friendly remembrance of those excellent men, Miessner
and Neumann, Söchting and Tagge.

I found the Foreign Secretary, von Marschall, in a very bad
humour. The *Norddeutsche Allgemeine Zeitung* was spread out in
front of him and he read me a malicious paragraph in which that
highly authoritative paper announced my summons to Berlin. "It
is reported that the Imperial Ambassador, von Bülow, is leaving
Rome to-day for His Majesty's Court. We may safely assume
that the journey is not unconnected with the state of health of the
Foreign Secretary, Freiherr von Marschall." This brutal reference
to his health, which had been undermined by work and by the attacks of his opponents, had naturally hurt Herr von Marschall's
feelings. He suspected that his intimate enemy, Kiderlen, was
behind this perfidious paragraph. Marschall cared neither for the
"rude" Bavarians nor the "malicious" Swabians. He knew that
Kiderlen had made fun of him in the Berlin Casino and elsewhere
by relating in his own comic vein that Marschall, who did not know
a word of French or English when he took office, went for walks in
his garden with a French governess on his right and an English
governess on his left ever since, thus to penetrate the secrets of
those two languages. Kiderlen had also taken pleasure in spreading Prince Bismarck's cruel remark about the *"Ministre Etranger
aux Affaires."* Having relieved his feelings with respect to such
"crudeness", Marschall gravely declared his satisfaction that I

and not Kiderlen or Monts had been chosen as his successor. I
would fare better than he in many ways. He had, he said, been
brought to fall because the force of circumstance had thrust him
into sharp opposition with the Bismarcks, both father and son, in
spite of his old intimacy with the family (an intimacy which,
like my own, reached back to the years of our youth in Frankfort),
and in spite of his inward admiration for the great man. I, he said,
could approach the Bismarcks with a clean slate. Although he,
that is to say, Marschall himself, had begun his political career in
the Conservative Party, he had nevertheless been compelled to
fight many a skirmish with just this Party which looked upon him
as an apostate and treated him accordingly. In spite of his Conservative past and although he had, for example, been a pronounced
bi-metalist, he had also been compelled to support commercial
treaties that dissatisfied the Agrarians very much. He said I could
take office with the conviction that everything would be easier for
me than it had been for him, and that I would render the country
more substantial services than he had been able to render, owing
to the unhappy consequences of Prince Bismarck's dismissal and under the direct unpopularity of this dismissal itself. Besides, he continued, I was more of a diplomat than he was by reason of my whole
career, and then I knew foreign countries better. He declared
that in any case he knew that for me, as for himself, the welfare of
the Fatherland stood above everything. He urged me to accept
pro patria. With a quiet dignity he gave me to understand that
his health had been affected by overwork but that he was not so ill
as to be incapable of doing any more good work : he would be
glad to take over an Embassy. He did not feel confident that St.
Petersburg would be the right thing for him. It was too slippery
ground. Besides, under the influence of Holstein, he had taken a
large part in the non-renewal of the "Re-insurance Treaty" with
Russia and had even been compelled to defend it in the Reichstag.
London too was out of the question because he would not repudiate
the responsibility for the Kruger telegram, whatever he might have
been able to say in self-defence about the origin of this telegram. He
supposed the Count Philipp Eulenburg was irremovable in Vienna.

There remained Rome and Constantinople, for which he thought
he was most fitted. He knew that there was active opposition
against his continued employment in the service, but he counted
upon my good will and support. After all, our parents had been
friends in the good old days of the Bundestag.

I was able to assure Herr von Marschall, with a good conscience,
that not only the remembrance of the past, but also the interests
of the service, made it seem desirable to me that his abilities should
be employed in the service of the country and that Constantinople
would be presumably the post where these services would be of
most account. He had better not press the matter. I would keep
it in mind and strongly recommend him to the Kaiser.

Having made the two most important calls in the Foreign Office,
I went to the Imperial Chancellery. Prince Hohenlohe impressed
me, at least outwardly, as being older and weaker than he was at our
last meeting. Self-engrossed and with bowed head, this old man of
seventy-eight sat in his deep armchair. A pretty and pale-brown
dachshund was rubbing up against him, as his aged hand with
its very prominent bluish veins caressed the charming little creature. The Chancellor received me with a quotation : *"Hier steh'
ich, ein entlaubter Stamm."* [1]

He did not seem greatly concerned over the departure of Marschall.
He said that Marschall was an opportunist who would always trim
his sails to the wind, and that he had gone much too far in his obstinate, envenomed hatred of the Bismarck family, just because
he could never forget a few sarcastic remarks which Prince Bismarck
had made about his incapacity as a leader of foreign policy, nor
could he forget the unpleasant scene Herbert Bismarck had made
after the downfall of the Bismarck family in his presence at the
house of the Bavarian Ambassador Lerchenfeld. On that occasion, as often before, Herbert Bismarck's behaviour had been too
passionate and too extreme, but he had really been in the right as
far as the matter itself was concerned, for Marschall did not understand much about politics, at least not about high politics. He
was, so the Chancellor continued, more of a jurist than a diplomat.

----

[1] "Here I stand, a leafless trunk."

When I suggested that, in my opinion, Marschall could do good work in several diplomatic posts, for example, in Constantinople, the old Prince replied that as far as he was concerned I could send Marschall where I wished, only not to Paris or St. Petersburg, for he was really not the right man for those capitals. Prince Hohenlohe emphasised the paramount importance of cultivating good relations with Russia most particularly. "We must do all we can to make some amends for the consequences of the biggest piece of foolishness in the whole of our last seven years' policy, namely, the termination of the Re-insurance Treaty with Russia."

Prince Hohenlohe then gave me a picture of the international situation. He spoke in a whispering voice, but his ideas were clearly expressed, and he proved to me that he was still in the possession of those qualities that had always given his judgment a high standing in my eyes — a calm and thoroughly sober consideration of all divergent interests and a clear-sighted estimate of the strength and the aims of the different European Powers. These qualities were upheld by almost eighty years of experience and by an aristocrat's breadth of view, an aristocrat who had not only seen much but (what was at least as important) was not easily impressed. Whereas the Chancellor parted company with von Marschall without excessive regret, the separation from Bötticher touched him very deeply. Bötticher was an official after his own heart — industrious, and always ready to obey the higher command; that is to say, to gallop to the right or to the left whichever way he was ordered at the moment. Besides, with his somewhat subservient ways, Bötticher had won the heart of the old Prince, who did not forget that his house had once been a royal house and that his own grandfather himself had appointed and dismissed ministers. He was never happier than on those two days of the year — his birthday and the birthday of the Princess — when he wore his own dynastic decoration, the Hohenlohe "Order of the Phoenix", which Philip Ernest I, Prince of Hohenlohe, had founded in 1757, and which with a pun on the name of the illustrious race, bore the device *Ex flammis orior*. Bötticher had won his Highness' whole heart because he always called him "sire." He was unwilling to sacri-

fice the good Bötticher to the stormy Conservative sea that raged
behind the so-called "Bismarck Fronde" and the Farmers' League.
Hohenlohe asked me what I thought of Posadowsky. He was,
he said, regarded as a pusher and mischief-maker. I replied that
I had not as yet made Posadowsky's acquaintance, which rather
pleased the Chancellor. I added that, judging by all I had heard,
Posadowsky was an extraordinarily capable official.

The Prince seemed particularly preoccupied by problems of
domestic policy that clearly presented themselves to him under a
double aspect — he was extremely anxious not to forfeit the halo
of Liberal statesmanship which he had acquired in 1848 and had
carefully retained and cultivated ever since and, at the same time,
not to lose the Kaiser's favour. He asserted again and again that
at some future time he wished to part in peace from the Kaiser.
He did not want a rupture with him like Bismarck, nor did he want
to be dismissed like Caprivi, who, getting on his employer's nerves
by reason of his stubborn obstinacy, was simply shown the door
like a head valet. The relationship between the Prince and the
Kaiser was not quite simple. The Kaiser called him "uncle" on
the grounds that the Kaiserin's mother had been a Hohenlohe. But
the Empress never called Prince Chlodwig "uncle" in the presence
of other people, but only "dear Prince" and never emphasised any
relationship. If the Kaiser did so, this never prevented him from
talking very bluntly about Uncle Chlodwig, whom he used to call
"Germany's old woman." The Prince was a little deaf and rather
monosyllabic and the Kaiser did not like to be seated next to him
at banquets, for conversation with Uncle Chlodwig became more
and more difficult as time went on.

In our first talk, the Chancellor and I agreed in the conviction
that we ought not to allow the Parties to tear each other to pieces
in domestic quarrels but should try to unite them in a common
task as far as possible. I also agreed with him in thinking that anti-
socialist emergency legislation would lead to no result. But, on
the other hand, he spoke eloquently against the idea of modifying,
and still more of abolishing, the laws against the Jesuits, laws which
the Centre Party was fighting with renewed ardour. Although he

was a Catholic, he was filled with a distrust and a dislike of the Jesuits such as I had rarely found even amongst zealous Protestants. He was full of stories and anecdotes about intrigues and crimes that had been committed by the Society of Jesus in previous centuries. He was convinced that there were no measures from which the Jesuits would shrink even to-day. He was sure that it was they who had poisoned the Secretary of State, Franchi, in Rome, who, so he declared, had been suspect in their eyes because of his liberal inclinations and his efforts to promote an understanding with the Kingdom of Italy. After a mass which he had read in a Jesuit church, a priest of the order handed him a sherbet and, having drunk it, he died soon after in great abdominal pains. Prince Hohenlohe also confided to me that his brother, the Cardinal, was so afraid that the Jesuits would do away with him in the approved manner of the House of Borgia in the sixteenth century that he never allowed the wine destined for the chalice to be poured out except by his manservant out of a sealed bottle. One of Prince Hohenlohe's favourite maxims was that there were three Powers whose enmity was uncomfortable for every politician — the Jesuits, the Freemasons, and the Jews. The ideal would be to have all three on one's own side, an ideal that was not, however, easily realised. On the other hand it was dangerous to surrender entirely either to the Freemasons, or to the Jews, or — and most of all — to the Jesuits. The latter course would lead to a sure catastrophe, as was proved by the fate of Charles X of France; the mistakes made by Napoleon III towards the end of his reign under the domination of his bigoted wife, the Empress Eugènie; the submergence of Poland; the end of the reign of Queen Isabella of Spain; the result of the Jesuit experiment in Paraguay; and above all, the history of Austria, especially in the period of the Counter-Reformation and during the Concordat.

Before we separated, Prince Hohenlohe dropped me a gentle and friendly hint that he assumed the Kaiser had chosen me as his successor. I did not deny that this might be so, but added that his Majesty often changed his plans and intentions and, should he do so in my case and refrain from appointing me his, Prince Hohen-

lohe's successor, then I could assure the Prince that I would gladly
return to Rome.   But if the Kaiser should persist in regarding me
as the future Chancellor, then I would be grateful for every day
the Prince would remain in office and I would do all I could to make
it easier for him to remain, for, quite apart from my personal attachment to himself, I was convinced that his stay was in the
country's interest.

He had been called the "living bridge across the Main" [1] in the
days between 1866 and 1870.   Considering his whole past and his
personality and, notwithstanding his seventy-eight years, he could
still be called a clasp that held the Empire together.   The Prince
told me in parting that we would see each other again at Kiel on the
yacht *Hohenzollern*, and, as I left, I met his son Alexander in the
anteroom.   The young Prince would have liked to have played that
same part next to his father which Count Herbert played during the
last few years of the Bismarckian era.   Alexander Hohenlohe was
neither without ambition or ability.   But he lacked strength and
constancy as well as firm principles and firm, unshakable patriotism.   Not that he did not strive to do his duty by his country, but
the international outlook, displayed by so many German princely
houses, whether sovereign or mediatised, was especially marked
in him.   Alexander Hohenlohe was quite ready to become a Russian in exchange for Verki, the huge Lithuanian estate which was to
fall to the house of Hohenlohe through his grandmother Radziwill
and his Wittgenstein mother, in so far as this was compatible with
xenophobe Russian laws.   And as a Russian he would have become
a Russian diplomat without misgivings.   After all, his great-
grandfather, Prince Louis Adolph Peter zu Sayn-Wittgenstein, had
risen to the rank of Field Marshal General in Russia, not to speak
of the endowments that had fallen to his share.   The day on which
I introduced myself to his father as future Secretary of State and
successor of Marschall, the Prince tried to convince me that the
latter had no claims to an Embassy: "If you persuade the Kaiser
to give him Brussels it will be more than enough."

When I left the Foreign Office I had the impression that it would

---

[1] *I.e.* a link between North and South Germany.

not be quite easy for me to assert myself in this "den", as the Foreign Office was called by its members.   My brother Alfred, who had a repugnance for all intrigue and trickery as well as for ambition and jealousy, used to say, in his quiet manner, that over the Foreign Office there lay in dense swathes the exhalations of the intrigues that had been spun there for years past.   Even in Bismarck's time, intrigues of this kind had not been lacking, but, just as the sun breaks through the mist, so his genius overcame these dark shadows and lit up the shady side of politics and of mankind.   And during the six years my father worked as Secretary of State under Prince Bismarck, his temperament, which was rooted in a deep and true Christian faith and was averse to all vanity and superficiality, did not fail to exercise a beneficent influence upon the internal state of the office under his charge.   It was not without reason that he received the nickname of "the holy power."   After the departure of the great Prince, Holstein and Kiderlen doubtless often intrigued under the honest Caprivi as well as under the lofty-minded Hohenlohe, but in their own way and with all their faults, they felt concern for the welfare of the country above everything else.   Holstein was a thorough Prussian.   The mere thought that Prussia and Germany might lose their place in the world, might be injured or abused by other Powers, roused him to the depths of his soul.   It could truly be said of him that he was devoured by zeal on behalf of our dynasty, a zeal that sometimes robbed him of his whole sense of reality and converted his vigilance into an exaggerated distrust.   In these things Kiderlen was to Holstein what Sancho Panza was to Don Quixote.   He was incapable of enthusiasm and of any idealistic conceptions.   His feet were always firmly on the ground, but he had a very strong feeling for the prestige and the advantage of the firm and he watched the competitors with great vigilance.   With the advent of Bethmann, the leading position in the Empire fell to a man who knew nothing of foreign affairs and who, unfortunately, altogether disappointed those who hoped that he would gradually feel his way along and grow to an understanding of them.   And when Kiderlen also vanished from the scene to be replaced by Von Jagow, who was as small in body as he was in mind, our Foreign Office became more and more a bureaucratic playground for mediocrities where the work that was done became more and more inadequate and where, in the end, hardly a single political intellect was left. Thus the Foreign Office of 1914 was the incubator in which the evil egg of the ultimatum to Serbia was hatched. It was here that nearly all the errors through which we entered the war and lost the war were committed.

On the twenty-sixth I arrived at Kiel. I stayed at the Hotel Germania and at once went on board the *Hohenzollern*, where I was immediately received by the acting aide-de-camp, Colonel von Loewenfeld. Herr von Loewenfeld came from the First Regiment of Foot Guards, the "First Regiment of Christendom", as its officers used to say in the old days, a regiment which covered itself with glory in all Prussian campaigns, a regiment in which many bearers of historical Prussian names had sealed their faith for King and Fatherland with their blood, a regiment at the head of which Colonel von Bismarck fell, sword in hand, a little before the end of the World War. When the officer's corps of the First Regiment of Foot Guards once again saw the Kaiser and the Empress in the Regimental Casino, before proceeding to the front, the Empress gave each one of the officers a rose with her blessing. Hardly one of the heroes who received this distinction came back unwounded, and most of them are buried in alien soil. Prince Eitel Frederick of Prussia, the Kaiser's second son, who had himself served in the "Tall Potsdam Regiment", as it was called in the army, and had led it manfully in the war, writes in his fine tribute to the regiment which was founded in 1678 by the Great Elector, the founder of the Brandenburg-Prussian State:

The First Regiment of Guards fought at Oudenarde and Malplaquet, at Mollwitz and Hohenfriedberg, at Prague, Leuthen, and Torgau, at Grossgörschen, Leipzig and Brienne, at Königgrätz, Saint-Privat and Sedan. It stood before Paris twice in one century, in 1814 and 1870. But even these brilliant feats of arms must give way to the terrible struggle in the World War, a struggle that began with the battle of Namur-Charleroi on the 23d and 24th of August, 1914, and ended with the last attack on the Meuse position on the 10th of Nov. 1918. Between these two dates lay four years of unbroken active fighting, the march through France and Belgium on the Marne, the battle of Rheims, the action in Artois, the battles in Flanders, the defensive actions in Champagne, the Galician Polish campaign of 1915, the autumn battle at Arras and La Bassée, the trench battles at Roye and Noyon, the two-fold action in the battle of the Somme, the double battle of Aisne-Champagne, the fights in the Argonnes, the break-through in Eastern Galicia, the battles at Riga and on the Dvina, the "great battle" in France, the renewed trench battles at Rheims, the battle at Soissons, the Battle of the Marne in 1918, the defensive actions between the Marne and the Vesle, the Oise and the Aisne, the Argonnes and the Meuse, from which the last embittered struggle on the Aisne developed to become the retreat to the Antwerp-Meuse positions in November 1918. In fifty months of unbroken active warfare against enemies in the east and in the west, 124 officers, 418 N. C. O.'s and 3,208 trusty grenadiers and fusiliers of the First Regiment of Foot Guards sealed their faith with their death.

This was the finale to the heroic history of the Potsdam Guards. The German people would be unworthy of its name, unworthy of one-time greatness and one-time renown if it ever forgot such heroism!

Colonel von Loewenfeld was not only an officer of great military ability but also of high education. His mother was English and because he spoke English well, the Kaiser once sent him to Oxford, the English university of ancient fame, to be his representative at the jubilee. On the evening of his arrival there was a banquet in his honour at which he astounded the English professors by the abundance of his knowledge. On the following morning there was to be a fox hunt in which a large number of professors took part in red coats and immaculate breeches. One of the English professors pointed to the field and said to the German Colonel: "We are not as learned as the Germans but you, on the other hand, haven't got professors who ride with the hounds." The difference between the two great Germanic peoples could hardly have found more pregnant expression. Colonel von Loewenfeld loved to use the Potsdam-Berlin officer's jargon, but even in this humorous form he often uttered telling truths: "I could tell you," so he started a talk with me on the 26th of June, 1897, "what that old robber

chieftain said to the founder of our religion when he was summoned
to Worms to give an account of himself. What did he say? I
think he dropped a hint that things looked rather glum for Luther.
Well, you'll soon know whether you're in for it or not. The job
they've got in mind for you certainly is n't a soft one. I always
think the Ministers and the Parliament are like the lion-tamer who
has to enter the wild beasts' cage. If he can't manage the brutes,
he gets the sack. But if they tear him to pieces, our most gracious
Sovereign, who's looking on from the royal box, won't shed too
many tears for his sake."

Our conversation was interrupted by the Emperor's huntsman,
Schulz, who summoned me to His Majesty's presence. The Emperor Frederick died in the arms of this faithful man, who looked
after the son and successor with the same faithfulness. A heart
of gold beat in his broad chest.

Kaiser William II received me on the upper deck of the ship
where he was walking up and down all alone. He held his hand
out towards me and said, "My dear Bernard, I'm sorry for you
and even more for the Contessina (for this is what the Empress
Frederick and her children had always called my wife) but you must
go to the front. The Badener has betrayed me." He then gave
me an exposé in which, with his sentences tumbled helter skelter
over one another, he informed me that Marschall had intrigued
against his master with the Centre and with the Democrats behind
His Majesty's back. What the recent Secretary of State's ultimate
idea had been, he said, was still obscure, but his intentions towards
his master were certainly not good. There was evidence that
Marschall wanted to diminish the prerogatives of the Crown with
the help of the enemies of the realm and to establish a parliamentary
system. Punishment, the Kaiser said, was necessary and Marschall
would have to vacate his post. I could not refrain from expressing
my surprise at this melancholy revelation. Could Marschall really
have pursued such diabolical plans? The Kaiser struck the left
side of his chest with his strong right hand. "I have the proofs
here," he said with great emphasis. I suggested that it would be
of interest to me if I could have some knowledge of these proofs, so

that I could guard against similar snares. The Kaiser evaded my question. "I'll show you the proofs some time later on," he said, "at present I'll just tell you one thing above all, that you must go with me to St. Petersburg at the beginning of August. You've been active there as Counsellor of Embassy and you will be particularly useful to me. The English are behaving so disgracefully toward me that we must cultivate relations with Russia all the more assiduously."

I replied that I was at His Majesty's disposal so far as the journey to St. Petersburg was concerned, but I asked him if he would not let me go on leave until then. "Dear me!" said the Kaiser, "I thought we were going to be inseparable from now onwards." I replied that until I had thoroughly informed myself about our international situation by studying the documents of the Foreign Office, I could not possibly give a definite answer as to whether I could conscientiously accept the post offered to me or not. Besides, I would have to collect my thoughts before I made the final decision, not through any kind of timidity, but because I felt my responsibility towards the country and the throne. I therefore asked for leave until the end of July and in the meantime I would go to my accustomed summer resort, the Semmering. The quietude of that place would best enable me, with the help of the documents and with calm reflection, to reach a clear decision. This much I knew from my experience as an ambassador as well as from history and from the newspapers, namely, that the problem which would confront me was essentially this — we were to build a fleet for our defence and security without becoming involved in a war with England through building this fleet. That was not a very simple matter. We must not "*propter vitam vivendi perdere causas.*" The Kaiser was amused by my quotation. He thought I was a great Latinist but he was not much interested in Latin, he said. In spite of all the trouble that Hinzpeter had taken in this respect, Latin had no particular attraction for him. Thereupon I told him that I did not know what Latin writer had coined the truth in question, but I remembered that the verse had been quoted sixteen or seventeen years ago by Gambetta, if I was not mistaken, in a debate about the system of proportional representation which he had proposed. After the Kaiser again insisted that he counted on my company when he visited St. Petersburg, he let me go in the friendliest fashion.

My impression was the same as before in Naples and in Venice, as well as in Berlin and Potsdam, namely, that hardly anyone could be more amiable, more simple, and more natural than William II. It was only after long navigation in the Imperial waters that the rocks of his nature were revealed. At the luncheon to which I had been summoned, King Leopold II of Belgium as well as Prince Albrecht of Prussia were present, and so were the officers with whom the Prince as the Kaiser's representative in London had attended the Jubilee celebration of sixty years of Queen Victoria's reign. King Leopold welcomed me as an old friend whom he had met at Ostend. In the German environment the sarcastic side of his nature showed itself more plainly. He tried to parody every conversation he had with our Kaiser by beginning somewhat in the following manner: "His Majesty the Kaiser and King was most graciously pleased graciously to tell me the following about his most exalted attitude towards the problem in question, the high value of the revelation of which was equal to the happiness of sojourning in his most exalted neighbourhood and was heightened by proceeding from his most exalted lips." The King spoke very good German even if with a slight French accent. But our Empress was not pleased by his visit. Her Majesty had heard all kinds of unfavourable things about his way of living and, kindhearted as she was, she would have no levity in matters of ethics and morality. Nor did it please her that the King of Belgium had endeavoured to persuade the Kaiser to take part in a number of considerable business enterprises, especially in Eastern Asia but also in Africa. "The Kaiser shouldn't listen to the plans of the horrible man," so the Empress said in her touching and somewhat motherly care for her husband. "Who knows whether he won't fall into a trap? God grant that he doesn't give the Kaiser bad advice in other matters as well." Our political relations with Belgium, incidentally, were at that time so full of confidence and so friendly that even a little friction could not spoil them.

The Kaiser was not gratified by what the gentlemen who came back from England had to say. When Prince Albrecht of Prussia passed by with his suite in the London ceremonial procession of the 22d of June, the crowd in the streets repeatedly shouted, with reference to the Kruger telegram, "If you want to send a telegram to Oom Kruger, you'll find a post office round the corner on the right." Prince Albrecht also related that a number of Englishmen who could speak with authority had told him that the Kruger telegram had made a very lasting impression in England, not so much on the Cabinet and on the Court, as on the broad masses of the people and on public opinion. The wound had gone deep because the Englishman, in his simple manner, always thought himself in the right and had never believed that his quarrel with the President of the Boer Republic would be thus judged in Germany. In England no one had expected this of us — the English would have taken the affront far less amiss had it come from the French or even from the Russians. Of all Princes of the Royal House, Prince Albrecht was the greatest, a true son of Enoch. He reminded old people of the Emperor Nicholas I as far as his figure was concerned, and he was particularly fond of talking about that Emperor. After the dinner on the *Hohenzollern* he drew a comparison between the English Court, which he had just visited, and the Court of St. Petersburg, which he had formerly visited, and told me how indelibly the figure and manner of the Emperor Nicholas had impressed him. He had been a young man of scarcely seventeen then and when he had presented himself to the Tsar, the latter had asked him if it were true that Prussian princes really wanted to go to Bonn University or had actually done so, for it was an unheard-of thing that not only Princes, but Princes of royal blood, should be allowed to move unhampered amongst students who were all infected by revolutionary poison. The Tsar had so few illusions about his own people that during a parade, when the Prince expressed his admiration at the smart bearing and the enthusiasm of the so-called Suitzkis, that is, the members of the Maison Militaire, he replied with his hard Russian accent, "Lip service, nothing but lip service!"

Prince Albrecht of Prussia was a sensible man with a simple, sober intelligence, a kind heart, and a noble disposition. The older generation called him "Prince Albrecht the Son", to distinguish him from "Prince Albrecht the Father", the youngest son of King Frederick William III and the beautiful Queen Louise. King Frederick William IV, who had a great deal of wit and brilliant humour, though he did not shrink from acid and indeed unjust jokes, once said of himself and of his brothers, "If we four had been born the sons of a petty official, I would have become an architect, William a sergeant major, Charles would have gone to prison, and Albrecht would have been a ne'er-do-well." The remark about Prince Charles referred to a serious conflict he had with his own huntsman when he was a young Prince, the huntsman having surprised him with his wife. Prince Albrecht's father was married to the beautiful Princess Marianne of Holland. The marriage was not a particularly happy one. The husband fell in love with the pretty daughter of the Minister of War, Von Rauch. The garden of the Ministry of War bordered on that of Prince Albrecht's palace, and Prince Albrecht (father) separated from his wife and married Miss Von Rauch, to the sorrow of the pious King Frederick William IV. He was expelled from Berlin with his second wife by the King and settled in Dresden, where he built the "Albrechtsburg" and where, a few years later, the Duke of Sachsen-Meiningen gave him and his wife and children the title of Count and Countess of Hohenau. Princess Marianne went on a voyage to Italy to comfort herself. In her entourage there was a virtuous lady in waiting, a worthy chamberlain, and a lackey who had been recommended as being particularly reliable. The journey went off very well at first. The chamberlain reported to Berlin that the Princess was enchanting the Italians by her amiability, and her entourage by her kindness. He was soon able to report that her Royal Highness was still in the best of moods and that she seemed satisfied with her whole suite, but that she treasured the services of her lackey in particular. These services and the adaptability of the lackey were further emphasised with praise until, suddenly, the dreadful news arrived in Berlin that the Princess had ordered the lackey to share in the noonday and evening meals. Later on, Princess Marianne married her favourite. She was treated badly by him, he seemed to have been a brutal fellow, but, pious as she was, she accepted chastisement from her husband as a salutary ordeal and remained his faithful and obedient wife until he died. The child of this marriage died young. The older she grew the more sincerely religious she became, but at the same time the old aristocratic pride returned and she was unsparing in her judgment on every misalliance in princely families. That she herself had married below her rank had simply slipped her memory.

I have forgotten which Greek historian it is who relates that a Greek sophist, who asked some Asiatic King what he wanted to learn from him, got the answer, "Teach me the art of being able to forget." Princes, generally speaking, need not learn this art. They forget of their own accord and do not like reminders. In harmony with her religious bent, Princess Marianne moved to the extreme Right politically and, when she visited her son, who had become General Commanding in Hannover, she expressed disapproval, so that all could hear and in the presence of Hannoverians, of the annexation of Hannover by Prussia. Prince Albrecht (son) had completely eliminated his mother's marital backsliding from his memory. On one occasion he told me how painful it had been for him when he visited Madrid to have to call on Queen Cristina who, in her second marriage, had espoused the Life Guardsman Fernando Muñoz. Such misalliances, he said, were as objectionable to him as they were incomprehensible. Prince Albrecht (son) too was in no need of special instruction in the art of forgetfulness.

I revert from Madrid to Kiel and to the *Hohenzollern.* When the Kaiser had withdrawn, Prince Hohenlohe took me aside and asked me if I thought that he would incur the Kaiser's displeasure if he seized the chance of visiting Friedrichsruh while he was at Kiel. I replied in all good faith that I did not think he would. If he had gone and asked the Kaiser for leave of absence for that purpose, the latter would have tried perhaps to dissuade him ; confronted with a *fait accompli* his imperial master could hardly be angry. The Chancellor asked me if I would care to accompany him. I answered that I would consider it an honour to go to Friedrichsruh with the Prince. I would in any case pay a visit there myself sooner or later. Considering the long friendship between my father and Prince Bismarck and the kindness which he had shown to me and to my brothers, I could not take up my new duties without having presented myself at Friedrichsruh. "Excellent," said the Chancellor, obviously much relieved, "then we shall go off together. Herr von Wilmowski will make any other arrangements that are necessary."

Wilmowski, who was then head of the Imperial Chancellery, was the son of the Wilmowski who had been so long head of the Civil Cabinet under William I, a typical well-proven Prussian civil servant of the best period who had devoted himself to maintaining a good relation between our old Emperor and his powerful Chancellor, and thereby done permanent service to his country. For many years the elder Wilmowski had contrived on the one hand to induce the irritable, somewhat suspicious, and not always accommodating

Chancellor to adopt a respectful attitude towards his grey-haired sovereign, and, on the other, ever and again to strengthen the confidence of the latter in his great servant. The son was worthy of such a father from whom he had inherited not only strength of character but also sound judgment and fine tact. He was a tower of strength to the aged Prince Hohenlohe, who was little versed in questions of administration and legislation, especially in office matters. Later he carefully initiated me into the methods and workings of the Imperial Chancellery; then he became Oberpräsident of two provinces, Schleswig-Holstein and Saxony, and, at the end of his days, was the courageous leader of the Conservative party in the Upper Chamber.

On June 28 we arrived at Friedrichsruh about lunch time. We were met at the station by the Prince's son-in-law, Count Cuno Rantzau. Both his sons were away, but in compensation there was staying on a visit at Friedrichsruh an old and loyal friend of the Bismarck family, Baron Ferdinand von Stumm, eventually ambassador in Madrid, a post from which he was driven by Holstein's intrigues. Prince Bismarck greeted Prince Hohenlohe with marked and, as it seemed to me, studied courtesy. He clearly meant to make obvious the distinction which he drew between the third Chancellor and the second whom he had vehemently fought. I found Prince Bismarck greatly aged, but upright in his bearing and keen-witted as ever, the eyes and glance as impressive, the voice as gentle as ever they had been. He greeted Wilmowski and me as old acquaintances with a cordial shake of the hand. At table the conversation turned on the Russian estates of Prince Hohenlohe, to which Prince Bismarck returned repeatedly, expressing the wish that the large and lovely estate of Verki might be left in the possession of his second successor. He was most assiduous in his enquiries after Princess Hohenlohe and asked whether she was as keen on bearhunting as ever. How many bears had she laid low at Verki? He had shot many a bear in Russia in his day, but there could be no more of that particular sport for him now. Towards the end of the meal Prince Bismarck asked me how my father was. His daughter, Countess Rantzau, quickly broke in with the remark that Secretary of State Bülow, as he had been, had died some years ago.   At the correction I saw the corners of her father's mouth twitch: it seemed to pain him, this little betrayal of himself.   "It was n't failing memory," said Countess Rantzau after lunch, "it was just absent-mindedness."   Later the Prince came over to me, gave me his hand and said in kindly tones, "I have forgotten neither your father nor you."

After coffee and cigars, Prince Bismarck went for a short walk with the Imperial Chancellor, at the end of which the general conversation was resumed.   Baron Stumm took a lively part in it and showed himself to be as charming socially as he had been able and zealous as a diplomat in London and Paris, St. Petersburg and Madrid.   Ferdinand Stumm had only one weakness: he was a *malade imaginaire*.   He enjoyed the very best of health and at an advanced age was still to retain unusual vigour of mind and body and a youthful appearance.   Nevertheless he was constantly bemoaning the fact that no long life would be his.   His charming daughter, Princess Maria Hatzfeldt-Wildenburg, once sent him on his birthday a beautiful frame carved by herself on which she had engraved in parody of that well-known and lovely saying of the Emperor Frederick on his death bed:

"Learn to complain without suffering."

During our visit on June 28, Prince Bismarck had no opportunity to speak to me alone and I had the feeling that Prince Hohenlohe would not have liked it if he had.   Not from jealousy, of course, for that emotion was entirely foreign to that great nobleman, but possibly because he wanted to be able to say truthfully at his next meeting with the Kaiser that I had had no chance to speak alone with the ex-Chancellor.   Particularly did he want to be able to assure Holstein, of whom Prince Hohenlohe was scared, that nothing of the kind had happened.   Since the dismissal of Prince Bismarck Holstein had, with the greatest bitterness, stoutly upheld the principle that under no circumstances should it ever be allowed even to seem that the "new course" was taking advice from the greatest exponent of the "old course", or needed instruc-

THE VISIT TO BISMARCK IN FRIEDRICHSRUH,
JUNE 28, 1897

*Prince Bismarck between Prince Hohenlohe and the newly appointed
Secretary of State von Bülow*

tion from him. While Prince Hohenlohe was conversing with Countess Rantzau and Baron Stumm, Prince Bismarck nevertheless found a chance to say to me with a side-long look at Prince Hohenlohe, " It is just as well to make him keen about Verki so that he may deal gently in St. Petersburg with the young man Absalom whom we have no occasion to put out of humour or irritate."

It was my first visit to Friedrichsruh. I was struck by the simplicity of the house, the modesty of the furnishing, the complete lack of adornment, in a word, with the inartistic character of the whole establishment. Not a single fine picture hung in Friedrichsruh except a splendid portrait of the Prince by Lenbach. Of a library of any size there was not a trace to be seen : there was no sign of ornamental ceilings, tapestries, or eastern carpets. The sun of Homer had never smiled on that house, and of that glamour of the Italian renaissance which has made beautiful so many of the princely homes of Germany and which even yet casts some reflection of its radiance on Tegel and on the Goethe house at Weimar, there was no trace in Friedrichsruh. But surely this absence of all the seemingly beautiful was a worthy manifestation of the real spirit of Prussia, whose last and, since the days of the great Frederick, greatest representative was Prince Bismarck. The whole house, the whole style, seemed to reiterate the warning which the oracle of Delphi gave to the Spartans who came to ask about their country's destiny : "Wealth alone can destroy Sparta." And above all it was the house of the man who, as I was to say[1] four years later before his memorial in Berlin, had carried through to a triumphant conclusion that for which our people had longed through the centuries, for which our noblest spirits had striven, for which the Ottos and the Salian and Hohenstaufen Emperors had battled in vain, for which a long line of martyrs to the ideal of Germany had fought and suffered. All the great memories, all the good spirits of German history seemed to hover round this modest home.

While Prince Hohenlohe was with me in Friedrichsruh the follow-

[1] Prince Bülow's "Speeches" (large edition), I. 222; (small edition), I. 246.

ing announcement was published by the official Wolff Telegraph Agency:

Kiel, Monday, June 28.

As the state of health of Baron Marschall von Bieberstein has made necessary his replacement as Secretary of State in the Foreign Ministry, Herr von Bülow, the Imperial Ambassador in Rome, has, as we learn on excellent authority, been selected by the Emperor to be his successor as head of the Foreign Ministry. Herr von Bülow, who has been here for the last two days and has been repeatedly received by the Kaiser, will take over his new duties after the Kaiser returns to Berlin. Till then the conduct of Foreign Ministry business will be as heretofore in charge of the Under-Secretary of State Baron von Rotenhan.

Passing through Berlin on my way to Semmering I found both Holstein and Rotenhan in an equally contented mood. Holstein was pleased that he could mess about for some weeks yet before I took him in hand. Rotenhan was delighted that he was still to carry on *ad interim*. From the outset I was quite clear that Herr von Rotenhan would not suit me as Under-Secretary of State. He was, like all the members of that old Franconian family, a man of superior character and equally a man of experience and judgment, but he was what the English call " a slow coach." [1] Before he gave an answer he used to remove his glasses which, being nearsighted, he always wore, and slowly and carefully polish them. That gave him time to gather his thoughts and prepare an answer. This *modus procedendi* was not at all out of place for interviews with foreign diplomats with their artful questions. But work inside the office was not exactly helped by it. Later I replaced Rotenhan by Baron von Richthofen whom I encountered as Director of the Colonial Section. Herr von Rotenhan as ambassador in Bern and at the Vatican continued to do his country service. He died, if my memory serves me aright, from the effects of an accident in the street caused by the excellent man's nearsightedness. When I took over the business of the Foreign Ministry and thus not merely stepped into the limelight but, to use an expression of Prince Bismarck's, into the front line filth, I gave instructions that all carica-

[1] English in the original.

tures concerning me should be carefully collected. They contributed to my amusement when they appeared and even now I find
retrospective pleasure in leafing over the twenty-seven official
volumes of the caricatures devoted to me which adorn my library
in the Villa Malta. When I opened the collection I wrote on the
first page those lines of Goethe:

> *Sollen dich die Dohlen nicht umschrei'n,*
> *Musst nicht Knopf auf dem Kirchturm sein.*[1]

When I arrived at Semmering I condoled with my wife on the
possibility of what was, in my opinion, almost certain exile for her in
Berlin, a city which, as it happened, she came later to like immensely
and where she was to be very happy. Then I turned to what I
called my thinking labours in contradistinction to her occupation,
which was to read Goethe. I had brought with me some important
memoranda on our relations with other states, notably England and
Russia, and on the situation in the Far East. Also I had brought
the documents necessary for a proper appreciation of our commercial relations, especially with Russia and America. I once heard
Hermann Helmholtz say that his best thoughts came to him when
he was walking uphill and down dale over hilly country. I would
not seek to compare myself with that great scholar, but I arranged
my day so that I spent the forenoons studying documents and
the afternoons pondering over what I had read while walking along
the road to Mürzzuschlag or climbing the Sonnenwendstein. Thus
I strove to make the international situation clear to myself.

My mind was clear on one point long before my summons to
Kiel: that Germany had little to gain by a war and a great deal
to lose. Should we undertake campaigns of conquest southwards,
eastwards or westwards, annex new territory in the north? Should
we force smaller neighbours to join us? To the old foes of the
Empire should we add new ones? No far-seeing German patriot
could wish that. Still less could a conscientious German statesman
counsel it. Using a somewhat banal French expression which,

---

[1] If you do not wish the jackdaws to screech around you, then you must not be the
steeple on the church.

however, hits the nail on the head : *Le jeu ne valait pas la chandelle.*
Also I had not the least doubt that, as the whole stage of the world
theatre had altered during the last decades, a localised war on the
European continent was hardly conceivable ; on the contrary the
danger was that every European conflict might be transformed
into a great war, into a world war, with all the fearful risks attendant on such an event and with all its incalculable possibilities.
On the other hand, every year during which we kept peace with
honour was a gain to us. Our population and our economic
strength grew each year. Time was on our side, especially when
we made comparison with our most dangerous neighbour, France.
How were we then to maintain that peace which the German nation
wanted, which it required for its further progress in all domains?
The answer could only be : provoke no one, but, at the same time,
allow no one to tread on our feet. In the last instance we had to
bear in mind the old Pomeranian proverb which Prince Bismarck
was fond of quoting: "It's only the green shoots that the goats
eat." It was clear that, if we tamely suffered the attacks and
encroachments of others, then on the first disregard of our interests
would come a second, on the first violation of our rights a fresh and
more painful one would quickly follow. Meantime, and until philosophy takes a hand in reconstructing the world and until a system
is discovered and enforced which shall be ideally just, protecting
all rights and considering all interests — until that time, a nation
which once lets pass a real and a serious injury to its interests and
to its honour will have to reckon with further injuries and viola-
tions.

As I saw the picture of the international situation in 1897 it
seemed to hold many lights, but also shadows that were deep and
serious. Since the beginning of German history we have been, as a
result of our unfavourable geographical position in the middle of
Europe, more exposed to attacks than any other great nation. We
were encircled, to use a phrase used later in my "German Policy" [1]
as a matter of fact since the Treaty of Verdun, that is, since
August 11, 1843. Our neighbour in the west was the French

[1] Prince von Bülow: "German Policy" (popular edition, 1916), p. 293.

nation, the most restless, the most ambitious, the vainest, and, in the truest sense of the words, the most militarist and the most nationalist of all the peoples of Europe. Since the last Franco-German War this nation had been severed from us by a gulf which, as a well-known French historian wrote to me in 1913, would never and could never be bridged. In the east Slav peoples surrounded us, peoples filled with dislike of the German who had been their guide to a higher civilization, who, just for that reason, was pursued by their deadly hate, that hate which an unruly, unmannerly school-boy feels for an upright and able teacher. This is true not so much of the Russians as of the Czechs, and especially the Poles, who since the foundation of a great Polish kingdom by Boleslaw Chrobry, that is, nine hundred years ago, had laid claim to Germany's eastern territory. The relations between Germans and Englishmen had constantly changed in the course of the centuries. But it is generally true to say that John Bull stood firmly resolved to patronise and protect his poor German cousin, and even to let him do the rough work now and again but not to recognise him as an equal. As for the others, none of them really liked us, and this dislike of us existed before the envy, aroused by the power and prosperity created by Bismarck, had intensified it into hatred. The reason why we are disliked is that we underestimate the value of forms, of appearance, and as the Greek philosopher demonstrated long ago, mankind in the majority judges by appearances and not by the reality of things. Such a conception and appreciation of things could only be adopted by the German with difficulty, for he always goes to the heart of things and is therefore too indifferent towards the outer shell.

What was our position in foreign affairs seven years after Bismarck's retirement? What were the conditions at home?

Even before my summons to Berlin, during all my diplomatic service abroad, I had striven earnestly to keep in close touch with affairs at home. I had anxiously watched the development of the domestic situation at home and regularly studied the great European newspapers. I had particularly kept in touch with things through an exchange of letters with friends and colleagues. Particularly interesting were the newsletters of Count Monts which I had preserved. I had got to know Count Monts when I was a young attaché at the Foreign Ministry. Shortly before that he had passed his examination as assistant judge with distinction. He was three years younger than I and, like me, wanted to enter the diplomatic service. He tried to be intimate with me, which did not please me particularly. He had never been either an officer or a corps student and, whatever one may think in general of officers and corps students, it cannot be denied that it is in their school that the young German who is inclined to be uncouth, learns manners. Monts' manners were bad. He was extremely tactless. Also he was far too much of a "pusher" and too obviously bent on promotion. Overcritical and arrogant where he thought he could get off with it ; servile and obtrusive towards the great. When I was ambassador in Bucharest he discerned in me a "rising man", a coming man, and, from time to time, sent me letters in which he gave the most fulsome expression to his friendly feelings towards me. It was not very long before he presented the bill for all his compliments. As Consul General in Budapest he was not over-successful, just as unsuccessful, in fact, as he had been before as Counsellor of Embassy in Vienna. Count Szögyenyi, who was Austro-Hungarian ambassador in Berlin for so many years, used to say : "Cis-Leithania and Trans-Leithania are not usually in agreement ; on one thing only indeed are they united. Cis-Leithania and Trans-Leithania both find Monts damnable." After his failures in Budapest and Vienna, Monts was considered unsuitable for posts in Europe and was going to be transferred to Rio de Janeiro. He sent an appeal to me — ("Out of the depths I cry") — and besought me to use my good relations with the Foreign Ministry to save him from a post which in his bad state of health would be death for him — ("And I am so young, so young," concluded the letter, a letter not without wit). I was able to induce the Powers that Were in the Foreign Ministry to send him not to the other hemisphere but to Oldenburg, that little North German post which lies so pleasantly on the Hunte and was founded by Wittekind's grandson, Walbert, and called after his wife Altourga, where he needed to be less concerned about his health under the shade of the Church of St. Lambert than at the foot of that sugar loaf scorched by a tropical sun, the Pao de Assuecar. In Oldenburg Monts made his début with a jest which pleased me, for I have a weakness for a jest. At his formal reception by his Royal Highness the Grand Duke, Monts turned up, not in the regulation top-hat but in a bowler. His attention called by an outraged grand-ducal chamberlain to this gross breach of etiquette, the new ambassador replied: "Small courts, small hats." Once I had saved him from Rio, Monts wrote me more often. When I was promoted to be ambassador in Bucharest, he addressed to me on my birthday, May 3, 1888, a memorandum dealing with personalities in Rumania which ended thus: "Excuse these lines. They are occasioned by the desire to be of some slight service to you on your entry into the rather ticklish Rumanian situation so far as my weak powers can help you. Take them in friendship and with indulgence, and with them my best wishes for you in your new position. From your very devoted Anton Monts." Monts knew Bucharest, where as secretary of legation he had been just as impossible as in Vienna and Budapest.

As far as my meditations at Semmering were concerned only a few letters were really relevant in which this busy and lively observer gave me details about the increasing difficulties with which our home and foreign policy had to struggle, not least because of the growing tendency of William II to autocratic intervention in the orderly conduct of affairs. The prospect which these letters — effective and enlightening in their freshness and candour — opened out to me was not particularly happy. On the situation in Austria-Hungary which in all our political conceptions occupied an important place since the time when Prince Bismarck had sought union with Austria in 1879 and had concluded a defensive alliance with the Hapsburg monarchy, Monts wrote to me as follows from Budapest on November 16, 1891: "Honoured patron: This dualism on closer acquaintance is the most miserable piece of botchery ever created by frivolous amateurs. How long will the army succeed in maintaining a precarious unity? What way of escape will a successor who does not enjoy the universal reverence enjoyed by Francis Joseph find from his insuperable difficulties? The Magyars

are Magyarising only the Germans and the Jews; that is to say,
those elements which, in the interests of the Empire, ought not to be
deprived of their German tongue, and they are powerless against
Rumanians, Croats, and Slovaks. If the Magyars realise their
aim, the personal union, the collapse of Austria-Hungry is certain.
At that moment Hungary will be stripped of half her territory.
Whether we are strong enough to maintain the influence necessary
for our own existence on what is left of Austria without annexing
this Catholic lump, and retaining a hold on Hungary, Croatia, and
Siebenbürgen is a thing I doubt. And then we are left isolated
between the two millstones, France and Russia, and are lost. Numbers are against us even now. We cannot at all count on Italy, and
France's army alone exceeds ours in numbers. As Clausewitz very
rightly deduced, when conditions are otherwise equal, numbers
must decide. And how many men must we leave behind on the
eastern frontier to give the Austro-Hungarian army moral support?
Besides, do you know that in the negotiations for a commercial
treaty Rudini threw us overboard? If Austria didn't let Luzzati
concede that 'linen duty' so desired by his electors, then he, Rudini,
would go and it would be all up with the Triple Alliance. You
can't imagine what a panic it caused in the Foreign Ministry in
Berlin. Just at the critical time I was in Vienna. Dispatches
simply flowed and the comedy ended, of course, with the acceptance
by us of the Italian demands. Bismarck's jest about having two
irons in the fire still has point. Logically we must now invariably come off second-best in the Triple Alliance. We have two
avowed and deadly foes; Austria has only one. Italy's position
is the best of all, for her enmity with France is quite easily got over,
and if things came to the worst, England, who is not ready to help
Germany or Austria, would protect Italy from any invasion. Besides Russia can't get at Italy and the Alpine passes can easily be
defended against France. In this state of affairs the internal
situation of the Empire must be a real comfort to the patriot. *Re-
gis voluntas suprema lex.* Where will it all lead to? Just fancy,
making an entry of this kind in the guest book, and, what is more,
in the Munich guest book. Stablewski's appointment as Arch-

bishop of Gnesen also makes a painful impression. The Poles won't be cajoled, and if there is war with Russia, they will be on our side in any case: why then so dangerous a concession? The German element in Posen and West Prussia is, alas, losing ground permanently. The Germanisation of that region is none the less a matter of life and death for us, considering the geographical position of Berlin and the necessity, which is bound to come, of annexing territory up to the Vistula. All the same one must not, as you rightly say, despair of the future of the Empire. With a collapse of Germany the whole of European civilisation is lost; a united Slav Empire would stretch to the Oder against which what is left of France and Germany would not count. If the All-Highest would but get a clear picture to some extent of the danger of his situation! Besides, he still thinks that the Tsar has some regard for him. And yet this Tsar, our one guarantee of peace, hates our Kaiser, as I learn from a very good source, because he doesn't love truth! *Sed haec hactenus.* My most humble respects to your charming wife and do not you be too severe a censor of this salad in letter form, from yours very cordially, Monts." On April 6, 1894, Monts, who was paying assiduous court to the triumvirate Holstein, Kiderlen, Phil Eulenburg, wrote about the campaign which *Kladderadatsch* was then making against the oyster-fiend Holstein, the Spätzle-eating Kiderlen,[1] and the Troubadour (Eulenburg). "Honestly, in my humble opinion this *Kladderadatsch* business is becoming steadily more embarrassing. We must set the public prosecutor against *Kladderadatsch* without the least hesitation. Now we are only earning ridicule. Please give Phil my cordial greetings and be assured of the grateful loyalty of your proconsul in Pannonia, Anton Monts."

On November 1, 1894, Monts, answering a short note which I had sent him from Palermo where I was visiting my brother-in-law Camporeale, wrote: "While you're wandering under the palms as ambassador there's been some scene-shifting at home. At the risk of telling you what you have known for a long time, I'll tell you

[1] Spätzle are small pastries eaten with meat dishes in Swabia, Kiderlen's home, though also throughout southern Germany and Austria.

what I believe to be quite true though it is but the prologue to the real drama. The Prussian Prime Minister, Botho Eulenburg, had worked out the draft of an Anti-revolutionary bill in which *inter alia* there was mention of preventive police measures against the press. In that connexion he insisted that it was the protective regulations in the Empire and not those of Prussia that needed amendment. During the manoeuvres in East Prussia he got a plan that was opposed to his own put aside, the plan that Prussia should go on with an associations and assemblies bill. He had it rejected with the help of the King of Saxony, and the Kaiser declared that he agreed in principle with the idea that Botho Eulenburg should work out most drastic proposals for submission to the Federal Council. The proposals were, however, of such a nature that his Majesty thought they could not be carried without a *coup d'état*. Besides the States declared they would not support the plan. As a consequence, so we learn, H. M. called on Caprivi on the 23rd and told him that he had ordered Botho to work out his bill according to Caprivi's programme. This is all I know. Probably you already have later news of the swift-approaching catastrophe. I went to Brunswick on the 25th; and at midday on the 26th I was at Blankenburg to welcome H. M., whose baggage was already on the special train. He was leaving for Blankenburg immediately after the intercessory service at Schuvaloff's for the Tsar. This was the turning point. At two o'clock came a wire saying that State business which could not be put off made his Majesty's coming impossible. In the course of the afternoon all sorts of folk turned up, including Stolberg, Lehndorff, and Waldersee. Everyone believed that the Tsar had died, although no one would commit himself before the first special editions arrived from Berlin. Waldersee in particular would not give the Hohenlohe combination longer than Saturday and even three days later he was not sure. The gentlemen in Berlin pointed out how old the Prince is. Of course a good number of them were mixed up in the East Prussian Agrarian intrigue which, as is well known, was led by the Chief Marshal of the Court and Imperial Household, August Eulenburg. On the other hand, all the non-Prussians were overjoyed. I think that we can be extremely satisfied with the outcome. We have to thank: (1) Hohenlohe himself and his patriotism, and (2) the wide outlook of Holstein, who at that time stood by Hohenlohe and without whom Hohenlohe would hardly have pulled it off. If Köller does his duty, that is to say, if he rises to the height of his task, then Hohenlohe can stand firmly on three legs — Holstein (diplomacy and the more delicate bits of internal politics), Marschall (Parliament, trade questions, and the heavy work), Köller (administration and man of confidence in the Prussian ministry which needs reforming so sorely). In mind and body, he is as hale as ever, so that we can count on him for another three years. But three years is a long time. Then possibly you'll have to step into the breach. Although I should pray and hope that you may get anything except this, yet, *supremo loco*, it is impossible that the conviction should not steadily grow that a diplomat is the right man for the highest post. And whom, then, would we have? The Hohenlohe régime can go on existing; only he must husband his strength and be more sparing of his own personal efforts. But however much our class will provide him with supporters, however Marchall and Holstein strain every nerve, the unfortunate fellow will not lack enemies. The East Prussians, Waldersee, the *maison militaire*, perhaps soon the whole of the generals' corps (for in the end they will follow a leader just like sheep), and, last but not least, that much travelled Ulysses Miquel. If God would but grant that the Conservatives understand the signs of the times aright! One can't get a majority without them, for to deal with the Centre and Radicals [1] means a renewal of that wandering in the maze which Caprivi thought was the art of government. It may seem frivolous, but none the less a socialist or anarchist outbreak might rally the moderates and all loyal constitutionalists, including a section of Radicals and the Centre. And then *il faut battre le fer pendant qu'il est chaud*. That means to 'amend' not to transform the electoral law, for you won't get the necessary two-thirds majority for transforming it. But you know all that better than I with your clearer insight and greater knowledge of the men involved. Meantime let us rejoice in the sun which is

[1] Freisinnige.

clearly breaking from the clouds to shine over the Fatherland. Public opinion is so decidedly for Prince Hohenlohe that even the God of Thunder[1] in the Saxon forests sounds hymns of peace in the 'Hamburger Nachrichten.' As to what concerns our profession more especially, it seems to me to be more desirable than ever that, after Marschall obtained the title of Minister of State which he has so greatly coveted, something should be done for Holstein. We are now gathering the fruit of his wise conduct of foreign affairs (Russia, England, etc.). Some naïve folk ascribe all that to Caprivi and the real leader stands aside unnoticed and unhonoured. If Phil could only make it all clear to the Kaiser! Couldn't he? It would certainly be very difficult. H. M. thinks he himself, and he alone, conducts policy. Will Werder remain ambassador in St. Petersburg under the new Tsar? The fellow is hardly equal to the new situation. I have great trust in the new Chancellor and am confident that, just as he knew how to keep Botho Eulenburg out of Alsatian affairs, so he will be able to keep the military from interfering in St. Petersburg. There is another consideration it seems to me, and that is, whether it would not be advisable to build a golden bridge for the beaten foe and help the most dangerous of the East Prussians, the fool of the family, August Eulenburg, to a long-desired embassy. Otherwise Alvensleben is the man, although he is fundamentally a weak character. And as everyone, of course, has to look out for himself, although I can scarcely count on Brussels (which would be just the thing for me), I'd hope if there were any shuffling of posts to get out of my present really unworthy position. What do you think of Deines as Governor General? I don't say it out of personal dislike, but it really is a bit too thick, entrusting the Crown Prince to such a narrow, one-sided creature. Does H. M. really know his people so ill? Besides one more bitter opponent for Holstein right on the spot too and always near the Emperor. *Sed haec hactenus.* Go on enjoying the beautiful Roman winter — no one knows how long you'll be allowed to. My most humble respects to your wife. And think sometimes on an odd bad day of your friend veiled in northern mists, Anton Monts."

[1] *I.e.*, Bismarck.

The depreciatory remarks in that letter about Botho and August Eulenburg, two unusually able men and full of character, were unjust. This is equally true of the scornful judgment on General Deines. My old wartime friend Adolf Deines was an idealist, too much an idealist to be of any use in the diplomatic service. But for the future King and Kaiser and his brothers, no better tutor could have been found than that able, upright, and honourable gentleman, Adolf Deines. Monts did not show himself so much of an honourable gentleman after the fall of Prince Bismarck when he at once turned his back on the man whom he used to call "our hero", and threw himself into Holstein's arms. At the same time he naturally cut adrift from Herbert Bismarck, whom he used to compare to the young Siegfried.

On January 26, 1895, I received the following lines from Monts: "I agree *in toto* with the political essay in your last welcome letter. Peace and steadiness above all things. Gradually the Prussian mill will again attract the water of our national aspirations. Hohenlohe's last speech was extremely good *meo voto*. In how kindly a manner does the Bismarck press prepare a shelter in an embassy for Herbert Bismarck! It might be all right if the old man could be propitiated with the sacrifice and be made to keep his mouth shut. But that could not be done, this dart cannot be stuck in the sides of Marschall and Holstein. In the happiest circumstances he would be an unsuitable representative. Presumably he would only go in for the most infernal intriguing."

After Monts had become ambassador in Munich, thanks, not least, to my appeals to Hohenlohe, he wrote me from there on February 24, 1895: "The news from Berlin does not sound good to me. H. M. is very upset about the course of events between ourselves and England and about the estrangement, for he can hardly go to Cowes. And so he is running after these people again, which is exactly the opposite way to what he should do. He sends entirely superfluous deputations of guards, a private letter to his tippling old grandmother, and a message as unknown to the Foreign Ministry as the letter is, to be delivered personally to the old huckstress by his aide-de-camp Arnim. This inclination of his Majesty to make the Conservatives smart is wrong. Instead of building a golden bridge for these beaten folk he seems, alas, to mock at them still. I am told that the ill humour of these people on whom we are, after all, dependent, is now very great. The Jewish bankers and financiers are very sick about the cancelled procession at the subscription ball: there are no court balls because H. M. is going to pay back Berlin society for the Kotze affair. In short, as in the days of Frederick William IV, the outlook 's pretty gloomy. Only in foreign policy are things going excellently. The Kruger dispatch gets all my approval. If only we don't climb down! Our Far Eastern policy is likewise universally applauded and also our attitude at the Golden Horn. All this must be put principally to Holstein's credit. Certainly he is powerless without Hohenlohe, but the Commander in Chief and his Chief of Staff are working together marvellously. Only matters of internal policy are not coming quite up to scratch. In Munich particularly things aren't going too well. Bavaria is, as always, consciously working towards augmenting her position in the Empire. We hesitate between giving her complete freedom of action and a regular blaze-up. It is typical that at Munich in the summer H. M. opened the carriage door for Prince Louis and now wants to forbid him to display his flag on the cadets' barge. The house of Wittelsbach is now above everything making sure of the army which I can only characterise as purely dynastic. We lost our last hold over it when we gave up the right of inspection. Where the Bavarian army would stand if it came to a war is dubious. I can't help laughing at the illusions Berlin has on that score. Crailsheim's attitude is characteristic. Lerchenfeld's picture of the confusion in Berlin must have so impressed him that he now takes up a quite uncompromising attitude. He appears to me to be hauling the old Bavarian seesaw policy out of the lumber-room. Everywhere I am up against his efforts to make himself independent. His tone with me is far stronger: his deference to aristocratic and clerical wishes is unbounded. The court is more stubborn than ever. Ill feeling on both sides, despite despatches, ceaselessly envenoms the atmosphere. Lerchenfeld does his utmost to fan the glow into a blaze. To his confidants he declares that he is extremely angry with me and it is not at all impossible that he will suddenly and successfully bring me to fall, for his influence in Berlin goes far, at least a good deal farther than mine. Happily Marschall seems to be no longer quite so credulous. If one had only the Foreign Ministry to consider, one could conduct policy towards Bavaria quite well, but, unfortunately, one is never secure against surprises from the All-Highest and never knows what influences are decisive in that quarter. Bavaria is so important a factor, the cornerstone of the whole German edifice, that everywhere the utmost care must be taken. Hohenlohe's real Bismarckian policy is working well. I have just been talking about it with Schwenninger, who told me that Bismarck was pleased with it and had expressed himself in a most conciliatory manner. But at the same time he said that he felt great concern over the growth of particularism, indeed separatism, in the country. As our friends in the south are entirely liberal, only a moderate liberal Imperial government can take any firm hold here. At present we have one. Fortunately H. M. has again poured water into the autocratic wine of his speeches. One speech can wreck the work of many months and more than that. If anything is published here about H. M.'s regatta griefs, then all the ground gained by the Kruger dispatch is lost in a trice. Lerchenfeld is always foisting something or other on the national newspapers here. The most important of them, the *Münchner Neueste Nachrichten*, I have so far tamed that it deals very cautiously with contentious stuff from Berlin and even asks for my advice. But you can't choke up every channel of news. If Lerchenfeld manages his agitation against the civil code law cleverly, I haven't much hope of its reaching port this session. The situation of our allies hasn't much that is pleasant about it. Italy's financial weakness makes me very anxious : 50,000 men in Africa is too great a burden for the poor Italian state. And Austria ! The renewal of the customs and commercial alliance makes the whole structure unsteady. Then there is the coming crash in Hungary. The prestige of our friends in Cis-Leithania is dwindling more and more and that's where our friends are. In Hungary we have actually no friends. In his inmost heart the Magyar hates the German scarcely less fundamentally than he hates the Muscovite. And what's to become of Bulgaria? Apparently Lobanoff will, for a while, leave the wretched Coburger *in suspenso*, for he can hardly find a more servile satrap. Eventually it will be the same old game again and the two millstones, the self-esteem of the Bulgars and the arrogance of the Russians, will grind Ferdinand as they ground Alexander. Thus everywhere — I don't speak of Egypt, Japan, and suchlike — seeds of entanglement are visible. The exaggerated love of peace which we display will not avail much in the hard world of reality, for we are far from being 'saturated', and we will in the long run make ourselves and the pipe of peace that we carry the mock of ambitious neighbours. But in this sphere it is very difficult to find the *juste milieu*. Above all, we must get England involved. If Russia, England, and Japan were fast embroiled, then we could in God's name let loose on the French. Even then, though, we wouldn't have peace, for in the long run without a foreign war we could never set Germany free from her present constitution which cannot possibly remain. With this parliament and the particularism of the states the whole affair will eventually go to bits. God bless you! My respects to your honoured wife. Always your devoted and grateful Anton Monts."

Monts at that time greeted his Majesty's telegram to President Kruger with jubilation and wished that William II would soon tread on England's pet corn once more. His judgment on the situation in Bavaria, in which he abused Crailsheim and Lerchenfeld, the grey-haired Prince Regent and Prince Louis, was equally unstatesmanlike. The doubts of Count Monts as to the national feeling of the Bavarian army, which stood by the Empire in devoted loyalty from the first day of the World War to the last, have been answered by history.

His impressions on a visit to Berlin Monts sent to me on May 20, 1895: "As far as the Foreign Ministry is concerned my impressions were excellent. Holstein is hale and hearty in mind and body and works most intimately with Hohenlohe. Marschall is entirely occupied with Parliament and does well there. Pourtalès with the help of Professor Kruger carries out very satisfactorily Holstein's personal instructions and goes on hoping that a small post will fall to him sometime. Mumm looks after himself. As reporter on German and ecclesiastical affairs Counsellor of Embassy Klehmet is active. They say he is a good worker, seems to be intelligent, but, in appearance, dress, and the like, is yards below Mumm. Unfortunately I did not get to know Alexander Hohenlohe. The Chancellor is extraordinarily hale. I told the Princess of my anxiety that actual exertion such as cabinet-meetings involve would finally prove harmful to her husband. And then there are his social duties. As before, relations with H. M. are excellent; little billets-doux pass between them. Marschall will stay on until further notice, but behaves as though he were resigned to everything. You know that Holstein wanted to make a Cabinet matter of Marschall's immediate departure. On the other hand if H. M. wants a change later on, Holstein won't oppose it. I hope, however, that the waves will calm. The apothecary Lucanus as well as the pro-Bismarckian Imperator's camp followers are none the less very down on the wretched 'public prosecutor.' Very serious now is the roaring of the Agrarians. Hohenlohe told me that he would unconditionally oppose their motions. Marschall, alas, has a bi-metallistic tendency. If the Agrarians were better tacticians, they could soon capture the Kaiser. Marschall is the obstacle in the way. Round him, however, the aristocracy, the court, and the most influential sections of the civil service pursue their sapping tactics. Even people so able as Leo Buch have gone quite mad over the Kanitz motion. The tone of the Conservatives in the Reichstag is becoming more and more bitter. In the Casino, Mirbach-Sorquitten preaches every evening to a little circle of microcephalics. I hear from well-informed sources that the Socialists are now likely to gain still more adherents from the lower ranks of the civil service, postal clerks, policemen, and office servants. It is hoped, though, that they will gradually transform themselves into a radical Left party. In their own way the Socialist members even now are a support to the Government on many questions. In many quarters the keenness and zeal of these deputies is made the occasion for not very flattering comparisons with the Conservatives. What do you think of Bill Bismarck's appointment as Oberpräsident in Königsberg? I had a talk with him; he seems very pleased about it. The public is very favourably impressed thereby. As I hear on excellent authority, the ex-minister Botho Eulenburg refused the appointment, as well as August Dönhoff. Köller did not make a very favourable impression on me and Bötticher seems to have sadly deteriorated. In the Foreign Ministry they are not satisfied with Schenck and are going to replace him by Heyking, who is too smart for Cairo. To Buenos Aires a new man will go by the name of Müller-Raschdau. If I get free of this place, may I burden your good lady with the request to get some silk for me; her taste is as renowned as her kindness, which is the reason why I rush my request in in good time. Of your brothers I saw only the Uhlan, Karl Ulrich, in Berlin. I played skat with him one evening. He impressed me as a thoroughly good and able fellow. Long live the *gens Bülow!* With that prayer and with warmest greetings and complete devotion to your wife I close this Italian salad which I had to compound as best I could amid constant interruption. Your devoted Monts."

On the impressions he got on a second short visit to Berlin, Monts wrote me on March 27, 1896: "H. M. greeted me rather perfunctorily. The Chancellor, on the other hand, had a long and exhaustive discussion with me. He is still the same as ever, clear, calm, unexcitable. Only he complains a little about the Emperor and the burden of business. In the Foreign Ministry Holstein is acknowledged master. His powers of work are simply marvellous. Unfortunately his nervousness and his sensitiveness are increasing. His relations with Alexander Hohenlohe, the next most influential person, are regular again, but the latter seems to be creating enemies for himself, and so for his father, by his rather nonchalant methods and his too obvious contempt for the mandarins. Mumm (extra dry)[1] floated on the Nile. Pourtalès is a little too devoted to dinners and his own greatness. Klehmet is active on his feet but is mediocre at the best. Rotenhan seems to be showing signs of

[1] Mumm is also the name of a German brand of champagne.

independence. But nobody takes them seriously. Meanwhile he counts the days of old Otto Bülow and makes a mess of Vatican matters. Marschall is much elated by his success in Parliament. How he stands now with Holstein, I 'm sorry I can't tell you. The small favour shown him by the Imperator oppresses Holstein a good deal. So much for the Foreign Ministry. My impressions elsewhere were much less favourable. Society shows signs of decomposition : the manifold indiscretions of the Kaiser are bearing fruit. Outside his Court retinue and military courtiers he has no true friends, and these are just what you would expect. Through his unfair treatment of the little Princes the Emperor has now lost the last vestiges of sympathy amongst the higher aristocracy. The Agrarian minor aristocracy, already deeply embittered on its own account, is still more angered by his occasional social tactlessness. The world of Jewish bankers and financiers is much hurt by the activities of reactionaries, the hypocrites. The official class cannot flourish if men like Bötticher are not dropped and if open opposition to the regulations of the Ministry finds secret but powerful support from every conceivable person of importance among the reactionaries of Berlin. And yet there are among the Berlin bureaucrats just as excellent men as ever there were whose wings are clipped simply by their superiors and by the parliamentary system. Finally the feeling in military circles is n't good. In the Guards they think they are being simply made toys of. Everywhere, too, doubt is growing about the capabilities of the high command. The officers' corps as a rule lives above its means. The poison of Socialism is corroding the ranks of the common soldiery more and more. I need n't say anything about the wretchedness of Parliament. I often meet old friends of the Conservative party and am horrified at the views they hold, even the ablest of them, Leo Buch, Heydebrand, and the like. Here too there is openly expressed dislike of H. M. I also saw Engelbrecht, who used to be your military attaché. He seems out of humour and resigned, hopes for a brigade, and then for speedy retirement on a higher pension. The lesson to be drawn from all these unpleasantnesses — from which we must deduct Hohenlohe's not to be underestimated policy of pacification at home — is that we must *meo voto* go carefully.   So long as Hohenlohe and Holstein hold the helm of foreign policy firmly in their hands, despite occasional intervention by the Kaiser, we shall get along all right.   But what is to follow?   As far as home politics are concerned, the court and the generals talk of a *coup d'état*.   If you say, ' Well, that will be the end of the Empire', then you are answered : ' All the better, for then we shall have a Great Prussia again with thirty-five to forty million inhabitants instead of an Empire with ten to twenty million unreliable inhabitants in it.'   Thank God H. M. feels entirely German and Imperial.   He is also firmly opposed to the imbecility of bi-metallism, the Kanitz motion, and that sort of thing.   I saw in Berlin Phil Eulenburg, but he was, alas, worn out and miserable.   I met him again last Sunday and thank Heaven found him looking much fresher and more cheerful.   Always your devoted Anton Monts."

CHAPTER III

*More Letters from Count Monts on the Injury Done to the Imperial Idea
and the Authority of the Imperial Crown by the Latest Eccentric Speeches
of William II to the Provincial Diet of Brandenburg on March 22, 1897 —
Monts' Personal Impressions Gleaned during a Visit to Berlin — Monts'
Account Confirms the Anxious Fears which have Tortured Bülow since the
Dismissal of Prince Bismarck — How the International and the National
Situation Appeared to Him on Taking over the Work of the Foreign Office
— Return to Berlin — Changes of Personnel — Letter of Baron von Mar-
schall (July 4, 1897).*

I HAVE related how deeply the personality of William II, his lively
and original mind, his amiability and kindness to me on the few
occasions on which I had come into official contact with him, had
impressed me. These occasions had, however, all been of the formal
official kind. Now things were different; now it was my lot to be
near the Kaiser in the routine of daily political work, to protect him
from hasty decisions, to guide him step by step on the way of continuity of policy. How great the difficulty would be with a ruler unusually gifted, but becoming more and more self-willed and, on occasion,
quite uncontrollable, I realised from a further letter of Monts about
the extremely unfortunate speech which William II delivered on
March 22, 1897, at an official dinner of the Provincial Diet of Brandenburg, a speech that exceeded all the earlier oratorical efforts of
his Majesty in sheer tactlessness. After a bombastic eulogy of his
grandfather, who was referred to with as much reverence as though
he had lived in the Middle Ages and as though in these pious days
pilgrimages had been made to honour his mortal remains, William II
declared that eminent counsellors had, by God's gracious providence,
stood by his grandfather. Theirs had been the honour of executing
the ideas of that great man, that noble king, their sovereign Lord.
And yet compared with himself these counsellors of his were but
pygmies, mere agents of an all-powerful dominating will. At the
end of his speech, William II called his audience to fight against the

revolution "by every means", for now it did not shrink from "the sacred person of the All-Highest himself." Anyone who read or heard this speech must have been greatly astonished, seeing that the monarch who made such an appeal to his Brandenburgers was the same monarch who a few years before had dismissed the strongest opponent of revolutionary movements, Prince Bismarck.

On the impression which the speech made in Munich Monts on March 2, 1897, wrote me the following pertinent letter: "The fears I expressed of late about an Imperial centenary speech have been realised in a way I could hardly have anticipated. Our enemies here scarcely find it necessary to conceal their great joy and give a hypocritical shrug of the shoulders over the exalted orator who is clearly no longer a responsible person. The people with really national sentiments are like a lot of scared hens. The average cultured South German politician, even the clerical, is furious over the falsification of history so beloved by H. M. and the characterisation of Moltke and Bismarck as mere agents of the ruler. It is also generally felt that the attack on the Socialists was very tactless. As to the canonisation — what a conception for a Protestant ruler! — the particularist clerical Munich paper, *Vaterland*, remarks that it would be an excellent thing if the bones of all the German Emperors were worthy of being the goal of pilgrims. What are we coming to? The little plot of ground still unsubmerged on which the representative of the Empire in Bavaria stands is getting steadily smaller. A flood like the Brandenburg speech will swamp it altogether. Meantime the trump-card of the late and honoured Emperor which we had in our hand has been thrown under the table, for here a William the Great is simply not accepted. Forgive me if to your many anxieties over the powder magazine of Crete I add this as *hors d'œuvre*."

On June 4, 1897, Monts wrote me: "Your excellent and very shrewd brother Alfred — I should like to be very emphatic on this that Alfred is and will be one of our best people — will have reported my idea of the situation to you. To-day I shall only recall in relation to the internal political situation in Germany a *mot* of the late Count Eugene Kinsky. He was once asked what the Vienna government would do at a critical moment, and answered, 'How do I know what's the stupidest thing to do?' You don't live in Germany. In spite of your farsightedness and your many relations you can't really have a quite exact picture of what is going on in people's minds, especially here in the south. The one consoling thing is that, in spite of everything, the material arguments for unity are so strong that no one wants to be disunited. But that is the only good thing about the situation. The most important thing is that the Kaiser has raised the personal dislike of himself to a really serious pitch, so serious indeed, that the House of Wittelsbach is pleading extenuating circumstances in a manner you would hardly have expected of it. The speeches and attitude of Prince Louis in that sense are very typical. He brings out the feeling of solidarity that unites the German princes and the conviction that, if there is a crash in Berlin, then down inevitably come the monarchist card castles here in Munich as well as in Stuttgart and Greiz. Besides, people here are fully informed on the Emperor's mental condition. I hardly think that it is in such serious case as the pessimists declare, but it is my impression, even from my latest observation, that delay is dangerous." On his visit to Berlin Monts at a private interview found the Kaiser amiable and so far reasonable:

"Then several other people came. The Emperor boasted, was obscure and unpleasant: besides his fixed ideas emerged persecution by Bismarck, excessive praise of the old William, and the like. Here, whatever people may say, is the rub. I gather, and you can't imagine what you can hear in Berlin, from doctors' hints that the Emperor can still be cured, but that every day's delay makes the chances of cure more unlikely. One shouldn't talk to Phil about these things. He's too much the man of feeling to be exposed to such ideas. Besides, he believes against all the evidence, though, as I think, in all good faith, that there isn't a word of truth in all the rumours. My one hope now is in the Emperor himself. If only he would get a glimpse of the truth, realise the position he is in, and see to what he has brought his fatherland. If he were surrounded with decent people, the psychological moment would, given H. M.'s high intelligence and his many calm and lucid intervals, have arrived long ago. But there is too much ambition, too many bedazzled people, and good impulses get stifled on the spot. The chasing from place to place, from banquet to banquet, the intercourse with Tom, Dick, and Harry leave no time for self-examination. None the less my conviction is that a year of peaceful life in the country with only the most necessary functions and duties would restore his mental balance. But if H. M. won't consent to that, I foresee a hand-to-mouth policy of force and *coups d'état* which will undoubtedly recoil on their originator and finish with the end of Kaiser William II. Meanwhile much both in home and foreign policy will be irretrievably lost. Caprivi and his adjutant Ebmeyer were unable to swim against the current. The nation, which is as easy as a child to lead, easier than any other nation, won't stand the leading strings of the absolute monarch, the aristocrat, and the priest. The German demands the peaceful enjoyment of civil liberty; then he is quite content to have a strong monarchical power ruling him. The internal situation would be so favourable. The Social Democrat is becoming a radical Philistine; his leaders are just as disunited as the coryphees of the Centre; the covetousness of the Conservative Agrarians is exceeded only by their stupidity. One could *peu à peu* achieve a policy of *divide et impera*, and gain the people without any concessions at all, and yet one constantly does just the opposite of what would gain one's ends. Think of that Associations Law! How the aged Hohenlohe ever consented to it is quite obscure to me, for I have been without news for some time. And then the blockhead, the warrior who stands deep under the level of Köller! His behaviour was deplorable. I could sing you yet another pretty song about the Chancellor's second 'promise' — the criminal proceedings business. The worst of it all is that the standpoint of the so-called Berlin government always changes after a sudden blaze-up. Twice Bavaria has been conceded her own Court of Appeal; twice the concession has been taken back. The patriot verily must veil his head. The man of vision sees the abyss to which we are hurrying but can't alter things a whit. Holstein thinks the same. Meantime the opinion is held within Germany by many, and in view of the incursions of the Kaiser into foreign policy, that the successors of the great Chancellor in his own particular department, the Wilhelmstrasse, are doing their jobs nobly. I can say so without the slightest hesitation. Only this explains that the general disillusionment over the Associations Law, which, in spite of the Landratskammer, was widely felt among the Conservatives, did not find vent in invectives against the aged Chancellor. Everywhere, at least by the 'Kreuzzeitung' and its wretched agrarians, Hohenlohe was treated with indulgence. Equally from no side except from the usual intriguers was the fulfilment of the second promise demanded. Thus I think we can hope that the Hohenlohe Chancellorship will last three years. But then what? Alfred will tell you what ill will H. M. bears to Marschall, and how Alfred and I urgently impressed on Phil that he should protest against it. Phil agreed with us and freely recognised that at present Marschall is indispensable. If Marschall goes, then Holstein goes, perhaps also Hohenlohe, who very rightly complains that he has sacrificed Bronsart without doing Marschall any good. All we can say is: *utinam dii immortales hanc rem bene vertant.* I hope I shall see you this summer. God guard you. My respects to your dear, good lady. Always your devoted Anton Monts."

Monts' reports on the situation gave me a picture of the state of things in Germany which if not always just in many details, and particularly in its judgments, was founded on acute observation. In view of the task in front of me it was not a very encouraging picture. But the worst thing of all was: Monts' accounts agreed in the main with what, coming as it did from very different standpoints but agreeing in its conclusions, had been said or written to me by Herbert Bismarck and Phil Eulenburg. What I heard from them of the rapidly declining prestige of the Kaiser and therewith, alas, the prestige of the Throne, of the badly shaken authority of the government, the general unsettlement and discontent in Germany, justified only too well those anxieties and fears which had been aroused in me by the dismissal of Prince Bismarck, a dismissal carried out in the most disrespectful, brutal, and clumsy way, a dismissal against which I had, in my letter of March 2, 1890, from Bucharest, warned

Phil Eulenburg in vain. "I see the future in dark colours," Bismarck had said to Frau von Spitzemberg as early as 1891. Frau von Spitzemberg, who was the wife of the Württemberg ambassador in Berlin and had long been intimate with Bismarck and his wife, told me this herself. The really terribly dangerous trait in the Kaiser's character was his constant readiness to yield to any passing influence and his reluctance to submit to any permanent one, and to do everything on impulse so that there was no continuity. In addition to this he had no sense of fitness and no insight. He neither respected nor considered the rights of others and always overshot his mark. So said Prince Bismarck to Frau Hildegard von Spitzemberg a year after his retirement.

My meditations and reflections had to be principally devoted to foreign policy, the conduct of which I was to take over. The burden I inherited from Marschall was neither pleasant nor light. Russia, highly offended at our refusal to renew the Bismarckian Re-insurance Treaty, had thrown herself into the arms of France. England had been deeply wounded by the Kruger telegram; Japan by the Far Eastern triple alliance made by Holstein. Although the English government and the leading Japanese statesmen felt these things less than did the broad masses of the English people and the Japanese intellectuals, France had not been reconciled by the occasional tactless advances of the Kaiser, while the alliance with Russia had powerfully raised France's self-esteem and therewith the hope of the great reckoning — *la grande revanche.* While the Froschnitz brook murmured nearby, I surveyed the international chess board as it lay before me. I soon recognised that the decisive point for us lay on the Neva. Long ago Frederick the Great had written in his last testament: "Of all Prussia's neighbours, the Russian Empire is the most dangerous in its strength as well as in its position. The rulers of Prussia in my opinion have sufficient reason to keep friendly with these barbarians." The great king during the Seven Years' War was saved only by a change of rulers in St. Petersburg at a critical moment. Our revival and salvation after Jena was made possible by the fact that Frederick William III, Queen Louise, and Prince Hardenberg had not been deluded by the sad drama of Tilsit into breaking the bonds which united Potsdam and St. Petersburg. In the last years of the reign of Frederick William III and especially under Frederick William IV, whose nervousness and weakness was overimpressed by the crude strength of the Tsar Nicholas and whose febrile imagination the brutal realism of the Tsar too greatly influenced, we were in what was often an unworthy dependence on our eastern neighbour. But Bismarck had all the indifference of true genius in the face of mere emotion and especially where the Polish question was concerned; he assured us of Russia from the day he came into power and so was able to free the Elbe duchies in 1864, expel Austria from Germany, and assure the Prussian hegemony in North Germany in 1866, and in 1870–71 create Kaiser and Empire.

Only once in the field of Russo-German relations did he make a mistake, a big one. Who is infallible? Who is always successful? At the Congress of Berlin in 1878, Bismarck dealt severely with the Russian chancellor Gortschakov, whose vanity and affected French manner he abominated, and who in 1875 had annoyed him, with the result that he drove the Russian statesman to resume his campaign of stirring up the Emperor Alexander II and the Russian intelligentsia against Germany. In 1879, under the mistaken impression that at Alexandrovo the Tsar had tried to put the Emperor William against his great minister, Bismarck completed his volteface to an Austrian alliance *ab irato* and therefore too hastily and violently. But after the mistakes had been committed the Prince used every resource of his inventive and supple intelligence to heal the breach with Russia. In this he found complete comprehension and support on the part of his aged master, who, on his death bed, whispered to his grandson and successor: "Keep on good terms with Russia: we have profited greatly thereby." These words contained not only decades of experience; but the whole history of Prussia.

Nevertheless Kaiser William II allowed himself to be led by Caprivi, Marschall, and — last but not least — Holstein to denounce the Re-insurance Treaty with Russia, although, after the dismissal of Bismarck, he had personally declared to the Russian ambassador Schuvaloff that the Treaty would be maintained by us. The denunciation was made in a wounding and unskilful manner.

It had, as Bismarck had foreseen and prophesied, automatically produced the Franco-Russian alliance, which had meantime passed much too deeply *in succum et sanguinem* of the two allies to allow any thought of exploding it. The great majority of the French feared war, but Alsace and Lorraine, Metz and Strassburg were not forgotten. Only a few enlightened minds in France dreamed the fair dream of a general reconciliation of the nations and of universal peace by that means. *"Qui dit alliance russe dit revanche,"* said in the eighties of last century a deputy who feared war to the leader of the League of Patriots, Paul Deroulède. The latter answered, pacifying his anxious interlocutor: *"Qui dit alliance russe, dit sécurité de la France."* The vast majority of the French people saw in the alliance with Russia, if not the one invincible guarantee, at least a very powerful guarantee, against a German attack. In Russia likewise there was no thought of an abandonment of the alliance and severance from France. No Russian government could dare, especially under a weak ruler like Nicholas II, to break the alliance with France. All that we could do, therefore, was to recognise the fact of the alliance and, in spite of it, maintain with Russia such an understanding as would protect us from a conflict with that Power. That was a question of diplomatic skill. "That in the west the pot may boil over is certainly possible, but I do not think that we need fear attack from the east, if our diplomacy is as skilful as it could be." So on July 10, 1892, had said the grand old man in the Saxon forests to a deputation of Württemberg admirers whom he greeted with the words from Schiller's *"Glocke"*: "Let peace be the first message of the bells."

The maintenance of peaceful and friendly relations with Russia was possible only by careful vigilance over those points where we had to stand in irrevocable opposition to Russia. We had to make it quite clear to Russia that we neither could nor would sacrifice Austria-Hungary. But Russia must also be given the feeling that in the Austro-German alliance the leadership lay with Germany, and that German policy desired and would honourably strive for a good understanding with Russia on the lines laid down by Frederick and Bismarck. *In specie* Russia must be made aware that, in spite of our economic interests in Turkey, we would not stand in the way of Russia in the Dardanelles question. This was Russia's most sensitive point and we must offer no opposition there : that we could quietly leave opposition to others. The opening of the Dardanelles to Russian warships was quite reconcilable with the maintenance of Turkey ; the appearance of the Russian fleet in the Mediterranean might be unpleasant for France, Italy, and England, but it left us quite indifferent. Further, we must convince Russia not merely by words but by deeds that we were aware of our community of interests with her in the Polish question and had no intention of playing the Polish card against her. A French historian, Albert Vandal, who had made the Russo-German and the Franco-Russian relations his special study, coined the phrase that the partition of Poland has been " *le berceau sanglant* " of the Prusso-Russian friendship. Finally, we must make it clear in the most suitable way in St. Petersburg how many common dynastic interests united both governments and empires against the dangers of revolution. For it was clear to anyone with vision, that however a conflict between the two northern nations might end, it was the dynasties that would pay for it.

Our relations with England were also of supreme importance to us. Unlike Russia, England could not assail the German oak at its roots, but it could lop off many a noble branch and destroy much beautiful foliage. It could deprive us of our colonies, destroy our shipping and our commerce, and so cause us loss running into thousands of millions. I was always convinced that so long as we maintained friendly relations with Russia, England would not attack us. But I never had the least doubt that if we came to loggerheads with Russia, English policy, which, with almost infallible instinct, does the right thing for England, would not, in the case of Russo-German conflict, lose the opportunity to destroy the strongest power on the Continent and so the traditional foe of England, but also and more especially her most serious rival in shipping and trade. In the summer of 1897, great English newspapers had attacked Germany, and these attacks could not be dismissed as passing opinions and as mere newspaper excitement, for they clearly expressed that

English selfishness and unfailing policy of realism which, in the final instance, has always characterised and determined English foreign policy. When in the eighties German industry expanded to a degree far greater than the English monopolists liked, the average Englishman showed his uneasiness. The Kruger telegram of January 3, 1896, tore down the veil of friendliness which had for so long concealed what were in reality the not very cordial relations between the two Germanic cousins. When I was called upon to assume the direction of foreign affairs, the situation as between the German and English nations was quite clear. The immediate but terribly difficult task which lay before us was to build up to such naval strength that an attack on us would be a serious risk for the attacker. We must build up our sorely needed defences against England to protect those thousands of millions which we had entrusted to the seas. But at the same time we must build so as not to attract attention.

Our connection with Italy had lost much of its glamour to the eyes of the Italians as far back as 1897. When Bismarck and, after him, Caprivi and Holstein had coldly refused to accede to the wishes of Crispi to come to a real reckoning with France, who was then so hated by Italy, the Italians generally recognised that, in the eyes of the Germans, the Triple Alliance was a partnership for insurance and not one for profit-making, and that they would have to adjourn their plans for expansion in the north of the peninsula and on the coasts of the Adriatic as well as in the west and on the north coast of Africa. From the unfortunate end of the expedition to Abyssinia and the painful consequences of the commercial war which Crispi began with France, many Italians had drawn the further lesson that to be on bad terms with the great Latin sister would be of evil consequence to Italy. The Italian is a realist in politics. Generally speaking, the Italian together with the English nation is politically the best endowed in Europe, whether one thinks of the monsignori who operate through the international hierarchic apparatus of the Catholic Church in the oldest and noblest palace in the world, the Vatican, or of the ministers who on the Tiber guide the foreign policy of the Kingdom of Italy. We should have to handle Italy cautiously, tactfully, and subtly and with very careful attention to these imponderabilia which are of great importance in a land in which great worth is ascribed to *gentilezza*.

Since the dismissal of Prince Bismarck our foreign position had been seriously injured with regard to Japan, whom we had gravely offended by Holstein's unlucky experiment of an Eastern Triple Alliance and still more perhaps by that most unfortunate picture of the Kaiser's to which he had given the title "Peoples of Europe! Defend your Holiest Possessions." No one understood how the holiest possessions of Europe could be threatened by the mild teachings of Buddha. But William II, with all the stubbornness that was his on occasion, was so full of this mad idea, the product of his own wayward perversity, that even the individual Japanese had become antipathetic to him. In spite of my representations and those of others, he treated Japanese diplomatists and soldiers discourteously, and compelled Ballin and Wiegand, the directors of the Hamburg-Amerika Line and of the Norddeutscher Lloyd, whom he treated with the greatest distinction, to carry that grotesque picture on all their ships sailing to the Far East, to the great joy of the English who, right to the last day of the Kaiser's reign, were to draw no insignificant profit from such an outrage on Japanese feeling.

Of my quiet survey of the world-situation the final conclusion was that the most valuable possession of the German people, an honourable peace, could surely be maintained, even if we built the fleet which we needed for our protection and for defensive purposes. That line we ought not to overstep by a hair's breadth, but we could only advance to it if our policy was conducted with steadfastness, with courage and determination, and also with caution, with tact and — last but not least — with cleverness.

Although the work of the Secretary of State for Foreign Affairs is as a rule confined to the field of foreign policy, I was none the less of the opinion that an intelligent and sound foreign policy could only be carried on if we rightly estimated our inner strength and kept in contact with the ideas and feelings of the nation. I therefore tried in these quiet weeks to get a clear idea of the situation at home. The uncomfortable and uneasy feeling which had prevailed in Germany since the dismissal of Prince Bismarck had received new life in the first half of the year 1897. At the banquet of the Provincial Diet of Brandenburg the Kaiser delivered the more than eccentric speech to which I have already alluded. In that speech the Kaiser had made other errors. He confused Sir Francis Drake with Balboa and the Pacific with the Atlantic. Such small slips he often made in the heat of his eloquence. But this time when the Imperial orator had finished, anxious aides-de-camp ran from chair to chair, asking the guests present not to mention the salient parts of the speech. This request was complied with by nearly all the guests present except one indiscreet gentleman, as it is asserted, a Radical deputy, who was pleased to spread abroad the most drastic of the Kaiser's utterances. The impression they universally made was deplorable. From many quarters came the complaint that if things went on in this way, the rich heritage that had fallen to Kaiser William II, the rich bequests in respect, credit, and popularity which had been conferred upon the young Emperor now on the throne, by a long series of Prussian kings, especially William I, would, within measurable time, be exhausted. In Conservative circles the Brandenburg speech was most sharply criticised. Adjutant General Karl von der Goltz, a man over eighty years of age, who had passed half a century in attendance on William I, gave me his verdict in the following words: "The Emperor wants to celebrate his grandfather and exalt him. If the old gentleman could come out of his grave and read the Brandenburg speech he would shake his finger at his grandson, and with that homely common sense of his, say, 'But, William, you 're cracked, man.'" The friends of the ruling Kaiser, many of them from conviction and with good intentions, others simply out of selfishness and with that tendency to sycophancy which from the beginning of the world has flourished at courts and which will probably be noticeable in cruder form around the men who have held power in the Republic since 1918, explained the speech of the Kaiser by the pain which he felt because his grandfather had been so completely put in the shade by his great counsellor. Perhaps in justifiable reaction to the underestimation of the grandfather he so respected and so passionately loved, the Kaiser had rather overshot the mark.   Only the Socialists got any advantage from the speech, and to some extent the Radicals, who did not let the chance slip of making capital from that latest extravagant oration.

The failure of his speech could not remain unknown to the Kaiser and he was so disillusioned thereby that, for the first time since his succession, he had a nervous breakdown and had to spend several days of rest and recuperation in his hunting box at Hubertusstock. He had expected his "powerful" speech to be a great success.   What actually happened, had happened neither to William I nor to his son : the speech of the Kaiser was made the subject of ridicule.   All Berlin laughed over the story of how in the Friedrichstrasse a Hungarian who, like many of his countrymen, used to mix up his articles, went to a policeman and meaning to say "Where is the Brandenburg gate?" actually asked, "Where is the Brandenburg fool?"[1] to which the honest policeman angrily replied : "If you make fun of His Majesty again I 'll run you in.   D' you get me?"   The special delivery office for such disparaging humour was Harden's *Zukunft*, which under William I would never have been able to get into society, much less find a crowd of readers.

Shortly before I was summoned to Kiel, the great English weekly, the *Saturday Review*, reviving the aggression and envy of Cato, flung down its *ceterum censeo Germaniam esse delendam*.   At the same time a Reichsgerichtsrat, Otto Mittelstädt, seeing the rising flood of the Socialist movement, published his *"Vor der Flut"*,[2] which was a cry of anguish and despair.   But above these threatening phenomena there stood before me, as a result of my impartial survey of the home and foreign situation and my final conclusion thereon, the necessity of maintaining our people in honourable peace within the Empire that Bismarck had called to life.   This, despite all the rocks and shallows in the way, seemed to me to be possible.   I remembered the beautiful words which my beloved Homer puts into the mouth of the brave Hector, when he calls to his charioteer Polydamas, who, in his terror over the bad omen of a flight of birds, beseeches him to leave the battlefield :

[1] A pun on the words "*das Tor*" (the gate) and "*der Tor*" (the fool).
[2] Before the flood.

I reck not of them, nor have I any care
Which way they fly, to right, into the daylight,
And the sun, or, passing left fly down
To evening's darkling shadows and into the night.

An omen indeed for the salvation of the Fatherland! I prayed to God that he would grant me strength and ability for my task, and at the end of July I returned to Germany.

During my absence Herr von Bötticher had been replaced by Count Posadowsky, until then Secretary of State for the Treasury; Miquel had succeeded Bötticher as vice president of the Prussian Ministry. Lieutenant-General von Podbielski had been appointed Secretary of State of Posts. Fourteen days later Prince Adolf of Schaumburg-Lippe resigned the regency over Detmold after the court, appointed under the presidency of King Albert of Saxony to determine the succession, had declared Count Ernst zu Lippe-Biesberfeld able to succeed! The Kaiser, who had, unfortunately, taken up a personal attitude in the Lippe question from the very first, sent his brother-in-law, on his departure, and his sister Victoria a telegram in which he passionately and far too emphatically declared that Detmold would never have better rulers than the princely couple who now had, alas, to leave that country. This pronouncement, which politically was quite out of place, roused astonishment and annoyance in the German courts and even in wider circles. In their opinion to the whole manner in which the Kaiser had treated the Detmold question, the French expression could be applied, *tant de bruit pour une omelette.*

Mindful of an old verse in the guest-book of the Bülow family, that he who comes of a noble house or possesses wealth and riches is not necessarily a nobleman, but that virtue and courtesy make a man noble, I wrote a few amiable words from Kiel to my predecessor, Herr von Marschall. He knew only too well that, like anyone else who has spent some years in office, he had made many enemies. He knew above all that he had lost the Kaiser's favour and that the All-Highest disfavour was the signal for the many rats among his former colleagues and underlings to leave the sinking ship. I wanted to soften this departure from a high position and at the same time reassure him as to the future. I received an answer which is not only interesting by reason of its defence of his policy and attitude during the seven years in which he held office as Foreign Secretary, but also by reason of its warm and genuinely friendly tone towards myself. To this tone Baron von Marschall held firmly all the years I was Secretary of State and Imperial Chancellor. I confess to my simplicity, for then I did not have the experience and the knowledge of men which fate has given me since, the fate that Goethe calls a wonderful but expensive teacher. I really believed that Herr von Marschall was grateful to me for having against opposition got him a fine embassy and so a field for new and profitable activity, although even if not in the first rank of those responsible, he still bore a good share of the responsibility for the denunciation of the Re-insurance Treaty with Russia and for the Kruger telegram. In later years I was even able to persuade the Kaiser to grant him the Order of the Black Eagle, which this one-time "traitor" wore with proud joy. Alas, I must add that his friendship for me lasted only until the day when I retired from office.

" For the spirit of men upon the earth is even such as the day which the father of gods and men brings upon them."

So, three thousand years ago, the wanderer Odysseus said to wise Amphinomos. I append the letter which Baron von Marschall sent me :

Dear Friend,

Please accept my warmest thanks for your friendly letter. No one can appreciate better than I do how hard it must have been for you to decide to accept that difficult post which the confidence of his Majesty assigned you, but I must add how genuinely glad I am from the point of view of the general interest to be able to greet you as my immediate successor. You will remember that I prophesied at our last meeting in autumn two years ago, that things would turn out like this and indeed in the interest of the Kaiser and of the Empire it had to turn out this way though I then had doubts whether the intermediate stage of the Secretary-ship might not be spared you.

In your new office much will undoubtedly be easier for you than for me. You bring to your task a knowledge of foreign politics which I could possess only in a general and really in an incomplete manner.   For home politics you enjoy the incomparable advantage that you have never been identified with any side in the fierce war of parties.   Through a peculiar chain of circumstance I not only appeared in the foreground in these questions which to-day rouse the fiercest passions, namely, questions of economic policy, but I generally found myself in a position which forced me to fight my parliamentary battles with front reversed against the Right to which I once belonged as a party member, and amid the applause of the Left whose political principles I have fought from the first day I was capable of political thought.   You too, and in the very near future, will have to take up a position against Agrarian desires and demands, but that won't unchain the storm against you, as against me, the author of the hated commercial treaty policy.   And I am convinced that under you the only healthy system will be restored, that is, that the parliamentary defence of economic policy will be entrusted permanently to the Secretaries for Home Affairs and for the Treasury, while the Foreign Secretary will retain a decisive voice in all matters that concern international relations, but will not concern himself publicly with commercial policy and programmes, that is to say, he will not need to intervene in the party strife.

For your friendly wishes about my health I am deeply grateful.   I confidently expect that within a few weeks I shall be so much better that my services can again be made use of, if there is any desire to do so. My own wishes go no further than to be able to serve the Kaiser and the Empire for a few more years in whatever post is assigned to me.

As I am sure you would like me to get out of the official residence and let the necessary alterations and improvements be done, I shall come to Berlin about the end of August and do what is needed.

With the request that you remember me most kindly to your wife, I remain with friendly respects, yours very sincerely

                                                                Marschall

Neuershausen, Station Hugstetten in Baden,
July 4, 1897.

CHAPTER IV

WHEN I got to Berlin in the beginning of August, I sought out Prince Hohenlohe, the Finance Minister von Miquel, and Herr von Kiderlen, who had hitherto been detailed to accompany the Emperor when he travelled. Prince Hohenlohe told me that, as the sea voyage was too unpleasant for him, he would go by land to Peterhof : besides he wanted to spend some time in Vilna and Verki. He advised me to accompany the Kaiser on board the *Hohenzollern*. I asked Kiderlen if he was going with the Kaiser to St. Petersburg and he said he was not. I urged him to do so : *Qui va à la chasse perd sa place.* If he would come, I would promise to restore his good relations with the Kaiser which had been unsatisfactory for some time. I still had the charm of a novelty for the Kaiser and I would work a reconciliation. Kiderlen, however, held to his refusal and said to me in his rough way : "If your Excellency had had to put up with the unpleasantnesses of these trips for as many years as I have, the whole thing would stick in your gorge as much as it does in mine." I found the Finance Minister worried over a telegram which he had received some minutes before from his Majesty from Kiel. There had been serious floods in Silesia, Saxony, and the Lausitz, and unfortunately over a hundred persons had lost their lives. Thereupon the Kaiser had sent a telegram to Miquel in which, by a bold association of ideas, his Majesty saw some connection between that serious catastrophe which Heaven had ordained we should suffer, and the opposition of the Reichstag to his Majesty's naval policy. Miquel regained his calm over this revelation of the All-Highest's ideas which had at first stupefied him, when, out of my ampler knowledge of the Kaiser, I pointed out how, when the latter was so full of a thing as he was of the Navy Bill, he would snatch at any argument which might help to realise his ambitions — a process greatly helped by our Imperial Master's much too ready imaginative bent. Thus, when on July 30, 1897, the English government announced the denunciation of the Commercial Treaty of May 30, 1865, and at the same time suggested a most-favoured-nation treaty which would merely regulate Anglo-German relations to the exclusion of the English colonies, the Kaiser saw in this step a direct threat to vital German interests, which could be balanced only by speeding up the creation of a German fleet, and sent off excited telegrams in that sense to the Imperial Chancellor and the Prussian Minister of Finance. The telegram which he sent *en clair* to the aged Prince Hohenlohe, which was to scare him out of his well-earned summer holiday at Alt-Aussee, ran : "From the depths of my heart I deplore this sudden denunciation of the commercial treaty, which implies a heavy blow to our poor folk so sore afflicted by the flood disaster. This unqualified step is equivalent to the beginning of a war to the knife against our just-developing production. The nation will now know what valuable time has been lost in these last ten years in spite of my warnings. If the Socialists had not for years fought against naval construction with the utmost bitterness and in their incomprehensible infatuation defeated it, we would not now be practically defenceless at sea and exposed to attacks on our commerce. If we had had a strong fleet that commanded respect, the denunciation would not have happened. As answer thereto we must now see to a rapid and substantial increase in the building of new ships."

Before I left Semmering I received from Palermo the following telegram from Francesco Crispi, to whom I had written expressing my regret that it had not been possible for me to take a personal farewell of him : "I thank you for your good wishes. I recall with the greatest pleasure that during your period of duty in Italy, we have been in agreement on everything that concerned the well-being of our countries and the peace of Europe."

On August 3, 1897, I again reported to the Kaiser at Kiel. The Kaiser asked in that frank, winning manner of his, which he always

IMPERIAL CHANCELLOR PRINCE CHLODWIG ZU
HOHENLOHE-SCHILLINGSFÜRST

had when he was in good form and so long as the person with him was sympathetic, "Now, what about my ships? What did you devise in the hills of Austria?" I knew that William II disliked lectures and, particularly, long lectures. To save the conversation from a premature end I answered his Majesty that to deal with this matter would require a talk of an hour or two. The Kaiser sighed and indicated that we could have that conference while taking a walk. From his mother William II had inherited a wholesome and healthy passion for fresh air. In the first years of his reign he had sorely taxed the strength of all the dignitaries of his grandfather's time by receiving their reports during a quick walk or on a heaving ship. But I was hardened to physical exertion and welcomed the suggestion of "a good walk." The Kaiser went ashore with me and cut right across country. He was at that time the picture of health and vigour, not so stately as his father, not so awesome as his grandfather, but full of life and enterprise, a very attractive figure. Here and there on our wanderings, mostly over sandhills and along the Holstein hedges, we met workmen and labourers. I noticed, and it pleased me, how indifferent and unconcerned the Kaiser appeared at the possibility of an attempt on his life when there were neither police nor detectives nearby and when no measures of any kind had been taken for his protection. Critical observers and judges of his Majesty, of whom there was no lack in his entourage, declare that this was just the foolhardiness of ignorance. The Kaiser had no fear of anything which he could not see before him; but if danger suddenly did appear, the impression it made was all the stronger. That judgment, I hold, is entirely wrong. There is no doubt at all that the Kaiser did possess physical courage. The fact that with only one useful arm he was used to getting on horseback, riding recklessly, and even taking hedges and ditches shows his fearlessness. When some years later a growth showed itself in his throat that might have terrified any man who remembered that his father had died of cancer, William II never lost his nerve. After great mental disillusionments he had nervous breakdowns, as he had when he saw himself confronted with some great political peril, or believed something had happened to tear him from the paradise of his imagination. He was no fool, but he often lived in "a fool's paradise." I often feared for his mental balance, and one of the chief reasons, though not the most important of all, for my steady maintenance of a policy of peace for Germany was the conviction that unlike his father and his grandfather, and still more unlike the Great Frederick, William II was not mentally equipped to stand the heavy test of the vicissitudes and ordeals of a great war. I am convinced that the Kaiser realised this himself and that that was one of the reasons why he undoubtedly hoped that he would be spared the test of a great war.

As we continued our walk the Kaiser again asked me, "What about my ships?" I therefore explained to him the main lines of my opinion on that subject. I said that there was not the least doubt that we must protect the wealth, amounting to thousands of millions, which we had little by little entrusted to the high seas, our merchant fleet, our commerce, our rapidly increasing industry. The industrialisation of Germany had proceeded with an energy to which there was no parallel save in the United States. Even at the end of the 'seventies German agriculture had supported as many people as industry and trade put together. When Prince Bismarck retired, agriculture employed rather more than one million persons less than industry alone. It would always be one of the extraordinary things of history that the statesman who as no other had been a product of the German countryside, the squire of Schönhausen, and the dyke reeve of the district of Jerichow, the man of whom his wife could say, long after he had become Imperial Chancellor, that a cabbage interested him more than all his policies, the man who at the end of his life cared about every detail of estate management, that it was this man who more than any other had been the instrument of German industrialisation. As the proverb has it : " What he weaves no weaver knows." Prince Bismarck had not *ex post* failed to recognise the dangers of too extensive industrialisation and he had sought to balance it to the best of his ability by his strong action for the protection of agriculture. After his retirement Prince Bismarck had, and in my opinion rightly, blamed Caprivi for his dropping of the grain duties and equally was right, in my opinion, in his present demand for the increase in protective measures for agriculture. We could do nothing to alter the gigantic, perhaps excessive, present development of industry, commerce, and shipping. We must assuredly protect better than we had done these industries on which the welfare and life of millions of Germans depended. Was that possible without coming to blows with England? It would certainly not be easy, as the policy of England towards her economic competitors and especially her seafaring competitors in the past had clearly shown. The best assurance of success would be a quiet, careful, and, if I might use the expression, elastic policy on our side. "Now, that's your job," interrupted the Kaiser. I begged his Majesty not to doubt my good intentions. But that would not be sufficient: I must have his support. He clapped me on the shoulder and declared that I could count on his full support and his full confidence.

I hinted that it was not merely a question of my getting his active help, but also, and quite particularly, his "negative support." He ought to do nothing and to say as little as possible that might endanger peace at home and, in certain circumstances, peace abroad. "Aha!" laughed the Emperor, "now the curtain-lecture's starting. But go on with it." I quite frankly emphasised the very unfavourable impression which the Brandenburg speech had had even on absolutely loyal elements and pointed out that it was not very wise, and in any case that it was not necessary, on the occasion of the unveiling of the Emperor William memorial in Cologne on the anniversary of Waterloo, to shake in England's face the trident which ought to be in our hand. I was quite aware that we in Germany, as conditions were at present, could only proceed to build the fleet needed for our defence if the necessary national sentiment were aroused. Marschall and Bötticher had sought to attain that end by negotiations with the parties and party leaders, a work as productive as the labour of the Danäides — the labour of carrying water in a sieve. So far the Conservatives had no particular inclination for the creation of a fleet. The Centrists would agree to it but would demand a big *douceur* for their consent. We could be sure only of the National Liberals and a section of the Radicals, the "courtiers" under Rickert and Barth, but hardly of Eugen Richter, with his narrow and somewhat Philistine ideas. We could naturally reckon on the violent opposition of the Social Democrats under any circumstances. The parties, and especially their leaders, would only consent if we could arouse in the country a strong wave of feeling for the idea of a fleet. We would have to beat the national drum. "Agreed, agreed!" cried the Kaiser, pleased and delighted. I told him that the Navy League, professors and patriots of all shades, would do their duty. But it assuredly would not do to ruin our relations with England in any irreparable way. I was quite convinced that we could succeed in our aim of building a fleet sufficient for our needs, that is to say, for our security and for defensive objects, without getting into a war with England if we avoided all eccentricities, and did not thereby expose a flank for England to attack successfully by getting into hostility, or, worse, into serious conflict with Russia.

The Kaiser assured me in tones of complete sincerity that he wished nothing more earnestly than to restore that friendship with Russia which in the days of his grandfather and great-grandfather had united the two courts and the two countries. "And then the English would burst with envy." I answered that in politics one should never let oneself be guided by the desire to spite this country or that. We should not make advances to Russia merely in order to annoy England and *vice versa*. A calm, positive policy on both sides, without any attempt by either to outstrip or take advantage of the other, but equally without allowing the other to take precedence — that was how we would obtain the best results. I felt that I already must seem a little too much a mentor to the Kaiser, a mentor who plagued his Telemachus with hoary wisdom instead of handing him the fruits of the tree of life. "Our people must have aims set before them," he declared. "Unless we do this, and unless the people see that we are achieving something and that we are having our say, you will never stir up the right feeling. Bismarck, after all, acquired colonies too."

I admitted the justice of this argument. We might possibly gain something in Polynesia by diplomatic action. In the Far East, too, there lay open a wide and marvellously fruitful field for German enterprise. I had seen in the documents I had studied at Semmering that, the naval authorities were thinking, we must think of a number of bases on the potentially rich coasts of the Pacific. We would just have to wait for the right moment and take possession of them. The Far East, on the one hand, and Asia Minor, on the other, were lands from which we could not allow ourselves to be excluded. But we must walk warily.

My repeated reference to the need for caution, especially in what was said, annoyed the Kaiser, who had, besides, been put out by my disparagement of his Cologne trident-speech. I begged him not to think me timid; I hoped I would be able to show him that I was not that. But we could not forget the lessons of German history. The most tragic thing about German history was its lack of continuity. Very justly had Treitschke spoken of the absence of the sunshine in our history, of that German Imperial splendour of the Middle Ages which passed away like a midsummer night's dream. We, in Germany, looked back on no such steady, clear, uninterrupted development as they did in France, where in France's dark hour, Thiers, in February, 1871, in the National Assembly, could speak consolingly of the *"admirable unité de l'histoire de la France"* or as they did in England where, even to-day, the descendants of the statesmen who under Elizabeth and with William III had guided the policies of the country and were still ruling and where the men in power to-day carried on their tasks from the same standpoint and nearly by the same methods as their ancestors. When we regarded our often so unfortunate and contorted history, we must never forget the danger of a relapse. This, too, Prussian history taught us, with its brilliant periods of greatness which were often followed by periods of terrible decline. My former chief in St. Petersburg, General von Schweinitz, took personal charge of his eldest son's history lessons and devoted especial, meticulous care to the catastrophes of 1806 and 1848. Such lessons of our history warned us to be cautious.

Among the many good qualities of William II was the unusual quickness with which he comprehended an idea, to an extent, indeed, which I have seldom met. Where he had no preconceived notions to which, in certain circumstances, he would stick with the obstinacy he had inherited from his Guelph mother, and if there was no personal rancour to influence him, he was always open to sound argument. "Yes, a man should be capable of self-mastery," he declared with a sincerity that deeply moved me, it was so heartfelt. "He who prevails over himself, conquers! My wife had painted that saying in blue letters on parchment for me, she had it framed and placed it on my desk in Berlin. I will never forget our talk to-day. *Pro pace et imperatore.*" The Kaiser had little affection for the Latin authors, but he was very fond of expressing his thought in Latin tags: *Tamen, semper talis, nunquam retrorsum, pro rege et grege,* and the like.

Meantime we got back to where the *Hohenzollern* lay at anchor. Lunch was already waiting for the Kaiser on board. On the evening of August 4, she resumed the voyage to Peterhof. On this voyage the Kaiser was attended by the chiefs of his three Cabinets, Herr von Lucanus, General von Hahnke, and Admiral Baron von Senden, by the Chief-Marshal of the Court and the Imperial Household Count August zu Eulenburg, by the Commandant of Imperial Headquarters, General von Plessen, and by myself as Secretary of State for Foreign Affairs. Herr von Lucanus had been recommended to the Emperor while he was Crown Prince, as Counsellor to the Cabinet by Prince Bismarck himself, with the words, "He'll get you out of any mess."

His predecessor was Herr von Brandenstein, the scion of a noble and very conservative family, a Saxo-Borussian of Heidelberg, a corps comrade and friend of Leo Buch, who later led the Conservatives in the Upper Chamber with resolution and ability. Brandenstein was of the extreme Conservative wing, a fact of which he occasionally made public betrayal. Some time later he was to arouse the indignation of many good Philistines by a speech in the Diet in which he complained that in these modern days a "gentleman" might be placed in the awful position of having to share a second-class and even a first-class compartment with people who wore detachable cuffs! After his clashes with the Conservatives, which had begun at the end of the 'sixties and became much more serious in the first years of the 'seventies, Prince Bismarck had no love for the extreme Conservatives, although he himself had come from that wing and retained many of its ideas till the end of his life. When a certain Herr von Seydewitz was proposed as *Präsident* of Breslau in the Prince's later years of office, he wrote on the margin of the recommendation although Seydewitz was qualified for the position not only by being a Silesian, but by other recommendations: "No, he is one of the *Kreuzzeitung* gang and they put party views above reasons of state." To the great Chancellor Brandenstein did not appear at all a suitable counsellor for the future Kaiser. Consequently that able man was removed from the presence of the Crown Prince and sent as *Regierungspräsident* to Hannover. In consideration of his industry, his knowledge of affairs, and his uprightness of character I endeavoured, later on, to make his activities useful to the Prussian State. I had him in my eye for *Oberpräsident* of Königsberg, perhaps with an interim appointment as *Regierungspräsident* in Düsseldorf, but could not persuade the Kaiser to agree.

When I suggested Brandenstein for Düsseldorf, the Kaiser declared, with a smile: "That won't do at all. Brandenstein's too fond of tippling and there's too much good Rhine wine in Düsseldorf. When he got there he'd get drunk and fall into the Rhine and I would be blamed as well as my *Regierungspräsident*." Nor would the Kaiser hear of his going to Königsberg. "That won't suit at all; the grog's too good there." Whence these misgivings? Years before the Kaiser had attended a celebration of his 13th Regiment of Uhlans, the King's Uhlans. During the dinner, as sometimes happens, there was a sudden silence after a general and lively conversation, or, as is sometimes said: "an angel is passing through the room." At that moment one of the diners was heard to speak in an unusually loud voice. The Kaiser asked his neighbour, Field Marshal Count Alfred Waldersee, who had commanded the 13th Uhlans after the Franco-German war, who was shouting so

loudly. Waldesee did not like Brandenstein, whom the extremely
religious Countess Waldersee, otherwise a distinguished lady,
American born and with Puritanical ideas, considered fast. "That's
Brandenstein," Waldersee replied to his Majesty, "he's drunk
again already." All who have to live near a man of power, whether
the latter is a monarch or the head of a republic, a minister or an
influential Parliamentarian, should take warning from this instance,
and carefully avoid depreciatory remarks about those who stand
outside their circle. Expressions of praise or appreciation seldom
find much echo : disparaging, spiteful, and mocking words, on the
contrary, have a long life.

> Men's evil manners live in brass; their virtues
> We write in water,

says Queen Katherine's marshal Griffith to his hapless queen in
Shakespeare's "Henry VIII."

But taken all in all for so important a position Herr von Lucanus
was undoubtedly the more suitable of the two. The Centrists did
not like him because they could never forget that during the *Kultur-
kampf* Lucanus had held a post in the Ministry of Education under
Falk. The Conservatives too did not like him, for they held him to be
a liberally inclined official. Actually he did belong to that school of
old liberal bureaucrats who administered Prussia under Frederick
William III, and who, under Frederick William IV, had been superseded mainly by romanticists, pietists, and extreme Conservatives,
had been disliked by Bismarck, but under his rule had been elevated
again to those positions for which, because of their devotion, energy,
and incomparable knowledge of government, they were indispensable. Herr von Lucanus not only possessed powers equal to any
demands made upon them and devotion to duty and unusual knowledge of every branch of civil law and administration, but (and
herein consists his highest merit) his guiding motive was the good
of the state. He had no illusions on the point that some of William
II's peculiar characteristics held potentialities of danger for the
ruler himself and for his country. And therefore he made it his
task to strive with all his might that the rule of this monarch

might continue without doing permanent harm to himself and his house, to Prussia and to Germany.

Herr von Lucanus had a knack of drawing up documents with a speed which I have seldom found elsewhere. When the news of the death of Prince Bismarck reached the *Hohenzollern* in the summer of 1898, Herr von Lucanus sat down on a seat on the Imperial yacht, a pocket pencil in his hand and a pad of paper on his knees, and in a quarter of an hour drew up the Kaiser's message to his people and to the Princes in connection with the passing of the great German statesman, a message which met with universal approval, a thing that rarely happens in Germany. After his retirement Prince Bismarck was angry with Herr von Lucanus because, in that disastrous March of 1890, he had brought him the Emperor's request to resign with all possible speed. The Prince himself jested over those mediaeval monarchs who used to hang the bearers of bad news on the nearest tree.

The public saw in Herr von Lucanus, above all, the official who carried the silken cord to ministers ripe for dismissal. One might compare him to Hermes, the conductor of souls, who in the twenty-fourth book of the " Odyssey " escorts the souls of the slaughtered suitors down to Hades and the fields of asphodel, in his hand his staff made of gold and the souls twittering as they follow. With that comparison Eugen Richter had, and not without wit, made great play in his "*Freisinnige Zeitung.*" Kiderlen, who had a reckless tongue, tried often but in vain to make Lucanus ridiculous in the Kaiser's eyes by saying that he was the son of a chemist in Halberstädt. He made not the slightest impression that way on William II. The Kaiser was much too unprejudiced to throw the origin of anyone in his face, especially an origin derived from a pharmaceutist, a member of a profession which requires much care, caution, and knowledge, which was held in high honour among the Greeks, and by the Arabs, in Italy in the earlier, and in Germany in the later, Middle Ages. The death of Cabinet Counsellor von Lucanus, who died in harness in August, 1908, at the age of seventy-seven, was a very serious loss to William II, especially when the experienced and skilled statesman who for twenty years had rendered steadily distinguished service to the Throne and to the nation was succeeded by the junior and quite mediocre Herr von Valentini.

The chief of the Military Cabinet, then General-adjutant and later General-field marshal von Hahnke, was a worthy representative of the glorious infantry of our old army. He rose from a foot guardsman and felt a deep attachment to his regiment. For many years he had been the closest of friends with another typical representative of the Prussian guardsman, Major-general von Pape, who, on August 18, 1870, had led the attack of the 1st Guards Infantry Division at St. Privat. The military critic may as he likes make all sorts of criticism from the point of view of tactics of that famous charge, but every guardsman and every good Prussian looks back with pride to that feat of arms which is commemorated in a painting in the Hall of Fame. The Guards had been ordered to fire a volley and then lie down, so that the enemy's reply would pass overhead. Instead they remained standing and waving their helmets with the loud cry, "Forward, forward." Under the hottest of fires General von Pape had ridden along the front. Of his numerous staff every officer was killed or wounded except Lieutenant von Esbeck-Platen who, later on, was for many years master of ceremonies, a really fine courtier whom one would not have suspected of passing through that ordeal by fire. He reminded one a little of the Aramis of the famous book by the elder Dumas, "*Les Trois Mousquetaires*", a book which in my youth was the delight of all the boys who could read French. According to the ideas of these days the losses in that attack at St. Privat were disproportionately great; the *Kreuzzeitung* said that the Prussian nobility would be a year in mourning, and *Kladderadatsch* published a beautiful poem by Ernst Dohm on the harvest which death with sweeping sickle had reaped of the flower of the army. Since then we have had to accustom ourselves to more and far heavier losses, and the prophecy of Prince Bismarck that the next war would, as the French say, be a cause of *saigner à blanc* had received fearful fulfilment. On August 18, 1870, at St. Privat the Prussian infantry had its greatest day of glory since Leuthen. Just as at Leuthen all gave way before it when it stormed on in full flood:

Als ging durch alle Glieder der Front ein eisern Niet,
Trat sie vernichtend nieder in Staub, was nicht entflieht.[1]

Old Suvaroff used to say that the bullet was a fool but the bayonet was a fine fellow. From the highest ranks to the lowest there were many folk in the Prussian army, and especially in the Guards, who agreed with him before the great war. From the point of view of strategy, tactics, and military economics they were certainly wrong. But all honour to them who then as now in the World War showed the finest heroism which the world had seen since Marathon and Plataea!

General von Hahnke had held his head high in civilian life also. For many years he was adjutant to Ernest, Duke of Coburg, the Duke of whom Frederick William IV ironically asserted that he had the ambition to found a kingdom of "Eastphalia" in Central Germany, and in the first half of the 'sixties enjoyed a good deal of popularity as "Rifleman Ernest." Then it was generally believed that Ernest II sought to become German Emperor by popular election, but the year 1866 put an end to all that sort of nonsense. The Duke joined Prussia with enthusiasm, took part even, if rather in the background, in the battle of Langensalza and made his peace with Bismarck. For a moment Ernest II had hoped to take the place of the Albertine house in Dresden and so be able to take on behalf of the Ernestine line of the House of Wettin a somewhat belated revenge on the Albertines for their treachery in 1547.

General von Hahnke used to tell a story about the court of the Duke who was not too particular about matrimonial fidelity, which the great good nature of his Duchess, a Princess of Baden, made easy for him. The somewhat loose morals of the court at Coburg and the character of the Duke is said to have been present in Gustav Freytag's mind when he wrote "The Stolen Manuscript." In this milieu Captain von Hahnke maintained his upright and independent attitude. After he had seen and experienced a good deal

[1] When like a rivet of iron it sped
Through the lines and tramping to dust
Of destruction all but the foes who had fled.

which did not meet with his approval, he refused to allow his wife, a sister of General-adjutant Adolf Bülow, who later commanded the 8th and 14th Army Corps, and of the Otto Bülow who for many years was the Emperor William I's travelling companion and later ambassador to the Vatican, to go to court. The Duke tackled him on the point. When, scenting the real reasons for this stiff attitude on the part of his adjutant, he sharply bade him remember that the Duchess was pleased to be present at the ducal banquets and never objected to the guests. Herr von Hahnke answered curtly: "What is fitting for the Duchess is not yet fitting for my wife." General von Hahnke has often told me how much William II reminded him of the Kaiser's uncle Ernest of Coburg. Not, naturally, as far as morals were concerned, for the family life of the Kaiser was a model one; his marriage without stain, his domesticity which was seen in the relations between himself and the Empress and to their children might serve as a model for every German home. But when General von Hahnke observed how the Kaiser, when he was not on ceremony, walked with somewhat tripping steps, when he saw the shrug of the shoulders, above all, when he listened to the Kaiser telling a story and on occasion drawing the long bow, then General von Hahnke was forcibly reminded of Ernest II. The Duke had joined the Schleswig-Holstein army when the Elbian Duchies rose against Denmark and was in Eckernförde when it was bombarded by the Danish warship *Christian VIII*. The way in which he described that day went through many variations or, rather, it went from height to height. At first he had been only a spectator, then from a commanding altitude he had directed the defence and, in the end, had himself fired a shot which hit the Danish ship. About his part in the battle of Langensalza he also had many a fantastic story to tell, and during the Franco-Prussian war he incurred a good deal of unpopularity by the criticising of what was done in the field (which he wrote in his criticisms in the security of the "Hôtel des Reservoirs" in Versailles where the German princes were housed during the siege of Paris), criticisms which abounded in insinuations against the Royal Saxons who were not exactly in the good books of the Duke of Coburg. *Kladderadatsch* at the time devoted the following neat little poem to the Duke:

> *An einen hohen Schlachtenbummler*
> *Variationen über das Thema:*
> *" hätten die Sachsen besser einggriffen "*
> *Zwar hast Du diesmal Dir den Kriegermut,*
> *Die Heldentaten meisterlich verkniffen;*
> *Bei manchem hübschen Kind, manch jungem Blut*
> *Hast ehmals Du viel besser eingegriffen.*
> *Gesichert, wo der eh'rne Würfel fiel,*
> *Und fern der Wahlstatt, wo die Kugel pfiffen,*
> *Hast einst im lustigen Komödienspiel*
> *Als Bolingbroke Du besser eingegriffen.*
> *Die armen Sachsen, die Du rezensiert,*
> *Mit einem Takt, so zart, so fein geschliffen!*
> *Hätt'st Du statt dessen selbst sie angeführt,*
> *Meinst Du, sie hätten besser eingegriffen?* [1]

Scandal, especially in England, has spread the story that the real father of Ernest, Duke of Coburg and his brother, later Prince Consort in England, was not Ernest I, Duke of Coburg, but a Jew called Simon Meyer. This scandal was made the occasion of many more or less bad jokes turning on the double significance of "S. M." There is, of course, admittedly a good deal to be said which rather tells against Ernest I being their father. But at the Thuringian court, as a Thuringian prince told me once, they were convinced that there could be no question of a Simon Meyer but at the worst there might be question of a Herr von Ziegesar, and "his," said the Thuringian prince, soothingly, "is a very respectable noble family." I have never found anything more futile than this sort of

---

[1] "To a royal battlefield tourist:
  Variations in the theme:
  "if the Saxons had intervened more effectively."

" It is true that this time thou hast shirked warlike courage and heroic deeds in masterly fashion. In the past you often intervened to much better effect amongst pretty children and young folk. Safe, where the iron dice fell and far from the fateful place where bullets whistled, thou hast intervened to better effect as Bolingbroke in a comedy. The poor Saxons, whom thou hast censured with such fine, polished tact, dost thou think that if thou hadst led them thyself, they would have intervened with better effect?"

research into paternity. Not only because such nosing about is thoroughly disgusting, but because, whatever our parentage, we are all equal in the sight of God, all poor mortals with human imperfections and weaknesses. That too was the view of Kaiser William II who once told me of a lovely story of his aunt, the Princess Henrietta of Schleswig-Holstein-Sonderburg-Augustenburg. In the tragedy of Struensee the relations of that unhappy creature to the Queen Caroline Matilda of Denmark played a great part. The Queen had been induced by a base fraud to confess her illicit relations with her former physician and later Minister of State Struensee. Not long after the execution of Struensee and the banishment of the queen, the latter was delivered of a daughter who later married the Duke of Augustenburg, the grandfather of Princess Henrietta and the great-grandfather of the Empress Augusta Victoria. In the nature of things it was to the greatest extent improbable that Princess Louisa Augusta of Schleswig-Holstein-Sonderburg-Augustenburg, born after the Struensee tragedy, was the daughter of Christian VII of Denmark. When, as the Kaiser told me, Princess Henrietta was twitted once by another princess on her possible descent from Struensee, she retorted : "I'd rather be descended from a respected doctor than from an idiot king." Kaiser William II considered this a splendid answer. Certainly he was no Philistine, as I once declared in answer to August Bebel in the Reichstag.

The head of the Naval Cabinet, Admiral von Senden-Bibran, was the son of a Silesian nobleman who had been in Austrian service. He himself when a young man entered the German navy to which he was devotedly, one might almost say fanatically, attached. Outside the navy there existed nothing at all for this old fellow who had neither wife nor child and had only a few friends. Such devotion was fine in itself and might have had useful results if it had not ended in complete onesidedness. Amongst the many things which, apart from the fleet, Herr von Senden did not consider at all, were, unfortunately, political caution and wisdom. Admiral von Senden's love for the navy went so far that, in its interests, he stuck to Admiral von Tirpitz and supported him, whom he personally detested, because he thought he was the only man whose organising ability and energy would ensure the swift and necessary expansion of the fleet.

At the time of Admiral Hollmann, who from 1890 to 1897 was Secretary of the Navy and belonged to the so-called "friends" of the Kaiser and, like most of these gentlemen, was very compliant towards his Majesty, William II, despite all the representations of Admiral von Senden, meddled far more than was good with the laying down and construction of warships. The Kaiser loved to design houses, castles, churches, and, especially, ships. This talent for designing and his passion for draughtsmanship William II inherited, like so many other things, from his mother. As in many other spheres, his ability was smaller than his enthusiasm. While Admiral Hollmann was Secretary for the Navy it constantly happened that the Kaiser tried to exercise a direct influence on the construction section of the department. He was determined to intervene personally everywhere and on every occasion in constructional matters. In the 'nineties, the Kaiser, in the course of a visit to Italy, made the acquaintance of the Italian Minister of Marine, Admiral Brin, who was considered to be one of the ablest naval architects in Italy and even in Europe. After long discussions about the best way of building ships, and especially capital ships, the Kaiser had asked Admiral Brin if he might send him a plan for the construction of a battleship which he, the Kaiser, had had worked out with especial care and as the result of long study, constant diligence, and much thought. Some weeks later, Brin received from Potsdam the design in question. He returned the design to the Kaiser with a letter which was a masterpiece of Italian delicacy and also of quiet irony. "The ship which your Majesty has designed", ran the letter, "would be the mightiest, the most terrible, and also the loveliest battleship ever seen. It would have a speed which has not yet been attained, its armour would surpass anything now afloat; its masts would be the highest in the world; its guns would outrange any others. And the inner appointments are so well arranged that for the whole crew, from the captain down to the cabin boy, it would be a real pleasure to sail on her. This wonderful vessel has only one fault: if she were put on the water she would sink like a lump of lead."

The Kaiser was not at all angered by the Admiral's reply. It was one of the Kaiser's most sympathetic traits, and one which differentiated him from many princes, that he was never annoyed at criticism wittily made — so long as it did not get abroad. His personal friends could be jovial with him, for between them and his Majesty things could go on in privacy. But it was difficult for ministers, since they, and the Kaiser with them, had to work in full publicity.

For the reasons indicated, because Admiral von Senden in his zeal for the fleet took nothing else into consideration, the admiral had a deplorable influence on the relations between the Kaiser and his uncle Edward VII and thus on Anglo-German relations generally. Senden was what the North Germans call *"stur."*[1] He was also, unfortunately, extremely tactless. The gentlemen who formed the entourage of William II with very few exceptions were men of distinguished qualities. They lacked neither loyalty nor love of truth nor independence of thought, but tact was not the hallmark of the new generation. At the court of William I tact was general. Of the milieu in which William II lived one could not, with the best will in the world, say this much. Even Philipp Eulenburg and Kuno Moltke could not and would not deny it, but they found a formula to cover it : "Tactlessness is manliness."

Admiral von Senden was constantly sent to England by the Kaiser on special errands and scarcely ever came back without having incurred hostility from lack of tact. He loved to talk in the London clubs of how we would build a monster fleet and, when it was ready, then we would talk seriously to England. An incident which happened shortly before my appointment as Secretary of State had particularly unfortunate results. The Kaiser had sent Senden to London with a present for his uncle, then Prince of Wales, a present which, to the Kaiser, seemed nice and tasteful but which the fastidious and refined uncle did not particularly relish. Besides, as the Prince was engaged with all sorts of other business, he could not find time for a long interview with the Kaiser's messenger. When the touchy Admiral got back to

[1] obstinate.

Potsdam, he reported this to the Kaiser, probably embroidering the story a little and making the thing appear more pointed. The Kaiser flew into a rage and wrote to his grandmother, Queen Victoria, a letter in which he complained strongly and with considerable embellishments of the vexation caused him by the abominable treatment his messenger had received. The Prince of Wales declared that all Admiral von Senden's story of improper treatment was untrue and never forgot what he called "a detestable bit of scandalmongering." Every time the Kaiser went to England or his uncle came to Germany there were always long and painful negotiations as to whether or not the uncle would receive Admiral von Senden.

It is sad to say that such personal differences had often far-reaching and even political results in the end. Supported by other intelligent people I made the greatest effort to remove from the political path such rocks of offence as lay between two people so important as the Emperor and his uncle.

Publisher's Note. The following text printed in small type contains inaccuracies and certain serious misstatements which call for correction. It is totally untrue that Lord Lonsdale "stirred up trouble and offence between the Kaiser and his English uncle "; or that King Edward VII expressed the views attributed to him; or that Lord Lonsdale was a bankrupt. The high esteem in which Lord Lonsdale is held by the general public as well as by all who know him, will insure universal acceptance of his own comment on this passage: "This is absolutely imaginary on the part of von Bülow."

Senden was not the only nor the most dangerous rock. There was still another man who constantly stirred up trouble and offence between the Kaiser and his English uncle, and that was the Earl of Lonsdale. The Kaiser was tremendously keen on this man, who in many respects was the typical jovial English nobleman, tall, broad-shouldered, with light red hair and ruddy complexion, strong as a giant, always as ready for any physical exertion as for any good company. Always with a gold coin in his hand for anyone who asked anything, and with a jest always on his lips. He was the best horseman in England. He was also a fine yachtsman. It was a delight to see him on the yacht *Meteor*, on which the Kaiser often took him sailing, in his correct English yachting suit, his sleeves rolled back, the muscular arms and the bare strong chest, tattooed all over with pierced hearts, small flags and double initials, his feet in embroidered slippers so as not to slip on the smooth deck, surpassing any of the sailors in strength and skill. He was indeed a jolly good fellow, but he was also the *bête noire* of Edward VII, who called him "the greatest liar in England" and did not think it at all proper that the Kaiser should be intimate with a man who had for long been in a state of bankruptcy. As far as this was concerned the Earl of Lonsdale was in the same position in which another friend of the Kaiser, Prince Max Fürstenberg, found himself later, for the Prince too got into financial difficulties. It was a fine trait in the Kaiser that he was loyal to his friends, but he should not have been loyal at the cost of policy, as was the case with his friendship with Lonsdale. Also he should have made some distinction between German friends, like Senden, who could be addressed, treated, and guarded as good comrades, and a frivolous foreigner who could not be expected to stand by his Majesty if the drums beat to war with England. When in 1914 England declared war on Germany, it was reported in the newspapers that Lord Lonsdale, who had been present with the Kaiser at many German manoeuvres on sea and land, had turned all the pictures of the Kaiser which he had in his castle with their faces to the wall.

Admiral von Senden did not escape the reproach that in contrast to his colleagues of the Civil and Military Cabinets he liked to meddle in foreign policy and naturally, in accordance with his whole inclination, in an anti-English sense. In this respect he had much destruction to his credit. It is, according to Goethe, the nature of the dilettante to underestimate the difficulties which he has to face. Proceeding from the simple and highly dangerous conception, which in its simplicity was naïvely applied, that Russia should be played off against England, Herr von Senden made friends with the Russian naval attaché Paulis, with whom he was fond of discussing a common Russo-German action against England. Paulis was a shady sort of person. No one knew whether he was a Russian, a Belgian, or an Italian, and against him even the Russian ambassador took precautions. But in his loyalty to his "friends" the Emperor never permitted himself to lose faith in his Admiral and Chief of Cabinet.

CHAPTER V

The Cabinets — Court Ceremonial — The Adjutants — First Differ-
ence with William II and Swift Reconciliation — Arrival in St. Petersburg
— William II's Impressionable Nature.

UNDER William II the Cabinets played a much greater part than
they had done under his grandfather. Of the latter's Chief of Cabinet, Herr von Wilmowski, the public knew practically nothing, for
he never appeared in public. Herr von Lucanus, on the contrary,
was among the most discussed personalities of the time. His
name was in every mouth; his caricature was constantly in the
comic papers, which had taken no notice of the existence of the
worthy Herr von Wilmowski. The ideal of William II would have
been a system of Cabinets *sans phrase.* In the honest belief that
he would thus in the swiftest manner get rid of all the difficulties and
obstacles which stood in the way of his efforts for the prosperity
of his land, the Kaiser would have preferred to have regulated and
settled everything military through his Military Cabinet, even
in opposition to the War Minister and the General Staff — to have
built up his fleet through the Marine Cabinet, so as to be its sole
superintendent, and to rule at home through the Civil Cabinet.
Like many other plans and wishes of the Kaiser these ambitions
which filled the first years of his reign were wrecked by the power
and the deceitfulness of circumstance. To rule as William II
dreamed he might after the dismissal of Prince Bismarck would,
as things were in Germany and the world in 1890, have been impossible even for a Frederick the Great.

Since then the Kaiser had been compelled to mix much water in
his wine. But undoubtedly all through his reign the Cabinets
exercised great influence. That was the case so long as the able and
serious Herr von Lucanus was at the head of the Civil Cabinet, and
the excellent and worthy General von Hahnke was at the head of the

Military Cabinet, and it was so from 1901 to 1908 when Count Dietrich von Hülsen-Haeseler, who had had a clear, unprejudiced, and sound understanding, was chief of the Military Cabinet. It was so even with Admiral von Senden, who, with all his whimsies, had a holy zeal for the fundamentals, that is, in his case, for the Fleet, which was so dear to him, and for its honour and glory. But it was no longer so when Herr von Valentini was at the head of the Civil Cabinet, Admiral Müller at the head of the Naval Cabinet, and General von Lyncker, a man of stainless honour, but a small and narrow-minded man, was head of the Military Cabinet. This Cabinet system has its share in our defeat in the World War. When Grand Admiral von Tirpitz in his letters to his wife called it the "Hydra" and the three chiefs of Cabinets as the three heads of a new Lernaean serpent, when he raged against "the strong plaster wall around the Kaiser", against the "accursed gang in Pless", when he spoke of "government by the Cabinets as before Jena" and declared that the Hydra must be sharply attacked and the chiefs of cabinets swing on lamp posts, this cry of anger on the part of the builder of the fleet can be understood by anyone to be the very human result of all of the intrigues of Admiral von Müller he had been forced to put up with and of the observation and knowledge which he had acquired at closest range of the wretched Herr von Valentini. *Facit indignatio versum.*

Although the Cabinets, which were a sort of focal point for great and powerful circles and interests in political life, could give me trouble here and there, and actually did in some measure, I faced the world of courtiers that surrounded the Kaiser without any embarrassment whatever. Certainly the influence neither of the *Maison militaire* nor of any of the genuine courtiers was to be underestimated. To deal with the military, who scarcely ever meddled in politics and were sent back to their own places by William II on the occasions when they did, and who, as a result of their whole military training and their birth were men with a high standard of honour, did not seem to me difficult. As far as the occupants of court posts were concerned, I understood matters there too well to fear very serious difficulties from them. The agonised fear of "the great court" in which my wretched successor lived was far from me. *" Ayant vécu dans le sérail j'en connaissais les détours "*, that crowd could not impose itself upon me. Besides, in the immediate proximity of their Majesties, I had an absolutely reliable friend in the person of my old war-comrade, Bodo Knesebeck, who was in the Empress' Cabinet. But it was above all in the personality of the Chief Marshal to the court and the Imperial Household, Count August Eulenburg, that my main guarantee lay that the court would not trespass beyond its own sphere.

He was a worthy scion of that East Prussian noble family which for centuries had given many distinguished men in war and peace to the service of the Prussian state. When in 1813 the province of East Prussia rose against the French and carried the King and the whole land with it, as Heinrich von Treitschke has described in imperishable words in the first volume of his German history, the Prussian nobility stood at its head. Unforgettable are the beautiful lines which Max von Schenckendorf dedicated in his "Song of the Three Counts" to the first victims of the holy war, Counts Kanitz, Dohna, and Groben. Count von Schweinitz, who for many years was our ambassador in St. Petersburg, used to say that every Prussian king had had "his East Prussians." One of the truest paladins of our old Emperor was the man who had been his adjutant for many years and had ridden by his side at Königgrätz and Gravelotte, Count Heinrich Lehndorff. This tall man with the "Emperor William beard", as it was then called, was one of the most remarkable sights of the Prussian court. The story went that in his youth he had broken many hearts. When no longer young, he married the beautiful Countess Margarete Kanitz, with whom he lived in the happiest of marriages, and who presented him with three children, one of whom was an unusually gifted boy. He was intended for a diplomatic career and had a great future before him, but fell in the World War, leading his Cuirassiers of the Guard. The father, Count Heinrich Lehndorff, had with endless tact and absolute loyalty looked after the official and personal relations of the old Emperor and Prince Bismarck. Men like Count Lehndorff, General von Lindequist, Count Fritz and Count Louis Perponcher, General von Albedyll, Count Stillfried, Count Pückler, General Count Alten, Prince Anton Radziwill, General von Steinäcker, and many others gave the old court its noble appearance. Count Heinrich Lehndorff in political matters, too, had a good and shrewd judgment. I shall always account it to my honour that this man, a nobleman in the best sense of the word, was a friendly protector of mine in my youth and my good friend in later years. The beneficial rôle which Count Heinrich Lehndorff had played in the court of the old Emperor was destined to be played under the latter's son, then Crown prince and later Emperor Frederick, by Count August Eulenburg. Even in his youth, when he was captain in the 1st Regiment of Foot Guards, he had been assigned to the Crown Prince as adjutant. When his predecessor, Major von Schweinitz, later the ambassador to St. Petersburg, was replaced by Eulenburg, he persuaded the Crown Princess to maintain the most friendly and confidential relationship possible with Eulenburg. A better guide and adviser in the labyrinth of Berlin intrigue as in the problems and riddles of policy she would find with difficulty. Time passed; then the gifted but impulsive and so, rather naïve lady let herself be influenced against Eulenburg by her chamberlain, Count Seckendorff, and never rested until she had driven him from her court and had passed him on to the great court as Chief Master of Ceremonies.

In this position Count August Eulenburg found himself at the coronation of William II, who promptly promoted his then Court Marshal, Herr von Liebenau, to be Chief Court Marshal. Herr von Liebenau had become the military equerry of Prince William after my brother Adolf and then his Court Marshal. He had accompanied Prince William to the University of Bonn and had also been with him during his service at Potsdam with the 1st Regiment of Guards and with the Hussars of the Guard. Externally Herr von Liebenau was rather the rough soldier and without the manners of a Court Marshal. The ladies of the court complained about his "sergeant-major's tone"; they complained still more of the fact that he refused them so many drives in order to prevent exhaustion of the Imperial horses. The Empress too found him quarrelsome. So Herr von Liebenau had to go. All the same, despite his martial exterior, he was an able and, in his own way, a clever courtier who had affiliations with the Normann Stosch-Roggenberg circle and was inclined to liberal ideas. I have often had occasion to notice that liberally-inclined Chamberlains, adjutants, and Court Marshals are more complacent and actually more servile to the "greatest" than stout Conservatives and true Junkers. Liebenau left the court profoundly hurt and went back to Wiesbaden, where he swelled the troop of higher officers and officials who had been replaced, and who in that charming resort, at the foot of the Neroberg, meditated on how very much better the state and the army would be managed if they were still in the service. Liebenau was succeeded by Count August Eulenburg, who brought with him all those qualities of mind and character which made him able to render good and profitable service to the Kaiser as to the court and so, as things were, to the country. In what was for me an unforgettable conversation in October 1879, Prince Bismarck said to me that there were many good and some clever folk, but only a few who were both good and clever. Of these few, of these *rarae aves*, August Eulenburg was one. His intelligence was as clear and acute as his character was firm and reliable. He never lost his head or his poise either as Court Marshal on the slippery floor of the court or as Minister of the Household in the storm of the November revolution. He did not belong to that class of men, of whom William II was one, who fail in tact. After the revolution he was able by his dignified and cool calmness to tame the democratic parvenus with whom he had to arrange the problems relating to the property of the Royal house. He regarded things as from a lofty keep; he saw the great as great and the small as small; he was conscientious and noble minded. He was a keen Prussian patriot through and through, and at the same time he had the best and most conciliatory manner. I would have much liked to send him as ambassador to Petersburg, Vienna, or London, but the Kaiser would not be deprived of "this pillar of his court." It was not for the good of either Kaiser or country that Count

Eulenburg was transferred from the court to the royal household, a post in which he saw the Kaiser less often and no longer accompanied him on his travels. It was certainly not for their good that Eulenburg was succeeded by the shallow and empty Herr von Reischach, whose actions, thanks to his inordinate conceit, were almost comic, and that, too, not long before the War when the Kaiser had double need of an able man of character as adviser who would be in direct contact with him. In the Ministry of the Household, and especially after the November revolution, Eulenburg rendered distinguished service to the Emperor by his self-possession and insight. But he was not at Coblenz or at Luxembourg, at Charleville or at Pless. Above all he was not at Spa in 1918. If Count August Eulenburg had been at his side, the Kaiser William II would never have fled over the frontier. The commandant at General Headquarters, General von Plessen, later Major General, had been adjutant to the old Emperor and had the good manners, the calm demeanour, and the discretion which were characteristic of that circle. He had married the daughter of the great surgeon, chief medical officer of the Army, Bernhard von Langenbeck.

From his post as adjutant to the old Emperor, Plessen was transferred to become adjutant to the latter's grandson, who soon after his accession made him commandant of General Headquarters. Under the old Emperor, who had conducted two wars, there was no headquarters in peace time. Kaiser William II had made the acquaintance of this organisation in Russia. The idea of clothing his suite in peace time with the garments of war gave him pleasure. Our royal master loved to play at war in peace time. But when peace-time war became a real, a bloody and a terrible war, his deepest nature, his fundamentally tender nature, and his whole sensitive makeup shrank from it. In his well-known novel "*Der König*", the Vienna journalist Karl Rosner has drawn too malicious a portrait of Major-General von Plessen. Rosner had been attached to Great Headquarters as representative of the *Lokalanzeiger*. His flowery war bulletins which regularly appeared in this *Scherl* paper pleased the Kaiser. Rosner's style was of the true Viennese kind. When Prince Bismarck wished to get an article into the papers, an article which he wanted written with lively colours and with an undertone of sentimentality, he used to give a short summary of the contents and write on the margin: "In the Austrian manner." It is quite humanly comprehensible that Rosner judged the gentlemen around the Kaiser by the attention which they paid him, and thus depicted them. Major General von Plessen quite obviously did not trouble much about him. Consequently Rosner depicted him as a physically exhausted, intellectually limited, rather simple, and, in addition, a gluttonous man. Right up to the last year of his service General von Plessen was, as far as physique was concerned, elastic, tireless, and resistant to hardship; he had excellent manners and was of normal intelligence. I knew him as such for many years. He was neither an intriguer nor a flatterer.

How far are the reproaches just which have been levelled against Major General von Plessen in connection with the flight of the Emperor William II to Holland? After that terrible catastrophe it was related that it was General von Plessen who had advised the Kaiser to flee, that he had counselled that fatal decision of escape to Holland or, at least, had made it possible for his Majesty to commit that error which could never be repaired. On the evening of November 8, 1918, Kaiser William II dismissed Field Marshal General von Hindenburg and the gentlemen with him, with the remark that they would continue the discussion next morning. On the morning of November 9, when the gentlemen who had been summoned to the council had appeared, they found that the Kaiser had escaped to Holland in the night. General von Plessen, it is said, had given all the necessary instructions to the servants and to the railway officials and had thus assisted the flight. The full truth of that unspeakably sad business will only be known later on. But even if General von Plessen did carry out the Imperial order to this effect, it would be unjust to censure an officer of such long service for so doing. For nearly thirty years he had never refused to obey an Imperial order; for nearly thirty years any attempt on his part to express his own opinion had been jestingly or indignantly prevented by the Kaiser. Certainly Plessen would have done well to have seized the Kaiser by the sword knot and, at that terrible moment in Prussian history, told him that an honourable death on the battlefield — for they were still fighting at the front — was in the interests of the country, of the dynasty, and of the Kaiser himself, and was a hundred and a thousand times preferable to flight. But such initiative on the part of one who had been so long in the position of an obedient attendant was not to be expected nor to be demanded.

"Zeus whose voice is borne afar takes away half his worth from a man when the day of slavery comes upon him."

So says the noble swineherd Eumaeus to Odysseus in Homer. The Kaiser was fundamentally friendly, amiable, and benevolent by nature. He was kindly disposed towards all the people in his immediate neighbourhood; he was always delighted when he could secure some pleasure for any of them. In intercourse with them he was amiable and even easy-going. There was really nothing of subservience in the usual sense of the word in the Kaiser's entourage. But opposition annoyed the Kaiser, and as the general feeling was that the Kaiser must be kept in good humour, most of the people around him renounced all initiative, and even, to a certain extent, their own opinions. Man does not alter from one day to the other. It would be a scandalous lack of objectivity, it would be more than unjust, if I did not freely add that I am far from believing that such intellectual subservience exists only, or especially, at Courts. Nowhere is it seen more prominently than in the Social Democratic crowd. A Socialist, but a Socialist of genius, the Frenchman Proudhon said : "On my honour and faith, I would rather be ruled by our old kings who represent centuries of honour and prosperity than by demagogues who secretly despise the people and the state and who flatter the former simply to get control of the latter." And Voltaire declared that taking things all in all, he would prefer to be ruled by one lion who *après tout* is a gentleman of good stock, than by a hundred rats. When we were going to Russia with Kaiser William, anyone who prophesied that the Empire would have such an end as it did actually have twenty-one years later, would have encountered just as many unbelieving faces as did the prophet Micaiah in the twenty-second chapter of the first Book of Kings : Micaiah, Imlah's son, who prophesied that the king of Israel would be defeated and fall from his throne. The king of Israel gathered all his prophets together, some four hundred of them, and asked them whether he should go up to fight at Ramoth-Gilead or should leave it alone. All the prophets, like good courtiers, answered his Majesty, "Go up, for the Lord will deliver it into the hand of the king." Micaiah alone expressed a decidedly unoptimistic view and declared that in a vision he saw all Israel scattered like sheep that have no shepherd. Then the Chamberlain Zedekiah, a high court official, struck him on the cheek and the king ordered Micaiah to be thrown into prison and to feast on the bread and water of affliction until the king returned, crowned with victory. But the king never came back at all.

Undoubtedly in the first years of the Kaiser's reign many hearts were deeply anxious. The growling Titan in Friedrichsruh made no secret of the fact that his dismissal and, above all, the manner of his dismissal, the almost simultaneous denunciation of the Re-insurance Treaty with Russia and the circumstances attending that denunciation, that the many eccentric speeches and acts of the Kaiser and the young monarch's whole method of government filled him with the deepest anxiety.

When the Empress Frederick in the 'nineties came to Palermo while travelling in Italy, she visited my mother-in-law, Donna Laura Minghetti, who had settled with her son by her first marriage, Prince Paolo Camporeale in his lovely villa on the Olivuzze. Together the two ladies took a drive to Altavilla, which lies between Palermo and Termini, and which belonged to my wife and had been for centuries in the possession of the Camporeale family. The little place is proud of its famous church built in 1277 by the Norman duke, called La Chiesazza, Robert Guiscard, the conqueror of Sicily, which possesses a miraculous picture of the Madonna. From La Chiesazza one can survey a long stretch of the coast of North Sicily. When the widowed Empress, even in presence of the lovely landscape before her, maintained that look of sadness which had been hers

since the death of the Emperor Frederick, Donna Laura asked her
if the wonderful blue sea which stretched away before her, the
picturesque Monte Pellegrino with the chapel of St. Rosalie in
the background, the orange trees, and the olive trees did not
bring other thoughts to her and alleviate her sorrow. "I do not
mourn simply for my dear husband," the Empress answered, "I
mourn also for Germany." And with fixed stare she continued,
"Remember, Donna Laura, what I say to you to-day. *Mon fils
sera la ruine de l'Allemagne.*" Horrified by this ill-omened
prophecy, Donna Laura, who was of an optimistic nature, and also
had the highest opinion of the strength and power of Germany,
earnestly besought her not to give way to such gloomy forebodings.
But the Empress refused to withdraw her prophecy. Long years
still separated us from the terrible catastrophe in which in November 1918 land and dynasty were involved. Of all those who in
those August days of 1897 were on board the *Hohenzollern* only
two, the Kaiser and General von Plessen, were twenty-one years
later to be actively concerned in that catastrophe. Nine years earlier I had been dismissed in complete disfavour. All through the
war Count August Eulenburg was detained in Berlin by his duties
as Minister of the Household and so at the most critical moment
of Prussian and of German history his wise counsel and his equable
and noble character were, alas, not at the Kaiser's service. Lucanus, Hahnke, and Senden had departed this life long before the
collapse came in the dark days of November 1918, and I count
them happy that they were not required to live to experience the
calamity which in those August days in 1897 was hidden from
our eyes and still in a distant future.

The atmosphere on board was cheerful. The Kaiser was, as
usual, in good form, for he was on his travels and was anticipating
an interesting experience. I once asked the Kaiser how it happened
that he, who was in so lofty a position, with everything at his disposal, took such delight in travelling, paying visits, and having
interviews with potentates. I told him that a plain man like myself
did not set much store by them. I liked to be with his Majesty,
but these travels and interviews I considered rather like what the

French called a *corvée*. The Kaiser declared that this was easily explained, for I, even in my youth, and then later as a diplomatist, had been able to go all over the place, and could travel where I liked and had seen much. But he, in the early days of his life had travelled practically not at all, and made the acquaintance of hardly any court, save the English court, and was not accustomed to meet with potentates, so that now he had a great desire and need to make up for lost time. Besides, he considered that more was to be attained by direct conversations between monarchs than by the most excellent notes between ministers. This sad overestimation of the influence which a monarch can bring to bear on foreign sovereigns and ministers the Kaiser had also inherited from his mother who, in the days when, against the wish and will of the old court, the Emperor William I and the Empress Augusta, above all, against the decided opposition of Prince Bismarck and to the grief of her husband, she strove with the most passionate obstinacy to bring about the betrothal of her daughter Victoria to Prince Alexander of Battenberg, was convinced that an hour's interview with the Tsar Alexander III would suffice to win the Tsar to that marriage project. The visit which she paid to Paris shortly after the dismissal of Prince Bismarck, and which ended in a fiasco, was undertaken because of the same exaggerated overestimation of the personal power of princes which many years later was to lead her son into the tragi-comedy of Björkö.

Right on the first day of our cruise to St. Petersburg the Kaiser excitedly declared to me that he had some interesting and joyful news for me. The King of Belgium had proposed at Kiel to go into partnership with him in the Far East where great wealth was to be made. The King had held out the prospect that he would use his influence in England and France so that the Powers should agree to a German as governor of Crete, which would be a good stroke for Germany. I did not conceal from his Majesty my opinion that I did not find the idea of financial speculations with the King of Belgium a very pleasant one. Perhaps in this sort of thing I was rather old fashioned but, in my judgment, such transactions did not become kings and especially did not become the King of Prussia.

As far as Crete was concerned we had every reason to keep our finger out of that pie. In the Mediterranean we had only minor interests. Whatever happened to the island of Minos was all the same to us; let Russians and English, Turks and Greeks fight over it as they liked. To have a German as governor of Crete would be a burden and an embarrassment for us, not a pleasure or an honour.

With a rather disillusioned air, the Kaiser came out with his second and more important proposal. Philipp Eulenburg had passed on a most excellent idea to him which had first been conceived by the much-travelled Wurttemberg Duke of Urach. This excellent Duke was the same Urach who, during the World War, was Herr Erzberger's candidate for the throne of Lithuania. Twenty years before that he tried to make the Kaiser take notice of the Bear Islands, tiny islands in the North Arctic Ocean to the north of Spitzbergen, scarcely 600 square kilometres in size. They had been discovered at the end of the sixteenth century by the Dutch sailor, Willem Barents, who had been trying to discover a way to China through the Arctic ocean. Urach declared, and Phil believed, that there were great coal deposits on the islands. So Phil had made to his Majesty the proposal that we might suddenly occupy the Bear Islands which appeared to be *res nullius* and then offer them to Russia as compensation for the harbour which we desired in China. The Kaiser had already given Admiral Senden notice to have a ship ready to sail for the Bear islands whenever an order by telegraph was received. When I declared this idea, which would have disturbed the three Scandinavian nations and might easily upset Russia and England, to be impractical and fantastic, the Kaiser got angry and excited. He had never expected this when he summoned me, when he longed for me as Minister. He had expected that we would understand one another in everything. But the contrary seemed to be the case. I was just as dogmatic and difficult towards new ideas as Marschall had been, on whose account he had had enough vexation. He would not put up with this sort of thing. I felt that my whole future relationship with the Kaiser, the possibility of a collaboration profitable to the country and so, in the actual state of things, to a good part of our political future, depended upon my not losing my nerve but sticking to my guns. I had the feeling which came over me when I was a young lieutenant of hussars and was riding at the head of my troop on a restive horse on parade. I said to myself then that if I did not stay in the saddle and keep the noble beast under control, he would bolt, throw the squadron into confusion, and ruin the whole parade. So calmly and in respectful tones but quite firmly, I answered his Majesty that I was not glued to my job. At any moment I was ready and even willing to go back to Rome and, if his Majesty did not wish me to have Rome again, I could retire without regret or complaint into private life. I could find plenty to do; I was very fond of reading and there was an endless number of good and interesting books which I would like to know and did not yet know. On the shore in the distance the towers of Memel were visible.

I pointed them out to the Kaiser and asked him if he would like to have me rowed ashore now. It would be very interesting to me to have the chance to make the acquaintance of a historic town where the Prussian monarchy had seen its darkest hours but also the beginning of its glorious resurrection. With that kindly and noble expression which he could assume, the Kaiser laid his hand on my shoulder and said to me: "Don't take it amiss. Only people who like each other quarrel. We're reconciled already. I'll abandon Phil's and Urach's Bears."

Now I was able to proceed to expound to the Kaiser, who listened with friendly attention, the line I thought our political conversations in St. Petersburg should take. Above all we must be very circumspect in St. Petersburg in our allusions to France and still more in our allusions to England. The French were actually the allies of the Russians, and to criticise them would be of as little use as to tell scandal about his wife to a husband who was deeply in love with her. Still more dangerous would be adverse comments on the English. Because of the numerous connexions between the English and the Russian courts every opinion of ours expressed in St. Petersburg and unfavourable to England would at once and with special joy be carried to Osborne, Windsor, and Sandringham by female agency. On the other hand, we must resolutely and candidly express our solidarity with Russia as regards Poland and the revolution and revolutionary dangers. We need volunteer nothing, but if the Russians brought up the Dardanelles question, we could say calmly that we thought that a settlement of this question, in a sense favourable to Russia, was quite compatible with the independence of Turkey. As far as the Far East was concerned, it would, in my opinion, be best if Russia, at the same time, practically, with Germany, sought a harbour on the coast of China. Then we should stand covered against England. Thus British jealousy against any competitor on any point of the globe, any emanation of the usual "dog in the manger" attitude of England, would to a certain extent be diverted from us. We should hold on to Kiaochow, which the Navy declared, and rightly, to be, with its hinterland, Shantung, the most suitable base for us, but we had no reason to oppose any establishment by the Russians at any point on the Liaotung peninsula, the region to which apparently their ambitions were directed. Kaiser William was in complete agreement with the programme as I sketched it and did not take it at all amiss, when I said to him that the Tsar might not, at a personal meeting with the older, more experienced, and stronger-willed Kaiser, like to be put too much in the background, especially before his own subjects.

During the next few days similar conversations were repeatedly held by the Emperor and myself, in which his amiability and his kindness were always the same. Meantime we had entered the gulf of Finland :

> *Currit iter tutum non secius aequore classis*
> *Promisitque patris Neptuni interitum.*

The weather was beautiful; the Baltic as calm as an inland lake, which was just what the Kaiser wanted. He was filled with a passionate love for the sea, but, like his mother, the Empress Frederick, and also like Admiral Nelson, he was plagued with sea-sickness. The Empress Frederick used to say that the sea was an unhappy love of hers.

Peterhof lay before us. The excitement of the Kaiser reached its height. When he saw before him a meeting with another mon-

PRINCESS MARIA VON BÜLOW
In her Viennese days
(*Portrait by Hans Makart*)

arch, when he set foot on foreign soil, he had that feeling of mingled impatience, joyous anticipation, and nervousness not unlike what a young girl feels when, with her bouquet in her hand, she first enters a ballroom. How will it turn out? How will I get on? But once the first round of dances is over, when at the cotillon bouquet on bouquet is heaped up over her chair, then gradually the feeling of having completely realised her dearest wish overcomes her. In this mood the Kaiser was naturally exposed to foreign influence. A feeling then came over him which, if it was not quite *hybris*, was one in which he easily crossed the boundary between the desirable and the possible, between illusion and reality. There was also the fact that, with his unusual intellectual impressionability and versatility, he felt himself at home wherever he went. It was said of Alcibiades that he discussed art and philosophy with his Athenian fellow-countrymen, ate black soup with the Spartans, and wore the long Asiatic robe with the Persians. The same could be said of William II, although, as I conceive, Alcibiades had a motive in his mimicry. In William II's case it was more the desire to please and to that end assimilate himself to his surroundings. In Russia he felt like a very worthy Russian adjutant general of the old type, or like a prince who had wandered to Russia from Oldenburg, Altenburg, or Strelitz. In England he felt like the Queen's grandson and "admiral of the Fleet"; in Vienna he thought in terms of black and yellow, and in Budapest like a Magyar. In Italy he shone in various colours. In the Quirinal he was completely *Casa Savoia;* in the Vatican he saw himself in the guise of the protector of the Roman Papacy, as once the Roman Emperors of German race had been, or had wished to be. In Sicily he followed in the tracks of the Hohenstaufen.

CHAPTER VI

Conversation with Muravieff — The Question of Kiaochow — The Gala Banquet (August 7, 1897) — William II's Extravagant Speech — Prince Radolin — The Finance Minister Witte — Audience with Nicholas II — Empress Alexandra Feodorovna.

WHILE William II and Nicholas II were exchanging kisses on both cheeks, as sovereigns usually do, kisses which in the course of history have prevented neither wars nor betrayals, Muravieff approached me, greeted me as an old friend and told me that Prince Hohenlohe, who had meanwhile arrived in Russia, expected both him and me for a conversation in his apartment in Peterhof. The monarchs withdrew for their first confidential exchange of views, while their attendants sat down to a sumptuous luncheon served on that gold service which in the reigns of Nicholas I and Alexander II had aroused the astonished wonder of the German guests of those days. Since then we ourselves had grown richer and fairly luxurious and we were not so easily dazzled. From the windows of the room where we ate we looked out on the park of Peterhof, which, like the palace itself, had been constructed by Peter the Great on the model of Versailles, with beautiful plantations and lovely waterfalls which ran over broad steps to leap high in the air in a great fountain, famed in all Russia as the Simson fountain. Versailles and the court of Louis XIV had not been a model to German princes only. The rays of the *Roi Soleil* had shone even to the far Neva and even to the town where the Grand-Duchess Helene Paulovna complained that the streets were wet and the hearts were cold. The influence of the French character, of French brilliance, and of the refined French civilisation on the rougher but therefore more receptive Russians, goes very far back. In the park of Peterhof bloomed the rose of which Prince Bismarck loved to tell. He told how once while walking in the park the Tsar Nicholas I noticed a sentry standing in front of a bare rose bush. The Tsar asked the sentry why he stood there, but the worthy grenadier could not tell him. The Emperor had enquiries made and it was found that in the time of the Empress Catherine II that rose bush had once borne a lovely rose. So that it should not be plucked the Empress had established a sentry post over it, which, half a century and more afterwards, still had this duty to perform. This characteristic story of Russian subordination and mechanical obedience pleased Prince Bismarck. Particularly since his departure from office he rarely agreed with his sovereign; he was also of the opinion that much is permitted to Jupiter which is not seemly in Bos, and on occasion laid claim to a very extensive right of criticism. But democracy and everything connected with it was distasteful and almost obnoxious to the Prince because of his upbringing and youthful impressions, his whole character and mentality. He was not above administering democratic poison now and then according to his own measure and in doses regulated by himself, but the Prussian state and the German people and character must not, in his opinion, be corrupted by it.

We met in the course of the day, Hohenlohe, Muravieff and I, for a conversation in the drawing room of Prince Hohenlohe, in which a great picture of the Tsar Nicholas I looked down on those present, proud and severe. When Prince Hohenlohe immediately turned the talk to the Far East, Muravieff interrupted him with a friendly laugh to say that the Kaiser William in his first conversation with the Tsar had disclosed the fact that he had no intention of establishing himself in Kiaochow. He would gladly hand over this fine port to his Russian cousin and friend and only begged permission that German ships might call and coal there. Old Hohenlohe had one splendid quality; he never let himself be bluffed. In a parliamentary debate he was never able to speak except with a piece of paper in his hand on which he had carefully noted all the points. Since the November revolution nearly all the Ministers and Chancellors had been accustomed to read their speeches. Sometimes it also happens that they mispronounce words of Latin or Greek origin. The Socialist Chancellor, Bauer, once read a speech prepared for him by *Ministerial direktor* Rauscher, a typical November Socialist, in which the word *"Politiker"* occurred. With expressive pathos Bauer, on reading this foreign word, put the accent on the third syllable. When Rauscher in despair cried the correct pronunciation in the Chancellor's ear, Bauer replied crossly, "What's the matter? I read it off all right." A Chancellor who would speak in the manner of Prince Hohenlohe to-day would make no sensation. Twenty-five years ago greater demands were put on people, and thus the prestige of the Prince suffered, although despite his oratorical shortcomings he possessed so many distinguished qualities. One of his finest qualities was that he never let himself be imposed on by his equals, Ministers or Princes. Sovereigns, he promptly replied to the Russian minister, were rather inclined to follow the noble desire of their own noble hearts. *"C'est aux ministres qu'il incombe de mettre d'accord ces nobles élans avec les réalités politiques et les nécessités économiques."* Muravieff laughed and answered that this question like many others should be left for discussion between him and me as soon as it was possible. We were old and good friends and would find a solution.

Later I had a two-hour conversation with Count Muravieff. Count Michael Nikolayevitch Muravieff, who was a year or two older than I, came from a Russian boyar family. A scion of his house, Count Muravieff-Apostol, was one of the leaders of the Dekabrist movement in 1825. Condemned to death, he was sentenced to be hanged. At the execution the rope broke and Muravieff fell to the ground. While the hangman was preparing another rope the young reformer called to him, *"En Russie on ne sait rien bien faire, pas même pendre."* Very different from this idealist was the so-called "Lithuanian Hangman" who had the same Christian names as the Minister of Foreign Affairs. During the great Polish rebellion of 1863, of which Bismarck took advantage, and, by adopting a strictly anti-Polish attitude, won Alexander II's confidence for many years and so carried through the policy of 1864, 1866, and 1870, conditions in Lithuania became ever more threatening and the flames of the rising spread to Dvinsk and nearly to Pskov. Alexander II, full of anxiety, had the then Minister of the Imperial Domain, Count M. N. Muravieff, summoned, and entrusted him with the restoration of order in the wide Lithuanian area. Muravieff declared his readiness to go, but demanded a free hand. Alexander, who had a noble nature and a kindly heart but could easily fall into the ways of his father and grandfather if it was a question of his autocracy, nearly had a regular fit of rage at this answer. He caught the Count by the arm and asked him if he wanted to be shot as a rebel and a traitor. But when the general who had been selected as dictator held fast to his point that a dictator without dictatorial powers is nothing at all, the Tsar gave way, as every autocrat gives way when he is frightened. Forty-eight hours later Count Michael Nikolayevitch went off to Vilna. As adjutant he took with him a young officer who became the adjutant general of Alexander III, Tcherevin by name, who told me much about his former chief and his doings when we were in close relations during my period as Counsellor of Embassy in St. Petersburg from 1884 to 1888. When the two of them, Muravieff and Tcherevin, arrived at Vilna, the dictator ordered the usual Russian supper for midnight and invited the chief of police of Vilna to join them. The supper and the chief of police appeared at the appointed time. The dictator demanded the list of suspects, which contained about one hundred names. While he was eating Muravieff marked some twenty names with a cross which he drew with his pocket pencil. The chief of police remarked diffidently that the people marked out by his excellency and so destined to the gallows were those who were least guilty. "That's all right," answered Muravieff, "when judgment comes like lightning from a cloud no one knows whence it comes, where or why it is going to strike, and that is what causes the greatest terror." When it was announced to the dictator the next day that Polish women had adorned with flowers the graves of the executed, he had the corpses dug up and brought to the parade ground. There they were barely covered with earth and over them two Cossack regiments were drilled until the bodies were only shapeless lumps and fragments. Half a century later the Russian Revolution and Bolshevism gave the answer to such cruelty. The Hegelian law of the swing of the pendulum is ever valid. Even in his own lifetime, noble-minded men recoiled with horror from dictator Muravieff's brutalities. When, after the quelling of the Lithuanian insurrection, the Tsar Alexander II asked what honour should be given as reward to Muravieff, Prince Suvoroff Italiisky, who from 1848 to 1861 had been the mild governor general of the Baltic provinces, answered: "Your Majesty should present Muravieff with a golden axe or miniature gallows and make him wear it on his breast beside his other decorations." The dictator Muravieff died completely out of favour. He had forgotten that pregnant remark of Alexander I, who once said to an overzealous minister of police, "Don't forget that princes sometimes approve of savagery but seldom of those who are its agents."

The foreign Minister, Count M. N. Muravieff, was no monster like the Hangman of Lithuania, and the fanaticism that had distinguished the unfortunate Muravieff-Apostol was also alien to his character. He looked a real Russian, big and broad-shouldered, with sea-blue eyes and short nose, although he had a German mother — according to his enemies and rivals in Russia, a German-Jewish mother — who in her old age escaped from the cold and damp of St. Petersburg to the warmth of Wiesbaden. He himself had studied in Heidelberg and been a corps student. He spoke German quite as well as he did French, which every educated Russian speaks as well as his mother tongue. For many years relations between Muravieff and myself were on a most excellent footing. Having pointed this out, he plunged straight *in medias res*. Things were very different now from what they had been in the first half of the 'eighties when we had been colleagues in Paris, and in the second half when he had been Counsellor of Embassy in Berlin. Since then, on our initiative and in brusque manner, despite all the Russian representations and entreaties, Germany had denounced amid lamentable attendant circumstances the treaty of alliance between Prussian Germany and Russia, which went back to the days of the Holy Alliance and actually to that memorable scene in the Garrison Church at Potsdam, where Alexander I, Frederick William III, and Queen Louise had embraced by the tomb of Frederick the Great. We had cut old and valuable ties. *"Tu l'as voulu, Georges Dandin,"* *i.e.* not myself but *"ce pauvre Caprivi"*, who, by his own confession, felt himself incapable of juggling with more than two balls at a time, and Marschall, the *"ministre étranger aux affaires"*, who after hitting Russia over the head, had with the Kruger despatch struck the English a blow as well. Thus the Franco-Russian alliance had come about of which he, Muravieff, from the point of view of Russian domestic politics and the security of the dynasty had had grave doubts, and still had. But there it was, and there was naturally no use in thinking of its removal. He said quite frankly to me now that during the forthcoming visit of the President of the French Republic in a few weeks' time, the alliance concluded between France and Russia would be alluded to in the toasts exchanged on that occasion. In the toast mention would not be made of friendly nations but of allied nations. Muravieff again repeated that for various reasons he would prefer to be allied with us rather than with the French. But nothing could be altered. He could not let himself be parted from *Marianne* and return to his former German wife. "But," he continued, "we can do this; each of us, you and I, can within his group work in a peaceful sense. The supposition is that we will keep the French from being stupid, and you, the Austrians, that is, from being stupid in a way that is irreparable. People will always be committing stupidities, but stupidities that cannot be repaired ought not to be made. With deepest earnestness I assure you that the Emperor Nicholas and I desire peace, peace everywhere, but especially in Europe, and in Europe more especially between Germany and Russia. You know that I am a monarchist through and through. I consider that for Russia autocracy is the only possible form of government. Not of course that in Russia reform is either impossible or unnecessary, but in Russia, considering the character of the Russians, who always go to extremes, a pure parliamentary system, a Radical system, would end in anarchy and dissolution."

A European war, the Russian Minister of Foreign Affairs further declared to me, would involve very serious dangers for the internal state of Russia. Those who thought that by a great war the dynastic sentiment would be strengthened among the Russian people and that there would be increased reverence for the Tsar and the

autocracy, were gravely mistaken.   As history showed, the contrary
would be the case.   The Dekabrist conspiracy, whose leader had
absorbed revolutionary ideas in Paris, followed the war with France
under Alexander I.   After the Crimean War Alexander II had to
make the concessions which his father had refused, and after the
Russo-Turkish war which he had waged, the same Alexander II
fell a victim to the Nihilist movement caused by that war.   With
these opinions I could only agree and declare that, given the conditions internal and external at present existing throughout the world,
a war would be a risky business for any monarchy.   Kaiser William
entirely realised that; he was for peace through and through.
He would naturally not submit to any encroachment on his rights
or any wounding of his honour by any one.   But he would certainly do his part in maintaining peace, peace in Europe and particularly peace with Russia.   Consequently we were much pleased
with the joint notes which the cabinets of St. Petersburg and Vienna had, on April 29 of the present year, addressed to the governments of the Balkan states.   These little brawlers were not worthy
to be the cause of setting great Powers and old dynasties against one
another.   Muravieff did not conceal from me the fact that relations
between Russia and Austria were much more complicated and
delicate than those between Germany and Russia.   These things
must be handled with cleverness and a certain amount of tact.   In
spite of all the glamour of the Slavophiles, the Russian government
did not want war with Austria, with whom indeed Russia had
never yet crossed swords.   Equally it did not want to bar Austria
from the Balkan peninsula.   By the Treaty of Reichstadt of 1876,
it had voluntarily recognised the Austrian rights in Bosnia and
Herzegovina.   The Minister in this connection added that after
the Treaty of Reichstadt letters had been exchanged during the
congress of Berlin by Gortschakov and Andrássy and at the meeting
at Skierniewice by Giers and Kalnoky in which Austria was considered authorised, if she should think it in the interest of peace in
the East and of European peace in general, to turn the occupation
into annexation.   Russia would raise no claim against this.   But
there was a tacit agreement that Austria would interpose no curt

veto on certain Russian ambitions with regard to the passage of ships through the Dardanelles. *"Nous avons fait la croix sur la Bosnie, et cela depuis longtemps."* Naturally, of course, Austria was not to undertake anything hostile to Russia in the Balkan peninsula. Russia was, and would remain, a Slav and an Orthodox Power. She could not repudiate her whole history. Besides, as regards the Balkan peninsula, Austria was in a far better position than Russia, which had no particularly dominating influence either in Belgrade or Sofia, never to mention Roumania.

A further delicate point was the Polish question. Austria must abstain from all agitation among the Poles of the Kingdom, that is to say, the Russian Poles. He was well aware that the Emperor Francis Joseph disapproved of such an agitation. The attitude of Goluchovski, although himself a Pole, was quite correct. But from Galicia a considerable subversive agitation was carried into the Kingdom of Poland and grave injury was being done. Now, as before, the joint opposition to the Polish irredentists was a very strong bond of union between Germany and Russia. I reminded Muravieff that years ago in Paris we had both been present at a Polish wedding, the wedding of George Radziwill and Bichette Branicka, at which Russians, Poles, and Germans had met. On the way home he asked me on the Boulevard des Italiens what the Poles had said to me. I replied quite truthfully that they had with the greatest amiability and true Polish vivacity declared that Germans and Poles who were both civilised peoples could easily understand and love one another but never the Poles and the barbarian Russians. But he, Muravieff, had told me at the same time that the Poles, both ladies and gentlemen, had said to him that between Poles and Russians who were both Slav peoples there was no unbridgeable antagonism, but never could the Pole love the German. We would certainly be very simple, I declared, if we tore each other in pieces for the *beaux yeux* of the Poles. Nor did the Balkan peoples deserve the honour that the destinies of great kingdoms should be put in jeopardy on their account. Not long before the Congress of Berlin, when I was a youthful *chargé d'affaires* in Athens, the Greek Minister for Foreign Affairs, when I had declared to him Prince

Bismarck's love of peace and desire for peace, had answered with a pleasant air: "*C'est bien, c'est bien, va pour le prince de Bismarck, mais, moi, je vous déclare qu'une grande guerre européenne fera un bien énorme a l'Hellénisme.*" When, during the Congress of Berlin, I told this to Prince Bismarck, he declared: "So we are to set the world ablaze simply to let the Greeks annex Larissa or Trikkala or some such pigsty of which I don't even know the name."

I avoided opening the subject of the Far East with Muravieff after Prince Hohenlohe had with scarcely surpassable tact retrieved the Kaiser's lapse during his first conversation with the Tsar. Count Muravieff, on his own initiative, turned to that subject with the remark that, considering our great and increasing commercial interests in the Far East and our naval policy, he quite understood our wishes in connection with Kiaochow. Personally he was inclined to believe that the important point for Russian interests was the Liaotung Peninsula. But he could not say anything definite to me, for in that matter there were conflicting opinions and desires at the Russian court.

On the same day I was received by the Grand Duchess Maria Paulovna. She was no longer the brilliant beauty whom I had known in by-gone days, but although she was forty-three, she had a most attractive appearance. I soon received the impression that the loyalty and attachment of this Mecklenburg princess was not so complete as it used to be. She had become "Russified." At the same time she had maintained her old dislike of the ruling Empress of Russia and the "great" court of St. Petersburg. She had not loved Maria Feodorovna and she had no more love for Alexandra Feodorovna, for the Hessian as little as for the Dane. She complained about the English stiffness of the Empress which was making both herself and the dynasty disliked. Nothing could be more anti-pathetic to Russian society than a cold and unapproachable manner. The Empress thought to make up for her hauteur and her "English stiffness" by her excessive zeal for the Orthodox Church, which only induced contempt on the part of the indifferent Russian society. The Grand Duchess appeared to me in particular to be somewhat disturbed about the further developments in Russian internal conditions. In complete contrast to the days of Alexander III, under whose strong and powerful rule court circles and the upper ten thousand hardly considered the possibility of a revolution, I thought I saw in the Grand Duchess, as in other ladies of Petersburg society whom I saw later, a fear that a revolution in Russia was something which, if not probable, was at least quite possible. I shall leave undecided how far the Grand Duchess, in the event of such a revolution, thought her sons (not her husband, whose unconditional loyalty she recognised) might play a part analogous to that played by the Orleans against the older line of the Bourbons in France. The Grand Duchess spoke disapprovingly and not without acerbity on the developments of Germany during the last ten years. The dismissal of Prince Bismarck had been a gigantic blunder. The "rough and clumsy" denunciation of the Re-insurance Treaty, to which the Emperor Alexander III as well as the whole Imperial house and all royalist and conservative-minded people in Russia had held fast, was a second, and quite as gross, a "*sottise.*" At that moment the Grand Duke came in, heard his wife's last words, and said in tones of kindly sarcasm: "*Pourquoi abreuves-tu de reproches cet excellent Bülow pour des gaffes dont il est parfaitement innocent?*" In earnest tones he added that, if there were many things in life whose consequences were irreparable there was nothing left to be done but to make the best of everything. What was needed was to keep calm both in Berlin and St. Petersburg and not commit new stupidities. "*Du sang froid et de l'habilité, voilà ce qu'il faut.*"

On the evening of August 7 the gala dinner took place at Peterhof. Before the banquet the Tsar had made the Kaiser an admiral of the Russian fleet. It was the Kaiser's way to take such externals *au grand sérieux*. He gave them greater significance than others attached to them. Formalities he took far too seriously and, to a certain extent, drew on himself the reproach which Beaumarchais levelled at the courts of the ancient régime, that they took *les choses sérieuses avec frivolité*, but *les choses frivoles avec sérieux*. Very soon after his accession, William II had astonished Prince Bismarck by his wild excitement at being made a British admiral, a "Rear-Admiral of the Fleet." He explained to the great Chancellor that the appointment was of great significance in a political and military sense. He would now be able and entitled to intervene directly in the construction, organisation, and management of the English fleet. He could, whenever he stepped on a British vessel, take command of it. The Kaiser was, of course, very far from conceding to others those rights which he claimed for himself as a result of his honorary position in a foreign navy. Some years later the Imperial minister in Lisbon reported that the King of Portugal had gone to Vigo bay, to inspect the British squadron which was lying there, as an admiral of the English fleet, a title of honour which he also bore. The Kaiser exclaimed: "The fathead! It's nothing but an honorary title which gives him no rights at all." The great French historian, Hippolyte Taine, in his brilliant and profound *"Philosophie de l'Art"*, was fond of using the expression *"qualité maitresse."* He meant that a nation, like an individual, has a dominating trait, an especially prominent characteristic. The *"qualité maitresse"* of William II was his lack of logic. That made him entertaining and even brilliant in conversation, for he was no Philistine, but what the French call a *"prime sautier."* But it also made the conduct of affairs and consistent policy very difficult.

When the Kaiser proposed his toast in the palace of Peterhof, he was under the influence of the delight he felt over his appointment as Admiral of the Russian fleet, which had already inspired him to offer the Tsar Kiaochow. In the toast he spoke of the "gracious words" with which the Tsar had so "affectionately" welcomed him. He laid "at the feet" of the latter "his deeply felt, most joyful thanks" for the surprise of enrolment in "your Majesty's glorious fleet." That was an especial honour which he knew how to treasure in all its significance and which in an especial sense was also a distinction to his own navy. He placed in "your Majesty's hands" the "renewed pledge", and in this he knew that "his whole people" stood behind him, that he would give the Tsar his strongest support against anyone who should seek to destroy the Tsar's edifice of peace. Before our arrival at Peterhof Prince Hohenlohe and I had already drafted a banquet speech for his Majesty. But by his additions the Kaiser had so altered our idea of it that the original text was scarcely recognisable and he shot off his own speech without any previous consultation with us. The same thing happened only too often later to the drafts of letters to the Tsar which I submitted to his Majesty. The Kaiser was a remarkable orator. In all the parliaments known to me and, especially in the German Reichstag where oratorical ability was always moderate and since the revolution has sunk to a level below that of any representative assembly in a civilised state, I have known few speakers so effective as William II. His speeches were forcible and striking without ever being banal, picturesque and colourful without being bombastic; the words came lightly and clearly from his lips : he never was in any danger of losing his thread. What a contrast to the Tsar, who read his speeches off a huge white sheet with difficulty and hesitation !

After we rose from table the shorthand reports of the speeches exchanged were brought for correction to Prince Hohenlohe, Lucanus, and myself in the Imperial Chancellor's apartment. I pleaded for the excision of the "gracious words" and the expression "lay at his feet" and also for a softening of the end which could be interpreted as a hit at England. I also said that the Tsar's speech had been courteous and correct, but colourless and conventional. Lucanus objected to any alteration of the Kaiser's words, which would only irritate him to no purpose, and before we separated he said to me : "For Heaven's sake, don't start right away by putting the Kaiser out. What will happen then?" I said nothing, for this was my first experience of the kind, but I resolved to keep a more watchful eye on the Kaiser in the future.

While Kaiser William was present at a great parade at Krasnoye Selo, I went from Peterhof with Prince Hohenlohe to have lunch in St. Petersburg with our ambassador, Prince Radolin. Prince Radolin was of pure Polish descent. When he was seventeen years old, his mother, a clever woman of the same family as her husband, asked whether he wanted to remain a Pole or be a German. She gave him full liberty of choice. But he must not be a sort of halfbreed, like the bat in the fable which did not know whether it was an animal or a bird. When he had made his choice, he must be either entirely a German or entirely a Pole. Hugo Radolin decided for Germany and remained loyal to his decision to the end of his life. Curiously enough, though not surprising when one considers the low state of national feeling which is natural to us Germans, his second wife, née Countess Oppersdorf, the sister of the renegade Hans Oppersdorf, who after Germany's downfall went over to the Poles, became steadily less German and more and more half-Polish and half-French. Her mother had been a Frenchwoman, a Talleyrand. Once when he was ambassador of Prussia at Weimar in the first half of the 'eighties, a Russian lady, the Baroness Olga Meyendorff, who had settled at Weimar, asked Hugo Radolin whether as a Pole he would like to go with her to a performance of the oratorio composed by Liszt in honour of Poland's patron saint, St. Stanislaus. She received the angry answer : "*Sachez, j'exècre tout ce qui est Polonais.*" When, during the nine and ninety days, the dying Emperor Frederick raised Count Radolinski, who had meantime become Chief Marshal of the Court and of the Imperial household, to the dignity of Prince under the name of Radolin, he thanked the Emperor with the words, "Above all I thank your Majesty for freeing me from that accursed '-ski.'" Prince Radolin was extremely clever, a perfect gentleman, of a flexible, somewhat supple nature, which was the reason why Prince Bismarck called him the "Pole with the india-rubber back." He was too sensitive and touchy for a diplomat. When he was ambassador at Petersburg, he not only had deadly quarrels with a good number of influential Russian dignitaries, for instance, with the Chief Master of Ceremonies, Prince Alexander Dolgoruki, but even with the Grand Duchess Vladimir. In that connection, Prince Hohenlohe, with all the wisdom of a highly experienced man of the world, said to him in my presence after the dinner at Peterhof : "My dear Radolin, one ought always to be on good terms with the ladies, especially if they are pretty, and very especially if they are grand duchesses as well." The witty Countess Kleinmichl once said to me in the same connection : "*Pourquoi avez-vous envoyé à St. Petersburg un Polonais qui a tous les défauts des Allemands?*" Abroad the German is considered to be easily offended.

At this lunch I made the acquaintance of the Finance Minister Witte, who at that time was the most influential man in Russia. The son of a Baltic German sergeant major who had emigrated from the Baltic provinces to the Caucasus and there had married a Russian, the sister of the well-known Slavophile, Ratislav Andreyevitch Fadeyeff, Sergei Yulievitch Witte had inherited from his German father a capacity for work, ambition to learn and to educate himself and to get on in life, and from his Russian mother that indispensable ruthlessness and, wherever it was needed, that brutality without which no success was ever possible in Russia. The Russian people are perhaps the most good-natured and in certain respects the most docile in the world, but ever since the days of the Varangians history has shown that they have to be ruled with an iron hand and possibly will always have to be so ruled. In this respect, there is no real difference between the days of the Tsar, Ivan the Terrible, that is, the second half of the sixteenth century, and the methods of Lenin's government. In appearance Witte was completely Russian, a tall, sturdy figure with coarse but intelligent features and a snub nose. His strong chin betokened strong will; the big mouth, love of pleasure; the expression in his sharp eyes was not in the least sentimental. He spoke German but indifferently, perhaps with the intention of concealing his German origin; French he spoke passably. He had worked himself up to the heights from a lowly position. This, to my mind, is always in a man's favour. He was thoroughly acquainted with the whole Russian bureaucratic machinery, its cumbrous and also complicated mechanism. He had special knowledge of the railway system. Chance had drawn upon him the notice of important people in Russia. At the beginning of the reign of the Tsar Alexander III another plot against his life was discovered, news of which penetrated to the provinces. Witte, in the first flood of patriotic indignation over these constantly repeated attempts on the Tsar, drew up a memorandum in which, with sound human understanding and a certain motherwit, he made proposals for the organisation of comprehensive measures to protect the sacred person of the autocrat. Witte sent the memorandum to his uncle, General Fadejeff, in St. Petersburg. The latter

brought it to the knowledge of the Grand Duke Vladimir. Thereupon Sergei Yulievitch was ordered to Paris to watch the Russian
exiles there. He himself described to me in an amusing way how the
principal use he made of this mission was to get acquainted with the
joys of Parisian life — by day and by night — though also to extend
his political horizon. Apparently he sent good reports. From
that time onwards he was *en vue* and advanced rapidly in that
country of which, as I said in relating my meeting with the Imperial
secretary Polowzew in July, 1884, a French observer had said, more
than a century and a half ago, that it was the easy chances of getting
on that preserved Tsarist Russia from a general revolution. When
I made Witte's acquaintance he was at that time of life which, for
an ambitious man, is perhaps the most attractive time of all.

> *Wie gross war diese Welt gestaltet,*
> *So lang die Knospe sie noch barg!* [1]

In 1897 Witte had not quite reached the heights, but the world
was quite confident that he would. He was famous already. People turned round to look at the Minister of Finance. Envy and
hate, those attendants whose presence is the surest sign of success,
were already being shown him. Witte stood in high favour with
the Tsar Nicholas; so far nothing had disturbed their relationship.
Witte also enjoyed the confidence of the two banking houses of
most importance for Russian credit, the Rothschilds in Paris and the
Mendelssohns in Berlin. Not long before the visit of our Kaiser
to Peterhof, Witte won a great personal and social success. For
many years he had been on intimate terms with a lady of the St.
Petersburg *demi-monde* called Mathilde. When she presented him
with a daughter he married her. She was, on the whole, considered
a decent sort of woman and she had, in particular, never omitted to
use her great influence on the Minister for the benefit of her many
previous admirers in the two crack regiments of the Russian army,
the *Gardes à Cheval* and the *Chevaliers-Gardes*. This she did out
of downright kindness of heart and without making any charge.
After long opposition on the part of the two empresses, Madame

---

[1] How grandly this world was formed as long as the bud still concealed it!

Witte, at the wish of the Tsar, was received by his mother and his consort. At that luncheon with Prince Radolin, I had a long conversation with the Russian Minister of Finance which was to lay the foundation for our friendly relations later on.

On August 10 I was received in audience by the Tsar Nicholas. Scarcely above average height, slender, and small-limbed, the Tsar gave one the impression of being a delicate, but not in any way a sick man. He was very different in appearance from the gigantic Alexander III, as from the stately and tall Alexander II, his grandfather. He had beautiful, rather melancholy eyes, long and slender hands, a clear and sympathetic voice. He had the best possible manners. Even if one did not know him, one would have recognised him in a London, Vienna, or Paris drawing room or at St. Moritz or Biarritz as a gentlemanly young fellow, perhaps an Austrian count or the son of an English duke. Everything about him was refined, especially the way he dealt with the people around him, with whom he was as considerate and courteous as if he were dealing with grand dukes or foreign crowned heads. He invariably wore only a colonel's uniform, the rank he had reached when his father died. He wore as few orders as possible. When William II (who was tireless in inventing medals, aiguillettes, and clasps of all sorts which he exchanged with his fellow monarchs so as to strengthen the friendship between them), bestowed decorations of this kind upon him, the Tsar thanked him in the most courteous manner and put the presents away in a drawer to take out only when he was going to meet the German monarch.

The Tsar made me sit down opposite him at his desk, expressed his delight at the Kaiser's visit, and then in broad outline and without going into particulars repeated what Count Muravieff had said to me. What he said revealed the traditional distrust of Austria with which the Imperial house had been filled since the Hapsburgs took up that attitude of theirs in the days of the Crimean War, the attitude which, according to the Russian version, had by its ingratitude and treacherous cunning broken the "great heart" of the Emperor Nicholas I. Still more frankly did the Tsar express himself on the "little Japanese", whom obviously he had not forgiven for the wound which a Japanese fanatic had dealt him during his travel in the Far East. Very genuine did the Tsar's assurance ring when he declared that he desired peace as earnestly as Kaiser William, of whose pacifism he was convinced. He was not quite so convinced of the love of peace of the French. He clearly believed that they would let slip the dogs of war as soon as they thought there was chance of success. But he would make it his business to see that the French did not jump over the traces. Germany, he said, had the same duty to perform with regard to Austria. For the Balkan peoples he had no special sympathy; they had cost Russia much blood and treasure and Russia got neither real gratitude nor true loyalty in return. The Balkan peoples thought only of themselves; they were absolutely selfish. But, of course, Russia, an Orthodox and a Slav Power, could not throw over her kindred by religion and race in the Balkans altogether. *"Ces petits peuples doivent être sages, mais, naturellement, nous ne pouvons pas les laisser écraser."* As regards Russia's internal condition, only a few remarks were made, which showed that the Tsar had little inclination to consent to reforms. Like Muravieff, he thought that it might be possible to consider a general extension of the *Zemstvos* and of communal and provincial representation, but a real parliamentary system would mean the end of Russia. In contrast to his usual practice, he quoted a Russian proverb: "If you want a clean house don't have the pig at table." The Tsar showed interest in all I said. Later on I often saw him follow a conversation, even at large gatherings with courteous and admirable attention. And yet I had the impression that a great, a very great, indifference was the fundamental trait in his character. *"L'empereur Nicolas"*, the Russian ambassador in Berlin, the aged Count Osten-Sacken who had seen four Tsars, once said to me, *"a une indifférence qui frise l'héroïsme."* This indifference bordering on heroism Nicholas II certainly showed when abdication was wrung from him in a railway carriage. May it also have remained with him in that terrible hour when he was murdered in a Siberian cellar after having seen his wife and children slaughtered before his eyes.

From the windows of the Tsar's apartments at Peterhof, which were in the upper part of the palace, one could see not only the gilded cupola of the Isaac church but also the lofty tapering spires of the church of Peter and Paul, where the rulers of the House of Romanoff sleep, not far from the low, wretched, narrow, cold, and damp prison cells in which were languishing many of those who twenty years later were to overthrow the Tsarism that so long had been held unshakable.

After the Tsar the Empress Alexandra Feodorovna gave me a short audience. She was the youngest daughter of the Grand Duchess Alice of Hesse-Darmstadt, the second daughter of Queen Victoria of England. Together with the traditional and genuine family affection which existed in the English royal family there was a certain rivalry between the two sisters Victoria and Alice. The elder was Princess Royal of Great Britain and Ireland; the latter and younger was not. The elder was to become Queen of Prussia and German Empress; the younger only Grand Duchess of Hesse-Darmstadt. The husband of Princess Victoria, the Emperor Frederick, was one of the fairest and noblest figures in German history; the Grand Duke of Hesse was a brave, thoroughly good fellow and an able ruler, but not above the average. The Grand Duchess Alice was as liberal in politics and especially in religion as her sister, the Crown Princess. The Grand Duchess had with delight and gratitude received from the hands of David Friedrich Strauss the book on Voltaire which that great scholar had written and dedicated to her. As there is compensation for most things in this world, the daughters of the Grand Duchess in compensation for her lower rank in the princely hierarchy were more beautiful than the daughters of the Crown Princess. The Grand Duchess Elizabeth Feodorovna who married the Grand Duke Sergei was really the "Pre-Raphaelite Beauty", as the ambassador von Schweinitz had described her in his report on the wedding. Princess Alix, who was now Tsarina, was, as her grandmother of England had once called her, "very showy"; her expression was majestic; she had a beautiful figure; her carriage was superb. *Incessu dea patuit.* Anywhere she would have been rated a princess, a real princess. Horrible calumnies have been spread about this unfortunate and noble woman whose end was so dreadful.   Unnatural wickedness was imputed to her; shameful intrigue laid to her charge.   It was alleged that she had been the prey of an ordinary impostor, the monk Rasputin.   It was said that she had dishonourable relations with his accomplice Vyrubova, a Russian woman of the people of his own class.   I have no belief in these scandals.   In secluded Darmstadt the Empress Alexandra Feodorovna had been carefully and strictly brought up like a court lady and almost like a *bourgeoise*, as is customary in these small palaces.   Apart from Darmstadt she knew only the great English court, the court of her grandmother, the old Queen Victoria, round whom moved princes and princesses like tiny planets round a great central sun. In Darmstadt, as in Osborne and in Balmoral, a thoroughly sound and moral atmosphere pervaded the house of her noble grandmother.

In youth it was foretold that Princess Alix would marry the heir to the Russian throne and become Empress of Russia.   While she was still young she was sent "on approval" to the St. Petersburg court, as had been the case with so many German princesses since the Empress Catherine II.   The first attempt miscarried. The Hessian princess did not please the heir to the throne.   She had to go back home unsuccessful.   The future Tsar Nicolas was under the influence of a beautiful Polish dancer, who had been provided for him on his arrival at manhood *pour le déniaiser*.   During the winter of the inspection most people kept away from the young Princess as soon as it was apparent that the wind of court favour was blowing away from her.   Only the aide-de-camp, Count Orloff, did not vary in the attention he paid her.   When he was taking leave of her just before her departure from St. Petersburg, she gave him a flower and told him she would never forget his friendliness.   From this absolutely innocent remark, which revealed only the Princess's goodness of heart, a regular romance was concocted later on and it was whispered that she had been passionately in love with the aide-de-camp and that, after her betrothal, Orloff had been banished and had committed suicide abroad.   A fairy tale from beginning to end!   Still more abominable are the slanders about the Empress Alexandra Feodorovna and her alleged abnormal preference for women. In this case too there was nothing more than the emotion of a heart which was in the best sense receptive to friendship. Among the friends of her youth was a Countess Rantzau, a sickly and somewhat overdeveloped girl, but good at heart and what people used to call "a beautiful soul." Princess Alix, even after her marriage, corresponded with the young countess, and when the latter, who had been sickly from childhood, died young, the Empress of Russia did not hesitate when travelling to Darmstadt on her first visit to take the roundabout way via Kiel in order to lay flowers on the grave of her friend.

The Empress Alexandra Feodorovna finally owed her marriage, which for long was uncertain, to the initiative of her cousin, Kaiser William. On the occasion of the wedding of Princess Victoria to the Grand Duke Ernest Louis of Hesse there was a great family gathering at Coburg. At the celebrations the sister of the bridegroom, Princess Alix, was present. Her cousin german, William II, and Nicholas of Russia, the nephew of the Dowager Duchess of Coburg, were also attending this union of the houses of Wettin and Hesse which had been arranged, or it would be more correct to say ordered, by the grandmother of both of them, Queen Victoria, a union which was to be by no means a happy one. After the heir to the Russian throne and Princess Alix had been in each other's company for some hours and not without embarrassment, Kaiser William in his cheery impulsive way took him by the arm, led him to his room, made him take off his sword, and carry his fur cap in his hand, stuck some roses in his hand and said to him, "Now go and ask for Alix." The betrothal was announced that evening. But as so often happens in life it was a case of

> *Sic vos non vobis nidificatis aves,*
> *Sic vos non vobis vellera fertis oves,*
> *Sic vos non vobis mellificatis apes,*
> *Sic vos non vobis fertis aratra boves,*

as the greatest of Roman poets Vergil wrote on the gate of the Emperor Augustus to the dishonour of his plagiarist, the wretched Bathyllus. For this cousinly and successful intervention in her life the Empress Alexandra Feodorovna was in no way grateful to Kaiser William. She hated to be reminded of it, and, as Empress of Russia, could not abide the German Kaiser although her sister, the charming Princess Irene, was married to Kaiser William's brother, Prince Henry of Prussia. During the short audience which I had with the Empress Alexandra Feodorovna she confined herself to conventionalities. She seemed to find some difficulty in uttering them and only showed animation when I told her that I had passed my boyhood at Frankfort-on-the Main, quite near her beloved Darmstadt.

CHAPTER VII

Return — Discussion of the Naval Problem — The Kaiser's Education at the Hands of Hinzpeter — The Latter's Verdict on William II — Return to Kiel (August 14, 1897) — At Wilhelmshöhe — Tirpitz Reports — Conferences on the Naval Question.

ON August 11 the two monarchs parted. Both of them were in excellent spirits: Kaiser William because he felt that things had gone on well, Tsar Nicholas because he could now go back to his peaceful family life. There can scarcely have been a man who felt happier within his own four walls than the last Tsar, the last, that is, for the time being.

Où peut-on être mieux
Qu'au sein de sa famille!

as runs a pretty song of good old Grétry. So think many worthy fathers of families when they get back home in the evening, and so felt the autocrat of over one hundred and twenty million souls. He liked to be disturbed as little as possible in this peaceful domestic happiness. Every visit, and especially every royal visit, seemed a disturbance to him. Sometimes the Tsar had no outsiders at his table for weeks, not even his nearest relatives, so much did he like the company of his own family. This was very respectable, it was even moving, but it was not the way to rule a gigantic empire and a people of whose revolutionary elements Karl Marx had written in the early 'eighties that they were the advance guard of the international proletariat. If the shade of Peter the Great strode through the gardens he had planted in the park of Peterhof in those August days of 1897, he would not have been edified by the action or rather the inaction of his descendant. I did not leave Peterhof and Petersburg in the same exalted mood as Kaiser William II, but with the renewed conviction that our relations with Russia depended on diplomatic skill.

The Kaiser used the voyage back to Kiel, which took several days, to discuss the question of naval policy with me, in the utmost privacy. With the help of the tables showing relative naval strengths, tables he had himself drawn up and submitted to the Reichstag (probably more to astonish than really to please or genuinely convince it), the Kaiser explained to me hour after hour how weak we were and how necessary was the strengthening of our fleet as contemplated by him and his henchman, Tirpitz. He took great pains to equip me for the forthcoming campaign in Parliament and in the country with oft-repeated arguments. Meantime a hot sun beat down on us; there was not a breath of wind; the Baltic lay still as a mirror. In order to spare both the Kaiser and myself unnecessary loss of time and energy in the oppressive heat, I explained that for years I had been convinced of the necessity of having sufficient protection for the thousands of millions of money and for the national energy that we had entrusted to the high seas and that *il prêchait un converti*. But he would not let himself be put off. It was in the Kaiser's nature to devote himself personally to whatever interested him.

He was essentially active and energetic. This excellent characteristic which nature had given him, had been developed and stimulated by his tutor, Professor Hinzpeter, in every way. In educating the future King and Kaiser Hinzpeter took the personality of an especially capable and meritorious Thuringian prince of the past for model. I have forgotten the name of that ruler: John Frederick the Magnanimous or Ernest the Pious, or something like that. Anyway it was a prince who intervened in everything; at all times had looked after his rights and never failed to be present when anything was doing. Young Prince William was to take him for pattern and make himself just like him. The only thing that Hinzpeter forgot was that the conditions in a tiny Thuringian duchy of the sixteenth or seventeenth century are naturally very different from those of our day. Given the character of the Kaiser and also the present-day impossibility of even a Frederick the Great or a Napoleon I being able to superintend and decide everything personally, this incitement of the Kaiser to activity could easily do more harm than good. I do not know what French historian it is who said of Prince Talleyrand that "*sous Napoléon I, dont l'activité exagérée était devenue un fléau, le prince de Talleyrand avait élevé la paresse à la hauteur d'une vertu.*" No one has ever reproached me with idleness and I am very far from seeking to compare William II with Napoleon or myself with Talleyrand. But it is quite correct that the excessive activity of William II had its grave dangers. Once in an hour of depression Miquel expressed his opinion on the point thus : "The Kaiser," he said, "is interested only in things he can personally take part in and if he does, he spoils them all." That was too severe. But even to-day I think that what I once told the Kaiser to his face is quite just, namely, that his plans, ideas, and intentions were not always, but generally right, good, and even masterful, but that he often went astray in the ways and means of attaining these ends. The ways and means, I said, were not his strong point. The Kaiser who was in a good humour agreed with me, and declared that I was quite right but that the two of us together would therefore repair the mischief. Was Hinzpeter the right tutor for the Kaiser? He had been recommended to the Crown Princess Victoria at the beginning of the 'seventies by Sir Robert Morier, who was then English minister in Darmstadt, who had known Hinzpeter when he was tutor in the house of Count Goertz. It was a curious dispensation of Providence that the man who should have sponsored the person who was to be responsible for the education of the future German Kaiser was Morier, later English minister in Munich and then ambassador in St. Petersburg, who was inwardly one of the bitterest and, because of his full knowledge of German conditions and weaknesses, one of the most dangerous enemies of the new, the Bismarckian, the strong Germany, and who was politically a forerunner of Edward VII. Hinzpeter was, above all, greedy of power. He wanted to have his say in everything. Although not without vanity, he attached less importance to outward signs of distinction than to real influence. To him the end justified the means. He might be described as a Protestant Jesuit, that is to say, if the Jesuits are what their enemies conceive. Hinzpeter, who had great influence over William II even when he was an adult, as was clear from the many proofs of Imperial favour, had intelligent ideas on many subjects. Like myself, he thought that the hostility of William II to the classical languages and humanist education, which at that time was violent, was an aberration. The true German education is based on the classical languages. Humanist schools are the nurseries of our culture. Nothing can take the place of the examples and the lessons which ancient history and the ancient writers give of patriotism, courage, and all the manly virtues. One of the leading men in the economic life of Germany, Albert Ballin, once said to me: "If I had two candidates for a post in the Hamburg-Amerika Company and one could read Homer and Vergil in the original and the other knew all the intricacies of double bookkeeping and was experienced in stock business as in exchange discounting, I would prefer the former." Yet Ballin was in the best sense of the word a "self-made man." Hinzpeter also understood the gravity of the social question and of the Socialist movement, but on these his views, in my opinion, were too pessimistic. He rightly fostered in the Kaiser his interest for social policy, but he was himself quite convinced that all that would be of no avail and that the victory of the Social Democracy was as certain as the bad weather prophesied by the meteorologists or the eclipse of the sun calculated centuries ago by astronomers. Hinzpeter was very original. He told me that when he went for a walk with the young Prince William, he made him give a quick, definite judgment on every one they passed. This sort of instruction was only too effective, for even then the young William was inclined to overhasty judgment of men and things. Hinzpeter also sought to strengthen the self-consciousness of the young Prince, which in any case was developing fairly well. He assured me that he had been no out-and-out opponent of Prince Bismarck. He once took his young pupil on a visit to Prince Bismarck so that William could see what a great man looked like. But none the less I have no doubt at all that Hinzpeter played his own part in the fall of Prince Bismarck in 1890, whether his motive was opposition in principle to the Prince's anti-Socialist policy or, what seems to me to be more likely, that he considered himself to have been too little considered and honoured by Prince Bismarck.

Besides, Frau Dr. Hinzpeter was a Frenchwoman who had taught William II's sisters. Hinzpeter was unpleasant in that he often spoke very sarcastically of the Kaiser behind his back while writing him letters which were models of sycophancy. The Kaiser often showed me such letters, a fact which, of course, Hinzpeter did not know. Privately Hinzpeter told me that in his opinion his pupil lacked all philosophical, all higher, and all deeper endowments. He was fit only for mechanical or for manual work. "He ought to have been a mechanic." Now every naval officer would tell me that no one knew the naval signals better than the Kaiser, that no one knew the technical vocabulary of navigation so well as he, yet he was quite incapable of sailing the tiniest vessel from Kiel to Eckernförde. On land it was the same. He could criticise manoeuvres but was quite incapable of leading an army himself. This was fortunate, in so far as the Kaiser shrank from war in consequence, and if there were a war, would certainly leave the conduct of it and the responsibility to others. The utmost he would do would be to interfere in naval affairs. I shall not conceal the fact that since the revolution I have met many "great men" of the republic to whom the witty words of Leibniz apply: "There are few men who know everything, but there are many who know everything better."

Hinzpeter was almost cruel in the way he ascribed the Kaiser's strong inclination to impress others by appearances and to take appearances for realities to that left arm of his which had been withered since birth. Even as a child he had heard Prince Frederick Charles, who could really be a boor, let fall the horrible remark that a one-armed man should not be king of Prussia. This had made him feel intensely the need of impressing his army and his people by the greatest possible insistence on externals, by uniforms and orders, by lifeguardsmen tall as trees behind him and his Field Marshal's baton in his outstretched right hand. This verdict is incorrect. The energy with which William II, without in any way concealing his crippled arm, mastered all the difficulties that it caused, was one of the many things about him that evoked not merely sympathy but admiration and respect. Hinzpeter's humour was bitter. Once when a younger son of the Imperial couple was confirmed, a dinner was given in the Imperial palace at which the Kaiser proposed a toast which concluded with a fervent expression of gratitude to our Lord and Saviour. After dinner Hinzpeter said to me : "You know, I was sure the Imperial toast was going to finish up with the words, 'I ask you to drink to our Lord Jesus Christ. Hip, hip, hurray'." Sometimes Hinzpeter expressed himself so savagely about the Kaiser that I, who knew those sycophantic letters of his, often had the feeling that he was playing the part of an *agent provocateur*. In one point undoubtedly his influence on the Kaiser was anything but good. Hinzpeter had no tact. Shortly after the Kaiser's accession there appeared his book, "Kaiser Wilhelm II", which began roughly as follows: "The young Kaiser, who is a mixture of Hohenzollern egoism and Guelph wilfulness, was by no means easy to educate." When the whole older generation in Berlin read these words from the pen of a royal tutor and a high official, a shudder passed through their limbs, just as poor Gretchen shuddered in her tiny room that was so close and stuffy, and sang the immortal song of the King of Thule. The older generation had a foretaste of the tactlessness which we were to endure after having for thirty years been accustomed to the most tactful of all princes, William I.

When we got back to Kiel on August 14, 1897, my confidential talks with the Kaiser on naval matters terminated to his satisfaction, and he demanded that I should come to Wilhelmshöhe as soon as possible whither he had summoned Tirpitz. I got through all the work that was awaiting me in Berlin as quickly as I could and went off to the old castle which the Hessian Electors had built in the Habichtswald in a noble park with beautiful fountains.

I was always particularly glad to be at Wilhelmshöhe. Not merely because of the beauty of the country, but also because this castle, as hardly another, induces reflection on the vicissitudes of German history, its heights and also its depths. Here after the battle of Sedan, the culmination of recent German history, Napoleon III was held prisoner and for seven months was treated with true knightly courtesy by our old Emperor and with almost excessive attention by the Empress Augusta. Sixty years before, King Jerome had dallied here with his favourites, some of whom, alas, belonged to the German nobility. Here, so it was said, he bathed in red wine, here in the evening he dismissed his courtiers with the famous words "More fun tomorrow." The castle itself had been built by the Hessian Electors with the blood money which, to their shame, they took from England as payment for their own subjects whom they sold to serve in England's American wars. Friedrich Kapp — an exile of 1848 and also the father of the organiser of the "*Putsch*" of 1920, which not only revealed the complete political incompetence of its framer, but also gave a chance to the rulers of the young Republic to make themselves ridiculous by their precipitate flight to Stuttgart — wrote an excellent book on the German princes' trade in soldiers. I once gave it to the Kaiser to read so as to let him see how low German princes could sink. He read the book with interest and genuine indignation.

Admiral Tirpitz had preceded me to Wilhelmshöhe. The Grand Admiral von Tirpitz was one of the most eminent people whom I ever met. Even his outward appearance was impressive. His opponents, and he had no lack of opponents, used to declare that, if he shaved off that huge long beard, everyone would shrink with horror from the ugliness of feature and expression that would then be revealed. I refrain from expressing any opinion on that point for I never saw Tirpitz without his beard and I do not attach much value to political conjectures of any kind. Whatever Tirpitz may have been he never failed to draw attention upon himself. The tall, broad-shouldered man, with the calm, steadfast look in his expressive eyes, never could have gone unnoticed. He had a naval officer's walk that even on dry land shows its possessor accustomed to keep his balance in a rolling sea. Even among a people which has so great a talent and desire for organisation as the Germans, Admiral von Tirpitz stood out as an organiser of unusual greatness. He was capable of great conceptions, even of the greatest, and yet the least detail did not escape him. To daring imagination he joined cool calculation.

Tirpitz, as I have said, had many enemies. It was natural that he should be hated by Herr von Bethmann-Hollweg later on, for inadequacy does not love superior merit and the mediocre readily see in the great their personal enemies. It was equally comprehensible that Admiral Müller whom William II unfortunately chose as the head of the Marine Cabinet during the war period should be an opponent of Tirpitz, for Müller belonged to that type of official scarified by Bismarck who, careless of the consequences of what they do, peacefully slumber on as long as they are covered by some expression of the All-Highest's desires, which in one way or another they have covertly secured. It is also comprehensible that the son-in-law of Admiral von Müller, Admiral von Holtzendorff, a swaggerer and a boaster, but, alas, a favourite of the Kaiser, had no liking for the practical and earnest Tirpitz. But even among decent, well-meaning folk, Tirpitz had many opponents. He was distrusted. He was considered an intriguer and unreliable. He was held to be untruthful. It is true that Tirpitz with his aim always steadily before him, bending all his powers to achieve it, did not, in certain circumstances, shrink from devious and doubtful ways of gaining his ends. His aim — the fleet — was everything to him. He could say with the Psalmist, "For the zeal of thine House hath eaten me up." Jealousy for the fleet consumed him.

Among his comrades and colleagues he was considered unsociable. That in itself is not so very reprehensible. His tendency to sacrifice other and even important interests, even interests that claimed attention, to his own aims was more serious. Prince Bismarck often used to complain of the "squadron patriotism" that prevailed in Germany and among German officials. By this he meant the mentality of the squadron leader who, as long as the horses of his squadron are sleek and shining, does not care if the horses in the other squadrons have any fodder or not. There was a real danger that Tirpitz in his complete concentration on the fleet might be misled into promoting the fleet at the expense of the army. But the army was still the Atlas on whose shoulders Prussia and Germany rested, precisely as it was in the days of Frederick the Great. And if Léon Gambetta once said to the French army that it was the pride of France and the foundation not only of her greatness but of her existence, "*notre dernier salut et notre suprême espoir*", this was none the less true of Germany. Tirpitz had one fault, he had really no head for politics. Like most military and naval men he lacked a sense of *nuances*. He was inclined to assume that things were either thus or thus. But often they were now this, now that, and sometimes both this and that.

He too often went on the assumption that there were only two courses of action. But there are usually middle ways that may be usefully followed for a time or permanently. These faults of the admiral are the usual faults of martial thought which permits the supposition that a good soldier seldom makes a good diplomat or a successful statesman — and vice versa. Those qualities which are indispensable for the commander-in-chief are just those which can be dangerous in the politician and diplomat, and the method by which the diplomat most frequently gains the day would utterly ruin the general. Nor was Tirpitz the man to conduct or influence foreign policy, for the passionate nature which was concealed behind a placid exterior made him judge things and settle his course of action on personal grounds of like or dislike. He entirely lacked that cool, icy detachment which, undisturbed by love or hate, permits a man to see in moments of crisis only what is best for the nation. This lack caused him to judge incorrectly and criticise unjustly not only things but people as well ; for example, our ambassador in London, Count Paul Metternich. Equally it led him to entertain occasional illusions about Russia and even about France, countries in which he sought support against England, the land he especially hated.

If Caprivi at the time of the "new course" and Bethmann-Hollweg, after my retirement, had come to the conclusion that war with Russia was inevitable, the superior intelligence of the Grand Admiral was above any conceptions of this kind. Certainly in England as in Russia there were very malignant and very dangerous currents of feeling against Germany and much envy and hate of her. It was absolutely true that we must ever be on the *qui vive*, as Frederick the Great long ago impressed on his successor. But we also had to take care, as we did after the restoration of the Empire in 1871, not to expose a flank to our foes, but, with dignity and ability, to avoid a great war. That was what Tirpitz expected of me, as the man responsible for the conduct of foreign policy. In my endeavours to that end, he supported me as far as his jealousy on behalf of the fleet would allow. The premises of what I held to be a strong, self-conscious and yet cautious policy were that we should not regard *a priori* that a war, be it with England or with Russia, was unavoidable. The theory of fatality and every admission of inevitability cripples energy, lessens the resources of will power and intelligence, and, in the end, produces that state of mind in which the chicken runs right into the poisoned fangs of the snake. That is what happened to us in the fatal summer of 1914.

Tirpitz was an excellent writer — clear, logical, and convincing. He was not so good a speaker. His voice was thin because, I believe, of asthmatic trouble, for which he had to go and breathe the pure air of the Black Forest, where he had a house at St. Blasieu. This man of might spoke without force, and this fine intellect expressed itself without irony, although pathos and sarcasm are the great *vehicula* of the orator. For this reason, and also because he was really without true political talent, he did more harm than good, despite the very best intentions, when he created and led the Fatherland Party later on. From my first day of office to my last, I supported Tirpitz personally and politically, a fact which he recognised at my retirement in a letter of warm sympathy. After our victory at Jutland, a famous but belated victory, the Grand Admiral in answer to my congratulations said that my share in the victory was as great as his. I supported the Secretary of State not merely out of personal friendship but because I was convinced that by so doing I fulfilled my duty to my fatherland and was of use to the German people. It is my firm conviction that, if the German fleet had been concentrated immediately after war was declared and sent against the enemy in August, 1914, not only would Germany never have found herself in the position that she is to-day, but also the verdict on Tirpitz would be different.

The fatal reluctance of the Kaiser to risk his darlings, the giant battleships which were so dear to him, the servility and weakness of the head of the Marine Cabinet, Admiral Müller, and finally the

ADMIRAL VON TIRPITZ

blindness of Bethmann, whose guiding idea — after a war of life and death had burst on us — a war that should have been avoided but, once it had begun, should have been fought with all our strength — was to do nothing that would "irritate" England, prevented the naval battle which, fought at the right moment, would, in the opinion of the vast majority of our naval officers, have offered us good chance of victory. A friend of mine, an Italian naval officer who is an American by birth and speaks English like an Englishman, once told me that in 1918 or 1919 he was present at a great banquet in New York which American officers gave to English comrades. The talk was quite free in the presence of my Italian-American friend, who was not suspected of being anything but a pure American, and he observed that there was agreement between the English and the Americans that, if immediately after the outbreak of hostilities in August, 1914, Germany had sent out her whole fleet in a great offensive, the war might have gone very differently. This much is certain, that worse could not have happened than what did happen to the fleet and to us through the tactics of Bethmann, of Herr von Müller, and, alas, of the Kaiser also, tactics which led to the disgrace of the surrender of the German fleet. Thus no one can read Tirpitz's "Memoirs", which he wrote with his heart's blood, without deep emotion. Had Tirpitz not been paralyzed at the outbreak of the war by the jealousy and meanness of some, the weakness of others, and by the Kaiser's fatal mistake, and had he not been prevented from exercising any influence on the conduct and activities of the fleet, many things would have happened differently and he would have stood out as the Scharnhorst of our navy.

The fate of Admiral von Tirpitz is a tragedy, tragic as his book on the war is tragic, above all, as is the fate of the German people, the fate of our fatherland, which is and abides one of the greatest tragedies in the history of the world. But in spite of the final destruction of the fleet with all the horror of the circumstances that accompanied it, the German people will never, never forget its earlier heroic deeds, the battle of Jutland and the battle of the Falkland Islands, Count Spee and his two sons, Otto Weddigen, and all those who cruised and fought on the submarines. They will live in the hearts of the German people as do the heroes of the German sagas, as do Siegfried and Roland, as do the heroes of our early history, as do Totila and Tega and Arminius the Cheruscan. And so too will Tirpitz live in German history. All the abuse that overwhelmed him after his retirement will not change this. The attacks of a retired naval officer like Captain Persius will be forgotten, forgotten just as will the censures and the insults of the Radical deputy Peter Struwe, M.D., specialist in skin and urinary diseases, who got all his nautical knowledge by strolling in the port of Kiel and by listening to what the sailors and marines who came to him for medical aid told him. And first of all to be forgotten, and rightly so, will be those clumsy and silly attacks which Professor Dr. Hans Delbrück directed against Ludendorff just as against Tirpitz, Delbrück who in his younger days was nicknamed "John Clumsy" by his friends because of his lack of tact and balance. After Delbrück, by supporting the wretched and sanctimonious Bethmann (whose inadequacy had long been evident) and the predatory plans of the Poles, had damaged the interests of the fatherland more than any other, the late deputy Bassermann said of him to me that he would rather call him "John Clown." All of them will be forgotten in time, while the name of Tirpitz will never cease to move and to hold German hearts.

The relations between Tirpitz and William II went through many phases.

In 1897, at Wilhelmshöhe, the Kaiser was devoted to Tirpitz and when he went for a walk with me in the beautiful park of the castle could not find words sufficient to express his admiration, gratitude, and amazement. The Kaiser at that time nicknamed Tirpitz "Master", a nickname which, as a young officer, he had received from comrades who realised his superiority. But later on there were periods when the relations between the Kaiser and the admiral were not so pleasant. On the one hand, the Kaiser overwhelmed him with marks of distinction and honour — Tirpitz became Secretary of State, he was ennobled, he received the high order of the Black Eagle, he became Grand Admiral — but at the same time unfriendly expressions of opinion were heard from the All-Highest, and even when the admiral was in audience, the Kaiser was often ungracious and irritable. The fear that Tirpitz and not he himself would be considered the creator of the increasingly majestic fleet worried the Kaiser, and his fears in this respect were fostered by the jealousy or meanness of Tirpitz's enemies.

In that very Wilhelmshöhe where I heard the Kaiser say so many nice things about the "Master", Tirpitz, I went for a walk to the Farnese Hercules with the Kaiser some ten years later in just such another lovely summer. We walked to our destination by a narrow, rather stony path. The Kaiser went first; I followed. I cannot remember now how our talk turned to the Secretary of State for the Navy, but I do remember how the Kaiser reproached me vivaciously for making him keep Tirpitz. I would, he said, regret this on my deathbed. I had forced Tirpitz on him, he declared. I answered that I hardly knew Tirpitz when, before I came into office, the Kaiser had selected him to succeed Admiral Hollmann. I had always been of the opinion that we must be anxious for an extensive protection of our interests at sea once we had been forced on to that element by the natural economic expansion of the German nation. But the Navy Bills had been the work of Tirpitz, work that had been greeted with joy and repeated recognition by the Kaiser. After we had embarked on this path since the end of the 'nineties, I had been entirely of the opinion that Admiral von Tirpitz, with his supreme powers of organisation and his enormous capacity for work, was the best man for the difficult and responsible task now involved. This opinion of mine was never changed by the frequent, substantial, and sometimes sharply formulated differences of opinion about the measure and extent of our naval construction between Admiral Tirpitz and myself. I added that in any case, he inspired me with greater confidence than many another who talked bigger than Tirpitz but did less with his hands and still less with his head. Annoyed by this allusion to one of his favourite admirals who was hostile to Tirpitz, the Kaiser rather angrily retorted: "You won't admit having forced me to keep Tirpitz? With clenched fist you compelled me to do so." I always made it a rule to keep all the calmer, the more excited the Kaiser got. So I answered, respectfully but firmly: it was certainly possible that on occasion I had argued with his Majesty in too heated a fashion and that I had a habit, with which my wife sometimes reproached me, of interrupting others. But such an unseemly attitude as the Kaiser now ascribed to me was quite unlike me. The Kaiser turned, shook me by the hand, and went on, laughing. In personal intercourse he had an unusual faculty of retrieving his slips and repairing his faults. He was rather tiresome in the long run, but very kind-hearted, and as natural as could be.

After my resignation the relations between the Kaiser and Tirpitz went through many ups and downs. Not long before the World War the Kaiser expressed himself to one of the members of the Federal Council with whom he was on friendly terms as follows: "One Tirpitz is worth ten Bethmanns." During the World War their relations grew worse and in the end Tirpitz, after nearly twenty years' activity as a minister, was dismissed in complete disgrace, because, as some one in the Imperial entourage told him, his relations with the Kaiser simply "could not be restored." Tirpitz was not the only one of William II's ministers to suffer this fate. Prince Henry of Prussia, the brother of Frederick the Great, erected a monument in the park of the castle of Rheinsberg and engraved the names of those who, in his opinion, had been unjustly treated by his brother the king, upon it. If such a monument were to be put up for the victims of William II, it would bear a far bigger list of names. At the head of the list there would be the great name of Prince Bismarck; then the names of Caprivi, Waldersee, Miquel, Tirpitz, Bronsart von Schellendorf, our best War Minister since Roon, Ludendorff; and many another would follow, nor would my name be missing. We were all, some of us for a time, some for ever, called traitors by William II, although there is no intelligent man in Germany who is not convinced that though one or other of those named may have made mistakes in this or that question, none of them had ever any other aim but the welfare of the state, the dynasty, and of the Kaiser himself.

The Navy Bill due to come before the Reichstag was constantly discussed at Wilhelmshöhe in 1897, by the Kaiser, Tirpitz, and myself, sometimes *à trois*, sometimes in private discussions between the Kaiser and myself, and sometimes between myself and the Secretary of State for the Navy. Tirpitz submitted the main outline of the bill which was to be made public some months later. The bill was to make it clear that the federal states would not pursue plans of limitless expansion, and in any case would not violate the rights of the Reichstag. Our aim was within a certain time to create a German navy, capable of action and strong enough to represent the Empire's interests at sea effectively. Quite a different sentiment animated this bill as compared with all other navy bills. It breathed definite purpose and strong will. The whole scheme and its individual provisions were all of a piece. It was certainly only a provisional project, but a project which opened to us wide, very wide horizons. In these horizons, in this projection into the future, lay the greatness but also the political danger of the Tirpitz Navy Bill. I repeated to the admiral and often told his Majesty that I had no doubt that the great majority of our people could be convinced as to the necessity of a stronger fleet. I was also convinced that, if the government acted and spoke rightly in the committees and at the full session of the Reichstag, they would carry Parliament with them. I had still no parliamentary experience, but I had a feeling that the bill would pass the Reichstag. What I was more doubtful of was whether England would give us the chance and the time to carry out these extensive and far-reaching plans of Admiral Tirpitz. This was the critical point of the whole matter and of our whole position. Many years ago, almost half a century, our old Ernst Moritz Arndt, assuredly a true patriot, wrote: "What triple jealousy will England reveal whenever Germany reaches a position in which she can begin to be a naval power!" We ought never to come into a position of dependence on England, for if we were completely bound to her, she would never let us put up a barbed-wire fence to protect our economic development, which was already giving our British cousins just uneasiness, and to make us independent of them. We ought neither to challenge England nor yet ally ourselves to her. Between that Scylla and this Charybdis lay the danger zone which we had to traverse. The political situation would be much relieved for me if,

in our new building, we did not put battleships into the foreground
and laid stress rather on cruisers, torpedoes, and coast defences.
The contrary was decided. Tirpitz was expressly willing to give up
new armoured ships for coast defence.

My arguments met the excited opposition of the Kaiser who was
much put out by them. He let himself go so far as to tell me to my
face that they had been suggested to me by "the wicked old man in
Friedrichsruh." He had also advised Tirpitz not to build big
battleships but only cruisers. I could assure the Kaiser with entire
truthfulness that Prince Bismarck had never discussed the navy bill
or naval policy in general with me. The admiral in Wilhelmshöhe
defended the demand for battleships with such technical knowledge
and with such unrivalled mastery of documents, that it was very
difficult for a layman to contradict him successfully in this domain.
But I made it quite clear that I had sufficient good taste not to play
the part of the bungler who botched the work of the skilled worker.
Only I could not but say that the political safeguards for the carrying
out of the naval plans would be more difficult to obtain, the more
the attention of England was drawn to battleships. I was not, at
the moment, of the opinion that England would be driven to a
coup de main, by our naval construction, to an ultimatum, or to
such a procedure as Albion, ninety years before, had taken towards
Denmark. Our political relations with England would become
extraordinarily difficult : if we allied ourselves to England by treaty
that would, more or less, mean that we would renounce the execution
of our naval plans, for they would scarcely be reconcilable with a
really definite Anglo-German alliance based on mutual confidence.
But even if we retained complete freedom of action, we must avoid
everything that might become an occasion of unnecessary mistrust
and friction between us and the greatest naval power. Our conception of the "risk" must exclusively guide us in German naval
construction and must remain well in the foreground. We must
never fail to insist that our naval construction had no offensive
purpose behind it, but was intended only to create a steady increase
in the risk which any power threatening our peace must take to
attack us.

Tirpitz promised me that I could count on his support in this respect and he kept his promise. He steadily made every endeavour to keep the launching of ships from being too brilliant a function, a thing which, considering the Kaiser's preference for outward pomp and circumstance, was often extremely difficult. He tried to keep the Navy League to a calm and reasonable attitude, a task which was also full of difficulties. During the Boer War he took especial pains to prevent the enthusiasm for the Boers which was general in Germany from taking too exaggerated a form. On my side I promised that it would be my part to carry the naval bill of my colleague through the Reichstag. Our policy must be conscious of its aims and be firm, clear sighted, and courageous, in keeping with the greatness of the Empire, with the glory of our past, and the strong character of our nation. We could not, and must not, take our hand from the plough at the moment when it behooved us to till our fields.

CHAPTER VIII

*William II at the Autumn Parade of the Troops at Coblenz — Würz-
burg Manoeuvres of the Second Bavarian Army Corps — Journey to Nurem-
berg with the Bavarian Ministers (September 2, 1897) — The Premier von
Crailsheim, the Minister of Finance von Riedel, Minister of War Baron von
Asch — The Prussian Minister at the Bavarian Court — Count Monts —
Imperial Manoeuvres in Hesse — King Humbert and Queen Margherita of
Italy — General von Schweinitz — Gibraltar.*

I LEFT Wilhelmshöhe as soon as I could in order to get back to the
work of my office in Berlin. The Kaiser left his Hessian seat at
Coblenz at the end of August for the manoeuvres of the Eighth
Army Corps. Here at a military banquet on August 30, 1897, he
gave a toast which, as a piece of oratory, was one of his finest efforts.
There have not been many people who could speak as well as he
and with as much charm. The eulogy which he paid the former
general commanding the Eighth Army Corps, Baron Walter von
Loë, a general whose name has become a synonym for valour, whose
character serves as a pattern of chivalry, and whose life incarnated
loyalty in war and in peace, not only went to the heart of every old
hussar who like myself had looked up to Loë as his colonel on the
battlefield and loved him, but was received with enthusiasm throughout the Rhineland. But when William II, at this banquet given him
by the Rhine Province, spoke of his kingship by the grace of God
with "that terrible responsibility to the Creator alone from which
no man, no minister, no parliament, no nation, can free him", when
he congratulated the Rhine Province that the "blessed foot of the
great Emperor" had trodden its soil, he spoke in a manner intolerable to our age and to our modern habits of thought. It reminded
one of Frederick William IV with the difference that behind the
brilliant and glittering periods of William II there was a stronger
will than behind the speeches — oratorically just as fine — of his
great-uncle.

It is disappointing to me, but I must say that my efforts to get the Kaiser to bring his style of rhetoric and his attitude more into harmony with the present day and with the realities of German life and thought had had, so far, not much success. All my advice dropped from him like water off a duck's back, to use an expression Bismarck was fond of. Or rather to speak in the language of Goethe, you cannot forbid the silkworm to spin.

On September 1st I again was with the Kaiser in Würzburg, where the great autumn manoeuvres of the Second Bavarian Army Corps were to take place. The old episcopal town, over which towers the fortress of Marienburg, lies picturesquely on the banks of the Main, whose valley is formed of vine-clad hillslopes. With its charming red episcopal residence, adorned with the inspired work of the famous Italian master, Tiepolo (which Napoleon I, not without malice, called *"la plus belle cure de l'Europe"*), and the palaces of its cultured nobility, it offered a most suitable setting for the Kaiser's meeting with the noble regent of Bavaria, who had been born in Würzburg and was particularly attached to his native town. The Prince Regent Luitpold who was then in his seventy-sixth year, and was to go on living for another fifteen years, looked like a mediaeval knight who has stepped out of a picture into our present-day world. Anyone looking at him could at once have an idea of what a Franconian or a Bavarian or a Swabian Duke looked like in the twelfth or thirteenth century. His appearance was always stately whether, as Grand Master of the Order of St. Hubert, he wore the brilliant robe with its eight-pointed silver star, on which was depicted the saint and the stag, with the dark red and green belt of the Order, which was founded as long ago as 1444 by Gerhard V of Jülich and Berg, or whether he rode through the Spessart in a simple hunting cape. Among the many German princes who have revered the patron saint of hunting, Prince Regent Luitpold was certainly one of the most zealous devotees of him, whom a stag carrying a cross between its antlers had summoned from the chase and the world to the monkish cell. Hunting indeed regulated the Prince Regent's life. He spent most of the week at it ; on Sunday he went to mass and on Sunday afternoon attended to the business of the state. Nor did the business of the state go badly. The Prince Regent Luitpold had unusually able Ministers, who were distinguished not merely by industry and ability but also by the length of time they had held office.

Three of them — Count Crailsheim, Herr von Riedel, and Count Feilitzsch —had been in office thirty years. The Prince Regent gave his Ministers a free hand, but was very far from letting himself become dependent on them. He was a deeply religious man, but held the clergy at a careful distance, stood firmly on the platform of equality, and in ecclesiastical questions had real confidence only in his personal friend, the Prior of the Chapter, von Turk, who each year on Maundy Thursday heard the old gentleman's confession. Even in his dealings with the Papacy itself, and for all the personal reverence he paid it, he always energetically defended the sovereign rights of his house, as may be clearly seen in a letter in which he emphatically refused to accept Pius X's secret pressure to approve certain alterations in the constitution. When the Minister, Count Podewils, whom he greatly liked, fell foul of him politically, he got rid of him just as he would have got rid of a huntsman who had led him astray on a hunting expedition. On the evening of the day when Count Podewils went (and he did not go willingly), the old Prince Regent was having his corns cut. When the worthy Münchener, who was entrusted with the care of the aged feet, for the Prince Regent was then into his ninety-first year, asked him how things were with him, the prince answered, "They go well. I dismissed all my Ministers to-day. And yet people say I'm getting old."

The Prince Regent had an iron constitution. Every day he took a cold bath, and so as to take it in winter he had a hole cut in the ice on the pond in the castle of Nymphenburg. It often happened that all heated with the chase, he had to drive home, a one- or two-hour journey, in rough autumn weather and pouring rain, and refused to wear any overcoat or cap, or anything of the kind, but would first open his jacket and then his waistcoat and then his shirt and then with obvious delight let the rain stream over his broad chest. Half dead with the cold, his Minister Podewils would sit beside him although Podewils was very delicate and it was only by an unusual strength of will and extreme sense of duty that he was able to force his body to do the work demanded of it.

I was conducted to the palace of the Freiherr von Würtzburg, a finely made renaissance building of Würzburg's best period from the artistic point of view. Baron Würtzburg was the picture of a Franconian nobleman, a typical representative of the old knightly families of Franconia whose coats of arms, united on a shrine of silver placed before the altar in the lofty cathedral, bear witness to the glory of Würzburg in its prime. In the first Bavarian Chamber, to which he belonged as a hereditary member, Baron Würtzburg had upheld the idea of the Empire with warmth and strength of conviction and conducted himself as a patriotic but moderate and reasonable politician in the Navy League. He was to be the last of his race. His only son, Edmund Baron von Würtzburg, fell gloriously on the Western front in 1914, while leading a patrol with especial gallantry.

From Würzburg we went on to Nuremberg on September 2, 1897.

> *Wenn einer Deutschland kennen*
> *Und Deutschland lieben soll,*
> *Wird man ihm Nürnberg nennen,*
> *Der edlen Künste voll.*[1]

William II was particularly fond of staying in this lovely town. Here his family had long held the office of Burgrave. The King of Prussia has four titles — Kaiser, King, and Margrave of Brandenburg. His fourth title is Burgrave of Nuremberg. It is fairly well known how difficult it was for Prince Bismarck after the Prussian victories in Bohemia to persuade his old King to a moderate peace in 1866. The King would willingly have kept lovely and rich Bohemia; he especially wished to recover the Franconian principalities lost in 1806, the Margravate of Bayreuth, which the Hohenzollerns had possessed since 1248, and the Margravate of Ansbach, which they had held since 1362. William I also

---

[1] If a man wants to know and to love Germany, then Nüremberg, full of noble arts, must be mentioned to him.

raised claims to the city where his house originated, to Nuremberg where the Hohenzollerns had been elected Burgrave as far back as 1190. After the thunder-stroke of Sadowa there was great anxiety in Munich lest Franconia be lost to the Bavarian crown. Filled with gloomy forebodings, the Premier of Bavaria, Baron von der Pfordten, appeared at Prussian headquarters. The first greeting by the Count von Bismarck-Schönhausen was not calculated to remove the Bavarian Premier's anxiety. Count Bismarck began by saying to Herr von der Pfordten that his visit was a surprise, that he had given orders that he should not be admitted, and that he would have the officer who, in spite of that order, had admitted him, court-martialed. The Prussian Premier then recalled to Herr von der Pfordten's memory all the services which in the course of history Prussia had rendered to Bavaria; the preservation of Bavarian independence by Frederick the Great in the hour when an Electoral Prince of Bavaria, because Belgium, a rich and cultivated country, attracted him more than Bavaria, which was rather undeveloped, thought of handing Bavaria over to Austria. Count Bismarck then recalled that in 1866, just before the war, a condominium had been proposed to Bavaria on the basis that Prussia should assume the leading rôle in North, and Bavaria in South Germany. The Bavarian Premier in fancy saw Ansbach and Bayreuth and the lovely Nuremberg lost to his country. Then Count Bismarck suddenly turned and declared to the Bavarian minister that, if Bavaria expressed her willingness to enter into an offensive and defensive alliance with Prussia, it would escape with only trifling loss of territory and a very reasonable indemnity. Herr von der Pfordten, who felt as if he had been translated to Paradise after a brief taste of purgatory, was so overcome with emotion that he embraced the great statesman before him, who besides had been his colleague in the Frankfurt Bundestag, with the words, "I see that you too have a German heart." Laughing, Bismarck answered, "Did you take me for a wild Indian?"

As a little salve to the wounded dynastic feelings of old King William certain honorary rights in the Castle of Nuremberg were later conceded him in the Prusso-Bavarian treaty. He was granted the right to live there in a wing assigned "for all time" to the Prussian Royal house and to display his family flag. I do not remember whether William I ever made use of these privileges. William II, who attached great value to such honorary rights, never came to Nuremberg without hoisting the black and white flag and using the rooms assigned to him. That of course hardly pleased the House of Wittelsbach, but it went on without arousing any serious feeling. The German princes felt that they had never been so well off as in the German Empire which Bismarck's policy had restored. In the days of Napoleon many of them, and especially the houses of Wittelsbach, Württemberg, and Zähringen, had suddenly advanced greatly in importance, but things had not been entirely comfortable for German Serene Highnesses under the rule of the terrible Corsican. In 1848 they had all trembled for their thrones, and some of them were not far from being ready to abdicate voluntarily. Only after the great epoch 1866 to 1871 did the German kings, granddukes, dukes, and princes feel themselves in complete security, guaranteed by the four-square edifice of the constitution of the Empire. The genius of Prince Bismarck was never more clearly seen than in the constitution of the North German Bund, out of which arose the constitution of the German Empire, that constitution which came from the brain of his genius like Pallas from the head of Zeus. He dictated the main lines of it to two of his colleagues in one night in 1866. One of these was the later *Oberpräsident*, Minister of the Interior, and Premier, Count Botho Eulenburg, who from the cradle to the grave was the true type of the higher Prussian official, conservatively inclined but thoroughly unprejudiced and enlightened, a statesman distinguished alike in character and ability. The other was Lothar Bucher, one of those who refused to pay taxes in 1848, was condemned for so doing, and had to flee to London, where he stood in close relations with Karl Marx in exile. Thus did Bismarck know how to use all men's powers to attain his great end, the unification of Germany and her evolution to a really great power. Bismarck succeeded in accomplishing what centuries had failed to accomplish; the compromise between the justified particularism of the German peoples and German regions on the one hand, and the

much-needed unity of the nation on the other, between the traditions handed down for centuries and the indispensable innovations.
He transferred to the realities of politics the fine saying of the old
father of the church : *in necessariis unitas, in dubiis libertas.*   Compared to this stroke of genius the laborious patchwork of Professor
Dr. Hugo Preuss is like the bleating of the clerk Beckmesser in
Wagner's immortal "Meistersingers" as compared with the divine
inspiration of the song of the knight, Walter von Stolzing.

On the journey to Nuremberg I travelled in the company of the
Bavarian ministers.   The Premier Baron, later Count, von Crailsheim was the scion of an old Franconian knightly family, a tall, thin
man who always held himself straight as a ramrod, of agreeable
manners and very pleasant intellectually, the best premier Bavaria
has had in the last hundred years and one of the most distinguished
men of the New Germany.   He was absolutely loyal to the Empire,
but just as carefully and ably as he looked after the national unity
did he look after the constitutional rights of the second greatest
German state.   The Imperial Secretary for the Post Office, General
von Podbielski, who wished, by a brilliant *coup*, to rejoice the heart
of William II, one of whose friends he was, had the idea, shortly after
his appointment, of inducing Bavaria to surrender her right to have
her own postage stamps.   He went off to Munich and was received
by the Premier in his study with the dignity characteristic of him,
but a little reserved in a friendly, but not in an enthusiastic manner.
Podbielski, who was jovial by nature, seldom felt resentment, and
liked people to call him "Pod", went right up to the Bavarian Premier who had risen from his chair and said in a jesting tone : "I'm
an old hussar and would like to charge your ranks.   What about
giving up your white and blue stamps?   They really mean nothing
to you and you'd be doing us a favour."   Calmly and firmly Crailsheim answered, "Shall I surrender a right reserved to Bavaria?
Only over my dead body."   Pod returned with his task unaccom-
plished, but did not take his defeat tragically.

Next to Herr von Crailsheim the Finance Minister Riedel was the
most prominent member of the Bavarian cabinet, one of the best ministers of finance I have ever known.   He was unusually ugly, knew

it, and liked to joke about it. Once when Riedel was in Berlin and was present at a big court ball, a wonderfully beautiful woman was pointed out to him. He gazed at her, bemused with admiration. In the end she made him exclaim that he could hardly bear to look on such beauty. Unless I am in error she was the wife of the Argentine or Mexican ambassador, whom he got to know shortly after, and who, even more than Riedel, was the opposite of an Adonis. Greatly consoled, Riedel declared, "I'm as good-looking as he is." Baron von Riedel had an unusually quick and clear intelligence. I can say without exaggeration that it only took half an hour's talk with him in a window seat of the great Federal Council Hall, in the Ministry of the Interior, to arrange the fundamental ideas of the tariff bill and settle the directions for his handling of it in the first reading of the bill in the Federal Council. We understood one another at once. When I became Imperial Chancellor, the Bavarian ambassador in Berlin, Count Hugo Lerchenfeld, a man of sound understanding, said to me: "You'll get on all right. There are plenty of people in Berlin who know every tree in the wood, every trunk and every bough and every leaf, can reckon them up and write them down. But there are not many who, over and above the trees, can see the wood, and to these few I think you belong." To these few in any case belonged the Bavarian Minister of Finance, Riedel.

During our railway journey to Nuremberg the Minister of War, General von Asch, a brave soldier who had proved his worth in the war of 1870, called my attention to the fact that among the ministers of Bavaria who were present, Franconians and Protestants predominated. "And that's a good thing," added the Minister, "for Franconians and Protestants are better than we are. I say this although I'm a Catholic and a real old-Bavarian." In a grave, dignified manner and not without acerbity the Premier protested. Of course it was a fine testimony to the wisdom of the House of Wittelsbach, that for centuries it had taken pains to bind the non-Bavarians and non-Catholics to the ruling house by especially friendly treatment. But neither equity nor equality had ever been outraged thereby. Everyone present agreed with him.

The Prince Regent delivered a short but warm address at a gala banquet. William II was as oratorically effective as ever and, like his host, spoke (with a warmth that came from the heart and went to the heart) of the old and so essentially German town of Nuremberg. He recalled that during his expedition to Rome the German Emperor Henry VII had on the same day and on the meadow by the Tiber near the Milvian bridge knighted the Hohenzollern Frederick V and Louis of Bavaria, subsequently German Emperor. I sat beside Count Crailsheim. No Teiresias could have foreseen then and no Cassandra could have prophesied that the seat of Count Crailsheim would one day be occupied by an adventurer who had been expelled from Galicia and had come to Munich via Berlin, Kurt Eisner, and that in the period of Soviet supremacy the Ministers under him would be men like Catiline, men who, like the Hébertists of 1794 and the Paris Communists of 1871, ought to have been if not in prison, then at least in an asylum. And who would have thought that twenty-one years after this festive occasion in Nuremberg the German Kaiser, then at the very height of his power, who, in this most German of all German towns, had, with the Prince Regent of the second greatest German state by his side, celebrated "the beautiful, the so essentially German old town of Nuremberg", in a lofty speech, would be superseded by a saddler lad who had drifted from Heidelberg to Bremen, where he opened a tavern and, on that very September 2, 1897, was probably giving his guests foaming beer or a stiff grog on credit and arguing with them about the golden age which Socialism, liberating and uniting the nations, would bring to Germany if it could get into power. This worthy taverner was Fritz Ebert. Social Democracy has come into power. But its promises and its pledges have not been fulfilled. The victory of Social Democracy in Russia, in Hungary, and, where their Left Wing got the chance, in many parts of Germany, produced bloodshed and every sort of atrocity. Even the moderate majority could produce neither a better understanding among the peoples nor yet bring true freedom.

The more pleasant and soothing were the impressions which I got from personal contact with the Bavarian statesmen on my first visit to Bavaria, the more reassured I was by the loyal declarations which the excellent Count Crailsheim had given me and revealed how true he was to the Empire, the less agreeable did I find the attitude which Count Monts, the Prussian minister at the Bavarian court, had taken up towards the Bavarian government and had expressed all too volubly in the letters I have already quoted. The Prussian ministers accredited to Munich since the founding of the Empire undoubtedly often had to contend with difficulties, but they did enjoy personal esteem, and the palace in the Türkenstrasse was one of the centres of Munich's social life. In contrast to his predecessors and his successors, Monts was not at all liked in all circles in the Bavarian capital. His standing among them was but mediocre. After my visit to Würzburg and Nuremberg the Royal Minister in Munich, Count Monts, wrote to my wife as follows:

"In Franconia I have just had the opportunity to see with what deftness your husband knows how to handle people and how brilliant he is in other ways as well, and, last but not least, how his constitution is wholly equal to his difficult task. Even if this did not surprise me, it was a comfort and a joy to watch it, and I hasten to tell you about it. Don't, of course, tell Bernhard about this letter I am writing. It is for his wife alone, whom I respect so much, in the hope that it may contribute something to your peace of mind. I don't tell you anything new when I speak of your husband's brilliant qualities. But you can't help being glad and comforted and filled with pride when I tell you that all Bavaria is singing the praises of your Bernhard. The sense of proportion, the calm, the goodwill that he shows in all he does has captivated everyone. Those who, like Crailsheim, begin to talk business to him are amazed at the swiftness with which your husband brings his mind to bear on a thing and at his profound culture in all domains of knowledge. Your husband is well equipped for his task. May the immortal gods now look with favour upon him as he takes it up!" The request not to tell me anything about the letter was of course not meant seriously. The letter was really intended for me, but was, by that neat phrase, meant to seem like the spontaneous overflow of a full heart. For the next twelve years the homage of Count Monts was to accompany me as in ancient tragedies the chorus follows the action. For the benefit and edification of all climbers and sycophants, I append a few of the endings to his letters with which he sought to make his letters to me more impressive:

"Be assured of the most grateful devotion of your . . . "

"I remain with the utmost gratitude always your loyal servant Monts."

(To my wife): "Be assured, most gracious protectoress, of the unchangeable, most grateful respect of your loyal servant A. Monts."

At New Year (also to my wife): "Once again I greet you at the *capo d'anno* and, in the new year as in the old, remain your and Bernhard's ever loyal and gratefully devoted A. Monts."

"Daily do I count myself fortunate to be in Munich (Rome) and realise that I have only and solely Bernhard and nobody else to thank for it."

"God guard you in every way."

"May God have you in firm and sure keeping."

"*Gratias quam maximas ago, semperque agam.*"

"In most grateful devotion, your diplomatic little artist."

"Your true proconsul in Pannonia (Munich, Rome)."

The commencement was: "Most honoured protector (to my wife: "Most gracious Protectress")."

"*O tu praesidium et dulce decus meum.*"

When Count Anton Monts had been allowed to visit us, he wrote to me as follows: "When associating with you I recover my belief in humanity. Good people are nearly all stupid, alas, and all the clever people are bad, as a rule. But you and your wife are clever and good; every pettiness is far from you. Thank you once again for all your kindness. I understand more and more why all the Secretaries of Legation who have the good luck to be under you and, in your home, learn gentility, propriety, and elegance, then become quite different." The expressions of his unchangeable gratitude crop up particularly time and again, in his letters. "In Bülow", he wrote to my wife, "I honour the spiritual father of my Munich ministry (my Roman Embassy) and so I have every reason to be grateful to him. God reward him for his friendship!" When he gave utterance to his joy at my appointment as ambassador in Rome he wrote me: "Besides, I assure you my delight is not in the very least mixed with envy. Just as I have always readily recognised your superiority, and have often defended you when I saw you were not *persona grata* with certain gentlemen (a hit at Marschall, Holstein, and Kiderlen to whom none the less he had earlier paid assiduous court), so am I now glad at heart that a good man is getting his deserts."

"Association with two such rare souls as you and your wife is always real delight for me."

"But you, my dear old Bülow, are the refuge and hope of the good."

To my wife: "I beseech the favour of all the fairies for the fairest and sweetest of all ambassadresses. *Servitore umilissimo Monts.*"

To myself: "I desire always to abide under the shadow of the Bülow banner."

"*Gratias* from a full heart, for your and your wife's New Year wishes. I send you the same with all my heart and beg to be allowed to lay my humble good wishes at Donna Laura's feet. More than any others do true Italian women, to my mind, embody the maternal and the filial with their perfect kindness, their wit, and their decorative touch of Italian graciousness. But your wife possibly possesses herself more goodness of heart than one could justly hope to find even in the noblest of Italian ladies."

And a few days later he wrote, also to my wife: "I thank Bernhard so much and am not able in any way to pay him back for the kindness he has done me in difficult times. But let him count on my devotion and on any service asked of me, Your truly devoted Monts."

There is a poem by Chamisso called "Cousin Anselmo" that so brilliantly delineates the soul of the climber and the toady that the wise poet might have been a statesman or a minister who had opportunity to study such vermin around him. Prince Bismarck commented profoundly on the moral of the poem:

O Dankbarkeit, du süsse Pflicht,
Du Himmelslust, du Himmelslicht!
Wie hab' ich dich mir eingeprägt,
Wie habe ich stets dich heilig gehegt![1]

So spoke to the magician Yglano his humbly importunate cousin Anselmo. So too spoke Count Anton Monts to me so long as he needed my support and favour. To recall our old association and so let gratitude gleam through he began his letter after I had become his superior with his usual "dear Bülow", but then proceeded: "Forgive me if I make use of this friendly mode of address, but I know that in you the superior will never overcome the friend." Then follow some political disquisitions and then comes the consoling sentence, "But you know all this better than I, and there, perhaps, where I only see a blank wall you, with your keener insight, have spied an exit. At any rate my best wishes go with you as you can firmly count on my unconditional devotion and loyalty."

The rest of my reminiscences will, alas, show that when the day of my official activity drew to a close, there was no trace of the troth and devotion, nor of the respect and affection, and, least of all, of the loyalty of which Monts had so often and so hotly assured me and of which he gave me the very quintessence when, in the spring of 1909, he said to William II in Venice, "I never thought much of Bülow."

On the Bavarian manoeuvres followed the Imperial manoeuvres in Hesse. At this war-game the King and Queen of Italy were also present as the result of a special invitation from the Kaiser. Some mishaps, such as usually occur at these large-scale Imperial manoeuvres were this time sharply criticised in the press and especially in the Bismarckian *Hamburger Nachrichten*. The over-exertion of the troops in nothing more than parade was condemned, and so were the great cavalry attacks which were not at all like real war. The military drill, it was argued, should not degenerate to a sensational exhibition based on sheer improbabilities, and producing false ideas of war. The individual actions in the fighting should all be

[1] O gratitude, sweet duty, heavenly delight, heavenly light! How I have impressed thee upon myself, how I have always sacredly treasured thee!

suited to real war. More attention should be paid to the effect of the enemy's fire in serious warfare, better use should be made of the ground, and each engagement should be carried out more deliberately and slowly. The comfort of the royal and non-royal guests at the manoeuvres was not what mattered, but the training of officers and men for serious warfare. This, particularly, was the opinion of the great Hamburg newspaper which had very close relations with Bismarck, whose days were drawing to an end, but whose eyes, still penetrating and anxious, looked into the future. The great official dinner was held at Homburg-on-the-Hill, a favourite residence of William II's, where, during the Franco-Prussian war, he had stayed with his mother and his brother Prince Henry, for some considerable time. If the eternally youthful Chidher sung of by Friedrich Rückert had found leisure during his wanderings to pass through the pleasant land of Taunus and had entered the great hall of the chief hotel at Homburg, he who had known this hall with its long and broad green-covered tables with the single-noted whirr of the roulette and the monotonous triple call of the croupiers: *"Faites vos jeux, messieurs! Le jeu est fait! Rien ne va plus!"* he would have seen in this very same hall the Imperial banqueting table. Three queens sat at it. Queen Margherita of Italy, Empress and Queen Frederick, and the ruling German Empress Augusta Victoria. My seat was opposite the queens and the Kaiser asked me in jest if ever before I had sat opposite three queens. Of course I said "No." Which of these three had the most unfortunate fate? The Empress Frederick, who had lost her noble husband and so the possibility of carrying out all those lofty schemes and ideas which she had nursed for years, while waiting for his reign to come? Or Queen Margherita, to whom a few years later they brought the blood-stained corpse of her knightly husband into the castle at Monza and into the very hall from which she had parted from King Humbert an hour before? Or was it the ruling German Empress who would be held the most unfortunate, she who twenty-one years later was to live through the downfall of the fatherland and the flight of her husband and then to die a slow and painful death in exile?

Denn das Herz wird mir schwer in der Fürsten Palästen,
Wenn ich herab vom Gipfel des Glücks
Stürzen sehe die Höchsten, die Besten
In der Schnelle des Augenblicks! [1]

After the banquet I met my old and honoured chief in St. Petersburg, General von Schweinitz, in front of one of the open folding doors. He had retired to Cassel after he had left St. Petersburg, where he had had a long and distinguished career as ambassador. He told me jestingly that I, as "an active ambassador and minister", should go *before* him through the door. I refused with the phrase of Martial: "*Cedo majori.*" Laughing, Schweinitz said with a smile, "Aha, at last I again see some one who knows the ancient writers and speaks a learned language." I can swear that I did not get that quotation from Büchmann.[2] Even when I was at school I had a taste, or a weakness, for quotations. When an idea came into my head I preferred to leave it in the form which some great prose writer or poet had discovered before me. While I was in office the comic papers were constantly portraying me with Büchmann in my hand, which afforded me much amusement. As a matter of fact, I never had a Büchmann in my hand until, after my resignation, his publisher sent me a beautifully bound copy with a friendly letter in which he said that the gift of the most famous of all his publications would have been misinterpreted while I was in office. The publishers had therefore waited and took the liberty now of sending me the volume in which, meanwhile, one or two utterances of mine had been embodied.

General von Schweinitz made an appointment with me for next day so that we could talk without being disturbed. Accordingly we met in a shady corner over a glass of Moselle in the garden of a Homburg hotel, and thoroughly discussed the home and foreign situation. Personal feeling made Schweinitz incline to England rather than to Russia. In his early years he had stayed in England,

[1] For my heart grows heavy in the princely palaces,
When, from the pinnacles of happiness
I see the highest and the best fall down
In the twinkling of an eye.

[2] A German book of quotations.

spoke English excellently, and liked the English individually. But he agreed with me that Russia was now the pivot of our foreign policy. As long as we were not embroiled with Russia, France would not attack us and still less England. But if we got into a war with Russia, then assuredly France and, perhaps, England, too, would go for us. In the course of our discussions I recalled a remark which Prince Bismarck had made in my presence towards the end of the 'eighties: "There's a boiling and a heaving in the Russian barrel and it may burst one of these days. The best thing for the peace of the world would be if the explosion were to happen not in Europe but in Asia. Then all we must do is to avoid standing in front of the bung hole and taking the risk of getting the bung in the belly." Herr von Schweinitz eagerly seized upon that saying of Prince Bismarck: "And there the grand old man was right again. Russia needs an outlet for the juice that is fermenting inside her. Once the Balkan Peninsula, the Near East, served that purpose. To-day, now that we have become the ally of Austria, this is too dangerous, especially if our policy was to be governed by a not very skilful and not very strong hand. Only the Far East, Eastern Asia, is left for Russian expansion." In connection with what I had to face in home politics, and especially my first appearance in Parliament, Schweinitz reminded me of that wise saying of Socrates. When the youthful Alcibiades was about to make his début in the Pnyx, he had a slight attack of stage fright. The sage asked him if he would be frightened to talk to Ariston the sausage seller and Leander the cobbler individually. For if that were not so, then he had no need to be afraid of addressing them collectively. I only had to separate the body of deputies into its constituent individual parts and regard them close at hand and they would find it difficult to cause me embarrassment. "But," continued Herr von Schweinitz, "we haven't yet touched upon the hardest part of your task, that is, your relations with the Kaiser. Now, when I was a young officer at Potsdam before 1848, we lived very simply, so that a circus aroused great interest. There was a mule called Gibraltar at the circus. One hundred thalers were offered to anyone who could ride Gibraltar thrice around the ring. Many uhlans, cuirassiers,

and hussars had a try.   Many of them rode Gibraltar around once
and were thrown off at the second round.   A few accomplished the
second round, but no one succeeded in the third.   To get on permanently with our most gracious sovereign seems to me to be quite
as difficult."

I was often reminded of the mule Gibraltar.

CHAPTER IX

*Gala Banquet in Homburg (September 4, 1897) — William II's Enthu-
siasm over Queen Margherita — His Letter to Philipp Eulenburg on His Visit
to St. Petersburg — First Meeting with the Future King Louis III of Bavaria — Return to Berlin — Contact with the Foreign Ambassadors: Count
Szögyényi, Count Lanza, Sir Frank Lascelles, Count Osten-Sacken.*

AT the gala dinner in Homburg on September 4, 1897, Kaiser William II proposed a toast in which he referred to Queen Margherita in
so flowery a vein as had never before been observed in any of his official speeches. "In the deepest gratitude," said William II, "and
in the name of my people I welcome the noble queen who did not
disdain to leave her quietude and her artistic and literary pursuits
to honour our soldiers' camp with her gracious presence. Your
Majesty is especially beloved and honoured by us Germans because
you are like the lofty star to which your country and your people
look with trust, because the artist, the sage, the musician, the scholar
have free access to your Majesty." In my long life I have met
few princes who strove so zealously, whether by addresses, toasts,
presents, visits, congratulations, telegrams, and attentions, to afford
pleasure of every kind and to win hearts as did William II. No
doubt this was part of the kindness and simplicity that made William
so humanly attractive. But it was also a result of his overestimation
of externals. Although there was scarcely room on his broad chest
for any more of them, William II took the greatest delight in any
new decoration, and every title or rank in a foreign army seemed to
him a personal success of which he was as proud as the Greek who
could crown his head with the victor's laurel at the Isthmian games.
The consequence was that he thought there was no better way of
attracting and influencing others, especially foreigners, and foreign
monarchs in particular, than by paying them the greatest possible
attention. In this he not seldom overstepped the bounds of good
taste and laid on the colour far too thickly, involving loss of dignity

to himself and so to the Imperial Crown.   Once when he opened the carriage door for Prince Louis of Bavaria, who was paying him a visit — when he met ex-President Roosevelt at the gate of the royal and venerable castle in Berlin and personally took him to the apartment which had been assigned to him, he simply went too far. Thus it came about that not long after he had honoured them so vigorously he often succeeded in offending the very same people in a sudden burst of ill humour, or more or less justified irritation.   The final result was that at the end of his reign among the princes, his colleagues, as he loved to call them in jest, he did not possess one real friend because he had got on the nerves of all of them, and because fundamentally none of them liked him.   "*Juvenile consilium, latens odium, privatum commodum, haec tria omnia regna perdiderunt*", so, as he lay on his deathbed, said to the nobles around him, Mathias Corvinus that King of Hungary who had fought victoriously against Turks, Poles, and Bohemians, who conquered Silesia, Moravia, and Lausatia and made his residence in Vienna.   He had also founded in Budapest one of the most valuable libraries in the world, the famous Corvina, a feat which I rank still higher because I am a confirmed book lover.   Kaiser William, alas, violated the wise words of the King of Hungary in all three particulars.   In his youthful folly he had with *juvenile consilium* chased Prince Bismarck away, to use his own bitter expression, like an unworthy servant.   That *latens odium*, that hate which accumulated against him in many places, in many lands, in many men, he did not perceive. He was subjective to a degree that otherwise I have only encountered in the virtuoso.

The Homburg toast to Queen Margherita, as far as that lady was concerned, was perfectly justified.   Equally gifted in intellect and character, distinguished for sweetness as well as for dignity, Queen Margherita was in truth a true daughter of the House of Savoy, which has given the world many brave soldiers and able rulers, many a proud queen and even women who were canonised by the Church.   As Shakespeare's *King Lear* was "every inch a king", so it could be said of King Humbert's consort that she was every inch a queen.   In a talk which I had with her at Homburg-on-the-

Hill I said that in contrast with my work in the Palazzo Caffarelli the task now before me promised more thorns than roses. As a result of that remark the queen next day sent me the following lines written in German which reveal her noble character, her wit, and her charm:

Gather the roses bravely. God has given them to you so as to delight your heart and mind with the beauty of their colours and the sweet scent of their petals. And do not let yourself be frightened by the thorns. The joy which each tiny and perhaps seemingly insignificant rose can bring into your life is worth a hundred thousand thorn-pricks. For the smart of a prick is soon cured and forgotten, but the sweet scent of the rose even when it is faded remains for long, all your life perhaps, in your memory, and the thought of it can still brighten the soul. Many people spoil their lives because through their cowardly fear of thorns they will not gather the roses which the angels of God have planted on their paths. Pity them. They are the real unfortunates of this world. They are unhappy because they choose to be so.

Margherita

Homburg September 9, 1897.

In reply to the Kaiser's enthusiastic speech on that Fourth of September King Humbert read a speech which had obviously been provided by his Foreign Minister, an unoriginal, rather conventional, but a quiet and sensible speech. The King put emotion and enthusiasm into the passages in which he spoke of his friendship with the Kaiser and his admiration for the German Army. The day after the banquet the German Imperial couple went on an excursion around the district with their Italian Majesties and their suites, an excursion that lasted several hours. We took the road by Ursel, Kronberg, Königstein, Höchst, and Frankfort and so back to Homburg.

I had invited the Italian Minister of Foreign Affairs to share my carriage. The Marchese Emilio Visconti-Venosta was not of an expansive nature. He was cold, cold to the heart, in his attitude towards Germany and all that is German. He was a Milanese and in that great city (which in the old Roman Empire was called Roma Secunda) there had been strong sympathy for France ever since

General Bonaparte, a few days after he, tricolour in hand, had stormed the bridge over the Adda at Lodi, had entered Milan all radiant with the sunlight of his tremendous fame. The enthusiasm of the Milanese for the French in those days has been depicted by Stendhal in his great novel, "La Chartreuse de Parme." Sixty years later, after Magenta and Solferino, the enthusiasm for France once more rose so high that Milan resolved to erect an equestrian statue to Napoleon III, the nephew of the great Corsican, in front of the wonderful cathedral which a German, Master Heinrich Arler of Gmünd, had built. But a long alliance with the Powers of Destiny is seldom granted. When, eleven years after Magenta, Napoleon III lost both a battle and a throne at Sedan, his statue had just been finished. It was never set up and, unless I am mistaken, is still in a shed at Milan.

But in spite of all *discrimina rerum*, sympathy for France remained a living thing in Milan. Emilio Visconti-Venosta never got rid of it. When he still held republican views, he had, as private secretary to Mazzini, often visited Paris on secret missions for the great plotter. As Minister he was often seen at the Tuileries when Napoleon III and the Empress Eugénie lived there. He was still drawn to Paris after Italy joined the Triple Alliance. Only unwillingly and under the influence of the Premier, Marco Minghetti, did Visconti-Venosta as Minister of Foreign Affairs accompany King Victor Emanuel II in 1873 to Berlin where by his all too reserved manner he displeased Prince Bismarck just as much as the latter was pleased with the candid upright Minghetti, who with all his cleverness was thoroughly honest and magnanimous.

During this excursion in the Taunus, which Visconti and I made in September, 1897, we went over the best roads in the world, which greatly astonished our Italian guests, accustomed as they were to the bad roads of Italy, through friendly prosperous villages and past charming country houses, deep meadows, and long rows of beautiful fruit trees. The land looked like a garden. I could see how the first indifference of the Italian Minister was more and more transformed into astonishment and even amazement. *"Que ce pays est beau, qu'il est riche! Quel bien-être! Comme tout est bien tenu!*

Quel ordre, quel propreté! Tout respire le travail, le bien-être.
Ah, vous êtes un grand pays, un pays bien gouverné." In my early
youth I had myself lived in this district. I too was astonished at
the progress which had been made in the interval, the more so as
since the day I left Frankfort and Taunus the larger part of my life
had been spent abroad. How beautiful Germany was then! In
the depths of my being there rang the words which in the period of
bloom and glory in the history of the German People, in the age
of the Hohenstaufen, our own Walther von der Vogelweide had
sung, that there is no land to compare with Germany. The pleasant and comfortable but decidedly provincial Frankfort of the
days of the Federal Diet and Biedermeier had become one of the
richest, most lively, and most splendid cities in Europe. Here was
revealed what German energy was capable of.

> *Das war die deutsche Treue,*
> *Das war der deutsche Fleiss,*
> *Der sonder Wank und Reue*
> *Sein Werk zu treiben weiss.*[1]

Here was shown what German culture meant, this German culture which, through our boastfulness and stupidity, though even
more through the perfidy and malice of our enemies, has fallen into
ill repute beyond our frontiers as *"culture allemande avec un K."*
On that excursion in 1897 long, long ago I felt how true it was of
us Germans that culture really is derived from *"colère"*, that our
culture means fundamentally the preparation, cultivation, and
development of the land with tireless energy, the tending of trees
and plants and indeed of a whole land, and, resulting therefrom,
the development of all that is embraced in the life of the spirit,
religion and philosophy, science and art. The Germany of those
days lies like a lost Paradise before eyes that, filled with sorrow,
look back into a fairer past.

How was it we fell from such greatness? Why did we collapse?
With the Capucin monk in Wallenstein's camp we can but admit:
"the offence came from above." As a man William II possessed

---

[1] That was German truth, that was German industry, which, without wavering or
regret, knew how to carry on the work.

many, very many sympathetic, attractive, becoming, and worthy characteristics. But to his own destruction and ours he lacked precisely those qualities which make a successful ruler. In earlier centuries many "Mirrors for Magistrates" were written which described the model prince and all the qualities which a good prince should have. In William II, alas, many of those faults and weaknesses were visible which a prince must avoid if his rule is to be successful, if like William I he is to look back on his reign with satisfaction, if he is to have the right to say, as did the dying Augustus to his friends around him: " *Plaudite amici, bene egi actum vitae.*"

While I was with the Kaiser at the manoeuvres in Hesse Philipp P. Eulenburg sent me the copy of a letter which William II had addressed to him after his return from Peterhof. Although I had known the Kaiser for years and had now for months had the opportunity to study him closer at hand, I was thunderstruck at this letter. What exaggerations! What illusions! What an extraordinary way of seeing things just as in one's conceit one wants to see them. I was still more painfully impressed with the naïveté with which the Kaiser made free not only with realities but with the truth itself, how he put words and sentiments in my mouth which I had not only never uttered but which were absolutely the opposite of my wishes, of my advice, and of all my explanations to him. Like a searchlight this letter showed up all the difficulties of my task. How, with this in many ways highly gifted, likeable man, who as a ruler was so inclined to false logic, exaggeration, and illusion, was I to protect the Empire from the dangers which threatened us at home and abroad! Dated August 20, 1897, from Wilhelmshöhe the Kaiser's letter to Philipp P. Eulenburg was as follows:

Dear Phil,

Most sincere thanks for your most useful and interesting letter with the enclosed memorandum of which I have a sufficiently good recollection. Your frank expression of opinion on the conduct of naval matters rejoiced me and I am particularly grateful to you for it: for if *you* don't speak from the heart who will? *In rebus maritimis* you seem to be particularly anxious about the alleged feeling in the south of the "united"

German fatherland. It will therefore interest you to hear what is happening here. The naval or "Fleet" bill is practically ready; it has received my approval and in principle that of the Chancellor. It provides for the strength of the fleet to be attained by 1905, and which must and can be obtained. It stipulates for an increase in the ordinary budget of 28,000,000 marks and for a yearly expenditure on construction of 56,-000,000 instead of the present 30-40,000,000. That is the whole affair. The good German people were prepared for thousands of millions and if the bill goes to the house they will look mighty foolish, all the more so as the first instalment asked for will be just the same as what was asked before and will not be increased. That is, in sum, the bill and its purpose. Now as to the methods. Tirpitz has just organised a huge office which both directly and through intermediaries will look after *maritima* in some 1000 to 1500 newspapers and magazines. In the great university towns all over the country the professor-class has met us willingly and is going to coöperate by speaking, writing, and teaching Germany's need to possess a strong fleet. Furthermore Tirpitz took advantage of his stay in St. Blasen to get in touch with Uncle Fritz of Baden[1] and tell him all about it. The result has been that the Grand Duke, who, like the majority of our princes and people, was completely without knowledge or understanding on the matter, was quite surprised at the modesty of the demands, at the dangerous aspects of our present position, and at the revelation of the national necessity that the bill should go through. He has thus become an enthusiastic defender of my ideas which have been carried out by Tirpitz. The admiral brought me this message from Uncle, namely, that he was quite convinced of the rightness of my policy and with all his energy would support and help in the "battle for the fleet" (sic!). He would manage the Baden press but even more and at once would he explain to the "assembled princes of the Empire" that it was "their duty and obligation" to support the Kaiser in this matter. And if as a result it should come about that the envoys to the Bundesrat should make energetic declaration in Parliament, what shadow of doubt would remain that the princes stand united behind the Kaiser. Jagemann will get instructions to this effect. Tirpitz is proceeding from here to Friedrichsruh to have a talk with "the wicked old man" about the launching of our programme and then goes on to Munich, Stuttgart, Dresden in order to discuss things with the princes and put them *au fait*. Uncle Fritz

[1] The Grand Duke Frederick of Baden.

has given him introductions all over the place and will also prepare the ground for his visit.

So much for Tirpitz and the German princes. You can understand that with such an advocate in prospect I naturally keep my mouth shut and use it only for eating, drinking, and smoking. What a noble harvest is beginning to grow and what a reward God is giving me for all the care and anxiety that I have experienced over this business! As for the conduct of naval policy and the cabinet there is unanimity there. But I still worry a good deal over coming struggles and over deputies and the like. To my sorrow the most panicky of all is that smooth wriggler Miquel. This gentleman, whose character reminds me of a reed, has been stampeded into firing inspired articles off in the *"Norddeutsch"* and the *"Post"*, against Tirpitz's proposals which are not known at all to the general public, nor in all their detail even to his colleagues. The result was a sharp telegram from Tirpitz to Hohenlohe and a peremptory order to the *"Norddeutsche"* to remember once again that as a government organ it must n't play such tricks. Besides Bernhard (splendid fellow!!!) has given the Foreign Office and the newspapers what for. He has, in particular, taken it on himself to say nice things about me to the "characterful" Vice President of my Ministry of State and to punch his head at the same time. He is even empowered to tell the ministry that whoever of the gentlemen does not wish to obey my orders and does not subscribe to my policy will have to clear out instanter. It is high time that this lobby intriguing stopped and that once the Kaiser's will is expressed, obedience automatically follows, like Frederick the Great's orders to his generals before Leuthen!

As to the anti-revolutionary legislation, I have already expressed my view that we will attain our ends much quicker if we inspire terror by heavily punishing strikes, boycotts, etc., and at the same time protect the willing worker from intimidation than by the so-called "Socialist Law", that is to say, by the tightening up of the criminal code by which everything which the Socialists can now do with impunity will earn them imprisonment of no less than ten years. This would be very effective, for people don't go to prison — it damages their halos too much. Bernhard entirely shares my view on this matter.

The visit to Russia turned out far better than I expected, and in several exhaustive discussions I reached *complete agreement* with Nicky on all important political questions, so that together we have, so to say, disposed of the world. A restoration of Alsace and Lorraine to France by

Russian aid is an *absolute and downright impossibility*. Thus a war between Gaul and us and Russia and us is, God willing, *no longer* to be feared. The *Continental blockade* against America and, *it may be*, England has been *decided upon*. Russia has *pledged* herself to bring France over to the idea *bon gré mal gré*. It will be your task to separate Vienna from London. Nicky and I again parted as friends who are united by a sincere affection and *absolute* confidence in one another. Our relations are now as they *never were under Bismarck*, perhaps what they were at first under Nicholas I, and Grandpapa. Bernhard has done clever work and I adore him. My God! What a difference to the South German traitor! What a pleasure to have to deal with someone who is devoted to you body and soul, and can understand and wants to understand! Kiderlen is played out after trying to set me against Bernhard by intentionally disregarding the dispatches on the Crete governorship on the journey north. And we are to fall out with Goluchowski! *Doux pays!* The Foreign Office is working full pressure.

Wilhelm I. R.

When I read that letter I realised why Prince Hohenlohe had twice, since I became his colleague as Minister of Foreign Affairs, deliberately and gravely asked me if I considered William II to be quite normal. Once before in his life, so the old Prince declared, he had the misfortune to be the Prime Minister of a sovereign whose mind had given way. He did not want this to happen to him a second time. I had stood in close relations to him and his family for many years. He begged me, and he certainly expected it of me, that I should not dilute the wine but tell him the absolute truth. I answered at once without a moment's hesitation, what I would answer to-day in reply to the same question: "No, William II is perfectly sane. The parallel with Louis II is not exact because the unfortunate king of Bavaria was sexually abnormal, was devoted to alcohol, and was in a high degree unsocial. Our Kaiser is physically quite normal, absolutely healthy, and morally a pattern of purity. But he is neurasthenic and so is always oscillating between excessive optimism and equally excessive pessimism. This is the case with many gifted and important people who are neurasthenic. It is also clear that in marked contrast to his father, grandfather, and great-grandfather our young Kaiser is inclined to *hybris*, which has been a common and highly dangerous trait in princes for centuries, aye for millennia. In William II *hybris* is shown in his passion for boastful talking, which not only makes him unpopular but is politically dangerous. It arises simply from the desire to conceal his feeling of insecurity and of anxiety, a feeling which the Kaiser has much more often than people think. Fundamentally, his nature is not bold but timorous. And finally William II is very tactless, and tact, as you know, is a quality that is born and cannot be acquired. Now that I have so frankly and plainly answered the difficult question asked me, I may hope that I may be believed when I say on my honour that to the best of my knowledge William II is not insane. William II, so far as human experience can judge, never will be insane."

The old Prince was silent for a long time. Then he declared: "Insane or not, there's many a subtle distinction. In any case the young gentleman needs abler and cleverer advisers at his side than any other sovereign."

And while there stood at the head of the Empire a monarch who in his misfortune fully deserves the compassion of all men of feeling and the tears of the tender-hearted as a man, but who, as a ruler, will be found too light when weighed by the scales of history, the Socialists pursued their fatal task of digging the grave of the proud Imperial edifice of empire erected by Bismarck. Their work resembled that of the termites, that extraordinary species of ant in the tropics which nature has endowed with such complete capacity for destruction. These insects live under the ground, build strong dwellings of clay, feed on wood, and, by their astounding technical skill, cause the strongest woodwork to collapse. They form regular communities and proceed systematically, methodically. If instead of woodwork we substitute the grandeur, the strength, and welfare of the Empire, the analogy is complete. At the head an incalculable personality; in the depths a tenacious resolve to destroy. Certainly the result was not in any way unavoidable. It was, above all, clear that no amount of underground work would bring down the strong edifice as long as war was avoided with dignity, with foresight, caution, and tact, and, of course, with the necessary skill. Only a war, indeed only an unsuccessful war, would allow revolution to succeed in Germany and so bring Socialism into power. That was what Bebel meant when at an international Socialist conference he reminded his French colleagues that they owed their republic to the German victory at Sedan, and added: "Besides, German Social Democracy does not object if their French comrades help it in the same way." No French, no English, no Italian Socialist ever spoke like this. But German Socialism had been instilled by Karl Marx with unpatriotic sentiment, with complete indifference, in fact, hatred towards patriotic interests, traditions, and sentiment.

During the days spent in Homburg I had a chance to secure the confidence and the gracious patronage of Prince Louis of Bavaria, who was later to become King Louis III. At a chance meeting on the first day I found the Prince very much put out, even angry. When I inquired after the causes of the princely ill humour, I got the answer: "Am I to show myself good humoured when the Russian Grand Duke who is also here rides in the royal carriage driven by a Prussian royal coachman with a cockade of nobility in his hat, while I, a Prince of Bavaria, ride in a carriage hired in Frankfort, and all that my coachman has on his dirty top-hat is a number?" I at once replied that, of course, some lamentable mistake had been made. A word from me to the extremely punctilious and amiable Chief Marshal of the Court and of the Imperial Household would be sufficient to give his Highness satisfaction. Next morning the Prince greeted me with the words, "Everything has been put right. I will never forget what you did." Happy days when German princes and royalties had no more worries and needs than this! King Louis III was a most friendly patron and remained so even after my retirement. He showed his friendship for me in Homburg when we met at the Kaiser's in the evening, by conversing with me on his favourite theme, the past glories of his house, which, as a matter of fact, is one of the oldest and most famous princely families. "You know," he said, "I could be king of Italy, for we are descended in direct line from King Berengar, the son of King Eberhard of Friuli and grandson of the Emperor Louis the Pious, who after Charles the Fat's death in 888 was crowned king of Italy but was, unhappily, murdered in 924. All the same I'm quite glad I'm not king of Italy," pursued his Highness, "for between the claims of the Italian people to Rome as the capital of the kingdom and my reverence for the Holy Father I should be in a pretty pickle. I am also descended from the Stuarts and every year I receive a telegram of homage from English Jacobites on my birthday. But there'll be no declaration of war on the Hannover-Coburg dynasty as a result. Of course you know that my house reigned in Sweden and therefore in Poland also. The Austrian Netherlands, that is, the present-day Belgium, were offered us in 1786. But we have also lost fair lands. I never go to Ludwigshafen but I think that Mannheim once belonged to my house, and without looking towards Heidelberg in the distance where we once resided. Well — it is all as God wills!" As a result of such thought and feelings the King of Bavaria's ambitions were bent towards Alsace during the World War. The King even thought of a personal union between Bavaria and Belgium because he believed himself a peculiarly suitable person to carry through the assimilation of Belgium to ourselves. Louis III was, of course, not the only German prince who wished to aggrandise his kingdom. Hardly had Bavaria made public her claims to Alsace, when Saxony demanded at least Mülhausen, Thann, and Altkirch as "compensation", while Württemberg demanded Mömpelgard (Montbéliard) on the ground that this county had belonged to Württemberg until the beginning of the nineteenth century. Only Baden was "saturated" and wanted Alsace to remain an Imperial domain. Desire for aggrandisement and land hunger had for centuries been characteristic of all the German princes and dynasties and was still active up to the eve of the catastrophe not only in the West but also in the East where Courland, Finland, and Lithuania appealed to the ambitious.

While Kaiser William was still busied with the manoeuvres, I returned to Berlin. I thought it desirable to get into personal contact with the ambassadors accredited to the capital. In 1897 the Austrian ambassador — he remained at his post till the outbreak of the World War — was Herr, later Count, Ladislaus Szögyényi-

Marich, then sixty years of age, who earlier had been Hungarian Minister at the Imperial Court, and, before that, head of a
section in the joint ministry of Foreign Affairs, a knight of the Golden
Fleece, like his father, who played a great part in the narrower field
of Hungarian domestic politics while his son, while still quite
young, had entered the diplomatic service of the Dual Monarchy.
Count Ladislaus Szögyényi was an excellent man with little peculiarities and great qualities. He was thoroughly reliable, a patriotic
Magyar, who, however, perceived that Hungary in her own interests
could not do better than maintain connection with Austria in the
spirit of Andrássy and Franz Deák and maintain a joint foreign
policy and a joint army. The maintenance of the alliance which
had been created by Bismarck with the help of Andrássy was not
to him simply a matter of intelligence but also a matter of sentiment. He was none the less fully conscious that the circumstances of the alliance entitled Germany to the leadership and,
indeed, that this was in the interests of the weaker and disunited
Austro-Hungarian monarchy. He found my standpoint quite
correct as I formulated it to him on more than one occasion : Germany ought not to and will not sacrifice Austria, but she will under
no circumstances be drawn into war with Russia. More than once
Szögyényi said to me of his own accord that from his point of view
he regretted that Caprivi, Holstein, and Marschall had rejected the
renewal of the Re-insurance Treaty so brusquely and with such unpleasant accompanying circumstances. "That treaty was in Austria's interest as well, for its existence prevented us from committing
stupidities to which there is a distinct tendency both in Vienna and
in Budapest." It was a misfortune that in the summer of the fatal
year 1914 Count Szögyényi, under the pretext that he, who, in fact
was physically still strong and of clear intelligence, was "too old",
was removed from his post and replaced by Prince Gottfried Hohenlohe, a gentleman whose motives were those of a courtier, whose outlook was narrow, and who was, to boot, careless and superficial.
The new ambassador in his dispatches stressed the black and yellow
note so as not to render himself an object of suspicion to Vienna court
and aristocratic circles because of his Imperial German origin.

Besides, through his ties of kinship to several leading personalities in Berlin, notably to the vain and garrulous Court Marshal Reischach, he was in a better position than other Austrian ambassadors to promote Austrian at the expense of German interests. Many things would have turned out differently if Count Szögyényi had been Austria's representative in Berlin during the World War instead of Prince Gottfried Hohenlohe. Szögyényi's little peculiarities hurt no one. He was very zealous and his visits usually lasted from one to two hours. He was very inquisitive and after he had discussed things with the Chancellor and the Secretary for Foreign Affairs he rarely omitted to seek out the head of the relevant political section to inquire of him also. He also had the little foible of pocketing any pencil he happened to see, which gave rise to much raillery and jest. But take him all in all he was a loyal and far-seeing go-between between the two Central Powers.

Like Count Szögyényi, the Italian ambassador Count Lanza was a straight-thinking man of proved reliability. He was originally a soldier and was for many years adjutant to King Victor Emanuel I and to King Humbert. For some years he had been military attaché in Vienna, had been amicably received there, and had successfully striven to improve Austro-Italian relations. In the German-Italian Alliance he saw the foundation and corner stone of Italian policy. Lanza respected and liked the Kaiser, who returned his feelings and very early gave Lanza the order of the Black Eagle, but later, after the murder of King Humbert, often caused Lanza anxiety and even despair through his dislike of Queen Elena. This dislike was only too often revealed in injudicious speech. While able men and men really devoted to William II deplored such "*écarts de langage*", Professor Theodor Schiemann, who was outdone in the art of flattering the Kaiser only by Adolf von Harnack, pointed out that even Frederick the Great had allowed himself malicious jokes at the expense of the Empress Maria Theresa, the Empress Elizabeth of Russia, and the Marquise Pompadour, a circumstance which had not prevented the appearance of these three ladies in the allegorical decoration over the new palace at Potsdam as supporters of the victorious Prussian crown. The *si duo faciunt idem, non est idem* of Terence remains, however, an unchallengeable truth.

Relations of great friendship over a long period bound me to the English ambassador, Sir Frank Lascelles. For many years we had been colleagues in Bucharest and had daily wandered together down the "Chaussée", the Champs Elysées of the Roumanian capital. Sir Frank was a fine type of English gentleman to whom one may be opposed politically but whose numerous and excellent qualities only prejudice and partiality can deny and to which the German should not blind himself, even after the most terrible of all wars, in remembrance of the Roman maxim: *Disce ab hoste.*

The Russian ambassador in Berlin, Count Nikolai Dimitriyewitch von der Osten-Sacken, was the incarnation of those qualities which distinguished the old Russian diplomacy. He spoke and wrote French excellently and knew enough German to understand what was said in German in his presence, and thus was able to pick up much that was interesting, particularly as he always behaved as if German were quite beyond him. He combined the best of good form, a dignified appearance and an absolute correctitude with a good deal of cunning. His favourite anecdote was of the famous remark which the Prince de Talleyrand, the model of all diplomats of "the good old days", made to his successor when he was deprived of office by Napoleon I: "*Mon cher Duc,*" said the prince of diplomatists to his successor, the Duke of Bassano, "*je vous présente le personnel du ministère, tous gens de mérite et surtout, grâce à moi, réellement zélés. Il y a peut-être parmi eux quelques jeunes attachés qui en cachetant une lettre exécutent cette opération délicate avec un peu trop de precipitation. Mais j'espère que vous les corrigerez de ce léger défaut.*" Count Osten-Sacken had been minister at Munich during the reign of Louis II for a long time. One of the peculiarities of this hapless monarch was that receptions were very distasteful to him, particularly receptions of diplomats. Consequently he did not, for a long time, receive the Russian minister at Munich. By chance Alexander III learned of this. The robust Tsar had little regard for minor courts in any case. To the annoyance of his cousin, Queen Olga of Greece, the daughter of the Grand

Duke Constantine Nicolayevitch, he had once said to her, banging his fist on the table: *"Tous ces petits rois de droite et de gauche ne me disent absolument rien."* As his minister in Munich could never see the King of Bavaria he resolved to do away with this quite unnecessary post. Hence great excitement in Munich, where great store was set on having as complete and brilliant a corps of foreign diplomats as possible, the Nuncio shining at their head with ambassador's rank.

The Spanish ambassador in Berlin also belonged to the Munich diplomatic corps even if only in the second instance, and was received with tremendous dignity when he paid his yearly ceremonial visit to the Bavarian capital. It is very characteristic of the far-seeing policy of Prince Bismarck, which always took account of the traditions, even the paltry traditions and vanities of the German courts, that he took diplomatic action at St. Petersburg to ensure the maintenance of a Russian minister in Munich. This action was ill-rewarded, inasmuch as the Russian Ministry made itself unpleasantly felt at the outbreak of the war in 1914 by its anti-German machinations. Should Prince Bismarck in Elysium be reproached for this he will probably reply that with him and under him the World War would not have happened at all.

When I took over the conduct of foreign affairs in Berlin, Count Osten-Sacken was nearing his sixtieth year. He still had lively recollection of the reign of Nicholas I, whose favourite his father had been, a brilliant cavalry general who had distinguished himself in the wars against Turkey, in the Polish war, and even in the Crimean War. His great-uncle, Fabian Wilhelmovitch von Osten-Sacken, had become a prince and a Russian field marshal and, in 1813, commanded the right wing of Blücher's army at the Katzbach. The Russian ambassador in Berlin had not inherited much from this martial hero. He was a drawing-room diplomat. The difference between our ways of looking at things and the old-Russian mentality was never made clearer to me than by a little anecdote which the ambassador once told me of his youth. He had had an elder brother who was a delicate boy. The Emperor Nicholas I happened to notice the boy with his father and said to the latter that he wanted the youngster for the corps of cadets or the corps of pages. The father begged him not to think of that as his son was delicate, but the monarch insisted. "Naturally," continued Count Osten-Sacken, "my brother was dead in a few weeks. And now see how kind-hearted, how sympathetic the Emperor Nicholas was! To console my father and to reward him for his obedience he followed the coffin of my little brother on foot."

CHAPTER X

Two questions were to the fore when I returned to Berlin in the early days of September, 1897: the menace of a conflict between Spain and the United States and the aftermath of the war between Greece and Turkey. In both cases William II had acquired a definite opinion. Events which seemed to herald armed conflicts between foreign states worked with especial force on his lively and fantastic imagination. In his case there was nothing, indeed, of the selfish standpoint of the citizen in "Faust":

> Nichts Bessers weiss ich mir an Sonn- und Feiertagen
> Als ein Gespräch von Krieg und Kriegsgeschrei,
> Wenn hinten, weit in der Türkei,
> Die Völker aufeinanderschlagen.[1]

Still less did he hold the Machiavellian conception: *Duobus litigantibus tertius gaudet.* Kaiser William II followed the wars of other people with all the excitement of the playgoer before whose eyes there is performed a piece which holds his liveliest interest but in which he has himself no part. He reserved only the right of the critic and, as Kaiser, the privilege to award the palm to one side or the other in accordance with his verdict. When foreign war threatened, he could hardly wait for the curtain to go up. In the threatening Spanish-American war his sympathies were all on the side of Spain simply because Spain was a monarchy and America a republic. He came to the conclusion that it was the duty of the European monarchs not to leave the Queen Regent Christina of

---

[1] I can think of nothing better on Sundays and holidays than talk about war and warlike clamour when, far away in Turkey, the nations are met in battle.

Spain, "our gallant colleague", in the lurch.   It was, therefore, my
business to take care as far as possible that the Kaiser in his visit
to Budapest, which was planned for the middle of September, did
not express himself too emphatically in an anti-American sense.
The Queen Regent of Spain, besides being an excellent wife and an
able regent, was the daughter of the Archduke Charles Ferdinand of
Austria, niece of Archduke Albert, the victor of Custozza, and
a sister of the Archdukes Charles Stephen and Eugene, who of all
the Austrian archdukes were most liked by the Kaiser.

During the hostilities between Greece and Turkey which had
ended before I took over the conduct of foreign affairs, the Kaiser
was entirely on the side of the Crescent.   Here, too, personal considerations which determined his judgment on most occasions decided the matter.   I have known few natures more versatile and
more sensitive than William II's.   He so yielded to every impression that he was quite capable of changing his views twice or thrice
a day.   But, on the other hand, I have known scarcely anyone whose
character was so constant in its broad lines.   In his fundamental
traits, the exile of Doorn is, I believe, absolutely the same as he was
when, in 1897, after learning of the heavy defeat of the Greeks under
the Crown Prince Constantine in Thessaly, he sent a telegram to his
mother, who was a passionate philhellene, so that she should learn
of the "disgrace" of her son-in-law and his hoplites as soon as possible.   So many people were mistaken about William II, and even the
penetrating gaze of Prince Bismarck did not quite attain complete
understanding of his character because for the most part it was
not recognised that he took action solely on personal considerations.
In 1897 he was anti-Greek because he wanted to annoy his mother
whom fundamentally he admired for her wit, her culture, and also
for the obstinacy of her character, and whom, at certain moments,
he even loved (he certainly loved her more than she loved him), but
to whom none the less he was in deepest opposition.

Many people have never understood the sudden change of attitude which William II adopted not long after his accession towards
his grandfather's great Chancellor, whom during the nine and ninety
days he had dithyrambically celebrated as the standard bearer of the

Empire, in order soon after to treat him, insult him, and threaten him as insubordinate and rebellious.   This change of attitude was unreasoning and stupid in its manner and harmful to the country as well as to the Kaiser himself.   The reason for his enthusiasm for Bismarck during his years as Crown Prince was less his own intelligence than his desire to take this stand against his parents and especially his mother.   He knew that that was the way to annoy her.   When William II came to the throne, Bismarck as mentor, or as he once put it in a conversation with his confidant, Phil Eulenburg, "as private tutor or rather mayor of the palace", became a burden to him.   It was not very different in the case of another great genius, Richard Wagner.   The Crown Princess had no sympathy for the mighty master of Bayreuth.   She preferred the tame music of Handel and Mendelssohn and unfortunately prevented her husband from doing honour to the genius of Wagner.   Had it not been for his wife, the Emperor Frederick, by reason of his love for everything truly German, for the romantic, for the great memories of the nation as they are expressed in "Lohengrin", in the "Meistersinger", in "Tannhaüser", in the "Ring der Nibelungen", would certainly have been converted to Bayreuth.   After his accession William II's opposition to his mother became ever more defined and his Majesty's admiration for Wagner very much and very noticeably cooler.   When he was Emperor, he once (to the indignation of the solemn house of Wahnfried) made the trumpeters of his Bavarian Uhlan regiment, who were stationed at Bamberg, blow a noisy fanfare at the tomb of the master.   But he himself went no more to Bayreuth.   He no longer had any liking for Bayreuth, and finally, in open opposition to Bayreuth, preferred to have Auber and Lortzing and composers of that type produced in the Royal Theatres of Berlin and Wiesbaden.   Not to speak of Meyerbeer's "Huguenots", which once set William II aflame with enthusiasm and which had to be produced at great expense.   To the composer of the opera "Zar und Zimmermann", the honest Albert Lortzing, a monument was erected in the Tiergarten at the command of the All-Highest.

When I was back in Berlin, I gave instructions to observe neutrality and great reserve in the Spanish-American quarrel that was becoming steadily more serious and to show indifference in what was left over of the Greco-Turkish war, namely, the Cretan question. At my first summons to Kiel Kaiser William had said to me that he wanted me to accompany him to Budapest as I had done to Peterhof : he was going there to attend autumn manoeuvres. On September 18, 1897, I arrived with the Kaiser, who was lodged with his suite in the lofty castle of the King of Hungary in Budapest, the castle where, it is alleged, Attila lived after the first occupation of Pannonia by the Magyars, the *prima occupatio*, as it is called in old official documents of Hungary. From its windows we enjoyed a lovely view of the superbly beautiful Pest and the majestic Danube. Noble embankments penned in the stream of the great German river which was spanned by great bridges. The most famous of all lay just below us, the Kettenbrücke, where in 1848 the mob, incited by Kossuth, murdered the General commanding in Pest, the Count Palatine Franz Philipp von Lamberg, — the same bridge from which, in the reign of terror under Bela Kun and Samuely, the Hungarian Bolsheviks flung many innocent people into the Danube. When the reaction which is bound to follow revolutionary excesses came, not a few innocent folk, especially Jews, were murdered and their bodies flung into the river.

The day after my arrival I was granted an audience by the Emperor Francis Joseph which lasted nearly two hours. The mighty ruler was amicably disposed towards me. He knew that while I was in Rome I had maintained good relations with his representatives there, Baron von Bruck and Baron Pasetti. He knew, particularly, that during my term of duty in Bucharest I had been in close official and personal intimacy with my Austro-Hungarian colleague, Count Agenor Goluchowski, who since then had become Imperial and Royal Minister of Foreign Affairs, and had made myself useful to Austria. The Austrians were not quite pleased that, while in Bucharest, I had secured for Germany a favourable German-Roumanian commercial treaty which Austro-Hungarian competition considered to be an attack on their former monopoly. But of much greater political consequence for the Hapsburg monarchy and for the aged Francis Joseph was the fact that I had decisively and, if our policy was rightly conducted, permanently brought Roumania into the orbit of the Central Powers.

These memories assured me a gracious welcome from the Emperor, Francis Joseph, in 1897. His goodwill to me remained the same during all the period of my work as Minister. Particularly and repeatedly did the Emperor show his unreserved approval of the way in which I solved the Bosnian crisis of 1908–9. Not long before my retirement he said to Count Szögyényi, the Austro-Hungarian ambassador in Berlin: "Bilof — the Emperor Francis Joseph always pronounced my name the Vienna way — managed that affair excellently. On the one hand, he carried our claims on Bosnia and the Herzegovina through to a successful issue — claims that were just, and founded on treaties and conventions of many years' standing. On the other hand, he did not let things go as far as war. I must give him all the praise, for an old man like me does not want to have a war again." At the same time the old monarch sent me his highest order, the Order of St. Stephen in diamonds, with a congratulatory telegram. I also possess a photograph of the old Emperor in the uniform of his Prussian regiment, the Emperor Francis' Second Grenadier Regiment of Guards, with his autograph, in a beautiful gold frame, and also a life-size oil-painting of him, which, as it is the work of a famous painter, is of no little value. The Emperor Francis Joseph did not want a war and he knew why. He had gone to war in 1859 over Italy and Italy had been lost. He had gone to war in 1866 over Germany and his House had lost the hegemony in Germany. A dark presentiment told him that if in his reign it came to war a third time, this time over Balkan questions and in opposition to South Slav aspirations, this war too would be disastrous and might be the last war which the Hapsburgs and the old Austria would ever wage. In the autumn of 1914, soon after the outbreak of war, the Emperor said to his friend, Frau Katherina Schratt: "I shall rejoice if we come out of it with no more than a black eye." In the second year of the war the old monarch sighed, "The struggle is getting beyond our strength." He did not live to see the end of the World War, but, if everything does not conspire to make me wrong, he departed this life with sad forebodings.

I only lost this gracious goodwill of the Emperor Francis Joseph during my mission to Rome in 1914–15. He was angry that, in order to avoid a conflict between the Central Powers and Italy, I urged for timely concession on Austria's part to Italy. He did not understand that by the amputation of a finger his and his Empire's life might be saved. As I shall show later, Berlin intrigues had something to do with this. Under the benevolent gaze of Bethmann, the ambassador, Von Tschirschky, as well as failures in diplomacy like Count Monts, set out to discredit me in Vienna. The question whether Germany, fiercely engaged on all the fronts, could take on another enemy, and a strong enemy at that, seemed a small thing to these gentlemen compared with their fear that a success in Rome would make possible my return to the Imperial Chancellery, a post for which, so far as my own personal feelings were concerned, I had no ambition whatever.

At that audience in the castle at Budapest twenty years before the almost simultaneous dissolution of the Hapsburg monarchy and the collapse of the new, strong, and prosperous German Empire created by Bismarck, the old Emperor never dreamed of the calamity hanging over his realm in the future, nor of the annoyance which I was later to cause him in my effort to avoid this complete catastrophe. In his plain, always correct, and ever dignified way, he at once asked me to be seated. One cannot think of any greater contrast than that between the Emperor Francis Joseph and the Emperor William II. Perhaps it was just for this reason that the Emperor Francis Joseph was practically the only sovereign in Europe with whom the Emperor William II never had friction. The strongest friction which William II ever experienced was between himself and his own mother, whom he so resembled in many ways and particularly in his talent, in his charm, in his naturalness of manner, in his sensitiveness and vivacity, yes, even in his self-will, in his caprice, and in his preconceptions. "There are only two people," the chief of the Court of the Empress Frederick, Count Goetz Seckendorff, once said to me, "so alike as the Empress and her eldest son. The only difference is that he wears trousers and carries a sword, while she has long dresses and wears a veil." Once when the Empress Frederick was especially complaining to me about her eldest son, the Kaiser, I retorted that all the misunderstanding and friction between their two highnesses was due to the fact that they were so alike. They were as like each other as are two billiard balls which spring violently apart on contact. The Empress protested vehemently. She wanted to have nothing in common with her son, nor to be like him in any way. If the difference between William II and Francis Joseph I was possibly the reason why they got on so well together, this unlikeness revealed a difference in character which could hardly be greater. William II was constantly and in everything personal; subjectivity was the keyword to his character; he was, if one may use a hateful modernism, egocentric. The Emperor Francis Joseph was as impersonal as a shadow and indeed the verse could well be applied to him:

> Through world history a shadow wanders,
> But who casts it no one sees.

William II was greedy of fame and here and there let himself go in the most unrefined boasting. He always wanted to be in the centre of the stage. The Emperor Francis Joseph did not shine; he kept himself, so far as his duties as ruler allowed him, well in the background and never spoke from the stage. William II loved display; he used, as already mentioned, to wear as many orders as he could. His self-esteem rose when he took a field-marshal's baton in his hand or on shipboard, the admiral's telescope, which on the high seas replaces the marshal's baton. The Emperor Francis Joseph wore orders other than his own only when he had to receive or visit foreign sovereigns, and even these he wore only in miniature. I do not think I ever saw him with a marshal's baton in his hand. The thought of having to wear full court hunting dress, top boots, spurs, and feathered hat, which William II bestowed on all his friends and servants who loved hunting, would have filled him with horror. The Emperor Francis Joseph went to hunt in the same simple outfit as any Austrian sportsman. The German Kaiser's manner of speech was what the French call *saccadé* — jerky and abrupt; the Austrian Emperor's was sober, even, monotonous, almost soporific.

THE KAISER WITH PRINCE MAX EGON
ZU FÜRSTENBERG

Inwardly the German Emperor never forgot his high position, but he was easy and familiar with people who were sympathetic to him, a habit that sometimes had awkward consequences. He used the intimate second person singular to all the German princes, not only to members of sovereign houses but also to those of non-sovereign families. The Emperor Francis Joseph kept the second person strictly to his nearest relatives and the princes of his house. The idea of using the second person to a Lobkowitz or an Esterházy would have seemed to him a breach of etiquette for both parties.

I may add that Kaiser William never addressed me in the second person as has been widely said and believed. I did not wish to be so addressed. It is no help to business if a Minister is on too familiar a footing with his sovereign. The English say, "Familiarity breeds contempt." Too great familiarity makes it easy for a sovereign to refuse to take his Minister *au sérieux* or to treat him wrongfully, while it leads the Minister to see in his sovereign no longer the ruler of the land for whose welfare he is responsible but just one of his personal friends whom one does not wish to put out of humour or annoy. In the second half of his reign William II had a great partiality for Prince Max Egon Fürstenberg, who as a result of inheriting property was domiciled in Baden, but in his nature, traditions, and inclinations was an Austrian. The Kaiser paid a visit to Fürstenberg each year, took him with him on his travels, and even, as he also did with the Earl of Lonsdale, took him to the German manoeuvres. From the Austrian Fürstenberg the Kaiser had no secrets either personal or political. He showed him confidential reports, made a jest of his own ministers and foreign potentates, let himself go completely in his presence. The Emperor Francis Joseph did not understand such intimacies. "I can't be too astonished," he said once to another Austrian prince, who repeated it to me, "how the German Kaiser can treat as he does Max Fürstenberg, who knows nothing and is not a serious person at all. Why does he admit only Max Fürstenberg to his intimacy? Of course it is all the same to me." The intimacy between Max Fürstenberg and the Kaiser could indeed be a matter of indifference to the Emperor Francis Joseph, for Fürstenberg, as far as his intelligence and his ability permitted, did his best to promote Austrian interests at the Prussian court. Thereby he influenced our relations with Russia and also with Italy repeatedly and unfavourably. Fürstenberg sent a report to Vienna of all he heard at the Prussian court that was of political interest. This was quite comprehensible in an Austrian, who by birth and sympathies through his mother and his wife was an Austrian, *pur sang*. The Austro-Hungarian ambassador in Berlin, Count Szögyényi, told me *proprio motu* that his duty as an envoy, as a man of good feeling and decency, was to tell me frankly about this.

With all the gravity which was natural to him and which was naturally heightened by the tragic destiny which in his reign of more than sixty years so oppressed him, the Emperor Francis Joseph preserved the Austrian bent for humour, kindly and innocent humour. Even in his old age he rose very early, between four and five o'clock in the morning, and in compensation, went to bed at night as early as possible and never after nine o'clock if he could manage it. His Foreign Minister, Count Goluchowski, had exactly the opposite habits. He went to bed long after midnight and so got up as late as he could in the forenoon. When he accompanied the Emperor on a journey to Roumania, the former said to him with a smile, "My dear Count, I know that you like to sleep in the mornings. So please don't trouble to bring reports to me at five; come about six." A remark the Emperor made in 1866 (its authenticity was guaranteed to me) shows a grimmer humour. It was at a hunting party. The Emperor, as was natural after a war which he had lost, was in a depressed mood. His adjutants thought that they might improve his Majesty's temper if they abused the Prussians and, of course, Bismarck in particular. One of them went too far by declaring that he knew from a sure source that Bismarck got drunk every day on schnapps. "Heavens," cried Francis Joseph, "if my ministers would only take to schnapps." The Emperor Francis Joseph once summed himself up : he thought, he said, that he would have made an excellent court official. His grandfather, the Emperor Francis I, had already said something similar about himself. There is something tragic in the fact that the monarch, who was attracted by the laurels of a subordinate official and whose most intimate feelings showed a kindly and harmless nature, seemed, in the imagination of whole nations, a cruel executioner. The Italians called him the "*gran Impiccatore*" (the great hangman), and right up to his death a great part of the Hungarian nation could not forgive him the many death sentences which he had allowed to be carried out in Pest, in Temesvár, and in Arad after the crushing of the Hungarian rebellion in 1849. The last years of his reign were again to be saddened by the executions — some of them cruel ones — in Galicia, in Dalmatia, on the Save and on the Narenta, in Bosnia and the Herzegovina. And in Rome a marble tablet opposite the Palazzo Venezia, which was so long the home of the Austrian Embassy to the Vatican, as well as a marble bust on the Pincio, commemorate the cruel execution of the burgomaster and deputy of Trent, Cesare Battisti, who was captured, arms in hand, by the Austrians and, although severely wounded, was hanged by them. When the Emperor Francis Joseph died, the English and French newspapers remarked that never had a monarch, unless indeed an Asiatic or African monarch, during his reign signed so many death warrants. That remark, "But we 'd better hang a few first", which was made by Austria's one statesman of genius, Prince Felix Schwarzenberg, to the Lombard and Hungarian noblemen, who asked for milder treatment of the Magyar and Italian rebels in 1849, holds good from the beginning to the end of the sixty-eight years of the Emperor Francis Joseph's reign, one of the longest reigns known to history.

But the biggest difference between him and the Emperor William consisted in this, that the ruler of the Dual Monarchy refused to entertain any and all of those feverish phantasies which nature had so prodigally bestowed on the German Kaiser in his cradle. Francis Joseph I was therefore incapable of understanding the tendencies of his age, the ideals and deepest aspirations, the good as well as the bad qualities of his many peoples, not to mention his inability to turn them to political profit. Just as he often saw the present in a false light, so was he lacking in the intuition of what was going to happen in the future. William II very often saw things in a false, an absolutely false, light, but he had vision, he had ability to see into the future, he had genius. If occasionally he was too impulsive,

Francis Joseph had no impulses at all.   It is possible to go too far
in saying that he was without feeling, but only to a very few
had he shown his feelings.   It scarcely ever was in his power
to turn an enemy into a friend, to secure a politician by a heart-to-
heart talk.   He was no captivator of man or souls, whereas William
II, with the undeniable charm of his nature, captivated more than
one person who had come with an inward opposition to the plans
and ideas of the monarch.   In contrast to his Austrian, and especially his Viennese subjects, Francis Joseph I had no sentimental
strain in his nature.   Just as he stoically endured what fate brought
upon him — and what blows both of a political and a personal kind
did not fate deal him ! — so he had no feeling for the fate and sorrows
of others and, at the best, could give to those overwhelmed by misfortune only a few quite banal, quite conventional words.   William
II was attractive because of his quick sympathy with people whom
he liked.   Francis Joseph I never unbent towards his ministers, at
least, not after he had passed his years of youth.   But he shed no
tears even over those whom he had liked.   William II was grieved,
he was upset and pained, when, in 1895, the Imperial Chancellor
Hohenlohe quietly but firmly insisted on the dismissal of the Minister of the Interior, Ernst Mathias von Köller, for whom the Kaiser
personally had a great liking.   While he was still Crown Prince,
William II had regretfully, during the nine and ninety days, seen the
dismissal (with the tacit consent of Prince Bismarck) of the Minister,
Robert von Puttkamer, who was his personal friend, and he gave
lively and public expression to his feelings on the matter.   Francis
Joseph I allowed his friend Taaffe to go with the same equanimity
as he saw the departure of Giskra, whom he had branded as a "bad
Austrian."   When the Emperor Francis Joseph at a chance visit to
Schwechat saw for the first time for many years among the assembled notables Count Bernhard Rechberg, who in the critical
years of his reign from 1859 to 1865 had stood by him and in close
contact with him as Minister of Foreign Affairs, he could find no
other greeting for the old statesman, who had been proved in many
a position and was now ninety-one, save the words, "We 've not
seen one another for a long time."   To no one was the German

Kaiser just indifferent. He took up a definite attitude *pro* or *contra*. Without showing any sign of emotion Francis Joseph submitted to the appointment as Premier of Hungary of Francis Kossuth, whose father, Louis Kossuth, as dictator of Hungary, had proposed and carried in the parliament at Debreczin in 1849 the deposition of the House of Hapsburg. During the whole of the World War and even in the summer of 1918 William II resolutely refused my return to office (although in my years of office I had done good service to him and to the country) simply because he had *ex post* taken amiss my attitude in the November days of 1908, an attitude which I had taken in the interests alike of the Empire and the Throne. On the other hand, William II revealed many fine and noble traits of character.

Besides, it would be a mistake to think that William II could have been personally sympathetic to the Emperor Francis Joseph. The Hapsburg treasured the loyalty of the Hohenzollern to the alliance; he placed his confidence in that loyalty, but personally William II got on the nerves of the much older Francis Joseph, although he did his best to conceal it. He looked forward with dislike to meetings with William II; he hailed his departures with a sigh of relief. He found William II original but not quite dignified. The jests and sallies of his German colleague seemed vulgar to him and his whole manner not quite that of a gentleman. As William II, despite his brilliant qualities, lacked flair and tact, he never noticed that, considering the great difference of age between the two monarchs, a greater reserve on his part would have been welcomed by the older emperor and that the latter would have much preferred not to see the German Kaiser appear quite so often on the beautiful blue Danube. Francis Joseph was human only in his relationship with Frau Katharina Schratt. I will add at once that the relationship was purely one of friendship. Frau Schratt was not merely a talented actress; she was also an amiable and agreeable woman, sprightly, gracious, and above all natural, as Viennese women are. She kept aloof from politics completely, a fact which did not keep the industrious envoys of the smaller powers from paying zealous court to her and with grave importance telegraphing her harmless chatter to Dresden and Munich. Frau Schratt stood in completely good relations with the Empress Elizabeth, who was genuinely glad that her exalted spouse found in conversation with Katharina relaxation and compensation for the checks to his policy and the terrible ordeals which he had to undergo in his private family life. In his letters to her Francis Joseph always addressed Frau Schratt ceremoniously. In her drawing room hung a large picture of the Empress Elizabeth, who had sent it to this friend of the Emperor's. The Emperor was very fond of playing tarock — one of the popular card games of the Danube valley — with Frau Schratt. The third in the game was an excellent official called Schulz. When one of the Emperor's daughters, who like her mother was very fond of Frau Schratt, called her father's attention to the fact that it was perhaps not quite the thing to play cards with a plain Herr Schulz, Schulz was made an excellency and this difficulty in the eyes of the Hofburg brilliantly removed. But whatever he may have been, the Emperor Francis Joseph was the last Austrian Emperor and was worthy to be the last of that long line. It would be an outrage on that old Imperial family to describe the Emperor Charles as the last of the Hapsburgs. This Ephialtes among the princes, who feloniously, cravenly, and treacherously went over to the enemy and betrayed his ally, who, alas, through Austria, had let herself be involved in the most terrible of all wars, was a blot of shame in the history of the Hapsburgs and of Austria. He cannot and ought not to be reckoned as that history's end.

The House of Hapsburg had sinned, very greatly sinned, against the German people. Through its false policy Switzerland and Holland were driven from the Empire. The counter reformation policy of Ferdinand produced the Thirty Years' War, the most terrible misfortune which overtook Germany before the World War. But Austria is and remains part of the body of Germany. Austrian and Hapsburg history are too closely connected with German history for us not to desire a worthy end to the old Danubian Monarchy. I have never stood in the presence of Francis Joseph, although I am a Prussian of the Prussians and cannot forget the sins of the Hapsburgs against Germany, without feeling emotion at the thought of the old connection between us and this house. How many and what great events, what heights and what depths are not included in those six centuries between the day in 1273 when Rudolf of Hapsburg left the Habichtsburg in the Aargau, whence the greatness of his house sprang, to ride to Frankfort-on-the-Main, and the day in 1918 when the Hapsburg empire fell to pieces, the election of Rudolf to be German king, the victory over Ottokar, King of Bohemia, the acquisition of Austria and Styria, of Carinthia and Krain, of Tirol and the Breisgau of Istria and Trieste, the marriage with Mary of Burgundy, the match with Joanna of Aragon. *Tu felix Austria nube!* From the German Imperial throne the sceptre of the Hapsburgs stretched over Spain, Holland, and Belgium, over all Italy from Milan to Palermo, over part of what is to-day France. The Hapsburgs ruled South America, Central America, and a great part of North America. They won Bohemia, Silesia, Hungary, Croatia. "Austria great in honours and in victories." Prince Eugene, the noble knight, Zenta and Belgrade; the Archduke Charles and the victory of Aspern, which Heinrich von Kleist greeted so joyfully, and in the last century even the old Radetzky. "In his camp was Austria." For history the Emperor Francis Joseph, who, despite all his weaknesses and faults, is worthy of reverence, not only for the length of his reign but also because of those blows which fate rained on him and which find their like only in the tragedies of destiny of Sophocles and the tragedies of the kings of Shakespeare, is an end which evokes sadness and the sense of the transience of all earthly things and makes vanish hateful memories. But may the future grant that the German-Austrian race may find its way back to be one again with Germany, its mother.

The Emperor Francis Joseph began his conversation with me in the Castle of Budapest on September 19, 1897, with a survey of the Balkan princes such as the *genius loci* invited. Prince Ferdinand of Bulgaria came out of it worst. In his early years Prince Ferdinand had served in the Austrian army. Like many other scions of the House of Coburg he was intellectually very gifted and undoubtedly of the stuff that reigning princes are made of. In

versatility, frankness, and fineness of intellect he surpassed most of
the monarchs of his time, but during his several years of service
in the Austrian army he had been an indifferent officer of hussars.
While the Emperor Francis Joseph even in his old age sat straight as
a ramrod in the saddle and took every ditch, Prince Ferdinand considered a horse a personal enemy.   That did not at all please the
old cavalryman, Francis Joseph.   Much, very much more did it
displease him that Prince Ferdinand, two years after a Roman
Catholic baptism, had let his eldest son, the Crown Prince Boris, be
received into the bosom of the "true believing" Bulgarian national church by a second baptism at the hands of the Metropolitan
of Rustschuk.   The Emperor Francis Joseph was a loyal son of the
Roman church, but neither intolerant nor bigoted.   "The Emperor,"
once said the aged Adjutant General Count Paar, "would give
all his bishops for three new regiments of cavalry."   Reasons of
state were supreme with him.   One could say of him that he was
the incarnation of the Austrian state although he was not intellectually able enough to conduct Austria's policy correspondingly.
He had very little of the glowing religious zeal of his nephew, the
Archduke Francis Ferdinand, who, after a sermon by a Jesuit priest
on the blessings of Ferdinand's counter reformation, told the preacher
with shining eyes and quivering voice that the sermon had been
one of the finest and deepest impressions of his whole life.   The
Emperor Francis Joseph was still further removed from the childish
simplicity of his nephew Charles, who, after he had ascended the
throne, to the woe of the Hapsburg monarchy and its German ally,
once asked a Capuchin monk to draft him a programme of government for the conduct of the most complicated and most difficult
mechanism in the world : to wit, for the conduct of the domestic and
foreign policy of the Austrian-Hungarian monarchy.   And this
worthy monk was but a little more scrupulous counsellor than those
members of other orders with whose help the Emperor Charles
and his intriguing wife, the Empress Zita, contrived the treachery
to the German ally, who on behalf and through the instrumentality
of the Hapsburg monarch had allowed itself to become involved in
the most terrible of all wars.

What Francis Joseph reproached Prince Ferdinand with in the matter of his son's second baptism was what the Emperor called lack of character. With relish he related to me some malicious stories of the Bulgar prince which he had heard from his Foreign Minister, Count Goluchowski, who judged the second baptism of the Crown Prince much more harshly even than his sovereign. With Serbia the old Emperor was quite pleased. There for nearly a century the house of Obrenovitch and the house of Karageorgevitch had fought each other by the methods which once distinguished the house of Atreus and the family relations of the Borgias. King Milan of the House of Obrenovitch had, by his heedlessness, given Austria plenty of trouble, but he had always held to Austria, from whom he received large subsidies. After long matrimonial quarrels with his spouse, Natalie Ketschko, Milan had left Belgrade, which long ago had become boring to him, so as to enjoy life in the Capua on the Danube, the beautiful and easy-going Vienna with occasional expeditions to Paris. His son Alexander followed in his father's footsteps politically and at that time they were quite content with him in Vienna. The Serbian Circe, Madame Draga Maschin, had not yet made the acquaintance of the young ruler. With real sympathy the Emperor spoke of King Carol of Roumania, who was genuinely sympathetic to him by his equable character, calm self-possession, and excellent manners. "All goes well between us and Roumania," declared the Emperor Francis Joseph. I knew only too well that everything was not going well between the two countries. I had worked too long in Bucharest not to know what great danger to the Hapsburg monarchy lurked in the over-severe Magyar policy towards the nationalities.

One of the ablest Hungarians, Benjamin von Kallay, who from 1879 to 1882 was head of a department in the Foreign Ministry and since had been Imperial Minister of Finance and so entrusted with the administration of Bosnia and the Herzegovina, and had written an excellent history of the Serbs, once in the 'nineties warned his fellow countrymen in an arresting speech against carrying the nationalities policy too far. He called to mind the *fata morgana* that is sometimes seen in the Hungarian prairie. The Magyar calls her "*Delibab*." She lures the unwary traveller who trusts her into a bog into which he sinks and is lost. In Bucharest I noticed only too well how boundlessly the Serbs and Roumanians were embittered by the mixture of megalomania and psychological shortsightedness, of fanatical intolerance and legal pettifoggery which was the hallmark of the Magyar nationalities policy. But contempt for the smaller peoples within the realm of the Crown of St. Stephen was so ingrained in the Magyars that no rational considerations would have accomplished anything against it. To the Magyar the Roumanian was the "*büdos allah*" — the stinking Wallach; to Serbs and Croat were applied the words, "The Slav is not a man." In vain did Franz Deák preach moderation and self-control to his fellow countrymen; in vain Count Julius Andrássy warned them that the Magyar ship of state was so loaded with prosperity that one ounce more of cargo, be it dross or gold, would capsize it. The Parliamentary and aristocratic government which held the tiller in Hungary pursued the phantom of complete assimilation or extermination of the non-Magyar nationalities in the Kingdom of the Crown of St. Stephen with a blindness from which none of the Hungarian statesmen who, after Deák and Andrássy, had any influence, can be absolved. The greatest of them was Count Stefan Tisza, who might have been reckoned among the really great statesmen had he possessed as much moderation as strength, as much reflection and foresight as glowing patriotism. But to this idea of the accomplishment of the absolute hegemony of the Magyar race he sacrificed every other consideration. Thereby Tisza was to do his land grave injury. But none the less as a man who at all times remained true to himself he was a great historical figure. He was the only one of the influential Hungarian and Austrian statesmen who was opposed to the mad policy which was introduced in the summer of 1914 with the ultimatum. He was also not in favour of just as senseless a step, the proclamation of the independence of Poland by the Central Powers. He was against exaggerated annexations, for they appeared to him to endanger the predominance of the Magyars in the Dual Monarchy. He maintained order with an iron hand. When the Emperor Charles, to whom Count Tisza as a Protestant was already unsympathetic, dismissed him soon after his accession, after he had for some time been declaring that "the Calvinist Pope" would not be long in office, the bells of doom sounded for the Dual Monarchy and the House of Hapsburg, the clock ran down, the hand fell; its day was done. Stefan Tisza did not survive the downfall of his nation. He died by the hand of an assassin as fearlessly as he had lived.

Count Julius Andrássy the younger, and Count Albert Apponyi were just as unintelligent in the handling of the nationalities as was Tisza, but they did not possess the strength that was his characteristic. But Apponyi had certainly the greatest oratorical gift of any man I knew. He spoke brilliantly and equally well in any language: in Magyar, in German, in English, in French, probably also in Italian and Latin. He could speak on any subject: politics or music, education or agriculture. But he had the ill fortune, perhaps because of his versatility, to be disliked by the Emperor Francis Joseph. The latter left Apponyi in no doubt of his dislike, and the sensitive Apponyi was from that day a very bitter opponent, not only of the old Emperor, but also of the Austro-Hungarian compromise of 1867. On the other hand, no effort was made in Vienna to win back Count Albert Apponyi, who sprang from an extremely conservative family which until then had been completely loyal to the Emperor. When Apponyi delivered his first anti-Austrian and, in a certain degree, anti-dynastic speech, the ambassador, Count Szögyényi, who had been a great friend of Count Albert Apponyi's father, said to me: "When I read Albert Apponyi's speech, I was as thunderstruck as if I had seen my dead mother dance a cancan in the churchyard." But it was also Szögyényi who told me that when Albert Apponyi began to play a part in Parliament, Vienna could have won him over by giving him a minister's post in Athens to be followed by an ambassador's some years later, but that now nothing could content him but the deposition of the old Emperor. Count Andrássy shared in all the extravagances of Count Albert Apponyi. He was not quite so filled with rancour against the Hofburg, but he was at least just as ambitious.

When I was in the Emperor's presence on September 20, 1897, I could have said a lot to him against the Magyar nationalities policy, founded on my experiences and impressions at Bucharest. But to give a lesson to an old Emperor, to a prince who had seen so much, experienced so much, struggled so much, suffered so much, as had the Emperor Francis Joseph, who was on the throne when I was born, is not so easy or so simple as to give an answer in Parliament or at a Cabinet council. "I should like to see the man who can direct the attention of the Emperor Francis Joseph to a matter that he wants to avoid," had said once an Austrian, the Finance Minister Kaizl, after an audience with Francis Joseph I in which he had found it impossible to put forward what he wanted. And above all, the German-Austrian alliance had been concluded by Bismarck with the Magyar Andrássy, who with the Hungarian nation behind him had prevented Beust, the Archduke Albrecht, and the Emperor Francis Joseph from joining France against Prussia and Germany in the summer of 1870. In the summer of 1884, when in connection with my transference from Paris to St. Petersburg I stayed at Varzin, Prince Bismarck pointed to a map and said: "There between the Danube and the Carpathians live the Hungarians. For us it is just as though the Germans were there, for their destiny is tied with ours — they stand or fall with us. That is the fundamental difference between them and the Slavs and Roumanians. The Hungarian factor is the most important for us in the whole Balkan region, which really begins with the roads round Vienna." Prince Bismarck resolutely refused, as I did later, to let us be dragged into a war with Russia through the Magyars, but he also did not want to interfere with advice in what were internal Hungarian politics. But as far as the Emperor Francis Joseph is concerned he who judges rightly will not overlook how difficult it must have been for him to put himself in opposition to Hungarian public opinion, to Hungarian passions and Hungarian prejudices, to the wishes of Hungarian ministers. Most of the tasks of his government were strongly negative; of the few positive tasks that he accomplished, the first in importance was that of reconciliation with the Hungarian nation.

It was dearly, perhaps too dearly, bought. Consequently he did not wish to forfeit this gain, and he knew that he ran the risk of endangering it whenever he ran counter to the exaggerated nationalistic feeling of the Magyars. The Magyars were an aristocratic nation of magnates for which a then very obsequious but chauvinistically pro-Magyar Jewish class provided the necessary lawyers, doctors, journalists, and financiers. Fundamentally, all Hungarian domestic policy, which created so much furore, was simply the expression of a struggle between a few noblemen and their followers, Count Julius Andrássy, Count Albert Apponyi, Count Bánffy, Count Khuen Hederváry, Count Michael Károlyi, and, the greatest of them all, Count Stefan Tisza, and amongst them a few scions of the gentry like Koloman von Szell, Wekerle, Féjerváry were included.

CHAPTER XI

DURING the long interview with which he had honoured me, the Emperor Francis Joseph had been extremely amiable. But the impression which I had previously received from all the Austrians and non-Austrians who had closer knowledge of him that his chief characteristic was calm indifference could only be strengthened by the audience I had with him. This made me wish that the temperamental William II would not shock too sorely the refined taste of his host when the time came for speech-making at the official banquet arranged for September 21. When I expressed this wish to the Kaiser he answered very pleasantly, in tones in which there was only friendliness and not the slightest indication of taking offence: "My dear Bernhard, you are far cleverer than I. But I know much more about speech-making than you do. As far as I know you 've never yet made a public speech. I 've made plenty of them and I 'll say without conceit that my speeches were n't bad. Don't get excited, but let me speak in my own way."

At the banquet the Emperor Francis Joseph painfully, hesitatingly, and in a tired voice read out the very careful, but cold and characterless speech which his Foreign Minister had composed for him. Kaiser William at once got to his feet and delivered one of the best speeches I have ever heard him make. I know hardly any other of his speeches which was so characteristic of his manner. He began with the assurance that the splendid reception given him in beautiful Budapest had overwhelmed him. Talleyrand said of the first

Napoleon that he was "*le moins amusable des hommes.*" William II, on the contrary, was easy to entertain, easy to win, and particularly easy to make enthusiastic. During my term of office I seldom went anywhere with him without his declaring to me after his entry that it was the most wonderful reception of his life. That was the case at Peterhof and at Windsor, in Budapest and in Vienna, in Constantinople and at Venice, in Rome and in Jerusalem, at Naples and at Palermo, at Damascus and at Beirut, at every visit, at all manoeuvres. Napoleon was happy only in the storm and stress of gigantic destinies. The son of the arrogant isle of Corsica appeared first to France and the world amid the smoke of gunpower and the thunder of the cannon of Toulon, and he ended that short meteoric career of twenty years in the sunset of a lonely island far, far out in the Atlantic. William II's case was different.

> *Jung ward ihm der Thron zuteil,*
> *Und ihm beliebt es, falsch zu schliessen,*
> *Es könne wohl zusammengehn*
> *Und sei recht wünschenswert und schön:*
> *Regieren und zugleich geniessen.*[1]

The verses which Goethe in prophetic mood puts into the mouth of Mephisto about the emperor in the second part of "Faust" in the most pregnant way reveals the disposition of William II. And although Faust replies:

> *Ein grosser Irrtum. Wer befehlen soll,*
> *Muss im Befehlen Seligkeit empfinden,*
> *Ihm ist die Brust von hohem Willen voll,*
> *Doch, was er will, es darf's kein Mensch ergründen.*
> *Was er den Treusten in das Ohr geraunt,*
> *Es ist getan, und alle Welt erstaunt.*
> *So wird er stets der Allerhöchste sein,*
> *Der Würdigste — geniessen macht gemein —* [2]

---

[1] He was young, when the throne was conferred upon him. He loved to come to the false conclusion that it was both fine and desirable to govern and to enjoy simultaneously.

[2] A big mistake. He who is to command, must take pleasure in commanding, his breast is full of high resolve but no man may fathom what he wills. What he has whispered into the ears of his most faithful is done and all the world is surprised. Thus will he ever be the highest, the worthiest — enjoyment lowers.

These words are eternally true. But William II felt and thought otherwise. Sensitive to every pleasant and interesting impression, he was one of the men most capable of enjoyment whom I ever met, but I must specially add that low pleasures, particularly those of a sensual kind, had no attraction for him at all.

To return to the Budapest speech. Then came a positively dithyrambic eulogy of the Magyars. People in Germany, he said, followed with sympathetic interest the history of the chivalrous Magyar nation whose love of country had become proverbial, who had never refused to sacrifice possessions and life for the Cross. Names like Zriny and Szigeth made the heart of every German youth beat higher even to-day. With astonishment Germany had watched how the loyal Hungarian nation had with "surprising brilliance" celebrated its thousandth birthday after it had secured a place of equality among the great cultured nations by its proud architectural works, its artistic sense, its formidable public works, its progress in trade and commerce. I was sitting opposite the two Emperors and could see in the face of Francis Joseph that this burning enthusiasm on the part of his guest for the Magyars, which as a matter of fact had no forbidden political design behind it, but rose right out of the warm expansive heart of the German Kaiser, went too far for his host and did not please him. With obviously deep emotion William II at the end of his speech eulogised the Emperor Francis Joseph, for whom in Europe and especially among the German people there was "glowing and unbounded enthusiasm", an enthusiasm in which he, William II, made bold also to share, for "in the manner of a son" he looked on Francis Joseph as his father's friend. That, also, was too emphatic. Fundamentally Francis Joseph liked the new Germany as little as he liked the new Italy. Possibly he liked it rather less, for in 1870 he was ready to go hand in hand against Prussia-Germany by the side of France with the Kingdom of Italy, that "robber of churches", which had grown great in its fifty years' struggle with Austria. Such a development had been prevented first by the brilliant resolution and skill of Bismarck's policy and then by Andrássy, who, finding support in our swift and crushing military success, carried through the maintenance of Austrian neutrality against Beust, against the Archduke Albert, and against the Emperor Francis Joseph. General von Schweinitz, from 1867 to 1876 minister and ambassador in Vienna, has often told me that one of the most painful interviews of his life was that which he had in January, 1871, with the Emperor Francis Joseph, when he announced to him officially the election of the King of Prussia to the German Imperial throne, and the restoration of the German Empire. But it was scarcely an interview at all. For a long time the Austrian Emperor could not bring himself to speak or utter a single syllable. In the end he curtly asked Schweinitz if the Kaiser's Prussian regiment, the Emperor Francis' Second Grenadier Regiment of Guards, had had heavy losses, and dismissed him as coldly as he had received him. Ultimately it was fear of Russia, fear of her pan-Slav propaganda, of her measureless reserves in men and her extraordinary strength in material resources, which induced the Emperor Francis Joseph to give his consent to the alliance which in 1879 Andrássy had concluded with Bismarck. And even while the World War was raging, an Austrian nobleman, who was intimate with court circles and had long been a friend of mine, told me that the best times the old Emperor had since the war began were those when he heard or read that the "Prussians" had received another good beating.

After the banquet on September 21, 1897, a long reception took place. I was struck by the large number of archdukes. They formed what the French call *tapisserie*, that is to say, they stood up, one beside the other, along the wall, most of them with rather dull faces and bored looks. Only the Archduke Francis Ferdinand, with his strong features and his manly bearing, pleased me. Although there was in his eyes something of that malice, even cruelty, that distinguished his grandfather on his mother's side, the last king but one of the Two Sicilies, the famous Ferdinand II, whom the Italians called "Re Bomba" because he had ordered a bombardment of his own city, Messina. The general impression which I got of the heir presumptive was certainly that he was a man of unusual strength of mind and intelligence. A clever Austrian princess, who had long been one of my friends — incidentally

she was said to be completely "black and yellow" [1] politically —
once said to me: "A Hapsburg must keep to the old paths; otherwise he will come to a bad end. The only two Austrian sovereigns who were not mediocrities were Charles V and Joseph II, but
the former died in the monastery of St. Just and the latter of a
broken heart. The brilliant Archduke Rudolf killed himself; the
dreamer Maximilian was shot in Mexico; the gifted Johann Orth
was swallowed by the sea off Cape Horn." The princess ended with
the words: "The archdukes ought therefore to keep nicely to the
old ways. The witty lines which in Metternich's day Nestroy
wrote on Austria apply doubly to them:

> *Wenn einer alles kann,*
> *Stellen's ihn erst recht net an.*
> *Das muss einen antreiben,*
> *Ein Esel zu bleiben."* [2]

Besides, the old Emperor simply could not stand his nephew and
heir, the Archduke Francis Ferdinand. It was comprehensible
that he should have no love for the nephew, who now stood in the
place of his dearly loved son. His nephew's morganatic marriage
only strengthened the dislike.

After the banquet was over, Kaiser William invited his ambassador in Vienna, Count Philip Eulenburg, and myself into his apartment. Phil was so excited with the brilliance of the Kaiser's speech
that in my presence he ran up to the Kaiser when he came in and
kissed both his Majesty's hands with the words: "I am overcome,
I am overwhelmed." As a result of William II's over-emphatic
praise of the Magyars, the Emperor Francis Joseph, forty-eight
hours later, sent a rescript to the Hungarian premier, Count Bánffy,
in which he announced that he proposed to erect at his own expense
memorials to ten Hungarian heroes. The old Emperor was not going
to let himself be outdone in love and honour of the Magyars by the
German Kaiser. All the silly rumours which appeared during the
next ten or twelve years in the French and English press that one

---

[1] The Austrian colours.

[2] If a man can do everything, they are all the less likely to give him a job. This
must encourage everyone to remain an ass.

of the sons of the German Emperor had been marked out for the throne of Hungary had their ultimate source in that speech of William II's on September 21, 1897. It was even said that it was the second son of the German Kaiser, Prince Eitel Fritz, who was thus designed to wear the crown of St. Stephen, and that his name "Eitel", actually an old Hohenzollern name, was only the German form of the Hungarian "Attila."

In October, 1897, William II visited Wiesbaden, as he usually did at this season of the year. By the beauty of its surroundings, its warm climate, and its theatre it specially attracted him, although the relatively small château there was not a very pleasant place to live in. While the German Kaiser was at Wiesbaden, the Tsar Nicholas of Russia came to Darmstadt with his wife to pay a visit to his brother-in-law, the Grand Duke of Hesse. Nicholas II liked living in a small South German palace rather than anywhere else. First of all, his wife, who was deeply attached to her Hessian home, felt in good health there. Then in Hesse the Tsar knew that he was safe against attempts on his life, which were always possible in Russia, and then on the banks of the pretty stream of Darm, he could live the free, quiet life of a private gentleman. Is there a better proof of the worthlessness of all royal pomp and circumstance than the fact that what the autocrat of all the hundred million Russians loved most was to go in a slow train with his brother-in-law, Ernest Louis, to travel second-class from Darmstadt to Frankfurt, incognito as far as possible, and there buy ties and gloves on the street?

In this unpretentious, but, in the nature of things, comprehensible pleasure, the Tsar did not like to be disturbed, and therefore was averse while he was at Darmstadt to interviews with other royal personages. None the less his peace was twice broken into in 1897. Kaiser William did not rest until he had more or less forced the Tsar to agree to visit him at Wiesbaden. After suggestions by letter had produced no result William II, without any preliminary discussion with me, sent his adjutant, Scholl, to Darmstadt. Scholl so worked on the Grand Duke there, and so persistently, that the latter consented to bring pressure on the Tsar with the result that on October 20 the Tsar appeared at Wiesbaden. I saw him only for a moment or two before and after luncheon. He appeared listless and smiled at me half with embarrassment and half-pathetically. At an interview thus extorted, like some of its predecessors and many of its successors, naturally nothing like the expected success was realised. Prince Bismarck had recognized that much long ago. When, not long after his accession, William II triumphantly announced, after a visit of Alexander III to Berlin, that he had been invited by the Tsar to attend the Russian manoeuvres at Narva, the Chancellor was silent. When William II, put out and annoyed, asked the Prince why he did not congratulate him on his "success", the Chancellor answered that he did not think that the presence of the Kaiser at the Russian autocrat's manoeuvres would be really welcome to the latter. The Prince was absolutely right. Alexander was taciturn; William loved to talk. Alexander rode at a trot; William at a flying gallop. Consequently the former did not want the latter at his manoeuvres and the participation of William II in the Narva manoeuvres, which did happen despite the Chancellor's earnest warnings, led not to an improvement but to an impairment of the relations between the two Emperors. But the opposition of Prince Bismarck on this occasion contributed substantially to the estrangement between him and William II.

The Tsar's visit to Wiesbaden had a sequel in that same month of October, 1897. There was no princely couple more worthy of respect than the Grand Duke Frederick and the Grand Duchess Louise of Baden. The Grand Duke was the real type, and a fine type, of the popular German ruler, of princely appearance, kindly heart, fluent speech, and also, in great things and small, of model loyalty and conscientiousness. To every German the Grand Duchess Louise, as the only daughter of our old Emperor and the sister of the Emperor Frederick, could not but be dear, and she merited that love not only by her noble character, her untiring care for all in distress and in need of aid, but by her fine culture. The grand-ducal couple of Baden belonged to the old régime in the sense that they were very correct. The thought that the Russian Imperial couple could stay in Germany, indeed not far from Karlsruhe, without a meeting with them was almost unbearable to the Grand Duke Frederick and the Grand Duchess Louise. Then there was the relationship between the two courts. When the court at Karlsruhe had taken some gentle and tactful sounding of the court of Darmstadt, but without success, the Baden monarchs resolved to go straight to Darmstadt, an intention which they announced the evening before their departure. At the eleventh hour there came an answer to this announcement from Darmstadt that the Tsar had engagements for every day up to his departure and could not receive the grand ducal couple. That was the announcement made next day to an astonished world by the "*Karlsruher Zeitung*." Over this rejection of the noble princely pair Germans generally were deeply indignant and, theoretically, with clear justification. But the Tsar Nicholas said in Darmstadt that it was intolerable if he could not come to Germany "*sans être embêté*."

While I was with Kaiser William in Wiesbaden, my definite appointment as Minister of State and Secretary of State for Foreign Affairs was announced. My successor in Rome was the ambassador in Constantinople, von Saurma, who was succeeded in Constantinople by Baron Marschall von Bieberstein, who was to find a wide field for his diligence and for his equally great ambition. On my final appointment to the Secretaryship of Foreign Affairs the then German Ambassador in Madrid, Herr von Radowitz, who twenty years before had been my instructor in the Foreign Office in Berlin and under whom, seventeen years before, I had worked in the Paris Embassy, wrote me as follows: "I can quite understand how deeply in your hearts you and your wife must dislike exchanging Rome for Berlin. Certainly we all owe you gratitude that you have not hesitated to sacrifice your own pleasure to take up the burden and the responsibility of the Berlin office. Twenty-four years ago, in the late autumn of 1873, I returned from Varzin to Berlin with the final report to the Kaiser on the appointment of your father as Secretary of State. On October 8 he took over his post, about which I had to report to him during his first days of office. On October 15 the Chancellor also arrived and after his first conversation with your father, he said to me: 'Herr von Bülow has settled down as though he had been Secretary for ten years.' Now, when after a quarter of a century you succeed your father, whom none of us can ever forget, memory will go back to the days with which his name is permanently associated and whose traditions, I am sure, will be safe in your hands. The conditions, the personalities, the duties have all altered, and new aims are set before us. But the spirit and the noble methods which characterised the management of foreign affairs in those days still remain the best."

To the Kaiser, Wiesbaden and Homburg were especially dear because they gave him the chance of constant visits to the Saalburg. This frontier fort of the Romans in the Taunus had been the quarters of the Second Rhaetian cohort in the second and third Christian centuries, a cohort on which the proud appellation of "*cives Romani*" had been bestowed. In the quarters farther back the Eighth and the Twenty-third Legions had been lodged with a goodly number of auxiliary troops. Even in my childhood in the 'fifties, people were digging about on the site. Since the 'seventies regular excavations had been carried on under the conduct of the eminent Baurats Jacobi, who was later director of the Saalburg museum at Homburg-on-the-Hill. In these excavations William II took a lively interest. The history of the Roman emperors had an extraordinary fascination for him. As was natural from the subjectivity of his outlook he was convinced that a glorification of the Roman Emperors would have a good influence on the status of monarchs now reigning. He was of the opinion that the teaching class was too content to glorify the heroes of the Republic, Marcus Porcius Cato and Marcus Junius Brutus, the brothers Tiberius and Caius Gracchus, at the cost of the Emperors. That tendency ought to be combated by the most thorough exposition possible of the services rendered by the Roman Emperors. For the great men of republican Rome appeared to William II very much like contemporary Radicals or even accursed regicides. A few days before my arrival at Wiesbaden the Kaiser got up a sort of ceremony on the Saalburg (ostensibly as a preliminary to the initiation of restoration work on a large scale) with the personnel of the Wiesbaden theatre, who, for this purpose all appeared, all of them actors and supers, dressed up in Roman

SECRETARY OF STATE BARON MARSCHALL
VON BIEBERSTEIN

costumes in the characters of legionaries and lictors, centurions and prefects. At the celebration the representatives of the old Roman Empire, the Rome that nearly two thousand years ago had vanished beneath the sea of time, were to show honour to the ruler of the new and mighty German Empire. The theatricality of this display astonished the old ladies of the court.

Such little episodes were quickly over, only it was necessary that they did not occur too often. It was a more serious matter, however, when the Kaiser in his suddenly awakened passion for the Caesars of old Rome suddenly had the idea of basing the historical teaching in the high schools on his preferences. He had said some time before, to the Minister of Education, Bosse, an extremely conscientious, able, and tried official, that the greatness and merits of the Roman emperors should receive a great deal more attention in the curriculum than they actually got. Dr. Bosse, who was naturally opposed to this, asked me for my support which, although the matter was really outside my competence, I gladly gave him. On an excursion to the Saalburg I expounded to the Kaiser in detail that under the Roman emperors, taking things all in all, the evil surpassed the good. No regulation could prevent a teacher from pointing out to his scholars the atrocities of Domitian and Caracalla, the worthlessness of Vitellius and Marcus Salvius Otho, nor from branding the monster Nero as semi- or totally lunatic. Even Titus and Trajan would come off badly. The civilised world saw the history of imperial Rome through the eyes of one of the greatest and most impressive historians of all time, a historian distinguished alike by the strength and the depth of his genius, Cornelius Tacitus, out of whose pages there still spoke to us to-day the virtues which had made republican Rome great. The Kaiser argued a little, then let his opposition drop and did not return to the matter again. But there remained for long in his excellent memory that last and noble word of the Emperor Septimius Severus, which I had told him on the Saalburg. On his death bed Severus dismissed the legions with the word "*Laboremus.*"

The French saying about the days *qu'ils se suivent et ne ressemblent pas* holds good for the moods of Kaiser William II. His enthusiasm for the Caesars melted like snow in the sun when a year later he came so deeply under the spell of Houston Stewart Chamberlain's "Foundations of the Nineteenth Century" that he read it every evening to the Empress and her ladies, one or another of whom went off to sleep at such serious and heavy reading. That is not said as a reproach to the noble idealist who, from unselfish love of German ways, as revealed to him at Bayreuth, had transformed himself from an Englishman into a German, and equally no reproach to his most significant book. With the passing of his enthusiasm for the Roman emperors, the Kaiser's desire to interfere with and upset high school curricula, especially on the classical side, passed away. There came a time when far more serious dangers were to threaten the humanist schools from a party which, simply because its material conception of history allowed only economic effort to count in the life of a nation, was bound to be opposed to the humanist education built on the old languages and the world of ideas of the ancients, and so be opposed to real and true culture. It is to be feared that the abandonment of universal military service, which was forced upon us in the Versailles peace, will have no very favourable results on the physical strength and appearance of the Germans. On the other hand, the more the classical languages are excluded from our school curricula, and the more the humanist schools are diminished in numbers, the nearer comes the danger that the German, in front of whom Goethe and Schopenhauer, Wilhelm Humboldt and Friedrich Hölderlin once bore the torch, will become a clod and a churl. Can socialist policy and administration offer any suitable alternative for such a downfall of our education?

On the day of my appointment as Minister of State and Secretary of State for Foreign Affairs there took place in Wiesbaden the unveiling of the memorial to the Emperor Frederick. William II was not particularly interested in monuments to his father. He took no delight in looking back on those nine and ninety days of his father's painful illness. He wanted his father to live in history and in the thoughts of his people simply as "Crown Prince." He felt himself the direct successor of his grandfather and the completer of the latter's work. What William I had done for the army

he wished to do for the navy. If William I had been blessed with
the unification of Germany, he wanted to establish Germany at
sea and so her position as a world power. But always with the
qualification and the vital difference that he was not going to allow
what, in his completely wrong conception, he believed had happened
to his grandfather to happen to himself; he was not going to let his
own glory be dimmed by minister or Chancellor, admiral or general.
The reign of Emperor Frederick must be considered as an interlude;
he must be renowned simply as "Crown Prince."

But as long as there were no tactless reflections on the son, William II was not so set against the glorification of the Emperor
Frederick as victor of Weissenburg and Wörth or, better still, as
the patron of the sciences and the arts, as he was against anything
that seemed to do honour to Prince Bismarck. Lucanus, although
he was full of rancour against Bismarck, because the Prince had
treated him badly and as a matter of fact unjustly as the bringer
of the bowstring at his fall, regretted (for reasons of state) that
the Kaiser would hear of no distinction for any of those who, either
as designers, committee-members, or donors, had helped in the
erection of Bismarck memorials or Bismarck towers; while on
those who had busied themselves with the erection of monuments
to William I orders and photographs of the All-Highest were
showered. But the Kaiser did not object to the erection of the
Bismarck monument in Berlin in front of the Reichstag in 1901,
for this monument was erected under his eyes and in accordance with his own wishes. The nonchalant attitude of the great
man, his (in military eyes) almost untidy dress, displayed the
Prince as the Kaiser wished the nation to see him, as the resolute
Junker who turned his back on the Reichstag, who knew how to
deal cavalierly with popular assemblies and adopted the right tone
in dealing with the people's representatives. What a difference
between that and the noble, dignified, and serene bearing, also
executed according to the wishes and ideas of his Majesty and
also by Reinhold Begas in 1897, of the great monument to the old
Emperor in Berlin, which shows him returning as victor, attended
by Victory, to the castle of his ancestors! William II had no

liking at all for the fine Bismarck memorial which rises on the Elbe heights and overlooks the port of Hamburg. The Kaiser knew this memorial only from pictures which he had seen in the illustrated papers. But that was enough to show him that the masterpiece of Lederer had let the Chancellor appear just as he did not want him to appear to the German people, that is to say, as the incarnation of German strength and German character, as the genius of the German nation, as the mighty figure who reminded the seamen and the travellers, who sailed from distant lands back up the Elbe to the port of Hamburg and the fatherland, of Roland and Siegfried, of Arminius, of Charlemagne and Barbarossa, of Odin himself, of the mythical or semi-mythical figures of German epic and of German history. William II never consented to go to see this memorial and always refused all the invitations to see it, from the Burgomaster of Hamburg, Burchard, whom he otherwise greatly respected. Once when the two of them were driving through Hamburg together, the Burgomaster succeeded, without the Kaiser noticing it, in bringing the latter to the Heilige-Geist-Feld, which is quite near the Bismarck memorial, but when he pointed it out to the Kaiser, William II obstinately turned his eyes in the opposite direction and only looked out on things with a kindly gaze when the Bismarck memorial was well behind him.

The oration at the unveiling of the Wiesbaden monument to the Emperor Frederick was delivered by the theatre manager of Wiesbaden, Georg von Hülsen. He and his brother Dietrich, then aide-de-camp, later Adjutant General and chief of the Military Cabinet, played a big part during the reign of William II. They were the sons of Botho von Hülsen, who had for years been theatre manager under William I and had died in 1886. He was the *bête noire* of the Wagnerians, for he was considered an opponent of Wagner's music and indeed produced Wagnerian operas but seldom and unwillingly. This was certainly not to his credit, but it must not be overlooked how unintelligently in the 'fifties and 'sixties of last century Wagner's immortal genius was disliked by the widest circles, especially in Berlin. Anyone who to-day reads the articles with which practically the whole body of Berlin's music critics greeted "Tannhäuser", "Lohengrin", and "Tristan und Isolde" might well cry with Faust :

Methinks I hear a whole choir of a hundred thousand fools a-speaking.

Botho von Hülsen and his wife, *née* Countess Haeseler, were not only beloved and honoured in the artistic world, but in the 'fifties, 'sixties, and 'seventies of the last century they kept in Berlin a house which all who knew how to treasure culture, wit, and kindliness will be glad to remember. The second son of this charming couple, Count Georg von Hülsen-Haeseler, followed in his father's footsteps and, after several years in Wiesbaden, became general manager in Berlin in 1903, a post he held until the November revolution. It was held up against him in jest that he was much too complacent to the Kaiser's taste toward mediocre music *à la* Meyerbeer, Lortzing, and Auber, but he was none the less a man of wit and a man of heart. Of more importance was his brother, Count Dietrich von Hülsen-Haeseler, from 1894 to 1899 military attaché in Vienna, from 1899 to 1901 chief of staff of the Guards Corps, and since 1901 chief of the Military Cabinet. He was a man who in the most humorous way — he preferred to talk in the authentic Berlin dialect — could make very shrewd remarks. He was quite frank with the Kaiser, full of sound human knowledge of men, and of a fine nature. His death, which was the result of a sudden stroke at Donaueschingen on November 14, 1908, was a heavy blow to William, who keenly felt his absence before and during the World War.

The 18th of October, which is held doubly sacred by every good Prussian and every German who is truly patriotic as the anniversary of the Battle of the Nations at Leipzig and as the birthday of the Emperor Frederick, was to be celebrated in Wiesbaden in 1897 by a gala performance at the Royal Theatre. At the command of the All-Highest the piece selected was Joseph Lauff's "Der Burggraf." I do not believe that ever a piece has appeared on the stage of any German theatre which so little satisfies the most modest claims which the modest audience of a modest little town is rightly accustomed to make. In a land which calls its own the immortal masterpieces of the greatest poets, a Goethe and a Schiller, a Lessing, a Kleist, and a Hebbel, such a piece ought not to be offered to the public. I sat in a pit-box with Lucanus and Philip Eulenburg. I did not conceal my opinion from either gentleman. "In this great and lovely theatre," I said to them, "there is, as we all three know, not a single soul except the Kaiser who does not think this play flat and silly. And the Kaiser is applauding enthusiastically! I don't like it at all." Lucanus laughed in his cool way. "Naturally, your Excellency is absolutely right. But the public is delighted to see the Kaiser and to hear the fanfare of trumpets which heralds his arrival. The play that is on is a matter of relative indifference. And so far as his Majesty is concerned it is better for him to busy himself with this sort of childishness than to embarrass your Excellency by meddling in foreign policy." Eulenburg said softly, "And while muck of this kind is put on here, my beloved Kaiser will not give the order for my wonderful play 'Der Seestern' to be put on the repertory, although it was performed years ago with the most brilliant success." In the foyer the author, Joseph Lauff, was wandering about receiving congratulations on his rank of major, which he had received in payment for his play. "Der Burggraf" was given only in Wiesbaden so long as the court was there. Later it was staged in the Royal Opera in Berlin for two days with the authorisation of the court, which meant that all court society had to go to see it. As soon as the courtiers fell away, no one at all went to see it, and "Der Burggraf" disappeared into that Orcus in which the mournful shades of dramatic abortions sadly wander.

The counterpart of the dramatist Lauff was the painter Hermann Knackfuss, who was as great, or rather as miserable, a botcher with palette and brush as was Lauff on his Pegasus. I think that few things damaged William II more in the eyes of the cultured section of the German people than his one-sided, blind, and nearly always intolerant attitude in matters of art, which are taken seriously by every German, than the Emperor's preference for painters who should have confined themselves to illustrating coloured picture-books, but whose works should never have got into royal museums and galleries, and for poets who had never been kissed on the brow by any one of the nine Muses. After I had some arguments with the Kaiser on this subject, arguments which were disagreeable because the Kaiser naturally took interference with his personal tastes much less quietly than he took opposition on policy, I had to return to the charge in November, 1908, and point out that the ever-rising tide against his personal rule was not least of all the result of autocratic intervention in purely literary and aesthetic affairs. The Tschudi case and the imperial boycotting of the painter Liebermann created much bad blood. The Kaiser yielded then, but he resented more my intervention on behalf of modern painters and poets than he resented my former representations. That on this occasion I was guided by regard for the general welfare and by reasons of state, can be seen from the fact that in all my acknowledgment of the talent of Max Liebermann and homage to the genius of Gerhart Hauptmann, my attitude to modern tendencies in art and poetry was quite unprejudiced but not especially enthusiastic.

From Wiesbaden I went to Frankfort-on-the-Main with Gustav von Kessel, then general *à la suite*, later general commanding the Guards Corps, and finally governor of Berlin, to visit my brother Adolf, who was then commanding the 21st Cavalry Brigade. During supper the talk turned to the excitement which the succession strife in Lippe had induced in the Kaiser. The deputy, Eugen Richter, roused by the stupidly exaggerated conception of the equality of birth which the conflict revealed, felt himself compelled to throw light on the descent of the reigning Empress in the "*Freisinnige Zeitung.*" He had consequently pointed out logically that if the Schaumburgers reproached the Biesterfelders with their Fraülein Modeste von Unruh, a Countess von Wartensleben, and even a bourgeois Fraülein Halbach, the Biesterfeld house could reply that even the reigning Empress counted among her ancestors ladies of the so-called inferior nobility and even *horribile dictu* daughters of parsons and sextons. This article came to the notice of the Kaiser, who declared that if the Deputy Richter went on busying himself with the circumstances of the Imperial family, he would send two aides-de-camp who would compel him, "revolver in hand", to apologise and retract. Kessel thought it was not at all impossible that the All-Highest would give such an order. The issue would depend on whether the officers selected would have sense not to obey or to make only a pretence of obeying. My brother was less pessimistic and declared, "With our excellent Kaiser there is a long step between word and deed." I recalled that one of the ablest ambassadors of Bismarck's time, whom Bismarck himself had called "the best horse in the stable", Count Paul Hatzfeldt, had in the 'eighties impressed this instruction upon me: "Always in carrying out Bismarck's instructions, be satisfied with carrying out three-quarters of them. The Prince is always pleased afterwards if you don't carry out orders to the last letter." To that my brother added, "Well, in the case of our present Kaiser it is better to carry out only one quarter. I'll give you that advice if ever you find yourself on dangerous ground."

During the evening meal at my brother's I received a ciphered telegram which, when deciphered, told me that in Port-au-Prince, the capital of Haiti, the German merchant Lüders had been illegally arrested and had been kept many weeks in prison under a false accusation. Our representative, Count Ulrich Schwerin, though still a young man, behaved with firmness and circumspection. His protest was supported by his American colleague with whom he was on good terms. I at once told Berlin to demand compensation and satisfaction from the Negro republic and, if need be, to give emphasis to the demand by the dispatch of warships. Although this incident was in itself of no importance, it clearly supplied a useful argument for the necessity of our naval requirements.

Next morning I went from Frankfort-on-the-Main to Schillingsfürst, where I had announced I would report to Prince Hohenlohe. My brother Adolf accompanied me to the station. It was the last time in life that I saw him. Schillingsfürst, the ancestral seat of the then Imperial Chancellor, lies, like so many Franconian castles, on a low hill with a wide prospect over fertile country. The rooms of the castle gave an impression of grandeur but not particularly of comfort. The Prince attached little importance to the external comforts of life. He never used a *chaise longue*, which I can also say of myself. When he was ambassador in Paris Prince Hohenlohe was attacked by heart strain that was not without danger. The doctor urgently advised him to lie down each day on a sofa for a long period; he carried out the reclining treatment on three hard cane chairs. The Princess, who was far happier hunting bears than in her drawing room, put not the slightest value on comfort. When the Prince took me to my room, he called my attention to a bas-relief on the staircase depicting Leda and the swan most realistically. He told me a story connected with it. Some years previously his brother, the Cardinal Gustav Hohenlohe, had announced that he would visit Schillingsfürst and had added that he would bring with him a very distinguished Roman prelate. At Schillingsfürst they discussed whether the bas-relief should not be concealed, but did not know how it could be done properly. The Cardinal arrived and was steered past the danger spot without noticing the relief. The Roman visitor however promptly stopped in front of it. The ladies of the house were in some embarrassment. The prelate made a careful and detailed inspection of the work of art and then with all the calm dignity of a Roman prelate remarked: "*Questo basso-rilievo è fatto con molto giudizio!*"

I found Prince Hohenlohe much concerned about the speeches — in parts eccentric enough in all conscience — which William II had delivered in the course of the summer and which were followed not long after by the absolutely extraordinary speech at the recruits' parade on November 18. The old Prince, who was clearly haunted by dread recollections of Louis II of Bavaria, asked me if I considered that the Kaiser was really absolutely sane. I answered for my part with full conviction and good knowledge that the Kaiser was very impulsive, completely lacking in foresight, and unfortunately often tactless; that he had been spoiled because, thank God, things had so far always gone well with him; that even as a young man he was given to boasting; that, in order to boast, or in order to get out of a painful situation, or to avoid any awkwardness, he was not too careful of the truth — but mentally unsound he certainly was not. There was not the slightest resemblance between him and Louis II.

Not very long before my visit, a little domestic drama was played in the castle of Schillingsfürst which was very characteristic of the Prince and Princess. The Princess had been away travelling for some time. There came to stay with the Prince and to console him in his grass-widowerhood a lady who in spite of his great age was his intimate friend, Frau von H. They sat together in intimate union when Princess Hohenlohe's arrival was announced. Frau von H. wanted to fly. The Prince, who did not for a moment lose his wonted calm, told her to remain. The Princess entered; the Prince introduced the ladies. Frau von H. made a fresh attempt to leave the room, but the Princess cried out to her in a friendly way. "No, no, my dear! *Qui va à la chasse, perd sa place.* Chlodwig is a butterfly: once you've got him, you must hold him tight." Prince Chlodwig von Hohenlohe-Schillingsfürst was then approaching his eightieth year. In the late afternoon of the day of my departure the Prince and Princess took me to their mausoleum. I kept some twenty or thirty paces behind them. In the clear autumn air, fanned by a sharp east wind which blew over the Franconian hills and valleys, the frail old couple looked on the tomb which was so soon to receive them both. That is the picture of them that I still see to-day, the picture of two people beside whom I spent so many of the years of my life.

CHAPTER XII

General Adolf von Bülow's Fatal Riding Accident — His Character — William II's Candidates for the Imperial Chancellorship — Murder of Catholic Missionaries in China — I Go to Rome to Present Letters of Recall — Speech to the German Colony; Back to Berlin — Letter from Theodor Mommsen — The Russian Ambassador on Kiaochow — Dispatch of the German Squadron to the Far East — Prince of Wales's Letter to the Empress Frederick on Germany's Naval Ambitions — The Empress Frederick; Her Friendship with Fräu von Bülow — Opening of the German Reichstag by William II (November 30, 1897) — First Reichstag Speech.

FROM Schillingsfürst I went straight to Rome in order to present my letters of recall as ambassador. A few days after my return I was sitting at my desk one afternoon when I received a telegram from a major whom I did not know, telling me that my brother Adolf had had a serious accident while at a paper chase near Darmstadt. A few hours later came news of his death. The refractory animal he was riding had shied at a high fence. Brought to the leap with knees and spurs, he reared up and fell over, crushing his rider beneath him. My brother Adolf was only a year younger than I and was my companion until 1869, when he entered the 2nd Guard Dragoons as volunteer, while I continued my studies. Physically and mentally he was a strong man. Everything about him was of a piece, so that when brought into contact with the often contradictory events of this complicated world, he was too single-minded. No one denied his military talent. He had one enormous asset: he was entirely without fear, and rightly there is engraved on his tombstone in the Church of the Twelve Apostles in Berlin, the words of the prophet Isaiah, "Fear not, for I am with you; blench not, for I am thy God." In 1870 when he was a lieutenant in the 2nd Dragoons Guard he had distinguished himself by conspicuous bravery at Mars-la-Tour: later he was equally distinguished as regimental adjutant and in the War Academy, commanded the Royal Uhlans in Hannover, and again drew attention to himself as

chief of staff of the 4th Army Corps at Magdeburg. Complete
confidence was placed in him, and despite his youth, he earned the
respect of the brilliant Count Alfred Schlieffen — later Chief of the
General Staff — under whom he served in the 1st Uhlan Guards.
As aide-de-camp he had served three Emperors, William I, Frederick,
and William II. As first personal aide-de-camp to William II —
a post he held from 1879 to the middle of the 'eighties — he had had
considerable influence on the development of the future Kaiser.
My brother was devoted body and soul to Prince William. His
friendship made him rather overestimate the young Prince, who
aroused many hopes which later years were not to fulfil. In my
brother's will is the clause, "Wherever I may die I ask that
Prince William be told that in death and in deep gratitude for his
trust and friendship my last and deepest wishes are for the greatness of my Fatherland, for the glory of the Army, and for the star
in peace and in war of the Prince for whom I would gladly give my
life."

Of the many tokens of sympathy at this premature death I give
only the letter of Count Herbert Bismarck, which does as much
honour to his heart as to my brother's abilities :

Schönhausen-on-Elbe, November 2, 1897

Dear Bülow,

I am so deeply shocked by the dreadful news I have just read of the
sudden death of your brother Adolf, that I cannot but give expression in
a few heartfelt words to my feelings of deep sympathy and sincerest grief
at this tragic misfortune. I do so, mindful of the good friendship which
goes back, back as far as I can remember to our very earliest years in
Frankfort; in age I stood between you and the brother you have lost,
and always followed your careers and development with the greatest
interest and with heartiest goodwill. How often we have spoken of the
brilliant gifts and the distinguished work of your brother, and to me there
was always something wonderful in the fact that you in your modesty
always ranked him higher than yourself. All the more do I realize how
cruel this unexpected blow must be to you just at a time when, in your
difficult and exposed position, you more than ever need sure and true
allies in the homeland. In that connection a brother's loss is irreplaceable,
especially the loss of one with qualities so high as everyone recognised

Adolf to possess. May God comfort you and strengthen his sorrowing widow. In times of such grief words fail even the best of friends; I would only say to you that in spirit I press your hand, and know better than most what you have lost by his death.

In true friendship as of old,
Yours,

H. Bismarck

That the influence of my brother on Prince William was entirely for the good I cannot, for all my love for the mentor and all my recognition of his great qualities, admit. In his pupil he implanted many of his own qualities and roughnesses. His steadfastness, his earnestness, and his complete fearlessness he did not succeed in transmitting. Kaiser William II had great schemes for my brother. He thought of him as future Chief of the Military Cabinet, even as Chief of the General Staff, as Minister of War, particularly as my brother possessed an unusual gift of oratory. He had even thought of him in certain eventualities as a possible Chancellor.

But what are hopes? What plans can man, the passing child of time, build on the shifting sands of fate?

My brother Adolf certainly was not equal to all the tasks that fall to the holder of the highest office of the German Empire, but in hours of difficulty he would have stood his ground. The list of those of whom William II during his reign considered for the office of Chancellor is a long one, longer even than the famous Leporello list of the ladies loved by Don Juan. On it one found men so thoroughly and seriously possible as Count Posadowsky, Baron von Marschall, Baron von Rheinbaben, the later Chief of the General Staff Hellmuth von Moltke, the minister von Miquel, Baron von Schorlemer, Count Johann Bernstorff. But on it are found also the oddest vagaries of his phantasy. At the wedding of Prince Hugo Radolin with Countess Johanna Oppersdorff, which took place in the presence of the Kaiser in Ober-Glogau in Silesia, the bride's brother, Count Hans Oppersdorff, who later wandered from one party to another and finally went over to the Poles, addressed the Kaiser in a speech more remarkable for its enthusiasm than for its contents. When he had finished proposing the toast, William II said out loud,

"That 's the Chancellor for me." This was in 1892. When King George of Greece visited me in Rome in 1911 he told me that once, at a meeting in the Achilleion in Corfu, the Emperor had in all seriousness said of the ambassador in Athens, Baron von Wangen-heim, "There 's a future Imperial Chancellor." Wangenheim was not without talent, but he was unstable, unbalanced, incautious, and easily carried away. He might have done much mischief. That is still truer of the ambassador in Rome, Count Monts, in whom the Kaiser's announcement that ambassadors to Rome were specially fit to be Chancellors, as the example of Bülow showed, had raised great hopes. Even in wider circles William II loved to say that a prince ought to have two or three successors in reserve for any minister and especially for the Prime Minister, so that no one should think himself indispensable. At certain moments William II even thought of Prince Lichnowsky, whose nerves would not have stood the strain of office for a fortnight, not to mention his shortcomings as administrator and orator. I must add that, for the most part, this sort of thing was no more than sudden impulse, notions rising like soap bubbles and bursting whenever responsible people spoke seriously to the Kaiser. Since those days we have experienced ministers and chancellors chosen by party intrigue, from purely sectional or personal considerations, whom no one had recommended to the parties or to Parliament: "Masters Tailor and Shoemaker", who were still less fit for their difficult tasks than the least suitable of William II's candidates, who really had but a brief phantom existence in that ever chang-ing imagination of his.

My brother Adolf lacked all unhealthy ambition. I think that nothing was so attractive to him as a purely military career, if possible, away from the capital, for he did not like court life and knew that at court he would often come into collision with the Kaiser. This actually happened at the time of Prince Bismarck's fall. When the Kaiser had resolved to dismiss the Prince, my brother — as the later Prince Karl Wedel, in 1890, general aide-de-camp to the Kaiser, told me afterwards — came into the room of the aides-de-camp, and went straight through the door leading to the

Kaiser's study. When Wedel told him that the Kaiser had given strict orders that he was not to be disturbed and would speak to no one, my brother answered, "That 's all the same to me. He must n't send Prince Bismarck away." My brother knocked three times at the Kaiser's door, then opened it and walked into the study. After half an hour he came out calm as was his wont, but with an expression of deep sorrow, and said to Wedel, "There 's nothing to be done. This is the greatest misfortune we have suffered since Jena." How magnanimous William II could be if he did not feel personally put out, is shown by the fact that he did not take my brother's loyalty to Bismarck amiss. "I understand," he once said to him, as he said more than once to me later, "you sticking by the old fellow. You were all children in his house. I don't grudge you your preferences, but you must let me have mine."

On the day on which I received the news of my brother's death, I left Rome for Berlin for the funeral, which the Emperor and Empress attended. After hearing the news the Kaiser had sent me the following telegram to Rome: "Deeply grieved at the news of the death of your dear brother who since boyhood has been always near my heart and to whose military career I looked forward with happy anticipation. I offer from the Empress and myself the deepest sympathy to yourself and your family. With our army I mourn one of our best officers who was loyally devoted to me and my house and whose memory I shall ever hold in a grateful remembrance. Wilhelm I. R." The Empress was particularly friendly to my brother. Subalterns of his old regiment, the 2nd Guard Dragoons, carried the coffin.

Scarcely had I returned to Rome ere I received a very long, very rhetorical, somewhat excited telegram from the Kaiser, occasioned by the news of the murder of German Catholic missionaries in the Chinese province of Shantung. The Kaiser threatened the heathen folk of China in constantly recurring phrases, which breathed forth rage and fury, that he would defend the Cross and its servants and ambassadors, and he therewith resolved that the German cruiser squadron should demand the punishment of the assassins and steam into Kiaochow Bay meanwhile. Like the Kaiser, I was of the opin-

ion that we should use this chance to make of Kiaochow the base —
a base selected as suitable after long and thorough investigation —
for the greater development of our very considerable interests in the
Far East.   But I held of course that this object could be gained
not by sounding phrases, but only by proper diplomacy, especially
towards Russia and England.

I speeded up the formalities of resignation from Rome as much as I
could, but I wanted to receive the representatives from the German
colony before my departure, for I had been on very cordial terms
with them.   The colony was kind enough to present me with a
replica of the statue of Augustus which is in the Capitoline museum.
I returned thanks in a short speech in which I said that I seemed to
myself to be like Odysseus, the Homeric wanderer, having to leave
a friendly haven to fare out on a stormy voyage on the open sea.
Well did I know what rocks and shallows that sea held, yet I found
courage in my resolve, whatever happened, to hold fast to two
principles — one, to do my duty and accept my responsibility in the
spirit of the categorical imperative on which the Prussian State was
founded, and, two, never to forget the claims of justice, equity, and
true humanity.   A letter I received after my return to Berlin seems
to me like an echo of that leave-taking in Rome.   It was from
Theodor Mommsen, the greatest German scholar then living, in
answer to the congratulations my wife and I had sent to him on his
eightieth birthday.   He wrote: "Your excellency, you and your
wife have been so kind as to remember in friendship an old man who
had the good fortune to enjoy your protection and your hospitality
in sunnier days.   It is a joy to me to remember those days in Rome;
it is a particular joy to have them recalled by this double greeting,
and I keep in loyal remembrance the friendship with which you
honoured me.   I ask your excellency to accept my grateful respects."

While press, public, and parliament in Germany received me with
a mixture of distrust and depreciation, the "*Times*", on the strength
of an article by a "non-German observer of high standing", wrote,
"According to all probability Herr von Bülow has before him the most
successful career of any German minister since Bismarck."   When
I got back to Berlin, I sought out the Russian ambassador.   Count

Osten-Sacken, first of all, in accordance with the old and by no means stupid practice of Russian diplomacy always to begin by shouting and complaining, at once asserted that our procedure in the Far East would make the worst possible impression in Russia and would encounter the strongest opposition. I answered that Russian policy towards us had now reached a turning point. "*Vous vous trouvez devant une bifurcation.*" We could not possibly ignore the scandalous murder of German missionaries (and Catholic missionaries at that), not merely for reasons of internal German policy and in regard to the honour and prestige of the Empire, but also in the interests of all nations who had relations with China, and certainly also in the interest of Russia, which bordered on China. If, in this sphere and at this moment, Russia made difficulties for us, we should naturally turn elsewhere, that is, to the West. If I might put myself in the position of a Russian Foreign Minister, I would rejoice to see Germany strengthen her position in the Far East, but for my own part would seek out and occupy that base which would be useful to Russia, that base which Russian newspapers had for a long time indicated to be Port Arthur. Osten-Sacken, who was a stylist — "*la grande plume du cabinet de St. Petersburg*", as Gortschakov in his pompous way phrased it — in my presence drew up a telegram to Count Muravieff which he showed me. At the same time I telegraphed in like sense to our ambassador in St. Petersburg. That same day I had a talk with the English ambassador, to whom I expounded the necessity of our procedure in the Far East. My old friend Lascelles knew his country well enough to know that the English press would hold firmly to the "dog-in-the-manger"[1] policy, *i.e.* to the old English conception that in political matters, and even more, perhaps, in matters of trade and industry, no power in the world had the right to seek any advantage except England. Nevertheless, he thought that the English government would not raise any serious objections. But of course there was a possibility that England, too, would look for a base in the Gulf of Tschili. England decided for Wai-Hai-Wai, right opposite Port Arthur, not far from Cape Shantung.

[1] English in the original.

The situation was critical, and at a difficult hour it was made more difficult for me by the intrigues of Holstein, who, with all his unusual qualities, was an incomparable intriguer because he was filled with pathological mistrust. *"C'est pour des hommes pareils qu'on avait bâti jadis le Bastille"*, Donna Laura Minghetti, who was proud of her excellent French and her wit, remarked about Holstein. Negative rather than positive, destructive rather than constructive, Holstein was just the man to consider himself the more indispensable the less sure of security his principals felt. Not without reason did he believe that frightened folk are in greater need of support than men who stand stoutly, strongly, and unshakably on the solid enduring earth. With such a conception in his mind, the Kaiser's friendly feeling towards me made him uneasy. So he conceived the idea of encouraging Chancellor Hohenlohe while restraining Secretary of State Bülow in Far Eastern affairs. While in excited private telegrams to me Holstein painted all the risks of the Far Eastern venture in the most lurid colours, he urged Prince Hohenlohe to speak confidently and boldly to the Kaiser. But I saw through Holstein's game and was much too sure that my policy was right to be entrapped. And Prince Hohenlohe was too honourable and too old to lend himself to such intrigues.

On this occasion as on many others Holstein was like the watchdog which is very good at protecting the house against thieves and burglars but of which one can never be sure whether he will bite his master's legs or not. Holstein had long ago been authorised by Prince Bismarck to deal directly with chiefs of missions by the so-called "private telegrams", which went out ciphered but unregistered. Such telegrams of Holstein's were marked "Private" at the head. Naturally they gave Holstein a big influence on the course of policy, for they were not handled in the ordinary run of diplomatic business and were not always laid before the Chancellor or the Secretary of State. By means of "private telegrams" Holstein was in constant intercourse with Count Paul Hatzfeldt, Prince Philip Eulenburg, and Prince Radolin; and occasionally with Monts, Eckardstein, and other *dii minorum gentium*. To be just, I must add that though Holstein through the peculiarity alike of his character and his position certainly did much damage to many during his thirty years' work in the Foreign Office, yet he never did such mischief as Mathias Erzberger by his indiscreet handling of the Czernin report, his unskilful and senseless conduct of the armistice negotiations, his sabotage of the mission of Count Brockdorff-Rantzau at Versailles, his entire political conduct — a mixture of self-seeking and ignorance, of mercenary ambition and frank demagogy, although his intentions were not altogether bad during his years of power.

The extravagant hopes and claims of our nationalist and, more especially, of our colonial circles gave me graver anxiety than the intrigues of Holstein (to which I had been accustomed for years). For by dispatching our fleet to the Far East, a visible sign had been given that the government felt an obligation to protect our great and ever-increasing overseas interests. The gods who gave our people so many productive, great, and noble qualities denied them political sense. Once when I was leaving a Reichstag session I made this complaint to Ministerial Director Althoff, and that distinguished man answered with his own peculiar Westphalian wit : "Now, now ! What are you complaining about? We Germans are the most scholarly nation and also the nation most fitted for war in the world. In all the sciences and all the arts we have done wonders ; the greatest philosophers, the greatest poets, the greatest musicians are Germans. To-day in the natural sciences and in practically every technical domain we stand in the first rank and have accomplished a prodigious economic development. How can you be surprised that politically we are asses? There must be a fly in the ointment somewhere." The especial gift denied to us in the domain of politics, it seems to me, is moderation. We are too ready to go to extremes. Our history is therefore somewhat disjointed. The tradition and continuity which marks the history of other great nations are lacking. Even so able and experienced a man as Admiral Tirpitz lost himself in what were at the time fantastic plans before actual experience taught him the necessary limitations which Germany had to impose upon herself in overseas policy as a result of her central position. I offer in proof a note which Counsellor of Embassy Klehmet sent me from the

Foreign Office in March, 1898, on a conversation which he had had
with Admiral Tirpitz on his overseas projects :

Berlin, March 16, 1898

Very confidential.

In the course of my conversation to-day with Admiral Tirpitz about
the sale of ships, the Admiral began to speak on Germany's overseas
policy of his own accord.   He began with the remark that, politically
speaking, the Spanish-American War had come too soon.   He would have
considered it much more fortunate if it had not broken out until we, as a
result of the Navy Bill, could have intervened decisively.   Things being
as they are, we must nevertheless, in his opinion, send out some ships in
order to show that we too had something to say over there.

For Spain the outcome of the Spanish-American War would inevitably
be the loss of Cuba to the United States.   He had just come into possession of most interesting news about the extraordinary activity of American
chauvinism to this end, so that for us the last chance to acquire Curaçao
and St. Thomas by purchase had come.   North America could do nothing
to prevent this, for she was at that moment occupied with Cuba and had
enough to do there.   England could only welcome our getting a foothold
in these regions.   In his opinion our diplomacy would have no difficulty
in proving such a German step to be a real service to England.   But if
we neglected to use present circumstances, then we should assuredly lose
South America as a region for economic expansion, especially after the
completion of a Panama or Nicaragua canal, which was sure to come.
In any case, as he thought, we should not long be able to maintain the
North American market.   In the Far East he had two wishes in connection with the occupation and commercial development of Kiaochow.
First we ought to have a settlement on the Yangtze, preferably in Woosung,
for the time must come when, as a result of still keener German-English
competition, German firms would no longer be allowed to remain in the
English concessions and would have to look for settlement on what would
be German territory.   Further, it was absolutely essential to show the
German flag on the Yangtze conspicuously far inland.   The German mail
steamers must be officially ordered to do this.   The Admiral asked me
expressly to put these ideas of his before your Excellency and added that
he had prepared special memoranda on the American affair which your
Excellency might inspect if you wished.

Klehmet

In those decisive days which followed the dispatch of our cruiser squadron to the Far East the Empress Frederick called on my wife when I was present. She read me a letter from her eldest brother, the Prince of Wales, which was concerned with the German Navy Bill and the despatch of German warships to Kiaochow. The letter betrayed with naïve candour the masterful spirit of the English which is based on a proud history of success and on a secure insular position. Germany had a good army; let that content her. The sea belonged to England. In the Far East especially the Germans had nothing to seek. In any case, and not without reason, there was much "ill feeling" in England against Germany, who was becoming England's trade rival more and more and was even now a greater inconvenience to England than France was.

It is possible that the Empress Frederick in a more responsible position, that is to say, as consort of an Emperor who was not mortally ill but in sound health and reigning for many years, would have identified herself more with German interests and would have been more considerate of German feelings. I would certainly concede that the responsibility resulting from a higher position would, especially as the high places were surrounded by danger, have had an educative effect on a nature that was self-willed but neither shallow nor arrogant. As Emperor her husband, despite that tender love for his wife which sometimes made him too complaisant towards her, would have made no concessions at the expense of the honour of his throne, for the nobility and dignity of the throne filled his pious soul with almost religious awe. As Crown Princess, as a Crown Princess consumed with impatient longing for the throne and therefore misunderstood, and then as the hapless and embittered Empress Dowager, the Empress Frederick looked at things only with English eyes. An out and out rationalist of the temper of Herbert Spencer and John Stuart Mill, she believed that it was the aim as well as the task of man always to perfect himself. Such progressive self-fulfilment, she thought, could best proceed in accordance with English ideas and customs from England's political institutions down to Windsor soap. The best Germany could do was to make herself useful to England and England's high aims, and at the same time ennoble herself by keeping in the course of English policy like a tiny boat in the wake of a great frigate. Above all Prussia-Germany must be firmly and gladly prepared to go to meet the barbaric Russian bear for the interests of England, interests which were identical with the progress of humanity and the highest idealism.

Once we had settled down in the house allotted to the Secretary of State — a small one but most tastefully decorated by Hans Stob-wasser — which Count Paul Hatzfeldt, Count Herbert Bismarck, and Baron von Marschall had occupied before me and which, alas, Gottlieb von Jagow, Richard von Kühlmann, and other inadequates of that sort were to occupy later, the Empress used to visit my wife nearly every morning. Like her eldest son, the Empress was an early riser. She used to come at about eight o'clock. My wife was not an early riser, and at that hour she was still under the blankets. The Empress sat down on her bed to talk with her for about an hour. Never about banal things, still less about gossip, but about questions and affairs worthy of attracting the attention of men of intellect. When she went away, she would say, "I hope so much Bernhard will not be angry, that I come so often and stay so long." [1] In this too the mother was like the son in that they were perfectly natural in friendly intercourse for all their inward self-consciousness. Although William II only too often assumed the pose of the autocrat he was neither constitutionally nor actually an autocrat. It was something quite external. When his mother remembered that she was Princess Royal of Great Britain and Ireland, she promptly surrounded herself with all the pride of her England. In private life both were simple and unassuming. On the other hand, I have known many German officials, professors and, last not least, deputies, who were far stiffer, far more pretentious, far more "posed" than William II and his mother ever were.

On November 30, 1897, the opening of the Reichstag took place. The speech which the Kaiser had delivered a few days before when recruits for the Guards took the oath was no happy prelude to the coming decisive session. The Kaiser had exhorted the recruits to obey him "whether against a foreign foe or a foe at home." He

[1] English in the original.

spoke of the good God "Who never deserts us", called our army victorious and unconquerable, went as far as to say that "Whoever is not a good Christian is not a good soldier." This sentence Lucanus, without asking his Majesty's leave, changed in the proof of the shorthand note of the speech into "Whoever is not a good Christian is not a good man." As is usual in these cases the authentic sentence filtered through to the public. "*Kladderadatsch*" on November, 1897, published a cartoon which depicted the devil as a northern bogyman with horns, tail, and claws, looking at his long tail in which he had tied a big knot. In the clouds up above, Alexander the Great, Leonidas, and Napoleon were laughing over a newspaper. Frederick the Great came up to them with the familiar crooked stick in his hand and carrying a paper. Above him with his wig and his ironical grin hovered Voltaire. Satan speaks: "Now I remember why I made that knot in my tail. I wanted to fetch old Fritz because he is neither a good Christian nor a good man nor a good Prussian soldier and can in no circumstances do what the Prussian army demands of a soldier. Well, perhaps I'll succeed in getting a revision and make up for lost time and free the heavenly hosts of these bad Christians and bad soldiers." For this jest the then editor-in-chief of "*Kladderadatsch*", Johannes Trojan, an attractive poet, an amiable man, and a good patriot, was sentenced to two months' detention in a fortress.

The speech from the throne which William II delivered on November 30, 1897, had been *more solito* drawn up in the Ministry of State, the passage on foreign policy by myself: "The murder of German missionaries and the attacks on mission stations in China, which are under my protection and which are near to my heart, have compelled me to send my East Asian cruiser squadron to the Bay of Kiaochow in the neighbourhood of the scene of the outrage and to have troops landed in order to demand full reparation and a guarantee against such regrettable incidents in the future. Political relations with foreign states are entirely friendly. My meetings with the allied and friendly monarchs as well as the brilliant and cordial welcome which I received on my visits to Peterhof and Budapest, have given me new guarantee of this. All the signs of the times confirm our hope that, with God's help, we may look forward to the peaceful development of Europe and our German fatherland." This composition was not rhetorical enough for the Kaiser. After he had read the speech from the throne, he went on to a speech of his own in which he called to mind the oath which he took two years before on the famous colours of his first Regiment of Foot Guards, to perpetuate the creation of William I. The Parliamentary deputies had "with moved hearts and wet eyes" accepted his oath and thus had become his "partners" in it. Before God Almighty and in remembrance of the great Emperor, he asked them to help him to keep his oath so that he could guard the honour of the Empire for whose maintenance he had not hesitated to imperil his only brother. How often must those deputies, for the most part dull and prosy bourgeois, have heard amazed those improvisations of the Kaiser without rightly comprehending the real meaning of that unusual interlude in the White Hall before the Imperial throne.

The debate began on December 6 when Prince Hohenlohe read his speech in an almost inaudible voice; it contained many fine and just observations which were not heard. Tirpitz and the Secretary of State for the Treasury, von Thielmann, were nearly as unintelligible and both were dull. Schönlank, the Socialist, made a personal attack on the Kaiser's after-dinner speeches, on our world policy, and the political impotence of the Chancellor. I had the feeling that if the parliamentary début of the Navy Bill was not to end in a fiasco, something different must be heard from the Government bench. I saw that none of the Ministers and Secretaries of State present had any desire to undertake it and that no one could expect the aged Chancellor to make such a reply. On the other hand, I was confronted with an entirely unfamiliar task. I had been accustomed in Paris and Rome, in Bucharest and Athens, to be a spectator of parliamentary debates, but not very often, and of course without having any real share in them. I had been in the German Reichstag only once in my life and that was thirty years before, when from a platform open to the public I heard Bismarck speak on the Luxemburg question. Before the debate on the estimates in 1897, I had received all sorts of good advice from my colleagues and collaborators in case I should have to speak. Some of them had advised me to speak well out, as otherwise no one would hear me. Others, on the other hand, thought that to shout would irritate and annoy the deputies, who preferred a clear and distinct tone. I had made no sort of preparation for my speech for I had been assured that in no case would I be called on the first day of the debate; at the very earliest it would be on the second day and most probably the third or fourth. The papers of the Left before my first appearance in Reichstag had let the public know with more enjoyment than wit that I was a mere novice and consequently as an orator not up to my new position. The "*Lustigen Blätter*" on my arrival in Berlin published a cartoon on their front page, showing the Government as a nurse presenting a baby to three elderly gentlewomen. The ladies were the Centre, the Conservatives, and the Liberals; I was the baby. The Government said to the Parties: "There, look, that's the latest little Minister, a fine boy this Bülow, isn't he?" The Parties replied: "Ah, well! We must wait and see. You can't know anything about him until he begins to *speak*." This pretty picture began the collection of caricatures of myself that in the end filled thirty stately volumes. I was pictured as a baby in long clothes and with a little dimple in the chin and the hair parted in the middle, just as the caricaturist's pencil portrayed me until the end. The dimple remained, the parting vanished with my youthful hair.

On the day before my début in the Reichstag August Stein, the Berlin correspondent of the "*Frankfurter Zeitung*" (who was later, in spite of many divergences of political outlook, to become a good personal friend of mine), published an article of greeting upon me, in which he wrote, not without malice:

"Herr von Bülow, the new Head of the Foreign Ministry, comes before the Reichstag as a complete parliamentary novice. It remains to be seen whether an uncommonly witty conversationalist will prove to be a parliamentary debater as well. Ludwig Bamberger was probably the last who had thoroughly mastered this manner. Since his time much has changed in the Reichstag, including the debating style. If Herr von Bülow should speak in the Reichstag in the style which has won him such laurels in company and in private conversation, he would be likely in the Reichstag of to-day to meet with more astonishment than acceptance." Now that I look back on the first public speech I made in my life, I think it was perhaps a good thing that I spoke entirely without preparation. Since then I have spoken a great deal, perhaps too much, but I have always found that I spoke best *ex tempore.* There are painters whose sketches are more successful than their carefully finished pictures. I closed my speech of December 6, 1897, with the words: "We do not want to put anyone into the shade, but we demand a place for ourselves in the sun," without dreaming that the phrase would become historical, a new experience altogether for me up to then. At one moment during my speech, when there was laughter in the House, it occurred to me that perhaps the style of my speech, its matter or manner, was exciting the risibility of the popular assembly, a thing which would not have been so very surprising in the case of a parliamentary *homo novus.* As I went on speaking I reflected — for it is quite possible to speak and meanwhile be thinking of other things — what I should do if the laughter continued or even grew. I recalled how in a similar situation Disraeli, the great English parliamentarian, shouted to the House at one point in his maiden speech that if they laughed now they would listen later, and I resolved to say something of the sort if the need should arise. Fortunately I desisted from any such apostrophe; it would, as things were, have been entirely out of place and quite absurd. So I carried my speech through to the end as calmly as I had begun it. When I sat down, I was able to see from the gloomy faces of my colleagues that I could not have done so badly. My old friend Villers, of Vienna, once said that as far as envy and jealousy are concerned there is nothing to choose between the *corps diplomatique* and the *corps de ballet.* For diplomatic corps one might with no less justice substitute the corps of Ministers and Secretaries of State. So it used to be, and it is no more likely nowadays, that Ministers would be found living together "in kindly affection, in brotherly love and harmony." Any doubts were set at rest when I hear Miquel say behind me : "Bülow *primus*." This, from the mouth of this old parliamentarian, this great speaker and man of genius, did the novice good.

Next morning I read in the most widely circulated of the Berlin newspapers, the *"Lokal-Anzeiger"*: "The maiden speech of Secretary of State von Bülow was altogether a surprise. Whatever one might think of the activities of Baron von Marschall, even his bitterest enemies admitted that he was an orator of the first rank. One was prepared in advance to make every allowance in this respect for his successor. Herr von Bülow has no need to ask for any tenderness when judgment is passed on his oratorical gifts. He is, beyond all question, a born orator." Next day the Kaiser telegraphed to me : "I congratulate you most heartily on the magnificent speech with which you made your début in the Reichstag. Most cordial thanks also in the name of my navy. The impression made seems to have been remarkable." Before this and a few hours after my maiden speech in the Reichstag, Herbert Bismarck wrote to me :

Berlin, December 6, 1897

Dear Bülow,

I was most heartily glad of your splendid success in the Reichstag to-day and must give expression to my feeling by sending you cordial congratulations. In the House I preferred to refrain from greeting you personally, although it would have been a pleasure to me to do so; but as matters stand it could only have done you harm, in more than one direction. You will understand me, but I wanted nevertheless to explain my reserve to you personally and to tell you that it was due purely to consideration for your position, which no one can be more desirous than I to see established and made a pleasant one. You will not regard it as flattery or bad taste in an old friend if I tell you without reserve that you did brilliantly. Everything was just as good as it could be — the contents, the diction, tone and phrasing. I only came to hear you, and I was fully rewarded. It will interest you to hear that several members near me, men who are strangers to you, cheered you loudly and shouted out: "There at last is a voice from the manly days of long ago. In his style and his striking phrases Bülow forcibly recalls Prince Bismarck."

I am going home this evening, but shall attend one or two sessions before Christmas, and hope after Christmas to be able to shake hands with you somewhere or other.

I received with many thanks your kind letter from Rome, and was very touched by its cordiality.

Yours always sincerely,

Herbert Bismarck

My old chief and benefactor in Petersburg and Vienna, Prince Henry VII of Reuss, wrote to my wife:

Trebschen, December 11, 1897

Carissima,

From my quiet corner in the countryside I must send you a sincere "Bravo!" Bülow has made a grand beginning, and that is a great thing: he will know how to maintain his position in the place he has won for himself. The whole tone of his speech was refreshing and encouraging to me, it reminded me of the good old times! Now I only hope he may have a little luck — luck is always useful in everything — and then he will go ahead — as, for that matter, I never doubted that he would.

Needless to say, there was an enthusiastic message of congratulation from my "eternally devoted Monts." On the chaffing pretext that he had no intention of complimenting me to my face, he wrote as follows to my principal secretary, Prince Lichnowsky, who, as he well knew, showed me everything:

First of all, let us congratulate one another on Bernhard Bülow. He is doing his job admirably. Besides, his extremely human manner is winning great and small alike. To-day he is the most popular man in Germany. I only hope everyone may be as free from envy as you and I in looking up at his greatness, including the gospeler! I grow in my own esteem when I think how such a man as Bernhard Bülow honours me with his friendship.

By "the gospeler" Monts meant the Kaiser, referring to Prince Henry's speech at Kiel, in which the latter had praised his brother and said that he intended to preach to all the world "His Majesty's gospel."

Monts wrote to my wife:

I simply must write to you and send you my heartiest congratulations on your husband's great successes. I expected much of Bernhard, but my expectations have been surpassed. You should hear the judgments which are being passed here by men of all parties. Parliament, they are saying, has not experienced such a day since Bismarck's time. Our real friends are absolutely triumphant, and not least among them your most obedient undersigned. I cannot possibly express to you how proud I am of my chief Bülow. After the long time during which the diplomacy of the Empire has had to make the best of such inferior Prefects as Caprivi and Marschall, we are once more really coming to life in foreign affairs. I pray that Heaven's favours may fall on your head and your husband's, and conclude with grateful regards as always,

Your most devoted
Monts

A sincere message of congratulation was telegraphed to me by the noble Grand Duke Frederick of Baden: "Accept my warmest and heartiest congratulations on the excellent speech you made in the Reichstag on the Navy Bill. It was a real pleasure to me to observe your clear and thorough exposition. I hope it will be rewarded with success."

CHAPTER XIII

Parliamentary Eloquence in Germany: Bennigsen, Stresemann, Miquel, Bassermann, Eugen Richter, Hertling, Bebel, Heydebrand, Naumann, Paasche — With William II at Kiel — His "Mailed Fist" Speech (November 15, 1897) — Prince Henry in London — His Report on His Far Eastern Voyage — William II and Salisbury — William II Visits Prince Bismarck at Friedrichsruh — The Kiaochow Lease Agreement (January 5, 1898).

THE thing that had pleased me most was that, during my maiden speech, I had felt no trace of embarrassment or nervousness. Since then I have made many a speech in three Parliaments and also outside Parliament. I do not flatter myself that this would enable me to write a book like Cicero's "De Claris Oratoribus", but I think I have acquired a considerable measure of experience in this field. Why is it that in France and Italy, in England and America, in fact, everywhere, they speak better than we do? It was so during my period of office, and in the Republic, as I have been assured by adherents of all parties and as can be seen from the Parliamentary reports, the level of German parliamentary oratory has sunk distinctly lower still. The German's poor sense of form may have something to do with it, for one thing. In French schools special importance is attached to "rhetoric", and almost all the great French parliamentarians have distinguished themselves ever since their school days in this important branch of instruction, while nearly all British Ministers and Members of Parliament have been capable debaters at Eton or Harrow, Oxford or Cambridge; but in Germany the art of oratory is almost entirely neglected. Bismarck said that good speakers are generally bad politicians. For that reason Right-wing politicians feel they have a good excuse for attaching little importance to the form of their speeches. The Left-wing groups, especially the Socialists, are more interested in training their party members as orators. This, however, is often carried out in a cheapjack style and is confined to instilling into them out-of-date catch phrases and eternally recurring terms of expression. There is a Latin saying, *"Poeta nascitur, orator fit"* — the poet is born, the orator is made. I think the truth is that every man is a born speaker, for everyone has a tongue. It is quite true that the most fluent tongue is of no avail without clear thinking and some sense of logic. These are and will remain essential for any permanent effect. But when Faust says that intelligence and good sense need little art for their presentation, we must not be too ready to let the matter rest there. His servant, the dry Wagner, the arid crawler, is not altogether wrong in his comment that the speaker's manner makes the speaker. Some grains of inspiration, a little originality, are desirable gifts. *"Tous les genres sont bons hors le genre ennuyeux."* The German can stomach an interminable meal of boredom. But I think the most admirably orthodox of Social Democrats would quail at the task of reading through a collected edition in many volumes of August Bebel's speeches, filled from end to end with an unquenchable fire of anger and a perpetually boiling indignation, with the present always as Hell and the future as Heaven, with humanity always divided up into wolves and lambs, with never a touch of humour or originality or wit, an immeasurable Sahara with a Fata Morgana on the horizon. How different was Bismarck! From the first speeches made by the young Bismarck, from his junker standpoint, in the United Diet and in the Erfurt Parliament to the powerful speeches addressed to the nation after his dismissal in the market place of Jena and from the balcony of the modest house in the Saxon forests, they are all to this day a storehouse of undying thoughts, thoughts that tower over changing times and over every division of party, a storehouse rich in picturesque phrase, in happy inspiration, in striking simile, drawn from nature and life and permanently impressing themselves on the memory. How different from Bebel was even Ferdinand Lassalle! And yet August Bebel was not less inferior to Lassalle than, say, Scheidemann to Bebel, as I know from ample evidence *de visu et de auditu* gathered during my last days of office in the Reichstag. And since we have been living in Republican

Germany I have everywhere heard that in comparison with the
Communist leaders Scheidemann makes the impression of a Gladstone or a Thiers.   To say nothing of Leichenmüller, or Adolf
Hoffmann, whose prominent position in his party is due mainly to
his happy-go-lucky way with German grammar, his capricious use
of "*mir*" and "*mich*" — or of Max Hölz, who is familiarizing us with
the niceties of the convict prison.   British, French, and Italian
statesmen count good intellectual equipment, and often even scientific and literary distinction, amongst their titles to fame.   I need
only recall Disraeli, Gladstone, Balfour, Thiers, Guizot, Hanotaux,
Marco Minghetti, Massimo d'Azeglio and Vincenzo Gioberti,
Bonghi and Luzzati.   It does not matter greatly that Bismarck
on occasion made fun of men of this type, such as Bunsen and Pro-
kesch, when he found them in the ranks of his opponents, opponents
who, indeed, counted for little.   It may be questioned, for one
thing, whether his occasional display of his rather low opinion of
culture and intellect was the happiest side of Bismarck's character.
It brought down upon him Thiers' phrase "*un barbare de génie.*"
But then our greatest man was his own refutation, for he was a very
distinguished author, speaker, journalist, letter-writer, and philosopher.   No less a man than Mommsen once said to me when he
visited me in Rome in 1896, that after Goethe, Lessing, and Schopenhauer he counted Bismarck as the greatest of German prose writers.
During my period of office, from 1897 to 1909, I met few speakers in
German parliamentary bodies who could bear comparison with the
coryphaei of our western and southern neighbours.   The German
speaker loses himself in details too easily, when the effect of a
speech depends more than anything on bearing Voltaire's phrase in
mind, *que le détail est une vermine qui ronge les grandes choses.*   The
German expects everything of common sense, which, to have its
full effect, must be reinforced with rhetoric.   How different, during
the World War, was the impression created abroad by the thoroughly
rhetorical French propaganda from that of the purely matter-of-
fact German propaganda!   How differently Viviani and Briand
stirred men's emotions from the most learned German professors and
the best-informed German parliamentarians!

Among German orators the strongest impression left on me was that made by Bennigsen, although when I entered German parliamentary life in 1897 he was rarely heard any longer in debates, and he died barely two years after my appointment as Chancellor. What made Bennigsen so impressive was the sense he inspired in everyone of having a life full of hard work and hard thinking at the back of his words, the sense that what he was saying had not been got up for the occasion four-and-twenty hours before, but that his utterances were the outcome of years of observation, study, and, above all, thought, and that at all times he abjured every sort of empty phrasemaking. His disciple and ultimate successor in the leadership of the old National Liberals, now the German People's party, Gustav Stresemann, is, if not the only orator, far and away the finest the German Parliament has known since the revolution of 1918.

A great orator in the European sense was Miquel. I shall never forget a scene in the Reichstag which I witnessed when I was Secretary of State. Miquel was not very popular in the Reichstag then for several reasons. He had been a member of the Reichstag from 1867 to 1877 and from 1887 to 1890, but for some years had no longer been seen in the monumental building in the Königsplatz. Now, however, Ernst Lieber, leader of the Centre party, a Nassau man and for many years a friend of the ex-mayor of Frankfort-am-Main, but subsequently estranged from him, had directed violent personal attacks against Miquel as Minister of Finance, charging him with having moulted his Communist skin and emerged as an Agrarian and reactionary. Miquel had to reply and came to the Reichstag the following day, taking his seat next to me. When he began to speak, the feeling in the House was plainly hostile to him ; the whole Left wing regarded him as a renegade and enemy, the Centre as unreliable ; and the Right wing was determined not to compromise itself for his sake. Anyone could see that the Socialists were only waiting for a suitable opportunity to interrupt his speech with heckling and laughter. Johannes Miquel dealt first, speaking rather low, with the charge of flagrant apostasy. "I have never denied," he began in effect, "that in my early years, before I was

capable of withstanding the dialectic of a great intellect, I declared
myself an adherent of the ideas of Karl Marx." He said this in so
insinuating a tone, and the expression on his face, turned towards
the extreme Left, was so fascinating, that even the stalwarts around
Bebel were unable to escape his influence entirely. Miquel then
proceeded to show, in strong and striking phrases, how practical business, acquaintance with actual life as member of the Reichstag, as
mayor, and as director of a great bank had gradually drawn him out
of the world of abstract ideas into the real conditions of our national
existence and our practical needs. He read a letter from a friend
of his youth, the aged creator of the Civil Code, Gottlieb Planck, a
blind man who had done immense work; Planck pointed to Miquel
as a fine type of the man who strives always towards perfection.
When Miquel came to the end of his speech of defence against Lieber,
his audience was as though transformed; there was nothing but
cheering to be heard. Before the violent attacks from Herr Lieber
had compelled the Prussian Minister of Finance to come before the
Reichstag, "*Vorwärts*" did Miquel the disservice of publishing a
letter which he had written as a young student in 1848 to Karl
Marx. It began with some such words as these : "As a Communist
and atheist like you, I share your belief that a new and better world
can only arise on the ruins of present society." On the publication
of this letter Miquel had submitted his resignation. William II
received the letter of resignation while staying in Hohenzollern
Castle. After reading it he sent Miquel the following telegram :
"From rock to sea, from youthful exuberance to statesmanlike
activity. That is the answer of your King to your submission."
A reply which did honour alike to Kaiser and Minister.

Ernst Bassermann, another member of the National Liberal
party, had neither Bennigsen's depth nor Miquel's charm, but he
was effective through his noble personality, of which his speeches
were the expression. He was not infallible, and made mistakes
like everyone else now and then. But he had qualities to which
so many lay claim without acting up to their professions; for
Ernst Bassermann the country did really stand above party, and
far above personal ambition. Eugen Richter I found disappointing

as an orator. Much as I valued his industry, his mastery of all questions of state, and his unselfish character, I found him as a speaker barely second-rate. He spoke with a long slip in his hand on which he had noted down not only his points but the jokes he meant to make. One could see from his face when the joke was due to come. And the same joke would come too often. Thus, in every budget debate he used to cast a sly look at the Ministerial bench and quote the verse from Psalm 103 in which man is likened to the flower of the field : the wind passeth over it, and it is gone ; and the place thereof shall know it no more. Eugen Richter irresistibly recalled those professors whose audience can sense the approach of the joke : it is carefully noted down in the speaker's manuscript, so that the listener shall later be able to see plainly that the professor is saying nothing but what the book contains. Richter as speaker was decidedly surpassed by a professor, Baron von Hertling, later Chancellor. Hertling had as a young man been a lecturer in residence at Bonn. He was compelled by extreme nearsightedness to speak without notes. He not only spoke entirely without notes, but also with entire confidence, often very finely. But he lacked warmth, there was nothing about him that evoked enthusiasm or carried away his hearers. Here lay Bebel's strength ; his speeches were better to hear than to read — he was effective more through temperament than through depth or even clarity of ideas. At bottom Bebel had only one unchanging speech.

The best debater, in my view, in the German Parliaments was Heydebrand, a clear, incisive, ready speaker. It is true that this member exemplified Bismarck's dictum, just mentioned, that good speakers are generally bad politicians, and that party leaders with a good gift of oratory are so much the more harmful. If a strong attack had been made against the Right wing in the Reichstag, its members offered the spectacle of a fowl-run above which a bird of prey was circling. Members looked at one another, but none could be found prepared to reply at once. Then a cry for help would go to the Prussian Diet, where Herr von Heydebrand was oftener to be found than in the Reichstag. The "little man", as his party called him, would come in, quickly get details of the attack that had been made, throw a confident glance at his party colleagues, and reply often smashingly, generally with telling effect; sometimes, but occasionally, with much hair-splitting. Wilhelm von Kardorff, for many years leader of the Conservative Radicals, was scarcely inferior to Heydebrand in readiness, and surpassed him decidedly in political insight and statesmanlike gifts. The most tedious speaker I ever met with was the Radical, Gothein. If he spoke at length, and he almost always spoke at great length, the keenest and usually most attentive members of the House sank into a gentle slumber. There was a riddle current among members and journalists: "What is the most reliable opiate?"

"Chloral?"

"No!"

"Veronal, then?"

"No!"

"Cocaine?"

"No!"

"Not strychnine, surely?"

"No, not even strychnine, but Gothe-ine. Nothing can withstand it."

The most banal speaker I ever heard was Philipp Scheidemann. Never did there issue from his mouth a phrase, an argument, a joke that had not appeared countless times in "*Vorwärts.*" His speeches, pretentiously delivered, were like small change that had worn down in passing through hundreds of greasy fingers. Friedrich Naumann only came into the Reichstag towards the end of my period of office, at the elections of 1907. He was counted an orator, but I can only agree up to a certain point. When Naumann was under discussion August Stein, who for many years was on the staff of the "*Frankfurter Zeitung*", used to quote a couplet of Faust's servant Wagner:

> *Ich hab' es öfter rühmen hören,*
> *Ein Komödiant könnt' einen Pfarrer lehren.*[1]

Naumann's speeches always betrayed the former pulpit preacher; the delivery was splendid but the accents were rather too parsonic,

[1] I have often heard say, a comedian can teach a parson.

and did not always ring quite true. If volubility were all that counted, the National Liberal, Paasche, would have taken first place. It was calculated that he could send a hundred words a minute scampering over the hurdles of his teeth. What he had to say was usually of very little importance. Before the revolution he was the only member who, to use a *terminus technicus* then unknown but now in general currency, was regarded as a "*schieber.*"[1] Before the revolution members who had engaged in illicit or even merely risky business (I remember one or two cases) were unostentatiously but resolutely edged out of their party. The time was to come when a man who had been proved in court to have mixed up private deals with his political activities in a disreputable way was to play a leading part in our public life, when Chancellors in office were to praise this man during his life and elevate him to national canonization after his death. It was significant that when the exposure of Mathias Erzberger began and had, indeed, gone very far, Herr Paasche publicly did honour to him in a speech as one of the most splendidly endowed and hard-working members of the German Reichstag. It was Herr Paasche, too, who, about the same time as he was lavishing enthusiastic praise on Erzberger, greeted Secretary of State von Kühlmann at the Anhalt station in Berlin, on his return from Roumania, as victor in the diplomatic struggle in Bucharest — at the very moment when Herr von Kühlmann, by his diplomatic incapacity and by his manner in the Roumanian capital, had painfully embarrassed our friends and supporters in Bulgaria, Roumania, and Turkey.

William II had promised his brother, Prince Henry, that he would pay him a farewell visit in Kiel before he sailed for China, and had summoned me to accompany him to Kiel. On the morning of our departure, December 15, 1897, I received a telegram from St. Petersburg from which I could see that my conversation with Count Osten-Sacken and my instructions sent to our Embassy in St. Petersburg at the same time had borne good fruit. The Russian Government was abandoning its opposition to our landing at Kiaochow, and was itself sending a Russian squadron to Port

[1] Profiteer, dishonest dealer.

Arthur to occupy that port, which was an important acquisition for it. This was a load off my mind. It sometimes happens, however, that at the very moment he has a piece of good fortune a man does something stupid. Instead of keeping the good news to myself for the time being, I imparted it to the Kaiser on our way by rail to Hamburg. If William II had not, as was his way, at once been pleased and excited by this good news, he would probably not have made his unfortunate "mailed fist" speech that evening. We stopped off at Hamburg, where we visited the bourse. The great hall of the bourse was thronged. The "honest merchant" of Hamburg had come in his legions to express his satisfaction at our action in the Far East. In the name of the bourse Adolf Woermann, one of the ablest of the business leaders of Hamburg, made a speech in stentorian tones, amid enthusiastic cheers from the business men assembled, thanking the Kaiser for having taken our commercial relations with the Far East, where great prospects were unfolding themselves for Hamburg and Germany, under his powerful protection. With its hopes and aspirations all Hamburg stood behind the Kaiser and his Government. At that moment everyone felt the pulsation of the greatest German commercial city, which, before a German Empire had come into being, had struck out paths for German energy and enterprise in every corner of the world, including those very shores of the Pacific.

The banquet at Kiel took place in the Castle. Filled with the impressions of that day, and in high spirits over the successful diplomatic handling of our enterprise, for which he thanked me in the warmest terms, the Kaiser proposed a toast, speaking with much spirit and really finely, and, with his remarkable assimilative capacity making various useful points based on things that I had had the opportunity to mention to him on the way to Kiel, but also making some very unfortunate observations. The phrase about the German Michael, with his shield, adorned with the Imperial eagle, firmly planted on the soil, might pass, for the Kaiser had used it often enough before in his rhetorical and impressionist fashion. A more serious matter was the statement that if anyone should set out to injure us, Prince Henry should hit out at them with the

"*gepanzerte faust.*" The phrase "*gepanzerte faust*", especially
in its English version of "mailed fist", was destined to crop up
endlessly for many years to come in all the attacks made by the anti-
German press, and to turn William II, good-natured and well-
intentioned as he is at bottom, and certainly unmilitaristic, into a
new Genghis Khan. The Kaiser added to this regrettable threat
with the "mailed fist" an invitation to his brother to weave a
laurel about his young brow, which no one in the German Empire
would grudge him. At these last words Lucanus, who was sitting
next to me, whispered to me softly: "He means to set his brother
at rest in case the Prince should be afraid that any success of his
might arouse the Kaiser's envy."

The Kaiser's address to his brother only contained one or two
regrettable passages; Prince Henry's reply from beginning to end
was terribly out of place. Prince Henry had not only inherited his
noble father's good looks. He had, like him, a nature that was
noble through and through. He also had a heart of gold. A man
of uncommon physical strength, he was equal to every call on his
energies. Had he been born a plain citizen, he would have been
a splendid sailor, mate, master, and would have been equal to any
storm. Nor was he wanting in sound common sense. But his
simple decency and modesty failed to reckon with the evil always
in mankind, and in the maze of politics he was no adept at picking
his way. Hinzpeter once said to me, in his caustic way: "You
can see in Prince Henry what the Kaiser would have become if I
had not taken him in hand." Which does, indeed, raise the question
whether, all in all, the German Empire might not have been better
served with Prince Henry as Kaiser than with his much more gifted
but also much more difficult, capricious, and unreliable elder brother.
The burden of Prince Henry's speech on December 15 was the hardship it must have been for the Kaiser not to be able to lead the
China expedition in person. "Your Majesty," the Prince said,
"has made the great sacrifice of entrusting this command to me."
For this the Prince thanked him from his "most faithful, brotherly,
humble, and obedient heart." He realized very well what His
Majesty must be feeling, and knew how great the renunciation must

have been when His Majesty entrusted to him so fine a command. This it was that moved him most deeply. But he assured His Majesty that he was not caught by the lure of fame or laurels; the one thing that he looked forward to was "to proclaim, to preach the gospel of Your Majesty's sacred person to all who will hear it, and also to those who do not want to hear it." That was what he wanted inscribed on his standard, and he would inscribe it wherever he went. The speech closed with an "Ever and aye, hurrah, hurrah, hurrah!"

When we got up from the table I went with Lucanus to a vacant room to look through the speeches that had been exchanged before releasing them for publication, and I told him that neither the "mailed fist" phrase nor the eccentric passages in the Prince's reply must be published. The head of the Civil Cabinet strongly opposed this. He had now had nearly ten years' experience, he said, which had shown him that to hush up blunders of this sort only made matters worse, for it was exactly the striking declarations that always found their way into the papers somehow or other. To suppress, moreover, just the passages in his speech which he regarded as the finest, and above all to mutilate his brother's tribute, would deeply irritate the Kaiser. "We have taken immense trouble," said Herr von Lucanus, "to bring Your Excellency along—Hahnke, August Eulenburg and I, and plenty of others. We regard you as the only man capable of manoeuvring the ship of state in the stormy sea into which our Kaiser has now led her, without running her upon the rocks or sandbanks. We regard you as the only possible Imperial Chancellor when old Hohenlohe is past work. If you spoil your relations with the Kaiser in advance, your career will be a short one. You may answer that in that case you would just go, but I tell you that if you were to go for such reasons and under such circumstances I would regard your withdrawal as a desertion of the colours. Be guided by the example of the Chief of Staff, Count Schlieffen, who allows the Kaiser to do any silly thing he likes at the manoeuvres, so long as he is able to keep a free hand in big questions and grave emergencies." The criticism of the toasts at Kiel made by a great part of the German press confirmed everything that I had said to Lucanus only too strongly. Even the *"Kreuzzeitung"* pointed out that there was only one gospel that could be preached, the gospel which would be the object of a festival in a week's time — "There is born this day a Saviour unto you." Much more severe was the judgment pronounced by the German liberal and clerical press and the whole of the foreign press. The *"Times"* declared that it was quite comprehensible that Prince Henry should wish to preach his brother's gospel to any who wished to hear it. But to preach it to those who had not the least desire to hear it — that was really going too far.

About a week after those high-flown speeches at Kiel, the Kaiser received in my presence a letter from his brother, who had made a short stay in England on his way from Kiel to the Far East, in order to visit his relatives, especially his grandmother, Queen Victoria. The Kaiser expectantly opened his brother's letter, curious to see what had been said at the British court about the festivities in Kiel. His face grew longer and longer as he read his brother's note; on the other hand, having begun reading it aloud to me he did not want to stop, lest I should end by imagining even worse things than the Prince had actually written. Prince Henry reported to his brother, with his customary frankness, that the speeches which the two of them had made at the splendid Kiel banquet had not aroused the admiration they had hoped for. "Grandmamma", clearly of set purpose, had avoided the subject altogether. "Uncle Bertie" had made sardonic remarks about the speeches; the other uncles and aunts had set them down as unfortunate. It was evident from Prince Henry's letter that he had been greatly impressed by this family criticism. His mother, the Empress Frederick, had written to my wife about his speech: "Henry is such a dear boy, but his speech was very foolish." It was part of Prince Henry's simple upright character that, unlike so many other royalties, he clung to all his relatives with touching loyalty.

I must add that the letters which Prince Henry sent to the Kaiser during his voyage to the Far East, and which the Kaiser regularly passed on to me, were very sensible. He wrote on July

11, 1898, in exultation over the behaviour of Shantung coal: "A few tons of Chinese coal that I had as samples from the much discussed coal basin, and with which I made parallel trials against British coal, have yielded a surprisingly good result. The best Poshan coal is equal to Cardiff! The poorer quality is incomparably better than the Japanese." On the many differences between the various naval authorities the Prince wrote to the Kaiser:

I hope that by the time these lines reach you all questions of organization will have been cleared up and that you will have remained firm in holding on to the organization we have had hitherto. Your will can only be expressed through a single medium of command. Trust Tirpitz as always, but don't be led astray by him in cutting down the authority of the supreme command in the slightest. No one has fought harder in his time for such a supreme command than Tirpitz himself. And he has done so out of conviction! God bless and preserve you. I include you and yours every day in my prayers. Your deeply loving and always loyal and obedient brother, Henry.

In spite of his warm friendship for his brother-in-law, Tsar Nicholas, Prince Henry always had warmer feelings for England than for Russia. Thus he wrote to his brother from Tsingtao on October 28, 1898:

I still regard Russia's slow but continual advance in the Far East as a regrettable factor which may easily endanger German and British interests in China. Since her seizure of Port Arthur, Russia has come regrettably close to Peking. Manchuria is already coming under her influence and is being slowly Russified. Korea may be only a question of time! . . . I have repeatedly laid stress on your friendly relations with Nicky, and I think I may say to the general satisfaction, although my declarations were made at a time when you were thinking of our old comradeship in arms with England, which I myself welcomed with joy from the bottom of my heart.

In those December days of 1897 William II at once attributed the frowns over his Kiel celebrations to the personal hostility of Lord Salisbury to the German Empire and the German Emperor. The Kaiser, as is well known, had had a brush with the British Prime

Minister during one of his first visits to England after his accession, long before I came into office. Lord Salisbury had found the Kaiser restless and exacting; William II found the British Premier pompous and arrogant. English friends told me that the antipathy of the powerful British statesman to the German Emperor, regrettable and politically injurious as it was, but undeniable and increasing as years passed by, was also attributable to the honest indignation of the Marquis of Salisbury, who in spite of occasional friction had been an admirer of Prince Bismarck, at the ungrateful and contemptuous way in which William II had got rid of the great Chancellor. Another distinguished British statesman had a similar sentiment — the Earl of Rosebery, who was a personal friend of Herbert Bismarck. After the fall of the Prince, Lord Rosebery sent Herbert the woodcut of "*Punch's*" striking cartoon "Dropping the Pilot", showing Prince Bismarck in pilot's uniform slowly and heavily descending the companion ladder of the ship Germany, looking exceedingly grave, while William II, with his crown on his head, looks superciliously over the rail. William II knew that Lord Salisbury had no love for him. In his annoyance over the news which Prince Henry had sent him about the bad impression created in England by the events in Kiel, the Kaiser wrote a long letter to his grandmother, Queen Victoria, without saying anything about it to the Chancellor or to me; in this letter, without mentioning the Kiel speech and its unfortunate reception in England, he complained that Lord Salisbury gave him annoyance and upset his plans whenever he got a chance. The Kaiser showed me later his grandmother's reply. She had confined herself to transmitting to her grandson the communication which Lord Salisbury had sent her on receiving the Kaiser's letter to her. I remember the British Premier's letter because it is characteristic of the gravity of British politics and of the sense of duty both of Queen Victoria and of British statesmen. Lord Salisbury thanked the Queen in very respectful terms for graciously bringing the Kaiser's letter to his knowledge. He added that the Queen would agree with him that he was not a German but a British Minister, and that, although he was keenly desirous of maintaining good relations between

Germany and Britain, he simply had to protect British interests. The Kaiser did not seem to appreciate this fully; he was clearly unacquainted with British traditions and the British Constitution. The Queen would certainly be the first to blame her Prime Minister if he were to pursue any other but a purely British policy. That had been his course hitherto, and he would continue to pursue it in future, confident of the approval and support of the Crown. The Kaiser did not take the reply tragically. He merely said:

"Now at least we know where we are."

Needless to say, I read to His Majesty or placed before him all the adverse comments of the German and foreign press on the Kiel speeches. The day after the farewell banquet at Kiel, the Kaiser and his retinue paid a visit to Prince Bismarck at Friedrichsruh. On the way to Friedrichsruh I told Lucanus I hoped the meeting might pass off well; Lucanus, with the utmost cynicism, said: "*Ach*, you know, the Kaiser only wants to see for himself how far the old Prince's candle has burned down and when his death may be expected." On receiving the news of the Kaiser's impending visit, Prince Bismarck sent him the following telegram, which touched me in its simplicity: "In gratitude for the high honour of the Imperial visit, I beg Your Majesty graciously to forgive the shortcomings in external appearances which result from my illness." We did in fact, when we arrived at the modest house in Friedrichsruh, find the Prince in an invalid chair. Mentally I found him unchanged. The Kaiser sat next to Countess Rantzau, the Prince's only daughter; I sat on her other side, and the Prince faced us. He led the conversation from the first moment, endeavouring to turn it to serious subjects. The Kaiser, with a deliberation that alienated me, evaded every political subject and took up none of the threads which the old Prince, almost ingratiatingly, offered him. The Prince spoke of his activities as Prussian Minister at the court of the Emperor Napoleon III in 1862. He described, in his rich, low voice, how the Emperor Napoleon had "graciously shown confidence" in him, and had asked him on one occasion what were his views as to ministerial responsibility, personal rule, and the advantages of the various systems of government. He had replied to the Emperor that personal rule had many attractions, but could only be maintained so long as the monarch could rely on his guards and so long as they were entirely in a position to assure order and loyalty in face of any possible incident. Where there was no such absolute assurance, it was advisable for the Crown to place the Ministers as a buffer between itself and every sort of opposition, in order to absorb and neutralize the impact of any blows aimed at it. The Kaiser listened absentmindedly, and replied with one or two old barrack room jokes which for many years had always aroused the same laughter at every garrison banquet in Potsdam. During the conversation after dinner the Kaiser again avoided any sort of intimate talk with Prince Bismarck. When the Kaiser brought the visit to an end, comparatively early, the Prince's bath chair was pushed into another room, so that we might all take leave of him. The Prince cordially shook hands with most of us. When Lucanus bowed to him, he looked past him as though he were thin air. As I came to him he gave me his hand and said: "May God abide with you!" It was the last time I saw him and heard his voice.

On January 5, 1898, the *"Reichsanzeiger"* published the text of the German-Chinese treaty leasing the Bay of Kiaochow. I reported the conclusion of the treaty to the Kaiser in a short telegram, in which I expressed my satisfaction at the successful completion, with God's help, of the course on which we had entered in November. The Kaiser was all the more pleased since he had received a curt answer to a telegram which he had sent shortly before this, on his own initiative, to the Tsar Nicholas, and had half given up the matter as a failure. He had then telegraphed to me somewhat impatiently that Prince Hohenlohe, the Chancellor, considered the occupation of Kiaochow an infringement of the Peterhof agreement. It was "deeply humiliating" and "derogatory" that we must get a "quasi-permit" in St. Petersburg when, three years before, we had had the opportunity of occupying Kiaochow and had missed it. The Tsar's answer was "cold and reserved." Kaiser William now telegraphed me: "My dear Bernhard, what a New Year's present! I am quite beside myself with joy! You are very right when you remark how great has been the Lord's help and mercy to us; without it we would never have succeeded. But it was done for the sake of the Cross and so He was with us. Deepest thanks for your loyal and self-sacrificing work. What a splendid first success for you! A good innings![1] For the rest — *in hoc signo vinces!*" So William II telegraphed to me when the seizure of Kiaochow, so ardently desired by him, and an operation not without danger and a delicate matter, anyhow, had succeeded. On that very day he honoured me with a visit and personally handed me the Order of the Red Eagle, first class, with the words: "This is only meant as a beginning; there are better things to follow."

Nine years later, on January 11, 1906, the Kaiser made this marginal note on an article in a Paris paper, in which the acquisition of Kiaochow was attributed to the joint labours of the German political leaders and the Ministry of the Navy: "Hohenlohe was the man who *alone*, with keenness and decision, helped me and warmly supported me in the Kiaochow affair; the Foreign Office . . . in its trousers; Tirpitz stood aside, dissatisfied and growling. Hohenlohe, Hollmann, and I! We acted in entire agreement and unison, and the two of us were surprised at the cool determination and courage of the old gentleman. It is to him that Germany is indebted for Kiaochow." Respect for my male and especially for my female readers makes me suppress an excessively coarse word in the All-Highest's marginal note. When it was shown me, after passing through all departments, I gravely and very emphatically called the Kaiser to account. With a sharpness both of words and manner that I never had occasion to use with him before or after, I recalled to his memory how the whole affair of Kiaochow had been put through by Tirpitz and myself. Prince Hohenlohe, for whom I had the greatest admiration, and at whose side I had stood through a quarter of a century, was a very old man in 1897 and, as the Kaiser must have known, had been able to do no more than lend his name to the Kiaochow move. As for Admiral Hollmann, he had told me, before I was summoned from Rome to become Secretary of State for Foreign Affairs, not to let myself be tempted to Berlin:

[1] English in the original.

though I might speak with the tongues of men and angels, I should fail to win over the Reichstag to the Kaiser's naval plans and would equally fail to carry it with me for any action in the Far East; in both directions the Kaiser was deceiving himself. The Kaiser, very much embarrassed, replied to me that he had, of course, not been thinking of me at all when he wrote his marginal note; he knew very well that he was indebted primarily to me for Kiaochow; he had only been annoyed at the way Tirpitz wanted to take all the credit for the Kiaochow expedition and for the ship-building programme. "Tirpitz always wants to thrust himself into the foreground. He is just like bad old Bismarck, who pushed his way up at the expense of my grandpapa." As for Hollmann, he was, the Kaiser said, such a good fellow. "Little Hollmann" had been hard hit because Tirpitz and not he had had a hand in the increase of the navy and in the seizure of Kiaochow. I reminded His Majesty that Hollmann had retired because he felt quite unable to carry the Kaiser's plans and desires into realization. "Your Majesty will not get far," I concluded, "if time and again you prefer the bad to the good musicians, simply because the former are in your good graces — that is, you find them more amenable." I had almost been more irritated at the coarseness of his marginal note than at its falsification of history. I demanded and received authority to express to the Foreign Office, and in particular to the Under Secretary of State, Baron von Rotenhan, and Geheimen Legations-rat von Holstein, His Majesty's deep regret at his note, which had been due to an erroneous judgment of the circumstances. I mention this unedifying episode *anticipando*, because it throws up particularly clearly the Kaiser's constant fear of being put into the shade by his advisers, ministers, generals, admirals. He wanted to make out *ex post* that he alone had acquired the navy and Kiaochow with Hohenlohe's and Hollmann's help because he said to himself that no one would credit either of those worn-out old gentlemen with any serious hand in such achievements. It is the same mentality which impelled William II, while the ship of state was being tossed to and fro by wave and storm in the frightful years of the World War, to send one inadequate steersman after another to the helm. Field Marshal von Hahnke told me on one occasion that some months after her son's accession to the throne the Empress Frederick had said to him: "If you should ever suppose that any other motives could determine my son's action than purely personal ones, and above all personal vanity, you will find yourself mistaken." Gloomily the old Marshal added: "Unhappily she was right."

One small touch will, on the other hand, suffice to show how human, generous, and good-hearted this same monarch could be. Our Minister in Copenhagen, Herr von Kiderlen, had reported a conversation with King Christian IX of Denmark, then an old man of almost eighty, after a dinner at court. The King had said to him, after "a few flattering words" about me: "I must have seen Secretary of State von Bülow as a boy at his father's house. That was a man of mark, a fine character; unhappily he was not listened to in Denmark, and as no one would pay attention to him he left the country in the end, going first to Mecklenburg-Strelitz; there, it seems, he did not get on with the Grand Duke, and he went on to Berlin. I remember still how I met the old Emperor William shortly after Herr von Bülow's death, and the Kaiser expressed to me his grief at the irreplaceable loss that he had suffered, both in the Minister and the man." When this report was placed before His Majesty, William II wrote *ad marginem:* "The judgment is entirely just, and very heartening and comforting for the son of that excellent man." The question whether William II has a heart has often been discussed, even in the days of his power and good fortune, and widely varying answers have been given.

I remember a curious conversation on this point dating from my time as Imperial Chancellor. One evening, when my wife was at a concert or the opera, I invited to dinner the then Minister of the Interior, Theobald von Bethmann-Hollweg, and General Hellmuth von Moltke. We were *à trois.* The conversation turned, as often, to the Kaiser, and the question was raised whether he had a heart. I said Yes, definitely and with conviction, just as I would to this day. General von Moltke opposed my view with equal decision: William II, he said, was much too selfish to have any heart; and in any case too fickle for any reliance to be placed on his heart. Hellmuth von Moltke adhered to this view to the end of his life. He came to see me a few days before his sudden death, and spoke bitterly of the way in which, as soon as Fortune had deserted him, the Kaiser also turned his back on him. The Kaiser placed all the blame for the unfortunate initial course of the war on him, and took virtually no notice of him anyhow; at his last birthday, instead of the usual, almost excessively cordial congratulations, he only telegraphed him a few cold words. At that dinner in my home, during which Moltke had argued that the Kaiser had no heart at all and I had urged that he had a good and a noble heart, Bethmann-Hollweg took refuge, as was his wont in such cases, in an embarrassed silence. How vividly I remember that meeting — on my left sat the unfortunate General, who was later, by a mechanical and uninspired application of the Schlieffen strategy, to lose the battle of the Marne and so, if not the whole campaign, at least the prospect of any complete victory. On my right sat the yet more deeply responsible Minister, who, in the ultimatum to Serbia and his clumsy diplomatic treatment of it, was to make the most dreadful mistake in all the history of Prussia and Germany, and one of the worst in the history of the world.

CHAPTER XIV

The Passing of the Navy Bill (March 26, 1898) — Letter from Grand Duke Frederick of Baden — Prince Bismarck on Bülow — Baron von Richthofen Becomes Under Secretary of State vice Baron von Rotenhan — Helfferich, Ludwig Bamberger, and Georg Siemens — The Spanish-American War — The Succession Question in Lippe — The Tenth Celebration of the Accession of Kaiser William II (June 16, 1898) — His Telegram to Philipp Eulenburg — The Latter's Relationship with the House of Bismarck.

THE great Navy Bill, which had for years been the subject of long and careful preparation and had excited public opinion pro and contra more than any other, was passed on March 28, 1898, by 212 to 139 votes. The opposition vote was made up of the opponents of all German national claims and aspirations — the Social Democrats, the Poles, the Guelphs, and the Fransquillons of Alsace. The Centre was divided : the majority of the party followed Spahn and Hertling in voting for the Bill. Most of the Bavarians voted against the Bill, including Schädler and Pichler, and with them a few Prussian extremists like Roeren. In the course of this winter session I several times found the opportunity I wanted of expressing in the Reichstag my views of the aims and the necessary limitations of our naval ambitions and of our overseas policy. I voiced the hope that the seed we had sown at Kiaochow would bear fruit. We would proceed without undue haste, but also without petty narrowness of spirit, not as *conquistadores* and not as schemers, but as a prudent and capable trading folk who, like the Maccabees of old, held a weapon in one hand but in the other the trowel and the spade. The acquisition of Kiaochow would thus itself promote the economic progress and the political power of the German nation. This anticipation was fully confirmed up to the midsummer of 1914. As lately as April, 1914, German travellers back from the Far East were telling me that, thanks to our base at Kiaochow, German economic interests in the Far East were making splendid progress;

Shantung justified the highest hopes and Kiaochow itself had become an important commercial and distributive centre. Even as far back as 1897 I had deliberately and emphatically set limits to our policy in the East.[1] We would pursue, I said, no aims, would not even take up offers made to us, that did not fit in with "our cautious and reserved Eastern policy." I made use of a figure from the world of music, a world normally far from my thoughts, as unfortunately I am entirely unmusical. It was not necessary, I said, in a concert, even in a European concert, that everyone should play the same instrument. One could beat the drum, another blow the trumpet, a third hold the great kettledrum. In Constantinople we were merely blowing the flute of diplomatic advice and persuasion. We were exerting no pressure; if trouble arose, we quietly stood aside; if differences grew strident, we put down our flute and left the concert hall. This was in harmony with our disinterestedness in Eastern affairs. I kept to this policy of caution and reserve in all Balkan, Eastern, and Mediterranean questions, right up to my retirement, and was especially careful not to allow myself to become entangled in the politics of Austria-Hungary, which abounded in snares and traps and pitfalls. This applies very specially to the Bosnian crisis of 1908–09, during which I saw to it that Germany kept the reins in her hand, neither abandoning Austria-Hungary nor allowing herself to be drawn by her into a war with Russia.

After speaking in February, 1898, on the aims and limitations of our foreign policy, I received a letter from the Grand Duke Frederick of Baden on the 16th:

Most estimable Minister of State,

I feel I must write to you and express my gratification in observing your public usefulness at the time when you were defining the policy of the Imperial Government in the Reichstag. I congratulate you from my heart on the far-reaching successes which you then achieved. You have not only won great confidence for yourself, but have also helped the nation to regain its own confidence in itself. That is a gratifying suc-

---

[1] Prince von Bülow's speeches (large edition), I. 24 *et seq.;* (small edition), I. 50 *et seq.*

cess, from which not a few further fruits may ripen. I wanted to send you my congratulations as soon as I saw the first impressions in the press, which paid such homage to you. I waited, however, in order to see what was the attitude of the foreign press, and there up to the last day or two I found so many comments on your political speeches that I followed these up and wanted to gain further information. Everywhere I found nothing but lively recognition and increasing growth of a renewed confidence in the Imperial policy. Now my congratulations are still warmer and deeper, for that is a success through which you have done the country a very great service. You have so substantially increased Germany's prestige and the significance of her power that the Powers are taking note of her true strength and estimating its value in their own interest. What used to be called her fitness as an ally is now undoubted. I am highly gratified that you have been accorded this very ungrudging recognition, and wish you from my heart continued success in agreeable labour. I remain with sincere respect,

Yours very faithfully,

Frederick, Grand Duke of Baden

The course which I pursued in foreign policy met with entire concurrence in Friedrichsruh. After my speech of February 8, 1898, on Kiaochow and Crete, on our policy in the Far and Near East, Count Cuno Rantzau, Prince Bismarck's son-in-law, wrote from Friedrichsruh to Herbert Bismarck, who passed the letter on to me, as follows:

Bülow really spoke very well, both form and content are quite irreproachable. Your father was very pleased with this speech; if you have an opportunity of saying so to Bülow, add that your father would have liked to write him a few words of congratulation, but refrained, lest his doing so should expose him to misconstructions.

Apart from these kindly recognitions of my work, Prince Bismarck continued to view the future with concern, and his eldest son did not conceal the fact from me. Herbert told me as early as the spring of 1898 that he had put the direct question to his father, why, in spite of his confidence in me, he continued to be pessimistic. His father replied: " Certainly Bülow is a clever youngster, and so long as he is in charge of foreign affairs all will be well, he will

PRINCE BISMARCK

On the balcony of his house in Friedrichsruh

not blunder into war. But sooner or later the Kaiser will fall out with him, and then there will be disaster."

Since his retirement the grand old man had feared that we might allow ourselves to be drawn by Austria into a war with Russia. He was almost more afraid that we might let ourselves be egged on against Russia by Britain.

On April 29, 1898, Herbert wrote me:

Yesterday in the Reichstag the gravest political rumours were being bandied about. It was being said that our policy, owing to a personal deviation, had fallen completely under the influence of Britain, and would be pushed along the path of Russophobia; that Britain had offered us Zanzibar, Witu, Walfisch Bay, and had promised to approach America for the cession to us of Samoa; we, in return, were going to turn our back entirely on the Transvaal and enter the British-American grouping against that of France and Russia. A year ago anything of this sort would have been no surprise to me; under the incompetent limpet from the Breisgau one was prepared for anything extraordinary. Yesterday, however, I energetically pooh-poohed these canards, as I do not suppose that you will let yourself be pushed by perfidious Albion into an anti-Russian attitude. The Centre and its adepts naturally would like nothing better than to bring us into conflict with Russia. Rome (*i.e.* the Vatican) is working in the same direction, with Britain and France, though for different reasons. The concessions from Britain would be very fine, but *never* worth the risk of an embroilment with Russia.

A few days later Herbert wrote me, visibly relieved:

I read your communiqué yesterday with great satisfaction, and saw with pleasure your adroit hand in its admirable wording. It will have an excellent effect, and knock the bottom out of all the mischievous drivel. For in a few short sentences, especially at the end, it contains the golden rule for the right conduct of our relations with Russia and Britain, those politically antagonistic but dynastically intimate countries. If you are only allowed a free hand all the time, I have no fear of mistakes being made.

The "incompetent limpet from the Breisgau" was Baron von Marschall, who was held in low opinion at Friedrichsruh. Herbert

Bismarck had inherited a capacity for hatred from his great father, and indeed he was a good hater. Herbert's ill-will was directed even more against two of my subordinates, Holstein and Hammann. The former was known in Friedrichsruh as the "blind worm", and Herbert let no opportunity pass of warning me against the trickiness and malice of this man, forgetting the indisputable fact that for a whole generation Holstein had been the confidant of the Bismarcks, father and son. Geheimrat Hammann, Head of the Press Department in the Foreign Ministry, had on behalf of Count Caprivi been responsible for the newspaper campaign against the grand old man in the Saxon forest, and had not always conducted the campaign in good taste. In the years that followed Hammann turned his capable and certainly industrious pen with no less ardour to the support of old Hohenlohe and of myself, and he was later to use it enthusiastically on the side of Bethmann-Hollweg. Herbert Bismarck knew him as early as 1897 as "the rat" which leaves every sinking ship and smartly jumps on board another one. At this time the "rat" and the "blind worm" were on terms of intimate friendship. But the time would come when they would be sworn and mortal enemies.

After my appointment as Secretary of State for Foreign Affairs, I replaced Baron von Rotenhan, the former Under-Secretary, by the former Head of the Colonial Section, Baron von Richthofen, who until his too-early death supported me with uncommon industry, never-failing loyalty, far-seeing vision, and great conscientiousness in things great and small alike. Oswald, Baron von Richthofen, son of a diplomat, brought up in a diplomat's home, well acquainted with life abroad from his youth up, a fine linguist, added to his knowledge of the world and its ways the traditional excellent qualities of the good type of Prussian official. He had always been interested in economic questions, and, in particular, he had a more thorough knowledge of the commercial relations between the great trading countries and with the financial conditions of the Great Powers than the majority of the members of the diplomatic service. His death was an almost irreplaceable loss for me. A fit of apoplexy, brought on by overwork, laid him low on January 17, 1906.

When, in the autumn of 1897, Herr von Richthofen became Under-Secretary in the Foreign Office, I looked round for a successor in the Colonial Section. I wanted a Hansa man and above all one acquainted with conditions overseas, if possible, a merchant. But all merchants to whom I turned declined appointment to an official position. "I would be a fool," an able Hamburg merchant replied to me, "if, instead of earning good returns on the stock exchange and driving out in the evening with two fine chestnuts to my country house on the Elbe, I were to slave away as an official in the Wilhelmstrasse in Berlin and sit in the Reichstag to be jeered at." In the end we decided on a distinguished lawyer and an able man, the Conservative member von Buchka, whose qualifications for the Colonial Section Richthofen humorously based on the fact that his home at least was by the sea, namely, at Rostock.

Soon after my appointment as Secretary of State I met Ludwig Bamberger in the Tiergarten. Born in Mainz, he was a hothead in his youth; in Frankfort-on-Main on September 17, 1848, the day before the rising in which General von Auerswald and Prince Felix Lichnowsky were murdered, he harangued the populace in a fiery speech and urged them to act instead of talking. At a later date he took part in the rising in the Palatinate, whence he fled to France; in Paris he made a fine fortune by means of lucrative banking deals. His brother Heinrich, who followed him to France, was naturalised there and became the head of the *Banque de Paris et des Pays-Bas*, and a thorough Frenchman. The two brothers were related to the prominent Brussels banking family of Bischoffsheim, and so to the well-known Türken-Hirsch, one of the first really great millionaires. Ludwig Bamberger returned to Germany, and spent the winter of 1870–71 in Versailles, editing for Prince Bismarck a newspaper published in French which carried on propaganda for our cause; later he fell out with the Prince, with whom he had controversies in the Reichstag which he carried on with neat rapier work, but which the Prince carried on with too much use of the bludgeon. Ludwig Bamberger was a well-informed man of courtly manners and a fine intellect. When I met him, he was already ailing, and in the dark autumn days he sometimes used to go round the Rousseau

Island and the goldfish pond in the Tiergarten leaning on my arm. One day he said to me : "In your Colonial Section you have a novice in whom I am interested. His father is on the committee of the Radicals in the Palatinate. He himself is a democrat and a mono-metallist. But though you yourself are more conservatively in-clined, you have no prejudices. Send for young Helfferich, he will not displease you."

A few days later, in this same Tiergarten, by the Rousseau Island, I met the founder and head of the Deutsche Bank, the Radi-cal member, Georg Siemens. He said to me : "In the Colonial Section you have under you a young man in whom I am inter-ested. His father is a worker for our party in the Palatinate ; he himself is on the Left wing, in politics as in economics. But I don't think you have any preconceived notions ; let the young man present himself to you, you will like him."

I sent for young Helfferich and found him a man of quick decision, very pushing, very ambitious, what the French call *"un arriviste"*, a beginner who means by hook or by crook to "get there." I helped him on and also brought him before the Kaiser, with the latter's assent. This gifted debutant was, in course of time, to become an excellent financier in the eyes of the politicians and an excellent politician in the eyes of the financiers ; he was to become a tolerable Secretary of State for the Exchequer, a mediocre Secretary of State for the Interior, and a failure as Ambassador in Moscow. For a time he was to strive after the highest office in the Reich ; ulti-mately, in a famous trial, he was to inflict moral defeat on Mathias Erzberger by his penetrating and merciless logic. Years later, a railway disaster was to put a sudden and tragic end to the schemes and aspirations of this gifted man.

Meanwhile the storm clouds which had been lying low for months over Spanish-American relations broke tempestuously into war. The war between the United States and Spain arose over Cuba, the pearl of the Antilles. I have already mentioned that the sym-pathies of William II—and it was his nature to be a hot partisan in every issue that arose anywhere — lay entirely on the side of Spain, partly through dislike of the republican form of the State in

America, and partly out of personal friendship for the Austrian brothers of the Queen Regent of Spain. William II was one of the many people who like to believe that things are as they would wish them to be. He was convinced that the Spaniards would emerge victorious from this duel. In a marginal note of April 3, 1898, he dogmatically declared: "The *hidalgo* will certainly cut Brother Jonathan to pieces, for the Spanish navy is stronger than the American." To my astonishment several of our military officers and even not a few naval officers believed in the superiority of the Spanish navy and army. It had long been customary among us to overrate the Austrians, Russians, and Spaniards, and to underrate the French, Italians, Americans, and, at least so far as their military efficiency was concerned, the British. I strove to convince the Kaiser that we must steadily pursue a strictly neutral course and stand carefully aloof for many reasons, one of them being that the ultimate victory of the Americans was certain. The Spaniards were a brave, chivalrous, noble people, with a glorious history and proud memories. They had given the world great poets and great painters, but the Americans were too far ahead of them in population and in economic resources to leave any room for doubt as to the ultimate issue. Throughout the Spanish-American War I steadily kept to the course indicated by this view of mine, against strong opposition and in spite of many wriggles from the highest quarter. Not that the Emperor made any secret of his preference for Spain or his expectation that the compatriots of the Cid would keep the upper hand. This view of His Majesty's was well known to our fleet in the Far East.

William II had no reason to make any secret of his sympathies; he knew that the great majority of the German nation shared them. Our nation has always been guided in policy more by its feelings than by cool consideration; it sympathized with the Spaniards against the Americans, as it was soon afterwards to espouse the Boer cause with all its heart against the British. In the same way it had once been enthusiastically on the side of the Poles and against the Russians, and was to be so again during the World War, in opposition to its own direct and vital interests — at all events in certain circles, with Bethmann-Hollweg, Friedrich Naumann, Hans Delbrück, and other ineffective players in the political orchestra at their head. There is a good reason why the word *"Kannegiesser"* (*pot-pourrir*) should exist only in the German tongue, conveying a purely emotional, entirely theoretical, and unpractical way of babbling and wrangling over political events, with no concern for realities, and none whatever for interests of the nation. In his fondness for this kind of *"pot-pourri"*, at all events, William II was entirely German. He telegraphed to me in April, 1898: "Tirpitz is as firm as a rock in his conviction that we must have Manila and that this would be of enormous advantage to us. As soon as the revolution has torn Manila from Spain we must occupy it." The Kaiser thought, on the strength of the reports reaching him from our cruiser squadron, that the Spaniards would be unable to quell the insurrection in the Philippines; but he also thought that the American fleet would be beaten by the Spanish. Then, he supposed, Manila would drop like a ripe fruit into our lap. The Spaniards, perhaps, might even ask us to restore order in the Philippines and then offer us Manila as our reward. A clean sweep was made of all such fantasies by the disastrous defeat of the Spaniards at Cavite. I was at the New Palace when the Kaiser received the news of the destruction of the Spanish fleet. His astonishment at this turn was great, and so was his disgust. He soon calmed down, however, and in the most gracious way asked me to get the country and himself out of this situation without injury. There was in the Kaiser's nature, as in that of many a German, a certain well-meaning, half-naïve obtrusiveness, and he had advised our squadron, in the event of a Spanish-American naval engagement, to sail up as close as possible, in order to gain useful lessons for us by observing the engagement. The Kaiser was already enjoying the news he expected would come. The consequence was that our squadron had approached much too close to the actual scene of the fight. This awakened concern and mistrust in America. The French and still more the English poured as much oil as they could on this smouldering American suspicion. The itch for self-advertisement of Admiral Dewey, the victor at Manila, did the rest.

With the aid of all parties in the Reichstag and of the excellent American Ambassador in Berlin, Mr. White, I was gradually able to end the German-American tension. Six months after the end of the Spanish-American War I was, in my speech in the Reichstag on February 11, 1899, able to show that there was no reason why Germany and America should not be on friendly terms. I saw no point at which German and American interests were in conflict, where the lines of their advance need cut inimically across one another. The German people had not refused to express human sympathy for the brave and sorely tried Spanish nation, but they had never been unfair or blind to the sound and brilliant qualities of the American people, and had been free from all prejudice against a people which for centuries had never met with better understanding or juster appreciation than in Germany. We had no desire or intention to let the bonds which united us with America be snapped. Our policy would continue in the future to follow the straight road marked out for it by national interest and national honour, without offering provocation and without showing weakness. In a telegram from Washington dated February 13, 1899, von Holleben, the Ambassador, reported that my speech had been received with great sympathy in America; the Kaiser remarked *ad marginem:* "Indeed, it was a masterpiece." I am glad I can say that our relations with the United States remained good, friendly, and secure, until the catastrophe of 1914 swept away with the rest this fruit of long years of attention, dating back to Frederick the Great.

About the same time a matter which bore to the great question of German-American relations the proportions of a mouse to an elephant, the controversy over the succession in Lippe, caused more stir in Germany than it need have done. Only the Germans could have racked their brains over the question whether in Detmold, a town of less than 12,000 inhabitants, the Prince of Schaumburg-Lippe or the Count of Lippe-Biesterfeld should rule something under 160,000 loyal subjects. On the other hand, by dint of continual and violent intervention, with particularly little tact, in this succession controversy, the Kaiser again and again managed to give offence not only to the German princes, who stood with few

exceptions on the side of Biesterfeld as the one supported by legiti-
mate title, but also to the general population, which in Germany
is sensitive to questions of legality. All the peculiarities of the
decidedly individual character of William II came to the fore in this
War of the Frogs and Mice between Detmold and Bückeburg.
He had only too often differed from his gracious mother; he had
offered harsh and violent opposition to his sister's desire to wed
Prince Alexander of Battenberg. Now he meant to show mother
and sister that, if he stretched forth his Imperial right arm to protect them, he would impose his will, *coûte que coûte*. The arbitral
award of the King of Saxony had placed Count zu Lippe-Biesterfeld as Regent in Detmold, and in the summer of 1898 the question
had been under discussion whether the officers of the battalion in
garrison in Detmold should accord him the honours customary for
the territorial ruler. The Regent claimed these honours and submitted his claim to the Kaiser in an entirely respectful petition.
The Kaiser replied with an uncivil telegram: "Give unto the
Regent that which is the Regent's. Nothing more!" The Kaiser
added that he objected to the tone of the Regent's submission.
This final sentence, especially, aroused general astonishment, for
it would have been impossible to write with more humility than
Count Ernst zu Lippe-Biesterfeld, Regent in Lippe-Detmold, had
shown in writing to His Majesty the Kaiser. Certainly it was all
just a storm in a teacup. It also recalled Goethe's phrase, that the
German nation could never compose its differences in comfort,
and always found stumbling-blocks in straws. It was a warning,
and a justified warning, of how things now stood, and how our
national character had developed through the centuries, when a
Bismarck organ, the *"Leipziger Neueste Nachrichten"*, wrote with
reference to the relations between the federal States: "That which
was created with blood and iron and tears can only be maintained
if all our energies are set to continuing in the path which Prince
Bismarck so clearly marked out, and never so plainly as in recent
years." A newspaper less friendly to the old man in Friedrichsruh,
the *"Hamburger Correspondent"*, pointed with concern to the
malicious glee with which Particularists and Socialists were warming

their hands in the comforting glow of the little blaze at Detmold. The youthful Kaiser still shut his eyes to such symptoms, for, in Prince Bismarck's phrase, he was still entirely in the young lord of Edenhall's frame of mind. William II himself was fond of drinking deep and sounding the loud note. Only too often did he have the clamorous festal trumpets sounded, and tempt fate, heedless of the warnings from the oldest vassal of his house.

On June 16, 1898, during the celebration of the tenth anniversary of his accession, the Kaiser made a speech to the officers of his regiments of guards in Potsdam. Rightly and in agreement with his great forefather, Frederick II, he declared that the army was the main support of the country and the central pillar of the throne, but added, not entirely in consonance with realities, that ten years previously, when he ascended the throne, the army alone had confidence in him; it had believed in him, and it would continue to follow him with "unconditional, iron, blind obedience." It is painful to recall to-day that such words should, twenty years later, have been followed by the flight into Holland.

On the same day William II sent the following telegram to the Ambassador in Vienna, Count Philipp Eulenburg.

For your loyal and painstaking friendship I thank you from the depth of my heart. May your person, with its striving after ideals, always be preserved to fortify my striving. This is my daily prayer. I have appointed you *Wirklicher Geheimer Rat*, with the rank of Excellency. Hoping to see you soon, if God wills.

Philipp Eulenburg was the more overjoyed at this evidence of the Kaiser's clemency and friendship, since he had suffered severely through the moral collapse of his only brother, Count Frederick Eulenburg. In the course of unedifying divorce proceedings between the latter and his wife, née von Schaeffer-Voit, later Countess Wartensleben, who had brought her husband a great fortune, he had been exposed as a man of unnatural tendencies. Philipp Eulenburg had been so shocked at the exposure of his brother that later on, when he saw me very sad at the sudden death of my brother Adolf, he said to me with entire sincerity: "How much easier is your grief to bear and how much purer than mine! Your brother died finely as a horseman. Mine is morally dead and inspires only disgust in the world." Anyone who had told me then that the time would come when Philipp Eulenburg would go the same way as his brother, I would have called a fool. After receiving the Kaiser's telegram, which reached him in Karlsbad, Phil wrote me:

If you know what I have suffered, you can gauge what I was bound to feel when this message of deep friendship and truly touching humanity from His Majesty penetrated to my heart. I feel as though I were in a dream, and, on the other hand, as though I were awaking from a bad dream. If you see the *dear* Kaiser, tell him that in all his life he has never done so good a deed. His words were balm on a deeply wounded heart.

Previously, in February, 1898, Philipp Eulenburg had written to me after my speech on Kiaochow and Crete:

I do not want to be missing from among the many who have come to you with congratulations. You know that my joy is *free from envy* and pure. In others you will have no assurance with regard to envy. It must have been already present in certain hearts, and on your shining way it will have seized others too. From now on you will need to be trebly cautious and trebly ruthless and feel that you have a *sure* guard round you. No one since Bismarck has had such success as you have had. It will not turn your head — but do not forget *le revers de la médaille*.

Phil resembled Holstein in his habit of representing my position as unsafe and menaced on many sides. He assumed that if I took this view I would have all the more regard for him. Hence the phrase about the sure "guard" which I was to provide for myself by caution and ruthlessness. In spite of my years of friendship with Philipp Eulenburg there had been a deep difference of opinion between us since the fall of Prince Bismarck with regard to the Prince's dismissal. In 1890, when the first rumours of the crumbling of Bismarck's position travelled round the world, they reached me at Bucharest, where I was Minister. I then wrote to Philipp Eulenburg, who was already the Kaiser's confidant, friend, and adviser, a **very** earnest letter which I have reproduced above, warning him of the unforeseeable consequences if the Crown were to turn against the greatest Minister Prussia had ever had. My letter was of no avail. Bismarck was dismissed. After that I took every opportunity of demonstrating to Eulenburg that the treatment to which the Kaiser was subjecting Prince Bismarck, partly out of his own thoughtlessness and impetuosity, partly under the influence of Boetticher and Holstein, was continually reopening the wound which Bismarck's dismissal had left in the national conscience. I do not think that Philipp Eulenburg had intrigued against and stirred up feeling against Bismarck before the Bismarck crisis. But he had done nothing to restrain the Kaiser and had at once, with the absurd exaggeration which often made his character repellent to the clear-sighted observer, taken His Majesty's side against the Prince. Immediately after Bismarck's dismissal, Philipp Eulenburg wrote on an open postcard to his friend Baron Dörnberg, then Secretary of Legation at Bucharest :

Bismarck is gone! Things will go better now than hitherto.

There were many who thought so in 1890, and not only among the three parties, Centre, Democrats, and Social Democrats, which had always fought against the great Chancellor.

But what Prince Bismarck and all his family never forgave was that Philipp Eulenburg, with Holstein's support, did not rest until Prince Bismarck's son-in-law, Count Cuno Rantzau, had been transferred, much against his will, from Munich to the Hague. Eulenburg made a great mistake in taking the post at Munich made vacant by Rantzau's transfer. Eulenburg had a particular liking for Munich, he felt at home in the artistic atmosphere of that city, where his "Rosesongs", his "Songs of the Skalds", his "Christmas Tales", and other products of his muse were admired in various quarters. He should, however, have known that Prince Bismarck, once injured or angered, never forgot, and that the removal of his son-in-law and his daughter from the Munich post to which they had both become attached would deeply incense the old Chancellor and that he would not forgive it. I once asked wise old Gerson Bleichröder why, after his dismissal, the Prince had turned so savagely on poor Bötticher. He answered, "The Prince is like our Jehovah, a jealous God, who punishes transgression and does not forgive." Rantzau was exasperated at his transfer, and I should be inclined to think that he passed on the evil rumours about Philipp Eulenburg, current in Munich from the time of his service as Secretary of the Prussian Legation there, to the Prince and that he then passed them on to Maximilian Harden. This is suggested at once by the expression "*cinaedi*" applied by Harden to Philipp Eulenburg and Kuno Moltke; the expression is a familiar one of Prince Bismarck's. The first act in the moral annihilation of the unfortunate Philipp Eulenburg came from the great hater in Friedrichsruh, and it was his hand that, nine years after his death, stretched out from his grave in the Saxon forest against the man whom he had regarded as an intriguer and cheat. On the other hand, with all my sympathy for Philipp Eulenburg, I am unable to deny that, in spite of my warnings, he again and again egged on the Kaiser against Friedrichsruh. At the funeral in Friedrichsruh, Eulenburg came towards Count Herbert with outstretched arms; the latter, in front of me and all the others, coolly and ostentatiously turned his back on him. Phil had a soft nature, but even doves can be poisonous. Philipp Eulenburg's rancour extended to the great father, the two sons, the daughter, and son-in-law Rantzau, and he sought to injure the whole family by making them ridiculous in the eyes of the Kaiser. I remember an "Egyptian fairy tale" written by Phil for His Majesty, in which the rage of a bull of Apis, plainly intended for the Bismarcks, father and son, was described. This bull had done good service in the past by tearing down fences that had divided up the realm of the old Pharaoh; it had then laid claim to divine honours, and, with the support of renegade priests and foolish philosophers, worked subtly and not without success to make life intolerable for the young and inspired successor of the old ruler, who had been a man of good heart but had grown senile in the end. The gifted "new master", however, refused to tolerate such shameless presumption. He drew an iron ring through the nostrils of the wicked Apis bull, and locked it with the two young bulls, its sons, into a stall where it could do no more harm. Then there were rejoicings in Egypt ! Then all loyal subjects of the young Pharaoh were jubilant !

The Kaiser laughed a great deal over this fairy tale, the ugly tendency of which could not have been compensated for even by a greater measure of poetic feeling and imagination. Still worse were the stories that Philipp Eulenburg retailed to His Majesty about the Countess Marie Rantzau, the kindly and innocent only daughter of Prince Bismarck, because he, Eulenburg, was after her husband's post in Munich. Among other things he said that she had conducted idolatrous rites with a guinea-pig. She had christened the animal, giving it the heroic name of Hermann. It died in her arms, and she then laid it in a miniature coffin and placed it on a bier in her bedroom between two tall silver candelabra with burning candles. Finally the guinea-pig was buried in a chapel in Friedrichsruh. In this whole story of the guinea-pig there was, of course, not a word of truth.

On the tenth anniversary of the Kaiser's accession, on June 16, 1898, the Empress Augusta Victoria wrote to me :

Seeing that man and wife belong together, I cannot but send you a word of thanks on this tenth anniversary of the Kaiser's accession, for your aid has saved him from many an annoyance and has, thank God, enabled him to carry out many plans for the good of the country. I send you this portrait as a sign that I too mean to try to do my share of work for the Kaiser, even if it is at times no more than to soothe him in his days of worry, when he is often overwhelmed with plans and decisions. How often in quieter past days did I use to consult with your poor brother Adolf for the sake of the Prince, as he then was; he too, I was always sure, only considered everything in so far as it would be best for the Kaiser. Always yours very faithfully,

Victoria

With this letter the Empress sent me her portrait, which I have — on my writing table — to this day, for it reminds me of a good wife, loyal in small things and in great.

CHAPTER XV

Reichstag Elections — Death of Prince Bismarck — Interment in Fried-
richsruh — Letter from William II to His Mother about Bismarck — Me-
morial Service in Berlin Cathedral — Nicholas II's Disarmament Proposal
— Announcement of a Bill for the Protection of Men Willing to Work —
Assassination of the Empress Elizabeth of Austria-Hungary — The Dreyfus
Affair.

THE elections for the Reichstag on June 16, 1898, brought fresh
progress to the Social Democrats, who increased their strength from
45 to 56 members. The Centre increased its former 98 by three
seats; the Conservative parties lost ten. Prince Bismarck made his
last official pronouncement soon after. At the end of July, 1898,
he wrote to Professor Kahl, who had courageously espoused the
claim of Biesterfeld to Detmold, and was now working to found a
provincial library in Posen which was to be called the Kaiser
Wilhelm Library. In his letter the Prince expressed the hope that
the famous name of his old master would bring success and prosperity to the patriotic undertaking in Posen, which had his warmest
sympathy. So the first and last acts of the greatest of Germany's
statesmen harmonized with one another. Half a century before, on
April 20, 1848, the young squire of Schönhausen had sent a letter to
the "*Magdeburger Zeitung*" in which he came forward to do battle
against the impudent claims of the Poles, and even more the tear-
ful and simple-minded German sympathisers of these hereditary
and mortal enemies of Germany, thus revealing the insight of the
genius who sees, far in the future, what remains hidden from the
feeble multitude. Bismarck, when he was a young man scarcely
thirty-five, had predicted that a restored Poland would "sever
Prussia's best sinews", and deliver up millions of Germans to Polish
caprice. An independent Poland would "become an unresting
enemy, always ready to attack us in the rear at every complication
in the West, much greedier for conquests at our expense than the

Russian Emperor." And the aged architect of the Empire's last entry on the scene was similarly occasioned by his concern for the Eastern provinces of Germany.

On April 1, 1898, I received the last written sign of life from Prince Bismarck. Replying to my congratulations on his eighty-third birthday, he telegraphed to me on the same day: "I thank Your Excellency most sincerely for your kind congratulations; please give regards to your wife." At the end of July the news spread that Prince Bismarck's condition was growing worse and there was great anxiety. On July 30, at 11 P.M., he passed into eternity. A friend of his and his family's, a lady who stood by his deathbed, told me later that in his delirium Prince Bismarck had mentioned Serbia, Russia, and Britain, had repeatedly cried, "Help, help!" and had again and again groaned: "But ah, Germany, Germany, Germany!" Were the ancients right when they believed that the gods reveal to the dying, in a last vision, the evil that impends, the approaching dangers? When the dying founder of the Empire cried, "Ah, Germany!" and "Help!" and named Serbia, Russia, and Britain, one after the other, did he see before him the rocks whereon what he created was to come to grief twenty years later? The last distinguishable word that Bismarck spoke was: "*Die Staatsräsen*[1]!" The thoughts of Napoleon as he laying dying in St. Helena dwelt on the battlefield; "*Tête de l'armée*" were his last words. Bismarck's last emotions, aspirations, and anxieties were devoted to the State which he had served as no other had served it.

When I received the news of his death I was at Semmering, which I regularly visited every midsummer, and I left immediately to meet the Kaiser at Kiel, where he was expected. He was on his Scandinavian tour when the sad news reached him. I stopped in Berlin for a few hours on the way through. Holstein came at once to see me. With feverish energy he endeavoured to persuade me that Bismarck's death left the nation entirely unmoved and not at all in mourning. He recalled the ugly phrase with which, seventy-seven years before, Talleyrand had greeted the news of the death of

[1] The good of the State.

his former patron, the great Napoleon : *"Ce n'est pas un évènement, c'est à peine une nouvelle."* He complained of the action of Richthofen, under Secretary of State, in having the Foreign Office flag lowered to half-mast. This demonstrative indication of grief would awaken general resentment amongst the liberally inclined middle classes, and still more so amongst the mass of the workers : apart from this, and worst of all, it would bring down on the Foreign Ministry the displeasure of His Majesty. In his blind and petty hatred, old Geheimrat von Holstein, who for over thirty years had stood closer to the great Prince than most others, seemed to me a cunning wolf who ought to be behind bars and not at liberty. In Kiel I found William II in a nervous state as usual in important and critical moments. He, of course, wanted to be present at the funeral in Friedrichsruh. He was specially anxious that the Prince should be laid to rest in Berlin Cathedral in a sarcophagus to be presented by the Kaiser and executed by Reinhold Begas. His excitement was increased when the Empress, his consort — she who, for all her goodness of heart and sense of duty, had never forgiven the great Prussian Premier his "dethronement" (as she termed it) of her father — steadily opposed the interment of Prince Bismarck in the Cathedral. On top of this the brother of the Empress, Duke Ernst Günther of Schleswig-Holstein, was intending to marry Princess Dorothea of Saxe-Coburg, at the very time of Prince Bismarck's death. The Empress particularly wanted the Kaiser to propose a toast to her brother at lunch on board the *Hohenzollern* on August 1, the day when the betrothal was to take place in Coburg. The Kaiser refused to do this, in none too measured language, and made Her Majesty go into mourning there and then for Prince Bismarck, for she had not yet done so. He took the opportunity to preach her a long homily, impressing on her in the presence of us all and with an emphasis that might scarcely have been expected from him, of all men, the fact that whatever looked at all like a stinting of homage or even of reverence for Prince Bismarck would find no forgiveness from the German people.

The Kaiser and Empress arrived in Friedrichsruh with their retinue on August 2. Count, now Prince, Herbert Bismarck met their Majesties at the railway station. The Kaiser embraced the Prince and kissed him three times on each cheek, as is the custom between sovereigns on solemn occasions. He then spoke of his desire that the dead Prince should be buried in the Cathedral in Berlin. Beneath its dome, where not a few Hohenzollerns rested, a "splendid" sarcophagus should be built for the Prince by Reinhold Begas. William II described it in hurried phrases, that came out helter-skelter, indicating strong suppressed emotion, constraint, and embarrassment. Herbert Bismarck declined with decision, indeed, almost curtly. His reply moved and impressed me. One could see the deep, passionate sorrow for the father whom he had loved, admired, deified. But there spoke also from his eyes a manly pride, there spoke courage and defiance. So may Hagen von Tronje have stood before Kriemhilde:

> *Du hâst ez nâch dêm willen zeinem ende brâht,*
> *Und ist ouch rehte ergangen, als ich mir hête gedâht,*
> *Nu ist von Burgonden, der edel künic tôt . . .*[1]

Emphasising every word, Herbert pointed out that he was bound to comply with the stipulations of the last will and testament of his father, who wanted to be buried on a little hill facing the manor house at Friedrichsruh. The Kaiser seemed to be put out, but did not insist further. At a later date when we were together Herbert told me that his father had himself chosen the place for his tomb. It was pointed out to him that the spot would be right along the railway line; his father replied: "So much the better! There will be life around me." Obliquely facing the tomb of Prince Bismarck is the bronze group representing a stag at bay with hounds. It was presented to the Prince by South German admirers. He had taken pleasure in looking at it, and had applied it to his long and bitter fights with the enemies of a strong Prussia and a monarchical, great, and powerful Germany. The mausoleum in which Prince Bismarck now rests from so many heroic contests is a copy of the mausoleum of Theodoric, near Ravenna, in my opinion the noblest of all tombs

---

[1] Thou hast brought it to an end according to thy will, it has gone according to thy prerogative as I thought it would. Dead is now the noble King of Burgundy . . .

in the world in its stark monumental simplicity, its solitude and world-eschewing silence. The funeral, simple and dignified, was one of the most unforgettable occasions in my life. When the clergyman had finished his short address, attuned entirely to the Christian note, in the room in which the coffin had been placed, Herbert took me alone with him into the Prince's bedroom. In this plain room, perhaps the most modest in the whole modest house, there hung only one picture, a simple woodcut directly facing the deathbed in which Bismarck had given up his great soul. It was the portrait of the poet who, in 1849, had said in the church of St. Paul in Frankfort, that no head would shine over Germany that had not been anointed with an ample pouring of democratic oil. And the conviction was impressed ineffaceably on me that only the union of the conservative energy of the old Prussian with the broad and liberal German spirit could happily shape the destinies of the nation.

At the funeral I saw once more, for the first time after many years, the Prince's only remaining sister, Malwine von Arnim-Kröchlendorff. She was then in her seventieth year. She had known her brother as student, as barrister, as squire and dyke-reeve, as a member of the extreme Right in the Reichstag, who was regarded as at least eccentric. Of the three children she was the one who most closely resembled the stiff, sensible, rather frigid mother. She must have been very glad when the wild young Otto became a delegate to the federal Diet. She must have entirely approved of his activities as Minister in aristocratic St. Petersburg and elegant Paris. And then she lived to find her brother, the "mad Bismarck", placed at the helm of the State of Brandenburg-Prussia, which his and her house had served for many centuries, and to which she, a woman of the Marches from birth and by her marriage with an Arnim, clung with every fibre in her being. Alardus de Arnim appears in the Marches of Brandenburg as early as 1204; Klaus von Bismarck was invested with the fief of Burgstall in the Altmark in 1345. The ancestral home of the Arnims is between Stendal and Arneberg; the little town of Bismarck is close to Stendal. Malwine von Arnim, like her sister-in-law Johanna von Bismarck, and like my own mother, who was a warm friend of both, was a Lutheran of deep piety and strong and active loyalty to the tradition of her faith. When I took leave of her after the ceremony she pointed upwards. Then she said in a firm voice, "I consider with Paul that the sufferings of this present time are not worthy to be compared with the glory that shall be revealed unto us."

The clergyman who had preached the funeral sermon told me that twenty-four hours before the Prince's death he had, at his wish, administered Holy Communion to him. The shadows of death were then already hovering round him. When he put the chalice to his lips, he had difficulty in swallowing. "On, on!" cried the dying man, with a break in his voice, and drank from the sacred chalice. Malwine von Arnim, who remembered her brother as an unpopular, hated Minister, struggling against immense difficulties, and then as the greatest in Prussia, the victor of 1869, the restorer of the German realm, the most powerful man in Germany and in Europe, and who had also witnessed his fall, now stood by his coffin, steady and erect. She did not weep. Next to her the loyal Pinnow stood sobbing — for twenty-four years he had been Prince Bismarck's manservant, distinguished less by elegance than by absolute reliability, not in the least like an English butler or a French maître d'hôtel, but all the merrier in Friedrichsruh, in Varzin, and in Berlin in the good days when he brought in the old Rotspon and poured out the fine Rhenish wines at lunch or dinner. On Herbert Bismarck's suggestion I found a situation for Pinnow after his master's death as porter at Schloss Bellevue. I do not know whether Pinnow lived long enough to see our terrible collapse. If in the last year before our disaster he was still on duty in Bellevue, where at that time William II used to hold most of his Cabinet meetings and give audience, the good Pinnow might be able to express views as to the correctness of his former great master's warning, that the audit of History is even more merciless than was that of the *Oberrechnungskammer* [1] at Potsdam.

Immediately after the burial of Prince Bismarck, Moritz Busch, who had made a name years before with his indiscreet book *"Bismarck und seine Leute"* (though it had been submitted to the

[1] The permanent commission that audits the German budget.

Prince before publication), published Prince Bismarck's letter of resignation of March 18, 1890. This document left no room for doubt that the final reason for the breach between William II and Bismarck lay in differences over the policy to be pursued towards Russia. Raffauf, the consul in Kiev, had transmitted a number of reports concerning Russian armaments, which showed more evidence of *"furor consularis"*, as Bismarck used to call excessive zeal on the part of the consuls, than of political experience and calm judgment. I have no evidence that Holstein had been encouraging the consul's alarmist zeal. I am inclined, however, to take it for certain that if Raffauf's messages, in themselves of no particular importance, came at once into the Kaiser's hands, Holstein had a hand in it, and probably, as I have mentioned in dealing with Prince Bismarck's resignation, Count Waldersee knew all about it. William II only wanted an excuse for getting rid of the Prince, who had become a thorn in his side — *quand on veut noyer son chien, on dit qu'il est galeux*, say the French — and on becoming acquainted with Raffauf's messages he sent the Chancellor an irritable, very exaggerated, and excited note, charging him in no gentle tone with concealing from his Imperial master the "frightfully menacing dangers" in Russia, and also with doing nothing to counteract them. After this Imperial letter of censure we continued to preserve peace with Russia for twenty-four years, and would have been able to preserve it for longer if in 1914 our policy had been directed along Bismarckian lines. Consul Raffauf, whom William II praised to the skies in his reprimand of the Chancellor, was transferred to Galatz after Prince Bismarck's fall; from there he came to me in Bucharest in 1892 or 1893 — I represented the German Empire there from 1888 to 1893. There was nothing about the insignificant little man to mark him out for a part in the great tragedy which had been enacted in Berlin in March, 1890. The move of a pawn hither and thither in chess may contribute towards checkmating the king. Raffauf was forgotten, and disappeared from the scene. It was a case of "the Moor has done his task, the Moor can go."

A few days after the benediction of the mortal remains of Prince Bismarck in Friedrichsruh, a memorial service was held in the

Kaiser Wilhelm Memorial Church in Berlin, attended by their Majesties. At the end of the service the Kaiser ordered the Ministers, with Chancellor Hohenlohe at their head, into the vestry and delivered an address to us, beginning with the words: "To-day the curtain has been rung down on a long act in our history. Now a new act begins, in which the chief rôle belongs to me." He then expressed to Prince Hohenlohe his confidence in him and exhorted the Ministry of State to support its President in order that he might be equal to his task. About a week after the death of Prince Bismarck William II received a letter from his most intimate English friend, the Earl of Lonsdale, which he did not show me, but gave to various gentlemen in his entourage to read. It read somewhat as follows: the Germans seemed greatly upset by Prince Bismarck's death. He, Lonsdale, was confronted by the thought that if Bismarck had not achieved German unity, "a far greater genius", William II, would have consummated that achievement. The Kaiser had written on this letter "And there are people who want to embroil me with a true friend like this."

Scarcely two months after the death of Prince Bismarck, Kaiser William wrote to his mother, the Empress Frederick, a letter on the relations of the great Chancellor with his grandfather, which is more revealing in regard to the mentality of William II than any other document known to me. The Kaiser asked Philipp Eulenburg to pass this letter on to me, adding the remark that care should be taken that our diplomats took every opportunity to express views in accordance with what he had written. Eulenburg, in passing the letter to me, gave me to understand that if it were to appear in the press "as though through an oversight", no harm would be done. During the whole of his reign William II felt on the defensive in regard to the dismissal of Prince Bismarck. He repeatedly suggested to me that the letter which he had sent to Francis Joseph after Bismarck's fall should be published. He felt sure that it would have a great effect. I was able to dissuade the Kaiser from doing this, and when that letter to Francis Joseph was published in Vienna after the revolution, in November, 1918, it did not, as William II had assumed it would, injure the memory of Prince Bismarck, but injured the

Kaiser himself, simply because it was too full of exaggerations and fantastic notions, not to speak of some palpable untruths. I have often asked myself whether the Kaiser was, in such cases, really aware of the untruthfulness of what he wrote. Philipp Eulenburg, who had a very subtle intelligence, once recalled a well-known and beautiful song of Uhland's about the singing bird that dwells among the boughs, and said that William II did not so much tell lies as let his fancy run riot, just as the bird that dwells among the boughs sings. Donna Laura Minghetti expressed it in her own drastic way when she said: "*L'imperatore dice molte bugie, ma non fa per malizia, fa piutosto per una certa naturalezza.*" I had prevented the publication of the Kaiser's letter to Francis Joseph I during my period of office, and I also refrained from publishing the letter to his mother; I give it below, however, as it is now only of historical interest, but is a document of value to historic truth.

Most beloved Mama,[1]

Your kind letter respecting the publishing of Prince Bismarck's "Reminiscences" reached me yesterday on my arrival in this lonely and lovely spot on the frontier! I fully agree with your judgment of the worth, the tenor and of the intentions which moved this man Busch to issue them. To us they bring nothing new. To the B.'s "*Clique à tout prix*" they seem a violation of the sanctity of their most cherished idol, and therefore — though they know perfectly well, that it is all plain truth — they kick up a row and try to disown them! But to the more sober part of the Germans, even of Prince Bismarck's friends and ad-mirers — these revelations will be an "eye-opener" and they will be deeply mortified, though they will not show it, and understand many things which till now perhaps remained more or less a riddle to them; and they will quietly recant! Busch himself has been best characterized by his namesake Wilhelm Busch, who once published a little poetical pasquill about the once famous book. "*B und seine Leute*",[2] where he recites:

> *Manchmal liest der Mensch bisweilen*
> *In den Büchern ein'ge Zeilen,*
> *Und spricht ohne Schmeichelei*
> *Für den Autor schon: Ei! Ei!*

---

[1] Written in English by the Kaiser.   [2] "Bismarck and His Men."

Aber was will das bedeuten
Gegen "B's seine Leuten,"
Wo uns wie mit Fäusten *packt*
Gleich ihr angeborener *Takt!* [1]

In this affair Moritz Busch once more shows the truth of Mephisto's angry disclaimer: "*Ich bin ein Teil von jener Kraft, die stets das Böse will und stets das Gute schafft.*" [2] His object is the same, the late B.'s was to be glorified and admired and worshipped by the People at the expense of our Dynasty and House, which he made the good People of Germany believe he was ever ready to die for and which he had raised to the German Imperial throne! But that is all without avail, the People will little by little find out all about him, and such manner of publications will only help to further the process of enlightening the masses. His ultimate ends are correctly stated by you, and the ways and means he adopted. But against one complaint you utter in your letter I must strongly protest! He is said to have turned away the hearts from their Parents of your three eldest children. What the two others have to say for themselves, I do not know, but for my part I simply but firmly and with a clear conscience am able to answer: "No!" He never dared and I never should have allowed him to talk about you or dear Papa in my presence! But if you mean to allude to the possibility of any lending a hand to the overthrow of the then almighty Chancellor in the days of dear Papa's Reign, I quite openly confess, that I was dead against it and for a very good reason. The death of Grandpapa had so fatally upset and even unnerved the country, that it was quite out of its mind; and in a state of hysterics. In this state it looked at Bismarck, not at us as the sole transmitter and keeper of the old tradition — it was wholly wrong and was his own crafty doing — but it was a fact! Had Papa, and I with him, sent Bismarck home, then such a storm would have broken loose against him and you, that we would have simply been powerless to stay it and you would have embittered poor Papa's last days, spoilt the spendid ineffaceable figure he had in his People's eye and — fancy — endangered your stay with us, yes perhaps made it impossible. For the moment Bismarck was the Master of the situation and the Empire! And the house of Hohenzollern was nowhere! Had we only even

---

[1] Often one goes to a book at odd times, reads a few lines, and says Bravo! without any flattery for the author. But what can one say of "Bismarck and His Men" when one is hit bang in the eye at once by their inborn tact!

[2] I am a part of that force which always sets out to do evil and always does good.

tried to touch him, the whole of the German Princes — I was secretly informed of this — would have arisen like one man and would have made us take back the Chancellor, to whom we and especially later I would have been delivered over bound hand and foot! The situation was simply impossible. I from that moment perfectly understood the terrible task you then did not foresee, which Heaven had shaped for me; the task of rescuing the Crown from the overwhelming shadow of its minister, to set the person of the Monarch in the first row at "his" place, to save the honour and the future of our House from the corrupting influence of the Great Stealer of our People's hearts and to make "him" atone for the way he harmed Papa, you and even Grandpapa! Appalling enough for a young man of 30! to have to begin a reign thus, after such a glorious one having just passed! I however felt what was my duty and thank God He helped me. Without Him I was lost. When the strife waxed hot and Bismarck began his most daring tricks against me, not recoiling before even High Treason, I sent a message to him saying: it seemed to me as if he was riding into the lists against the House of Hohenzollern for his own family; if it were so I warned him, that this was useless as in that case he must be the loser. The reply was what I had expected, and I felled him, stretching him in the sand, for the sake of my Crown and our House! Now since that terrible year I have had to bear up with the storm of Germany's feelings and the vilest tricks of the enraged and passionate B.! The same poor Papa and you would have had to bear! I bore it quietly, without flinching, the Royal standard firmly in my hand, the shield with the Black and White quarterings on my arm and God above, alone I bore it for eight long years! Where is he now? The storm has calmed, the standard waves high in the breeze, comforting every anxious look cast upwards; the Crown sends its rays "by the Grace of God" into Palace and hut, and — pardon me if I say so — Europe and the world listen to hear, "what does the German Emperor say or think" and not what is the will of his Chancellor! To my notion in one point Papa's theory of the continuation of the Old Empire in the new one is right; he always maintained and so do I! for ever and for ever, there is only one real Emperor in the world and that is the German, regardless of his Person and qualities, but by right of a thousand years tradition. And his Chancellor has to obey! Now goodby, dearest Mama, please forgive this epistle, but your letter had touched so many points of interest, that I ventured to dwell upon them a little longer; with best love I kiss your hands and remain ever Your most dutiful and devoted son,   Willy

The summer stillness of 1898 was broken by three political events. First by the Tsar's proposal for an international disarmament conference, made through a public rescript printed in the St. Petersburg Official Gazette and communicated by Count Muravieff, the Foreign Minister, to all Russian Embassies and Legations abroad and to the Ambassadors and Ministers accredited to the court of St. Petersburg. The original initiative that led to this Imperial rescript is said to have come from the Warsaw banker, Bloch, a worthy man who had long been an enthusiast for peace and goodwill on earth. Kaiser William II was so surprised and excited by this Russian rescript that, without consulting either Hohenlohe or me, he sent on his own initiative a telegram to the Tsar Nicholas throwing ridicule on his manifesto. He asked whether the Tsar intended to hang up the glorious standards of his regiments in a temple of peace, reminded him of the splendid victories of Russian arms in past times, and urged the necessity of keeping the Russian sword sharp, with as much zeal as though he were a Russian Minister of War. Our Empress, who deeply sympathized with all her consort's cares, told me that the Kaiser had not for a long time been so annoyed over anything as over the immature Tsar's sudden and stupid step. Philipp Eulenburg's comment was: "Our dear Emperor simply cannot stand anyone else coming to the front of the stage." I worked with Prince Hohenlohe to ensure that on this occasion the Russian Tsar, who was inspired by no ignoble aims, should not be met with a rebuff, and secondly and especially that the feeling should not be aroused in the world that the continuance of the armaments which were weighing heavily on all nations, and the undeniable tension in the international situation, were due to the German people, which, indeed, taken all in all, was and is in truth and in actual fact the most peaceful people in the world. I may quote in this connexion the word of advice for one's path through life which a witty woman, the Princess Elise Salm, née Princess Liechtenstein, had given me years before in Vienna: "Above all, avoid as much as ever you can taking the unpopular line."

At the parade banquet in Minden on September 5, during the

manoeuvres of the 7th Westphalian army corps, the Kaiser once more returned to the subject of the Lippe controversy, which, to use a not very pretty simile, was beginning to resemble a pimple that, through continual rubbing, had in the end begun to be dangerously inflamed. He enthusiastically lauded "the sons of Bückeburg", who had marched past "in splendid fashion", but made no mention of the unlucky Detmolders, as though they, now that they were ruled by a Biesterfeld, marched like heathens. On September 6, 1898, the Kaiser made a speech in Oeynhausen which had grave results; in it he announced a Bill for the protection of men willing to work. The protection of blacklegs, like all strike legislation, indeed like the handling of all conflicts between employers and workers, is one of the most complicated and most delicate of all legislative and administrative questions. Here, if anywhere, firmness must be united with reason and caution. In his Oeynhausen speech the Kaiser declared (in advance of the debate on the Bill which he had foreshadowed) very emphatically and in quite general terms, that everyone, no matter who or what he might be, who tried to prevent a German worker who was willing to work from doing his work, or who actually incited him to strike, should be punished with imprisonment. In speaking so the Kaiser himself very seriously jeopardized the fate of the Bill which he himself so eagerly wanted. Once more, to quote the favourite phrase of the Bavarian Minister, Count Hugo Lerchenfeld, he was killing the child in its mother's womb. The exaggerated harshness of the Kaiser's language was due to a long conversation which he had had a few hours before with his tutor, *Geheimrat* Hinzpeter, who had been urging the standpoint of the workers, with which he, Hinzpeter, was in sympathy. That had put the Kaiser out of humour, and in order to show Hinzpeter, who sat opposite him at the dinner table, that he still held to his own severe standpoint, he had charged his speech with its regrettable stiffening. William II had a rare gift of oratory; he could speak in a telling and rousing way as few others could, and with this gift he might have warmed many hearts, cleared many heads, and done a great deal of good. But he had an unlucky way of setting in circulation phrases which subsequently were turned against him and, moreover, against the German people. So it was with the "mailed fist"; so it was with the branding of the Workers Bill as a "Prison Bill"; so, later, with the "Huns" speech, with the "Pessimists" speech, and with many others of the Kaiser's speeches.

The Empress Elizabeth of Austria was assassinated in September, 1898, in Geneva by the Italian anarchist Luccheni, while I was at Semmering with my wife. Kaiser William announced his intention to be present at the funeral, and I travelled from Semmering to Vienna to await him there. Ten minutes before the arrival of the train from Berlin there appeared on the platform, with his never-changing distinction of presence, the Emperor Francis Joseph. On receiving the news of his wife's assassination he had said to a gentleman in his entourage: "Now nothing more can touch me, I have had to endure everything." In the Austrian Emperor's entourage there was a certain relief when the first telegram from Geneva, which had merely announced the death, was followed by another with the news of the assassination. It had been feared by the Emperor's retinue that the Austrian Empress, who had never recovered from the shock of her only son's death, who was of a melancholy nature and very much of a free thinker, might have taken her own life. Assassination was felt to be a lesser evil than suicide. Francis Joseph greeted me at once and kindly, and said: "I must not lament the Empress. She found the death which she had always desired — sudden and painless." After the funeral ceremony in St. Stephen's, the Austrian Foreign Minister, my old friend, Count Agenor Goluchowski, said to me: "Your Kaiser, spontaneous and generous as ever, not only expressed to my Kaiser in flaming words his indignation at the loathsome deed, but proposed immediate common action against the anarchists. I beg you urgently not to do this. It would be far from the Emperor Francis Joseph's wishes to make the painful personal tragedy which he has suffered the starting point of state measures and political steps; these might, moreover, endanger our relations with Italy and Switzerland." The assassination of the universally revered, noble, and beautiful Empress Elizabeth had no political consequences, yet in the late midsummer of 1914 the death of the Archduke

Francis Ferdinand, who was hated by a large section of those who would later have been his subjects, and who politically was a more or less incalculable element, was forcibly made the starting-point of the most senseless and dangerous steps. The telegram of condolence which the Kaiser William sent to the Emperor Francis Joseph — written and sent off by William II without consulting the Chancellor or me, but shown to me by Count Goluchowski — said that the German Kaiser hoped for an Austrian suggestion for common measures against anarchism, which he said arose from Liberalism, humanitarian slop, demagogy, and, above all, the cowardice of parliaments. The telegram ended : "Something must be done !"

Among the questions which specially occupied me in 1898 was the Dreyfus affair, which at the time of my summons to Berlin had split France into two camps for about a year past and was engaging the attention of the whole world. When I was summoned to Berlin I at once inquired what was the truth about this affair. I was told that we had never had anything to do with Dreyfus, and that he was entirely innocent ; the real culprit was probably Major Esterhazy. On January 24, 1898, Eugen Richter put a question to me in the Budget Commission of the Reichstag concerning the Dreyfus affair ; I replied that I must, of course, avoid everything which might be susceptible of being interpreted as interference in France's internal affairs. I confined myself, therefore, to declaring in the most categorical way that there had never at any time been any connection or relations of any sort between Dreyfus and any German authorities. This statement of mine displeased the Dreyfusards and the anti-Dreyfusards alike. In the Cercle de l'Union in Paris, the aristocratic club of the French capital, the Duc de Broglie, a former Prime Minister, stated that until then he had taken me for a personally reputable man. Since, however, I had taken up the cudgels for Dreyfus, he saw to his regret that I was no better than other Germans. On the other hand, my honoured friend Malvida von Meysenbug wrote to me, under the influence of the Dreyfus party, that she would be mistaken in me if I did not name the true culprit. *Judaeis scandalum, Graecis stultitia.* I felt it a duty both of humanity and of common sense to do everything possible to lighten the lot of the unfortunate Dreyfus. On the other hand, there could be no justification for denouncing Ester-hazy, for the simple reason that a Government which betrays its agents or spies will not easily find any more. I will expressly add that Germany expended much, very much less on her intelligence service, on espionage, and so on, up to the World War, and was much less active in this unclean but, after all, important field than any other Great Power. Our secret funds were ridiculously small in comparison with the sums commanded by Britain, Russia, and France and actually expended by them. This put us at a great disadvantage as compared with them. The Reichstag could not bring itself in time of peace to vote the necessary money for the intelligence service — partly from an unfounded fear lest the secret fund might be misused for the ends of home policy, partly from niggardliness, partly, and perhaps principally, because the German politician has a constant inclination to adopt a parish pump attitude towards all political questions and proceedings.

When — to use Tirpitz' expression — we slithered into the World War, we went to the other extreme with the intelligence service. It was through Erzberger in particular that millions on millions of marks were then poured out, generally in a clumsy fashion, and some-times stupidly and without any real benefit. The results which can be obtained even with comparatively small funds, properly used, became evident to me during the Bosnian crisis. At that time I gave a representative in Paris quite a modest sum, with the object of bringing about a sensible judgment of the Bosnian question. I im-pressed it on him that he was not to attempt to win over entire newspapers, but to limit himself to individual contributors, and not to ask for any support of Germany, but only that it should be pointed out how foolish it would be for France to pick the chestnuts out of the Balkan fire for others. Soon afterwards I read quite a number of French articles in which the European situation was sensibly discussed, and that was in return for small favors which all together hardly came to more than 100,000 marks.

The Dreyfus affair — *l'Affaire*, as the French called it — kept France crushed and crippled for years, until the admirable French patriotism, which we should do well to imitate, suppressed even this deep-seated and ugly difference, just as it overcame the passionate conflicts between the French State and the Catholic Church, finally reuniting all Frenchmen under the banner of the *revanche*, the policy of the recovery of Strassburg and Metz and of the reconquest of the old French hegemony on the Continent of Europe.

CHAPTER XVI

The Near Eastern Tour — Last Meeting with King Humbert — Their Majesties' Suite: Baron von Mirbach, Master of Ceremonies; v. d. Knesebeck, Cabinet Counsellor; Countess Brockdorff, Mistress of the Robes; Countess Keller and Fräulein von Gersdorff, Ladies-in-Waiting; Dryander, Chief Court Chaplain — Constantinople — Audience with the Sultan, Abdul Hamid — The Sultan's Harem — The Bagdad Railway — Herr von Siemens — Jerusalem — Damascus — German Secret Police.

ON October 12th we began the Near Eastern Tour to which the Kaiser had invited me when I was still Ambassador in Rome. We sailed from Venice, where a short meeting with the Italian King and Queen took place. There, against the background of the Church of St. Mark, the Palace of the Doges, and the Campanile, I saw King Humbert, the kindest-hearted and most chivalrous of men, for the last time. The Kaiser had been looking forward for months, indeed for years, to the journey to Jerusalem. The Orient with its brilliant colours, the Promised Land with its sacred memories, and not least the Sultan with his absolute government, which, as the Kaiser believed, was regarded as a blessing by all his subjects, except a handful of Armenians and international conspirators, attracted him powerfully. Originally, William II intended to visit Egypt as well as Constantinople and Palestine. But information of the alleged discovery in Cairo of an anarchist plot against the German Emperor induced His Majesty to abandon this idea. It was asserted in many quarters that the English representatives in Egypt, who had many reasons for not fancying a visit from the German Emperor, had purposely spread the rumours of a plot, in order to frighten off the distinguished visitor. On the Near East trip there were present in the entourage of the Imperial couple the heads of the three Cabinets, the Lord Marshal, Count August Eulenburg, Adjutant-General von Plessen, and, in addition, the gigantic von Scholl, General in attendance, of whom Philipp Eulenburg used to say that his relationship to his Imperial chief resembled that of a faithful Newfoundland dog to his master. William II had a weakness for big men, — in this, at any rate, not unlike his distinguished ancestor, King Frederick William I, the creator of the Prussian administration and of the Prussian army, although there was little about him resembling the earnestness, the discipline, and the unwearied energy of that monarch. One of the first actions of Crown Prince William on coming to the throne had been to telegraph to Captain von Scholl, of the 1st Regiment of Uhlans of the Guard, on June 16, 1888, that he had been appointed aide-de-camp to the Kaiser. Scholl was a native of Hesse-Darmstadt, and had originally been in the Hesse Dragoons, but was transferred to a Potsdam regiment of Horse Guards on account of his fine appearance. On receipt of the Kaiser's telegram, Scholl girded on his sash in great delight and rushed to the New Palace. Adjutant-General von Winterfeldt, who was on duty, asked the evidently excited Captain of Uhlans what he wanted in the Imperial Palace at that time of day. When Scholl replied that he had been appointed aide-de-camp to the Kaiser, Winterfeldt took him indulgently by the arm and led him into an antechamber, where, in an undertone, he asked two senior officers who were present to keep an eye on the Uhlan and not to let him go, as he seemed to have lost his wits in consequence of the exciting events of the last few days. General von Scholl, who from that day belonged to the constant entourage of the Kaiser, was a gallant man, and his Darmstadt tongue had a homely sound to the Kaiser whom so many youthful recollections bound to Hesse.

I took with me as Secretary a Counsellor of Legation from the Foreign Office, named Klehmet. The Kaiser, who in his good-heartedness quickly grew attached to individuals, was soon on friendly terms with Klehmet, who had raised himself by his ability from modest circumstances, and who was prized, particularly by Holstein, on account of his capacity for work. On the march from Haifa to Jerusalem, when we stopped for the night, Klehmet was fond of wearing a red Turkish fez, and the sight of the Prussian Privy Councillor with a Turkish head-dress was a constantly fresh delight to His Majesty. The Kaiser's favour for Klehmet was to have an unfortunate effect eleven years later, in November, 1908, in the affair of the *"Daily Telegraph"* article. The fact that Klehmet did not draw my special attention to the highly dangerous passages in this article was largely accounted for by his conviction that the Kaiser was anxious to see the addresses which he had given at High-cliffe to a number of Englishmen printed in the newspapers and by his not wishing to be suspected of having robbed His Majesty of this satisfaction.

Count Ernst von Wedel, Grand Master of the Horse, known as "Stable Wedel", to distinguish him from various other Wedels, was, like Scholl, remarkable for unusual stature, and also resembled Scholl in his absolute fidelity and trustworthiness. In view of the fact that the newly built Protestant Church of the Redeemer in Jerusalem was to be consecrated, Dr. Dryander, Chief Court Chaplain, also participated in the Emperor's tour. In the suite of the Kaiserin there were, besides her ladies, the Master of Ceremonies Baron von Mirbach and Cabinet Counsellor Bodo von dem Knese-beck. Herr von Mirbach was descended from an old Rhineland family, which had migrated from the Eifel to the Baltic Provinces and thence to East Prussia. Besides the Master of Ceremonies, the well-known parliamentarian and economist Count Julius von Mirbach-Sorquitten belonged to this East Prussian branch of the family. Other branches had settled in Austria and Bavaria. There was, finally, a Catholic line of Mirbach-Harff still living by the Rhine; from this line Counsellor of Legation Count Wilhelm von Mirbach-Harff was descended, perhaps the most conscientious and most capable of our younger diplomats, who unfortunately, as German representative with the Moscow Government, was shame-fully murdered by Russian revolutionaries in the summer of 1918. The Master of Ceremonies, Mirbach, was an excellent man, but one might have applied to him Bismarck's famous saying about Adoph Stöcker, that, as a politician, he had the drawback of being a cleric, and, as a cleric, that of dabbling in politics. His ecclesiastical zeal went too far for a high court official, while the church-builder Mirbach laboured under a disadvantage in being the leading personage at the court of the Empress. This was all the more the case since

Mirbach had not the necessary tact to smooth out these antitheses. He entirely lacked the "*génie de la juxtaposition*", which Anatole France praises in the Italians. Mirbach saw the shortage of churches in Berlin, and every means of removing it was right to him. With the zeal of a missionary, he passed round the collecting-bag to all his rich acquaintances and also to people who were merely well-to-do. He sent out printed circulars, in which only the name of the addressee was written in, and which stated something to the effect that the building of a church in this or that quarter of Berlin was urgently necessary, that the benevolent assistance of the addressee was counted upon, that Her Majesty, the Empress, was keenly interested in the building of this particular church, and that the list of the kind subscribers, showing the amounts contributed by each, would be brought to the notice of Her Majesty. And all that printed! Like all true apostles, the Master of Ceremonies, to reach his pious goal, did not even shrink from contact with persons not otherwise congenial to him. He had hunted up the chairman of the Social Democratic party, Paul Singer, an Israelite, and had warmly pressed upon his attention the shortage of churches and the need for building. Mirbach had an especial predilection for approaching rich Jewish bankers for a generous gift. He was the son of a higher administrative official, who was discharged by Bismarck in the 'seventies for holding views that were too stiffly conservative. Attached to the party of the Right in both religion and politics, Mirbach was, strangely enough, married to the niece of a democratic and anti-clerical Belgian politician, M. Frère-Orban, who was several times Minister, from 1878 to 1884 Prime Minister, and who had taken as his main task the struggle against ultramontanism. The Mirbach marriage was, however, a very happy one, and the last time I saw the Master of Ceremonies during the World War, I found him very disturbed over the German invasion of Belgium, which had destroyed his own and his wife's connexion with all her Belgian relatives, one of whom had been shot. Mirbach certainly did a lot of good, for the shortage of churches in Berlin was undeniable. But on the other hand his whole conduct deserved the blame it earned, and also a good deal of mockery, which was not to the advantage of court and monarchy. There was a favourite yarn about an elderly gentleman who had taken off his hat in a Berlin street and exposed a big bald patch, when a street urchin shouted: "Take care, ol' un, if Mirbach sees that empty patch, he will build a church on it." Mirbach was popularly known as "The Bell Clown." How far he was from possessing any political sense will at once be clear from the fact that at Colmar, on the last visit which our Royal couple paid to Alsace-Lorraine, during my term of office, he presented to the Empress one of the worst Fransquillons,[1] Herr Daniel Blumenthal, who was moreover a renegade, for Blumenthal's father was a native of Old Germany who had emigrated to Alsace. At the same time, one of the most prominent leaders of the Centre, Prince Aloys Löwenstein, was to be seen at the Catholic congress at Metz showing a preference for the company of the Abbé Colin, an ardent Galliciser. Both of them, Blumenthal and Colin, are said to have slipped off on a foggy night in 1914, on the outbreak of war, over the frontier into France, where they were afterwards fêted as "patriots." To such an extent are we Germans of all parties and of both sects lacking in patriotic sense, and only too often in the patriotic spirit as well. During my time as Imperial Chancellor the complaints against Mirbach mounted up until at last the Ministry of State and the Civil Cabinet made representations to the Kaiser. The latter had taken pleasure in pompously consecrating many of the churches built by Mirbach, but was at once ready to give up the Lord High Steward. Not so the Empress, who defended him with all her strength, and said to me, amongst other things, in a conversation about the case, with an emphasis which did nothing but honour to her loyal and noble character: "Would you think it nice if I threw over an old and faithful friend? Would you yourself throw over an old and faithful friend?" Mirbach's political simplicity was evident to me from one of the first conversations which I held with him during the Palestine trip. He zealously maintained that Frederick the Great was "a bad fellow", and that Frederick William IV was the best of the Prussian kings.

[1] Francophile Alsatians.

The Empress's Cabinet Counsellor, Bodo von Knesebeck, was my old war comrade whom I have already mentioned. We were together in the attack at the battle of the Hallue, and were to meet again twenty-seven years later in Berlin. There he was always and in all circumstances the best of friends to me, maintaining his loyalty to me even after my retirement. His death, which occurred not long before the outbreak of the World War, was a great loss to the Empress, and she felt it deeply. It was also a loss to William II, although His Majesty did not at bottom like Knesebeck, probably feeling that the latter, with his quiet scepticism, did not take him quite *au grand sérieux*. Knesebeck, however, was so suave that there was no getting at him.

Besides Knesebeck and Mirbach, the Empress had brought her three ladies with her: the Mistress of the Robes, Countess Therese von Brockdorff, and the Ladies-in-Waiting, Claire von Gersdorff and Countess Mathilde Keller. The last-named had been from her earliest days a close friend of the Empress, with whom she was already intimate when the Empress was still a poor and modest Princess of Augustenburg. The family of Keller was one of the many German families of which either the whole or some branches have settled abroad. At the beginning of the nineteenth century a Count Keller was Prussian Ambassador in St. Petersburg. The eldest son of this Count Keller entered the Russian service, and his descendants became so entirely Russian that the General Count Theodor Keller, who fell heroically in the Russo-Japanese War, once said to me, laying his hand on his forehead: "I am Russian right up to here, from toe to top." His sister was the Countess Marie Kleinmichl, who stood out even in the brilliant St. Petersburg society on account of her wit and intellect. The Prussian Lady-in-Waiting, Countess Mathilde Keller, had grown up with the Empress Augusta Victoria. As the one lady whom the Empress took with her to Holland, she was present at the latter's deathbed. Fräulein von Gersdorff was the daughter of a distinguished Prussian General, who had been prominent at Wörth, on August 6, 1870, at the head of the 22nd division, and was mortally wounded at Sedan, when leading the XI Army Corps; he died a few days after that splendid victory. On account of her half-singing, half-lamenting intonation, her innocence and inoffensiveness, she was sometimes made fun of, but she was intrinsically noble and good. When the first signs of the storm rising against the monarchy became apparent in the autumn of 1918, I met Claire Gersdorff. She was like a small bird at the moment when the first heavy raindrops of the coming tempest are falling. In the autumn of 1914, in the Kaiser's special train, but in the absence of the Royal family, a gentleman of the suite expressed his apprehension lest Bethmann-Hollweg, seen in the limelight, might show himself awkward and simple; she had guilelessly replied: "So much the better. The Sermon on the Mount says: 'Blessed are the poor in spirit, for theirs is the Kingdom of Heaven.'" Countess Therese Brockdorff was of different mould, strong-willed and energetic. She was a granddaughter of my great-aunt, Gabriele von Bülow, the daughter of Wilhelm von Humboldt. My great-aunt's biography, sensitively written by a young girl, her great-niece Anna von Sydow, has been widely read. Gabriele von Bülow was the wife of my great-uncle Heinrich von Bülow, Secretary of State and Minister of Foreign Affairs under Frederick William IV. Their daughter married Leopold Baron von Loën, Captain in the 1st regiment of Guards, a very good-looking but not otherwise particularly distinguished young man. On the day of the wedding Frederick William IV promoted him to Major and appointed him to be an aide-de-camp. Those were the good old days to which, as I have already remarked, Talleyrand referred when he said that no one who had not lived before the great French Revolution had any idea how sweet life can be. In the 'sixties, Leopold Loën went as Military Attaché to St. Petersburg, where he achieved fame by a report in which he described a series of fires from which the Russian capital had been suffering. The report closed with the words: "The Chancellor, Prince Gortschakov, whom I happened to meet, remarked with reference to these evidently systematically planned fires: 'We live in a swinish age.' I replied: 'Yes, Your Excellency, we live in a swinish age.' Signed, Baron von Loën, Major and Aide-de-Camp." General von Loën, who had had no experience of regimental service since he was a Captain, as an elderly man,

had command of an infantry brigade at Frankfort-on-the-Main.
He was given a particularly able adjutant. Before the first considerable formation which the general had to conduct, his adjutant
suggested that they should take care to keep close together all the
time, and he would prompt his chief with every order, and tell him
whether he had to ride right or left. Everything would then go
well. And everything went quite well, thanks to the adjutant's
assistance. When the General was riding back to Frankfort from
the drill-ground at the end of the drill, he said amiably to his
adjutant: "Well, the thing is much easier than people fancy. With
a bit of gumption and a good head it is a simple job." In the course
of my life, and especially since the revolution of 1918, I have seen
more than one politician who had the same idea of his field of
activity as the gallant General von Loën had of the Frankfort drill-
ground.

Countess Therese Brockdorff, the daughter of this General von
Loën, was very beautiful when young, and was still good looking in
her riper years. She kept clear of politics, or at least she did not
intentionally dabble in them. But she was "intense", and influenced her mistress as much as she could in the direction of her
own political convictions, which were conservative, Agrarian, and
rigidly Protestant. In this last respect she was surpassed in zeal
by Countess Mathilde Keller, whose brother-in-law, Count Wintzingerode, was for a long time president of the Evangelischer Bund.[1]
In view of my proposal to abrogate Article 2 of the Jesuit Law,
Count Wintzingerode sought an interview with me in the spring of
1904, at which he excitedly complained that in places that hitherto
had been purely Protestant, such as Stettin and Kiel, Catholic
churches were being built. I contented myself with replying:
"Then build two new Protestant churches alongside each new
Catholic one." Countess Therese Brockdorff was in strong agree-
ment with me when I protected agriculture by customs agreements
and commercial treaties. During the coalition period, however,
I had, at any rate politically, sacrificed her friendship, and when
I advocated the succession tax she told me, with a pained expression,

[1] Protestant Union.

that I was laying the axe to throne and altar. All the ladies-in-waiting were, like Her Majesty herself, very anti-English.

Meanwhile the white *Hohenzollern* carried us past Monte Gargano, past Zante, the flower of the Levant, past Cythera, the favourite dwelling of the golden Aphrodite. We passed through the Aegean Sea, whose islands had formed the bridge across which the civilization of Phoenicia and Asia Minor came to Europe more than three thousand years ago. The Cyclades and Sporades were settled by Ionians, the Thracian Islands successively by Athens and Sparta, Macedonia and Rome, Byzantium and Venice, and finally by the Osmans, and now a German ship was carrying the German Emperor past them to the former residence of the Emperor Constantine and Sultan Soliman. Time always passes very slowly on a sea trip, and to help us through, the Kaiser read us a description of a journey to Palestine aloud. I do not know what imp had put this particular account into His Majesty's hands, for it was couched in an openly rationalist vein. The Empress and her ladies were on thorns, but did not venture to criticize aloud. In his youth William II had often heard it said that in the house of his parents the wife dominated her husband and ruled the house. He did not intend having this said of him, and he kept his "poultry-run", as he once told me, respectful and in order. While the ladies were silent, Chief Court Chaplain Dryander demonstrated that in a faithful servant of the Word the possession of courage and firmness was quite compatible with the gentleness which won all hearts for the worthy pastor of the Imperial house. Dryander brought so much warmth and such decision to the defence of the standpoint of the believing Christian against the criticism of the Gospel as given to us by the Evangelists, which William II had been reading, that the Kaiser was touched and shook hands with him, and tears of emotion came into the eyes of the Empress and her ladies. Ernst Dryander, who, as the classicized name itself shows, descended from an old family of scholars — when I was at school at the "Pädagogium" at Halle, an uncle of his was the excellent master of our sixth form — remained true to the Kaiser, in contrast to Adolf Harnack, when William II, who as a student at Bonn had listened to Dryander's lectures, exchanged his

Imperial throne for exile. In the past, one thing and another have been said against the Court Chaplain, and many of them perhaps not unjustly. Chief Court Chaplain Dryander was a true bishop in the sense in which the greatest of the apostles counsels his righteous son Timothy to be a good soldier of Christ, remembering that God hath not given us the spirit of fear, but of power, love, and of a sound mind.

On October 18, 1898, we landed at Constantinople. I was so occupied with political work during our stay there — not only with conferences with the Turkish Ministers, but also with correspondence and interchange of telegrams with Berlin — that I did not even manage to visit St. Sophia. So restricted a life is perhaps a mistake. So much the greater was the satisfaction with which I was able after my retirement to devote myself to the enrichment of my knowledge and the widening of my mental horizon, which I had had to neglect during my twelve years of activity at headquarters, in the interests of concentrated and therefore necessarily narrow fulfilment of my official duties. Sultan Abdul Hamid did not impress me favourably during the fairly long audience which he granted me. Although he was known to the world as, and presumably was, the "Butcher of the Armenians", he looked more Armenian than Turkish, crooked, watchful, timid, and stooping. Munir Pasha, the Secretary for foreign correspondence, who acted as interpreter, had to touch the ground with his hand at every word he uttered. That amounted to saying: "I am but dust at the feet of your Majesty." The Sultan's replies argued great caution and much cunning. Both these certainly useful and even necessary qualities of his position were, however, swollen to a pathological degree by his morbid dread not only of revolution and outrages but of any press attack. It was a usual trick of all sensational journalists, especially in Paris, and occasionally in Germany too, to threaten Sultan Abdul Hamid with revelations about Turkish conditions. Blackmailers of this sort were almost always bought off by him with cash, and if they happened to threaten propaganda in favour of the candidature of some Turkish prince shut up in the seraglio for the Sultan's throne, they were silenced with large sums.

The first dragoman of our Embassy, Testa, one of the best authorities on Turkish conditions, told me that, before the grand parade which was held in Constantinople in honour of the German Kaiser and which I also attended, a peculiar incident had occurred. A Turkish captain of cavalry, who was to be present at the parade with his squadron, had telegraphed direct to the Sultan that he deemed it his duty to inform him that threatening movements of troops against the capital were taking place. When I asked Testa whether the officer had since been dismissed or sent to an asylum, our dragoman replied: "On the contrary; the Sultan gave him a present of money and appointed him his aide-de-camp."

The Sultan was especially distrustful of his missions abroad, of his navy, and of electricity. For his representatives in other countries Abdul Hamid had constructed an ingenious spy system. The head of the mission was watched by the secretary, the latter by the military attaché, the military attaché by his colleague the naval attaché, the naval attaché in turn by the ambassador. In the end they all deceived and betrayed the Sultan together. The navy was suspected and hated by Abdul Hamid, because his predecessor, Abdul Aziz, had been deposed by it. The Minister of Marine, Hassan Pasha, who passed for the greatest thief of all the Turkish officials (which is saying a good deal), enjoyed the special favour of his lord, because he left nothing undone to ruin the Turkish fleet thoroughly. I have seen lying at Kiel for years a Turkish warship which, if I remember rightly, had come to our beautiful Baltic port to bring the Kaiser a present from the Sultan. She could not make the return journey because the captain had no money to provide himself with coal and victuals. The sailors simply could not get their modest pay. The poor fellows tried to earn a few pence as labourers on the neighbouring Holstein estates, to keep themselves from starving.

Electricity was looked upon by Sultan Abdul Hamid with nearly as suspicious an eye as the navy. During our visit to Constantinople, the representative of a great German electrical company was staying there to obtain the concession for the electric lighting of the Turkish capital. The lighting was in urgent demand for reasons of safety by night. But all efforts to get the concession were in vain. The Sultan was afraid of electric sparks. All these things remained unseen by William II, or rather, in his predilection for the Sultan and for everything Turkish, he would not see them. *Il n'y a pas de pire sourd que celui qui ne veut pas entendre.* The Empress was less prejudiced, if only because she thoroughly objected to Turkish polygamy. It was only with difficulty that she made up her mind to pay a visit to the Sultan's harem. Rightly enough, she felt it beneath a German and Christian woman to visit such a prison, where, amid every luxury, women lived the lives of slaves. At last she complied even in this at the command of her husband, who insisted on the visit to the harem. Afterwards I asked the Empress what it really looked like in the harem; she said: *"Ach Gott!* A crowd of very fat women in Paris clothes, which did not suit them, eating preserves and chocolates and looking frightfully bored."

I do not imagine that in a few days I acquired any particularly deep insight into Turkish conditions. In this too I differ from Matthias Erzberger, who, in 1917, declared specifically to the editor of the *"Züricher Neuesten Nachrichten"*, which he subsidized, that, if he could have only half an hour's talk with Lloyd George, he would remove all the differences between Britain and Germany. And Erzberger understood not a word of English or French; I am not quite sure whether Lloyd George has any knowledge of German. However, I had exhaustive conversations with Testa and Marschall (who were both, indeed, very Turcophile) and with our officers who had been ordered to Turkey, and nearly all of whom looked at things in a more sober and critical spirit than our diplomats, if only because they were in closer touch with realities and visited the provinces; I also talked with old friends whom I found among the diplomatic representatives of other nations in Constantinople, and from all this I gained a good deal of insight, which during my period of office strengthened me in my efforts to moderate and keep in check the Kaiser's excessive enthusiasm and exaggerated zeal for everything Turkish and Mohammedan. I well remember the famous answer which Count Gyula Andrássy gave in the 'seventies, when he was

Austro-Hungarian Minister of Foreign Affairs, to a report from the then military attaché of Austria-Hungary in Constantinople, Count Alfred Uexküll. The latter, after looking around a little in Constantinople, despatched to Count Andrássy a long report, in which he demonstrated, on the basis of his impressions, the impossibility of the Turkish Empire continuing more than a very little longer. Count Andrássy replied that he had read this report with great interest, and that it contained much, very much, that was apposite. He remembered, however, having read in the Hungarian archives the report of a Hungarian representative with the Sublime Porte in the 17th century, in which the downfall of the Osman kingdom in the near future was prophesied with equal definiteness. He thought, therefore, that Turkey might survive the prediction of Count Uexküll. Count Andrássy's reply was clever, but not altogether to the point. Turkey was one of those political structures which Lord Salisbury, with British bluntness, had called the "dying nations", *i.e.* those States which accept losses of territory with equanimity, and thereby show that they have really deserved such losses and that there can no longer be any question of their recovery. Turkey had in the course of centuries lost Hungary, Transylvania, Greece, Serbia, Bulgaria, and the north coast of Africa, and nobody, least of all the Turks, believed that these broad territories would again come under Turkish dominion. Just as little as anyone has ever seriously assumed that Austria would regain Lombardy and Venice, or Belgium, or Further Austria, which she once possessed. For that reason I advised the Kaiser in the autumn of 1898 not to engage himself either for or against Turkish dominion in Crete; not to take any action against the Turks, but also not to take their part too vigorously, for Crete would in any case become Greek in time. The Kaiser at that time despised the Greeks, though later, after the reconciliation with his sister and Constantine of Greece, and particularly after the purchase of the Achilleion on Corfu, he was to become enthusiastic for them. He thus agreed only unwillingly to my suggestions, and in particular could not refrain from constantly attacking the Tsar in the interests of the Turks. I never really believed in pan-Islamism and the green flag, and did not imagine that its unfurling would bring serious embarrassment to either the British or the French or the Russians or the Italians.

I left Turkey with the conviction that we possessed there a wide field for economic activity, and in case of need also, a brave friend, about whose internal weaknesses we must, however, be under no illusions, and from whose green flag there was not much to be expected. Turkey was, perhaps, not so much the "sick man" of Tsar Nicholas I's phrase, used in 1853 to the British Ambassador in St. Petersburg, Sir George Hamilton Seymour, but an *old* man, who had already suffered a great deal, and who could no longer stand any drastic cure, let alone a series of drastic cures.

While we were staying in Constantinople, I had several conversations with the director of the German Bank, Georg von Siemens. This eminent entrepreneur, the real father of the idea of the Bagdad Railway, was always well aware, just as was later Herr von Gwinner, of the fact that the great scheme could only be carried through if Germany pursued a cautious and adroit policy, and especially one which kept the peace. Herr von Siemens, who made a very favourable impression on me as a Liberal member of Parliament by his keen intelligence and his wealth of knowledge, especially in all questions of banking and exchange, died prematurely when only sixty years old, scarcely a year after my appointment as Imperial Chancellor. I well remember the journey which I made with Georg von Siemens on a wonderful October morning from Constantinople to Haida Pasha, in the course of which he developed his project to me. Sixteen years of negotiations were needed, with many ups and downs, before the ideas of Siemens approached realisation. An agreement over the Bagdad Railway had just been arrived at between us and Britain when the flash of the ultimatum to Serbia struck. Our then Ambassador in London, Prince Lichnowsky, received the ratification of the Anglo-German Bagdad Railway Treaty, executed in masterly calligraphy and furnished with a wonderful seal, on the same day on which England declared war on us following our invasion of Belgium. If this symptom of the stupidity of our foreign policy at that time were not so tragical, I would quote Juvenal: *Difficile est, satiram non scribere.*

On October 26th we landed at Haifa. During the beautiful and quite calm sea voyage, we passed the coast of Troy :

> *Und Ilias und Odyssee*
> *Entstiegen mit Gesang der See.*[1]

With my old and boundless love for Homer I should have liked to disembark and look at the now quiet fields of Ilium with the rippling Scamander in the flowery Trojan plain. But — *Deus mihi non haec otia fecit*. At Haifa we stepped with high-pitched expectations on to the soil of the Holy Land. I had left the *Hohenzollern* a few minutes after the Kaiser, as I still had some telegrams to despatch to Berlin. I found His Majesty on a bench in front of a miserable dirty hut. The hut and he were surrounded with flies. These flies were very persistent. The heat was frightful. At that moment we were approached by the President of the Protestant Church Council, His Excellency Dr. D. Barckhausen, who with solemn countenance began a speech in which he pointed out that St. Paul, as is clear from the Acts of the Apostles, Chapter XXI, verse 7, stayed at this place. With the naturalness which was one of the best qualities of William II, and constantly reconciled one to him, he replied to the worthy President : "That is all very well. I have a great respect for Paul and for all the other apostles, but now I would rather have a glass of soda water, to wash the dust out of my mouth, than a sermon."

The journey from Haifa to Jerusalem was not made by railway, but on horseback or by carriage, and this pleased us all. A railway, with its cars, guards, and puffing locomotive, really did not suit the scene, nor yet the mood of those who had feeling for this country where events took place which were of more importance to the development of mankind than all the political proceedings, all the diplomatic trickery, and all the warlike conflicts of world history. When on the next day we saw on our road, not far in front of us, a woman riding on a little ass, and holding a child in her arms, while a robust man with a kindly face strode alongside, I remembered that a mother had once travelled this road with a child that was to redeem the world.

[1] And Iliad and Odyssey arose out of the sea with song.

On October 29th we rode into Jerusalem. The moment of the entry has been recorded in a picture, unfortunately by a very indifferent artist, Hermann Knackfuss, who accompanied us on the Near East tour, and got on the nerves of all his fellow-travellers with his silly lectures on art and nature. In front of the gate by which we entered, a deputation of Zionists wanted to address the Kaiser. At their head was Dr. Theodor Herzl, a clever Viennese journalist, filled with sacred zeal for the cause of Zionism. He had been presented to the Kaiser by the Grand Duke of Baden. William II was at first fired with enthusiasm for the Zionist idea, because he hoped by this means to free his country from many elements which were not particularly sympathetic to him. When, however, the then Turkish Ambassador in Berlin, who accompanied us on our Near Eastern tour, had made it clear that the Sultan would have nothing to do with Zionism and an independent Jewish kingdom, he dropped the Zionist cause, and refused to receive its advocates in Zion. On this day we went first to the Church of the Holy Sepulchre, where, unfortunately, the Easter celebration was in the habit of being desecrated by sanguinary fights between Eastern-Orthodox monks and Roman-Catholic Franciscans. These fights were only stopped with difficulty by the Turkish police, bamboo in hand. Then we went to the newly-built Protestant Church of the Redeemer, where Dryander delivered a sermon which was profound, well-constructed, and not too long, commensurate with the solemnity of the moment and also with the prevailing heat. Thereupon followed a second sermon from another, doubtless well-meaning cleric, who enlarged for an hour upon the New Jerusalem, and out of the powerful visions of the Apocalypse gave an exact description of the future city with its gates of pearl and its streets of pure gold, not even sparing the pious congregation the dimensions of the city and of its jasper walls. Next to me sat the gallant and gigantic General von Scholl. He was near fainting, and only held out to the end with the assistance of smelling-salts and a few drops of cognac.

When the second sermon, a sermon about the heavenly Jerusalem, was at an end, the Kaiser got up, rather unexpectedly, went to the

WILLIAM II

In camp before Jerusalem October 31, 1898

altar, and produced a big manuscript to read from. The Kaiser had put on over the gorgeous gala uniform of the Gardes-du-Corps a very artistic silk mantle, interwoven with gold threads, which Fräulein von Beaulieu, the Empress's chief waiting woman, had secretly embroidered for him. When William II suddenly stood before the altar in all this splendour, I saw that the Empress, who had previously known nothing of a speech by the Kaiser in the church, turned pale. She cast anxious looks at me. She was evidently seized with fear lest her consort, overpowered by the solemnity of the moment and under the influence of the frightful heat, might no longer be quite in his right mind. Her Majesty calmed herself, however, very soon, for the Kaiser read out a thoroughly dignified and excellent address, which Lucanus and Bosse had composed for him. At the end of the service, he received, in the vestry of the church, delegates from the Protestant churches of Britain, America, Holland, Switzerland, the Scandinavian kingdoms, from all the countries where the Protestant faith has secured a footing. The Kaiser gave the delegates a heartfelt address, in which he emphasised his unshakable fidelity to the "pure doctrine."

On October 31st we went to the site of the "*Dormitio beatae virginis*", which the Sultan had presented to the German Emperor for his free disposal. When the Kaiser had first spoken to me of his plan of a trip to Palestine, I had at once declared that he should not give this journey to Jerusalem any distinctly or exclusively Protestant character; I said that I personally was a loyal son of the Protestant church, but that it was only possible, and only right, to rule Germany, and Prussia, too, entirely on a basis of religious equality. Since the dynasty was Protestant, everything must be all the more carefully avoided which might in any way arouse anxiety lest the Catholic element and the Catholic church should be slighted. After hearing from various quarters that the possession of the Dormitio, where the Virgin is said to lie buried, would give pleasure to the German Catholics, I had the necessary steps taken with the Porte, through the dragoman Testa, and these quickly led to a favourable result. When the Kaiser visited the site revered by Catholics and in the custody of the Beuron Benedictines, he was received there by the Patriarch of Jerusalem, Monsignore Piavi, the type of a sagacious, refined, and able Roman prelate. The Patriarch delivered a very successful speech to the Kaiser, who was so pleased with it that with enthusiastic words he placed himself, his army, and his Empire in the service of the Mother of Christ, at whose burial place we stood. Monsignore Piavi on his part was so delighted at the reply that he said to me, speaking of the Kaiser : "*Il est plus grand que Charlemagne, plus pieux que Louis le Saint.*" I had later an interesting conversation with the very well-informed Patriarch, from whom I learnt that while completely devoted to the duties of his church, he nevertheless looked upon it as an important part of his task to defend the interests of his Italian fatherland and of the Italian people in all directions, when necessary even against the French. He complained bitterly of the Jesuits, who always championed French interests and injured Italian interests on principle. A very dear friend to me during our stay in Jerusalem was a pious Lazarist, Father Schmitz, a Rhinelander. He repeatedly visited me afterwards in Berlin, and talks with him were always a joy and edification to me. The excellent man died in consequence of an accident, if I am not mistaken, in Cologne, being run over by a tramcar.

On the evening of the day on which we had consecrated the Protestant church and taken over the "*Dormitio beatae virginis*", a great dinner was given in the Kaiser's tent. Our ladies had hoped that His Majesty's speech at this banquet would, as the crown of the solemn day, bear a distinctly religious character in the Christian sense. The Kaiser, however, toasted his host, the Sultan, the Mohammedans and Islam, with such enthusiasm that when the Turkish Ambassador asked me for the authentic text of this Imperial speech, which he wanted for his sovereign, I told him categorically that the speech would only become public in the version which appeared right to me. With his customary good sense and tact, the Ambassador refrained from pressing his request. As it turned out, Abdul Hamid was perfectly satisfied with the speech, even without the purple patches which my amendments had excised.

In Jerusalem we were accommodated in marquees, and the enjoyment of our stay was not exactly enhanced by the clouds of chalky dust that rose from the ground at the slightest breath of wind. How often did I not wish that I could have visited this land, with its sublime and hallowed memories, alone, unhurried, and undisturbed by the trivialities inseparable from the companionship of a numerous and ill-assorted entourage! But a moment came when every uncongenial experience, every obnoxious incident was forgotten. When we all assembled, with the Emperor and Empress, in the Garden of Gethsemane beneath the venerable olive trees, and, after listening to an address by Dr. Dryander, knelt down in prayer, the impression was profound. Before our eyes, on the far side of the deep ravine through which the Brook Kidron used to run, rose the same bare, grey hills on which Our Lord's glance had rested. It was the very soil His feet had trod, the Mount on which His cross had stood, and where He had said to the malefactor: "Verily I say unto thee, to-day shalt thou be with me in paradise." I have often looked down from the Capitol in Rome on to the Forum with deep emotion. I shall never forget the Acropolis, nor the view from there across to Salamis, Aegina, Sunium and the distant mountains of Peloponnesus, nor assuredly the aspect of Taygetus and Sparta. But that picture spread out before my eyes on the Mount of Olives — the shadowy Kidron Valley and the place called Golgotha, that is to say, a place of a skull — has left the deepest mark upon my soul.

The original plan of the tour had included visits to several other holy places in Palestine, but the Kaiser soon decided to restrict the itinerary, since the temperature continued to rise and he began to find travelling too fatiguing. Accordingly we took ship again from Jaffa on November 4th and went by sea to Damascus, arriving there on November 8th. Here the Kaiser's enthusiasm for Islam reached its height. It was the first time he had seen an Arab town, with its characteristic concealed courtyards and their plashing fountains, its fascinating bazaars, and the whole charm of the Saracenic architecture and the Arabs' mode of life. His impressionable temperament was struck still more forcibly by two particular experiences. For one thing, wherever he went the populace welcomed him with a peculiar cry of greeting, a long-drawn-out, repeated guttural bellow of "Lululu, Lululu, Lululu", and the monotonous noise intoxicated him as though it had been hashish. I recalled this imbecile refrain many years later, in very different circumstances, when I heard a somewhat similar chorus sung by Communist demonstrators marching through the streets of Berlin towards the end of December, 1918. They emitted a rhythmic chant composed of an incessant repetition of the words, "Up — Liebknecht ! — down — Ebert !" I gather that the German Communists had been recommended to adopt this type of monotonous but decidedly effective plainsong by the Bolsheviks, on the ground that it had proved to be of good propagandist value in Russia — a further demonstration, incidentally, of the strong Asiatic element in the Russian nature.

The second experience, and a source of even deeper satisfaction to the Kaiser than the persistent "Lululu" of the populace, was the provision by the Sultan of an Imperial bodyguard of two Syrian soldiers. The Kaiser used to say that the men had been ordered by the Commander of the Faithful to cut down anyone who might look askance at the German Emperor, the Khalif's friend. Be that as it may, the two warriors, majestic figures with gleaming eyes, accompanied him everywhere, sitting in front of his carriage, holding enormous muskets with fixed bayonets and casting ferocious glances around them in every direction.

A banquet was held at Damascus in the Kaiser's honour, at which Sheikh Abdobah Effendi welcomed him in a cordial speech. In his reply William II returned thanks in enthusiastic terms for the splendid reception the city had given him. He had been profoundly moved by the wonderful sights he had witnessed, and at the same time thrilled at the thought that he was actually treading the same soil which the great Sultan Saladin had once trodden, one of the most chivalrous rulers known to history, a *chevalier sans peur et sans reproche*, who had often given his Christian opponents lessons in chivalry. "Let me," he concluded, "assure His Majesty the Sultan and the three hundred millions of Moslems who, in whatever corner of the globe they may live, revere in him their Khalif, that the German Emperor will ever be their friend."

After the banquet I sent for the shorthand writer on our staff whose function it was to take down verbatim any public utterances delivered by the Kaiser, and told him that I could not allow him to circulate his transcript of this speech until I had made certain amendments in it. He displayed some embarrassment, and replied that His Excellency Baron von Marschall, acting, he said, on a direct order from His Majesty, had instructed him to despatch the report by telegram to the Wolff Agency, and the wire had been sent off some time ago. I thereupon went to Marschall and had things out with him in a frank discussion. I told him that, while I quite understood that he, in his capacity of German Ambassador to Turkey, tended naturally to look at events more from that angle, it was my duty to see that this "back-scratching" attitude in diplomacy did not get out of hand, for exaggerated expressions of sympathy might not only give rise to dangerous misconceptions in Constantinople, but also arouse suspicion and even coolness in Paris, London, and St. Petersburg, since each of these Governments had millions of Mohammedan subjects.

It was my policy during my whole term of office to cultivate cordial relations with Turkey, and I received every possible Ottoman decoration — and of the highest class — in recognition of my efforts. But I regarded our friendship with the Porte solely as a means to an end, and that economic rather than political. Moreover, I had no illusions as to the limitations of the Turks with regard to efficiency and endurance. Both Marschall and his successor Wangenheim, who looked on the Embassy as a stepping-stone to preferment in Berlin, were guilty of serious misrepresentation through the flattering tone of their reports on Turkish activities.

When I recall our Palestine tour, an incident comes back to my mind which, comical as it appeared at the time, was not without its grave aspect. Hearing rumours of a projected attempt on the Kaiser's life, the police authorities in Berlin decided to adopt special measures for His Majesty's protection, and the Minister of the Interior wrote to the head of His Majesty's Private Office that a particularly able and tactful officer of the Secret Police had been selected for this responsible task. We were on the road from Haifa to Jerusalem, and were just enjoying an al fresco lunch, when a gentleman in mufti came up to speak to the Kaiser. His whole appearance and demeanour, his very clothes, would have stamped him as a Prussian army officer a mile off, and to remove all possible doubt he wore, in as ostentatious a manner as possible, the 1870 Iron Cross. He stopped in front of His Majesty and proceeded to announce himself in a voice which Stentor might have envied — Stentor the mighty herald, whose trumpet tones resounded, as Homer relates, like the voices of fifty men together. "My name is von N., Your Majesty. Formerly Lieutenant in the —th Regiment, now employed under the Prefect of Police in Berlin. I have been honoured with the confidential mission of watching over the safety of Your Majesty's august person, and beg to present my humblest duty and respects to Your Majesty." The Kaiser was highly amused, shook hands with the "secret agent", and advised him to make his way back to Berlin as quickly as possible. The personal protection of the Emperor and Empress remained in the hands of the two Syrian warriors, who were certainly the equals of any police officials from Berlin.

The episode reminded me of a casual remark which Prince Bismarck had once made in my presence — that he had never once had at his disposal a really clever Prefect of Police in Berlin. Our race seems to lack those qualities for which so many of the Paris Préfêts de Police, from Fouché onwards, have been celebrated — an innate shrewdness and a profound acquired knowledge of human nature, combined with absence of scruples and, where necessary, a furious driving power. The only Prefect in Berlin who possessed these qualifications in some degree, Hinkeldey, was shot by a Conservative nobleman in a duel in the reign of Frederick William IV.

The homage of the populace, the courteous welcomes of the municipalities, the conviction that he enjoyed the real friendship and respect of all Turks, nay, of all adherents of Islam — all this produced such an effect on William II that almost every day he felt constrained to express his delight and gratitude to the Sultan by telegraph. I had the task of drafting these telegrams, and owing to the need for a certain variety of phraseology I gradually exhausted the whole available stock of expressions and idioms in the French language for the ideas of appreciation, pleasure, and gratification. Whenever the exclamation fell from His Majesty's lips, and it was a constant occurrence, that "that really was the finest experience we have yet had, Bülow. Send the Sultan a telegram of thanks" — I took up my pencil and flogged out a new variant. My friend Knesebeck said to me one day: "You know those pamphlets for lovers, 'The Model Letter-writer.' You ought to bring out a model letter-writer for polite correspondence with Sultans, for use during a Near East tour."

Thus William II went on from thrill to thrill, relishing to the full the magnificent Oriental scenery, the picturesque types of humanity, the glowing colours, the sublime memories, the far-reaching vistas. Meanwhile Herr von Lucanus, that hard-headed native of prosaic Halberstadt, was summarizing his impressions of the tour in a telegram to his wife, whom he had left at home at Potsdam. He read the poetical effusion aloud to the assembled company — naturally in the absence of the Kaiser. It ran: "Sick of this circus. Longing for you and roast hare." There was much amusement amongst those present.

CHAPTER XVII

Empress Augusta Victoria — The Journey Home — Malta — The Lippe Question Once More — Arrival at Wildpark Station — William II to His Ministers on Turkey — Arrival in Berlin (December 1, 1898) — Fashoda — The Windsor Treaty — Chamberlain's Attitude towards an Anglo-German Alliance — Letter from the Ambassador in London, Count Hatzfeldt.

I CANNOT close the pages dealing with our tour in the Near East and the Holy Land without paying my tribute of respect and gratitude to the Empress Augusta Victoria. Every member of the party agreed that it was very largely because of her kindness, her equable temperament, her unfailing amiability and good temper, that the many unpleasantnesses inseparable from a journey spent in such a large and varied company were smoothed over and eliminated. No small share of the credit for the reasonably satisfactory progress and conclusion of the tour rested with her.

Augusta Victoria was the very embodiment of all the sterling qualities of German womanhood. King Edward VII, when Prince of Wales, is said to have given currency to a silly phrase that German women had no interests in life beyond the three K's — *Kirche, Kinder*, and *Küche*.[1] In any case the Empress's chief interest, together with the Church and her children, was her husband, above all outward brilliance and all earthly goods. Her self-sacrificing devotion to her royal consort knew no bounds. Not that she was blind to the unprepossessing or weak spots in his nature, but her knowledge only enhanced her tender solicitude. In contrast to her mother-in-law, the Empress Frederick, who remained a thorough Englishwoman, and to her predecessor the Empress Augusta, who was a true daughter of Weimar in her cosmopolitan attitude, the Empress was German through and through. She disliked foreigners. She thought Russians were barbarous and lightminded, Frenchmen

---

[1] "Church, children, and kitchen."

immoral, and the Mediterranean races untrustworthy; the British, in her eyes, were a race of selfish and unscrupulous hypocrites, for whom she felt even less affection than the rest. Like all those who were connected by blood or marriage with the English court, she felt a profound respect for her husband's grandmother, Queen Victoria, but she detested Uncle Bertie, the future King Edward, if only for his reputation (which, apparently, was not entirely un-earned) for being a somewhat flighty husband.

Notwithstanding her excellent qualities, Empress Augusta Vic-toria displayed a stiffness and reserve towards foreigners that did not exactly tend to sweeten our foreign relations, either with Russia or, still less, with Great Britain or even with Italy. While her husband was, perhaps, inclined to overdo his affability towards foreigners, she often went to the other extreme.

She was a staunch churchwoman, and supervised her children's religious instruction with particular care, zealous to prevent any single deviation from the canon of strict orthodoxy, as inculcated in her mind by her father, Duke Frederick VIII of Augustenburg, and established at her confirmation in Dresden by the Court Chap-lain, Dr. Dibelius. Her children were taught to believe that the Prophet Jonah had spent several days in the belly of a whale and that, at the behest of the mighty Joshua, the sun had stood still upon Gibeon, and the moon in the valley of Ajalon. The Empress was not intolerant, but she could not help feeling an aversion for rationalists and an abhorrence for atheists, while the Roman Catho-lic Church filled her with much the same emotion as the "old Enemy", with his "awful weapons, Power and Cunning," as Luther puts it, still inspires in many a fervent Protestant. She told me once that Count Robert von Zedlitz, that brilliant Minister of Education and Public Worship, had said to her during his final audience on relinquishing his portfolio: "Your Majesty is not tolerant enough for my taste." I myself often used to try to ex-plain to the Empress the many sublime and beautiful elements in the Catholic faith and the Catholic outlook, but without achieving much success. She would never have approved of any injustice to Catholics or any infringement of the rights of the Catholic

Church, for she was too loyal to the Constitution, and also too kind-hearted, to do that. But she could never discipline herself to the idea of appointing Catholics as Chamberlains or Ladies-in-Waiting or to any post in her immediate entourage, although I frequently advised her to do so. She excused herself, certainly with some justification, by drawing comparisons with the procedure at the Bavarian court, where the Ladies-in-Waiting were exclusively drawn from Catholic families although two-fifths of the population of Bavaria is Protestant.

The Kaiser knew what a precious possession he had in his wife. He loved her, so far as the limitations of his naïve egotism permitted, and recognized and appreciated her loyalty, but she was always in his eyes, especially when he compared her with his mother, a Princess of a lesser breed. As he remarked more than once to me, "Things are always occurring which show that she was not brought up at Windsor but at Primkenau."

The Empress never ventured to interfere in politics. In so far as she took any interest in public affairs, her point of view was that of an orthodox Protestant Conservative, with instinctive leanings towards the Agrarian party as the most reliable supporters of the Throne and the Church. With her character and ideas, she would have made an admirable "*Commandeuse*", as we used to say in the army — that is to say, she would have gained universal respect and affection as the wife of a G.O.C. or Provincial Governor or Minister of State. In any such position, the world's verdict on her would have been : a model wife, thoroughly loyal and efficient, and German to the backbone ! She had none of the subtlety of temperament of a Russian woman, nor the verve of a Pole, nor the hard brilliance and still less the coquetry of a Parisienne — nor the passion and charm of a daughter of Italy. Nor was she anything of a sportswoman like the English, and no thought of flirtation had ever entered her head. Her alliance with the future King of Prussia and German Kaiser, then Prince William of Prussia, had been planned by Queen Victoria and her eldest daughter, the Crown Princess of Prussia, while both Princess Augusta Victoria of Schleswig-Holstein-Sonderburg-Augustenburg herself and her allotted

fiancé were children. William II once told me that, during a visit
he had paid as a boy to Venice, his mother had sent him to an island
near by to place a wreath on the grave of some Princess of Holstein,
long since dead. It was not until later that he had learned that his
marriage with a Holstein Princess had even then been a settled
matter. The Holsteins had been afraid that Prince Bismarck
would not give his consent to an alliance between the future king
of Prussia and a daughter of Duke Frederick of Augustenburg,
with whom he had had a good deal of political strife, but their
fears proved to be groundless : the Chancellor raised no objection.
Nevertheless, the Empress's relations with Bismarck were never
warm. She could never overcome that shrinking, arising from a
mixture of Augustenburg resentment, distrust, and fear, which she
had felt at her first meeting with the Iron Chancellor at the *levée*
held immediately after her wedding. The fact was that she had a
definite antipathy for Herbert Bismarck. She might have overlooked his occasional lapses from strict formality when he was in
a convivial mood, but could not forgive him for telling "improper"
jokes and anecdotes in the presence of ladies. I do not believe for
one moment that the Empress had any part in securing the Chancellor's dismissal ; she was too punctilious for that, and, besides, she
had no taste for intrigue. But, for all her general kindness of heart
and despite her sincere piety, she never really forgave the great
Prussian Minister for preventing her father and his line from ascending the throne of the sea-girt Schleswig-Holstein. In her eyes he
was a "bad man", and she remarked on one occasion in my presence
that God had evidently wished to spare the good old Emperor
William the direct burden of the sins and wickedness that were
doubtless indispensable to political success in this world of evil by
having them committed by Bismarck.

However, the Empress's particularist tendencies had not the
slightest influence on her husband. The first time he held manoeuvres in Schleswig-Holstein after his accession, he arranged for
his two brothers-in-law, the heads of the two branches of the House
of Holstein, Duke Ernst Günther of Schleswig-Holstein-Sonderburg-
Augustenburg and Duke Frederick Ferdinand of Schleswig-Holstein-

Sonderburg-Glücksburg, to ride in front of his carriage as orderly officers.

The Empress Augusta Victoria was of an optimistic nature. She was filled with a firm, unshakable faith in divine guidance, which never forsakes the pious and the upright, as we are told in so many beautiful Psalms. When dark days came, she hoped and believed to the last. She was indefatigable in the performance of her duties, in her care for the wounded, the sick, and the hungry. She kept up her husband's spirits and encouraged him when he hovered, as was his wont, between hope and fear. It is true that she shut her eyes to the real situation in the country right to the end, ignoring the crisis brought about by our clumsy diplomacy in the summer of 1914 and nerveless political leadership throughout the war. But, for one thing, she went on hoping against hope, as St. Augustine says (that is to say, against human common sense), for help from on high; and in the second place she was apprehensive lest the Kaiser, if he realized the gravity of the position, would suffer a complete moral collapse. Prompted by this motive, she did her utmost up to the last to prevent her husband from being told the undiluted truth.

But when the debacle came, she stood out like the *mulier fortis* of the Scriptures. She would never have abandoned the army and left the nation in the lurch if hers had been the choice. She kept her head high and maintained an attitude of dignified courage, even when the graceless mob penetrated to her apartments in the Castle on November 9, 1918, and reviled and threatened her.

One of the hymns sung on her wedding day by the congregation in the Castle chapel had been her favourite, that lovely poem by Count Nicholas Zinzendorf, known as "*Jesu, geh voran.*"[1] The second verse of this hymn was turned into living reality by the Empress:

> *Soll's uns hart ergehen,*
> *Lass uns feste stehen*
> *Und auch in den schwersten Tagen*
> *Niemals über Lasten klagen;*

[1] Jesu, lead us on.

Denn durch Trübsal hier
Geht der Weg zu Dir.[1]

Only a few days after the Kaiser had fled to Holland the Empress followed him. When she arrived at Amerongen, William II met her on the drawbridge which led into the tiny Dutch castle. She had not seen him since the day, early in November, when he had left the New Palace at Potsdam for the Front. He looked very woebegone, and not a little awkward. But the Empress, so I am informed by an eye-witness of the meeting, gave her husband a glance of boundless, deepest love, the look of a mother saying to her son: "Whatever you may have done, you can always rely on my love, my understanding, and if need be, my indulgence."

Before she found a last release, she was called upon to suffer much, both physically and mentally. I am sure she bore these sufferings with patience, as a penance imposed upon her, and with unshaken faith in the life to come. May this noble, virtuous woman experience the fulfilment of the prayer contained in the closing lines of her favourite hymn:

Tu uns nach dem Lauf
Deine Türe auf.[2]

Our return journey from Syria back to Germany was originally planned to include Malta and Gibraltar. The Kaiser explained his desire to include these places in the itinerary by saying that, to enable him to form a proper judgment of the political situation as a whole in Europe, he must gain ocular evidence as to the actual strength of the British position in these two Mediterranean strongholds. The Empress succeeded in persuading her husband to omit Gibraltar, pointing out that to proceed overland through Spain would take too long, while on the other hand there would be no sense in going as far as the Straits and then turning back. Accordingly, much to everybody's relief, any idea of extending the tour was abandoned, and we contented ourselves with visiting Malta

[1] If we should fall ill, let us stand fast and, even in heaviest days, never complain over our burdens, for, through sorrow here on earth, goes the way to Thee.

[2] When life's course is over, open Thy doors!

— the island held in turn by the Phoenicians and Carthaginians, by the Romans, by the Vandals and Goths, by the Byzantine Empire and by the Arabs, where the Knights of the Order of the Hospital of St. John of Jerusalem had held sway, followed by the First Consul, Bonaparte, until, like so many of the key positions in the world, it fell into the hands of Great Britain, the State which has revived the *imperium romanum* in other guise and by other methods.

Before we arrived, the Kaiser, in the course of dinner-table conversations, repeatedly stated that he meant to speak plainly to his English hosts in Malta, and more especially to any naval officers he might meet, without mincing his words, as he had reason to complain of a number of high-handed and unfriendly acts on the part of Great Britain recently. I may say that His Majesty's resentment on this score was keener than the facts justified; but in any case it never found expression, for history only repeated itself at Malta. As usually happened when he came into personal contact with Englishmen, the Kaiser once more succumbed to the charm he had always felt since his youth in the presence of a well-bred English gentleman, with his quiet manners, his self-possession, and his independence, combined with the utmost courtesy. Admiral von Senden, whose fundamental Anglophobia came to the surface more and more the nearer we drew to Malta, said to me as we entered the Grand Harbour, with a note of triumph in his voice, for he knew how concerned I was to maintain cordial relations with Britain: "Now you will see the Kaiser tick those English off. He 'll begin on the Admiral!" But when, half an hour later, I was pacing the upper deck with Senden, he suddenly pointed angrily to the bridge. There stood the Kaiser arm in arm with the British Admiral, who had come on board only a few minutes before to pay his respects, and he was treating him with every sign of cordial, comradely friendship.

After we had thoroughly inspected and admired all the sights of Malta, the whole party redoubled their efforts to hasten the return home, especially the Empress, whose maternal heart was longing to see her children again. The only one of us all who was anxious to defer the date of our return as long as possible was the Kaiser himself. He was looking forward with something approaching horror to the unpleasant and, still more, the tedious aspects of his life in Berlin and Potsdam—for such elements are, after all, inseparable from a sovereign's existence.

We lay off Syracuse for several days. The Kaiser showed no inclination to visit the famous quarries, with their luxuriant vegetation and their melancholy memories of the Athenian prisoners who beguiled their cruel captivity by reciting poems by Euripides. He could not be induced to visit the grave of the poet August Platen, nor even the Fountain of Arethusa. Instead of that he spent the whole day on the promenade deck of the *Hohenzollern*, walking to and fro with me, in order to discuss undisturbed what was for him the most urgent and outstanding political question of the day. Incited by his mother, who in her letters was always trying to set him against the unfortunate Biesterfeld family in the interests of her daughter, Princess Victoria of Schaumburg-Lippe, he was trying to discover ways and means, if not of removing Count Ernst himself from Detmold, at least of excluding his descendants from the succession on the plea that they were not of sufficiently high birth.

On this historic spot, which spoke so eloquently of the vanity of all human endeavours, where the fortunes of Athens had been shattered, it seemed specially trivial to be going over and over all the details of a typical case of German provincialism. Where of old Phoenician and Athenian war-fleets, Roman and Carthaginian triremes, Norman and Arab sailing vessels, and the galleys of the Crusaders had passed by, where Don John of Austria had triumphed after the victory of Lepanto, the relative degrees of status of the ancestresses of Prince Georg of Schaumburg-Lippe and Duke Ernst of Lippe-Biesterfeld were solemnly compared and evaluated. I pointed out that it would be contrary to the best interests of Prussia to declare the children of a lady like Countess Wartensleben to be "low-born", when the Wartensleben family had provided the Crown with so many first-rate officers and high officials; and that in fact the so-called "petty nobility" had served the nation in every field of public life far better than all the "mediatized" Princes and

most of the minor royalties put together. At this the Kaiser did
hesitate for a moment. But he came back again and again to the
same point, that it was not the business of public opinion, of the
Press, or even of the Reichstag to pronounce on questions of succession, to determine which was the sole concern and privilege of the
German reigning princes. He for his part intended to take the
opportunity of travelling back through Germany to consult his
royal colleagues and persuade them to endorse his views and plans
on this point.

A few days later we began to pass through the chief cities of
southern Germany, and the Kaiser made use of the ten to fifteen
minutes' stop in each place to urge his view of the Lippe question
on the Princes and Ministers who were at the stations to welcome
him. All the monarchs, however, especially the Prince Regent of
Bavaria and the King of Württemberg, replied that they could do
nothing except in conformity with the views of their Ministers and
after consulting their representative assemblies. Nothing annoyed
the Kaiser more than to hear reigning monarchs admit themselves
impotent in the face of opposition from their Parliaments or their
Ministers of State. It sounded to him like a sort of disloyalty to
their God-given office, for which they were responsible, as he himself had publicly affirmed, "to God alone and to none other."
William II held firmly to this conviction to the very end of his reign.
In the spring of 1915, when a German-speaking Roman prelate was
given an audience by the Emperor in Pless Castle, His Majesty
made a sharp attack on King Victor Emmanuel, who had declared
war on Austria shortly before. When the Monsignore pointed out
that the King of Italy had had no choice in the matter, since the
Salandra-Sonnino Government had insisted on war with Austria,
the Kaiser vehemently challenged this conception of kingship.
At the Day of Judgment, he said, King Victor Emmanuel would
not be able to evade the responsibility for his declaration of war
by shifting it on to his Ministers' shoulders. God would say to
him: "No, no, my little man, that won't wash with me! Who
made you a King, eh? Your Ministers? Your Parliament?
No, I placed you in that exalted position, and you are responsible

to me alone. Go to Hell, or at least to Purgatory!" The Roman prelate was distinctly startled at His Majesty's somewhat anthropomorphic outlook.

In Stuttgart and Munich all the Kaiser's rhetorical arts, all his brilliant dialectics, all his winning personal charm were powerless in face of the inertia of the reigning princes, who, in this matter of the Lippe succession especially, were more afraid of their Parliaments than of the Kaiser's displeasure, which they could assume, in view of their previous knowledge of that august individual's personality, would be only transient. It was only in Baden-Baden, where we stayed for twenty-four hours, that the Emperor found a more receptive listener. The Grand Duke Frederick, unlike most of the other German rulers, rather tended to favour the Bückeburg side, since he was related to the Schaumburg-Lippes, although, to be sure, his knowledge of the past history of the House of Zähringen ought to have inculcated a certain forbearance for "unequal" marriages. However, even the Grand Duke's sympathy for the Kaiser's point of view in the Lippe case was of a platonic nature, and he was unwilling to commit himself publicly to the solution favoured by William II.

A pleasing by-product of the journey was that I was able to take advantage of our short stay in Munich to reach a final understanding with the Bavarian Government over the troublesome question of certain reforms in court-martial procedure. The Prince Regent agreed to the appointment of a Bavarian Court of Appeal, to sit in Berlin in conjunction with the Supreme Military Tribunal there. On our side we agreed that Bavaria should be entitled to appoint both the chairman and the other members of the Court of Appeal, together with the Military Advocate. This settlement marked the end of a dispute which had caused a good deal of friction and had been allowed to drag on far too long. Prince Hohenlohe, for one, had been particularly anxious to see it brought to a definitive close. The Kaiser had stood out against the settlement for a long time, being fortified in his opposition by General von Hahnke, Head of the Military Branch of His Majesty's Private Office. He gave way finally on my representing to him, in the words of the Italian proverb, that "protracted disputes turn into snakes." I finally wrote the telling words ("*Le cose lunge diventano serpe*") on a piece of paper for him to keep. It was a peculiarity of William II's nature with its quickness of perception and fondness for all forms of wit — two of his outstanding characteristics — that pithy quotations or proverbs or apt *obiter dicta* of historical characters made more impression on his mind than the most exhaustive memoranda.

On November 26th we reached home again, arriving at the Wildpark Station in Potsdam. There the Prussian Ministers, headed by Prince Hohenlohe, had been directed to meet the Kaiser, and he proceeded to deliver an address to his constitutional advisers, containing an enthusiastic account not only of his reception in Turkey, but also of the wonderful conditions prevailing in the Ottoman Empire. He went so far as to say that Turkey might be taken as a model for other countries in the unquestioning obedience of her subjects to their Sultan, in whom they revered not only their sovereign but also their Khalif, that is to say, God's representative on earth. It was evident, he concluded, that the blessing of Heaven rested on the land of Turkey, the economic condition of which was extremely flourishing.

In the train which was taking us back to Berlin, Dr. Bosse, the Prussian Minister of Education and Public Worship, remarked to me that His Majesty's speech had disturbed him profoundly. He himself, with a large party of German churchmen, had visited Palestine and Syria about the same time as the Kaiser and had followed very much the same route. Everywhere he had seen nothing but poverty, mismanagement, and utter neglect. How was it possible that a man so highly intelligent as the Kaiser could harbour such illusions? Prince Hohenlohe remarked that he could not help being reminded of Louis II of Bavaria, who had conceived such a passion for the islands of the Aegean that he would gladly have given up his homely Bavaria in exchange for them.

In this connexion I feel bound to reiterate once more that I am firmly convinced that William II was not mentally deficient, but he was certainly superficial, hyper-sensitive to impressions, lacking in self-criticism and self-control, and hence frequently at the mercy of rapidly changing influences.

On December 1 the Emperor, accompanied by the Empress, made a ceremonial entry into Berlin. He was welcomed at the Brandenburg Gate by the Mayor, to whom he said that his tour in the Near East had brought him a rich harvest of sublime impressions in the fields of religion, art, and industry. He could assure the Mayor of one thing: that in every land, in every city, he had found Germany's reputation standing higher in general regard and esteem than ever before. Would the Mayor express his thanks to his "worthy citizens" for their welcome?

The Kaiser had done me the great honour and kindness to invite my wife and her mother, Donna Laura Minghetti, whom she happened to have staying with her, to witness his entry into Berlin from the balcony of the Dutch Palace. Donna Laura, a shrewd old lady who was very fond of the Kaiser, especially for his kindness to my wife and me, said to me, after witnessing the ceremony, that in her opinion a monarch would be well advised to confine his triumphal entries to such occasions as the victorious conclusion of a war. Very fortunately for Germany and for Europe, William II was peacefully inclined. But ceremonies such as this after a tour which had been arranged by Messrs. Thomas Cook and Son bordered on the ridiculous.

While I was in the Levant my wife had received several letters from Windsor Castle, from the Empress Frederick — always so fond of her — who was staying there on a visit to her mother. In one of them the Empress wrote:

Dearest Marie,

The only reason why I regret not being at Berlin — is that I can have no little chats with you! *L'inverno a Berlino mi pare sempre tanto triste, adesso più che mai!* I would be very grateful to escape one of these winters, if I did not just *miss you!* You must come again to Friedrichshof — Will you not? Your husband will return to Berlin now — and be glad to be home again I am sure! I expect to see the whole of Berlin Court with the "Fez" on their head, and the "Halfmoon" on their breast, since the friendship with the Sultan is so great! *Si potrebbe anche scegliere un amico piu nobile!* This modern Nero inspires me with nothing but disgust!

> Good-bye, darling *contessina*,
> Ever your devoted friend,
> Victoria

During the tour, under the influence of a clever but crafty Albanian officer, Turkhan Pasha, who had been allotted to him in Constantinople as his personal attendant, the Emperor had written, against my advice, a letter to the Tsar warmly supporting the Turkish claims to Crete. And while in Damascus he had been unable to refrain from expressing his enthusiasm for the Turks in a second letter to the Tsar. On his return to Berlin, he received from his colleague, friend, and boon companion, as he used to call him in fun, the following reply in English:

> Livadia, December, 1898

Dearest Willy,

It was very kind of You to have written two long and interesting letters during Your voyage — one from Constantinople — the second from Damaskus! I thank You heartily for them, I was particularly interested in hearing Your personal impressions, as unluckily I had not the chance of visiting Syria and Palestina during my voyage to the East. A few days ago I got a special report from Count Osten-Sacken, upon a conversation he had had with You the day he presented the picture of Your arrival at Cronstadt last year. Your usual frankness towards him made me happy and I beg You to continue to rely upon him even as much as You rely upon and trust me! Whenever You want to have a good explanation upon a question or if You want me to learn some news, which might concern us both, please, except writing to me (if You have got time) send for Osten-Sacken — in the future. I assure You the affair would in this way be quickly and noiselessly done. I hope England's arrogant conduct is not going to last long. She seemed to be very earnest in the beginning of her war-preparations, but now that she sees the effect she hoped to produce on the Powers — was not so great as she had hoped it would be, I am sure her martial mood will soon go down. I don't think there is much chance for England to form a real alliance with the United States against Europe in general, and Russia in particular — as there are so many divergent interests — Canada or the growing question of the Nicaragua canal. Of course they — (I mean the English) would like to push the Americans against us in China. This neither frightens me, because we sit firmly on land at Port Arthur — and above everything — Russia's borders touch the Afghan frontier! And England should not forget this! I am glad, that the Cretan affair is at last nearing its end. You know the reason why Russia had to take such a prominent part in its solution — at the risk of damaging our good and cordial relations with Turkey — the fear of another Power establishing itself on the island and of course the wish to put a final stop to the constant bloodshed. There was no other way of settling the question than sending George as High Commissioner of the four Powers — it is a radical measure, but therefore the only one in my opinion. Our troops shall remain there as long as England keeps her's on the island. We have both spent a most enjoyable time here; the autumn has been a real summer to us who come from the north. One does feel so well being out of doors all day, riding, playing lawn-tennis etc., and not having to receive daily tiresome ministers. Still they do not forget to belabour me with hills of papers, that I get twice a week. Alas! the end of our stay at Livadia is approaching, as we think of leaving about the 10–22 December. Alix sends You her best love; please give mine to Victoria and with warm thanks for Your kind letters,

> believe me dearest Willy
> ever Your most loving cousin and faithful friend,
> Nicky

During our tour in the Near East the Fashoda dispute between Great Britain and France had taken place. In April, 1898, the Sirdar, Herbert Kitchener — who was destined to meet his fate beneath the waves of the North Sea during the Great War — a stern, uncompromising soldier, full of energy, the embodiment of that bull-dog vigour of the English race which conquered India and South Africa, had routed the Dervishes at Atbara. About the same time a French force under Major Marchand had advanced from Abangki and occupied Fashoda, a town on the Upper Nile. This was the last feeble attempt on the part of the French to save a few remnants in the valley of the Nile out of their former important possessions in Egypt. They met with no better success in this than in the struggle for Canada in the eighteenth century.

In every clash with Great Britain in the colonial sphere France has always been worsted and thrown back on her continental policy. As soon as Kitchener heard about Marchand's expedition he resumed his advance southwards and inflicted a fresh annihilating defeat on the Dervishes, notwithstanding their preponderance of strength of fifty per cent. On September 5 Kitchener occupied Khartoum, and three weeks later hoisted the Union Jack at Fashoda, calling upon Marchand to evacuate the town. Marchand refused to leave Fashoda without a direct order from his Government. The Paris press blustered, but the French Government had not the slightest intention of quarrelling with Great Britain over any African question.

The foreign affairs of France, at that time, were in the hands of Delcassé, the most tenacious and skilful of all the protagonists of *revanche* — the idea which dominated his mind, his every thought, his very life. He made it perfectly clear to the British Government that France would not allow the *"affaire Fashoda"* to become the subject of any serious dispute, let alone a *casus belli*. I learned shortly afterwards, from a reliable source, that Delcassé had told the British Ambassador straight out: "So long as the Germans hold Strassburg and Metz, France has but one permanent enemy. It is from this point of view that we propose to deal with, and to liquidate, any and every disagreement that may arise between us and other Powers, whether Britain or Russia, Italy, Spain, or the United States of America." The Havas agency announced that the French Government had decided to dissolve the Marchand mission to Fashoda. This semi-official communiqué also gave a vigorous denial to all rumours of any strained relations between France and Great Britain, and stated that reports which had been circulated of emergency measures having been put into force at one of the French dockyard ports were entirely without foundation. A friend of mine, the representative in Constantinople of a country not concerned in the dispute, told me later that, when the news reached Constantinople that France had given way all along the line over the Fashoda incident, the French Ambassador, Paul Cambon (afterward Ambassador in London), said to him: "*Je suis ravi de cette bonne nouvelle.*" In Germany both public opinion and the Press, not for the first time and unfortunately not for the last, took up the very mistaken attitude of regarding the Franco-British dispute with great complacency, little wit, and less tact, in the light of a street dog-fight. I had this kind of ill-advised criticism, this kind of aberration on the part of the German public and Press, in mind when I referred eight years later, in my speech of November 14, 1906, to our misunderstanding of Bismarck — not, I think, without justification. During the nonage of the German Empire, at a time when the flood tide of jealousy, distrust, hatred of our growing power and our increasing prosperity had hardly begun to rise, Prince Bismarck, with his unique inventive genius, reaped shrewd advantage from the opposing currents between the other Powers; and many people in Germany inferred that the proper policy for Germany should be that based on the theory that *Duobus litigantibus, tertius gaudet.* On other occasions also I pointed out in the Reichstag that we could not live on the enmity between other Powers. In conversation tête-à-tête with more than one German politician or publicist, I demonstrated that the surest way to prevent disharmony between other Powers was to betray a longing on our part to see it and to make too naïve an exhibition of the satisfaction of the *tertius gaudens.* But the sons of Teut are by nature unpolitical; they are guided in their activities mainly by their emotions, seldom by cool reflection, and they fell again and again into this error. The feeling of the French towards us has never been better characterized than in the phrase which I have already quoted: "*La France désire la ravanche, mais elle veut la paix.*" Since 1871 France had never forgotten either Strassburg Cathedral or that of Metz, nor above all had she forgotten the dominating position which she had repeatedly held in Europe in past centuries. Aspirations of this sort persisted as undercurrents in almost every French heart. But to let themselves be carried by them into war, the French needed to be presented with a situation such as suddenly opened out before them through the clumsiness of our political leaders in the summer of 1914: our declaration of war on Russia, the declaration of war, again from our side, on France herself, the opportunity thus afforded to Italy and Roumania to escape *ex nexu foederis* under the wording of the treaties, the invasion of Belgium, which gave the British Government the opportunity, and, under British political traditions, almost laid on it the duty of taking up arms against us, and finally — last but not least — speeches delivered and phrases let fall by the German Chancellor Bethmann which made all the imponderabilia play at the very outset into the hands of our opponents.

As regards Britain, conditions in 1898 were different from those in France. There was no rankling sense of wrong. There was plenty of envy of us in Britain, and also mistrust and dislike, especially in high quarters. The Prince of Wales had no liking for the Germans, and hated his nephew, Kaiser William. On the other hand, there were large numbers of people in Britain, and among them many of the best and most honourable, in whose view a war between Britain and Germany would be a crime. In the summer of 1898 I had made an effort, in full agreement with our Ambassador in London, Count Paul Hatzfeldt, to come to an agreement with Britain in such a way as to avoid wounding the natural susceptibilities of others and, at the same time, to take account of the interests of the two contrasting parties. In this I was concerned not only for the actual subject of negotiation, the Portuguese possessions' in Africa, but also for the opportunity of establishing how far we could rely on British bona fides. The opportunity was a good one. Portugal, loaded with debts, was in a position of financial difficulty from which her creditors, Germany and Britain, had been suffering for years, as they were no longer receiving any interest at all. Portugal made to the two countries the offer to sell or pledge her possessions. Under our agreement Mozambique was to fall into the British sphere — Britain had long held a right of preemption in regard to the port of Mozambique, Lorenzo Marquez — and the Portuguese possessions on the West Coast of Africa into the German sphere. The Portuguese possession in the Sunda Archipelago was to be divided between the two Powers. The agreement was signed in October, 1898. I was able at the end of August to report to the Kaiser that in all substantial points the

British Government had declared its agreement with our proposals, and His Majesty telegraphed me:

I am very glad of this turn, which is all the more important since the peace and disarmament proposals and all the chatter about them add not a little to the prospects of war. I thank you, dear Bülow, for your devoted and successful labours, and for the ability with which you have induced Britain at last to give way to us. This is one more great triumph of your diplomatic adroitness and farsightedness.

About the turn of the century I learned, through the indiscretion of a foreign diplomat with whom I had been on terms of friendship since my youth, that Britain, a year after her agreement with Germany, had concluded a secret agreement with Portugal; this was confirmed by news which reached me from Paris banking circles. This agreement, the so-called Treaty of Windsor, expressly confirmed existing treaties, in which the powerful Britain and her client of many years past, the little Portugal, guaranteed one another's possessions, undertaking the reciprocal obligation to come in case of need to their defence. The conclusion of the Treaty of Windsor had largely been promoted by the then Prince of Wales, of whom the Marquis of Soveral, the Portuguese Minister in London, was a personal and intimate friend. This Treaty of Windsor was, of course, in flagrant conflict with the spirit of the British-German agreement concerning the Portuguese colonies. It was not only a guarantee for Portugal, but actually an encouragement to that country not to mortgage her colonies. It increased the old tendency of the Portuguese to give preference to Britain in all economic questions. To say nothing of the fact that the Treaty of Windsor further substantially increased the political dependence of the Portuguese on Britain.

In her interesting memoirs the Marquise de Boigne tells of the following episode of the time when she was living in England as the daughter of the then French Ambassador, before the great French Revolution. Her father was giving a dinner, and during it she suddenly discovered that her little lapdog had crept under the table. To get him to come out she held out a titbit to him. The little dog snapped at it and she was able to catch hold of him and give him to a servant to take away.   On this the British Foreign Secretary, who was sitting next to her, said to her very gravely : "That is very unjust of you, to abuse the trust of the good little dog.   You are spoiling its morals."   Touched and ashamed, the young lady told her father of the incident the day after.   He told her not to worry over it any more, for the self-same minister who was so rigorous in his views of our moral duties to little dogs had, so he said, deceived him so badly in an important political matter that he would probably lose his post.   In no country is the border-line between private and political morality drawn so sharply and so coldly as in England ; an Englishman of the highest personal probity will resort to the most doubtful expedients in politics as calmly as a doctor, if he thinks the case calls for it, will administer poisons. An English saying runs : "In love and in politics everything is fair." [1]   None the less, this grain of seed which I planted in 1898 with the British-German treaty concerning the Portuguese colonies would have borne fruit but for the War.   The time came when the House of Coburg-Braganza no longer sat on the throne in Lisbon, to be dealt with tenderly by British policy, owing to its close affinity with the British royal house, and when the elegant Marquis of Soveral, King Edward's intimate, no longer represented Portugal in London, but some Portuguese radical or other who had no entrée into English society.   Then Britain lost interest in Portugal.

The agreement of 1898 between us and Britain had been revived and was awaiting signature when the crisis which followed the ulti-matum to Serbia destroyed this hope for the future along with many other good things held and in prospect.   At the end of the last century, however, it was natural that after such an experience I should have felt, some time later, that caution was necessary when Chamberlain threw us the bait of an Anglo-German alliance.   He had not the whole of the Ministry behind him, and especially he had not the support of the Premier ; moreover, at the moment, as the man primarily responsible for the Boer War, he had every reason to desire to secure Germany as a buffer between himself on the one side

[1] English in the original.

and France and Russia on the other. I give below the important parts of a letter which Count Paul Hatzfeldt sent on June 27, 1898, before I got wind of the Treaty of Windsor, to his friend Holstein. The letter is not without interest on account of the light it throws on the relations between Lord Salisbury and his Colonial Secretary. It also shows how few illusions our cool and experienced Ambassador in London had : Chamberlain, he saw, would have been very glad to conclude with us a treaty directed against Russia, but had no more intention than Salisbury of according to us any real advantages.

London, June 27, 1898

Dear Friend,

I have been in bed for the last two days, with rather a bad cold. Nothing is lost by that, as even if I were well I should not feel it wise to show myself in too great a hurry in dealing with Salisbury in the Portuguese question. The people here, Salisbury and Chamberlain included, hate having to leave us a nice fat morsel. You ask whether I think any more can be got through Chamberlain; to the best of my knowledge I don't think so. *If I could offer him a political agreement directed against Russia*, he would certainly make me big colonial concessions, but, I am convinced, not otherwise. Salisbury is not anxious to give away anything to us, but we are in a better position with regard to him, in so far as he is not asking for a political agreement against Russia, and yet is alive to political considerations *the importance of which Chamberlain is unable to appreciate — at all events, he underestimates it.* As to my own view, you will gather it from what follows. In the course of one of my last conversations with Salisbury on the Portuguese question I said to him :

"It would be very regrettable if people here were to fail to recognize one fact, namely, that an unfriendly and negative attitude in this question would actually put weapons and arguments into the hands of all those in our country who are opposed to friendly relations with Britain and favour an intimate *rapprochement* with her opponents."

His face fell rather, and he replied :

"That is precisely the unpleasant dilemma in which we are placed."

He did not go any further into the matter, but these words show sufficiently, for all who know him, that he is burdened by the fear of driving us entirely into the Russian camp, and this consideration plays an important part with him.   This is not to be expected of Chamberlain, or not in the same measure.   I will take this opportunity of mentioning another statement of Salisbury's for your own and Bülow's confidential information, as it is not suited for a report.   I pointed out to him the services which we had rendered the British in regard to Egypt, and let him see that France and Russia — the latter because of the Suez Canal — would long ago have turned against Britain in African questions if we had not, up to now, stood steadily in the way of their ambition to absorb Egypt. He replied: *"Oui, tout irait encore bien si nous avions toujours Caprivi."* I asked him what he had to complain of in the present Imperial Chancellor, and he said: *"Il a une femme russe."*   I replied: *"Vous oubliez qu'elle est morte."*   His reply was: *"Oui, mais il a de grandes propriétés en Russie qui dépendent du gouvernement russe."*

I need hardly add that I described it as ridiculous to attribute to Prince Hohenlohe predominantly Russian sympathies because for a time the dead Princess had owned one single property in Russia.   You will see, however, from these confidential remarks of Salisbury's how greatly our aims are suspect.   This has its good side; for this anxiety of the British offers, as things are, the only lever we can apply here to secure colonial concessions.   You will have observed that up to now Salisbury has sedulously avoided giving any definite expression of opinion concerning the proposals which I have formulated, or indicating even tentatively how he would envisage the accommodation between us.   In consequence of this attitude he is in the pleasant position (1) of having no more to say to me in regard to every point than that we are' asking too much, and (2) of pointing out to us, and if occasion arises to others, that he is asking nothing whatever of us and also has made us no offer, but has merely listened to our far from modest proposals.   As things were there was nothing to be done but to answer his question by giving a full outline of our demands, but in my view we must not leave him a moment longer than can be helped in the position of advantage which he has taken up.   In other words, if the settlement between us comes up for further discussion at all I propose to turn the tables at once, to decline to give any further explanation of the points which I formulated, and to take up the standpoint that the next thing is to let me know what concessions they are prepared here to make to us in regard to the Portuguese colonies.   *In regard to Chamberlain I should like here to emphasize once more, and beg you to bear this in mind in case of need, that I have no means of doing any business directly with him*

*without breaking with Lord Salisbury and making my further official activity
here entirely useless.* From everything Salisbury has said since his return
it has constantly been perfectly plain that he thinks it quite natural that
I did not refuse to enter into discussion with Chamberlain in the past,
especially in view of the participation in the discussions of Mr. Balfour,
Salisbury's official representative, *but that he, Salisbury, desires that these
dealings shall on no account go any further, except in any case in which he
has given his consent beforehand.* I have, therefore, not the slightest doubt
that he would regard any attempt of mine to get into personal touch with
Chamberlain as a breach of faith. My position would thereafter, so long
as Lord Salisbury remains at the helm, become for all practical purposes
untenable, and you might as well recall me. How glad I should be of any
opportunity to see Herr von Bülow, I need not say.

With kindest regards,

Yours

Hatzfeldt

CHAPTER XVIII

Close of the Year 1898 — Prince Henry on the Far East — Acquisition of Samoa — The Grand Duke Karl Alexander of Weimar —Acquisition of the Carolines — Bülow Raised to the Rank of Count (June 22, 1899) — The Boer War — Cecil Rhodes in Berlin — Public Opinion in Germany and the Boer Conflict — The Canal Bill — Minister of Finance von Miquel — Letter from the Empress on the Canal Bill — The Canal Mutineers.

TOWARDS the end of the eventful year 1898, on December 12, I received the following telegram *en clair* from the Kaiser:

A year ago to-day we were standing on the deck of H. M. S. *Deutschland* and giving Henry his send-off. The future lay before us uncertain, and, in some respects, menacing. How splendidly, thanks to your able direction and God's help, everything has gone! The progress of our navy, especially, is assured, and our colonies have the prospect of the protection they need. May your prudent counsel and the Lord's support continue with me.

Wilhelm, I. R.

About the same time my predecessor, Baron von Marschall, wrote to me:

Honoured Friend,

I must send you my heartiest good wishes for the new year and especially say with what satisfaction I have noted your latest parliamentary success. You will let an old parliamentarian, who, as Bismarck expressed it to me once, has had experience of our Reichstag both as besieger and besieged, make his acknowledgment that your recent speech was extraordinarily fine both in form and content. Those subtle hints, that give members to understand that the Minister would have been glad to give information about the most varied questions in foreign policy, but is not in a position to tell all he knows, are just the thing to make an excellent impression in Parliament. In the shortest space of time you have won universal confidence, and so restored the natural relation between the Foreign Ministry and the popular assembly of which I did not have the benefit in recent years, much to the detriment of our foreign policy. I hope from my heart, for you and the Empire, that the new year may be as successful as the last, and may bring no more difficulties than are inseparable from your responsible office.

Herbert Bismarck wrote me on New Year's Eve, 1898:

I wish you, in addition to everything else that is good, continual satisfaction and more and more triumphs in your activity for the welfare of our country. An experienced reader of the newspapers can see between the lines of certain articles that you have plenty of difficulties. You have now to steer us out of the troublesome channel into which we were brought by the mistakes of navigation in 1890–91. I wish you "good speed",[1] and only regret that in your diplomatic army you have so few able assistants, so that you have to do everything yourself.

Before the end of 1898 I received a letter from Prince Henry of Prussia, dated November 28, 1898, and with the pregnant heading "China Sea", in which he wrote: "My dear Herr von Bülow, When we took leave of one another nearly a year ago now, you gave me permission to send you a few words now and then and to write freely of your subordinates."

In keeping with the Prince's goodness of heart, this bit of "writing freely" was a warm recommendation that Dr. Stübel, Consul General in Shanghai, should be appointed Minister in Peking. Stübel was an able official, but his official career recalls a melancholy verse which I found many years ago in an old album of the Bülow family. A Bülow of the sixteenth century had drawn in this book a zigzag line, and had written under it:

> *Sic eunt fata hominum,*
> *Ach, gingen sie doch nicht so krumm!* [2]

Dr. Stübel had at one time been chosen with Rottenburg in Prince Bismarck's final selection for the post of Head of the Imperial Chancellery, a fact which shows that he had qualities. He had then done well in the Consular service in the Far East, and had become

[1] English in the original.
[2] Would that they were not so crooked.

Director of the Colonial Section; there, however, he came to grief, owing to his inability to speak without notes. At the first speech which he had to make during the discussions of his budget in the Reichstag, I sat next to him. He was unable to find the words he wanted, came to a stop after every sentence, said the same thing over again, looked helplessly all round and up to the ceiling and down the Chamber, where the representatives of the German people sat listening with the mischievous pleasure with which the gallery in a theatre watch an actor who, in spite of the prompter's desperate whispering, is unable to get his lines out. I myself have never felt any embarrassment in speaking, but it is absolute torture to me when anyone speaking in public is unable to get ahead. I hope this little weakness may be counted as altruism and placed to my credit. As the good Stübel was of no use in the Reichstag, and, therefore, as Secretary of State, I found him the pleasant post of Minister in Christiania, now Oslo. There, during one of the Kaiser's Scandinavian journeys, Stübel had the ill-luck to "bottle" a telegram just when the Kaiser was expected in the Norwegian capital. This telegram contained the news of the birth of the Crown Prince's eldest son, who would some day be King and Emperor. There resulted a semi-comic, semi-tragic rumpus, the upshot of which was that, in spite of my intercession, Stübel disappeared into retirement. When a candidate was proposed to Cardinal Mazarin for an important post, the Cardinal used to ask: "*Est-il heureux?*" Once when Frederick the Great was riding along the outposts he came to a Captain who did not recognize the King in the simple dress which, as was his habit, he was wearing during his ride. The King entered into conversation with the Captain, who complained to him that, though he was a good officer and had been many times wounded, he had never been decorated. On his return the King gave one of his Adjutants an Order of Merit with instructions to take it to the officer standing at the particular outpost, of which the King gave an exact description. The next day, the King met the Captain again, noticed that he was not wearing the Order of Merit, and asked him why he was not doing so. "I am dogged by misfortune," the Captain replied. "When the Order graciously assigned to me by Your Majesty arrived here, I had been relieved just ten minutes before!" The great king coldly turned his back on the officer, saying: "Let him go, he has no luck!" The unfortunate Stübel belonged to the category of the people whom Mazarin and Frederick the Great could not endure because they had no luck. Luck is an element in character like any other. Schiller expressed this in a wonderfully fine poem:

> *Selig, welchen die Götter, die gnädigen,*
> *Vor der Geburt schon liebten.*[1]

This letter from Prince Henry of November 28, 1898, showed once more his old predilection for the English:

Our prestige stands high in the Far East. Relations with the British are good and are based on reciprocal sympathies; one can get many things done with these people if one knows how to take them and how to deal with them; coöperation with them is desired on both sides, because it is in our mutual interest. Both they and we fear and dislike the Russian, and the Frenchman is universally despised.

I shared the Prince's desire for friendly relations with Britain in all places, the Far East included. On China the Prince wrote me:

Think as one may concerning China and the Chinese, one is face to face with a people whose civilization dates back three thousand years, a people still little or not at all under the influence of European culture. In dealing with these people we shall do well to reflect carefully when the moment has come for severity and when mildness and indulgence is more in place. Incredible as the latest events in Peking may appear, they are in keeping with the history of this gigantic realm, just as are our own campaigns and battles at home. To make adroit use of such moments, to show the Chinese their weak side, and at the same time to inspire them with confidence in our Government, is the duty for which our representatives are here. What I have written is only a casual sketch, and I hope my burning interest in the continued advance of the German cause may incline you to make allowances for the contents of these lines. I remain, my dear Herr von Bülow, with the most sincere wishes for a

[1] Happy he whom the gracious gods loved before he was born.

merry Christmas and a happy New Year, your very sincere and always gratefully devoted,

Henry, Prince of Prussia

The year 1898 brought the opportunity of enriching our colonial possessions by two acquisitions which were of sentimental value to the German people. In Samoa and in the Carolines we had considerable economic interests. Both of these island groups offered our trade and our navy useful *points d'appui*. All informed opinion was unanimous that in 1885 Prince Bismarck had probably done well not to take possession of the Carolines, in face of the violent objection shown at the time by the Spaniards, as the impetuous Herbert Bismarck had wanted to do. Prince Bismarck had been equally right in 1889 to content himself with the condominium of Germany, Britain, and America which was set up by the Samoa Conference in Berlin, although this solution had not particularly served either peace in Samoa or special German interests. But in wide sections of the German nation the hope had persisted that both in Samoa and in the Carolines the opportunity would come of making good what had had to be foregone in the circumstances of the 'eighties. At the beginning of March, 1899, a telegram informed me that, after lengthy controversies between the German, British, and American consuls in Samoa, British and American cruisers had bombarded Apia. At the same time German colonists had been illegally imprisoned. When this Job's messenger reached me I was in Flottbeck, and I returned at once to Berlin. I was awaited at the station by Holstein, who had come to tell me, in lively but, it seemed to me, simulated excitement, that my only way out of this awkward situation was to send in my resignation, after a brick like that had dropped on my head. I replied to the incorrigible crank, perfectly calmly, that that solution had much in it that attracted me. If I did retire, I would advise the Kaiser that Prince Herbert Bismarck should be my successor, if only to propitiate the shade of his great father. Holstein, who since 1890 had feared the Bismarck family as the devil fears holy water, at once took a more sensible view of the situation. I was able to get British and American consent to a commission of inquiry into the unfortunate happenings, to restore order, and to work out proposals for the reorganization of the administration and the resettlement of the position of the islands with regard to the three Powers. Thus the way was paved for a solution satisfactory to us, through which we ultimately, after lengthy negotiations, brought the two principal islands, Upolo and Savaii, into German possession.

I still remember an incident, small but significant, in the Reichs-tag debate of April 14, 1899, a debate which took place amid some excitement not only in the House but in many quarters in the country. Tirpitz was sitting next to me, and while the opener was proceeding with his interpellation the Admiral said to me *sotto voce:*

"You really can do no good by speaking. It is clear that the action of the British and Americans points to the determination to go to war with us, in order to destroy us before our fleet has been hatched out of its shell. Otherwise one would have to assume that both John Bull and Jonathan had gone mad."

This view was characteristic of the military way of looking at things, with its tendency to disregard the relativity of things and of human beings, and its consequent aptness to run to extremes and so to come to mistaken conclusions in politics. The military mentality is not elastic enough to cope with political questions and see them in right perspective. "Ability to change course" was a quality that Prince Bismarck demanded above everything from his diplomats. I replied to my friend Tirpitz that neither the British nor the Americans had gone off their heads. Nor did they mean to take the very first chance of going to war with us. All that had happened was that some consuls and naval officers had got excited and kicked over the traces. Everyone would calm down if only we did not ourselves lose our balance. After a time the excitement duly subsided; it had not been without an element of danger, but there had been more of it in Germany than in Britain and America. Samoa was destined to be for fifteen years one of the finest brilliants in our colonial diadem. When our possession of Samoa was assured, William II sent me the following telegram:

Bravo! Am most pleased and delighted. You are a real magician, granted to me quite undeservedly by Heaven in its goodness.

In the name of the German Colonial Council, its president, the Prince of Wied, telegraphed me :

In its great pleasure at the good news of the happy acquisition of the two Samoan islands Upolo and Savaii, the Colonial Council, assembled here to-day, feels it must offer you, as the well-tried director of the Empire's foreign policy, its warmest congratulations on this splendid achievement in colonial policy, which is at the same time a genuinely popular one. Will Your Excellency permit the Colonial Council, in view of the very great difficulties which German diplomacy had to overcome in securing the acquisition of the Samoa Islands, once more to assure you of the full and entire confidence in Your Excellency of all the colonial interests in our country.

The Grand Duke Karl Alexander of Weimar telegraphed me :

The news of the acquisition of Samoa for Germany again makes me realize Your Excellency's enlightened and adept leadership, and I most cordially congratulate you on this achievement. Your Excellency is aware of the sincerity of this expression of my opinion, and of the pride which I feel in knowing that affairs are in your hands.

The Grand Duke Karl Alexander was, as is well-known, taken as the type of the *Serenissimus* who figured in so many farces, not always in good taste or even witty, which were staged in German theatres in the decades immediately preceding the World War. As a matter of fact the Grand Duke Karl Alexander of Saxony was one of the truest of aristocrats, the most cultivated and humane of princes who sat on a German throne. He was filled with the great tradition of his small realm, and was a kind and enlightened Maecenas, and not only in words, to authors and artists. He felt the greatness of Richard Wagner and gave him protection and support at a time when his genius was realized by very few and when the so-called intellectuals were ignoring "Tannhäuser" and "Lohengrin" or were making poor jokes at the expense of these masterpieces. He was united with Franz Liszt by a life-long and loyal friendship. He helped Adolf Stahr and Richard Voss. The Grand Duke was a true patriot. Though a brother of the Empress Augusta, who had for years been at daggers drawn with Prince Bismarck, he was a

staunch friend and admirer of the great Chancellor, to whom both
he and his courageous daughter, Princess Heinrich VII of Reuss,
remained loyal after his fall.   He was for himself a believing Christian, but retained the great scientist Haeckel in his chair at Jena in
spite of all attacks on him.   There were endless more or less true
anecdotes current about him and his sayings; they might move to
laughter, but were mostly merely the outcome of momentary
absent-mindedness or embarrassment.   I will mention one of these
innocent sayings, as I heard it myself.   While I was serving at the
Paris Embassy the Grand Duke stayed there for some days.   The
Ambassador, Prince Chlodwig Hohenlohe, gave him the hint that
he must call on President Grévy.   The Grand Duke refused to do
so because, as a cousin and friend of the house of Orleans, he could
not go to see the President of the Republic.   In the end he gave
way, and went with the Ambassador and myself to the Elysée.
As ill-luck would have it, the Grand Duke had to wait a bit before
he could go in to the President.   He began to get impatient, and to
soothe him Prince Hohenlohe said, with a smile alluding to the
well-known poem *"Der Wilde"* of the good Johann Gottfried
Seume: "Grévy is a Canadian, unfamiliar with — Europe's var-
nished politeness."   The Grand Duke, highly pleased, replied:
"Oh, he is from Canada, is he?   That at least makes him interesting to me!"   All things exotic attracted him, in common with
many Germans of the old generation.   During this same stay in
Paris the Grand Duke wanted, as he put it, to convey to the great
interpreter of Corneille and Racine, Sarah Bernhardt, the congratulations of Goethe's and Schiller's stage.   He was received in the
artist's home by a very well-bred young man, who was introduced
to him as the son of the house.   Rather taken aback, the Grand
Duke asked how it was that Mademoiselle Bernhardt had a son and
who the father was.   When he received the answer that the father
was a Prince de Ligne, Karl Alexander conceded that "That does
make matters better."   I will add one more anecdote, as it gives
a good picture of the ways of a better time that lies long behind us.
In the 'seventies the Grand Duke attended a mess dinner of the
proud 8th regiment of Cuirassiers, of which he was the honorary

colonel. He sat at the upper end of the table, and at the lower end were the younger officers; suddenly there was a shout of merriment from that end. A cheeky lieutenant, Herr von P., had proposed *sotto voce* the following toast:

> *Das Rindvieh säuft aus dem Eimer,*
> *Es lebe der Grossherzog von Weimar !* [1]

The Grand Duke asked what they were laughing at. An incautious cornet blurted out something about a toast. The Grand Duke asked what the toast was. Lieutenant von P. rose and in a stentorian voice, a true cuirassier's, shouted across the clubroom:

> *Besser als die Pappenheimer*
> *Reiten die Kürassiere des Grossherzogs von Weimar !* [2]

Very content with the toast, the Grand Duke invested von P. after dinner with the Order of the Falcon, 3rd class, of which Goethe had worn the Grand Cross. This same Grand Duke Karl Alexander who could so arouse hilarity had done in Weimar, — not in the same way as his great ancestor Charles Augustus, but with high ideals and with the same respect for intellect and genuine refinement — his full share in the observance of the traditions of his line and his capital and the nurturing and diffusion of true German culture. He had rather grand manners, but he possessed that *"politesse du cœur"* which has become regrettably rare in the new Germany. If the old Grand Duke had lived to see the luckless winter days in which the National Assembly met in Weimar, with Fritz Ebert giving none too tasteful ovations to the *genius loci* and meanwhile pouring out excessively ample libations to Bacchus in the Grand Ducal palace vaults, and with Mathias Erzberger entering in the guests' book of an inn the recommendation to Germans to comfort themselves for the dictated and shameful peace of Versailles by drinking and laughing, the barbarism of those days and the spiritual vulgarity of their matadors would have weighed **very** heavily on the Grand Duke Karl Alexander.

[1] The cattle guzzle from the pail,
Long live the Grand Duke of Weimar.
[2] The Grand Duke of Weimar's cuirassiers ride better than the Pappenheimers.

Our acquisition of the Caroline, Marianne, and Pelew Islands was the result of negotiations which I had carried on with the excellent Spanish Ambassador in Berlin, Señor Mendez de Vigo. Our acquisition was at once described by over-zealous adepts in colonial politics as more or less worthless. It is an old fault of the Germans that they do not take an honest pleasure in fortunate turns of fate, but chew the cud of them and work themselves into the belief that the good fortune is half or wholly a misfortune. And if misfortune comes, the average German is prone to trace back its antecedents ten, fifty, a hundred years, in order to establish "scientifically" the original cause of it. In politics the German does not sense realities with sufficient naturalness, simplicity, naïveté; his political emotions are often warped and distorted, and seldom spontaneous. Many years ago Queen Margherita of Italy, who as the daughter of a German mother knew both peoples, said to me with shrewd discernment:

"See how different Germans and Italians are! The Italian's emotional responses are simple, he loves or hates, usually for the simple reason that he finds a person or an idea to his taste or the reverse. Yet the Italian intelligence is supple and agile, ready and adroit, subtle and full of resource. The Italian does not apprehend things in isolation but in their relationship to one another, looks for a way out, and usually discovers a *'combinazione'* by means of which to reconcile the apparently incompatible and save the situation. The German is just the opposite. His intelligence is much too often that of the type known to the Italian as *'sempliciotto'* — pedantic, slow-going, doctrinaire, unable to see the wood for the trees; his emotions, on the other hand, are capable of endless modulations, from the tenderest love to stiff-necked recalcitrancy, from the very German moral indignation to the equally German readiness to take offence."

This diversity of character between the two nations is only too often perceptible in politics. The German critics who in 1899 carped at the acquisition of the Carolines and the Marianne Islands, and did all they could to belittle the value of these island groups, will to-day, if they are still living, probably hold exactly the opposite view. In any case, the haggling that went on after the World War between Japan, America, and Australia over certain of the Caroline Islands shows the value set on these particular islands by other Powers.

The acquisition of the Caroline and Marianne Islands turned our possessions in the western Pacific into a connected whole. With the Bismarck Archipelago and Kaiser Wilhelm Land in the south, the Marschall, Caroline, and Pelew Islands in the centre, and the Mariannes in the north, we now had a firm basis for our economic and general political development in Oceania. I was able also to point out in the Reichstag that the acquisition of the Carolines had in no way disturbed our good relations with Spain. For Spain they represented only fragments of a crumbled building, for us they were pillars and buttresses for (D.V.), a building with a future. It was impossible for me to foresee on June 22, 1899, that we were to lose the Carolines and Mariannes and Samoa, with the promising Shantung and Kiaochow, through letting ourselves be carried along by Austria, in spite of all the warnings which our greatest statesman had given from the time when he was a delegate to the federal diet in Frankfurt to the very last days of his life, and drawn into a World War over Serbia.

On receiving the news of the passing of the Carolines Bill by the Reichstag, William II telegraphed to me (June 22, 1899) :

I am pleased and delighted at your news of the passing of the Carolines Bill through its third reading in the Reichstag. I thank God that He has so disposed, and that the acquisition may also be regarded as a justification that does honour to the good ship *Iltis*. Next to Him I thank you most warmly for helping to acquire this pearl for my crown. In order to give special expression to my thanks for this, I am promoting you to the order of Count, since you have enabled me to keep the promise which I made to my loyal German people on ascending the throne, ever to be an "Augmenter of the Empire" in Peace.[1] God bless you for it, and our whole fatherland.

A few hours later I received a second telegram from the Kaiser, characteristic of his warmth of emotion and of his romantic sense

[1] *Allezeit Mehrer des Reichs* — traditional title of the Emperors.

and the poetical colour which he liked to give to his pronouncements in speech and writing :

In accordance with a signal from me, the navy has just given, in its gratification at the increase of territory acquired, three far-resounding cheers for the German fatherland, and these had scarcely died away when the sun, which had been obscured by dark clouds, suddenly broke through them. The bright rays seemed a sign from Heaven, and may it continue to be so with our dear fatherland.

Before this I had received from H.M. the Kaiser and all the gentlemen of his entourage the following telegram from the East Prussian manor of Prince Richard Dohna :

Secretary of State von Bülow, Berlin. Grateful thunderous cheers from us all to the ablest statesman, the wisest counsellor, the most amiable obtainer of the Caroline and Marianne Islands. Wilhelm I. R., Philipp Eulenburg, von Kessel, Eberhard Dohna, Dohna-Malmitz, Finckenstein-Simnau, Ilberg, Mackensen, Richard Dohna.

Kessel was the later Colonel General, Governor of Berlin and Commander-in-Chief of the Marches; Mackensen, then Colonel and A.D.C., later carved for himself a name for all time as a celebrated leader in the World War. Who would have been able then to tell me that that same prince who was encouraging me with such kind, perhaps excessively kind words on the completion of a heavy official duty of mine, would later include me in the long list of those whom he was to honour with the title of traitor ! "Put not your trust in princes," says the Psalmist, and it shows intimate acquaintance with courts when Adjutant General Leopold von Gerlach had this verse sung from time to time at morning prayers under Frederick William IV :

> *Verlasset euch auf Fürsten nicht!*
> *Sie sind wie eine Wiege;*
> *Wer heute "Hosianna" spricht,*
> *Ruft morgen: "Crucifige!"* [1]

[1] "Put not your trust in Princes !
    They rock to and fro like a cradle;
    Who cries 'Hosanna' to-day, cries
    'Crucify Him' to-morrow."

During the debates in the Reichstag on the settlement of the Samoa question and the acquisition of the Caroline, Marianne, and Pelew Islands, I laid down the principles which I regarded as irrefragable in dealing with international differences. In one of these discussions, in June, 1899, one of the noisiest speakers of the so-called Pan-Germans, the anti-Semite Liebermann von Sonnenberg, had spoken of the "scarcely enviable part" which we had played towards Britain in Samoa. I replied that we had omitted nothing to ensure that our countrymen should secure their full rights. We would not depart a hair's breadth from our just claims. But I added:

"But on the other hand we shall not forget that international differences in which there are not only clashes of various political and economic interests, but national feeling has been aroused, must be dealt with with calm reflection and in cool blood." [1]

The Spanish-American storm had passed by without damaging our territory or injuring our interests. But fresh clouds were coming up over South Africa. In 1899 the conflict broke out which had for long been latent between the Boer republics in South Africa and the British world empire. Like the petrel that precedes the storm, Cecil Rhodes appeared in Berlin in March, 1899. His visit was ostensibly connected with the laying of the British telegraph line through our East African protectorate. He was received by the Kaiser on March 11, 1899, and his visit was plainly made principally in order to see the Kaiser. After the audience he was invited to lunch, at which I was present. Cecil Rhodes could not but make a strong impression on any open-minded person. There was no pose about him; everything spoke of quiet strength. His manner was natural, with no attempt at effect. He showed respect to the Kaiser, but neither excitement nor diffidence. He gave His Majesty the broad outlines of his project of an all-British Cape to Cairo railway. The Kaiser's eyes shone, for every largely conceived plan in any part of the earth fired his imagination and worked strongly on his susceptibility to all that was out of the ordinary. Those fine and expressive eyes lit up still more brightly when Cecil Rhodes expressed the view that, while Germany had no vital interests in

[1] Prince Bülow's "Speeches" (large edition), I. 72; (small edition), I. 82.

Africa, she was entitled to be let alone in Asia Minor. Mesopotamia, the Tigris and Euphrates, Bagdad, the city of the Caliphs — there lay her future. I had begged His Majesty to do no more than listen attentively to all that Cecil Rhodes had to say, all the more since, as the British Ambassador had expressly assured me, Rhodes spoke only for himself, with no mandate from his Government. Thus, for the present we must preserve our freedom of action. But the desire to impress an Englishman, and one of such eminence, led the Kaiser to embark on a long and brilliant discourse, fertile in ideas and imagination, describing all his feelings and views and plans concerning world affairs in general — America and Japan, Russia, Italy, Austria, the Dardanelles and the Suez Canal, the Danube and the Yangtse-Kiang, — his whole programme for Germany's foreign policy. When the meal was over, William II, who had perorated incessantly and had scarcely allowed Cecil Rhodes to open his mouth to speak, imagined he had made a tremendous impression on him. Cecil Rhodes, for his part, had probably arrived at the opinion that the German Emperor was guided in his political judgments and projects less by reflection and insight than by his fancy. In the course of lengthy conversations which I had with Cecil Rhodes I was able to make plain to him that the Emperor, the Chancellor, and I wanted to live not only at peace with Britain, but on terms of the closest possible friendship with her, naturally on the basis of "*do ut des*" and above all of equality in regard to guarantees. As to the conflict between Britain and the Boers, we should be able to remain neutral the more easily the more Britain gave practical evidence of concern for our interests in the world, and avoided everything which would be felt to be provocative by German public opinion. The first result of Rhodes' visit was an agreement giving the Trans-African Telegraph Company permission to lay a telegraph line through our East African protectorate. We thus gave practical evidence of our desire to remain on terms of mutual accommodation with Britain in Africa. I replied to the exaggerated mistrust with which the Right wing in the Reichstag was filled with regard to Britain, that our interests were fully guarded in this agreement.

Both Cecil Rhodes' visit and Rhodes himself were treated by a large section of the German press in a petty provincial spirit. It was spread abroad by the narrow-minded in the press, in the lobbies of the Reichstag, and in society that Cecil Rhodes had gone to see the Kaiser not in a frock coat but a cutaway. The Empress had been infected with the excitement, and wrote me:

Your time must be entirely taken up, and I do not want to disturb you for nothing to-day. But I have got the impression from a conversation with the Kaiser that at the moment he is steaming full-speed ahead for England, so to speak. I should like to hear from you how I ought to treat Cecil Rhodes this evening, whether rather coldly or whether one ought to be particularly friendly to him. My own choice would be for the former. The Kaiser also tells me that he is going on the Queen's invitation to Cowes in August. This seems to me quite beyond belief! Perhaps he cannot be prevented from going to see his grandmother, but I do beg you to prevent him from sailing again at Cowes, especially on board the *Meteor*. He could quite well go in the *Hohenzollern*, pay a visit to the Queen, and then come back. After all that has happened, to mix again in that society, to expose himself to the risks of this sailing, and, last not least, time after time to let himself be beaten at the last moment by some trick of the English, this makes me too mad, both for the Emperor's sake and my husband's. I hope you will prevent it. Perhaps you will ask why this long letter to-day of all days. But I was afraid that at to-night's English dinner the Kaiser might let himself be carried away and make promises that it would be difficult to get out of afterwards. If you should see the Kaiser this afternoon, a word of caution from you might perhaps make the machine slow down a little. I have, of course, written this without the Kaiser's knowledge. It is rather like going behind his back, but when there is so much at stake, and you have so good an influence, you will understand how I look at it. I admit that yesterday, unfortunately, I got rather emphatic, and for that reason I would rather not return again to the subject to-day. So please leave me out of it entirely. Forgive this long letter. I should have preferred to speak to you, but that would have attracted rather more attention.

This intimate letter from the Empress shows once more the prudence and discernment which the royal lady united with the best of hearts. Unfortunately she had not the readiness in discussion needed in order to maintain her position against her impetuous husband. In this case I was easily able to set the Empress' fears at rest, and she met her English guest with her usual kindness and friendliness.

It was not so easy to calm German public opinion, on which Cecil Rhodes, like Chamberlain later, had the effect of a red rag on a bull. The attacks and sarcasms levelled against Cecil Rhodes were rather out of place at the expense of a man who was one of the great *conquistadores* who had built up the British world-empire. Since then an enormous monument has been erected in his honour on the endless grass plains of South Africa, a pyramid built up of giant stones in memory of the man who won the south of the Dark Continent for Great Britain. Apart from that, Cecil Rhodes was personally an advocate of good relations between Great Britain and Germany. After his visit to Berlin he placed in trust a considerable sum to facilitate the attendance of German students in the British universities, and of British students in the German colleges. The idea was well received in both countries. The German students at Oxford formed an Anglo-German Club, which numbers of Englishmen joined. In the spring of 1914 the young gentlemen were good enough to elect me honorary president of their association. I shall have to tell later how the Anglo-German Club in Oxford was on the very point of celebrating its founder's day, with many notable Englishmen participating, when the Berchtold-Bethmann ultimatum to Serbia and our diplomatic handling of the resulting crisis brought about the World War.

Never for a moment during the South African War did I doubt that Britain would carry the struggle through to a victorious end. With her enormous superiority in numbers, in money, and in resources of every sort, she was bound to gain and keep the upper hand if she was able to send troops to South Africa. This she would be able to do so long as she ruled the waves, and she did rule them. In this conflict, as in the Spanish-American War, a large section of the German public, even including military observers, was led astray by sentiment in its judgment of the situation in South Africa. His Majesty's military suite, including men usually of good sense, were convinced that the British would be no match for the Boers, and from time to time the Kaiser was inclined to think with them. The German public looked at the whole situation not with its head, but with its heart, and the German heart burned for the poor Boers. I was determined from the first to keep us clear of any steps for the Boers and against the British. I felt the more justified in this in that for months past, since the relations between Britain and the South African Republic had once more grown strained, I had advised the latter, and had especially urged President Kruger, to go cautiously and conciliatorily to work, and had left not the slightest room for any doubt in the minds of the Boers that, for all the respect and sympathy which were felt for them in Germany, they must not count on receiving any help from us. I knew that if it were to come to a conflict between Russia, France, and Britain, the French would not fight on our side against Britain but would fall upon us. What way Russia, which had been for eight years France's ally, would then turn could not be predicted with certainty. The French press poured out vials of wrath, contempt, and hatred over England. The newspaper kiosks along the Paris boulevards flaunted comic papers with indescribably vulgar caricatures of Queen Victoria. There was held, however, at the time a consultation between French statesman of every shade of opinion, and everyone of any weight agreed with Waldeck-Rousseau when he declared that coöperation with Germany in a big and serious question would be tantamount to a final endorsement of the cession of Alsace-Lorraine, and that was impossible.

My view was that neither Russia nor France had any intention of doing anything of importance for the Boers, and this view was shared by the most far-seeing of our diplomats, Count Paul Hatzfeldt, the Ambassador in London. He wrote to Herr von Holstein before the outbreak of hostilities in South Africa:

I learn to my astonishment that in the various departments of our Foreign Ministry there is some surprise, perhaps even dissatisfaction, at the fact that I am interested in the maintenance of peace in South Africa and am working for it. The next thing, I suppose, will be that I shall be declared to have some personal axe to grind in the matter. The truth is that at first I did have some doubt whether the outbreak of war would not have its advantages for us. You expressed a different opinion at the time, and I came round to your view. Even to-day I would consider that war is desirable from our point of view if I could see any hope of Russia or France taking action on behalf of the Transvaal and so bringing on a conflict with Britain. But I see no hope whatever of this, and, that being so, I am unable to see what advantage war could bring us. There is no reason to suppose that, with only the Boers to deal with, Britain would get into such difficulties as to have to make any great sacrifice for our friendship. It would be equally little to our advantage if in the end Britain were to annex the Transvaal, or if the end were to be the development of South Africa into a republic, which would be neither a pleasant nor a convenient neighbour for us.

The foremost question in internal politics in the summer of 1899 was the Canal Bill. No dispassionate judge will contend to-day that the Emperor William was not wholly right in envisaging the construction of two new canals, the Dortmund-Rhine and Central German canals. The development of our network of canals was equally desirable from every point of view, economic, strategic, and national. The arguments brought against it proceeded from particularist considerations, parish pump interests, and party politics, which unfortunately have always played so troublesome a part in German life, inspiring in our greatest poet the terrible dictum that individually the Germans are worthy of respect but that collectively they are a wretched lot. At the same time, the progress of the Canal Bill was greatly hampered, about the turn of the century, by the personal intervention of the Kaiser with speeches and telegrams and threats which, much as in the case of the Willing Workers Bill, slew the infant in its mother's womb. The more passionately he advocated the Bill — against all the remonstrances of his advisers, — the easier it was for the opponents of the Bill to represent it as the product of a caprice of the Kaiser's which in reality it was not at all. The Monarch's impetuousness made almost impossible the position of Miquel, the Minister of Finance, on whose shoulders, in consequence of the great age of the Chancellor Hohenlohe, and his inadequacy as a speaker, the task lay of defending the Bill.

Johannes Miquel was not only a great orator but a man of captivating charm in conversation. Like not a few old people — I do not except myself — he was inclined to discourse at length in private conversation, but in his case at least the discoursing was supported by the widest historical learning and by a wealth of experience. One of his favourite subjects was the gradual building up of the Roman world empire — he would give an admirable description of the process; another was the importance to the well-being of a country of a good network of canals, for which reason all good princes had built canals. William II had often heard this canal discourse in after-dinner conversations. His susceptible spirit was quickly fired, and with the student in "Faust" he thought:

> *Das sollt Ihr mir nicht zweimal sagen!*
> *Ich denke mir, wieviel es nützt.*[1]

The Kaiser had thus ended by demanding from Miquel a Canal Bill, and the very able Minister of Public Works, from West Germany, Thielen, seconded the plan with energy and conviction. Miquel was now in a dilemma. In his political nonage he had been an enthusiast for the communism of Karl Marx; but by now he had arrived at a conservative, even an extremely conservative and agrarian outlook. He knew that the Conservatives were against all canal plans, because they feared that they would facilitate the importation of foreign grain and the migration westward of the agricultural workers of the eastern provinces. Miquel, having failed to prevent the introduction of the Canal Bill, let the foregoing considerations temper his first speech for the Bill. Miquel was a great debater. "*Kladderadatsch*" said once that a Jesuit could adduce three arguments to prove that twice two makes five, Miquel could adduce five arguments, and I seven. That, by the way, was perhaps an exaggerated estimate of my powers. Miquel, however, every time he came to the Canal Bill, used such noncommittal, not to say ambiguous language, that one of the Conservative leaders, Count Hans Kanitz, opened his speech in reply with the words: "Finance Minister Miquel may be either for or against the canal plan; which of the two, we know just as little after the

[1] You need not tell it me twice over.

speech he has just made as before." The Kaiser, with his keen interest in the canal plan, read the newspaper reports of the debate with more attention than he usually spared for Parliamentary reports. Kanitz' remark aroused his mistrust; he sent for Miquel to meet him at the Potsdam station, and there, before he got into the special train which was to take him back to the New Palace, he gave him a vigorous blowing-up. After that Miquel became still more unreliable. His intimate friend Baron Oktavio von Zedlitz, the Radical Conservative member, known in Parliament as the *"chiaroscuro"* owing to his inclination for intrigue, joined Herr Viktor Schweinburg, an unreliable journalist brought from Vienna to Berlin to be Miquel's press mouthpiece, in all sorts of schemings, and after violent debates in the Prussian Diet Lower House the leaders of the opposition to the Bill, Count Limburg-Stirum, a Conservative, and Count Ballestrem, a Centre party man, won the day.

Great was the agitation of the Kaiser, who, as was his wont, took this blow as a personal affront. He bombarded me — though as Secretary of State for Foreign Affairs I had had nothing whatever to do with the Bill — with telegrams *en clair*, swarming with insults especially against Stirum. The Empress, as a loyal wife, shared not only her husband's difficulties and troubles, but all his feelings, but this time she suffered under the Kaiser's indignation against the Conservatives, as she was whole-heartedly on the Right in politics; she wrote to me on August 18, 1899, from Wilhelmshöhe:

I come to you in my trouble. Yesterday evening I had unfortunately to leave the Kaiser to go to Metz and St. Privat, though he was in great agitation and depression. This unlucky Canal Bill! If it is decided against on Saturday I do not know what is to happen. *Ach*, could not you write the Emperor a letter that might do something to calm him? It is really needed! It makes me very sad to be unable to be with him now. The doctor did not want all this travelling at all because of my foot; and on top of that I have a sick child here, my little Oscar. Ah, it has been a bad summer! May God continue to help us.

Yours very sincerely,
Victoria

As early as April, 1899, the Kaiser had sent a telegram to Herr von der Recke, the Minister of the Interior, commanding him to threaten the *Landräte* in the Prussian Parliament with "*Kassation*"[1] and with the cutting off of their personal relations with His Majesty if they did not vote for the Canal Bill. Count Limburg-Stirum was to be struck off the list of Privy Councillors for his opposition to the Bill. "The Conservative parties in their boundless narrowness and junker arrogance have thrown down a glove in challenge to me; I shall take it up." Miquel complained to me (I was not in the firing line in questions of internal policy), not without reason, that his position in the canal question was being made much more difficult by the impossibility of making His Majesty understand that the Conservatives as a party could not simply be the executors of the royal will, as if they did they would lose all hold over the electorate. "The Kaiser," said Miquel to me on one occasion during this period, "for all his great and many-sided gifts, is politically colour-blind." A neat phrase, which often recurred to my memory afterwards, and a just one. So much the greater, of course, and so much the more burdensome was the responsibility of His Majesty's advisers. In the course of the summer of 1899 the prospects for the Canal Bill grew continually worse, until in the end it was rejected in August. The Kaiser telegraphed to me:

This is rank stupidity, mixed with ill-will, and exploited by a young Jew. I am determined to make the party feel my anger through heavy *social* punishments, and so to compel it to do its work after all. No dissolution — that is what Centre and Radicals are hoping for. But exclusion of the Limburger and his associates from society.

In September, 1899, the following telegram from the Kaiser reached me:

The traditional pillars of throne and altar, who have always been spoilt by the royal house, have turned against their lord, and that under the lead of the Jew upstart Limburg. Let loose all your press-dogs and rain down cudgel blows on the party.

[1] Dismissal.

Count Limburg-Stirum, who for years had been the leader of the Conservatives in Prussia, was the son of a Dutch nobleman of long lineage and an Israelite. I have already mentioned the rather strong dictum of Prince Bismarck's that the union between a Teuton stallion and a Semitic mare sometimes gives good results; it certainly fitted Count Stirum. From his father's side he had inherited earnestness, tenacity, and industry, from his mother's a clear and acute intelligence. In the years which followed Prince Bismarck's fall, when so many deserted him, Count Limburg-Stirum stood loyally by the old man in the Saxon forests. This led during the Caprivi era to an uncalled-for and senseless disciplinary proceeding against Stirum, who, as Ambassador Z. D.,[1] had written a newspaper article opposing the Caprivi-Marschall commercial treaties. Honest Caprivi looked at the matter from the standpoint of military discipline, and Holstein, who did not like Stirum, egged him on. At the same time Count Stirum had on various occasions been cut and snubbed by the Kaiser, so that his feelings towards His Majesty may gradually have become embittered. However, it is due to him to say that his political judgment was not influenced by these experiences. He was not so able a party leader in the narrow sense of the term as his successor Heydebrand; he was less ready in debate and an ineffective orator, if only on account of a chronic hoarseness that made it impossible for him to raise his voice. But his horizon was wider than his successor's, he had a better sense of the inter-reactions between home and foreign policy, and above all he thought of State before party. Not for nothing had he passed through the school of Bismarck. Incidentally, the Kaiser's outbursts against his Jewish origin were the more surprising since William II was by no means an anti-Semite. A general dislike for Jews and Jewry was altogether strange to his nature. He was also on terms of personal friendship with many prominent Jews, such as Albert Ballin, Emil Rathenau, Eduard Arnhold, Paul von Schwabach, Robert von Mendelssohn, and many other excellent men. Needless to say, I did nothing at all to carry out

---

[1] Z.D. = "*Zu Diensten*", *i.e.* not actually officiating but at the Government's disposal for ambassadorial duties.

the instruction in regard to the "press-dogs", but, on the contrary, did my utmost to secure dispassionate treatment of the canal issue in the press.

In spite of his anger against the opponents of the canals, William II would not hear of a dissolution of the Prussian Parliament, though Prince Hohenlohe — who felt for the Prussian Conservatives something of the repugnance, built up of court traditions and insufficient understanding, which the South German baron sometimes feels for the North German junker — had been working for a dissolution, in the hope of so obtaining a Liberal majority in Prussia. But it was just this that the Kaiser did not want, and so he delivered a speech to the assembled Ministers of State in which, with the originality which he so often showed, he treated the whole matter from military points of view. When a regiment mutinies — such was the substance of his Majesty's pronouncement — it is not disbanded on that account, for that would be an injury to the army and an exhibition of ingratitude for the past merits of the troops in question. But the ringleaders are brought to the front and shot. On the analogy of this, all officials, especially the *Landräte*, who had voted against the Canal Bill must now be dismissed. All the Ministers except Prince Hohenlohe were opposed to this solution. Miquel foresaw that it would greatly anger the Conservatives, but he preferred that to a dissolution, from which he feared a considerable reduction of his influence and position. So a large number of honest *Landräte*, including some who, supported by the confidence of all their constituents, had administered their districts for decades, were dismissed as "Canal mutineers." It is true that among these "mutineers" there were several gentlemen, including Herr von Dallwitz, the future Governor of Alsace-Lorraine, Herr von Jagow, the future Oberpräsident of West Prussia, and some others, who were able later on to sun themselves in the full favour of His Majesty. If the departure of the *Landräte* had been a matter of small concern to the Kaiser, it was a different matter when the Chief Huntsman, the Duke of Pless, one of the richest and foremost Silesian magnates, sent in his resignation on the ground that he, too, was opposed to the canal scheme and had no desire to be treated better than the colleagues who shared his view. Prince Hohenlohe-Oehringen, the Head Chamberlain, asked to be relieved of his office on the same ground. The matter was getting serious. The Kaiser sent for me at once to the New Palace, and received me, in visible agitation, with the words:

"The great ones of my court are abandoning me."

In the course of the conversation that followed I was able to get an assurance that the most trustworthy of the dismissed *Landräte* should be given the prospect of reinstatement at a later date. The Kaiser propitiated the Duke of Pless by appointing his son-in-law, Prince Fritz Solms, Head Chamberlain in place of Prince Hohenlohe-Oehringen. It was only a few years before that the Kaiser had given the latter his appointment to the chief court office in Prussia, which from of old had ranked in the Prussian court order of precedence with the Prime Minister and the Field Marshals. The telegram announcing his appointment had been couched by the Kaiser in warm terms, very flattering to him, and addressed "Prince Christian Kraft von Hohenlohe-Oehringen." At the moment the Prince was staying incognito with lady friends in an Austrian spa — he was unmarried. He had given orders that all telegrams for him sent to Berlin or Slawentzitz, his Silesian château, should be telegraphed on to the spa, addressed to his valet, who had accompanied him. So it happened that, to the great astonishment of the clerk in the Imperial and Royal telegraph office in Kaltenleutgeben, near Vienna, the following telegram came in:

Hermann Schulze, valet. In grateful recognition of your eminent services rendered in war and peace, I appoint you my Head Chamberlain.
                                                            Wilhelm R.

The Canal Bill, which had got into a hopeless position through mistakes on all sides, came into my hands in later years when I was Prussian Prime Minister, and I was able to steer it into smooth water and bring it safely to port.

CHAPTER XIX

The Kaiser's Visit to Karlsruhe — Hohenzollern Castle — Queen Wilhelmina of Holland in Berlin (October, 1899) — Tsar and Tsaritsa Visit Berlin — Journey of the Kaiser and Empress to England (November 20, 1899) — The Empress Opposed to the Visit — Her Letter to Bülow — Hatzfeldt's Report — Landing in England — The Duchess of Connaught — German Princesses Abroad — Windsor — The Gala Banquet — British Courtiers and Statesmen — Prince Hohenlohe's Memorandum for William II.

In September I accompanied the Kaiser on a visit to Karlsruhe. It was always pleasant and refreshing to be with the Baden hosts. Grand Duke Frederick and the Grand Duchess Louise were both idealists in the best sense of the word, undeterred by the pettinesses and meannesses of the day in their contemplation of the great aims which should beckon like stars to the patriot. In spite of this patriotic idealism, the relations between the Grand Duke Frederick and Prince Bismarck had several times been clouded over. For all my admiration and love for the greatest of German statesmen, I must admit that the Prince was more to blame for the friction than the Grand Duke. Especially in the Roggenbach-Geffcken affair Bismarck had allowed himself to be carried too far by mistrust and rancour. This abates nothing from his greatness. Napoleon remains a great man in spite of his order for the shooting of the Duc d'Enghien, of which no one can approve.

From Karlsruhe the Kaiser drove with me to the manoeuvre ground and then for a visit to Hohenzollern castle. We were up at 5 A.M. and did not get back till 9 P.M., when we had still to go to the theatre and after that to a court soirée and reception. The Kaiser stood exertions of this sort easily. After he had been in the saddle three hours at the manoeuvres, he had a big breakfast in the carriage and then gave me a long audience during which I submitted to him a number of diplomatic transfers. These unfortunately included the return to the diplomatic corps of Counsellor of Legation von Schön, who had made a mess of it as Court Chamberlain in Coburg and wanted to get back into diplomatic life. There, as Ambassador in Petersburg and Paris, he was to gain no laurels, and none as Secretary of State for Foreign Affairs in Berlin. On the Hohenzollern (a visit to this hill always moved me as deeply as the sight of the Hohenstaufen — both these peaks in the Swabian country rise up as admonitions to the German people to remember its great past) the Kaiser gave me a fine picture of the castle of his forefathers, writing below it the date 9. 9. 99. On this occasion he told me that his grandmother, the Empress Augusta, had once said to him when they were talking of the fine view from the Hohenzollern : "Let it admonish you to acquire and retain a broad and unrestricted outlook." A saying in the spirit of Goethe.

In October, 1899, the Queens of Holland visited Potsdam. The Dowager Queen Emma, a Princess of Waldeck, impressed one as sensible, calm, and reliable. In 1879 she had married King William III of Holland, who was more than forty years older than she ; he had first been married, not altogether happily, to Princess Sophie of Württemberg, an able and intelligent woman, friend of Ernest Renan and other French luminaries, who had, however, become virulently anti-German, as unfortunately happens with many German princesses who marry abroad. There was only one son by this marriage, the Prince of Orange, who spent most of his time in Paris, where smart society knew the Prince d'Orange as Prince Citron. Excessive devotion to the service of Bacchus brought Prince Citron to an early grave, and at the wish of his people King William III resolved, to prevent the dying out of the famous house of Orange, to remarry. Queen Emma had borne the burden, no light one, of this union with devotion, patience, and tact. In spite of his eccentricities, William III had to the end remained popular with the people of Holland, who cling with unshakable loyalty to the house of Orange. The little stories which went about concerning the king and his many peculiarities only added to his popularity. Once the visit of a Minister for whom he had no liking was announced. He received him while bathing in a pond in his park and invited him to get undressed and come down into the water and there deliver himself of what he had to say. One day when he was entering Amsterdam with Queen Emma, the enthusiastic crowd lifted up into the carriage a fourteen-year-old boy dressed entirely in orange colours. It was meant as homage, but the King took it as importunity; he seized the boy and threw him far over the horses' heads back to the crowd, who hurrahed at this proof of royal muscularity.

Queen Wilhelmina, who at the time of the visit to Potsdam was scarcely nineteen, was then a fascinating young girl; she seemed still entirely under the influence of her mother. In honour of the guests from the Netherlands the Kaiser arranged in the New Palace an allegorical set of tableaux, which in well-composed pictures and not bad verses represented the intimate bonds between the houses of Hohenzollern and Orange and the latter's proud past. At the supper which followed I sat with the Kaiser and the two Queens at a table for four. The Kaiser led the conversation and spoke of the Boer War, which was then in full progress, in so anti-English a spirit, and with such heat and exaggeration, that the Queen Mother said to me after the meal that, though her sympathies were naturally with her people's blood-relations, the Boers, she thought it was doubtful whether the Kaiser's violent exhibition of anti-British feeling was not imprudent. If Queen Emma had dreamed of the enthusiasm with which the self-same Kaiser was to sail in British waters six weeks later, she would scarcely have worried about the matter so much.

On November 8, 1899, the Tsar and Tsaritsa came to Potsdam, with the Minister Muravieff, on a short visit on their way back from Darmstadt to St. Petersburg. After the evening meal Tsar Nicholas honoured me with a long conversation. He began by congratulating me on the Samoa agreement. What we had achieved was all the more notable since the British were *très durs à la détente* — very close-fisted — while we had no means of bringing pressure to bear on Britain on the seas. He was thus doubly glad to be able to congratulate me, as an old acquaintance with many friends in St. Petersburg. The Tsar then came to our Navy Bill, of which

he entirely approved. We could not do better than make ourselves a good strong naval Power. So long as the British navy
was so much stronger than the navies of all other countries, it
was difficult to stand up against Britain. The stronger the continental States became on the seas, the better for all of them and
for the peace of the world. The Tsar spoke with sympathy of the
Boers, but said with emphasis that Russia would not let herself be
tempted out of her aloofness by events in South Africa. These
events were a long way off from Russia and left her unmoved.
Russia wanted peace before all things, in order to consolidate herself in peace and to raise her economic and cultural level. Russia
also had no desire to see a conflict between France and Britain.
If Russia had desired that, war would perhaps have come a year
before between France and Britain over Fashoda, although the
great majority of the French now realized that Fashoda was value-
less, and M. Delcassé would not have it even as a gift. In any case,
Russia had no desire for any conflict between France and Britain,
and had for that reason urged moderation a year before on the
French. The Tsar said that, personally and politically, he had
been very favourably impressed in Potsdam. He wanted to maintain the very best of relations with Germany — *des relations cor-
diales, sûres et intimes*. There was no point at which the interests
of Germany and Russia clashed. Both countries could work together everywhere in friendship and for peace. There was only
one point, Tsar Nicholas added, where we must show consideration
and indulgence for Russian traditions, and that was in the Near
East. We must not let it appear that we wanted to drive Russia
entirely out of the Balkans politically and economically. She had
now for centuries been united with the Christian populations of
the Balkans by countless bonds of a national and religious nature.
Even though, said the Tsar, he personally might be a sceptic or
indifferent in his views in this connexion, he would still have to
maintain the Russian tradition in the Balkan peninsula. In this
matter he could not set himself in opposition to the traditions and
feelings of his people, or to their hopes, which, as he said, I knew
from my time in Petersburg, were directed towards the Dardanelles.

"*Les sentiments et les rêves du peuple russe vont dans la direction des détroits.*" The Tsar added that he hoped that mutual consideration and loyal frankness would succeed in obviating all occasions in this connexion for misunderstandings, friction, and conflicts between us.

Count Muravieff mentioned to me in conversation a visit which Delcassé, the French Foreign Minister, had made to St. Petersburg in August, ostentatiously avoiding Berlin, and said that Hanotaux had had a less narrow outlook than Delcassé, who was quite obsessed with the idea of *revanche.* "*Delcassé est un maniaque, qui subordonne tout à l'idée de la revanche. Il ne voit que Strasbourg sans penser aux intérêts supérieurs de l'Europe, ni surtout aux intérêts monarchiques, qui pour nous comme pour vous doivent passer en première ligne et qui unissent nos deux pays.*" Muravieff too congratulated me on the conclusion of our Samoa treaty with Britain and America, saying with emphasis that he rejoiced at all that tended to promote peace and quiet in Europe. Muravieff was plainly filled with anxiety lest there should be fresh revolutionary movements in Russia, and was still of his old opinion that nothing would do more to promote them than if Russia were to slip into a great European war.

An incident occurred at court when the Russian guests were leaving which was of no political importance in itself, but left behind it some personal ill-feeling that brought political trouble. Contrary to the expectation of the Russian Emperor and Empress and to the usage of courts, the Empress did not accompany the Tsaritsa to the station. The excuse which she put forward was her décolletée dress. The real reason was that as a good Protestant the Empress Augusta Victoria had not forgiven her Russian cousin her change of confession, and, apart from that, did not like her English ways.

On November 20, 1899, the Emperor and Empress set out for England. The majority of the Reichstag and still more the great majority of the German people regretted and disapproved of this visit. The Empress had done her utmost up to the last moment to prevent it. Only a fortnight before it began she wrote to me:

WILLIAM II AND THE EARL OF LONSDALE

(*Snapshot during Imperial Manœuvres*)

What is going to happen now? I hoped from your presence here yesterday that the English visit was falling through. We really cannot go there. I have done as you wished and said nothing to the Kaiser so far — very soon now our boats will be burned. I am afraid it will do the Kaiser any amount of harm in the country if we really go. Britain is only out to make use of us. Of course it is frightfully difficult for the Kaiser, but at bottom I think he would be glad to get out of it. I am anxiously awaiting your reply.

The ladies of Her Majesty's Court spoke of the sorrow and scandal of visiting England at the moment when British "Mammonism" was trying to strangle the brave and godly Boers. For a long time the Kaiser was undecided. I told him that I would take responsibility for the journey and defend it in the Reichstag.

A few days after my departure for England I received a letter from our Ambassador in London, Count Paul Hatzfeldt, dated November 11, in which he wrote:

Chamberlain is still a factor with which we must reckon, and we must keep on the right side of him; I think, therefore, it is of urgent importance that Your Excellency should give him the opportunity, if it is in any way possible, of a confidential discussion. I think, however, that in doing so we must bear in mind that Foreign Office circles show an unmistakable irritation at the independent negotiations, of which it is well aware, although Salisbury himself has so far made no sign of this to me. It would thus be desirable so to arrange any confidential conversation between Your Excellency and Chamberlain that it *does not come to the knowledge of Salisbury*. In regard to His Majesty's visit to England I may perhaps once more point out quite in confidence to Your Excellency how desirable it is in the interest of the matter that His Majesty should at least accept the invitation of the Duke of Devonshire.

Publisher's Note. The following passage contains allegations against the Earl of Lonsdale, K. G., which are entirely without foundation.

In this regard I cannot sufficiently stress the bad effect which is being produced by the Kaiser's intended visit to Lord Lonsdale in all quarters concerned, and especially with the Queen. Among his fellow-peers Lord Lonsdale is thought very little of, and one may sum up the general opinion of him, with which I have long been familiar, by saying that never in any circumstances does he speak a word of truth. Apart from that, the Queen is enraged at the idea that Lord Lonsdale, who is deeply in debt and is said to have spent a million marks on the last visit of the Kaiser's, should become involved in fresh indebtedness through the visit now proposed.   The Prince of Wales fully shares this view, and I feel that I ought to mention the fact, even though, perhaps, we need not pay so much deference to his view.   On the other hand I have been given definite assurance that the Queen would be reconciled to the visit if it is not the *only* one and if His Majesty also accepts the invitation to Chatsworth, the seat of the Duke of Devonshire.   This appears to me to be also particularly desirable, as I have already said, in view of the position of the Duke and Duchess and the friendly feelings towards Germany of which both have lately given evidence.   In any case I should like to press for the earliest possible decision by telegraph, since, magnificent as Chatsworth is said to be, the Duke has to make some preparations that would require a few days.

I have had no time for any official report on the situation of the war in South Africa, and I could only repeat that there is a fixed determination here to pursue the war to a victorious end, regardless of sacrifices in men and money.   It may be taken for granted that Lord Salisbury's declaration at the Lord Mayor's banquet the day before yesterday, that Britain would not tolerate any intervention, is completely representative of the attitude of the overwhelming majority of the public, and that, if, say, France and Russia were to try to intervene now or later in the settlement of the South African question, their overtures would be firmly rejected. I am only anxious, may I add, that neither France nor Russia nor both together should attempt anything of the sort.   If I may express my own view, it is that our task is defined in advance by our interests.   We must maintain as good relations as we can with both sides, Russia and France on the one side and Britain on the other, *without actively supporting either party, so long as they do not come to blows with one another*.   Should that happen, and as time goes on it will probably become almost inevitable, whether in Asia or elsewhere, it will be in the hands of His Majesty the Kaiser, as I have ventured several times to represent personally to His Majesty, to choose on our course and to lay down his conditions for it.

Over here both the Queen and her Court intend to show the greatest kindness to their German guests.   The only thing to bear in mind is that social ways over here are much freer than ours are and very different. Much less attention is paid, therefore, to the individual rank of any particular person, and a Colonel or General is treated no differently from a Lieutenant, if one wishes to be on friendly terms with either.   This is the custom of the country, and not the slightest harm is intended.   If Your

Excellency could get His Majesty's entourage to give no signs of unnecessary touchiness, this would contribute substantially to the success of the visit.

The Duchess of Devonshire, formerly Duchess of Manchester, was German-born — she had been a Countess Alten, sister of Count Karl von Alten, who for many years had been A.D.C. to Emperor William I and commander of his bodyguard. Count Karl von Alten had been a well-known figure in Berlin society in the 'seventies and 'eighties. His eldest sister was the wife of the Russian Minister in Brussels, Count Bludow; the next was married to General von Albedyll, who had been the head of the Military Cabinet of Emperor William I, an officer who had done sterling service and had been of great influence under the old Kaiser. The fourth sister had married first Count August Grote auf Breese, then my cousin Detlev von Bülow-Gorow, and finally Prince Luigi Colonna-Stigliano. She managed to become the subject of a great deal of gossip. The third sister had married the Duke of Manchester, and later the Duke of Devonshire. She had achieved social and political prominence in England, was intimate with the Prince and Princess of Wales, and her husband listened to her views and her judgments. The Earl of Lonsdale belonged, like Mr. Poultney Bigelow, Herr von Koscielski, Prince Albert of Monaco, Prince Max Fürstenberg, President Roosevelt, and the French Generals Lacroix and Bonnal, to the long list of persons over whom William II went into raptures, but who did not bring him much profit.

We landed in England at noon on November 20, and were received by the Duke of Connaught, the third son of Queen Victoria, a prince of noble ideas, of kindly manners, and filled with friendly feelings for his nephew, the Kaiser Emperor, and for Prussia and Germany. His wife, a daughter of Prince Frederick Charles of Prussia, was correspondingly hostile to all things German. I once asked the Kaiser what his cousin and aunt, the Duchess of Connaught, would say if at some British court function, or a distinguished garden party, a Prussian General were to come up to her and express his pleasure at meeting the daughter of the victor

of Düppel, of Königgrätz, and of Metz.   The Kaiser thought that
it would be horribly uncomfortable for little Louise.   I went on to
ask the Kaiser what the Tsaritsa Alexandra Feodorovna of Russia
would say if a German officer were to express to this cousin of the
German Emperor his pleasure in recalling that she was the daughter
of a German Prince and army commander who had done good service in the war of 1870.   "It would be beastly for Alix," said the
Kaiser.   I then told him a little story of the days when I was
Ambassador in Rome.   On one occasion the Duchess of Aosta, née
Princess of Orleans, was to receive the diplomatic corps in Rome
after her marriage to an Italian prince; I had been standing next
to the French Ambassador, M. Billot.   Billot told me he was
looking forward to his presentation with some curiosity, since —
to say nothing of the fall of the house of Orleans in 1848 — the
Duchess' brother, Duke Philippe of Orleans, had just been exiled
from France.   In due course the French Ambassador was presented
to this daughter of a dynasty exiled from France.   The Duchess
seized his hand and said : *"Je suis bien heureuse de voir l'ambassa-
deur de France, je suis Française et fière d'être Française."*   At the
end of the reception the Ambassador said, not without pride, and
justified pride : *"Nos femmes françaises sont patriotes, qu'elles soient
servantes ou princesses."*

I asked the Kaiser how it was that our German princesses were
often very different from the French, British, Russian, and Italian
princesses, the daughters of the princes of other countries.   He
suggested that it probably had something to do with the weaker
national sense of the German.   I have heard Herbert Bismarck
put it much more hotly on occasion : the patriotic shortcomings of
the German princesses and princes who found a home abroad were
due to the fact that the German people had never known how to
bring its princes to reason as the French had done on many occasions, the English in dealing with Charles I and James II, the
Italians during the Risorgimento, the Spaniards with Queen Isabella and Don Carlos, the Swedes with the Vasas, the Russians in
conspiracies and assassinations.   It is unhappily a fact that during
the World War, Queen Elizabeth of Belgium, a Wittelsbach, Queen

Marie of Roumania, a Wettin of the Coburg branch, Princesses Victoria, Elizabeth, and Alix of Darmstadt, daughters of the very ancient line of Brabant-Hesse, ostentatiously denied their German fatherland. Queen Mary of England, a Teck-Württemberg, the Duchess Helen of Albany, a Waldeck, Princess Elisaveta Mavri-Kievna, a Wettin of the Altenburg branch, at least did not make a parade of their opinions; Princess Marie Pavlovna, a Princess of Mecklenburg, only did so in the evening of her days. It is sad to have to observe that in the German nation, and in the German nation alone, just as widespread a deficiency of national pride is allowed at the top in age-old German princely houses as in the lower levels of Communism.

Next to the Duke of Connaught on the quay stood a gentleman in a blue evening dress with golden buttons, the sight of whom gave the Kaiser an unpleasant start. For in England William II felt himself, at all events in externals, entirely an Englishman, and as is well-known Englishmen do not wear evening dress in the mornings. The gentleman in diplomatic uniform was the German Counsellor of Embassy, Count Karl Pückler, a tactful, cautious diplomat, with experience and good manners, and in addition a fine musician, a gift which won him many hearts in society. But he was very nearsighted, and this gave him a quality of nervousness and uneasiness. I gave him a friendly tip to put on an overcoat — then his morning swallow-tails would not startle the Kaiser again. Unfortunately, however, he had lost his overcoat on the journey, and in the special train which took us to Windsor he met the Kaiser twice in his unlucky swallow-tails. At Windsor there was a great reception at the railway station, the Queen being represented by the Prince of Wales; then we entered the Castle. I bracket Windsor and the New Palace in Potsdam as the two finest palaces in the world. My Prussian heart is certainly lifted higher in the palace built by our great King after the Seven Years' War, the palace in which the noble soul of Emperor Frederick expired. But Windsor awakens yet more ancient and renowned memories than any German castle, and is incomparable in the luxury of its appointments, the beauty of the paintings hung in its galleries, and the charm of its surroundings. Every morning William II annoyed the gentlemen of his military entourage by pointing to Windsor Tower and saying to them : "From this tower the world is ruled." It was true that the tremendous memories of English history and the tremendous power of the British world empire find their embodiment in Windsor. After going through the apartments assigned to him the Kaiser asked me to see him and said to me with a delighted expression : "This is the finest reception and the most inspiring impression of my life. Here, where as a child I went along holding my mother's hand and marvelling modestly and timidly at the splendour, I am now staying as Emperor-King."

At that moment a telegram was brought to the Kaiser which contained the news that the Willing Workers' Bill had not merely not been referred by the Reichstag to a Commission, but, in spite of every effort on the part of Count Posadowsky, had been rejected *sans phrase* at the second reading.

William II's incautious oratory had provided the opportunity of nicknaming the Willing Workers' Bill the "Prisons Bill"; now the Socialists, in an ugly phrase, talked of a "burial" of the Bill. The Kaiser, who had gone to work all too impetuously in his advocacy of the Bill, took its rejection with equanimity amid the flattering impressions of Windsor. Meanwhile half a squad of Horse Guards had marched into the great castle courtyard, enormous, magnificent officers, on splendid horses, such as are only to be seen in England. While the Kaiser's admiring glance was travelling over these riders and their steeds, he noticed an unlucky man in blue swallow tails with golden buttons, who was trying to worm his way through the riders, disturbing some of the horses. It was Pückler, who had now definitely spoilt himself for England in the Kaiser's eyes. I took care to make sure that this amiable and able diplomat should be transferred elsewhere in the same capacity, *i.e.* as Counsellor of Embassy. He was sent to Vienna, where he felt happier than in England.

The banquet took place on November 21. When the guests had assembled, the Queen appeared, a little old woman, not of striking

appearance, brought in a priceless litter by four Hindus wearing
rich silkstuffs and bedecked with jewels. Alongside the litter
walked the Kaiser, showing every mark of deep respect and venera-
tion for his grandmother. At dinner the Kaiser sat facing the
Queen. My seat was near the Queen, and I was able to observe her
well. There was something touching in her whole bearing and
her way of eating and drinking. In these moments this woman
ruler of a world empire reminded one of some good old soul in Hannover, Hamburg, or Holstein as she carefully prodded the potatoes
on her plate to find the softest, or cut the wing of her chicken.
Behind her there stood the bearers of her litter, sons of Indian
princes. In striking contrast to the banquets in Berlin, where the
bands play our splendid Prussian marches with such a blaze of
sound that it is difficult to hear one's neighbour talk, though in
pauses between the marches the conversation goes on briskly, there
was almost complete silence at the dinner at Windsor, broken only
by the following short toast proposed by the Prince of Wales:
"The German Emperor and the German Empress" — replied to by
the Kaiser with "The Queen." The Englishman, not without
reason, considers the German, especially at meals, too noisy. I
remember a breakfast at Friedrichshof, not long before the death
of the poor Empress Frederick. None of the Court were present,
only the Empress, her eldest son, my wife, and I. Kaiser William
was speaking with his usual vivacity, but not particularly loud, when
his mother broke in in an aggrieved tone: "Please do not speak so
loud," adding, with a sigh, "Germans have such a habit of speaking too loud."

At the end of the meal Queen Victoria left the banqueting hall
with the same ceremonial with which she had come, and was taken
to a gallery, where the reception took place. Opposite the Queen
stood her sons and grandsons, and she beckoned to them one
by one, and gave them her hand to kiss, which the Princes did in
the most reverential way. Meanwhile I had long conversations,
some of them of much interest, with courtiers and Ministers whom
I had known years before, and with various of the diplomats
present. All of them agreed in saying that there was no doubt

anywhere in England as to the ultimate victory over the Boers, although the latest news from the front was unfavourable. Everyone in Britain was for a fight to the finish. There was a good deal of feeling against Chamberlain, who was primarily responsible for the Boer war. Lord Salisbury was said to have been reluctant to go to war, but now that Chamberlain had brought war about the Prime Minister would set all his pride, as well as the confidence in himself that he felt as an Englishman and as a Cecil, on fighting the war to the bitter end. The German guests were treated with special friendliness by the old Duke of Cambridge, who had for many years been the supreme army commander, though as a Guelph he had never forgiven us for the annexation of Hannover. He said very finely to me: "The war in South Africa is not going too well at present, and its origin and the political side of it are very open to question. But it is giving the British nobility the opportunity of showing that they still know how to die, and I am glad of that."

When I got to my room I found there the following letter from the Ambassador, dated Brighton, November 19:

I came here to get well and strong again, but I unfortunately caught a bad cold, which has kept me to my room for several days, and the doctor will not let me take a railway journey of any length. I need hardly say what a disappointment it is to me to have been unable to be present at the reception of the Kaiser at Windsor. I am, however, clinging to the hope that I may be able to pay my homage to His Majesty on Tuesday, or at latest Wednesday, and may then be able to call on your Excellency. In case I should have no opportunity of seeing your Excellency before your first meeting with Salisbury, I venture to make the following remarks, entirely in confidence:

1. So far I have noticed no actual sign of irritation in Salisbury himself over our relations with Chamberlain. If the irritation exists, it is with Chamberlain and not with us. Apart from that, I think it may be taken definitely that Salisbury was, after all, himself in favour of the accommodation with us over Samoa. He assured me once more in our last conversation, *after* the agreement had been concluded, that he was convinced that Samoa was of no importance to Britain. The only trouble, he said, with which he had had to contend at any time was

merely the disfavour with which Australia and New Zealand viewed the cession to us — an attitude which, as things were, had to be taken into account here. It appears, by the way, that the agreement was not due solely to Mr. Chamberlain's efforts. I have it *in strict confidence* from the Austrian Ambassador that Lord Salisbury told him shortly before the initialling that the agreement was being concluded *because Her Majesty the Queen wished it so.*

2. It is one of Lord Salisbury's traits with which, so long as he is at the helm, we are, after all, bound to reckon, that he has a positive terror of personal discussions and of claims on which he cannot count in advance. This applies particularly to any conversation with His Majesty, the idea of which fills him with anxiety, and it must also in my view be expected, though he will take great pains to conceal it, in his talk with your Excellency. I have done all I could to prepare the ground, giving him very plainly to understand, in the course of our last interview, that our purpose in the settlement of the Samoa question lay *simply and purely* in removing the possibility of further friction and so making good relations possible. *If there was no desire here for alliances (he agreed emphatically to this), that was entirely as we wished and as we viewed matters.* If your Excellency would speak a word in confirmation of this in the course of your interview, this will probably set Lord Salisbury entirely at ease, and he will talk openly and in a friendly spirit. Still more so if His Majesty the Kaiser would graciously take your Excellency's advice to let fall a word or two in the same sense.

3. From a remark which Lord Salisbury made in our last interview I got the impression that he does not consider there is any likelihood of an *early* conflict between Japan and Russia, but does not give up hope of it. He did not by any means scout the idea of its possibility, only remarking that Japan is not ready with her navy and needs another couple of years on this account.

4. The factor of whom we have especially to take account here — so far as I may venture to express a judgment — is, and will continue to be, Mr. Chamberlain, whose influence, if he victoriously overcomes his difficulties in South Africa, is bound, humanly speaking, greatly to increase. I do not attach any particular importance to his ill-humour at the moment at the attitude of the German press; I do not think this will deter him from trying to secure closer coöperation with us, and, if necessary, making proportionate sacrifice for the purpose. For this reason I should have considered it desirable for your Excellency to have a confidential talk

with him, *but not to enter into any definite obligations as to German policy.*
I should like to be able to talk further to your Excellency about this.

With sincere regards,

I am

Your Excellency's most faithful

Hatzfeldt

Hatzfeldt had thus advised me to have a confidential talk with
Mr. Chamberlain, but subject to undertaking no definite obligations in regard to German policy.   In the same spirit the Imperial
Chancellor had given the Kaiser an *aide-mémoire*, drafted by Holstein but carefully examined and approved by Hohenlohe, as a
vade mecum for the Kaiser's political conversations and his whole
attitude in England.   This "*pro memoria*", which came on to me
"for information and guidance", ran as follows:

Beyond any question your Majesty is more gifted than any of your
relations, male or female.   Your relations, however, do not extend to
you a respect commensurate with the brilliance of your qualities — quite
apart from the powerful position held by the German Kaiser.   The reason
is that your Majesty has always met your relatives openly and honourably, has initiated them into your plans and hopes, and has thus provided
them with the opportunity of putting obstacles in your way.   For the
most adroit of thrusts, if announced in advance, can be parried even by a
weaker fencer.   This English journey offers your Majesty the opportunity of righting this topsy-turvy situation and winning for your
Majesty at a stroke the authority which is properly due to your Majesty's
high qualities and great power.   All that your Majesty need do to secure
this is to avoid all political conversations.   This applies above all to any
talk with Lord Salisbury.   His habit for years past has been, whatever
discussion might arise, academic or practical, concerning the determination of British and German spheres of influence, to turn down the German
suggestions with the phrase: "*Vous demandez trop pour votre amitié.*"
He has also repeatedly, in talking to various people, expressed anxiety
lest Germany should profit by the occasion of your Majesty's presence
in England to come forward with impossible suggestions.   The impression
made on him will be all the greater if your Majesty does not express a
desire to receive him in special audience but, at any meeting with him at
Windsor or Osborne, merely disposes of him fairly quickly and with

immaculate politeness, but with everyday small talk and no more, asking how his wife is and so on. Lord Salisbury's goodwill is no longer an essential condition of successful negotiations, as is shown by the Samoa agreement, to which he was compelled to agree against his will by the use we made of the political situation and by Mr. Chamberlain.

The same reserve, combined with the utmost graciousness, is desirable with Mr. Chamberlain, though for quite a different reason. Mr. Chamberlain will try and rush matters, and, while ready himself to offer substantial concessions, will try to push your Majesty there and then into definite promises with their point aimed against Russia. If your Majesty, finding Mr. Chamberlain irrepressible, will just listen politely to him and then give him the reply that his suggestion merits careful consideration and that your Majesty will "give your full attention" to it, I have no doubt that the offers which Mr. Chamberlain will be ready to make by way of payment for Germany's diplomatic coöperation, and even for her firm neutrality, will grow in proportion as your Majesty exhibits quiet indifference and an absence of *empressement*. If the Minister's soundings remain without result, probably H. R. H. the Prince of Wales or perhaps H. M. the Queen herself will touch on the question where and how Britain and Germany might be able to coöperate politically. It would be precisely at this point, in my most humble opinion, that it would then be of far-reaching influence on Germany's political future if your Majesty were to decline to agree to anything definite, to permit no glimpses to be obtained of your Majesty's own plans, and merely to confine yourself to variations on this theme: "As things are, my neutrality is sufficient for the purposes of British policy, and at present this neutrality is a fact discernible by all. Of course the political situation may change any day, and I can conceive cases in which Germany and Britain might regard it as consonant with their respective interests to give a more definite expression to the fact of the similarity of their interests; but no such case arises at present."

If your Majesty speaks in these terms, it will be realized in England that your Majesty has no intention of making an offer at the first sign they make, but that they must make the first move, and must make a better offer than the mess of pottage Lord Salisbury is so fond of offering, if they want your Majesty to throw your political weight into the British scale. So long as the British imagine that they can get along without your Majesty, they will make no offer whatever. If, on the other hand, they think your Majesty is of service, or needed, whether for defence or for the support of a policy of acquisition, they will come along; and the conditions which you may then demand will be the more advantageous the less they know in England of your Majesty's ultimate views and final aims. I may remind you that Disraeli says somewhere in one of his books: "There is a consummate policy in never saying one's last word."

CHAPTER XX

ON November 22 I received a visit at Windsor from Sir Frank Lascelles, the British Ambassador in Berlin. He read me a letter from Lord Salisbury, the Prime Minister, of which the contents were as follows: Lord Salisbury greatly regretted that he would have no opportunity of seeing me. He had a pleasant memory of having met me once in my parents' home during the Berlin Congress, when I was a young diplomat. He was tied, however, to the sickbed, perhaps the deathbed, of Lady Salisbury, and could not leave her at present. (Lady Salisbury died a few days later.) Instead of seeing him, the letter continued, I would be seeing Chamberlain, the Colonial Secretary. Chamberlain was a great and gifted man, *but he spoke only for himself, not for the Cabinet.* In reading the Premier's letter to me, Sir Frank Lascelles emphasized the words indicating that the Colonial Secretary's views and proposals did not bind the Premier or the Cabinet.

I was visited by the Colonial Secretary in the afternoon. Joseph Chamberlain was then sixty-three years old, but I should have taken him for no more than fifty. His youthful appearance was the more remarkable since he was unlike most of his compatriots in that he had no interest in sports and games, playing neither golf nor lawn tennis, never hunting or yachting or even going for walks. Not only that, but he was in the habit of smoking very long and very strong Havana cigars. He was of medium height. Rather a long head, a smooth, clean-shaven face, a fine and lofty forehead, a prominent nose, cold eyes. Even in England, where everyone dresses well and Disraeli, in one of his novels, has a young man who is advised by an experienced elder to make it his first rule always to go to the best

tailor, Chamberlain stood out by the elegance of his cutaway and of
his evening dress, the fine orchid in his buttonhole, and his gold-
rimmed monocle. The first time Disraeli caught sight of him in the
House of Commons, he remarked that young Chamberlain wore his
monocle "like a gentleman." From those lips that was great
praise, and praise that went for much. In the German Reichstag,
with our tendency to *Ruppigkeit*,[1] a word for which other languages scarcely have an adequate equivalent, the façade of Chamberlain's great house and picture gallery would mark it down as a
"dandy" or a "buffoon", and it would be a subject for amusement
or contempt. The "practical" and "serious" German's carelessness of appearance and all externals, which often degenerates into
unceremoniousness, contributed not a little to the estrangement between Germans and Englishmen. Not long before the outbreak of
the war a very influential Englishman said to me: "A big German
fleet on top of the bad German manners is more than we can stand."
Chamberlain was the son of a London bootmaker; young Joe began
as a cobbler's apprentice. Later, Joe was sent by his father to his
maternal uncle to work in his screw factory. Lloyd George too is
the son of a respectable shoemaker in Wales. It is rather significant
that the proudest aristocracy in the world should have entrusted the
conduct of the country's affairs to the Israelite Disraeli and the
cobblers' sons Chamberlain and Lloyd George. It is also rather
significant that the two artisans' sons and the Jew were all eager to
assimilate themselves to the country's aristocracy not only by the
exhibition of unswerving patriotism and pronounced nationalism,
but also in their style of life and demeanour. There is no more
democratic aristocracy than the British, and no more aristocratic
democracy. Both Chamberlain and Lloyd George, like many
eminent British politicians, especially among the Liberals and
Radicals, were dissenters, *i.e.* members of sects which had parted
from the established church not so much on points of doctrine as of
ecclesiastical constitution and the ordering of the religious services.

In conversation Chamberlain conveyed the impression of an able,
energetic, shrewd business man, capable on occasion of ruthlessness,

[1] Shabbiness.

regarding and determining everything, even more than most of his compatriots, exclusively from the standpoint of British policy. He was entirely British also in his habit of being guided solely by the immediate end — in this case the winning of the Boer war which he had precipitated — in the conviction that everything else would settle itself somehow or other in due course. He began by giving me a lively and very candid account of his views and plans. His ideal, he said, was Anglo-German-American collaboration. That grouping would control the world. It would relegate barbaric Russia to her proper bounds and compel turbulent France to keep the peace. I replied with equal candour that such a grouping — Mr. Chamberlain had not used the word "alliance" and I would not be before him in letting it out — was possible in my opinion, subject to two provisos. The collaboration between the three Powers must, to begin with, not be directly aimed against Russia. Chamberlain said it was in the interest of the whole world to set a limit to the Russian plans of expansion. I pointed out to him that Germany was in a different and more precarious situation than Britain in regard to Russia. We had a common frontier with Russia; Britain was protected by the sea, and a Russian enterprise against India would be more difficult to carry through than a Russian advance on Königsberg or even Berlin. With such different risks to face we should in any case need guarantees from Britain and precisely defined assurances to cover the event of complications leading to war. The second proviso for friendship and the closest possible collaboration with Britain — which, as I repeatedly insisted, was eagerly desired not only by myself personally but by Prince Hohenlohe, the Imperial Chancellor, and by Kaiser William — was that, especially while the Boer war was still in progress, Britain must have regard to our public opinion and must avoid everything calculated to irritate it unduly. Mr. Chamberlain, speaking with politeness but not without some British arrogance, said that in Germany there is no such thing as public opinion. The German people had only the emotions which its Government required it to have. When the Prince of Wales thanked the Kaiser for coming to England in spite of the pro-Boer agitation in Germany, the Kaiser had replied:

"I am the sole master of German policy, and my country must follow me wherever I go."

The Kaiser, continued Chamberlain, was telling everyone who would listen that he himself was German public opinion, and that the Germans thought as he required them to think. I knew the Kaiser too well not to be aware that, though he might not have expressed himself so crudely as all that, he was certainly inclined to represent himself before foreigners, and especially before Englishmen, as virtually in a position to say, in the style of Louis XIV, "*L'état, c'est moi.*"

I made it clear to the British Colonial Minister that we had not in Germany so well-informed a public opinion as in Britain; we had not a public life with so long a past; our people, itself richly endowed in many directions, had endowed humanity with greater gifts than any other people in the world since the Greeks, but it was more gifted in the realms of philosophy, art, and science than in that of politics. But public opinion even in Germany had to be reckoned with by every Government, and by the Kaiser too, if he did not want to suffer unpleasantnesses. The Kaiser, I said, had shown not only political insight but strength of character as a politician in undertaking his trip to England now of all times, in spite of the sympathy felt for the Boers in Germany, as in every other country, and especially in France. I should take up a firm stand in the Reichstag and elsewhere against every attack on this journey, or on our entirely friendly policy towards England. But this was just the time when any incidents that might needlessly arouse irritation in Germany against Britain should be avoided. We should only have success if the German nation and German public opinion were not forced or rushed, but gently familiarized — *suaviter in modo* — with the advantages of a British-German understanding and a further and intimate *rapprochement*.

This conversation between Chamberlain and myself was carried on in the friendliest tone. Kaiser William had already had a fairly long talk with Mr. Chamberlain after the banquet of November 21. The Colonial Secretary had mentioned his desire for a comprehensive understanding between Germany, Britain, and America, and the

Kaiser had replied that a wide measure of collaboration of this sort had its drawbacks for both parties. It was not in accordance with British traditions to conclude formal alliances, while Germany's policy was confined within definite limits, at all events for the present, by her excellent relations with Russia. There were, however, a number of matters on which Germany and Britain could come to an arrangement, case by case. The two countries could further pursue the path of special agreements which had already been entered on with advantage in two cases. The Kaiser added that it was in Britain's interest to show consideration towards the German, with his sensitiveness, his dogmatism, and his tendency to be guided by sentiment; to avoid trying his patience, and to show him goodwill even in small things. The German, he said, is touchy; the more this was borne in mind in England the better for the relations between the two countries.

Mr. Balfour and Lord Lansdowne, the Minister of War, whom I saw later, dwelt less on the idea of closer association than Mr. Chamberlain had done. Both of them plainly viewed the idea of a comprehensive British-German alliance much more coldly. Balfour seemed to me the typical distinguished British statesman. He was of an old Scottish family, and on his mother's side a nephew of Salisbury, the Prime Minister — his mother was of the family of the Cecils, which has given England great parliamentarians and Ministers. Educated at Eton and Cambridge, he made his first speech when only twelve years old, at a meeting in East Lothian, and while quite a young man was distinguished among the members of the Lower House for his intelligence and wit. Mr. Balfour impressed one in conversation as a man of many-sided culture. There was nothing improbable in the tales that were told of his aesthetic inclinations, his liking for the Pre-Raphaelites and for Handel's oratorios, and his habit of philosophic contemplation of men and things. Yet nothing would be more misleading than to seek for any points of resemblance between Arthur James Balfour and Theobald von Bethmann-Hollweg. His philosophic speculations never dimmed the clarity of Balfour's political outlook, his aesthetic tastes did not abate from his will power and energy. Bethmann-Hollweg let us blunder into war when foresight and a wider vision might have prevented it; afterwards, when the explosion had come and only strength and energy could save us, he showed weak political leadership; Balfour was a cautious servant of his country in peace and a resolute one in war. Bethmann restored Poland, committing one of the grossest errors in the history of Prussia and Germany; Balfour as Secretary of State for Ireland mastered the rebellious "green isle" with an iron hand. His political judgment was calm, considered, and sensible. He seemed to be sincerely in favour of British-German collaboration, though he himself pointed out to me that, in view of the strong competition which we were offering to British industry and commerce, such collaboration would be more difficult than between Britain and France, who was scarcely a serious rival of Britain's. I mentioned to Lord Salisbury's nephew and confidant that what we wanted of Britain was rather of a negative than a positive nature; we had nothing special to ask or expect of Britain, but we were anxious that there should be neither misunderstandings nor friction nor needless provocation between Germany and Britain. Mr. Balfour replied that there was no British statesman who would not gladly subscribe to this programme. There was not in England the deep envy of Germany's economic expansion which many Germans imagined. Britain was too strong, too rich, had for long been economically too far ahead of all other countries, to have any reason for serious fear of German competition. The African agreement between Britain and Germany was a very useful arrangement, and its execution would be of service to both parties. In Asia Minor, too, Britain would put no obstacles in the way of German enterprises, and in particular would do nothing to obstruct the Anatolian Railway. Mr. Balfour complained, on the other hand, bitterly of the attitude of the German press, which was much more Anglophobe than the British was Teutophobe. I pointed out that Mr. Saunders, the very anti-German correspondent of the *"Times"* in Berlin, was making a hobby of raking up from the obscurest German papers every discoverable tactless phrase, and presenting them to the British public on the very day in an accentuated form. Mr. Balfour did not dispute the virulently anti-

German attitude of the leading British newspaper, but declared his readiness to bring about a change at least in the representation of the *"Times"* in Berlin. He spoke of France in a tone of pitying disparagement; he denied that there were any unbridgeable differences between Britain and Russia, Asia being big enough for both, but expressed his concern at the impending dissolution, as he imagined, of the Hapsburg Monarchy. He suggested that if that came the German Austrians would probably join the German Empire. I replied that that would amount in effect to a return to the status quo ante 1866, for the ending of which Prussia had waged a sanguinary war. We wanted the continued existence of the Austro-Hungarian monarchy, if only because otherwise the whole of the Balkan peninsula would fall under Russian influence. Kaiser William said to Balfour, whom he received on November 22, that he had not come to England as a "begging cousin", but sincerely and heartily desired to preserve peaceful relations with the British Empire, undisturbed by incidents.

Lord Lansdowne was reputed Francophile, because his mother was French. To me his attitude seemed matter of fact and reasonable. British national feeling is, moreover, much too strong and British pride too great for any admixture of foreign blood, whether on the mother's side or through marriage, to be able to weaken a Briton's patriotism. The Duke of Devonshire, who as an old friend of my mother-in-law's treated me with special kindness, was the true type of the British grand seigneur, to whom his hunting and horses matter more at bottom than any political scheme, but who, for all that, carries into his political activities British common sense and the firm conviction, born of the traditional pride of the Englishman, that in the last resort Britain is more than a match for all other Powers and has nothing really to fear. In evidence of the imperturbable equanimity of the Duke of Devonshire, King Edward once told me of the following small incident. So long as his father had been alive, the Duke of my time had been Marquis of Hartington and leader of the Whigs in the Lower House. As such, he was making in the course of a tedious debate an equally tedious speech, when in the middle of it he suddenly began to yawn. "He yawned over his own tediousness," said the Prince (later King Edward), "but after he had had a huge yawn he went ahead with his speech without turning a hair." The Marquis of Hartington was a great sportsman and was fond of foxhunting. Once in the hunting season he appeared at an early sitting of the Lower House in a red hunting coat and white breeches, as he intended to go straight from the sitting to the meet. To avoid soiling the impeccable whiteness of his carefully chalked breeches, he had made his valet tie on him a great white apron, and in this garb he took his seat on his party's front bench. One need only try to imagine Eugen Richter or Herr Friedrich Payer so attired to lead the Liberal Party in the German Reichstag, in order to appreciate the vast difference between the British and German mentality and British and German parliamentarism.

In contrast to this thorough English aristocrat, Mr. Goschen, in his shrewdness and plodding energy, reminded me rather of a German Permanent Head of Department. He had the same Christian names — Georg Joachim — as his grandfather, the Leipzig bookseller and publisher to Goethe and Wieland, but had changed his too German-sounding name of Göschen to Goschen, and set out to be a full-blooded Britisher. He was credited with having, as First Lord of the Admiralty, done more for the British navy than any of his predecessors. After the rather unfortunate Kruger Telegram of 1895, Goschen had taken the Kaiser severely to task in the House of Commons, speaking down to him from very much aloft. One of the great political qualities of the British is the gift of assimilating foreigners and foreign things. The Tecks (Cambridge) and Hohenlohes (Gleichen), the Bentincks and Barings, the Goschens and Bunsens of the second generation became entirely English. The French also have this capacity of assimilating foreigners. Marshal de Saxe, Marshal Rantzau, Kellermann and Luckner, Ney, Kleber and Rapp are distinguished names in French military history. Among the most trusted colleagues and friends of Gambetta were the Baden-born Spuller and the brothers Joseph and Salomon Reinach, born in Frankfort-on-Main. Clemenceau's *Chef de Cabinet* during the World War was Mandel, another man of German extraction, originally named Rothschild. Goethe says somewhere that the strength of a language lies not in what it sheds but in what it absorbs. The same is true of nations. Goschen (who for his services to the navy was made a Viscount) had a younger brother, Sir Edward Goschen, who before the war was British Ambassador in Berlin. Fifteen years later Bethmann-Hollweg, abandoned by all the guardian angels, was to coin in conversation with Sir Edward Goschen the phrase about a scrap of paper which, like Ollivier's phrase of forty-four years before, of the "*coeur léger*", was to have all the effect of a lost battle. As a reward for the promptitude with which he recorded in a sober and calmly expressed report this shocking lapse on the part of the German Chancellor, and so pinned it down for all future time, like a naturalist carefully preserving for the museum a rare butterfly which he has transfixed, Sir Edward Goschen was shortly afterwards raised to the dignity of a peer of England. When the Great War broke out, England was represented in two of the most important positions, Vienna and Berlin, by Ambassadors of German descent: in Vienna by Bunsen, the grandson of a Prussian Ambassador to the court of England, and in Berlin by Goschen, whose grandfather had published the first collected editions of the works of Goethe, Wieland, and Klopstock, and of the early poems of Schiller.

On the day after my arrival at Windsor, I was received by Queen Victoria in "the Queen's private closet," *i.e.* in the Queen's small drawing-room. She offered me a seat by her side, and enquired in the most friendly way after the health of my wife, who had been presented to her by the Empress Frederick during the visit which Queen Victoria had paid to her dying son-in-law, the Emperor Frederick, at Charlottenburg, in the spring of 1888. It was thoroughly English of the Queen to remark that her eldest daughter was in the habit of saying: "Marie Bülow is my best friend — on the Continent." Angeli, the artist, when he had to paint the portrait of the Queen, had said to Count Götz von Seckendorff, the Empress Frederick's Lord High Steward, with Viennese facetiousness and an artist's candour, that Her Majesty of Great Britain and Ireland looked "like a *schwammerl*." Let me add, for the benefit of non-Austrians, that "*schwammerl*" is equivalent to "mushroom." But in spite of her small stature, Queen Victoria had something really royal in her appearance and ways. I have seldom seen so much naturalness, simplicity, and dignity united in one personality as in hers. She had then already been sixty-two years on the throne, which she ascended at the age of eighteen. She told me that at her accession my great-uncle, Heinrich Bülow, was the Prussian Ambassador to England, "a most excellent man", to whom she had been much attached. She asked after his widow, my late great-aunt Gabriele von Bülow, the daughter of Wilhelm von Humboldt. She added, in a kindly way, that Lord Beaconsfield, whom she esteemed so highly, had mentioned my parents, as well as myself and a brother of mine, in a friendly manner in a letter addressed to the Queen during the Congress of Berlin. She would give directions for a copy of this letter to be sent to me. The letter addressed to Her Most Gracious Majesty by the Earl of Beaconsfield on July 4, 1878, during the Congress of Berlin, reads as follows:

I dined with the Minister of State, Bülow, a small party, about sixteen. An accomplished and apparently most amiable family. Bülow himself is attractive from his experience, highly courteous tho' natural manners; his wife, lively and well informed, and two or three sons at table, who I really think were the best-looking, the best-dressed and the best-mannered young gentlemen I ever met. They were all in the army, but she has seven sons, equally engaging, it is said." [1]

The Queen then turned to politics. Without going into details, she told me, with apparently entire sincerity, that she had always, in agreement with her ever-remembered husband, been for friendship and "good understanding" between Germany and England. Misunderstandings between the two were very regrettable, and real enmity quite unthinkable, both being good, civilized, Christian, Protestant peoples. The Queen seemed disturbed by the exceedingly spiteful utterances of the German Press against England in connection with the Boer War. She said it was undesirable to

---

[1] The letter sent to me by the Queen is printed in "The Life of Benjamin Disraeli, Earl of Beaconsfield", by George Buckle (London, John Murray, Albemarle Street, W., 1920, Volume VI, 1876–1881, p. 331).

irritate the English too much with Press attacks. The Englishman was slow and indolent, but if he was blamed too much, and, as he believed, too unjustly, especially by the Press of his German cousin, he might finish by losing patience. The Queen expressed great regret that I was not able to see Lord Salisbury, whom she described as an eminent statesman. Chamberlain she did not mention.

When Queen Victoria received me, she was looking back not only on an unusually long but also an unusually brilliant and prosperous reign, one of the most prosperous reigns in the history of the world. Anyone who has read her correspondence and the biography of her husband, Prince Albert, which she inspired, must look with admiration on such conscientiousness and such a high degree of tact. She had a strong will, and, with all her outward modesty, justifiable but uncommonly great self-reliance, but for all that she never attempted to go beyond the limits of the British Constitution and of British tradition. She had a great predilection for Disraeli and a strong dislike for Gladstone; but when the Parliamentary situation demanded it, she dismissed Disraeli and appointed Gladstone Prime Minister. In her home she was surrounded with the tenderest love, with the respect and blind obedience of the whole of her family. When she was staying at Osborne, her daughters and sons-in-law used to ask during the morning, not without agitation, whether and for how many hours they might receive permission to go out in the Royal Yacht "*Victoria and Albert.*" When King Carol of Roumania, after reigning nearly thirty years, paid Queen Victoria a visit at Windsor, Her Majesty, who was rightly pleased with his sagacious and yet candid manner, delighted him with two great proofs of her favour: she conferred on him the order of the Garter, which cannot be given to foreigners — apart from direct descendants of an English sovereign — unless they are crowned heads, and she handed him a small key to the mausoleum of her dead husband, Prince Albert, with permission to stay there for a time. The latter compliment appeared to the Queen to be the greater.

· The Queen would never have kept a Minister waiting who had to make a political report. But she once came half an hour late to a great State banquet to the diplomatic corps, because she wanted to receive a nurse of her granddaughter's, the Princess Charlotte of Meiningen, beforehand, to hear from her why she had been dismissed.   For all the voluntary self-command, which she imposed on herself as a constitutional ruler, her wifely, or rather her ancestral (for she had in time become a great-grandmother) scrutiny, penetrated into all the nurseries of her numerous descendants.   She was kind and unaffected, but always and in all circumstances she demanded the utmost correctness of form.   In the neighbourhood of Windsor there is a majestic gilt memorial to an English king of the house of Hanover which everyone calls "the coppered horse."   When on one occasion a German diplomat, who had been invited to dine with the Queen, remarked that he had taken a walk to the "coppered horse", the Queen said severely : "You mean that you have been for a walk to the memorial of the deceased King George III."   The Queen spoke as good German as English.   Her son, who was afterwards King Edward VII, spoke German with an English accent which was to some extent assumed.   Her grandson, King George V, speaks hardly any German.   The Queen had a German court-chaplain in addition to her English chaplain, and was interested in German schools and charities as well as in all reminders of Germany.   All this disappeared at her death.

Our Ambassador in London, Count Paul Hatzfeldt, had not been able to be present on the Kaiser's arrival in England, as his state of health made travelling impossible for him.   He had, however, had himself brought to Windsor, where he called on me and had a long interview with me.   In his condition of suffering he was only able to do this with a great expenditure of energy which called for my admiration.   He reminded me of a diplomat of the French *ancien régime* described thus in the memoirs of a contemporary : *"Criblé d'infirmités et de maux, presque mourant, mais d'une indomptable énergie et d'une parfaite lucidité."*   Hatzfeldt was persona gratissima with Queen Victoria, as well as with the Prince of Wales, and much esteemed by Salisbury.   Before our arrival the Queen had sent a telegram requesting her grandson to excuse "dear Count Hatzfeldt" from appearing at our landing in England and from all Court festivities, and generally to pay every consideration to his state of health, since everything must be done to enable "this most excellent man" to remain at his post as long as possible.

Hatzfeldt began by expressing to me his regret that I had not seen Lord Salisbury, whose will, so long as he remained in office, was paramount in the last resort. With Chamberlain we must be careful. Just now, the British in South Africa had suffered defeat after defeat; it would not prevent their ultimate success, but it had a very disturbing effect on the general public in England, and Chamberlain had only one thought, to bring the war against the Boers, by which he personally would stand or fall, to a successful conclusion. To this end he would, of course, like to make use of us against Russia and France. "We cannot take that amiss," said Hatzfeldt, "but we must not let ourselves be made use of beyond a certain point, as after all Russia is nearer Berlin than England."

Hatzfeldt was no opponent of an Anglo-German alliance. He told me smilingly that, if I brought about such an alliance on an acceptable basis, he would sincerely congratulate me, as even Prince Bismarck had not succeeded in that. It must, however, be an alliance which offered us real securities, and that in a twofold direction: in the first place, we must not expose ourselves to the risk, in the event of our being involved in a war, of the British Ministry which had concluded the alliance with us resigning and its successor not acknowledging the treaty of alliance. That was always possible in England, if we did not secure the assent of "Her Majesty's most loyal Opposition" beforehand. Further, I must be clear about one thing. He, Hatzfeldt, appreciated my gift of oratory. But even I would have difficulty in winning the Reichstag and the German people for a treaty by which we must come to the assistance of England whenever she was attacked in India or Canada or in some other of her numerous colonies and overseas possessions, while England remained with grounded arms if the Russians marched against Austria or the French against Italy.

The general impression which I received from my conversation with Hatzfeldt was that he regarded an alliance with England accompanied by firm guarantees and approximately equal obligations as a good thing, but an alliance without such guarantees and assumptions as very dangerous. As for the general world situation he was of opinion that we should have to use a prudent and intelligent policy to steer our ship of State past crags and sandbanks, until changes in the position in Europe, such as never fail to occur, permitted better progress in quiet waters. He expressed his confidence that I would succeed in bringing us past Scylla and Charybdis. We had, he thought, now only one primary interest, — to keep peace, as time was in our favour. Count Hatzfeldt was glad to be able to talk things out with me. In writing, even in private letters, it was not possible to say everything, since both the Kaiser and "our good Holstein" did not always keep within bounds, were altogether too impressionable, and overshot the mark now in one direction and now in the other. I seemed, he added to my pleasure, to have inherited good nerves and calm judgment from my father, among whose close fellow-workers he had been for many years.

The negotiations for an Anglo-German alliance were also conducted by me later, when Imperial Chancellor, from the same points of view which regulated my action as Secretary of State, — points of view which had the full approval of Prince Hohenlohe. We had to be sure that the whole Cabinet and above all the Prime Minister would support such an alliance bona fide and with inward conviction. We even had to desire that the Opposition should declare its agreement — at any rate in principle — to an Anglo-German alliance. For otherwise there was a risk that England, in the event of warlike entanglements, might free herself from the bonds of the alliance, so far as might appear to her desirable or convenient, by means of a change of Cabinet. We had to insist that, if we allowed the British Colonies, and particularly the Indian Empire with its three hundred million inhabitants and its frontiers exposed towards the north, to be included in the alliance, Britain on her part should recognize an attack on Austria by the Russians or on Italy by the French as a *casus belli*. Lord Salisbury had wrongly charged Prince Hohenlohe with a one-sided predilection for Russia. Such partiality was as far from being in the Prince's mind as in mine. Like myself, he valued very highly the advantage of friendly relations with Britain, and looked upon good terms with that country as doubly desirable since we had begun to build a navy. He enjoyed, moreover, the special favour of Queen Victoria as well as of her daughter, the Empress Frederick. I have myself read the autograph letter of condolence which the old Queen, who seldom took up a pen, addressed to Prince Chlodwig Hohenlohe after the death of his wife, a letter couched in the most cordial terms. But Prince Hohenlohe possessed in a high degree what Bismarck called "knightly perspective." He looked upon everything from a high watchtower. With his great political experience, extending over more than fifty years, with his knowledge of mankind, his flair, and the calm, somewhat sceptical — in political affairs icy cold — manner in which he regarded men and things, he seldom made a mistake in large questions. My successor as Secretary of State for the Foreign Office, Baron von Richthofen, and Mühlberg, the under-Secretary of State, had throughout their past careers been not anti-British, but pro-British, and both their political and their economic outlook confirmed them in this. Both were Liberals, both inclined in economic thought so much to the Manchester school that, during the struggles over the Customs tariff, although they conscientiously did their duty it was only with inner repugnance, in spite of their personal respect for me, that they followed me in my agrarian path. They were not so Russophobe as Holstein, but they were far from having any predilection or even special regard for Russia. Nevertheless, both Richthofen and Mühlberg, just like Prince Hohenlohe, considered that to yield to Chamberlain's blandishments would be highly dangerous without firm guarantees from the British side. I well remember receiving one morning a letter from Richthofen, which must be in the archives, in which he wrote to the effect that he had had a sleepless night, not having been able to free his mind from the Chamberlain offer, with its importance for the future of our policy and for the general world situation. He begged me not to agree to Chamberlain's proposals without *firm English guarantees*.

In the trade section of the Foreign Ministry, which also had a voice in political questions and was listened to, there were old sympathies with England and in favour of coöperation with England specially. But even here there was great hesitation about the manner in which Chamberlain was trying to lasso us. That a Dr. Fischer, who is not personally known to me, should have written a book with the sensational title "Herr von Holstein's Great No", in order to prove that the said Minister had held Germany back at the entrance into the Paradise of the British alliance, like the cherubims of old, who, as the Book of Genesis tells us, barred the way to the tree of life for our ancestors, Adam and Eve, with a naked-edged sword, only shows that people who are otherwise well-informed and intelligent can make mistakes if they write about men and matters with which they are not acquainted. Holstein, as I believe I have already said, was not anti- but pro-British, always had been, and, as much as his nature permitted, was warmly, almost passionately so. Although by birth a Pomeranian squire, he was as anti-Russian as any thorough-going Liberal. But he too was against agreement to the Chamberlain proposals without a firm bond and guarantee, although he long held to the hope that such guarantees would be forthcoming in the course of time. The whole Foreign Ministry, the political as well as the trade division, Holstein, Richthofen, and Mühlberg, all the controlling authorities would, like Hohenlohe and myself, have been readily prepared for a treaty with England, if the indispensable guarantees had been given. Everything was done on our side to obtain these guarantees.

How would events have shaped themselves if we had followed Mr. Chamberlain at the turn of the century? I should not like as an old man to lose myself in conjectural labyrinths, of which my good father had already warned me as a young attaché. But I may perhaps say that I incline to the view that, if we had followed Chamberlain's blandishments, we should have fared as Japan did, only with the essential difference that Japan was virtually out of Russia's reach, which we were not. Moreover, in the event of war, Japan had only Russia to deal with. We had to reckon that, if we were involved in war with Russia, the French would assail us in the rear. The chassepots would have gone off of their own accord, as Bismarck had warned us often enough. And, finally, — the main and clinching argument, — without yielding to Chamberlain's enticements, we lived in peace with England for another fifteen years, and we should have been able to live in peace with her still longer, if, in the fatal summer of 1914, Berchtold and Bethmann had not stumbled into war through their irresponsible and ill-judged handling of a Balkan question. The Great War, too, did not result from a collision with England. Scarcely a year before the outbreak of the war, a historian of such balanced judgment as Erich Marcks and a journalist in such close touch with Herr von Bethmann-Hollweg as Hans Delbrück were able to speak of the astonishing revulsion of feeling which had gradually taken place in England in our favor, although we had not accepted Chamberlain's proposals. In November, 1913, after a lengthy stay in England and a careful examination of the situation there, the conditions and the public mood, Delbrück expressed his conviction that neither economic competition nor our shipbuilding made any difference in the good relationship between Germany and England, and that, so far as the terms on which we stood with England affected it, the world situation was entirely satisfactory, peaceful, and calm. Two very important treaties with England, which were prepared by me during my period of office, — the treaty about the Portuguese colonies and the agreement over the Bagdad railway, — were on the point of being ratified. Then, as I shall narrate in detail later, the world conflagration broke out over a Balkan question. Casually and thoughtlessly, above all blunderingly, we had given the Viennese an unconsidered and unlimited blank cheque. We did not, in the summer of 1914, even take care that a safe and peaceful solution remained available in the event of our hope of localizing the Austro-Serbian conflict proving illusory.

CHAPTER XXI

Chamberlain's Character — Survey of the British Alliance Negotiations and General Impression — Letters to Hohenlohe and Holstein — Hatzfeldt's Report to the Imperial Chancellor — Visit to Sandringham — The Prince of Wales — Relations between Him and His Nephew, Kaiser William II — Lord Acton — Departure from England — The Empress Frederick on the Kaiser's Trip to England — Meeting with the Dutch Queens at Flushing.

IF we were not to commit ourselves to Britain, any more than Britain bound herself to us, then special caution was needed with regard to Mr. Chamberlain. There was hardly a British statesman who had changed so often in his political career, who had altered his standpoint so frequently and so suddenly, or with whom one must be so much prepared for surprises, for some unexpected divagation, as with Joseph Chamberlain. From a radical democrat he changed to a conservative tory, from a republican to a loyal monarchist, from a pacifist to an imperialist, from an enthusiastic free-trader and follower of Bright and Cobden to a passionate protectionist. He had advocated Home Rule for Ireland before Gladstone, but parted company with the "grand old man" when the latter brought in a Home Rule Bill, and thereby divided the Liberals, just as later he was to split the Conservative party by turning to Protection. He had been enthusiastic for the independence of the Boers, and had spoken in favour of it in Parliament and at numerous meetings, and then had pressed for war with the South African Republics more strongly than any other British politician. There was hardly a political question in which he had not, like the Sicambrian king, burned what he had previously worshipped and worshipped what he had previously burned. And, applauded by the majority of his fellow-countrymen, he defended each of these changes with the argument that it was not he but the circumstances that had altered.

There was yet another weighty reason against the inducements put forward by Chamberlain. Queen Victoria, who was without doubt peaceful, and within the limits of British interests outspokenly friendly to Germany, was in 1899 already in her eightieth year, and humanly speaking had only a short time longer to reign. Her successor, who had already participated personally and energetically in undermining the Anglo-German treaty over the Portuguese colonies, would, so far as could be foreseen, be no sure supporter of an alliance with a nation whose economic and political progress he observed with disfavour, whose ways were antipathetic to him, and whose ruler he hated. Would he have opposed the wrecking of such a treaty? For such underground work, he had at his command, in contradistinction to his venerable mother, craft and unscrupulousness. With his innate dislike of the German Empire and of everything German, with his strong predilection for France, Paris, and the French, would he, in the event of war, remain loyal and cheerfully true to the alliance with us? All questions which had to be seriously, very seriously weighed. And, finally, was it not comprehensible, in fact natural, that we should remind ourselves of the perfidious duplicity with which, by means of the insidious "Windsor Treaty", Britain had gone behind our backs to render ineffectual the treaty over the Portuguese colonies just concluded with us? Should not this suggest distrust, must it not inspire great caution? The harshness and ruthlessness with which Britain was handling all the incidents of the Boer War with regard to ourselves and only with regard to ourselves, the close-fisted pettiness which she displayed towards us and again particularly towards us in all colonial negotiations, were these encouragements to coöperate with Britain without firm and clear guarantees? We continued for some time longer to spin the threads of the Anglo-German alliance, although the casual manner in which Chamberlain dealt with this matter in public, and still more such British displays of ruthlessness as the seizure of the German mail boats, made its conclusion more and more difficult for the German Government. Chamberlain's speech at Leicester about Britain's relations with America and Germany was a *gaucherie*, I believe unintentional, but still a *gaucherie*, for, in view of the general world situation and of public opinion in Germany, such a delicate question should first have been discussed only *intra muros*, if it was intended to achieve the desired result. Chamberlain had far too much contempt for the force of German public opinion. With British arrogance he underestimated his unpopularity in Germany. He was probably also supplied with inaccurate information by Eckardstein, to whose pernicious rôle in the whole of the negotiations I shall return later.

Moreover, the statements which Chamberlain had made at Leicester about an Anglo-German-American *rapprochement* were received by the American Press more than coldly. It was inexcusable that the German Government, while striving to come to an understanding with Britain, should have had difficulties thrown in its way at a critical moment from the British side by the unjustified and absolutely brutal seizure of the German mail boats *"Bundesrat"*, *"General"*, and *"Herzog"*, of the German East Africa Line. I was told later by an English informant that this seizure was due to intrigues by the Boers, who had trapped the British local authorities in South Africa into it by anonymous denunciations. Holstein sometimes suspected that Chamberlain was never seriously in earnest in regard to closer relationship with us, but only made a show of its advocacy in order to intimidate the French and Russians and to compromise us, particularly with Russia. I do not believe that; but I do believe that Chamberlain, in his ruthless way, tried to attach us to himself at the moment when that seemed useful in order to ease his own position, in the conviction that, when the world situation changed, he would be able without great difficulty to free himself from the entanglements of his pledges. The Italians have an admirable proverb: *Passato il pericolo, gabbato il santo.* "When the peril is past, people mock at the saint."

Count Hatzfeldt continued to conduct the negotiations from the autumn of 1899 until the summer of 1901, especially with Lord Lansdowne; they were constantly and expressly designated from the English side as academic, confidential, and purely personal. Berlin adhered to the point of view that if Great Britain and her colonies, including India and Canada, were treated as a whole, the

Triple Alliance must also be treated as a whole, so that the *casus foederis* would then occur if Great Britain, the motherland, or any of the British possessions overseas were forced to take up arms in self-defence, or if the Triple Alliance were through an attack on any of the Triple Alliance Powers. That corresponded, moreover, with the Bismarck tradition and with the spirit of the Bismarck policy. I can imagine that, in a case of extreme need, Bismarck would have compounded with Russia at the expense of Austria. But I cannot imagine that Prince Bismarck, all the more after the dissolution of the tie which in his time bound us to Russia through the Re-insurance Treaty, would have left the endurance and efficacy of our alliance with the Hapsburg monarchy at the mercy of the whim of England. It was evident that, if Austria was not included in the Anglo-German alliance, it was not Germany but England that obtained the controlling influence in Vienna. The situation would then have been produced against which Prince Bismarck had given warning in his well-known conversation with the historian Sybel: Britain would be in a position in which she could leave us in the lurch at any moment that suited her, while we should be bound to follow on at her heels not only in defence but also in a fight against Russia. Even Prince Bismarck, in spite of his genius, and in spite of many efforts, was unable to secure an alliance with England in a form useful to us.

From the summer of 1901 onwards the alliance negotiations dragged out more and more, until in December, 1901, thanks to the ruthless energy of Lord Roberts and Lord Kitchener in forming the cruel concentration camps and in shooting numerous Cape rebels, the resistance of the Boers seemed finally broken, and King Edward VII wrote to the British Ambassador in Berlin, Sir Frank Lascelles, in a letter which the latter communicated to us confidentially, that he hoped that Germany and England would continue to coöperate on all points. To define this coöperation in a formal agreement was difficult, since a treaty to that end would undoubtedly encounter serious opposition and difficulties in the British Lower House. The King would not cease, however, to work in conjunction with the German Emperor for the welfare of the world.

I still believe to this day that Edward VII was keenly concerned to check both our economic progress and the growth of our political power as much as possible, that he was concerned above all to sow distrust between us and Russia and to set us at variance with Russia, and that he jumped at every opportunity of annoying his nephew personally. I am, however, just as firmly convinced that he did not want war with us. Even without any alliance with England, the peace between us and Great Britain was undisturbed up to the death of King Edward VII on May 6, 1910, and with his successor peaceful relations were still easier to preserve than previously. They had also become calm and peaceful when in midsummer 1914 the Great War broke out through the ill-judged handling on all sides of an incident in the Balkan peninsula.

Everyone knows the tale of the English traveller who, arriving at Calais after a short sea voyage, was there served with breakfast by a red-haired and not particularly polite French waiter. He wrote in his diary: "All Frenchmen have red hair and a disobliging manner." If I, after repeated but always only short stays in England, may form a general judgment, which perhaps has no other advantage than that of being the result of purely direct impressions, without any preconceived opinion, I would say that the physical, intellectual, and moral soundness of all classes struck me as the characteristic of English conditions and of English ways. England appeared to me a thoroughly sound country and nation. I found everything in England sound, from the English care of infants, which is incomparable, and the English nursery, which is the best in the world, to the grown-up Englishman, toughened by continuous bodily exercise, even in quite advanced years. With no more than such well-nourished, strong bodies, and such a strong national feeling something can be achieved. The English are in truth a nation of leaders, whose will to power is their political motive and aim, in contrast with the German, in whom the native hue of resolution is only too often sicklied o'er with the pale cast of thought. To a love of his country, which is not paraded so much as was that of the Romans, but which is perhaps still more unshakable, the Englishman unites "common sense" such as is possessed by no other nation known to me, with an intelligent and useful contempt for that grey wife, theory. The Englishman has not learnt so much as the German usually has, but his brain is the cooler on that account. The young German leaving a German place of instruction is certainly ahead of the pupil of an English school in information acquired. But, for the formation of character, for the education of the future citizen, more is achieved by the English school, whose paramount task, in view of the "struggle for life" among the peoples, is to provide the country with capable and manly citizens, having minds thoroughly national and patriotic. An Englishman once said to me that the "week-end" habit helped to prevent the British politicians from being as worried and nervous as those of the Continent. When in 1908 the Bosnian crisis entered on an acute stage, the then Foreign Minister, Sir Edward Grey, was out of reach for several days; he was fishing in Scotland, and had given orders that nothing was to be forwarded to him, as well as banning all visitors. He wanted to pursue his favourite occupation of fishing, undisturbed. I admit that only the Minister of a country protected by the sea can allow himself a protective crust of this sort. The fact that the Englishman forces his morals, his speech, his habits on the whole world, that he plays lawn tennis and golf at Homburg and Sorrento, in Ceylon and Sydney, is a sign of strength; his adherence to old habits, traditions, and systems is a proof of respect for the past, without which no great nation exists. Exemplary, above all, is the unity of the country, once there is strife with the foreigner, the sturdy conscience with which every difference with the foreigner is fought out with bulldog obstinacy on the principle of "Right or wrong, my country!" and the tolerance — more than that, the nobility in the internal party strife.

During my period as Imperial Chancellor, there was once a conversation in my house about music. A youngish German diplomat who was present delivered some admiring remarks on English concerts. Sidney Whitman, the author of the well-known books "Imperial Germany" and "The Habsburg Realm", was also present; he was well acquainted with Germany and, until the Great War, admired her, and had been a frequent visitor at the house of

Prince Bismarck. He said with a smile: "We English do not understand much about music; we are quite unmusical; in the most modest German home better music is made and with more real understanding than in all the 'after dinner' performances in English houses, or even in London concerts. But there are other spheres in which we surpass you Germans: we have a more tolerant and a much more gentlemanly political life than you." And then he related an incident of which he had been a spectator in the British Parliament. The son of Joseph Chamberlain was to make his maiden speech in the Commons. When the young man, evidently nervous, had spoken for some minutes, Mr. Gladstone looked up at the Speaker and asked for the next turn. Now Chamberlain's father was of course the man at whose hands Gladstone had experienced the cruellest disappointment of his life, who had most bitterly attacked and opposed him. Chamberlain's father moved uneasily in his seat, thinking that Gladstone would deal hardly with his offspring. When, however, young Chamberlain had finished his speech, the old man rose and in his melodious voice congratulated the House that again, as so often in English history, an eminent father had presented Parliament and the country with a son worthy of him; for in this, as in everything which promoted continuity, lay one of the foundations of English greatness. He hoped that Chamberlain's son had before him a career worthy of one of his name and of service to the country. It may, incidentally, be mentioned that this wish of old William Gladstone's was realized. When Gladstone spoke in this way, a tear ran down Joseph Chamberlain's cheek, the only one, it is asserted, which he had shed in his life. "And now," said Mr. Sidney Whitman in conclusion, "compare with this spectacle the scene when Herbert Bismarck made his début as Secretary of State in the Reichstag, and Progressives, Socialists, and members of the Centre, with Eugen Richter at their head, tried with interruptions and laughter to bring to confusion the son of the greatest German statesman of all time." When I heard this reminiscence, I thought of the remark made by the French Ambassador in Berlin when in 1895 the German Reichstag refused to congratulate Prince Bismarck on his eightieth birthday : *"Les Allemands diront et feront ce qu'ils voudront, ils ne seront jamais un grand peuple."*

Before I left England, I wrote to Prince Hohenlohe and to Herr von Holstein lengthy letters, in which I gave them my impressions. I wrote *inter alia :*

" The British politicians know little of the Continent. Many of them do not know much more of Continental circumstances than we do of the conditions in Peru or Siam. They are also, according to our ideas, rather naïve in their artless egoism, as well as in a certain blind confidence. They find difficulty in believing in really evil intentions in others, they are very calm, very phlegmatic, very optimistic. The South African war excites the people of Berlin more than it does London political circles. No one doubts that Britain will emerge well from the affair. The country exhales wealth, comfort, content, and confidence in its own power and future. It is clear that the people have never seen an enemy in their country and simply cannot believe that things could ever go really wrong, either at home or abroad. With the exception of a few leading men, they work little and leave themselves time for everything. It is physically and morally a very sound country. In general, there is no question that the feeling in Britain is much less anti-German than the feeling in Germany is anti-British. For that reason those Englishmen who, like Chirol and Saunders, know from personal observation the acuteness and depth of Germany's unfortunate dislike of Britain are the most dangerous to us. If the British public clearly realized the anti-British feeling which dominates Germany just now, a great revulsion would occur in its conception of the relations between Britain and Germany."

That revulsion took place in one of the most influential of the English, the then Prince of Wales, when, after ascending the throne, he set foot on German soil during the visit which he paid at Cronberg, at the end of February, 1901, to his dying sister, the Empress Frederick. A regular wave of deep dislike of Britain, politically foolish, but, in the German fashion, alarmingly intense, raged against him in the Press and even from the public assembled at the railway stations on his journey through Germany.

To conclude, I here give the official report which the Ambassador, Count Hatzfeldt, addressed to the Chancellor Hohenlohe, on the progress of the Emperor's visit to England, under date of December 2, 1899:

Your Excellency has already been informed of the course of the festivities in honour of His Majesty's visit to Windsor and Sandringham. All went smoothly beyond expectation. I must not, however, omit to express my firm conviction that the cordial intercourse between our Royal couple and their exalted relatives, which has been renewed under such happy auspices, will also have beneficial results in the future, and contribute towards strengthening the present confidence, to remove misunderstandings, and to prevent friction. After the many expressions of satisfaction, of pleasure, indeed of delight, which have been reported to me, I include in this confident expectation all the members of the Royal family, without exception, and above all, after the heir to the throne, his Royal Highness's son, the Duke of York. Not less lasting was the effect of personal intercourse with our exalted monarch on the Ministers of Her Majesty the Queen. Arthur Balfour stated that he had never experienced a more stimulating hour than that in which he was permitted to enjoy the honour of a long conversation with His Majesty the Kaiser and came under the spell of his personality. The elements at the Court of Her Majesty the Queen which are quite specially friendly to us, and the most influential members of the Foreign Office as well, greatly regretted that Lord Salisbury was prevented, by his deep mourning, from coming into direct contact with the Kaiser. It is believed in those quarters that Chamberlain and Arthur Balfour are looked upon among us as the real supporters of a policy friendly to Germany, while Lord Salisbury is credited, if not with a negative, at any rate with a passive part in this connection. A personal talk, these circles aver, would have dissipated on both sides the bias which perhaps exists, would have sown confidence and have had a favourable influence on later negotiations. I cannot refuse public opinion and the Press my testimony that they have tactfully respected the private character of the visit. Had His Majesty appeared in London, he could have been sure of the most spontaneous and enthusiastic homage. In the reserve which Press and public have had to exercise, they have, however, generally known how to avoid appearing too cool. This task was not altogether easy, inasmuch as any extravagance in expression might have provoked from the

German side the reproach that it was desired to bind the Kaiser politically to Britain, while a cold reception would have corresponded as little with the real feeling as to the rules of politeness, and must also have aroused displeasure in Germany. The essential feeling among the people, just as in the papers, was one of cordial thanks for a delicate attention paid to their exalted ruler and thereby indirectly to the whole nation. Had it been neglected, as a section of German public opinion seemed to wish, the expressions of annoyance and of disapproval of British policy on the part of German Press organs would have had an inevitable repercussion here, which would also have tied the hands of the Government and had an unfavourable influence on later negotiations, a result which, with the present inferiority of our naval power, no German patriot could contemplate without apprehension. After this, I can sum up my opinion of the feeling here by saying that the majority of the British people and their newspapers have not misunderstood the Kaiser's visit, and have not exaggerated its significance or exploited it in favour of their African policy; that, on the other hand, they rather respect our neutrality and gratefully acknowledge our non-interference and for the rest make no attempt to prejudice in any way our freedom of movement, but only wish to solve coming questions, whether colonial or European, in agreement with us. The visit of His Majesty the Kaiser to England, therefore, far from tying our hands in one direction, has left our liberty of action unaffected, whereas in the opposite case an estrangement would have arisen which could not be in any way desirable for us if only in view of our colonial interests. The moderate attitude which I have mentioned as being maintained in the Press here and in Court and government circles has, meanwhile, been departed from by Mr. Chamberlain, from whom this was least to be expected, in his speech at Leicester, in which he openly and without reserve raised the question of an alliance with Germany. I must refrain for the present from expressing a definite opinion on the motive for this proceeding, as, for the moment, I could only base it on suppositions, and I must therefore reserve the discussion of this question for a later date. Nevertheless, I should like at once to recall the view which I have frequently advanced, that Mr. Chamberlain, though a very capable and astute man of business, is by no means a diplomat who allows himself to be limited in his actions by definite rules. Great as is his personal ambition, it must not, in my opinion, be assumed that he allows himself to be exclusively guided thereby and not at the same time by definite political convictions. His idea of an alliance with Germany and America is, however, as your Excellency will remember, by no means a new one, and he long ago repeatedly discussed it with me in secret conversations, detailed reports of which I made at the time. If he now produces the scheme in public, this in my opinion shows that he thinks he has the majority of the Cabinet behind him in this question too, and that he considers, moreover, that the time has come to accustom the British public, which has hitherto shrunk from all alliances, to the idea of one. I consider it in no way out of the question that in this he may be pursuing, out of personal ambition, the object of precipitating a rupture with Lord Salisbury and of unseating him, in order to take his place. I am convinced that Lord Salisbury, in spite of many complaints made against him in his own party, must not yet by any means be regarded as politically a spent force, whom the Conservatives would promptly drop, provided that he does not himself show a desire to resign. Moreover, Mr. Chamberlain cannot have any doubt that even in the event of the resignation of the present Prime Minister it would be quite doubtful whether he could regard himself with any certainty as the successor to the office. When I recall all this, I am not at all disinclined to assume that when Mr. Chamberlain made his speech on the alliance he already had in his pocket Lord Salisbury's consent in principle, or else proceeded in the conviction that — as in the Samoan question — with the help of the majority of his colleagues, he would succeed in inducing the Prime Minister to agree to his wishes. For us it can, so far as I may permit myself an opinion, only be useful, if Mr. Chamberlain, *without us on our part undertaking any obligation*, adheres to the hope that we will ultimately allow ourselves to be induced to comply with his wishes as to an alliance, or, perhaps, an intimate understanding. So long as he retains this hope, he will have to show a spirit of accommodation towards us in the colonial questions which will probably yet arise, and, as in the Samoan question, to use his influence in the Cabinet, and especially on Lord Salisbury, in our favour.

Count Hatzfeldt.

The Empress, as her letters to me have already shown, had gone to England very unwillingly. She had never liked England, nor did she like it now. But with her strong sense of duty, she submitted, with great amiability and without the slightest sign of irritation, to the decidedly exacting demands of a princely visit of this sort.

From Windsor we went to Sandringham, the country house of the Prince of Wales, who had pressed his nephew to pay him a visit there. Sandringham is one of the most charming estates I know. Even in England, which is the land *par excellence* of beautiful manors, from the most splendid castles in the world to charming villas and comfortable cottages, it would be difficult to find a house combining the most refined luxury with so much comfort. The magnificent park with its fine oaks and beeches, its incomparably beautiful lawns, the rhododendron shrubs, the neat gravelled paths and quick hedges, made every walk an enjoyment. Johanna Schopenhauer, the splenetic and prolific writer who was the mother of the great philosopher, in one of her books makes the apposite remark that the English gardeners are true landscape painters on a large scale, and are indeed almost the only real artists in the English nation. The Prince and Princess of Wales were the most amiable of hosts, and everyone was looked after without being allowed to feel hampered in his freedom and independence of movement. Certainly one had to appear at breakfast in the morning and there ate bacon and eggs, porridge and jam, and on Sunday attend "divine service", but apart from this each guest could do what he liked. In the fine stables there was a famous stallion, whose name has to my regret slipped my memory, but which had gained for the Prince, in various races which he had won, nearly fifty thousand pounds, with which the magnificent greenhouses at Sandringham had been built. Another sight was the kennels, in which all possible kinds of dogs enjoyed life amid the best of care. In the chapel, memorial tablets commemorated dead servants and officials of the Prince of Wales, among them being German names.

Edward VII has often been wrongly judged. To some, especially to moralising German observers, he appeared to be a frivolous *bon vivant*, incapable of any serious thought, and from whom honourable fathers of families should keep themselves as far away as possible. At the first visit which William II paid to England after his accession, as soon as the Kaiser started a conversation with his uncle, the austere Baron von Mirbach, the Kaiserin's Master of Ceremonies, had murmured spitefully: "Now the 'pig' will have the upper hand again." Other Germans saw in the eldest son of Queen Victoria a profound politician of the school of Machiavelli, who pondered day and night how to set the world in flames and destroy Germany. The one conception is as foolish as the other. Edward VII was a man of much natural intelligence, of very great tact, of very good manners. He was always master of himself. He snubbed nobody, but allowed himself to be exploited by nobody. He had learnt little from books, but a great deal from life, which he knew from all sides, in all shades, in its heights and depths. As he had seen that his virtuous father, Prince Albert, in spite of his virtues or perhaps precisely on that account, had been looked upon in England as a stiff German and had never been really popular, he avoided everything which could in any sphere be accounted to him for pedantry, but observed all the more strictly all those English conventions to which the Englishman bows almost as deeply as to religious usages. Thus it was possible for an English statesman to utter a profound saying about the Prince of Wales: "Prince Albert was unloved, because he possessed all the virtues which are sometimes lacking in the Englishman. The Prince of Wales is loved because he has all the faults of which the Englishman is accused." It was the Earl of Granville who said this, the same who characterised the Empress Frederick in the apposite words: "She is clever, but she is not wise."

The Prince of Wales after his accession exercised more real political influence than most of his predecessors. But once when an honest squire asked the King's opinion on a political question which was troubling him a great deal, in order to base his own opinion on the King's, the King answered him through his private secretary that the King had always, on all political questions, and in all political matters, only the view which his Ministers put forward in Parliament. The future Edward VII was also a thorough Englishman in attaching great importance to faultless dress. It could rightly be said of him that, in the country in which unquestionably the gentlemen dress best, he was the best dressed gentleman. Uniform did not suit him particularly well, and the stiff and tight collar of his Prussian regiments annoyed him. But few men since George IV and his friend Brummel have worn civilian clothes better. In this, too, the Prince of Wales was very different from his nephew the Kaiser. The latter looked very well in the neat black "*attila*"[1] of our Hussars of the Guard, the brave Death's Head Hussars, and in the white jacket of his splendid Garde-du-corps regiment he charmed women and men, particularly in the South. Civilian clothes did not suit him, and he did not know how to wear them. His uncle, on the other hand, inspired great tailors in London, Paris, and Vienna. He took questions of toilet very seriously, he created new fashions, such as the Homburg hat and the trouser-crease. If mockery was at times heard in Germany about this, it was an emanation of German philistinism, and politically silly. That England should dictate the tone for men's fashions just as arbitrarily as Paris for women's, promoted English prestige, which the Prince of Wales served if he was in this sphere the uncontested *arbiter elegantiarum* in Europe and the world. I should like, incidentally, to mention that, during our stay at Sandringham, there was also among the guests one of the most learned of Englishmen, Lord Acton, a cousin of my mother-in-law, who, although an old man and a peer of England, still held lectures at Oxford. He enjoyed the particular and friendly respect of the Prince of Wales.

The prince was keenly interested in happenings at the Courts related to him, and especially, therefore, in Darmstadt, Coburg, and Berlin-Potsdam. He esteemed German diligence, German conscientiousness, German honesty, German accuracy, although he had no desire to compete in them. But like many of his country-men, he looked at Germany with a very jealous eye. The immense development of our industry, trade, and shipping aroused in him precisely those feelings which the owner of a great and ancient banking house experiences when a young, lower-class, and very active competitor, personally objectionable to him, appears in sight. In 1848, at our very first attempt at a navy, Lord Ellenborough in the House of Lords had contemptuously shouted at us Germans: "*Ephippia bos.*"[2] When now, fifty years later, we proceeded to

[1] The Hungarian braided coat, which is the uniform of German Hussars.
[2] "*Optat ephippia bos piger*" (Horace). The sluggish ox longs for horse-cloths.

build a fleet, Edward VII too found it superfluous and disturbing. Of all the children of Queen Louise of Denmark, his wife had most completely inherited the Danish-Hessian ill-will and antipathies of their mother against Prussian Germany. Long before the political relations between us and Great Britain deteriorated, the Princess of Wales in private conversation spoke of "those bestial Germans."[1] She was not without political influence on her husband, if only because the future Edward VII had not always a clear conscience as a married man, and consequently had to make up for this by compliance in other spheres.

All Edward VII's anti-German feelings were strengthened by the deeply-rooted dislike which he had for his nephew Kaiser William II. He had not cared about him as a forward boy, still less did he fancy him when he grew into a youth inclined to exaggeration and boasting, and the restless, loud — overloud — sovereign fairly got on his nerves. The inward and complete cleavage between uncle and nephew had been brought about by the events of the ninety-nine days of the year of mourning, 1888, by the attempt of the then Prince William to persuade his father to abdicate at San Remo, by the ugly scenes between son and mother at the father's death-bed, by the undutiful behaviour of the son to his mother after his father's death. Like the mother, her eldest brother, with whom close friendship united her during her whole life, had never forgiven this. Queen Victoria looked on these tragic dissensions with Olympic calm, seeing that she was equally respected by all, both by those who committed the wrong and by those to whom it was done. I repeat, however, that King Edward VII, with all his dislike of his nephew, which was perhaps all the more venomous because he often had to conceal it, with all his jealousy of the powerful forward strides of the German Empire, and all his hearty antipathy to Germany and the Germans, did not aim at or even wish for an armed conflict with us, and saw in the so-called encirclement only the means of forcing some slackening of pace upon our growth, and particularly of preventing the eventuality which he most feared, an agreement between Germany and

[1] English in the original.

Russia. It was psychologically interesting to see Edward VII associating with his nephew. In the main, the King impressed the Kaiser, although the latter did have moments when he hated his "wicked uncle." The occasions when he would have been only too glad for a heartfelt reconciliation were far more frequent. When the uncle talked politics with the nephew, I had an impression of a fat malicious tom-cat playing with a shrewmouse.

Our Empress and the then Princess of Wales had no sort of liking for one another. Between the houses from which they were descended, the house of Schleswig-Holstein-Sonderburg-Augustenburg and the house of Schleswig-Holstein-Sonderburg-Glücksburg, existed a relation similar to that which once ruled between the white and the red roses in the English royal family. Augustenburg and Glücksburg were both scions of the Oldenburg stock, the founder of which, Egilmar, was prominent as early as the eleventh century, and which gradually got possession of the thrones of Denmark, Russia, Oldenburg, Greece, and Norway. There had been frequent intermarriages between the houses of Augustenburg and Glücksburg, up to recent times. They had long lived peacefully together at the Danish court. Since the Schleswig-Holstein revolt in 1848 they had opposed one another in bitter political enmity. The then Princess of Wales — later Queen Alexandra of England — was one of those women who do not age. Even when seventy years old she still had the figure of a young girl. Having become quite English, she was infinitely popular in England, and deserved this affection by her amiability, her never-failing tact, and the way in which she overlooked many things in her husband and devoted herself entirely to the duties of her position. While the Empress Frederick remained an Englishwoman up to the last day of her life in Germany, Queen Alexandra became in every direction as English as it is possible to be.

King Edward, who had known me since my time in Paris, remained up to the end, through all political vicissitudes, well-disposed to me personally. On his last visit to Berlin, shortly before my resignation, he gave me bronze busts of himself and the Queen, accompanied by very friendly words. It was regrettable that Emperor William, who was self-willed and sometimes lacking in delicacy, particularly in small matters, should have forced upon his uncle at our visit to Sandringham, in spite of the latter's objections, two gentlemen of the German suite whom the Prince of Wales could not endure, namely, General von Kessel, whom the Empress Frederick accused of having behaved treacherously and ungratefully to her and her deceased husband during his sufferings at San Remo, and Admiral von Senden, whose breach with the Prince of Wales I have already mentioned.

Among the guests at Sandringham was also the attaché of the German embassy, Herr von Eckardstein. He had been a lieutenant of the 6th cuirassiers at Brandenburg on the Havel, and had been afterwards seconded to our Embassy in Washington, where by a little *coup* he attracted the attention of Herbert Bismarck. After a dinner which he had taken with diplomatic colleagues on the first floor of the restaurant, Eckardstein made a bet that he would be in the street sooner than the others. He succeeded in this, since they all ran down the stairs, while he jumped out of the window, spraining his ankle but winning the bet. This sample of his mettle pleased Herbert Bismarck, who had a fancy for jests of that kind. He had Eckardstein, who ought properly to have returned to his regiment, seconded for another year to the Embassy in London, where there was more doing than in the old town on the blue Havel, where Burgrave Friedrich of Nuremberg in 1412 had homage done to him, as the first of the Hohenzollerns, by the men of the Mark. In London the big prize in life's lottery fell into the lap of the young lieutenant of cuirassiers. Eckardstein succeeded in winning the hand of a pretty and amiable young lady, who was at the same time richly blessed by fortune. She was the only daughter of Sir John Blundell Maple, the greatest manufacturer of furniture in England, who, delighted to get a "German baron" for a son-in-law, made him his sole heir in his will, which made Eckardstein heir to two and a half million pounds — before the war, at all events, a sufficient amount.

By this marriage Eckardstein secured a certain position in English society. In particular, he had succeeded in acquiring an intimacy with Chamberlain, the Colonial Minister, and thus I hit upon the idea of having him promoted from attaché to Counsellor of the Embassy and making him Pückler's successor. This, as events proved, was not a fortunate stroke of mine. Had I then known how completely Eckardstein allowed himself to be dominated by the infinitely stronger Chamberlain, had I in particular guessed how much Eckardstein was inclined to speculation on the stock exchange, which was ultimately to be his financial and moral ruin, I should not have made this mistake. And yet Count Paul Metternich, then Ambassador at Hamburg, formerly Counsellor of Embassy and later Ambassador in London, had warned me. Metternich, who, with Count Paul Hatzfeldt, was one of the best authorities on English conditions, wrote to me on October 20, 1899, four weeks before the Emperor started on his trip to England, when the dispute about the advisability of this trip was still going on :

Eckardstein is said to have told His Majesty that the next British war will be against the Germans. From this, His Majesty is said to have drawn the conclusion that, if he did not now go to England, the British would make war on him. Eckardstein is useful as an informant, but he must have hurried to Berlin filled with the impression that the much cleverer Chamberlain has made on him. His utterances are to be taken not *cum grano sed cum copia salis*. The British are not thinking of attacking us, *i.e.* our colonies. They are, it is true, more annoyed at criticism from us than from others. If our papers could persuade themselves just to abuse something else than the British, while French and Russians are setting themselves up on behalf of the Boers, we should also have an easier job with Samoa. A European coalition is a sinister bogey to the Englishman, although he is right in not easily believing in it. Only *we*, I mean our Press, ought not to wave it in front of him. He must come upon it himself, through the behaviour of the French and Russians. If *we* meantime keep a smiling face, he will the sooner make a small sacrifice for us, in order to keep us in a good temper, which is of consequence to him; if we pull an angry face, or a threatening one, he will make the sacrifice for the others, and not for us. Eckardstein, whom otherwise I like very much, is in this case a fool.

When we left England, the Kaiser was, characteristically, in a most elevated mood. He telegraphed with some exaggeration to Count Metternich: "The visit to England has gone off excellently in every respect. Reception and atmosphere better than ever. The consequences for the future will in all human probability be very satisfactory and favourable. Her Majesty the Empress, and also Bülow, have had great success with the Royal Family. He was received by Her Majesty at a lengthy private audience."

From Friedrichshof there blew a sharper wind. At the Kaiser's wish I had written from Sandringham to his mother to say what a friendly reception we had had there and at Windsor. I had then dropped a word, since the Kaiser made me a direct request to that effect, that it was a satisfaction to His Majesty to give the British court a proof of his attachment and immutable friendship, precisely at a time when Britain was exposed to all sorts of unjust enmity and malice. The Empress Frederick desired nothing more fervently than the best relations between her adored English home and her German adopted country, with which she was less in sympathy. She would even not have been displeased to see German policy put entirely at the service of that of England. But on the other hand it tormented her that her son, whom she did not like at all, should have had a good reception in England. She wrote to me on December 1, 1899, from the South which she loved so much :

Imperial Hotel,
Trento.

Dear Herr von Bülow,

I am very much obliged to you for writing to me from England. The letter has just arrived, and I hasten to send you my best thanks. I did not at all expect that you, burdened with work as you are, would write to me, any more than that anyone would think of me during the visit to England. I hope that my son has enjoyed the stay, and that it has been a recreation for him and the Empress to be in my beautiful home and with my dear people, who have always received them in such a friendly manner. I have heard from England nothing but expressions of satisfaction about the visit, so that I hope that the impression made by the Kruger telegram will now be forgotten. You mention the fact that my country has unfortunately many enemies. It is only necessary to live in *Germany* to be quite clear as to that. Envy and prejudice are difficult to fight against, and it is a waste of trouble to hope for fair and just judgment in the public and the Press, in which blind hate and ill-will have so long been purposely preached and nourished. I will not take up any more of your valuable time, and with warmest thanks remain,

Yours

V., dowager Empress and Queen Frederick

Regrettable in my eyes was not only the irritable tone of the letter, but above all the fact that the royal lady, who was in constant correspondence with her eldest brother, the Prince of Wales, with her mother and all her sisters and many influential Englishmen, should so much accentuate and thrust into the foreground the German feeling against Britain which had been evoked by the Boer War, and which I deplored and combated.

In the Dutch port of Flushing, where the *Hohenzollern* took us from Plymouth, the two Dutch queens awaited us on the landing-stage. They seemed very pleased to see us again, and were greeted and embraced with cordiality by the Empress. The Kaiser, full of magnificent impressions gained in England, met his Dutch relatives with the coolness which many people display towards poor relations who cross their path at a not very opportune moment. Nineteen years later, in the same grey and foggy month of November, under an equally dark sky and in streaming rain, Kaiser William was to trust himself to the protection of these two queens, after crossing the Dutch frontier as a fugitive.

CHAPTER XXII

The Hague Peace Conference — The Kaiser's Scandinavian Tours — Reports and Letters of Count Philipp Eulenburg — The Kaiser Plans a Coup d'État — His Attitude towards the Social Democrats — William II on Cecil Rhodes — Cardinal Hohenlohe on William II — Bülow's Speech in the Reichstag (December 11, 1899) — Germany, Hammer or Anvil — Celebration of the New Century in the Berlin Palace — Murder of the German Ambassador in Peking — General Gündel in Command of the Expeditionary Force — William II's "Hun" Speech.

IN looking back on the events of the concluding years of the nineteenth century, I must not omit to mention the Hague Peace Conference. It was opened on May 13, 1899, under the chairmanship of von Staal, the Russian Ambassador in London. Von Staal, like Count Osten-Sacken, belonged to the old school of Russian diplomacy; he was already serving in the time of Nicholas I, and was quite friendly to Germany. He had married a Princess Gortschakov, a sister of the Baroness Olga Meyendorff, the friend of the great musician Franz Liszt. Both the sisters, equally distinguished in head and heart, had long been friends of my wife and myself. Before von Staal left London for the Hague, he called on me in Berlin, and we agreed in our opinions as to the problems of the Conference, as well as in regard to the best way to lead it to a result which should be useful to the peace of Europe. I held the view, and pressed it strongly on His Majesty, that we could accept and welcome everything that served the cause of world peace without jeopardizing our security, and that we must avoid taking up the position of setting ourselves in the way of the pacific and liberal efforts of other Powers. We were able, and were obliged, to act thus all the more because the German nation was in actual fact less ambitious and quarrelsome than the French, less imperious and hard than the English, and because the Kaiser in spite of many oratorical lapses and a too authoritative manner on ceremonial occasions, was neither an autocrat nor indeed a blusterer. On this occasion, too, His Majesty's efforts were unfortunately directed towards conveying the impression that he was the leader, and had in any case at least as much share in any eventual success as Tsar Nicholas. If he could not stand alone on the pedestal, he at least wanted also to lay his hand on the other's laurel crown as in the beautiful Goethe-Schiller memorial at Weimar. On the Tsar's birthday, May 18, 1899, at Wiesbaden, William II, in the presence of the Russian Ambassador, Osten-Sacken, proposed a toast in which he placed his representative at the Hague Conference, Count Münster, alongside Baron von Staal, and expressed the expectation that these two diplomats, "in accordance with the similar orders which have been issued to the two gentlemen by Tsar Nicholas and myself", would so conduct the conference that the result would satisfy the Tsar. Like so many of his pronouncements intended for the public, this toast of the Kaiser's, although he was at bottom good-natured and at all events peace-loving, was considered abroad to be intrusive and arrogant, and gave general offence.

My period of office as Secretary of State had already shown me that when, as often happened, circumstances separated me for weeks from the Kaiser and left me without direct touch with him, I was left in ignorance of what was moving in his vivacious and versatile mind. This was especially the case during the Scandinavian tour. It is true that the Kaiser was accompanied on all his travels by a representative of the Foreign Ministry. I had, however, more than once had to realize that this representative, whether he happened to be Tschirschky or Schön, was more concerned, when drawing up his report, to safeguard himself personally *à tout jamais* as regards the Emperor than to give me accurate information. I told myself that these gaps must be filled up in some way or other. I must keep myself up to date about William II's moods, about the influences to which he was subjected just at the periods when he was separated for some time from his responsible advisers. I made provision, therefore, for this, as in duty bound, by requesting Philipp Eulenburg, who was with the Kaiser, to keep me promptly informed about His Majesty's intentions and moods, so far as they appeared to be of political consequence, and especially if of serious import. Philipp Eulenburg was an excellent observer and wielded a first-rate pen. I reproduce word for word some of his letters of this period, since they give, better than any other explanations, a clear picture of the plans, moods, and ideas, which flashed kaleidoscopically through the Emperor's sensitive brain, and the often instantaneous transformation of which into a public gesture or deed more than once placed me in a difficult position.

During the Scandinavian tour of 1899, the Kaiser constantly gave evidence of indistinct but heated plans for a *coup d'état.* "When the telegrams," wrote Philipp Eulenburg to me, " announced trouble among the workmen at Augsburg and other places, followed by promenades enlivened by social philosophizing, we were sitting merrily together in the large dining-room, where breakfast was taken ; I was next to the Kaiser, Prince Albert Holstein on his right, and Consul Jenssen next to me. The Emperor got very excited over the Wolff telegrams. He took the workmen's agitation very seriously — and with complete contentment. 'That is right,' he said, 'just let them go ahead ! The moment will come for action. I shall not let myself be baulked by anything — not even by the Ministry, which will simply vanish if it does not go along with me. Be good enough to read my speeches which have appeared in print since my accession. You will see clearly that I have called the attention of the German people — at first gently, and then gravely — to the dangers threatening them from within. The German middle class is making a complete mess of it ! The Government must act, otherwise all is lost. Just imagine a serious external conflict, and half the army tied to the country by a general strike — we should be lost. And already England has had a finger in the pie, in the last Hamburg general strike. She did not succeed badly in the attempt. It is high time, therefore, to step in. I have already ascertained how far my military authority extends as regards the Constitution. The Minister of War has told me that at any time I can declare a state of siege throughout the Empire (!!!). Until the Social Democratic leaders are fetched out of the Reichstag by soldiers and shot, no improvement can be hoped for. We need a

law under which it is sufficient to be a Social Democrat to be transported to the Carolines.' I am giving you approximately word for
word what His Majesty said to me at table. Our neighbours heard
a good deal of it, probably also the sailors who act as waiters and
stand behind the Kaiser's chair. However, they did not hear
everything, as His Majesty said the worst things quietly. I replied
to the Kaiser that a state of siege was surely unthinkable without
cogent reasons. His Majesty said that reasons were not requisite
— but that, with the increasing unrest among the working classes,
reasons would find themselves at any time. That was yesterday.
To-day, during an excursion to the new health resort, on the mountains of Trondhjem, the conversation was continued further at
table. The line now taken was that pillage is hoped for, and that
then, but only after a couple of hundred citizens' shops have been
damaged, a *very* considerable blood-letting must be applied. I
only said that the organization of the Social Democracy was too
good for them now to start actual pillage in Berlin or other large
towns. 'Then there is simply nothing for it but to proclaim a
general state of siege,' was the Emperor's answer. Senden had the
tact to entangle Albert Holstein in a conversation and to divert his
attention. But the fat Consul Jenssen (thank Goodness, a good
honest fellow!) received the full impact of the Imperial speech,
which, this time, was delivered so loudly that at least six gentlemen
must have heard it." Prince Albert von Holstein was the son of
Prince Christian von Augustenburg, uncle of the German Empress
Augusta Victoria, by his marriage in 1866 with Princess Helena of
England, the third daughter of Queen Victoria. His elder brother
had entered the British service, and fell, if I am not mistaken, as a
British officer during the Boer War. The younger son, Prince
Albert, was sent to Darmstadt, where he joined the Hessian Dragoons. He spoke German with a distinct English accent, his ways
and manners were quite English, and the Kaiser's entourage believed that he reported to England all he heard. During the Great
War, however, he remained in Germany, the Kaiser having attached
him to the Governor of Berlin for special duties, and he complained
in his rather comic English-German about the unpleasant position

in which he was placed by the war between his "two fatherlands." Herr Jenssen was German consul in Christiania.

Thus spoke William II in 1899 about the Social Democratic party and movement. Up to my resignation, that is to say, during the next ten years, I learned directly and indirectly of many similar outbursts. I always answered the Kaiser that, if he wanted to proceed against the Social Democratic movement by exceptional laws and by resort to force, he should not have dismissed Prince Bismarck. The latter, the creator of the Constitution of the German Empire, the giver of the general and equal franchise, the architect of the Empire, would have been the only man who could have carried out such a violent cure with some prospect of success. Since Prince Bismarck had had to give up his position, nothing remained but to conquer the Social Democratic movement without violating the Constitution, without resort to violence, and, if at all possible, also without exceptional laws. This, in my opinion, was usually the best way to combat intellectual movements. Firmness and courage in face of any attempt of the Social Democracy to infringe the Constitution and the laws were obviously the first duty of the Government. In this respect he could rely on me absolutely. For the rest, however, a government calm, intelligent, and as skilful as possible: *In hoc signo vincemus*. These utterances of the Kaiser's, reeking of powder and blood, were, for that matter, not always meant seriously. They were intended more to impress the hearer, perhaps also, if reported elsewhere, to have a deterrent effect. There was no firm will, and especially no consistent one, behind it all. King Albert of Saxony, with whom I spoke on this point in my Secretary-of-State days, and who fully understood the danger of the Social Democratic movement, which he was able to observe at close quarters in Saxony in particular, said to me: "Do not indulge in any experiments in that direction, unless the Kaiser promises you in writing that he will stick to his guns. Otherwise he will slide out of it. And even then you are not quite sure of him." Eight years after these conversations on the *Hohenzollern*, I had reduced the Social Democratic party in the Reichstag from over 80 to 43 seats, had taken the wind out of their sails, and had assured the bourgeois parties a solid majority. A success of this kind, however, by no means unimportant to the welfare of the State as a whole as well as to the position of the monarchy, did not count with His Majesty against the personal rancour which, encouraged by the envious and ambitious, he cherished against me from November, 1908. I had to go. Under my successor the Social Democracy secured 111 seats at the 1912 election.

Other talks and incidents on the Scandinavian tour were communicated to me by Philipp Eulenburg, who possessed a talent — common in France, rare in Germany — for writing stimulating and entertaining letters :

Every day I imagine that calm has now set in. But the life of an Emperor of the type of our dear master is as changeable as the elements. It is a cloud, now white, now grey, now black, with rain and hail and storm in it — and especially plenty of electricity. . . . To-day the Emperor gave us a very interesting description of Cecil Rhodes. The task of the German Emperor, Rhodes told him, was to win and open up Mesopotamia. The Kaiser must build the railway through Asia Minor to the Euphrates and the land road to India. He, Rhodes, had arrived at this result by the study of history. And the Kaiser had certainly not gone to Jerusalem on account of the one or two holy places. He must have had other objects. " I confess," cried the Emperor, " that I was perplexed. I told him that my ideas too went that way. Dear Rhodes, you have guessed it ! I will build that railway and open up again to the world the homes of the ancient civilizations !" The Emperor continued : " Rhodes told me that he had never been afraid in his life, but his heart had beaten when he was coming in to see me. Then, however, he had recovered, when he found me full of comprehension for his plans. Rhodes has leaned so much towards Germany since his interview with me that during the Samoa dispute he went to Salisbury and was so rude to him that Salisbury still remembers it." I must confess that this long speech of His Majesty's made me quite wretched. Superficially the Kaiser has calmed down a lot during the eleven years of his reign. We who are now doing the Scandinavian tour for the eleventh time have too strong an impression of this alteration, but in his disposition not the slightest change has taken place. He is just the same in his explosive nature, the explosions are even more violent and more sudden, with his self-confidence born of ripe experience — which is no experience. His individuality is stronger than the effect of experience. That might be a circumlocution for something else — yet it is *not* something else. He does not belong to our age, just as there have at all times been natures which have stepped outside the framework of their epoch. *Real* genius shapes the age to itself, weaker minds are pulverized. At the head of a State, such strong, individual natures must produce convulsions — and we are heading towards a time when a decision will come whether the epoch or the Emperor will be the stronger. I am afraid that he will succumb, as his strength at the moment is founded more on the skill of his advisers, especially on *yours*. If he were to see that he can become great through you — he might bear the palm *malgré lui!*

Thus Philipp Eulenburg.

A great part was played in the conversations on the *Hohenzollern* by the *"Gedanken und Erinnerungen"*, which had appeared after Prince Bismarck's death, and which had greatly excited and upset the Kaiser although the third volume had not yet been published. Eulenburg wrote to me about this:

The Kaiser said that he would say nothing during his lifetime as to the real reasons for the dismissal of Prince Bismarck. He gave as his motive for this: "I cannot and will not rob the German people of their ideals." But when his reign had passed to some extent into history, on his death, the German people would learn *why* he had parted from Bismarck. The Emperor of Austria and the Queen of England already possessed in their private archives the reasoned statement which he had written to the two sovereigns as a sort of justification. He had dictated to Scholl the "Testament to the German people", *which contained the real facts of the dismissal and was to be published immediately after his death;* it was in his private safe. An idea passed through my mind of the effect which this testament will have, but I did not like to rob the good Kaiser of the illusion which he cherished. The people will be on the side of their hero even after the publication of the testament. Not for Kaiser William II but for Bismarck will the hill fires blaze, and not on January 27, but on April 1. I have had to stand in the front rank in the horrible battle with the dirt-throwers and the scandal-mongers, and it was hard for me to have to come to this view. *What* experiences they were that produced this sobering effect! . . . I did not conceal from the Kaiser the power of Bismarckism, a power of which the deepset roots lie firmly planted in German hearts in this day; but he listened unwillingly. He expressed the view that the Kaiser is more firmly planted in them than all else.

The Kaiser's anger over Prince Bismarck's posthumous work was shared by his mother, who on many subjects thought so differently from her son. She wrote to my wife about *"Gedanken und Erinnerungen"*:

I suppose, dearest Marie, you have read the vile book of Prince Bismarck, the one by Busch and the other by himself, truly disgusting. He has already so succeeded in poisoning the minds of half his countrymen that they will no doubt accept all his lies these books contain — and which emanate from him as sacred truths! One is truly ashamed of such vulgarity and low taste.[1]

Philipp Eulenburg told me, not without suppressed satisfaction, that the Kaiser had declared categorically that he would "never" and "in no circumstances" reëmploy Herbert Bismarck. Since the day of the funeral at Friedrichsruh, when Eulenburg had been snubbed to his face by Herbert Bismarck, he had felt almost as much hatred for the son as for the father. He was also aware that I should have been glad to see Herbert Bismarck Ambassador in London, Petersburg, or Vienna.

Eulenburg wrote repeatedly to me to say that he was continually preaching caution to the Kaiser, pointing out among other things that Cardinal Hohenlohe had written confidentially to him, Eulenburg, that the Kaiser must be *very much* on his guard, very cautious, very prudent. The Cardinal, he said, had written to him that he knew "positively" that the idea was being revolved in many minds of declaring the Kaiser not responsible for his actions; there were highly placed personages who would gladly lend their hands to the institution of a suit to that end. Eulenburg took pride in the statement that he had had a "serious and downright talk" with William II on this delicate subject, and had ended by saying that there was no danger for the Kaiser so long as I remained at his side and he kept careful. Contrary to his habit, the Kaiser had not, said Eulenburg, replied to this with a joke or "with an energetic

[1] English in the original.

verbal slash of the broadsword *à la* 1st Regiment of the Guards",
but had remained "thoughtful."

Such letters could not but gravely impress me, although it is in
human nature to get gradually used to everything, as to heat and
cold, hunger and thirst, so to peculiar characters. Man is not
always made of the commonest clay; but he rarely emancipates
himself, and never completely, from his wet-nurse, custom. I may
add, however, that custom never dulled my sense of the dangers for
the country which lay in the Kaiser's nature, and that even in my
earlier period of office I had never ceased to regard it as my first
duty and my most all-important task to take care that even with
this monarch the German Empire and the German nation should be
kept from harm. One anxiety after another arose, especially, from
the Kaiser's lack of discretion in carrying on political conversations.
He had often, very often, promised me not to repeat the mistake
of discussing B with A and A with B, if only because of the risk and,
indeed, the probability that A and B would confide the Kaiser's
indiscretions to one another and both would become distrustful of
him. More than once he told me that he meant always to bear in
mind that a monarch's incautious utterances are like a boomerang,
that Australian weapon which circles round to fall upon the thrower.
Again and again William II forgot himself, especially in conversations
with foreign Ambassadors, not out of any evil intention — there
was never any guile about it — but, as the French well say, *c'était
plus fort que lui*. When diplomats spoke to me of incautious utterances of His Majesty's of this sort, I would reply, as was the simple
truth, that any sharp sayings of the Kaiser's about this or the other
State or its head would only have been of any practical importance
if the Kaiser had been a man *à la* Napoleon I, who might conceivably
enter into a war of *aggression*. It would certainly be understandable then if those against whom his words were directed were to
prepare to defend themselves. In actual fact, however, the Kaiser
had no thoughts save for conservation and defence. His ethical
principles, his sincere Christianity, his fundamental common sense
forbade him to dream for a moment of a war of aggression. He
would never embark on one. His excited phrases attacking this or

the other State were always purely defensive in character, merely his reactions to reports made to him of hostile intentions of this or the other Government in the economic, political, or kindred fields. His views changed once more when after a little time he discovered that the hostile intentions which he had supposed to exist had vanished, or at least had been brought no nearer realization.

This unalterable characteristic of the Kaiser's amid all his changeability gave me deep anxiety when I looked back on the year 1899 and the whole decade that lay behind us, and amounted to a grave warning to me to remain *toujours en vedette*, as the Great King had advised Prussia. But I was filled with anxiety not only by the Kaiser's individuality but by our nation as a whole. In this retrospect I was unable to escape from the realization that the German people, on which, during the century then drawing to its end, Providence had showered so much good fortune, so many benefits and possessions, the people that had lifted itself out of the misery of Jena and Tilsit up to the glory of Dennewitz and Leipzig and had freed itself from French tyranny, the people which had been brought by Bismarck to the unity, power, and greatness for which our fathers had longed, but in a degree and with a fulness which they could scarcely have believed possible, was unhappily still far from having the patriotic pride or even the patriotic sense of other peoples. I had found very significant of this a short debate which took place in the Reichstag in 1899 over a Goethe monument for Strassburg. Prince Heinrich Carolath, the warm-hearted and highly cultured National Liberal member, himself a student and disciple of Goethe, had moved that the sum of 50,000 marks should be included in a supplementary estimate by way of contribution to the cost of a Goethe monument in Strassburg. The motion was debated in a thoroughly apathetic House. A Centre member with little sympathy for the project, Herr Schädler, asked: "Is there any particular reason why Goethe should have a special monument in Strassburg?" From the point of view of practical common sense he, Schädler, was opposed to the motion. The budget already contained far too many demands for science and art. The motion was also dangerous on account of its possible use as a precedent for other "great men", to whom it would also be proposed to erect monuments. In what country outside Germany would such an incident, so unworthy a speech, have been possible? Suppose that in the French Chamber of Deputies, now that, God help us, *"die wunderschöne Stadt"* [1] has once more been lost to us, the proposal had been made to erect a monument to Rouget de l'Isle in Strassburg, where the marching song of the French Revolution was first recited by him. Any deputy who were to attempt to speak against such a proposal would be torn down from the tribune. He would be a subject for universal contempt and be unable to show himself in the streets. But a deputy of that sort there simply would not be, in France or Italy or Britain or any country that I know of. That discussion of January 26, 1899, was more than symptomatic; a speech such as that of Canon Schädler was deeply humiliating. Bismarck had put Germany in the saddle, but was she really able to ride? As far back as the 'eighties the architect of the Empire had lamented that, barely fifteen years after the restoration of the Empire, the national idea had become clouded over; as early as that he had given in the Reichstag an exhortation to make the national idea shine forth over Germany.

In my speech in the Reichstag on the second Navy Estimates, on December 11, 1899, I said: [2]

Gentlemen, Recent decades have brought to Germany great good fortune and power and prosperity. Good fortune and growing prosperity in one quarter are not always greeted in others with pure satisfaction; they may awaken envy. Envy plays a great part in the life of individuals and in the life of nations. There is a great deal of envy of us in the world, political envy and economic envy. There are individuals, and there are groups of interests, and there are currents, and there are perhaps even nations, who feel that the German was a more comfortable and that the German was a pleasanter neighbour to live with in those past days in which, in spite of our education and in spite of our culture, foreigners looked down on us in political and economic respects as stuck-up aristocrats look down on a modest tutor. Those times of political impotence

[1] "The most lovely city." A line from the German song, "O, Strassburg! O, Strassburg!"
[2] Prince Bülow's "Speeches" (large edition) I, 88; (small edition), I, 96.

and economic and political insignificance must not return. We do not intend again to be, in Friedrich List's phrase, the bondmen of humanity. The one condition, however, on which alone we shall maintain our position is that we realize that without power, without a strong army and a strong navy, there can be no welfare for us. The means of fighting the battle for existence in this world without strong armaments on land and water, for a nation soon to count sixty millions, living in the centre of Europe and at the same time stretching out its economic feelers in all directions, have not yet been found. In the coming century the German nation will be either the hammer or the anvil.

Was this reference to the past, to our geographical situation, to the history of the sufferings of the German people, understood in the Reichstag or by the nation? When I spoke of the foreigner having looked down on us in the past as a stuck-up aristocrat looks down on a modest tutor, there arose in the Reichstag the laughter of the unintelligent and ignorant, although the mental attitude of foreigners towards the German of past centuries could not have been more pregnantly indicated. And how the foreigner now, since our collapse and the November Revolution, since 1918, once more looks down on our nation, once so happy and proud! *"Comme je vous plains,"* an old Italian friend who had remained a friend of Germany said to me after my return to Rome in 1920, *"de voir votre pays tombé si bas"* ("How I grieve for you, to see your country fallen so low").

On the last day of the old century I received from King Carol of Roumania the following telegram:

At the moment when a century rich in incident is drawing to its close, a century in which we have witnessed such great events and which has created the conditions of peaceful progress for States, I particularly want to wish you and your honoured wife a happy new year, and may God's blessing rest on it. At the same time I beg you to accept the assurance of my kind regards and to be assured of my contentment and satisfaction at knowing that the conduct of foreign affairs, in which you have already had such fine successes, is entrusted to your experienced hands.

The celebrations which Kaiser William arranged at the turn of the century in the Castle and the Hall of Fame (Ruhmeshalle) bore all-too theatrical a character. Cameras set up on either side photographed the Kaiser and all present at the moment when they were kneeling during the prayers of the priests and their blessing. And the Berliner, always ready for his joke, sometimes good-natured, sometimes malicious, spoke of the genuflexion of the century.

The first year of the new century brought the complete overthrow of the Boers. In March Lord Roberts took Bloemfontein, in June he entered Pretoria. But if the Temple of Janus closed for South Africa it opened its two doors very soon again for the Far East. On June 18 the German Minister, Baron von Ketteler, was assassinated in China. There followed in June the Imperial order for the equipment and conduct of an expedition to China, of which Lieutenant General Lessel was appointed commander. As Chief of Staff he had one of the best officers of the German General Staff, Colonel Gündel. It was this officer, since advanced to Infantry General, who was originally designated president of the Armistice Commission, a post for which he was admirably suited by his circumspection, his discretion, his tact, his thorough mastery of French, and his experience in dealing with French officers. The presidency of the Armistice Commission was, however, appropriated in 1918, in the violently pushing way natural to him, by the deputy Erzberger, who *manu propria* struck out General Gündel's name, with the assent of the weak Prince Max of Baden, and substituted his own. There can be no question that General Gündel would have been better, much better suited for the conduct of the Armistice negotiations than Erzberger, who possessed various of the qualities which help the demagogue forward, and was not without a certain naïve good humour, but lacked almost everything required for a diplomatic mission — knowledge and experience, tact and dignity. So it came about that in November, 1918, on that saddest day in Germany's history, the victorious French Commander-in-Chief was met in the Forest of Compiègne by the grotesque figure of the Member for Biberach. The World War, of which the appearance of Matthias Erzberger in the Forest of Compiègne was the horrible conclusion, was naturally something on altogether a dif-

ferent plane from the Chinese Expedition of 1900. But for the very
reason that the war against China was being carried on by William
II from a great distance, with comparatively little effort, with no
personal risk, and with good reason to hope that I should succeed
in righting the matter through political and diplomatic action, the
Emperor burst all restraints on this occasion. "Now," he said
repeatedly to me, "it is a pleasure to be alive!"

When the World War came I was no longer at the Kaiser's side,
but in my time I never saw him in so excited a state as during the
first phase of the Chinese imbroglio. He began by making speeches
in Wilhelmshaven and Bremerhaven, which were meant to impress
not only the Chinese but the whole world. In Wilhelmshaven he
spoke on July 2, 1900, of the crime of the Chinese, "unprecedented
in its impudence, horrifying in its brutality", demanded "exemplary
punishment and vengeance", and declared that he had foreseen this
atrocity but had not been understood. "The burning brand of war
has been cast into the midst of the deepest peace, not, unfortunately, to my surprise." This was a reference to the famous phrase,
"Nations of Europe, guard your most sacred possessions." Next
day, at a dinner in honour of the visit of Prince Rupert of Bavaria,
the Kaiser made a speech containing the rather unfortunate phrase
that no great decision should be made in the world in future without
the German Kaiser. He would ruthlessly employ the sternest
measures to maintain the position of the German nation as a world
power; that was his duty and his first privilege. Hohenlohe and I
were against the publication of this speech, but His Majesty passed
it at once direct to the representative of Wolff's Agency before
the dinner was over. To prevent Imperial outpourings of this sort
from derailing our foreign policy, I sent the following telegraphic
directions to the Foreign Ministry on July 2:

Even after the assassination of Baron von Ketteler our policy in the
Far East will remain carefully considered, calm, and unruffled. We shall
above all avoid anything that might disturb the harmony between the
Powers, shall continue in touch with Russia, shall not repulse England,
and shall deal on terms of friendship with Japan and America. The situation has, however, changed to this extent, that after the brutal murder

of our Minister it is of the first importance to show to the nation that those who are in charge of its affairs know how to take rapid and strong action to preserve German prestige and German honour. That is the policy which I have recommended to His Majesty the Kaiser and which he has approved.

The programme sketched in those sentences had met with the All-Highest approval in theory, but in practice the reckless impetuosity which characterized the Emperor's phrases and speeches continually carried him away and led him into regrettable outbursts.

The worst speech of this period, and perhaps the most harmful that William II ever made, was the speech in Bremerhaven on June 27, 1900. On our arrival at the port, Hohenlohe and I noticed a wooden erection by the quay, where the troops for the Far East were drawn up. Everybody was asking what purpose it could be intended to serve. Some were of the opinion that the Bremerhaven fire brigade was using this tower for fire practice; others, that sailors were going to perform athletic feats on it. Suddenly the Emperor appeared and clambered up it — evidently it had been put up as a temporary tribune for him. The speech which he made from this pulpit, in harsh tones that carried a long distance, contained this sentence: "There will be no quarter, no prisoners will be taken! As, a thousand years ago, the Huns, under King Attila, gained for themselves a name which still stands for a terror in tradition and story, so may the name of German be impressed by you for a thousand years on China, so thoroughly that never again shall a Chinese dare so much as to look askance at a German." While the Emperor was still speaking, I got into touch with Herr Wiegand, the able Managing Director of the Bremer Lloyd, in order to bind all the journalists present not to give out this speech for publication until I had provided a corrected version. This undertaking was given by them all and was loyally kept to.

When I returned to the *Hohenzollern*, a Berlin journalist who had taken a verbatim report of the speech came to see me; he had congratulated himself on being the first to telegraph it to his paper. On my putting the position to him he quite agreed to forego this priority and to suppress the strong passages in the Kaiser's address.

While the Emperor had been speaking, the face of the eighty-one-year-old Prince Hohenlohe had grown longer and longer. Scarcely three months before this he had telegraphed to me: "Be assured that, so long as I remain able to carry on my office I shall be glad to be able to count on your collaboration." Now he said, turning to me with resignation in his face, "I cannot possibly answer for this in the Reichstag; you must make the attempt." At dinner that evening the newspapers were brought along. The Emperor seized hold of them, and was much surprised to find his speech only in the form in which I had given it out, that is, with the objectionable phrases omitted. "You have struck out the best parts of it," he said to me, as I sat opposite to him; he was not irritated so much as disappointed and disturbed.

But there was a small newspaper published in Wilhelmshaven which had published the Kaiser's speech in full. A representative of this little paper had been sitting on a roof and had taken down the speech in shorthand and published it at once, without any possibility that either Wiegand or I could prevent it. He had also sent off copies of his paper already in thousands to Bremen, Hamburg, Hannover, Emden, and Berlin, glad of the good business that he was doing. The Kaiser was delighted to be able now to read the full text of his speech. He was less pleased when I called him to book for his indiscretions while he was smoking his after-dinner cigar. I reminded him first of all of the profession of Christianity which he was so fond of making. His outbursts would produce sorrow and mortification among good Christians. The Kaiser replied with his usual readiness that Moses, Joshua, and other Biblical heroes had used even harsher language in addressing their hosts of fighting men. I was able to reply to this that we were living not under the old but the new dispensation, the spirit of which was different from the mentality of the Israelites who had conquered Canaan thousands of years ago, and I went on to point out the political repercussions which the eccentric speech might be expected to have. It would be regretted and objected to by our friends in the world, and used by our enemies to sow mistrust and hatred of us. This speech would have devastating effects. The Kaiser was visibly taken aback.

He would count, he said, on my "friendship" for him and on my "famous eloquence" to "trumpet forth" the case for him in the Reichstag. I pointed out that I was not afraid so much of Parliament as of the judgment and feeling of the world outside. Such *faux pas* — I used the term several times — brought grist to the mills of all who were representing the land of Goethe and Schiller, of Humboldt and Kant, as a land of barbarians and heathen, and our Kaiser, who, I was still sure, was at bottom a good Christian and a good man, intending no evil at all, as a grasping and bloodthirsty conqueror, which, thank God, His Majesty was not in the least. Our discussion lasted until after midnight. When the Kaiser dismissed me, he gave me his hand and said: "I know you are only concerned for my best interests, but after all I am just as I am, and cannot change myself." I left the Emperor with the feeling that he was not likely after this conversation to have me as Chancellor, and the feeling brought me neither disappointment nor concern. In any case, everything that I had said to His Majesty proved, unfortunately, only too well justified.

A few months later I managed to dispose of the attacks made against the Kaiser in the Reichstag. What, however, was impossible for me to prevent was the use made subsequently, when we had been allowed to stumble into the war through the shortsightedness and the rank incapacity of our leaders, of this very "Huns speech" by French and still more by British and American propaganda, in order to set world opinion against us. If the good and noble German nation, a nation with humaner ideas and feelings, in the best sense, than any other nation, in either hemisphere, was called "the Huns" by millions, it was the result of the unfortunate speech which William II made in Bremerhaven.

CHAPTER XXIII

Bülow's Relations with His Colleagues in the Ministry — Count Alfred Waldersee — William II Becomes Field Marshal — His Emphasis on His Military Functions before the War — His Complete Withdrawal in the War — Field Marshal Waldersee Commander-in-Chief in China — The Kaiser's Melodramatic Leave from Him in Kassel — Count Metternich on the Situation — The Capture of Peking (August 15, 1900) — Summons to Hubertusstock — First Discussion with William II on the Succession to the Chancellorship — Candidates: Podbielski, Philipp Eulenburg, Karl Wedel, Botho Eulenburg, Hohenlohe-Landenburg — Summoned by Telephone to Homburg.

MY relations with my colleagues, especially Tirpitz and Miquel, were good. I was united to the Chancellor by old ties of uninterrupted friendship. In Miquel, whose character and abilities had attracted me from the first, but whom many, and those not the worst, distrusted, Prince Hohenlohe saw an element of unrest and insecurity; he wrote to me about him from Baden-Baden:

Dear Count,
    Miquel is determined to bring about a crash in the Reichstag. He is intriguing, a Member assures me, not only against me but also and still more against you, because you have the ear of the Kaiser more than he has. Accordingly he has been working on Herr von Lucanus, who is his very obedient servant and through whom he is able, unfortunately, to bring influence to bear on His Majesty, and has induced him to advocate the immediate introduction of the supplementary navy estimate, as a possible source of a crash. The Grand Duke of Baden is convinced of the necessity for removing Miquel. It was not my suggestion; I found him full of bitterness against the Minister of Finance, and I think he will write to the Kaiser. With kindest regards as ever, Yours very sincerely,
                                                                    Hohenlohe

About the same time the subject of this criticism, von Miquel, wrote to me:

I am thinking a great deal at present about you and your heavy cares and troubles, and how difficult it must be to steer the right course between too much and too little, not to come too much into the foreground, and not to retire too much into the background. But so great is my confidence that the controller of our policy will successfully bring the ship through the breakers. . . . May I send my most cordial respects to your wife, my honoured protectress? With sincere gratitude and respect and admiration, always yours most loyally and sincerely,

Miquel

About the same time I congratulated Tirpitz on a gracious All-Highest message on the occasion of the passing of the third reading of the Navy Bill. He replied:

Sincere thanks for your kind congratulations. In this great success the personal element matters almost nothing to me. I should be content with the knowledge that I have been able to provide for you the tools you need for the development and expansion of Germany. May this labour not be made too heavy for you, is the wish of yours very sincerely.

Tirpitz

I had no sooner taken office in 1897 as Secretary of State for Foreign Affairs than Holstein, whose suspicions never slept, had a collection sent to me of marginal comments of the Kaiser's concerning General Count Waldersee — three years before Waldersee was sent to China. The collection was the work of the excellent *Geheimrat* Mechler, who for more than a generation had been in charge of the Central Registry of the Foreign Ministry, an office which he had filled with exemplary conscientiousness. Before the fall of Prince Bismarck, to which both had contributed, each in his own way, Holstein and Waldersee had been good friends. After the Prince's fall they became enemies — the exact reverse of Herod and Pilate. Waldersee may have had hopes of the succession to Prince Bismarck, but, with a lightning volte-face of the kind characteristic of him, Holstein had turned against Waldersee after the Bismarck crisis had reached its end, and had gone over to Caprivi's side. On my appointment to be Secretary of State, Holstein, always distrustful, had feared that I might become too friendly with Waldersee. A perusal of the Emperor's marginalia on Waldersee might warn me and prevent the undesired intimacy. The Kaiser's notes were indeed not kind to the General. If ever his name appeared in any report or newspaper article, the Emperor found an ungracious word to write in the margin. The epithet "traitor" was the one that recurred most frequently, but there was no lack of still coarser expressions.

How had Waldersee lost the favour of William II? He himself told me several times how he spoiled his relations with the Emperor in the autumn of 1890, during the manoeuvres in Silesia. The Kaiser had himself wanted to lead one of the manoeuvring armies. He, Waldersee, had had to give his criticism as Chief of Staff at the end of the manoeuvres. He was well aware of His Majesty's touchiness and vanity, but had felt it his duty to the army and the country to expose the many gross mistakes in leadership which the Kaiser had made. Caprivi as observer had confined himself to remarking, in His Majesty's absence, that the planning of the manoeuvres by the Great General Staff had offered many traps, and the Kaiser had gaily fallen into every single one of them; he, the Chief of Staff, had been faced with the necessity of pointing out these mistakes to His Majesty in the presence of a considerable audience. That had been the beginning of the Kaiser's disfavour, and it had reached a culmination later during a war game in the General Staff building, in which the Kaiser had taken part and had again, as in the manoeuvres, made bad howlers; Waldersee's conscientious criticism of these mistakes had brought about a scene. Immediately after this he had been removed from his post as Chief of Staff and transferred to Altona, ostensibly as a great distinction, to be Commanding General, of all places, in the home province of Her Majesty the Empress. When he took leave of the Kaiser, the latter said to him that in a war he would not want a Chief of Staff, as he would himself take over the command and decide everything himself. "In war I shall myself be Chief of Staff. In peace the Chief of Staff is only one of my secretaries, and in that capacity you are too old for me." Waldersee observed, smiling, that his successor, Schlieffen, was only a year younger than he. All that the Emperor said to me on any occasion was that he had never seriously considered Waldersee for Chancellor, even when he was a young prince and an enthusiast for Waldersee and the Stöcker meetings. Bismarck, always suspicious, had, he said, imagined it, but mistakenly.   As Chief of Staff, the Kaiser added, Waldersee was constantly exposed to the temptation of putting a finger into the political pie.   He had intrigued against Caprivi and had agitated against him in the Press particularly.   As Commanding General in Altona, Waldersee reported to the Kaiser, in Hohenlohe's time, in favour of forcible measures against the Social Democrats.   After my appointment as Chancellor he quieted down.   He had already managed, at all events for a time, to get back into the Kaiser's favour.

Count Alfred Waldersee had an uncommon aptitude for managing minor royalties; he was a sly fox, and, as a young artillery officer in the Guards, had already earned the nickname of "The Fox." He knew how to get at the Kaiser's weakest spot, through his almost childish pleasure in outward distinctions.   By directly approaching the Austrian Military Attaché in Berlin, the Emperor had secured appointment by Emperor Francis Joseph as an Austrian Field Marshal.   Very soon after this Waldersee came up from Hannover in the company of Prince Albert, over whom he had a great influence, and asked His Majesty, "in the name of the army", to accept the rank of Prussian Field Marshal.   The Kaiser gladly acceded to this invitation, and after that took pleasure in seizing every possible opportunity of taking in his hand the splendidly decorated marshal's baton.   It is a deeply tragic circumstance that this same monarch, who took more delight in and attached more importance to his military dignities and privileges than anything else; who was taken up with the signs of his military rank, sometimes almost revelled in them, to a degree almost unheard of in any other prince; who never lost an opportunity of wielding the marshal's baton, never had his fill of parades and parade marches, cavalry charges and frontal attacks on the manoeuvre ground, drew back when Bellona turned her stern face towards him and real war began.   As early as the summer of 1914 it was semi-officially announced, by All-Highest command, that the Emperor had replied to a question as to the position of the military operations that he knew no more about them than anyone else; it was the business of General von Moltke. This was the William II who, after reading with breathless interest

the fine work of Heinrich Friedjung on the struggle for predominance in Germany, had declared in all seriousness in the presence
of a considerable audience that in the last resort the Prussian
victory of 1866 was attributable to the fact that at Königgrätz
King William had led the army himself, while the Emperor Francis
Joseph had left the supreme command of his army in other
hands.

During the World War any sort of serious military collaboration
on the part of the "Supreme War Lord", any interference or decision, gradually became scarcer and scarcer, and finally ceased entirely. He appeared more and more rarely at the Front, and when
he did come he was felt to be, and treated as, an inconvenient, almost
a troublesome intruder. Anyone who reads Rosner's book, "Der
König", which described only too vividly the part played by William
II in his army during the months of the final struggle, will be filled,
according to his temperament, either with distress or anger. In any
case, the impression created is painful when we see the descendant of
great soldier kings, of a Frederick II and a William I, the son of the
victor of Wörth and Weissenburg, gaining meagre scraps of information from an old ambulance attendant at the Ménil outpost concerning the movements of his struggling, bloodstained troops. A
Prussian king who witnessed the moment when Prussian trumpets
blared and Prussian regiments advanced under the glorious black
and white standard, in the critical attack, in which the iron dice
were cast for dynasty and nation, a Prussian king who in that
moment could do no more than apply his proved capacities to standing for hours at one spot in ignorance of all that was passing and
in complete passivity, impresses one as a mockery of all Prussia's
history. So frightful was the reckoning exacted of William II for
his ingrained habit of mistaking appearances for realities and play-
acting for achievement.

The devastating pictures which were to unroll before him, nearly
twenty years later in the great collapse of 1918, were still far in the
future when William II with pleasure and pride grasped the Field
Marshal's baton handed him by Prince Albert and Count Waldersee. With his real good-nature and unfailing pleasure in giving

pleasure to others, he very soon promoted five Generals, all of whom thoroughly deserved the distinction, to be Field Marshals : General von Loë, my former wartime Colonel, for many years an honoured friend of mine, the worthy General von Hahnke, the able Count Alfred Schlieffen, Count Gottlieb Haeseler, and the witty General Kolmar von der Goltz. Did the idea of appointing Waldersee to be Commander-in-Chief in China come in the summer of 1900 into the Emperor's head of itself, or did Waldersee put it there? I never found out. In any case, Waldersee was delighted at the prospect of once more appearing on the great world stage. He was so pleased that in Hannover, where he had been living since his retirement, and where the Emperor's telegram announcing the impending mission assigned to him reached him, he at once communicated the happy news to everybody, so that it got into the papers on that very day.

When I learned from Philipp Eulenburg of the Kaiser's intention to place the supreme command over all the Powers' contingents in Count Waldersee's hands, I telegraphically advised His Majesty to defer considering the whole question of the supreme command until the gravity of the military and political situation in China had been better realized by all the Powers. But it was already too late. In the Imperial special train which bore the Kaiser and me to Coburg for the funeral of Duke Alfred of Coburg, the second son of Queen Victoria, who had died on July 30, 1900, the Kaiser informed me that, assured in advance of the "glad" assent of the Tsar, he had proposed to him that Count Waldersee should be appointed supreme commander for China. The Tsar had assented. Would I, therefore, now see to it that the assent of the other Powers to Count Waldersee's appointment was obtained.

I pointed out that in order to do this I must return to Berlin as soon as possible, in order there to get into personal touch with the representatives of the Great Powers and at the same time to send instructions to our representatives in the European capitals; to this the Kaiser readily agreed.

On my arrival in Berlin Holstein, who was as excited over the Chinese complication as an old war horse who hears the trumpet and

PRINCE PHILIPP ZU EULENBURG-HERTEFELD

the signal "Gallop!" and who was now thoroughly in his element, said: "The Kaiser imagines that if he and the Tsar agree, our whole globe must roll on after them. It will not be so simple as he imagines. But if we go to work with a will we shall pull it off." In the end I managed to get the assent of all the Powers, not exactly with enthusiasm, and the French with a very bad grace, to the selection of Count Waldersee. In these discussions I took up the standpoint of my circular note of July 11 on the Chinese question; this note had met with pretty universal approval in Germany, and had had a not unfriendly reception abroad. In this circular I had pointed out that the events in China had menaced alike the successful work of the German missions, our prosperous trade, and the great economic enterprises on which we had embarked in Shantung. Military action in China was regarded as necessary by all the Powers. The Imperial Government would be guided in its policy by the conviction that the maintenance of unison between the Powers was the first condition for the restoration of peace and order in China. I was able in this connexion to point out that these guiding principles of our policy had had the full assent of the Foreign Affairs Commission of the Federal Diet.

Meantime Count Waldersee had arrived at Kassel, where the Kaiser took him from the station and drove him round the old capital of the Electors, which had grown greatly prosperous since it had become Prussian. During the drive, Waldersee, who not long before had been judged and treated with such ill-favour, had to take the place of honour on His Majesty's right. So Tsar Alexander I of Russia had once made Marshal Duroc sit on this right, when Napoleon had sent the Marshal to the Russian frontier to receive the Emperor before the Erfurt meeting. *"Car la gloire,"* the Tsar explained, with the Slav bent for delicate compliments, *"la gloire est toujours à la première place."* Next day in Kassel the Kaiser handed to Count Waldersee the Field Marshal's baton. Count Paul Metternich, who was then in His Majesty's entourage, wrote me:

Yesterday we did honour to Waldersee in the Stadtschloss at Kassel. His Majesty handed him the Field Marshal's baton, making a very fine little speech; Waldersee at once put it at the corner of his thigh in the regular pose of the old copper engravings, as though he had always carried the baton. My impression is that on arrival in China Waldersee will act very independently and with as little reference as possible to authorities at home, but with great caution both in the military and the diplomatic field, if, indeed, there is anything left for him to do. The capture of Peking has cast a temporary gloom over our otherwise happy circle. Count Schlieffen, who is staying here and is exercising a quiet, unobtrusive, excellent influence in the Council of the Mighty, considered that the allied troops should remain in occupation of Peking. This seems to me an obvious dictate of prudence, provided they can do it without danger to themselves. The thing that is most feared here is that others may develop inclinations to negotiate for peace before Waldersee gets his chance of a procession beneath triumphal arches with white-clad Chinese virgins at the gates of the towns somewhere in China. I am afraid others, if they are able to conclude peace before this, will not be deterred by such considerations. However, there does not seem to be anyone in Peking with whom to negotiate, and apart from this it seems very doubtful whether the Chinese would yet submit to the conditions of the Powers. The Imperial court has fled to Hsianfu, a place which even Count Schlieffen and his staff have not yet been able to discover on the map. Meanwhile fresh bands are continually coming up from South to North, and in a few weeks there may be plenty of kudos-bringing problems for Count Waldersee to work out. If, however, China should be ripe for plucking, we shall be unable to do anything to prevent others concluding peace if they stand to gain by it. There does not seem to me to be much prospect of advantage in our then making another expedition on our own account to Peking. We should also be diplomatically overwhelmed with tenders of the good offices of those who do not want everything upset again. However, there is no sense in trying to control events in advance when they do not depend on oneself. It has always taken two to wage war, and what one has to do oneself depends largely on what the enemy does. What that will be we do not yet know; so we must wait. Probably the capture of Peking and the intuition that there may not be much for us to do there are accountable for the fact of the resuscitation here in unofficial quarters of the fantastic plan of a march northwards from our leased territory. Count Schlieffen, who seems to have conceived great trust for me and discusses all these questions with me in advance, is against the plan. One more word, with my usual candidness, about the Yangtse-Kiang. The river basin is to remain open for the trade of all, under conditions equal for all. So far as I know, no one has anything to say against this. On the Yangtse, as in many other parts of the globe, German trade has prospered greatly in the past under the protection of the British flag. German and British houses work together there on excellent terms with one another. Nothing would less please the people whom we want to protect than if we were to fall out with Britain. It is perfectly possible for us to carry out the protection of our subjects in the Yangtse, in case of need, by landing troops for the protection of our settlements. But the need will only become apparent to all if other States also, under a like pressure of circumstances, proceed to the landing of troops, preferably after coming to a friendly agreement on the matter with the British. The North of China is being tacitly abandoned to the Russians; lower down we come, and right in the south the French are spreading themselves. In between there remains the Yangtse-Kiang, the best section of all, where from long ago and down to the present day, in spite of our rapid progress, British interests are altogether predominant. There is no reason why we should not go on conquering the Yangtse with our trade, but so soon as we show or suggest by political measures, such as a display of force without some compelling reason, that we want to play the paramount power there, there will at once arise an acute issue of prestige and power between us and Britain, of the type of the Transvaal issue in 1895, and probably with the same ultimate result. But *you* are not likely for a moment to let matters go so far. Britain will not let herself be squeezed out of her political position on the Yangtse without a struggle. Through our trade we can conquer more and more of the Yangtse, but not through political action. Two permanent achievements of our China policy in the immediate past are now apparent: we have learnt how to send considerable transports of troops overseas; and we have acquired the nucleus of a colonial army.

In all his busy activity in staging the expedition against China, and especially in getting Count Waldersee appointed Commander-in-Chief, Kaiser William was counting on his Field Marshal, whom the comic papers were already dubbing the World Marshal, having the advantage of a chance to deliver a smashing blow against the Chinese in a big battle, to storm Peking, and himself to liberate the Ministers there beleaguered. All the Emperor's addresses were shaped on this expectation. He made much of the splendid military qualities of the Chinese, plainly with the idea of adding to the lustre of the achievement when German victory overcame such brave fighters. All these expectations and fantasies, hopes and dreams were blotted out entirely by events. Count Waldersee did not reach China until September 27; but the Allied troops had entered Peking and rescued the Ministers on August 15. Since then the Chinese campaign had had much less interest for William II, and within very few months he no longer wanted to hear any more about the Chinese question at all, graciously leaving it to me to unravel the tangled skein. In his first transports of enthusiasm over his appointment, Count Waldersee had made the mistake of accepting ovations, not always in good taste, at various places during his progress through Germany; and in his addresses he had awakened very great expectations, so that the sober Eugen Richter was able to speak, not entirely without justification, of laurels presented to the Field Marshal on account. It is only fair to recognize that, once he reached China, Count Waldersee acted with ability and good sense, showing the needed energy and also the necessary tact; he achieved everything that was required, maintained his dignity as Supreme Commander, and at the same time avoided treading on the corns of any of the Powers.

To his faults Count Waldersee joined distinguished qualities. He was the son of the Duke of Anhalt by a morganatic marriage with a lady of middle-class origin, and sometimes recalled in the circle of his confidants that his forefathers rested in the family vault of the Ascanians, so that wide horizons opened before him. Like many ambitious people, he was inclined to intrigue, of which, indeed, a Disraeli said that it is indispensable in the last resort for an able man, if he is to negotiate the most difficult passages in his upward climb to reach the summit. Waldersee had, however, also some of the solid qualities which Disraeli postulated in addition to the capacity for intrigue. He was astute, but also able; crafty, but also reasonable; he could be sharp when this seemed called for, or smooth as an eel when he wanted to wriggle through. He knew how to seize Fortune by the forelock and how to bide his time.

Vergebens, dass ihr ringsum wissenschaftlich schweift,
Ein jeder lernt nur, was er lernen kann;
Doch der den Augenblick ergreift,
Das ist der rechte Mann.[1]

I think it would be safe to assume that in a great war Count Waldersee would have done well as Chief of Staff. As Imperial Chancellor he would have been unsuccessful, but as Chief of Staff he would have held the reins of the military leadership more firmly in his hand than the unfortunate General von Moltke, and his nerves would have stood the strain better. It was the terrible fate of the Empire to have, at the very moment when we were drawn into the war in 1914, the three most important posts, those of Chancellor, Chief of Staff, and Head of the Private Office, in the hands of men very different in mind and heart and character, but all, unfortunately, alike in being unequal to the situation.

At the end of 1900 I received, not without surprise, an invitation from the Kaiser to stay with him for a few days in his hunting-box, Hubertusstock. As I left my room and went down the stairs of the Foreign Ministry, past the two sphinxes which have kept watch there for half-a-century and longer, since my great-uncle, Christian Günther Bernstorff, was Minister of Foreign Affairs, I was stopped by a young diplomat, Secretary of Legation von Eckardt. During the Palestine tour I had learnt to value him as an industrious and intelligent official. I said to him that I was in a great hurry, as I had to be at Stettin Station in a few minutes, so at all events would he speak in telegram style, condense, condense! He replied that it was a question of his whole life's happiness. He had become engaged to a young Frenchwoman, whom he loved more than all the world and who had nothing against her except her nationality. His Majesty was refusing to consent to the engagement. He would not on any account give up his bride, and so his official future was at an end. I told him as I got into my carriage that I would see what could be done.

In Hubertusstock, the small, very modestly furnished hunting-box

[1] It is in vain that ye rove around with your science. Each one learns only what he can learn; but he who seizes the right moment is the right man.

in the Schorfheide, which the Emperor specially liked for its lovely surroundings, the marchland woods and lakes, I found His Majesty better disposed towards me than, after various occasions of friction during the summer, I had expected. I came at once to the marriage plans of Secretary of Legation von Eckardt. The Emperor replied hotly that he would not give his consent under any circumstances. He did not want a Frenchwoman in his diplomatic staff. I pointed out that Frenchwomen generally make good wives, and immerse themselves in the interests and the field of activity of their husbands. They dominate their husbands less than Englishwomen, Poles, or Russians. Then I added : "It is so seldom that your Majesty has the opportunity of really making a man happy. To-day you have the opportunity. If you give the consent that has been begged of you and I telegraph accordingly to Eckardt, this evening there will at all events be one human being completely happy. How long his happiness will endure, I do not know. His marriage may turn out unhappily. But in any case he will once in his life have been really happy, and that is an enormous thing, for even Goethe considered that in all his life he had not had ten entirely happy hours. Bismarck expressed himself even more pessimistically." The Kaiser's kindness of heart was accessible to an appeal even on behalf of a lesser brother; he laughed and gave his consent. A few minutes later I telegraphed to Secretary of Legation von Eckardt : "His Majesty the Kaiser accords to you the desired consent to marriage." Herr von Eckardt was not only happy that evening; the marriage then made possible by the edict from Hubertusstock ran a happy course. The lady became a good German wife.

Next day, in accordance with his custom, the Kaiser invited me to go for a walk with him. On his own initiative he brought the discussion round to the subject of the health of Prince Hohenlohe, who had told him by word of mouth and in writing that he felt absolutely unable to continue in office, neither well enough nor equal to the strain of business; he therefore begged for His Majesty's gracious dismissal. I expressed the view that it was in His Majesty's interest and the country's that Prince Hohenlohe should remain at his post as long as possible. Even if he was unable to do much more active work, he was a reassuring and steadying element. His wise counsel, his experience, and his balance were of great value. The Emperor agreed with me, but repeated that Hohenlohe could scarcely be kept on for long. Then he suddenly asked me, point-blank: "Would you accept the succession?" My reply was to ask whom else His Majesty thought of. The Kaiser did not seem altogether comfortable after my question; after a little hesitation he replied that he had thought of "Pod." I replied that I had pleasant memories of General von Podbielski as an old Hussar; and he had indisputable merits. He was vigorous and resourceful, two qualities seldom to be found together. He had, however, no experience of questions of foreign policy, and in home politics he was too much of a Conservative partisan. I could not say, more-over, whether his tact was as admirable as his energy.

The Kaiser went on to say: "Candidly, for me personally Phil Eulenburg would be much the most acceptable successor. He is my best friend. I am his 'Highest.' But I do not know whether he is equal to it. I have the impression that he himself doubts it. Quite recently he told me that he had neither the knowledge nor the energy wanted for carrying on an important office. He has also used up too much of his nervous energy in my service to be able to appear before Reichstag and Landtag. He would in any case only be able to take up the post of Chancellor if he had a Minister as his mouthpiece. He says that there was a case in which that was done under Napoleon III." The Kaiser was unable to recall the name of this French mouthpiece Minister. I suspect that Phil had been thinking of Eugène Rouher, who during the decadence of the Second Empire had been a maid-of-all-work for the defence of the Imperial policy in the *Corps Législatif.* The Kaiser proceeded: "Probably a mouthpiece of this sort is not to be had among us. Uncle Chlod-wig is no Cicero. But his parliamentary experience dates back to his time as Minister in Munich. He is thirty years older than Phil. He has a long political past, which Phil has not. Phil would be hardly likely to be able to count on the consideration and indul-gence in Parliament which is given to old Prince Hohenlohe." After a slight pause the Kaiser went on: "Many people have recommended to me Herr von Wedel-Piesdorf, my Minister in Attendance. He is an excellent Minister in Attendance. But he is almost more of a Conservative partisan than Pod, and after the impudent opposition which the Conservatives set up against me in the canal question they shall not come to the fore for the present." I asked the Kaiser whether he had not thought of one or another of the Generals. "Certainly," he replied. "I have thought of Bock, of the Guards, of Liegnitz, of the third army corps, of my old friend and Adjutant-General Wittich, of the eleventh corps. Also Lindequist of the eighteenth and Adolf Bülow of the fourteenth occurred to me. All blameless officers and fine comrades. But would they be equal to diplomatic problems? And I have none too pleasant recollections of Caprivi, a splendid soldier but hard of hearing and stiffnecked as a Chancellor, and, on the whole, a failure. Now, however, put forward your candidates."

I first mentioned Count Botho Eulenburg, a statesman, a thing that, with all the friendship one might have for them could not be said of either Phil or Pod. Count Botho Eulenburg was conservatively inclined, but without blinkers. He cared more for the Constitution than for any party ticket. The Kaiser objected to his candidature. He had a high regard for Count Botho Eulenburg, but considered him too much of a bureaucrat. He had got on his nerves as Prussian Prime Minister, and would do so even more as Chancellor. Moreover, Count Botho Eulenburg knew nothing about foreign politics, which he was too much inclined to regard and deal with in the spirit of an ex-administrative official. Nor did the Kaiser like the idea of having two brothers, one of them Chancellor, the highest official in the State, and the other Chief Court Chamberlain, the highest official at court. Prince Bismarck used to quote the Pomeranian proverb, "When the menials quarrel the masters are well served." Kaiser William II had no liking for intimacies between his various servants. I next drew His Majesty's attention to Miquel, the Minister of Finance. The Kaiser protested almost with heat. He had lost all faith in him. Bismarck, he said, had often judged men unjustly, but when he had described Miquel as a ward who was not to be trusted he had hit the nail on the head. I suggested Count Posadowsky, the Secretary of State for the Interior; he, too, the Emperor objected, knew nothing of foreign politics. He was just as much of a bureaucrat as Botho Eulenburg, only less diplomatic and with a less elegant presence than the East Prussian Count. The Ambassador in Rome at this time, Count Karl Wedel, was also considered by the Emperor out of the question, just as he was nine years later when I retired. He spoke of this excellent and high-principled man as full of "East Frisian obstinacy and dogmatism", and said that it would be impossible to work for long with him. Finally I mentioned as *proximus, sed longo intervallo,* the Statthalter (Governor) of Alsace-Lorraine, Prince Hermann von Hohenlohe-Langenburg. The Emperor made short work of this candidate too, saying that the Statthalter's cousin, Chancellor Prince Chlodwig Hohenlohe, had strongly warned him not to make Prince Hermann Chancellor. He had told Uncle Chlodwig that he was surprised that he would not have been glad to see his cousin at the head of the State; the old gentleman had replied: "Precisely because he is my cousin, I cannot possibly recommend him as Chancellor, for he would bring discredit not only on himself but on our whole house." Uncle Chlodwig had characterized his cousin Hermann Langenburg as "Of no use except as a façade." Let him remain Statthalter, he had said, in Strassburg, but he really was not equal to the office of Chancellor. Looking back to-day on that conversation with the Kaiser, I find that both he and I judged most of the candidates brought forward too severely. Professor Einstein is right — all is relative. Compared with most of the Chancellors whom we have had since the revolution, Botho Eulenburg and Miquel, Karl Wedel and Posadowsky were real demigods. People were more particular then.

The conversation between the Kaiser and myself led to no definite result. The Kaiser was only entirely with me in considering that everything must be done to facilitate Prince Chlodwig Hohenlohe's continuance in office. On the following day we had a walk alongside Lake Werbellin, which is close to the hunting-box. On the shore of this great lake, once full of muraenas, there stood long ages ago the castle of Grimnitz, where the Margrave Waldemar threw his disgraced Chancellor Nicholas von Buch into a dungeon and let him starve to death. To add to the pains of my unfortunate predecessor, the Margrave is said to have had fresh apples hung every day outside the barred window of his dungeon. In less fierce times there lived the Margrave Otto, the Margrave with the Arrow, who used to like to go across the lake in a stately ship with his wife, Heilwig von Holstein, and, surrounded by minstrels, to play the noble game of chess with her. In his fine *"Wanderungen durch die Mark"* old Fontaine has delightfully painted this marchland scenery for us. Now there stood by the shore of this storied Werbellin-See another Margrave of Brandenburg, who was also King of Prussia and German Emperor; and his wife, another daughter of seagirt Holstein, was roasting potatoes for us in embers, and we were eating her potatoes with an excellent appetite. When I left Hubertusstock that evening, the Empress gave me her hand with the softly spoken words: "Do accept."

Not long afterwards, on October 16, 1900, I was called to the telephone in Berlin, and the following conversation ensued:

"Secretary of State Count Bülow speaking."

"Kaiser William speaking. Hohenlohe has told me that he cannot possibly carry on any longer. Come to Homburg."

CHAPTER XXIV

Journey to Homburg with Lucanus (October 16, 1900) — Report to the Kaiser — Conference with Prince Chlodwig Hohenlohe — Appointment as Chancellor and Prussian Premier — Donna Laura Minghetti — Posadowsky Asks for Permission to Resign — Confirmation of Prince Adalbert — Return to Berlin — First Meeting of the Cabinet with Bülow as Chairman — Letter from Field Marshal von Loë — Herbert Bismarck to Bülow — Freiherr von Richthofen Secretary of State for Foreign Affairs — Letters of Congratulation — Changes in Personnel.

IN so far as I am able to think politically at all, I have always been an avowed enemy of the fatalistic theory. That is to say, I have never believed in the doctrine of an unalterable Fate, which is so powerful that all human effort is futile. World history shows that men, who have been defeated or have made fools of themselves, from the Austrian diplomats who failed in 1859 and 1866 to Bethmann Hollweg and his associates, always try to find a refuge in this fatalistic theory. "Why appeal to Fate? Politics are Fate," Napoleon said. I have already quoted similar words of his spoken on October 8, 1808, in the course of that memorable meeting with our greatest poet at Erfurt, words that should be framed in the room of every diplomat. Statesmen, who believe that some unalterable Fate controls a situation, have only too often led those who entrusted themselves to their guidance into defeat and catastrophe. Courage and ability may change the most difficult situations for the better. Within thyself are the stars of thy Destiny! It is true that in politics a studied reticence, the ability to wait and see, are often as necessary as boldness and daring are necessary at other times. I have never been able to understand that kind of passivity which causes a man to submit to an unfortunate situation in a cowardly manner, because he believes it to be hopeless. There is no political situation in which some advantage cannot be gained. *"Il n'y a point d'accident si malheureux dont les gens habiles ne tirent pas quelque avantage, ni de si heureux que les imprudents ne puissent tourner à leur préjudice,"* is one of La Rochefoucauld's most excellent maxims. The second half of this maxim, incidentally, is confirmed by the behaviour of the Prussian Conservatives and of the Emperor William II after my successful election in 1907. Anyone who is a fatalist and pays allegiance to an irrevocable Fate is lost before the battle has begun. As far as my country and my people are concerned, I have always been opposed to Fatalism, but in my private life, on the other hand, I have always assumed a different attitude. Perhaps it was a mistake, but the older I grow the less have I attempted to interfere with my personal Fate. I have confidently entrusted it to a Higher Power, to the gods who tranquilly rule the world, to use Homer's expression; to Our Father in Heaven, as the Christian believes: *Volentem ducunt, nolentem trahunt.*

When, upon my departure from Hubertusstock, I got into my carriage, which was to drive me to Neustadt-Eberswalde, where I was taking the train for Berlin, my future seemed more uncertain than ever. Because of the incalculability in Kaiser William's character, I was not certain even now, despite the fact that I had been associated with him for four years, whether I was to be appointed Chancellor, whether I was to act as Secretary of State under another Chancellor, whether I was again to be appointed Ambassador to some Foreign Power, or whether I was to be retired. I would have continued my work as Secretary of State for Foreign Affairs, if Count Botho Eulenburg, for whom I had the greatest respect and with whom I was associated when I was legal adviser to the District Praesidium in Metz, or if my dear friend Karl Wedel had been appointed Chancellor. I would also have remained if Miquel or Posadowsky had been appointed Chancellor, had they assured me that I would have a free hand in the conduct of foreign affairs. I would, however, have been equally willing to retire to private life without grief or bitterness, for I was sure that with my beloved wife and in the company of good books I should have been happy anywhere.

Almost simultaneously with His Majesty's request by telephone that I should leave Berlin for Homburg, I received the following telegram from the chief of the Civil Cabinet:

His Majesty, the Kaiser, has just ordered me by telephone, to join your Excellency to-morrow morning, so that we can confer with His Majesty together. I am spending the day in Potsdam because of a family matter and I shall be leaving the Potsdamer Bahnhof in Berlin for Homburg this evening at 10 o'clock. I would appreciate a word from your Excellency telling me whether you will travel by the same train.

We both left Berlin for Homburg on the evening of October 16, 1900.

Lucanus was an agreeable travelling companion. He was astute, almost cunning, but always easy going. At that time Ministers and other important men, with the exception of the Chancellor, did not travel in a special coach, as the leaders of the circus travel nowadays in the Republic. By a happy chance, brought about by a little tip to the worthy train conductor, Lucanus and I managed to secure a compartment to ourselves. As soon as we were seated, he squeezed my hand with some emotion. He was almost twenty years older than I was and a very experienced man, who knew the Emperor far better than I did. "I pray to God," he said, "that your marriage with the Kaiser will be a happy one. After all, he divorced Bismarck in less than two years. I have been accused of having had a hand in this divorce, but the accusation is unjust, for unfortunately I could not avert the breach. Caprivi was not at all successful: he did nothing but make stupid mistakes and he did not know how to deal with the Kaiser. Hohenlohe managed things a little better, but this was merely because he was completely passive. It is, however, very doubtful, whether it is an advantage in the long run for a Chancellor to be passive, for, after all, according to the Constitution, he is the only responsible official in the Empire. We need a Chancellor who can hold his own in the Reichstag, we need a man who can deal with his adversaries, and who can answer them back, so that the country as a whole will take notice of him. What we need is a personality."

Old Lucanus was silent for a moment and pulled at his cigar. Then: "The only problem is: how long can a Chancellor who has a

more or less brilliant personality get on with the Kaiser." The
experienced old gentleman did not speak for a moment. Then he
pressed my hand and closed the subject: "We must leave it to
God."

He then began to discuss less intricate problems. He told me,
not without humour, that my friend Philipp Eulenburg had done
everything he could to prevent my becoming Chancellor. He
— Eulenburg — did not in any way attack me directly, he did not
talk violently against me. On the contrary, he merely told the
Kaiser in most sympathetic terms that I was in very bad health
and he added sadly, that anyone who really cared for me could
only wish that the bitter cup of the Chancellorship would pass me
by. Eulenburg had told the Kaiser about a "terrible" eruption
of the skin which I was supposed to have contracted suddenly in
Norderney, while he, Eulenburg, was visiting me on the North Sea
— the fact was that I had merely suffered from a harmless rash,
which I had contracted after eating too many shrimps. The rash
passed as soon as I had taken two glasses of hot water with a solution of cooking salt. This is a prescription which, by the way, I
should recommend to anyone.

I asked Lucanus whether, by any chance, Phil wanted to be
appointed as Chancellor himself. "Oh, no," Lucanus told me.
"He would n't have that much self-confidence. He only encouraged Hohenlohe-Langenburg's candidature, so that he himself
could become the Stadtholder of Strassburg, a post that is the
acme of his desires." Lucanus took an article from the "*Pfälzische
Rundschau*" out of his attaché case, which contained the documents to be signed by the Kaiser in connection with the change
in the Chancellorship. This article described a mysterious journey
of Ambassador Eulenburg's to Baden-Baden. Eulenburg, according to this article, wanted to become Stadtholder of Alsace-
Lorraine. To create this post for himself, so the article continued,
he was trying to win Grand Duke Frederick over to his idea of
having Prince von Hohenlohe-Schillingsfürst replaced as Chancellor
by Prince von Hohenlohe-Langenburg. While Lucanus and I
talked about these things, midnight had come. Sleep overcame

us both, dispersing the unrest of our souls to-day just as it did in the days of the excellent Homer.

When we arrived at the station in Frankfort, Lucanus said that we should probably find His Majesty at the station at Homburg. Whenever the Kaiser had appointed a new Minister, he was always very impatient to see him and to fill him with his own ideas. Probably the Kaiser would begin the conference with a discussion of domestic affairs and tariff questions. He advised me to be careful what I said about these subjects. The Kaiser was bitterly opposed to the Agrarians, whom he blamed, and not without reason, for the miscarriage of his canal plans. Besides, so Lucanus pointed out, His Majesty had been told by his Hamburg friends that an increase or even the fixing of grain duties would make the conclusion of trade treaties impossible. The Kaiser was determined to conclude trade agreements at any price. I responded that I considered an increase in duties on agricultural products absolutely necessary, not only for economic, but chiefly for social, political, and for national reasons. I declared that I would not let my convictions in this matter be shaken. Lucanus looked at me doubtfully. He quoted a number of very drastic remarks which the Kaiser had made against the Farmers' Association and explained to me that, in keeping with his temperament and mentality, the Kaiser was much less interested in agriculture than he was in industry, trade, and shipping. We continued our conversation until the train arrived at the little station in Homburg, where we saw the Kaiser on the platform. He greeted me most heartily, took my arm, and asked me to go for a walk, so that, as he said with a smile, we could at once draft a Government programme together.

As soon as we were alone, the Kaiser did indeed broach the subject of trade and tariff questions immediately. He declared that I must above all see that the Agrarians "got what they deserved right away." They had earned this sort of treatment a hundred times, he said, because of their attitude in the canal question and because of the "insolent language" they had used. He said that there could be no question of increasing and much less of fixing agricultural duties. As we walked round the Elisabeth Spring, I explained to His Majesty why I considered an increase in protective duties on German agriculture an absolute necessity. I declared that I must be assured of an increase in these duties before I could take over the administration of our domestic affairs. I pointed out that agriculture was confronting the gravest difficulties and that the agricultural population was decreasing, while the industrial population was steadily increasing. The population of the cities, I said, was growing out of all proportion, like heads with water on the brain, whereas the country districts were becoming depopulated. This development, so I explained, was very dangerous not only from the point of view of our military strength, for the country districts provide better soldiers than the cities, but it was also dangerous for our entire social structure. In Germany there are far more large cities than there are in France or Italy and the disproportion between our rural and our industrial population is far greater than it is beyond the Vosges. Apart from Paris, which is the heart and the head of the country, France has only 11 cities with a population of more than 100,000 souls, whereas in Germany there are 30 cities of this size. The Kaiser replied that in England industrialisation was more highly developed than it was with us. I was obliged to tell him that England had reached a state of far greater social and governmental security than we had, because in England the political education of the people, the insight and wisdom of the aristocracy, and the patriotic sentiment of the masses were far more highly developed. The Kaiser was obviously surprised by the fact that I had contradicted him, but he finally asked, whether I did not realise that a failure to conclude commercial treaties would be "a terrible blow" for us. I quieted him with the assurance that, as I confidently hoped, even if we did increase agricultural duties, we should conclude advantageous commercial treaties with Russia, Austria, Italy, Roumania, and Switzerland. We must, so I told him, find the path between the two lighthouses: effective protection for agriculture on the one hand, and commercial treaties, which would effectively promote our industry, on the other. "The situation is, therefore, analogous to our foreign policy, in which we must steer a course between England and Russia."

In the end the Kaiser said, "Well, see how far you can go." I asked the Kaiser to permit me to call on my predecessor, Prince Hohenlohe. I was then dismissed near the Elisabeth Spring with a hearty handshake and the cheerful friendly words: "My dear Chancellor, we shall meet at luncheon."

Prince Hohenlohe received me with the calmness that never left him, but he was kindness and sincerity itself: "You will remember," he said, "that I prophesied to you twenty years ago in Paris, that you would be Chancellor one day. My friend Völderndorff made the same prophecy at the time when you met him on the Pont de la Concorde. He often told me so." Prince Hohenlohe, as he explained, realised that I would like to have seen him remain Chancellor a little while longer, not only for my own sake but for the country's as well. But his poor health made this quite impossible. On the journey to Homburg he had suffered two bad attacks of his increasingly serious heart trouble. He then read me a letter from his mother-in-law, Princess Léonille Wittgenstein, a lady for whom I had long felt the deepest respect. The Princess did not die until eighteen years later, when she was 102 years of age. The Princess wrote, urgently advising her son-in-law to retire. He could look back on a long and fine political career. She advised him to retire while the Kaiser and the nation still wanted him to remain in office and not to wait until he was urged to do so. "That is my intention," Prince Hohenlohe added, to me. "And you have my best and most sincere good wishes and hopes for your own success."

After I had retired to my room to change for the luncheon to which the Kaiser had invited me, there was a knock at my door. It was dear old Lucanus. "Well," he said, "you took the bull by the horns. The Kaiser was impressed by the fact that you contradicted him in such ticklish matters on the first day of your Chancellorship. Now, you must be conciliatory again and, above all, see that we conclude commercial treaties."

The Empress was the first to welcome me when I entered the old ivy-clad gateway of the Homburg Palace. Above the gateway there is a statue of the Landgrave with the silver leg, the victor of Fehrbellin and the hero of Heinrich von Kleist's famous drama, which is the finest glorification of Prussian military renown and of the Prussian spirit. The Empress pressed my hand in a kindly, affectionate manner. She said that she had great faith in me because she knew that I was loyal to the Kaiser. She promised to help me as much as she could. She admitted, with a sad smile, that her influence on the Kaiser was not very great. She expressed her pleasure at the fact that I had arrived just in time for the confirmation of her third son, Prince Adalbert. She always remained a good mother. After luncheon, the Kaiser signed the documents, which Lucanus had brought for him. As he did so, the Kaiser joked in a kindly and good-natured way. The documents included the consent to Prince Hohenlohe's resignation. The "Exalted Order of the Black Eagle with Diamonds" was conferred upon him. My appointment as Chancellor and as Prussian Minister of State was also among the documents.

During the afternoon I called upon the only daughter of General Friedrich Wilhelm Bülow, the victor of Dennewitz. She was at that time almost ninety years old and was spending the end of her life in Homburg. She was the widow of the refined novelist, Edward Bülow, the first biographer of Heinrich von Kleist, the apologist of the unhappy Dietrich Bülow, and the discoverer of the "poor man in Tockenburg." Hans von Bülow, the great musician, was her stepson. She could not remember her father, who died when she was only three years old. But she had been educated according to his ideas and she was filled with his spirit. She summarised her judgment of him in the following words: "He rested in himself. That is why he never lost his spiritual poise, either in fortune or in misfortune."

The branch of the Bülow family to which he belonged had for a long time upheld as their motto: "*In utraque fortuna ipsius fortunae memor*", which I translated at once: "Never forget that the weather, whether fair or foul, is always changeable." The old lady approved of my translation and expressed her conviction that the honour of our family, and particularly the honour of Prussia and of Germany, would not be tarnished during my term of office. My talk with this dignified old lady refreshed me. I felt as though the past were reaching out its hand to me, for generation should follow generation in the service of the Fatherland, and one generation should pass on to the next those patriotic qualities and that spirit which make the Fatherland great. *Quasi cursores vitae lampades tradunt.*

I then telegraphed to my wife that I had been appointed Chancellor. I prayed that God would grant me the strength to fulfill my task for the good of the people and of the Kaiser. My wife was not unreservedly pleased by the news, for she dreaded the excitements and the battles which this new position would entail. But she was greatly moved and at once informed my mother-in-law, who was staying with us at the time. My mother-in-law kneeled down at once beside her bed and prayed that the Mother of God might protect and guide me, for she loved me as though I were her own son. Donna Laura Minghetti had been educated in a Neapolitan convent. She spoke of the nuns as loving and kindly human beings, and she was always full of gratitude towards them. But the other clergymen and monks, whom she had seen in King Bomba's Naples, were not exactly edifying personalities. On the one hand, she had met with the crassest superstition, while on the other, she had found that many of the leaders of the Italian Risorgimento considered religious questions in a very sceptical manner. But the idea that death should end everything filled her with dread and horror. She compared herself, as she expressed it, with a wanderer, who had been pushed away from one shore of the stream, but who is unable to reach the other. After the death of her first husband, Prince Domenico Camporeale, who had died in Paris very young after a long and painful illness, she had found comfort and peace in the Dominican monk, Lacordaire, the great French preacher, and one of Saint Dominic's greatest sons. She was the intimate friend of a number of Catholic women, who were all very zealous in the Faith: Duchess Thérèse Ravascieri, a benefactress, who was loved by all Neapolitans as "Mamma Theresa"; Lady Craven, the author of "*Récit d'une soeur*", which was widely read by Catholics.

Her second husband, Marco Minghetti, was both an ardent Italian patriot and a convinced Catholic, emotionally as well as intellectually. She sought refuge in him in her moments of doubt and he showed her the way to Saint Francis, to François de Sales, and to Rosmini. In May, 1915, the last time I talked to my mother-in-law before I left Rome, I quoted one of the Apostle Paul's most beautiful utterances. She asked me to write it down for her. As she did not speak German, I wrote it in French: *Les choses visibles sont pour un temps, mais les choses invisibles sont eternelles.* (*II Cor. IV. 18.*) The slip of paper on which I had written these words was found on the little table next to her bed when she died on September 12, 1915, in her Villa Mezzaratta near Bologna.

On the evening of the 17th of October I sent the following telegram from Homburg to the Vice-President of the Prussian Ministry of State, the Minister of Finance Miquel:

As His Majesty has decided to appoint me Chancellor, I feel impelled to express the hope to your Excellency that you will continue to be benevolently disposed towards me and that you will assist me with your eminent knowledge and ability, which are invaluable to me. With old-time and loyal admiration, Bülow.

To the State Secretary of the Interior, Count Posadowsky, I telegraphed as follows:

Having been appointed Chancellor in accordance with His Majesty's wishes, I would like to tell your Excellency how sincerely I hope that your eminent knowledge of affairs and your strength will support me in my responsible post. In loyal devotion, Bülow.

Miquel's good wishes, in which he promised me his support, were gracious and spirited, but Posadowsky sent me a stiff and irate letter together with the following request to the Kaiser, in which he asked to be relieved of his post: "Your Majesty has most graciously decided to accept the resignation of Prince Hohenlohe-Schillingsfürst and to appoint Count Bülow as his successor. I think it is my duty as Vice Chancellor and as Secretary of State in the Ministry of the Interior most respectfully to ask your Majesty most graciously to permit me to hand you my resignation."

Had I presented this irate resignation to His Majesty with some unfriendly remark, the Kaiser would undoubtedly have accepted it. Lucanus, in fact, advised me to make some remark, for I would hardly find Posadowsky a loyal supporter in the difficult trade negotiations which were ahead. But I considered it my duty to retain the State Secretary of the Interior's unusual knowledge and ability for the good of the country. I therefore sent a telegram to Baron Richthofen, who was a personal friend of Posadowsky's, and told him that I had persuaded the Kaiser not to accept the State Secretary's resignation and that I had also persuaded the Kaiser to send him a gracious telegram. But Posadowsky, I added, ought now to come out of his sulking-corner and join me in useful work. He would hardly find a Chancellor who would be better disposed to him than I was, nor one who would be more appreciative or more obliging. A few weeks later one of those incidents, so frequent in public life, occurred, which the French compare with the proverbial brick, that suddenly falls on the head of a passer-by : *une tuile vous tombe sur la tête.* When the 12,000 mark affair suddenly fell on poor Posadowsky's unsuspecting head, he came to me as a suppliant and clung to me like a drowning man.

Prince Adalbert was confirmed on the 18th of October. Dryander's sermon was very dignified. It was free from all Byzantinism and pointed to the eternal stars which should shine before us on our stony and often dangerous pilgrimage. I was deeply moved when the congregation began to sing :

> *Ich weiss, an wen ich glaube,*
> *Ich weiss, was fest besteht,*
> *Wenn alles hier im Staube*
> *Wie Staub und Rauch verweht;*
> *Ich weiss, was ewig bleibet,*
> *Wo alles wankt und fällt,*
> *Wo Wahn die Weisen treibet*
> *Und Trug die Klugen hält.*[1]

[1] I know in Whom I believe, I know what firmly stands when here below in the dust all is dispersed like dust and smoke. I know what stands eternally where all sways and falls, where madness commands the wise, and deceit holds the clever.

I had seen and experienced enough in politics to realise that the author of these beautiful and profound verses, our dear old Ernst Moritz Arndt, one of the best Germans who ever lived, the faithful Eckart of our people, was only too right when he warned us against the delusions and the deceptions of human wisdom and knowledge. I often heard Bismarck say that his faith in human calculations decreased the longer he had anything to do with politics. I had read that Napoleon at the end of his reign said to his Arch-Chancellor Cambacérès, one of his most important collaborators in the reconstruction of French justice and domestic administration: "I have made so many mistakes during my life-time that I no longer blush when I am mistaken."

Heinrich Friedjung, the Austrian historian, who has been a friend of mine for many years, often told me and wrote to me that history above all teaches a certain modesty in giving political judgments. For history is concerned with intangibles; it is not an exact science chiefly because it deals with the riddle of personality at every turn. I believe to-day that a realisation of these facts will lead to modesty which is always useful, and never to faint-heartedness. I therefore joined in the second and third verses of the song with conviction:

Ich weiss, was ewig dauert,
Ich weiss, was nie verlässt;
Auf ew'gem Grund gemauert
Steht diese Schutzwehr fest.
Es sind des Heilands Worte,
Die Worte fest und klar;
An diesem Felsenorte
Halt' ich unwandelbar.

Auch kenn' ich wohl den Meister,
Der mir die Feste baut:
Es ist der Herr der Geister,
Auf dem der Himmel schaut,
Vor dem die Seraphinen
Anbetend niederknien,
Um den die Heil'gen dienen,
Ich weiss und kenne ihn.

When I say that I sang these verses[1] I am using a euphemism. I only hummed them. I am so unmusical, that even as a schoolboy in the Pädagogium in Halle on the Saale I was not allowed to join in the singing in church, because I disturbed the devotions of the congregation by singing out of tune.

On the 19th of October I travelled back to Berlin. On the journey, which was like a tour through German history, I passed through Fulda, where, in the Cathedral, the Apostle of the Germans lies buried. I passed through Gelnhausen, Barbarossa's old city in the Imperial Palatinate, which the Emperor Red Beard planned and where, on an island in the shade of chestnut and walnut trees, Kinzig held his court and summoned his parliaments. I passed the Wartburg, where, during the contest of the minnesingers, German poets and singers flocked together round Landgrave Hermann, where the Hungarian Princess Elisabeth became a German saint, and where Luther began his translation of the Bible. The train travelled through Erfurt, where Germany experienced the greatest humiliation she had ever known before the collapse in 1918. We passed Weimar, as small as Bethlehem in Judaea, but a great town none the less. The train journeyed on until the mighty church spires of Jüterbog rose before me. The village of Dennewitz and the battle fields are near Jüterbog, and here it was, where, on September 6, 1813, General Friedrich Wilhelm Bülow saved Berlin from the enemy and laid the corner stone of the liberation and the reconstruction of the Fatherland.

I arrived in Berlin in the evening and arranged a Cabinet meeting for the next day. I opened the meeting by emphasising my predecessor's achievements on behalf of the Fatherland through his untiring devotion to duty, his insight, and his wisdom, which his mature experience of life had instilled into him. I then explained

---

[1] I know what eternally endures,
I know what never abandons.
Built upon eternal foundations
this bastion firmly stands. It
is the words of the Saviour, the
words so firm and clear. To this rock
I cling unchangingly.

And well I know the master
who builds the stronghold for me.
He is the Lord of the Spirits
upon whom Heaven is looking, before
whom the Seraphim kneel in prayer, around
whom the Saints minister —I know who
he is and I know him.

that I planned to conduct Prussian affairs with full conviction and together with the Kaiser and King. The first thing to which I aspired, and which I demanded, was a united Government. Every member of the Cabinet was at liberty to express his opinions in the intimacy of these meetings and every member was free to give his opinions as much weight as possible. But once the Cabinet had come to a decision, with the approval of the Crown, these conclusions were to be defended in Parliament, in the newspapers, officially and privately by all members of the Cabinet alike. It was widely assumed that within the Ministry of State a number of opinions and points of view were represented. There must be an end of this assumption. An entirely united Ministry was the pre-requisite for the stable and clear-sighted Government which the country needed and demanded, and which was absolutely necessary for the effective representation of the rights of the Crown. I emphasised the necessity of complete agreement between Prussian and Imperial policies. The Kaiser knew where his power was rooted and he knew that the Prussian Monarchy was the basis for his position in the Empire and in the world. His Majesty expected, however, that the Prussian Ministry of State would do everything possible to support his position as head of the Empire and to facilitate the conduct of Imperial politics. I added that I did not share his Majesty's views only because I owed him this obedience but because it was my own inmost conviction. I should never permit the Empire to adopt any policies which would be harmful or even unfavourable to Prussia. But Prussian politics, on the other hand, must take the Empire's needs and political situation into consideration. The King and Kaiser particularly emphasised that the greatest secrecy must be observed concerning the discussions in the meetings of the Ministry of State. The Premier President alone was to decide which discussions, if any, were to be made known to the public. I closed with a request for unreserved confidence and for the support of the members in the fulfilment of my difficult task. I then assured them that I would always be mindful of the authority and the dignity of the Ministry.

Vice President Miquel replied in the name of the Ministry and expressed his complete agreement with all the points I had mentioned. He assured me of the members' loyal support. He particularly emphasised his approval of my point that disagreements, which are of course inevitable in meetings of this kind, should not in any way be known outside. The members were somewhat amused by this statement, though the solemnity of the moment made it impossible for them to give way to their mirth, because it was not unknown that Oktavio Zedlitz, the former director of the "Seehand-lung" and the leader of the Free Conservatives in the Prussian Diet, a very close friend of the Vice Premier, was very fond of intrigues; it was not unknown furthermore, that von Zedlitz' and Miquel's publicity manager, Herr Victor Schweinburg, was an evil scandalmonger. Miquel closed his remarks quite undaunted: "Each individual Minister must stand by the decisions of the Majority with equal determination." The next day when I went to my diplomat's desk, which had travelled with me from Paris to St. Petersburg and from there via Bucharest and Rome back to Berlin, I found it covered with congratulatory letters and telegrams. I cannot say that they moved me very much. It could have been foreseen that the rulers of the German States, the Emperor of Austria, and the King of Italy would send their good wishes to the new Chancellor. The office of German Imperial Chancellor at that time was different from what it became under Hermann Müller or Josef Wirth. In those days this office still had prestige, very great prestige indeed. The Kaiser, by the way, had himself informed the German rulers of my appointment and they had all whole-heartedly approved his choice. Being the son of a diplomat and having had long diplomatic experience of my own, I had many acquaintances and friends beyond the German frontiers. Goluchowski and Lambsdorff as well as my old patron, King Carol of Roumania, and many French and English friends, congratulated me most heartily. I was indeed moved by a letter from General Loë, to whom I was deeply devoted and who had been my commander in the victorious Franco-German War, when I fought in the splendid King's Hussars Regiment. Loë, who was then a Colonel-General, and was later promoted to the rank of Field Marshal, wrote to me as follows:

My dear friend,

Since the moment when a telegram first brought me the news of your long-expected appointment to the Chancellorship, my thoughts have been with you continuously. I felt the impulse to write or telegraph my sentiments to you, but I did not do so, because I did not care to send you a commonplace message like hundreds of others you must have received. I realised, furthermore, that, during the first few days after your appointment, you would be intensely busy. And my sentiments concerning everything that affects your public and private life are different from the sentiments of others, even from the sentiments of those human beings who are closest to you, with the exception of your wife. This may sound presumptuous — but it is my right to feel and speak this way about you. In your person are united the two most vital sentiments of which, at my age, I am still capable: my love for the Royal House and my country, for which I have laboured throughout my humble life, and my warm affection for you, which I have harboured ever since you were entrusted to my care as a young soldier. My affection for you has followed you in all the stages of your so fortunate career. I love in you the son of your father, my unforgettable patron; the officer in my Regiment, who takes first place in the memories of my long military career; the husband of your wife, whom you have given the happiness she deserves, the highly gifted, idealistic, and energetic, but moderate and circumspect statesman, who, in my opinion, represents the glad future of our country. You know that I do not speak in empty phrases — why should I speak in phrases at the end of a career which was truly not made successful by mere phrases? I speak sincerely and honestly, and I know you will understand my words. You will also understand why I have neither written nor telegraphed to you before. The fundamental impression which your message made on me is expressed in the double sentiment mentioned above: great joy, not unmixed with anxiety lest this hour of greatest outward success, this highest honour, which (as I have often prophesied) had to be conferred upon you for the good of the Fatherland, has come too soon. But there are certain decisive moments in which a resolute man must not look backwards. Since your appointment, I have thoughtfully considered all the circumstances, all the opportunities. The decisive moment came both for Germany and for yourself. There was no choice but to accept. Your predecessor had grown impossible, nor would it have been possible to appoint a provisional successor. You *had* to accept, and even if the time is a difficult one, the situation is all the more favourable to yourself, for the solution of the chief task immediately confronting you lies in a field of activity of which you are a master. You will unquestionably win the game, you will achieve a brilliant victory if you are given a free hand. You know that this consideration is the only shadow which, in my mind, has been cast on the shining light of your appointment. I hope that the memory of the greatest periods in our history, that the silent modesty of our heroes, will be as alive in *all* quarters as they are in you who have assimilated these grandiose impressions which are now the standard of your thoughts and actions. And now I wish you good luck, young knight. The main thing now is to trust in God and yourself and to go ahead. I enclose a letter for your wife. My joy at seeing you and Donna Laura again is unfortunately mixed with sadness. I cannot forget the Empress Frederick's terrible sufferings. I called upon her as recently as September 12th, and two weeks ago I received a letter from her. Until her last breath she will remain a gallant, wonderful woman. The fact that the Germans have not understood her, that they have not fully appreciated her, is a blot on their fair renown. She is extremely sensitive to the hate which surrounds her to the end. She longs to see her home once more. Will she ever return there? I hardly think she will! I hope to see you soon.

> In old friendship,
> Your Loë

Herbert Bismarck wrote to me from Heidelberg:

Well, at last! I send you a few lines and express my satisfaction that Chlodwig, the old mummy, has finally been removed and that you have been appointed Chancellor. I hope the responsibility will be easy for you to bear and a benefit for our country. I have been telling you for three years that this had to happen. I mentioned it again quite recently when you were visiting me in Friedrichsruh. I now congratulate you and the Fatherland. But I trust that you will get rid of all your weak colleagues and all the intriguers, otherwise you will be dragging along so much deadweight that it will tire you out. I am curious to learn whom you will appoint as your own successor. If Brauer were not the leading Minister in Baden, he would, in my opinion, be a suitable Secretary of State. Or could you choose Radowitz and thereby give the Centre Party a pleasure at par? In old loyalty,

> Yours ever,
> Bismarck

I should like to have had Brauer, who was then a Premier and later on Chief Superintendent of the Household in the "Muster-ländle",[1] coöperating with me as my Secretary of State for Foreign Affairs. We had been friends ever since we first met in St. Petersburg in 1875, when I was Third Secretary of the Embassy and he was Consul. Brauer united knowledge, a capacity for hard work, a most pleasing manner, and an entirely reliable character. Herbert suggested Radowitz' appointment because he wanted to play a trick on Holstein, for Radowitz had not really been popular with the Bismarck family ever since he assumed such a reserved attitude in 1890. Holstein and Radowitz were deadly enemies whom it would have been impossible to harness together in one team.

During my journey from Berlin to Homburg I had already decided to appoint Richthofen, who was now Under-Secretary, as Secretary of State for Foreign Affairs. Holstein had suggested several completely unqualified candidates for this post, as he hoped that the appointment of an ineffectual Secretary of State would give him a free hand for his swervings and his intrigues. It had not been easy to persuade the Kaiser to agree to Richthofen's appointment. His Majesty did not care for the traditional Prussian type of official with all his sobriety, his objectivity, his bee-like industry, his conscientiousness, and his loyalty. He considered men of this type stiff and dull, but, after sober consideration, he did admit that it was these men, together with the Prussian officers, who were the backbone of the Prussian State and that it was they who had navigated the State safely through many storms. I succeeded in getting *Geheimrat* von Mühlberg, who had been acting as the director of the Trade Department, appointed Under-Secretary. He was as distinguished a worker and official as Richthofen, and, like Richthofen, he had served his country with distinction in all the posts he had held.

Hugo Jacobi, the most gifted representative of the Bismarckian tradition in the press, wrote to me as follows after my appointment to the Chancellorship:

[1] Literally the "Little Model Country." The Federal State of Baden was looked upon as a model to others.

Great and difficult tasks await your as yet unbroken strength and the welfare of the country depends upon your success. You enjoy the greatest universal confidence. For ten years the Nation has been waiting for a political leader. Your appointment is surrounded by the auspicious and shining memory of the 18th October. I hope that the words "*nova vita incipit*" will apply both to your Excellency and to the Fatherland.

I might add in this connexion that when, a few months before my appointment, Herbert Bismarck expressed the hope that I would soon succeed Hohenlohe, he added: "My father said to me years ago: Young Bernhard Bülow is one of three or four men who must hold the Empire together after my death." Another intimate friend of the Bismarck family, Count Guido Henckel-Donnersmarck, who was made a Prince later on, wrote to me:

I congratulate you most heartily on the occasion of the great heritage which you have just received. If Caprivi and Hohenlohe had not held office meanwhile, I would congratulate you even more heartily and I would be even more happy. But there are no roses without thorns.

Dr. Hinzpeter, who had always struck me as being a rather candid person, wrote that he congratulated me all the more heartily as he realised how infinitely difficult it was to win the confidence and the affectionate understanding of his one-time pupil. As he himself had only secured the former and never the latter he could not but feel a certain admiration for a man who had secured both, and His Majesty was indeed fortunate "to have made such a rare find."

The congratulations I received from Josef von Radowitz, our Ambassador in Madrid, were very grandiloquent. He had been my chief while I was in Paris and before then while I was Chargé d'Affaires in Athens. I learned a certain amount from him, but I had not always found it easy to get along with him. He wrote:

Supported and carried by everyone's confidence, you have now reached the heights. Permit me to congratulate you and ourselves in devoted loyalty, even though I fully realize what a great and serious personal sacrifice it must cost you to give your entire vitality to this new post. I hope above all that the strong armour of perfect health will be granted to you. Then the old lines which so aptly unite the aims of the past and of the present with those of the future will be fulfilled:

Zu alter Wahrheit neue Liebe,
Zu neuem Leben neue Triebe,
Vor altem Bösen neues Grauen,
Zum alten Gott ein neu Vertrauen,
Ein neues Schwert zu neuem Kriege,
Im alten Kriege neue Siege! [1]

Herr von Mittnacht, who, for many years, had been a distinguished Württemberg Premier, and to whom on his resignation about this time I had expressed the well-deserved thanks which the Empire owed to his wise and characterful statesmanship, wrote to me as follows, thanking me for my letter: "I joyfully received the news that the highest post in the Empire has been placed in your hands where it will be wisely and safely wielded." The Lord Chamberlain, Count August von Eulenburg, who had heard about my appointment in advance from the Kaiser, sent me a telegram before I arrived in Homburg, which was as simple and as unassuming as he was himself: "Sincere congratulations and may God bless you." I was deeply moved by the good wishes from the clerks in the Cypher Department, whose loyalty was unequalled and through whose hands the most vital reports and instructions, and the greatest state secrets, passed every day. "Will your Excellency," Old *Geheimrat* Willisch, the chief of this Department wrote to me in the name of the entire department, "graciously allow your obedient servants, the clerks in the Cypher Department, most loyally to submit their respectful congratulations on the occasion of your appointment by his Exalted Majesty to the post of highest official in the Empire. Just as they have looked up to you as their Secretary of State in unchangeable loyalty and gratitude, they will always continue to harbour these sentiments towards you when you are their Chancellor. They will endeavour by unflagging loyalty to continue to deserve the approval which you have shown them heretofore." I replied: "I send you and the clerks in the Cypher Department, who have so loyally supported me with your devotion, my sincere thanks and the expression of my never

[1] To old truth new love, to new life new impulses, new abhorrence of old evil, new trust in the old God, a new sword for new war, new victories in the old war.

changing sentiments." Willisch was a unique sort of man. He had acted as head of the Cypher Department during Manteuffel's Premiership and he had been Manteuffel's confidential secretary. He belonged to some Protestant sect, I think it was the Moravian Brotherhood, he loved mystical meditations, and, because of his intensive study of the Apocalypse, he often had strange visions, which recalled the visions which the disciple whom Christ loved often had on the Island of Patmos. Willisch saw not only angels and trumpets and heavenly horsemen on white chargers, he sometimes saw the evil monster with the ten horns and the dragon on the throne as well. Then he would send me letters, marked "personal, highly confidential", in which he related his visions to current political events. This did not, however, prevent Willisch from being an extremely efficient and conscientious official.

Soon after my appointment to the Chancellorship I was able to fulfill the wishes of three of the younger diplomats. Kiderlen, then Minister in Copenhagen, was transferred to Bucharest. He had wanted this transfer, as the colourful and often tempestuous political life of Roumania interested him more than the quiet post in peaceful Copenhagen. Tschirschky, who was then Counsellor of the Embassy in St. Petersburg, was promoted to Minister at Luxemburg. Schön, who had formerly been a State Secretary, and who later became an Ambassador, was very eager to return to diplomatic life. I have already mentioned that I persuaded His Majesty to agree to his return on the 9th of September, 1899, on the journey from Karlsruhe to the *Hohenzollern*. When he was Counsellor of the Embassy in Paris, Schön had been badly treated by the Ambassador, Münster. Prince Münster had certain qualifications as Ambassador in Paris and London, where he had been before, but he was not always a considerate chief and by temperament he was a haughty Hannoverian aristocrat. He could not forgive Schön, who came from a Worms family which had become rich in the leather industry, for "smelling of leather." With the Empress Frederick's support, whom Schön had helped when she inherited a large fortune from the immensely wealthy Duchess of Galliera who had lived in Paris, Schön fled to the Court in Coburg, but here, too, things did not go very smoothly for him. Evil tongues say that when the Duchess Alfred of Coburg, Tsar Alexander II's only daughter, looked at him with favour, he preferred an actress at the Coburg Theatre to this high-born lady. The situation was, in other words, not unlike that of Lord Leicester and Monaldeschi, except that the outcome, thank God, was not as tragic. Schön was destined to do considerable havoc as State Secretary and as Ambassador. Shakespeare's King Lear asks his daughters which of them loves him the most. Regan and Goneril outdo themselves with expressions of ardent affection for their adored father, while Cordelia loves in silence. None of the three diplomats I favoured were like Cordelia. Kiderlen retained the greatest dignity and was content with no more than expressing his warmest thanks for the kindness which I had shown him now as heretofore and to assure me of his unchangeable gratitude and loyalty. Tschirschky asked permission to express his "deepest" gratitude for the "gracious" honour I had seen fit to show him. He asked me to rest assured of his "most loyal" devotion, and "constant" admiration. Schön wrote:

I beg your Excellency to rest assured that I fully appreciate the great honour conferred upon me and that I shall do all in my power to prove myself worthy of it. I am fully aware that I owe this post primarily to Your Excellency's friendly interest and mediation, for which I would like to express my most respectful, warmest thanks!

Kiderlen, who was generally considered rather crude, behaved relatively decently to me later. All he did was to attack me in his *billet doux* to Frau Kypke. Schön, the "faithful and obedient", turned against me when, in November, 1908, the storm broke round me. Tschirschky had intrigued against me even before that. I was not surprised by this change of attitude in any of them.

CHAPTER XXV

Count Waldersee Enters Peking — The Situation Abroad — Anglo-German Chinese Agreement — Austria-Hungary — Philipp Eulenburg on the Austro-Hungarian Heir to the Throne — Kaiser William's Relations with Archduke Francis Ferdinand — Our Relations with France — Army Demands — Regiments of Aristocrats — Russia: General von Werder's Letter on Russian Conditions —General von Schweinitz on Russia — Count Lambsdorff, Russian Minister for Foreign Affairs.

UNDER Prince Hohenlohe I had administered our foreign policy very much on my own. It was understandable, however, that, after my appointment as Chancellor, I became even more conscious of my personal responsibility for our foreign policy and that I felt it to be more and more my duty to make every effort to secure the future of the German people and to maintain a peace with honour and dignity by exercising the greatest insight and care of which a human being is capable. On several occasions Bismarck expressed the opinion that human beings (now that real prophets and the sons of prophets have died out) can only foretell the course of events four or five years ahead. In his famous order to Harry Arnim he pointed out that it was a mistake, particularly of German politicians, to plan too far ahead. I have also heard him say that in politics far-sightedness is more dangerous than short-sightedness. The main point is, he said, to take people and events as they really are. Ferdinand Lasalle, a man of genius, said: "Let us see things as they really are." All real statesmen, such as Cavour and Disraeli, Thiers and Francis Deák, agree with Bismarck that the main point in politics is to see things as they really are. I considered it my duty to pursue this method, all the more so because the Monarch whom I served had, unlike his grandfather, more imagination than common-sense and for this reason he tended to over- or underestimate persons and events and to vacillate between a sanguine optimism and a pessimistic despondency.

When the first crowds of well-wishers and visitors had disappeared and I had discussed the question of custom tariffs with my colleagues and with the leaders of the Centre Party, the National Liberals and the Conservatives, I endeavoured, in regular hours, to consider and to clarify the foreign situation in my own mind.

On the day on which I was appointed Chancellor, Field Marshal Count Waldersee arrived in Peking. This brought the Chinese question very much into the diplomatic foreground. The day after my appointment, President Kruger sailed for Europe from Lorenço Marquez in the Dutch cruiser *Gelderland*. It was obvious, now that Lord Roberts had occupied Johannesburg and Pretoria, now that the English Governor of the Cape Colony had stated in Parliament that the War was practically over and now that Lord Roberts had, on September 3, at last declared the annexation of the South African Republic, that Oom Kruger would make a concentrated effort to support the intervention of the European Continental Powers, especially of Germany, where sympathy for the Boers was widespread.

Guerrilla warfare continued in both Boer countries. The Boer leaders, De Wet and Delarey, reported continued success. The former penetrated into the Cape Colony and this success revived the hopes of Boer sympathisers in Germany, who were strengthened in their conviction that the Boer was not yet finally lost if only the German Government would decide to intervene in their favour. It was certain that my policy of strict neutrality and non-intervention would meet with great opposition in the Reichstag and among the German people many of whom were all enthusiasm for the Boer cause. The Empress who, in common with the great majority of the German people, had deep pro-Boer sympathies had written to me in the summer: "The Kaiser has just told me that the Boers have asked him to mediate for peace. As you, of course, already know, the Kaiser has only agreed to do so if England will do the same, but not otherwise. I telegraphed to the Kaiser expressing the hope that he would be able to secure favourable terms of peace for the Boers, because their bravery has certainly deserved this treatment. I wanted to write him this as well, so I added to my letter that the English must realise that the poor Boers have a right to live on their own soil and property. I am afraid that, otherwise, we shall again be forced to take sides with England. The Kaiser has been talking a good deal in favour of the English recently."

Untroubled by this violent sympathy for the Boers amongst the German people and amongst persons very close to His Majesty, I had concluded an agreement with the English about the Chinese question twenty-four hours before my appointment as Chancellor. According to this agreement, which outlined the policy to be adopted by both countries in China, the following points were agreed upon :

1. Open door to all ports on Chinese rivers and shores for citizens of all nations, especially in those districts of China where England and Germany could exert their influence.

2. Maintenance of the territorial integrity of China.

3. Should another Power exploit the Chinese situation to gain territorial advantages of any kind, Germany and England reserve the right to come to an agreement for the protection of their interests in China; both Germany and England, on the other hand, agree not to exploit the present difficulties to gain territorial advantages in China.

This agreement was to be submitted to all the Powers interested in China — France, Italy, Japan, Austria-Hungary, Russia, and the United States — with the invitation to adhere to the principles of the agreement. As an immediate result of this agreement the official newspapers in England welcomed my appointment as Chancellor. The Russian press, on the other hand, attacked me severely on account of the German-English Chinese agreement. The "*Novosti*" declared that I had lost my mind, the "*Novoye Vremja*" threatened a counter agreement signed by Russia, France, America, and Japan.

When I considered the international situation in the light of these events, I naturally turned first to our Austro-Hungarian ally. I had never doubted the fact that Austria-Hungary was internally weak and that the disintegration of the country—as a result of the pride of the Magyars, the arrogance of the Poles, and the presumptuousness of the Czechs, whom the high Austrian aristocracy favoured so unreasonably — could only be progressive. We could not permit a destruction of the Dual Monarchy, for, especially as Caprivi and Marschall had broken the link that connected us with Russia, we would then have been isolated and, in the event of a European War, England could not have helped us very much on land. If, however, we worked neither for the destruction of the Hapsburg Monarchy, nor so as to make her take sides with our adversaries because of any tactless treatment she might receive from us, it was certainly one of our highest duties to lead Austria and not allow her to involve us in an irremediable antagonism to Russia or to involve us in a war with Russia. The Hapsburg Monarchy had grown to resemble an old, half-ruined man-about-town, whose grim humour gradually prompts him to stake his all on one card. Austrian military men were particularly frivolous, just as they had been before 1856 and 1866. It was necessary to keep a close watch on them with regard to their attitude towards Russia, Italy, Serbia, and Roumania.

Emperor Francis Joseph's advanced years and his increasing feebleness of mind caused Archduke Francis Ferdinand, the heir presumptive, to become the chief factor in Austrian politics. At the time when I was appointed Chancellor, the Archduke's relations with the Kaiser were not very friendly. In a long private letter — the real course of politics comes to light much more clearly in private letters than in official reports, in which it is often necessary to exercise discretion — Philipp Eulenburg, in connexion with a proposed visit of Archduke Francis Ferdinand to Potsdam, wrote me a detailed statement complaining of the latent differences between the Archduke and the Kaiser.

Eulenburg's letter said: "The differences between Archduke Francis Ferdinand and our Master can probably never be smoothed over, because the Archduke's immeasurable arrogance would prevent his ever adjusting his old-fashioned views to the modern views of our Kaiser. Our Kaiser's deeply religious sentiments, which might form a bridge to a more objective Catholic like the Emperor Francis Joseph, are considered heretical by the Archduke, very much as Philipp of Hesse was a heretic in the eyes of Charles V.

For this reason the Archduke, when he is among his intimates, often expresses his dislike of our Kaiser's character, though he acknowledges the Kaiser's intellectual gifts; and it is on the basis of these that a certain understanding between the two might be possible, if, at the same time, the Archduke were received in Berlin with the highest honours. He has never forgotten a practical joke which the Kaiser once played upon him and which hurt him terribly. It happened a few years ago, when His Majesty received the Archduke at the station in Berlin and said: 'Don't imagine that I have come to meet *your* train—I'm expecting the Crown Prince of Italy.' (I think it was Crown Prince Victor Emanuel.) The sting of this 'insult' never left the Archduke's unusually proud memory. Duke Albert of Württemberg, his brother-in-law, who is a friend of mine, told me here that this affair is now forgotten —'practically forgotten.' Another remark made by our most gracious master the Kaiser was equally wounding, and has apparently been used to widen the breach between the two. After His Majesty's last visit in Pest, when he saw the Archduke informally, he made the following remark: 'I never realised that Francis Ferdinand was so intelligent.' When this remark was repeated to the Archduke he went pale with rage and said: 'Did he think me a fool?' I mention these incidents, because they are indicative of the atmosphere between the two. These incidents could not in themselves have produced such differences between them. Arrogance and envy are the real morbific agents and the facts will not remove these bacilli. A strong Germany with a ruler of genius is too favourable a soil for the evil character of bacilli that dominate the heir to the Hapsburg throne. All efforts to win him over will thus have only a slight effect. But a purely practical and sober judgment of all questions will not fail to impress the rather intelligent Archduke to a certain extent. And the incense of magnificent receptions will also have some effect. To these remarks about his personality I should like to add a few words about the Archduke's political views. Francis Ferdinand is like all discontented heirs. He will *never* forget anything that has offended his vanity, nor will he ever forget how foolish doctors and clumsy court officials counted him amongst the dead, whereas he had enough vitality to recover.   He will never forget that Goluchowski treated him as a *quantité négligeable*.   For this reason Francis Ferdinand always favours whichever policy Goluchowski is opposing.   For this reason he told others as well as his brother-in-law Albrecht of Württemberg with satisfaction that our most gracious Master had said, 'Goluchowski is a fool.' . . .   Despite his Catholic piety, Goluchowski is opposed by all the ultramontanes.   He is maintained by the confidence his Emperor has in him.   We should be making a mistake if we did not support him despite his various weaknesses, for the Russian anti-German party is rather strong here now. Our advantage lies in the fact that, because of Francis Ferdinand's hatred of Goluchowski, the latter cannot capitulate to this Russian-Feudal, anti-German party.   To complicate a situation which, at best, is no longer easy to understand, Francis Ferdinand, when he was on his last journey to the South, though he did not exactly incite the Southern Slavs (Slovenes, Croats, Dalmatians), did indeed agitate them very much.   Since then there have been strong Russian sympathies in the South, the 'Slovenian Empire' is heard of more and more.   When he undertook this journey, Francis Ferdinand played a perfidious trick on the Hungarians by opening the Slav question in Hungary.   I should not put it beyond him to have done this on purpose.   I cannot judge whether he has in mind a Slav transformation of the Hapsburg Monarchy, about which I have written several times.   But I do not consider it impossible that he may have been accessible to such a plan, in which a revenge for 1866, clothed in a Slav garment, may be featured as hopeful, if an alliance with Russia and France is concluded."

This letter indicates, incidentally, that, despite his weaknesses, Philipp Eulenburg was a man of sensitive political judgment and that he was able to express his judgment in a skilful manner.   But exaggeration and fantasies crept even into his letters and even into his sober and careful reports.   It was necessary to read his letters and his reports with "discernment", as old Prince Hohenlohe once expressed it.   The relations between the Austrian heir to the throne and our Kaiser were indeed not very friendly when I took over the conduct of our foreign policy. I was not able to improve these relations until some time later. I finally succeeded in the autumn of 1903, when William II went to Vienna, by persuading the Kaiser, not without an effort, to win over the Duchess of Hohenberg by adopting a friendly and gracious manner towards her. The Duchess held the key to the haughty and stubborn heart of her grim husband in her hands. After the relations between the Kaiser and the Archduke had become most friendly, the assassination in Serajevo ended the life of the Archduke and his charming wife and destroyed all the hopes and plans which had been centred round this unhappy couple. In a report, which I received from Vienna shortly after my appointment as Chancellor, Philipp Eulenburg stated that during a gala dinner at the *Hofburg*, the Emperor Francis Joseph had talked to him for a long time. My appointment as Chancellor had been the starting point of this conversation. The Emperor had said that Kaiser William could not have made a more fortunate choice. The Kaiser made a marginal note in the report concerning his Royal and Imperial Apostolic Majesty's remark: "You are right. I wish for Austria's sake that he also had such a Chancellor." Emperor Francis Joseph said to Eulenburg: "I telegraphed to Count Bülow at once. I felt a sincere impulse to do so. I was really very glad about his appointment." Emperor William added a marginal note to this remark: "Bravo." At the end of this report, Eulenburg mentioned the fact that Archduke Francis Ferdinand had discussed the intimate subject of his marriage with him: "The Archduke spoke in terms of 'perfect happiness' and 'physical and moral well-being.'" Kaiser William had, with good humour, written: "I congratulate you" *ad marginem*.

Our relations with France were the same as they had always been, except for a few relatively slight oscillations, since the Peace of Frankfort. The French did not want war, or better said, they did not dare begin a war. But they had not surrendered their claims to Alsace and Lorraine. Many Frenchmen, furthermore, still hoped to reëstablish the hegemony on the European Continent which France had held under Louis XIV and Napoleon. Prince

Radolin, our Ambassador in Saint Petersburg, wrote to me about a discussion he had with Prince Muravieff, who was peace-loving and, if anything, a German sympathiser. Radolin raised the question of a closer unity between Russia, Germany, and France, which would, of course, have been possible only if all three Powers could be sure that neither of the other two had any intention of diminishing the territory of the third. The Russian Minister of Foreign Affairs had said to Radolin that he could enter into an obligation of this kind as far as Russia was concerned, but not as far as France was concerned. No French Cabinet which agreed to Germany's wishes with regard to a guarantee of territorial integrity by the signatory Powers would last for 24 hours. I never wavered in the conviction that France would turn against us, as soon as we joined Russia, and my conviction proved to be only too correct. The German Kaiser, as well as the German people, were particularly glad to accept illusions about France. William II believed, just as his mother had once believed, that the French could be won over and soothed by personal friendliness, and this belief was a misjudgment of the passionate patriotism, the national ambition, and the national arrogance of our Western neighbours. With naïve good-nature, which is ethically a virtue, but politically a weakness of the German people, the great majority of Germans were filled with a sincere desire to be completely reconciled to the French, our interesting neighbours beyond the Vosges mountains, as soon as possible. This attitude led, among other things, to the great popularity among Germans of the Paris World Exhibition in 1900. They went to Paris in droves and they did not always make a good impression there. I had an old and good friend, Anna Lindau, who lived on the Seine. She was a daughter of David Kalisch, who founded the "*Kladderadatsch*", and her first husband was Paul Lindau, who was one of the most entertaining and brilliant, though not one of the profoundest, members of the Berlin press in the 'seventies and 'eighties. She had left her husband to go to Paris with a French journalist, who wrote on the Paris "*Figaro*" over the name of Jacques Saint-Cère. Actually he came from Fürth in Bavaria and his real name was Rosenthal. The dream of her life was a reconciliation between Germany and France, for she had never forgotten her old home. Not long after I assumed office, when she called on me in Berlin, I discussed the feeling in Paris with her and she said that it would have made a better impression if fewer Germans had come to Paris for the Exhibition. Many of them had not been exactly charming: their loud manners, the excessive sacrificial offerings they made to Bacchus in restaurants and bars, their vociferous bartering and their complaints about high prices in shops and places of entertainment, had been anything but pleasant. The French, so she pointed out, still implicitly followed Gambetta's advice: they did not talk of "La Revanche", but they thought of it all the time.

In view of the fact that the French, true to Gambetta's advice, were indeed augmenting their strong preparations for war year by year, it was obviously our duty at least to keep pace with them and not to neglect our increase of armaments. During my entire term of office, I therefore always approved of every military demand. Occasionally I tried to dampen the ardour of my friend Tirpitz for new armaments, particularly battleships. But I always made it clear to the Ministry of War and to the General Staff that I should always support new armament bills in the Reichstag and in the country, and that I would never shrink even from a dissolution of the Reichstag if it were necessary to make such bills become law. If the Reichstag were dissolved in connection with demands for armaments, on which the safety of the country ultimately depended, we could appeal directly to the people at any time. But I sometimes pointed out that military bills would pass all the more smoothly and easily, and that the Reichstag and the country would accept them and be willing to make sacrifices for them more readily, if certain defects were removed from the magnificent picture of our glorious army. I regretted the so-called "Aristocratic Regiments", that is to say, the policy adopted by some Regiments of accepting and appointing as officers only aristocrats. For reasons of tradition this custom was perhaps suitable for the two old Gardes de Corps Regiments, the First Foot Guards Regiment and the Gardes du Corps, but it was a bad mistake to let this custom gain ground in most of the Cavalry Regiments, in almost all the Guards Regiments, and in many Infantry Regiments of the line as well.

I also did not approve of the fact that Jews were never appointed officers in the Prussian army. In Bavaria conditions were better. Shortly before my retirement I had a long talk about this matter with my old friend Count Dietrich von Hülsen, the Chief of the Military Cabinet. We were discussing the case of a young Herr von Goldschmidt-Rothschild, a young man who was very well bred and who was eminently suited to become an officer or a diplomat. His father was a generous philanthropist. His grandmother, Baroness Willy Rothschild, who, I believe, came from the Neapolitan branch of the family, was a very distinguished lady, who had been a close friend of my parents' and my mother-in-law. William II admired her very much. The young man would undoubtedly have been well received in all clubs and salons in Paris and particularly in London. He knew that a special Imperial Decree had made it possible for his family to be received at Court in Vienna. As he was brought up in Germany he wanted to join our Army, but despite all my efforts I was not able to put this through. I later appointed him as an Attaché at our Embassy in London, where he soon made a name for himself. I must add that neither the Ministry of War nor the General Staff were unreasonable with regard to these matters. They admitted that I was right when I claimed that there was a certain amount of wrong in the system by which army officers were appointed personal adjutants to German Princes and rulers and were favoured when commanders and governors were appointed. They also admitted that Eugen Richter was not entirely wrong when in the Reichstag he criticised the famous stuffed-dummy Captain in the Regiment of Guards as well as the numerous military sinecures. This case, like most cases of discrimination against middle-class officers and the boycott of Jews in the Army, was really a matter of regular routine, which was particularly difficult to abolish, because this routine was based on ingrained prejudices rather than on the bad intentions of any particular person.

The Kaiser himself harboured no prejudices of this kind. His treatment of middle-class and aristocratic officers in his immediate entourage was exactly the same, and when middle-class officers were raised to the nobility, this was done because the officers in question had again and again emphasised their wish to be ennobled. Anti-Semitism of any kind was even further from the Kaiser's mind. I have pointed out this fact in connexion with the differences which occurred between William II and the Conservatives led by Count Limburg-Stirum when the Canal Question was being discussed. The Kaiser did not share the gentlemanly views which were rather widespread among our upper ten thousand. Herr von Tschirschky, who was then our Minister in Luxemburg, later our Minister in Hamburg, and a travelling companion of the Kaiser, and who was in the end appointed Ambassador in Vienna, was married to the daughter of a Budapest manufacturer, Stummer von Tavornock. On her father's side she was probably a Jewess and on her mother's side she was most probably of Semitic origin as well. Tschirschky had the weakness to tell His Majesty that his wife belonged to the high aristocracy, instead of realising that to a reasonable human being it was quite immaterial what blood an entirely respectable and very wealthy father-in-law had in his veins. During a dinner at the Austrian Embassy in Berlin, William II asked Ambassador Szögyényi in my presence: "It's true, isn't it, that Frau von Tschirschky belongs to a very old family?" The Ambassador replied in a very Austrian manner: "Your Majesty, Frau von Tschirschky comes from a good, a very, very good family, but there is no question of its being a Family." When the Kaiser the next day was informed (not by me) about Frau von Tschirschky's pedigree, he laughed and made the sensible remark: "Tschirschky should be thankful that he has a wealthy father-in-law and he should be happy that his father-in-law is an honourable man. It certainly doesn't make any difference whether he is of Finnish-Ugrish, Indo-Germanic, or Semitic origin." I repeat again: William II was really never a Philistine.

When I was still Secretary of State, I received a long letter from General von Werder, who for many years used to be our General à la Suite to Alexander II and Alexander III. General von Werder was probably the most popular German living in Russia during the last fifty years. In this letter of March 1, 1900, he described the feeling in Russia. Werder had been invited by Nicholas II to spend some time as a guest of their Russian Majesties in the Winter Palace. Werder wrote to me: "Emperor Nicholas, as usual, has received me in the most friendly and sympathetic manner. His health is better than ever, he has gained ten pounds and goes hunting even when the weather is bad. I have heard that, unfortunately, he is very annoyed with our Kaiser. The Grand Duke of Hesse is said to have egged him on. While I was visiting him, the Tsar did not ask after His Majesty. The Tsar was also offended because the heir (Grand Duke Michael) was not given the Order of the Garter in England. In general the Tsarevitch is not very pleased about the reception he had in London. His entourage, however, complains about our Kaiser as well, who is supposed to have treated them all very coldly and who turned his back on them in a noticeable manner. But one knows how pretentious these gentlemen are. Russian officers in particular are often excessively proud, and all this is unpleasant merely because one thing so often leads to another and talk about these incidents only pours oil on the fire. There is nothing tangible. It is all very difficult to understand: Who has been insulting? Who has been insulted? So often mere trifles cause all the misunderstanding. But it is too bad when these misunderstandings form a chain. I only wish to add that Alvensleben is received everywhere with confidence and that I am convinced that he will have a good position here." The Grand Duke of Hesse exercised a great influence on his sister, the reigning Empress of Russia, who was attached to her Hessian home with every fibre of her being. In common with most German rulers, he could not bear the Kaiser, even though he was his own cousin. It is not impossible that he said malicious things about the Kaiser. At that time (it was before Emperor Nicholas' son was born), the Emperor's brother, Grand Duke Michael Alexandrovitch, was the heir to the throne. On his way to England, he had passed through Kiel, where he had been received by His Majesty, but he had not been treated particularly well. This happened not infrequently when foreign royalty was visiting Germany, but it was not due to any malice or intention on the part of William II, but merely because of his mood at the moment. It is true, however, that, considering our relations with England and Russia, quarrels of this kind could be really harmful.

Another of our former Ambassadors to St. Petersburg, General von Schweinitz, hit the nail on the head regarding our relations with Russia, when he answered my question as to whom he considered the best successor to General von Werder as Ambassador to St. Petersburg, as follows:

Dear Count:

As I am in bed with influenza, I am dictating to my daughter the thanks I owe you for showing me your confidence by asking me to consider a topic which interests me very much. Before I resigned my post in the autumn of 1892, I mentioned three points which I considered decisive in the choice of my successor: he must be a professional diplomat, he must be a Prussian by birth, and he must have a personality which inspires confidence. Your Excellency will remember how inclined Alexander III always was to mistrust people, especially if they had intellectual distinction. I found that Count Alvensleben united in his person all the three points I mentioned. General Caprivi agreed with me, and if I remember rightly, His Majesty, too, agreed, when Vladimir's influence produced a change in attitude. Tsar Alexander, who did not want me to leave and who dreaded the appointment of some stranger, was delighted when he was told about the agreeable Alvensleben, whom he had met before. This, however, was Alvensleben *caelebs*. I agree with Your Excellency that Baron Stumm is the most suitable man; he is well thought of in St. Petersburg, he can lend a helping hand to the important men in the Ministries in the conduct of their affairs and, at the same time, he is popular among the ladies in the *haute société*. Baroness Stumm is elegant, clever, and rich and quite equal to Frau von Montebello. I am afraid, however, that Baron Stumm would not accept the post; one of the causes for his resignation has not yet been eliminated and, besides, he is not in very good health. He is restless — but who else is there? I must explain why I think it important that we are represented in St. Petersburg by a Prussian. The reverence for the traditions of Queen Louise, the Holy Alliance, Empress Charlotte, etc., which had considerable influence in 1866 and 1870, is now thoroughly obliterated, but there are, nevertheless, irrevocable ties such as the Partition of Poland with its endless consequences which unite Russia and Prussia. No such ties exist between Russia and the Empire. I should like to see our relations with Russia so carefully nurtured, that even if the worst happened (internal dissensions in the Empire) a Prussian-Russian alliance would be possible, regardless at whose cost. After Emperor Francis Joseph's death, there will be only two real monarchs. A firm Prussian should stand between them; a clumsy Swabian, a Liberal Badener, or a Catholic Bavarian would not be able to carry out the task. I am, furthermore, just as certain as I was in 1892 that a professional diplomat should represent us in St. Petersburg. I consider it particularly inadvisable to send a General there: the custom, which was so useful, of frequent meetings between our Ambassador and the Emperor has now been abolished. Now that the Marseillaise is being played, such a thing as Werder or myself, with Tsar Alexander clinking glasses with me in memory of St. Privat in the presence of General Chanzy at the Tsar's dinner table in Krasnoje seló and having the march of the Triumphal Entry into Paris played, would merely be a ghostlike anachronism. An Admiral might be better than a General. This third point I made in 1892: a personality who awakens confidence is no longer needed; the Empire needs a representative in St. Petersburg who can not only deal with Count Muravieff (which should not be difficult) but who is equally able to take a stand against Herr von Witte, one of the most remarkable statesmen of our day. Your Excellency could probably find such a man among people whom I do not know, but, unfortunately, the social position of the Ambassador, or the Ambassador and his wife, is so important in St. Petersburg, that this, in my opinion, is the most important consideration. The real intellectual study of the situation, though not the microscopic work, can be made in the *Villa* in the Königgrätzer Strasse; but the little accidents in the great *Morskoi* cannot be controlled from Berlin, and I therefore cannot think of any couple save Pourtales and his wife. I long for an hour's talk with you, but illness prevented me from attending the meeting of the Chapter of our Order and I find it difficult to make up my mind to undertake a journey unless there is some outward reason for it. With the request that you remember me to the Countess and your brother Alfred, I am, in true devotion, your very sincere   von Schweinitz

The remarks in this letter about Baron Ferdinand Stumm (who had been ambassador in Madrid under Bismarck) referred to his differences with Holstein. During the Caprivi-Marschall administration, Holstein had succeeded in making Stumm's post very distasteful to him by all kinds of intrigues. As a bachelor Count Alvensleben had been secretary of Embassy for several years in St. Petersburg, where he had acted as Chargé d'Affaires on several occasions and had made himself generally popular. His diplomatic standing had been somewhat harmed by his marriage with General Winterfeld's widow. She had been a Röder before her marriage. When Schweinitz mentioned the "clumsy Swabian", he meant Herr von Kiderlen-Wächter, his "liberal Badener" was Herr von Brauer, and his "Catholic Bavarian" was Count Berchem. Schweinitz hit the nail on the head when he emphasised that the Partition of Poland with all its consequences was an indissoluble bond with Russia as long as German politics were conducted in a sensible manner. He was also right when he demanded that our relations with Russia be so carefully nurtured that even if the worst came to the worst, a Prussian-Russian alliance would be possible, regardless at whose cost. This was true not only in view of possible differences within the Empire, but it was even more necessary to consider this matter in the light of our relations with Russia and Austria. If we wanted to be loyal to the spirit of Frederick the Great and of Bismarck, we could not afford to give up every possibility of coming to an arrangement with Russia at Austria's cost if the worst came to the worst.

During the summer of 1900, the Russian Foreign Minister, Count Muravieff, who was then 55 years old, died suddenly. His death was a loss to us, because he had two good qualities: he was clever enough to realise that a great war in the three Empires, especially in Russia, would be a serious danger to the monarchist form of Government, and he was filled with a deep distrust and dislike of the Poles. His death came very unexpectedly. Professor Renvers, who was my physician and friend for many years, told me that, shortly before his death, Muravieff came to him for an examination. Renvers, whose diagnosis seldom erred, found Muravieff's heart to be in perfect condition. Without making any definite statement, Renvers told me at the time that the Russian Foreign Minister's death had been a great surprise to him.   Fourteen years later, at the beginning of the World War, the Minister of Finance, Witte, also died rather suddenly and mysteriously.   Both Witte's and Muravieff's deaths were very convenient for the Pan-Slav revolutionary movement.   After considerable hesitation, Count Lambsdorff, who had been Muravieff's assistant, was appointed his successor on August 8, 1900.   Lambsdorff had been one of the most loyal disciples of Minister von Giers, who had been pacifically inclined and who had been very friendly to Germany.   Lambsdorff was one of the few officials in the Ministry on the "Singers' Bridge" at St. Petersburg, where Russian Foreign affairs were administered, who had been told about the German Re-insurance Treaty.   Giers had made use of Lambsdorff's abilities to prepare and draft the agreement.   *"C'est un homme de toute confiance,"* the Minister used to say about his assistant.   When Lambsdorff assumed office, he was very friendly towards us.   He was careful, discreet, a strict monarchist, and he wanted peace.   He had only one fault : he was of a very sensitive nature and he was not without vanity.   Our future relations with Russia depended a great deal upon how he was treated by us.

CHAPTER XXVI

Our Relations with England — Their Development since the Victorious Wars of 1866 and 1870 — Conference with Admiral von Tirpitz in the Wood at Düsternbrook — The Naval Bill Is Discussed by the Commission — Interpreting the Catchword "Weltpolitik" for Deputy Gröber's Benefit — Ambassador Count Hatzfeldt on the Subject of Salisbury and England — Count Paul Metternich's Memorandum on His Personal Impressions of England.

IT was with England that our relations were the most complicated and, therefore, the most difficult. When I took over the administration of the Foreign Office three years before, I had realised, as I have already pointed out, that our relations with Russia were even more vital than our relations with England. Our attitude towards Russia was a question of life and death. Our relations with England had passed through three stages during the second half of the nineteenth century. The Germans had never really been socially popular in England. For many years the Germans, who were considered harmless dreamers, were smiled upon more than they were hated or even envied, but our crushing victories of 1866 and 1870 caused astonishment and a certain amount of restlessness on the other side of the Channel.

I remember that the imaginative novel, "The Battle of Dorking", which fantastically but drastically described the sudden invasion of England, who had grown too careless, too lazy, and too pacific, by a wild Teuton Army, was widely read and discussed in the first half of the 'seventies by my English colleagues and friends, who, as a whole, took the book humorously, though some anxiety was already expressed in connexion with it. The French naturally poured oil on this fire, which, however, was so far only a small fire. It was in the 'eighties that Great Britain began to be actively jealous of Germany who had progressed economically in a brilliant and impetuous, perhaps too impetuous, a manner. It was soon proved that the order resulting from this jealousy, according to which all goods had to be marked "made in Germany", to show their country of origin, was a mistake. This enforced label did not prove to be a frightening deterrent; on the contrary, it became an enticement to buy and a recommendation to the buyer. German competition was not weakened, indeed it was strengthened, and so was England's jealousy.

I remember a conversation I had in Paris at the beginning of the 'eighties with the German Crown Princess. She was spending a few days in Paris on her return journey from London to Berlin. Because of Ambassador Chlodwig Hohenlohe's wisdom and tact this visit passed off without any unpleasantness. The Crown Princess had invited me (I was then second secretary of Embassy) and the Ambassador for luncheon at the Hotel Westminster, where she was staying. The Crown Princess, who was always entirely English until her death, complained to Hohenlohe, who smiled indulgently, that people in England, quite comprehensibly, were very dissatisfied, and this was very sad, because Germany was now competing "unpleasantly" and "excitedly" in branches of trade, in which England had heretofore controlled unchallenged markets. She said that the Germans should not be so "pushing." Her Royal and Imperial Highness's brother, the Duke of Connaught, who was also present, tactfully defended us poor Germans by saying that in this large world there was room for the Germans as well as for the English. But the Crown Princess persisted in asserting that our competition was too intensive and, as she claimed, not always "fair", and that it would cost us that English sympathy which we had enjoyed heretofore — a thing greatly to be regretted.

The Kruger telegram was the starting point of the second phase of Anglo-German relations. Baron Beyens, who was the Belgian Minister to Berlin before the World War, and who later became the Belgian Minister of Foreign Affairs, writes in his book about his stay in Berlin, which I shall mention again later, that Sir Edward Goschen, the British Ambassador in Berlin before the World War, told him a year before the war that the impression made in England by the Kruger telegram could never be entirely forgotten. This impetuous declaration shattered the friendly screen which, heretofore, had shrouded the discontent and dislike which had accumulated against us in England since the Franco-German War.

When we began to build our fleet, we entered the third and decisive stage of our relations with England. This development of our fleet, as I had emphasized in the Reichstag and in the country again and again and as I also pointed out in my memoirs, had become imperative because of our elemental economic development. I was transferred from Rome to Berlin to arrange the increase of our fleet, for such an increase had become a question of life and death to us. The problem was to see that such an increase did not lead to a war with England. I was to navigate the German ships through the danger zone, as the Kaiser and Tirpitz told me many times. From the very beginning I was fully aware of the difficulties involved in the task before me and every day while I was in office these difficulties became increasingly clear to me. I remember a grave conversation I had with Tirpitz in Kiel during the first few years of my Chancellorship. We were taking a walk along the charming grove which lies between Kiel and Düsternbrook. From the road, shaded by beautiful Holstein birch trees, we gazed down on Kiel Bay, which I had known as a Danish harbour during my childhood and across which I often sailed, on board the yacht *Meteor*, when I was Chancellor. The Kiel Fjord is the Queen of Baltic bays; it is as deep as the ocean and, on the other hand, protected against storms and wide enough to serve as a harbour for all the fleets of the world. It was here, on the same day in June on which, in 1897, I had been appointed as Secretary of State, that, in 1909, I was to receive my dismissal from Chancellorship on the magnificent yacht *Hohenzollern*, which, when I retired, was surrounded by the second largest navy in the world: the German navy. To-day the Kiel Harbour lies before us a quiet, empty, and dispossessed port. Once this port was our pride, to-day it is a sad, heart-rending reflection of our collapse and our downfall. In the course of our conversation, I asked Tirpitz when he thought that our fleet, which was in process of being built, would be formidable enough to make an unprovoked English attack too improbable for sensible people to contemplate. Tirpitz replied that, in 1904 or 1905, we should probably enter the critical phase of our relations with England. By this time our navy would have become so strong that it would cause anxiety and jealousy in England. After this critical period the danger of an attack from England would probably decrease. The English would then realise that any advance against us would probably imply an unreasonable risk for themselves. As we ourselves had no intention of attacking England, there would be nothing in the way of creating a basis for peaceful coöperation between the English and the German people.

As I mentioned in connexion with the Emperor's visit in England (November, 1899), Professor D. Hans Delbrück, who was an avowed pacifist, and one of the most zealous promoters of good relations between Germany and England and an admirer of von Bethmann-Hollweg, whose confidence he enjoyed, stated, after his visit to England in 1913, that English malevolence against Germany had vanished, that the building of the Fleet no longer troubled relations between the two countries, and that all was calm. The most terrible thing, in connexion with Germany's Fate, is the fact that we had really passed through the actual danger zone, that death had even taken the cards, which wily King Edward had shuffled so cleverly, from his hands when an almost unprecedented shortsightedness, thoughtlessness, and clumsiness on the part of Bethmann and Jagow made it possible for us to slide into the War.

In the spring of 1900, the year in which I became Chancellor, I had repeatedly discussed the aims and purposes of our new fleet in the Budget Committee of the Reichstag. Tirpitz asked me by letter and by word of mouth to take the responsibility for discussing the new Navy Bill in the Committee. Because of his age and his poor health the old Chancellor Hohenlohe was no longer able to attend the long meetings of the Committee. Though his voice was very low, Tirpitz was able to make successful speeches in the Reichstag if these speeches were prepared beforehand, but he was not sufficiently quick-witted to hold his own in the committee debates. In a committee meeting on March 27, 1900, I had made the following suggestions as the keynote of my statement:

The chief purpose of the Bill was to secure peace with England. As things were, a war with England would be very dangerous for us, because, in view of our present inferiority at sea, England might injure us very much, without any risk to herself. We, on the other hand, as long as our Navy was so small, would hardly find allies against England. And even if, in case of war, Russia were to come in on our side, the fact that we would be more open to attacks at sea would inflict the chief burden of a war upon ourselves so that we would suffer the chief losses. An unsuccessful war with England could throw back our political and economic development for generations, because our overseas interests, which have been increasing so markedly, could be destroyed, and because our export trade and industry could suffer infinite harm. We could only be sure of maintaining peace with England, as we sincerely wish to do, if an English attack on us seemed less dangerous than it does to-day. To-day the situation is such that we are well armed against attacks on land, but our defense at sea, in case of an attack by England, is very deficient. England is the only Power which could attack us without great risks to herself. There are two reasons why such an attack is possible : first, the fact that the Imperialist ideas, which have been gaining ground in England for years, will probably dominate after the South African Wars which will undoubtedly end in an English victory. Second, a general antipathy against Germany among the masses of the English people will surely find root in England because Germany is now a serious economic competitor in world markets as a result of our tremendous industrial development, our increasing trade, and our increasing overseas interests. In view of our weakness at sea, the majority of people in England consider a war with Germany as a relatively simple matter in which England would need only her Fleet and in which the English people would not be obliged to make any undue sacrifices, seeing that universal military service is not compulsory in England. Since a year ago, — so I went on in my confidential exposé, — our relations with England had twice reached a serious and critical pass through no fault of our own. It was not always possible to settle such incidents as the Samoa affair in the spring of 1899 and the case in 1900, when our postal boats were seized, through diplomatic channels. Both times England had been otherwise engaged, which had made a peaceful settlement more simple. And even in these circumstances, the feeling in England had made it possible to settle this difference only by using rather severe diplomatic pressure, but it would not be possible to repeat this pressure. If we do not take these warnings to heart, we might, the third time, find ourselves in a situation in which we must choose between grave humiliations and an unfortunate war. Just because we want to develop peacefully and side by side with England, because we want only peaceful industrial and economic competition, we must, at least, be in a position to defend ourselves against England.

In the course of the debate on March 27, 1900, I emphatically explained to Gröber, a Deputy of the Centre party, who had asked me for an authentic interpretation of the word *"Weltpolitik"*, that by this word I chiefly understood the tasks confronting us in view of the development of our industry, trade, and shipping. We could not check the increase of German overseas interests. We could not, furthermore, rebuke our own people for their industry, their ability to work, their alertness, and their intelligence. We have no intention at all of carrying out an aggressive policy of expansion. We intend only to protect the important interests which, through the natural course of events, we have acquired in all parts of the world. I could not understand the malicious opinion, so general in certain Centre Party circles, that we contemplated a "Protestant *Weltpolitik*." My policy in East Asia and in Asia Minor proved rather conclusively that I was quite as concerned with Catholic as I was with Protestant interests. My policy was neither Protestant nor Catholic, but German. Offensive tactics were entirely remote from our minds, we were not contemplating any adventurous or fantastic policies; what we wanted was to continue our economic and political development by peaceful means. I assured Deputy Richter that the behaviour of our officers in Samoa had been correct, careful, and controlled. In fact our naval officers had been unjustly blamed for not acting more promptly. Our consular

representatives had acted strictly in accordance with the Samoa
Statute then in force. English and American vessels had, despite
this fact, suddenly appeared at Samoa; they had bombarded and
destroyed German property and had violated the Samoa Statute.
Energetic diplomatic pressure had to be taken so as to make the
English agree to coöperate in the appointment of a joint Commission
appointed by the three Powers. The manner in which the Samoa
question was treated by English public opinion proved how
precarious our relations with England were at that time and
indicated the spread of imperialist and jingo ideas in England. I
only approved of sending our fleet to Manila to protect Germany's
great economic interests there. Any enmity against America was
distant from our minds. But in the United States also the Government and the people had, ever since the Spanish-American War,
become so chauvinistic that the mere presence of German vessels
had sufficed to bring about the tension which I had been fortunate
enough to settle amicably. These incidents went to prove to what
dangers peace was exposed in view of our present naval weakness.
I explained to the Deputy, Bebel, that the Navy Bill and my
peace policy towards England were not contradictory. Both had
the same purpose: the maintenance of peace. We wanted to
strengthen our Fleet because this would insure our safety against
the danger of an English attack; we were pursuing a foreign
policy which did not offend England's susceptibility because we
did not want to blunder into a conflict with England. I met the
criticism of those who maintained that the Kaiser's visit to England,
the South-Sea Agreement regarding Samoa, and the South African
Agreement showed too great a friendliness towards England, by
pointing out that the Kaiser's visit, these agreements, and particularly our absolute neutrality during the Boer War were in conformity with our necessary duty of maintaining friendly relations
with England. The European world situation as well as the protection of German interests made such a friendship with England
imperative. We could not sacrifice the greater and more important
interests in South Africa to smaller and less important ones.

I replied at once and emphatically to Deputy Bebel's interruption:

Even if our Navy were greatly increased, we would pursue a reasonable and thoughtful policy. I pointed out that I had, of course, never made the statement attributed to me that we would go for someone as soon as we had a powerful fleet. I was not a fool and did not talk nonsense. Even with a strong fleet, we would pursue just as pacific a policy. If we were more powerful at sea, other nations would respect us more highly and incidents such as the Samoa Affair and the seizure of postal vessels would, so we hoped, not be repeated. I finally emphasised — and not with the entire approval of von Tirpitz, who wanted, above all, to hasten the building of a large battle fleet — that I must lay great stress on the demand for ships in our foreign stations as these were necessary for the protection of our commercial interests. We were in need of greater protection, particularly in South America and East Asia, and this protection we would derive from an increase in cruisers. It was after the long and stormy meeting of the Budget Committee on March 27, 1900, that, as I have already mentioned in my book, " German Politics," Eugen Richter, the leader of the People's Party, stepped up to me and said to me privately : "You will put it through. You will have a majority for your Navy Bill. I would never have thought it." I tried, in the discussion which followed this remark, to explain to this man, who in many ways was very capable, why I could not understand his rejection of the Navy Bill, for German Democrats had for decades demanded that Germany's prestige at sea be properly maintained. Herwegh, I said, had composed the cradle song of the German Fleet and the first battleships had been constructed in 1848. I pointed out all the reasons why we must protect our trade and industries on the high seas. Richter listened to me politely and attentively and then he finally said : "Perhaps you are right. But I am too old to follow this turn of events." The turn of events, which Eugen Richter prophesied, occurred while the coalition "bloc" was in power.

In the spring of 1899, before the Imperial visit to Windsor and Sandringham, I had drawn the attention of our Embassy in London to Morocco. France's efforts to increase her North African possessions by Morocco became increasingly obvious and the idea that

Germany and England might come to some agreement about the future of this country seemed opportune. Count Hatzfeldt answered my suggestions by sending Holstein a long letter on July 8, 1899. He first pointed out that the English Prime Minister had not in the slightest forgotten the personal attacks which Kaiser William II had been rash enough to launch against him. Though Lord Salisbury pretended to be haughtily indifferent, he was really (as was obvious from various remarks he had made) still very much irritated by what our Kaiser had said. The political discussions about Morocco had given the English Prime Minister an opportunity to make some sharp remarks on the subject. He, the Ambassador, had serious doubts concerning the advisability of quoting these remarks in his official reports; this would only have poured oil into the fire. During his talk with Lord Salisbury he had not, however, hesitated to warn him about the possible results of his change of front towards Germany. He talked as few men in London would have dared to do.

When Lord Salisbury permitted a certain incredulity regarding other European alliances to become apparent, Hatzfeldt told him that he could inform him confidentially of a possibility which had come to his own notice, when the English Prime Minister's friend, Baron Courcel, the French Ambassador in London, had offered Germany French support in the second half of the 'nineties, if we would include Egypt in the list of claims to be made, which we had declined to do. And there were other countries, apart from France, which were making an effort to come to some understanding with us, probably at England's expense. Goschen, of the Admiralty, had recently remonstrated with Hatzfeldt, that Germany could not want to impair England's strength. Count Hatzfeldt had agreed that this was indeed the case as long as Germany's rightful interests were sufficiently taken into consideration by England. The danger of alliances, which would be hostile to England, would exist, however, as long as Germany was so badly treated and as long as there was no understanding or active support of German interests in England. Even though England's Fleet was so very powerful, it could not be denied that certain possible alliances might place England in an uncomfortable position, which could be prevented by a greater friendliness towards Germany.

Lord Salisbury, to whom the allusion to the conversation with Mr. Goschen did not seem very desirable, had not gone into the subject of other political possibilities. When Count Hatzfeldt urged him to express his opinion by pointing out the great uncertainty of the future, Lord Salisbury remarked that, in certain cases, England would be obliged to act according to her motto: *"Dieu et mon droit."* He added politely that he did not for a moment doubt the friendly intention of the Ambassador's probings. His personal irritation again became apparent at once, when Count Hatzfeldt mentioned Morocco. After Lord Salisbury had turned and twisted for some time in his efforts to avoid any exact statement, he said that the chief reason for his disapproval of the questionable agreement was a decided and fundamental aversion to all agreements, by which the property of living people was apportioned in advance. When Count Hatzfeldt remonstrated, pointing out that Lord Salisbury had done exactly the same thing in connexion with the colonies belonging to Portugal, a power friendly to England, the Prime Minister responded briskly that it was Mr. Balfour who had done this, but he was not blaming him for it; he, Salisbury, would not have concluded the Anglo-German Agreement regarding the Portuguese colonies.

The Ambassador immediately and emphatically protested, pointing out that, in 1899, the essential clauses of this German-English Agreement had been negotiated with Lord Salisbury himself. Whereupon Lord Salisbury had shrugged his shoulders and repeated that he would not have concluded this agreement with us. When Count Hatzfeldt emphasized further, that the chief point now was to restore good relations between Germany and England, which had been considerably darkened by various incidents, such as Samoa, and that a consideration of our interests in Morocco would be the best way to restore these relations, Lord Salisbury answered with a certain amount of bitterness: "You want to give your Kaiser a pleasure by arranging this, and I am to help you do it." In the course of his letter to Holstein, Count Hatzfeldt asked for my consent not to include personal irritable remarks of this kind on the part of the Prime Minister, especially remarks about His Majesty the Kaiser, in his official reports, because by including these remarks, considering the situation, the greatest harm might be done. He himself would do all in his power to change the English Prime Minister's irritation against His Majesty the Kaiser into a quiet, objective attitude in the face of the political situation. But time would be needed to accomplish this end. The Ambassador's opinion, based on years of experience, made him realise that he must do nothing at all for the present. Above all, he must avoid giving the impression that, despite the lack of friendship we had been shown by the English, we were running after their friendship. That was what our Ambassador in London had said before the Kaiser's visit in England.

A few weeks after that visit, Count Hatzfeldt wrote to Holstein on December 26, 1899: "If you tell me that public opinion in Germany will only accept Zanzibar if the English take Delagoa Bay, I am, of course, convinced that it must be so. But, on the other hand, I believe — and Eckardstein accepted this fact as agreed at our last meeting — that we are not nearly ready for Zanzibar here; neither the Government nor the people are ready for it. The reason is very simple. The public thinks that England can conquer the Boers under all circumstances, if a few million more or less are spent for this purpose and if enough reinforcements are sent. People here consider themselves completely protected against any European entanglements or against any dangers that might result from such entanglements. People hold this opinion, in the first place, because of the powerful English Fleet and, secondly and above all, because neither Russia nor France would ever decide to attack England. I cannot decide to what extent the second supposition is based on the truth. It is my personal opinion, which I have frequently expressed, that the French will certainly not undertake anything of this kind on their own and that the Emperor of Russia is not particularly belligerent. I do not believe, furthermore, that either of them, even together, would ever launch such an attack, if they were not sure of us. Our coöperation, however, would change the situation at once and might be very expensive for England. All we should have to consider would be whether such a coöperation was consistent with our future political interests, as such a step would seriously weaken England as a World Power. Even Prince Bismarck, despite his Russian sympathies, was not of the opinion that this was consistent, and I completely agree with him. As regards the next step in these matters, we must, I think, see our aims clearly. In my opinion we should discreetly give the English to understand that we are not at all hostile towards them, but that we, too, must take public opinion in our country into consideration, for public opinion would throw rotten apples at us if we let Delagoa Bay go without gaining distinct advantages from such a deal. Conclusion: If you cannot offer us advantages of this kind, keep your hands off and do as best you can without Delagoa, otherwise you will lead us into an undesirable situation, and public anger in our country would force us to adopt another line of action. If this idea is correct in principle, I should appreciate it if the Secretary of State would signify his approval to me, so that I can arrange the future discussions between Eckardstein, Chamberlain, Balfour, etc., along these lines (I myself shall have to keep in the background). I assume that Balfour particularly will understand the situation and that he will, therefore, be useful to us. Chamberlain, as I have always told you, is unaccountable. Regarding Salisbury, I have an intuition (so far it is nothing more tangible than an intuition) that he is again considering a *rapprochement* with the Russians and with the French to-day, that he wishes to pacify them by being friendly and conciliatory or, if necessary by real concessions, so that he can prevent them from undertaking any joint action against England. If he succeeds in preventing any hostile action in St. Petersburg, there would not be the slightest fear of France alone here, and there are people enough, like Chamberlain, who would greatly rejoice at an opportunity of destroying the French Fleet and shooting up a few French harbour towns. I consider Münster's reports about anti-English activities in France fantastic. Even if everything that our Ambassador in Paris reports about French movements is true, this does not by any means indicate

PRIVY COUNCILLOR FRIEDRICH VON HOLSTEIN

that the French will bite when the decisive moment comes and not, as at Fashoda, put their tails between their legs. I consider the latter possibility certain unless the Russians have expressly committed themselves to attack simultaneously, which I very much doubt."

In June, 1900, Holstein had told me that von Eckardstein, the Councillor of the Embassy, had written to say that the English would not put up with any German attempt to settle in the Yangtse Valley. Even the suspicion that Germany might be considering political acquisition in the Yangtse Valley was enough to cause the English to make the greatest efforts towards an understanding with Russia. Eckardstein was more and more becoming the mouthpiece of Mr. Chamberlain, who used this vain, somewhat weak son-in-law of Sir John Blundell Maple. Financial considerations had caused Eckardstein to become very Anglicised and Chamberlain used him to intimidate the Germans. As a matter of fact I had never even considered an acquisition of territory in the Yangtse Valley, much less had I thought of this in terms of a difference or a conflict with England. Eckardstein wrote to Holstein that Lord Salisbury was more inclined to come to an understanding with other countries than with Germany. The Prime Minister found all definite policies disagreeable and it would take strong pressure from his fellow members of the Cabinet to make the ill old man come to any decision. The rest of the Cabinet was inclined to be friendly towards Germany, but they would all unite against Germany if the Yangtse Valley had to be defended against any German annexationist plans.

Count Paul Metternich, who was still Prussian Minister in Hamburg, spent several months in England, where he had many personal friends, in the winter of 1900. When he returned to Germany, in the summer of 1900, he handed me a memorandum of his personal impressions of England. In this memorandum, he wrote among other things: "When I arrived in England early in February, I was told by a number of people that Lord Salisbury was an old and broken man, who would not be in the forefront of affairs very much longer. If I remember rightly, he is seventy years old. The long illness of his wife, whom he lost early last winter, and to whom he was very devoted, was a great grief to him and harassed him very much. The South African War, in which he became involved without his own participation, laid bare before the world many abuses and diminished England's prestige, particularly early in the winter. This probably affected him as well. He is, at heart, a proud patriot, and England's prestige is personified in him among living statesmen. But, as is the way of the world, when a human being sees disasters threaten, they often depress him more than the actual calamity itself, and his wife's death was really a burden off his mind (for time's healing power is greater in the old than in the young) and Lord Salisbury was more free to turn his attention to public life. The war, too, took a turn for the better. England's deep political depression was over and the harm done by the inefficiency of her generals seemed to be compensated for by her great resources in money and human material, which were now at the disposal of the country and the Empire. A happier, fresher mood filled people's minds. This fact, too, may have been responsible for shaking Lord Salisbury out of the lethargic state into which age, misfortune, and increasing obesity had plunged him. When I first saw him the middle of February, I thought that he looked better than he looked four years previously. Only his gaze is less clear, his manner is more uncertain, I might say more vague, than it was. He is now extremely careful what he says and when he believes that he has admitted anything he at once tries to weaken his statement. He was always known as a *cunctator*. His age, the war situation, perhaps also a distrust of us, may have sharpened this natural characteristic, though I know that personally he was very friendly towards me. After the death of his wife, it was said that he was going to resign. In February and March, he made some speeches in the House of Lords, which were so poor that his friends were embarrassed. Lord Rosebery picked him to pieces so sharply that it was considered unfair to treat the weak old man in so rough a manner. Later on, Lord Salisbury again made great speeches and to-day he is once more the chief speaker. His Party has always had a lot of fault to find with him, especially because of his inclination to make biting remarks about persons and movements, without any consideration of the voters. He never solicited favour from public opinion. He is considered the greatest living English statesman. No one, so his fellow countrymen believe, is equally experienced in the conduct of state affairs, especially foreign affairs. His prudence and reserve are considered virtues, even though there have been occasions, such as the open-door question in China, when he has been forced by public opinion to act and when he was reproached for his indecision. The English people do not like to plunge into inconsidered adventures, and they are grateful in the long run to people who hold them back from adventures of this kind. I do not see why Lord Salisbury should relinquish the reins of the chariot of state, and few men retire from important posts without some forcible reason.

"It is said that Lord Salisbury is against new general elections. Chamberlain is in favour of them. Salisbury probably feels that his post is secure for two years to come, whereas new elections would harbour a certain element of uncertainty. I consider Lord Salisbury too distinguished a statesman to believe that he would be influenced by personal sympathies. I do not believe, therefore, that he has preferences or aversions for this or that country. I do not consider him an enemy of Germany, but I am far from assuming that he would show us any special confidence. Earlier periods of history may have left the impression in his mind that, in case of war, we would prefer to join our powerful territorial neighbours rather than strive for an understanding with England, but that, in the meantime, we would like to derive colonial and other advantages from an understanding with England. But we shall not find it easy to deal with Lord Salisbury or his successor until the need for a special understanding with us is felt in England beforehand. It is to be assumed that Lord Salisbury is just as little a particular friend of France as he is of Germany. He is, however, just as likely to come to an understanding with France about current political issues, if it suits his general policy, that is to say, if it is in the interest of England. Recently, when I said good-bye to him, he brought up the question — and in a way

that seemed to show his wish to answer this question in the affirma-
tive — whether France, after the World Exposition, might not turn
against England. The elements of unrest seem to be coming stronger
and more dangerous in France.   Mr. Bertie, the Under-Secretary of
State, expressed the same idea.   He said that the increase of French
troops in Madagascar could only be interpreted as a demonstration
against England.   Lord Salisbury opposed the French with Fashoda,
that is to say, he suppressed the beginnings of an armed French
penetration into the upper Nile regions by force.   He would not be
able to offer the Russians a Fashoda so easily, because the Russians
can advance against England's power by land, whereas the French
must first cross the sea, where England's fleet is supreme.   English
policy, whether it be under Lord Salisbury or someone else's administration, will gradually and unwillingly tend to withdraw before the
Russian advance in North China and Persia.   At the Indian
frontier, however — where the Russians have not yet established
themselves, and where, contrary to a prevalent opinion, it would not
be so simple for them to establish themselves — the English would,
in my opinion, use armed force without any hesitation at all.   An
understanding between England and Russia is farther afield than
an understanding between England and France.   But neither is to
be expected at once.   Italy considers Lord Salisbury as a *quantité
négligeable*.   He, in turn, pays little attention to Italy's nervous
wishes and he is equally unafraid that she might unite with France.
He believes that Italy's interests lie within the scope of English
politics.   Among the masses of the English people Mr. Chamberlain
is the most popular man and is victoriously and confidently leading
England into new phases of Imperialism.   As the leading Minister
of Foreign Affairs he is, however, feared by the upper ten thousand,
because he is considered unstable and it is believed that, as horseman and charioteer, he will take wild leaps and bounds.   Mr.
Chamberlain would still like to coöperate with Germany.   He
would like to raise the colonial questions which could divide or unite
us according to the way in which they are handled.   He would like
to deal with the practical execution of the German-English agreement concerning South Africa.   After the consolidation of the

territories embracing Rhodesia and two Boer Republics, the need for access to the sea will soon become apparent and the Delagoa question may then become urgent. As regards the increase in the French forces occupying Madagascar, England would rather solve this problem with us than without us, regardless of our agreement. Apart from the fact that Portugal's approval must be obtained first, the difficulty in arranging our agreement lies in the stipulation that we are to proceed *pari passu*. Each party will jealously guard against any possibility of another party going ahead all alone, while the disorganisation of the Portuguese colonies and the natural conditions favouring the occupation by a third party might mature more rapidly in one colony than in another. It will be difficult to carry out a piecemeal disintegration in favour of both parties signing the agreement simultaneously, if certain sections are more firmly attached than others. If the Delagoa Bay question is to be raised first, we have the advantage, for England would be obliged to come to us with suggestions.

"In contrast to Mr. Chamberlain, Lord Rosebery is considered a prudent and reliable statesman in foreign politics. Conservatives as well as Liberals would be glad to see him at the head of the Foreign Office. I do not consider him a very amenable Minister of Foreign Affairs, although I believe that he would rather coöperate with Germany than with France or Russia. Lord Rosebery is very dependent on public opinion, that is to say, he would be little inclined towards any action that would not allow him to assume that he would have the immediate support of public opinion. From our point of view the best Foreign Minister out of the Conservative camp would be Mr. Balfour, from the Liberal camp, Sir Edward Grey. The relations between England and America have undergone a change. Even if we had had warlike complications with America one or two years ago, I should have considered them the only danger of war between England and ourselves. To-day the situation is different. The Americans have shown their dislike of England too clearly, and though the English will not admit this fact to themselves or to anyone else, they know it perfectly well. England will stand far more from America than from any other Power, and even in purely diplomatic issues it is more difficult to make England take sides against America than to make any other Power do so. I have never believed that England harboured an aggressive purpose against Germany. I do not consider her capable of such sinister intentions — to descend upon our ships and destroy our commerce only to be rid of a competitor. English capital is too vitally interested in Germany to want to destroy German prosperity, and the game is not worth the burden of Germany's eternal enmity. Contrary to the opinion held by many clever men and by the majority of European cabinets, I would like to make the heretical statement that English politics are not consciously aimed at laying plans for a European war. A Machiavellian policy of this kind is remote from the English mentality, and I cannot see why the English should consider it an advantage to see Europe go up in flames. They are very well off as it is. The more favourable war situation has greatly improved the feeling towards Germany in England. His Majesty the Kaiser's visit, the journey to Altona, the fund for the sufferers in India, and other expression of sympathy have made a deep impression in England and are paving the way towards reconciliation."

In connection with Metternich's report, I should like to mention that the perfidy with which the English, immediately after the conclusion of the German-English Agreement of 1899 concerning the Portuguese colonies, wrecked this Agreement by concluding another agreement, the Windsor Agreement, with the Portuguese at the same time, was not known to Metternich any more than it was known to Ambassador Hatzfeldt, Holstein, or the Kaiser. I had, on the one hand, given my informant my personal word of honour that I would mention what he told me in confidence to no one. It seemed politically wiser, on the other hand, not to unbalance such excitable natures as William II and Holstein by informing them about it nor entirely to discourage Ambassador Hatzfeldt, who was fighting against great difficulties in any case.

CHAPTER XXVII

The English National Character — Our Underestimate of England — Our Errors in Judging of Foreign Peoples and Our Mistakes in Dealing with Them — Hatzfeldt's Comments to Holstein about England — Holstein on the Subject of an Anglo-German Alliance — Events in Eastern Asia — Prince Henry's Report to Bülow — Japan — Herr von Mumm Becomes Ketteler's Successor — His First Report — Home Politics.

MY career brought me into official contact with many official personalities. As a subordinate, as a colleague, and as a chief I saw many Ambassadors, Secretaries of State, and Ministers at work. There are few German diplomats whom I have not known or about whose abilities I have not been able to form a personal judgment. I may say that no type of diplomat is unknown to me. If I frequently quote letters and reports by Count Paul Metternich, who for many years was our Ambassador in London, I do so not only because of the objective contents of his reports but also because I consider him a master of the thoughtful, calm, and well-considered exposé. Unlike many Germans, Count Paul Metternich did not make a painful effort to copy the English and to imitate the way they clear their throats and spit, he did not try to put his hands in his trouser pockets as they do, nor did he take off his hat (or rather not take off his hat) to people as they did (or rather did not) ; this was one of his virtues, for he did not try to degrade the honest and efficient German Michael to a monkey aping the haughty John Bull. At the same time he had an open mind for the good and great aspects and above all for the enormous latent power of the British Empire. Contrary to most Germans, Metternich estimated this power for what it was worth. The underestimation of this power was an error which was particularly deep-rooted in Prussia, especially in Prussian military and aristocratic circles. When, in August, 1914, General von Moltke, the chief of the General Staff, was told that England had declared war, he gave a sigh of relief and said:

"Thank God! I would rather have the English army in front of me, so that I can defeat it, than have England observe malevolent neutrality out of my reach." In Munich a statement made by King Louis III was publicly placarded: "England has declared war on us. We have another enemy, therefore our victory will be all the more glorious." In more than one German city, the population sang "Now thank we all the Lord" with reverence and enthusiasm after England had declared war. I do not believe that a statement said by the Northcliffe Press to have been made by William II about "the contemptible little British Army" is authentic. But it is a fact that William II, despite his English tastes and habits, underestimated England's resources at least as far as her military and moral strength was concerned.

Even those Germans who were familiar with England's long and successful history, and who were not so naïve in judging her unlimited political egotism as the majority of their fellow countrymen, had only an incomplete idea of the strength of the English people and of the English national character generally. The old German mistake of interpreting important questions of international policy and events on the world's stage and the peoples of the world in the light of narrow German Party politics also affected the Germans' judgment of the English. The German Democrat, and particularly the German Social Democrat, looked at Tsarist Russia with grim eyes; his thoughtful forehead grew red with "angry indignation" when good or still more intimate relations with this "barbaric country" were suggested to him. For a long time many democratic Germans judged all Frenchmen in the light of the Dreyfus Affair. In the book of Judges, Chapter Twelve, verses 5 and 6, we are told that the men of Gilead forced every fleeing Ephraimite who tried to escape through the fords of the Jordan to utter the word "Shibboleth." If he could not do so in common with all who were of Gilead, and said "Sibboleth" instead of "Shibboleth", he was killed, so that in the days of Ephraim forty-two thousand men fell in this manner. For liberal-minded Germans the individual Frenchman's attitude towards the Dreyfus Affair was, for many decades, as important in judging French conditions

generally as the little word "Shibboleth" was to the brave men of
Gilead. Every Frenchman who had sympathised with Dreyfus
was considered a pacifist or even a pro-German, despite the fact
that many of the most active defenders of Captain Dreyfus, for
example, Clemenceau, the Minister of War, Picquart, Senator
Scheurer-Kestner, and others were rabid jingoes and German haters.
German conservatives, on the other hand, regarded the "nation of
shopkeepers" with contempt. They looked with mocking eyes
upon Wellington who, when he was surprised by a sudden rain
while he was conducting a parade, quickly opened an umbrella
which someone handed to him, and they scorned a country where
the sons of dukes become clerks in banking houses.

During the World War, when the English gave much proof of their
strong patriotism as well as of their undeniable personal courage,
an eminent German scholar, Professor Werner Sombart, wrote a
war book which he called "Heroes and Shopkeepers." The English were, of course, the shopkeepers while we were the heroes.
This was a great lapse in taste as well as an injustice, because if the
Germans, despite their commercial and industrial abilities, did
indeed show themselves to be heroes during the War, the same
praise must be granted to the British. Even before the War German Conservatives and Liberals agreed in their aversion to the
English cult which, contrasted with the more comfortable, that is
to say, the more slovenly and more bourgeois habits of the Germans,
put greater stress on form. These Germans agreed in their dislike
of English servility under the dominion of fashion. Even Prince
Bismarck was not entirely free from this general underestimation
of England's power and of the moral resources of the British
Empire. During the 'eighties I heard him say more than once that
the British Bull was getting too lazy, and that it was desirable in
the interest of the European balance of power that this quadruped
should be kicked by someone or other until he rose from his bed of
straw and himself kicked about vigorously. At that time Herbert
Bismarck told me confidentially that his great father had educed
as the fundamental motive of German colonial policy, which he had
inaugurated, his wish to create "artificial surfaces of friction"

between Germany and England, so that the then Crown Prince and Prince William, who had been brought up to be very Anglophile, would not lead us into a too ·great intimacy with England, an intimacy that would make us dependent on that country.   Bismarck considered such a state of dependence a danger both to our foreign and to our home policies.

When I look back after twenty years it seems to me that the members of the pious community in the Homburg Palace on the Hill were not entirely wrong when, on October 18th, 1900, they sang of the madness which sometimes guides the wise and the deception which rules the intelligent.   If I have always estimated Albion's power and danger correctly, I have not such poor taste nor am I so foolish as to think that I am wiser than Bismarck.   I was brought up in an international environment ; from the time I was very young I associated a great deal with foreigners, especially with Englishmen and Frenchmen.   I belonged to a younger generation than the great Prince and it was therefore easier for me to see England and the English, the Holy See and Catholicism, and perhaps even Democracy and Social Democracy as they really were.   Personally my attitude towards England was a mixture of admiration and jealousy : admiration for the power and virtues of the English people, for their love of tradition, which is the surest criterion of great and strong peoples, for their unbending national pride and their unshakable patriotism, and for their almost unerring political instincts which the German people lack.   The inscrutable will of Providence created the German as a ζῷον ἀπολιτιχόν, as almost all German parliamentary debates, especially when they concern questions of foreign affairs, as the political expectorations of a Sombart, a Lasson, or a Haller, go to prove.   The prerequisite of all healthy politics is the realisation that might is the essential factor in any great state.   But when the World War was at its height and the final crisis was approaching fast, when Lloyd George was talking about a "knockout blow" and Clemenceau was preaching a *"Guerre jusqu'au bout"*, when both were rousing the pride, the ambition, and the might of their people, in Germany the Court Preacher, Dr. Adolf von Harnack, wrote a letter in which childish naïveté mingled with senile complacency. In this letter, which by some indiscretion appeared in the Munich *"Bayrischer Kurier"*, Dr. von Harnack said that he was coming to the conclusion more and more that the will to power is sinful. What this learned old gentleman's students should have called out to him is "Get thee to a nunnery, Ophelia." Or better still they should have used the words that the great English statesman Disraeli once used in the English House of Commons: "Professors and rhetoricians invent systems and principles. Real statesmen are inspired only by an instinct for power and by their love for their country. Great Empires are created only by emotions and methods such as these."

A considerable number of people, particularly among the educated classes in Germany, did not realise that the will to power is the main-spring and soul of any great state, nor did they appreciate the importance of good breeding in international intercourse. Some Germans made a repellent impression abroad because of their rough manners, their aggressiveness, and their loud boasting. The *miles gloriosus* contributed far less to our unpopularity (with very few exceptions, the German officer was well-bred and polite) than did the conceited "Herr Doktor" or "Herr Professor" or, to an even greater degree, the pioneers of our commerce who did not mind walking over corpses. We had never been very popular and now we began to be hated. This fact was mentioned to me by Swiss, Dutch, Italian, Scandinavian, and English friends every time I met them, after every international Congress. And William II, who was filled with a burning desire to win us not only the respect but the love of the world, failed unfortunately to help to make us more popular abroad, because he incorporated many of the weaknesses and the unsympathetic characteristics of the modern German. We were gradually getting on the world's nerves, only we ourselves did not notice this fact until the end of the World War.

Bethmann, Michaelis, Hertling, none of them were men of the world, they had not experienced a man of the world's training and they lacked worldly manners. Nor was this lack compensated for by any exceptional technical knowledge, as was the case with men like Posadowsky and Tirpitz. Nor were they conscious of their shortcomings, for, in common with the majority of their educated fellow country-men, they were convinced that a moral character, a few examinations passed with honours, and perhaps the title of *"Hofrat"* or *"Geheimrat"* were quite sufficient to ensure a welcome for a worthy German anywhere.

None of our post-Revolution Chancellors, such as Scheidemann, Fehrenbach and Wirth, Hermann Müller and Bauer, not to mention the most influential and the most active German politician of the first revolutionary years, Mathias Erzberger, were men of the world in any sense of the word. They had no knowledge whatsoever of good-breeding and worldly forms.

All these phenomena remained hidden from the Germans at the turn of the century. During the War they at first astonished the Germans immensely and then made them feel bitter when, with the dissolution and the disappearance of our glorious army, the respect for Germany, for the individual German, for the German intellect diminished everywhere by 80%. Very few of us realised that social antipathies as well as economic jealousy and political enmity separated us from other peoples. The ugly word "Boche", which the French have inflicted on our people, a people which has produced a Hölderlin and a Mozart, a Goethe and a Wilhelm Humboldt, a people which in its language and its poetry and in all the arts is more tender, more deeply sincere, and more sensitive in the best sense of the word than any other people, — this word signifies that the English do not consider us gentlemen, that the French do not think we are *gens du monde,* and that the Italians find us lacking in *gentilezza.* If I was able to realise these potential differences so long ago, it was because I had lived abroad the greater part of my life, because I knew foreign countries and foreign literatures and because I followed the foreign press. During the World War, German friends, honest and learned men in important positions, on the other hand, told me with a certain pride that they never, "as a matter of principle", took up any foreign newspapers.

The more I had become familiar with my sphere of activity since 1897, that is to say, during three years of work, the more I realised that it was my chief task to maintain peace with dignity and honour; it became increasingly clear to me that this task was, in part, identical with the problem of putting through the Navy Bill without any clash with Albion. Holstein, who liked to make pointed remarks, said that this idea reminded him of squaring a circle or of manufacturing a wooden knife out of iron. And even for a thoughtful, penetrating mind this task was, indeed, a very, very difficult one. Often, during the nine summers which I spent in Norderney as Chancellor, I looked with anxiety from our home, Villa Edda, on to the dark and turbulent North Sea, our German Ocean, and asked myself whether God would grant that I should solve this task. Before and after my appointment as Chancellor, I always urged calm and courage, particularly in dealing with England. When, on January 10th, 1900, I christened the Hamburg-America Line steamship *Deutschland* at the Vulkan docks in Stettin, I said in my speech that Germany, who had entrusted immense treasures to the sea, that the German people, who for a long time had been an inland people in the heart of Europe, but now occupied a leading place in world competition, must be fortified at sea, so that our peace, our honour, and our welfare could be maintained:

"Even if we must surmount difficulties and overcome obstacles on this road which Fate has prescribed for us, this will not dishearten us nor damp our courage. We must and shall progress courageously and steadfastly." [1]

Grand Duchess Louise of Baden, the daughter of the first and the sister of the second German Kaiser and the wife of a German Prince who harboured the sacred flame of the German national ideal with special depth and purity in his heart, telegraphed to me the next day: "I hesitate to take up your time, on which there are so many demands, even for a moment, but I cannot resist telling you what a grateful echo the patriotic, moderate, and enthusiastic words of the speech you made yesterday in Stettin found within me. I send you heartfelt good wishes for this remarkable speech, which was so encouraging and convincing at such a grave time."

The task with which I had been confronted had been solved

[1] Prince Bülow's "Speeches" (large edition), I. 98; (small edition), I. 131.

successfully beyond all expectation, yes, it had been brilliantly solved, when a World War, caused neither directly nor indirectly by our Fleet, nor started by England or against England, but due rather to the unskilful treatment of a chronic Oriental ulcer, brought my efforts of long and fruitful years to a close. I was like a physician, who knows that he has guided a beloved friend safely through many dangerous and critical illnesses, and then stands, utterly shaken, at the deathbed of his friend who has been killed by clumsy quacks.

The letters which Count Paul Hatzfeldt sent to Baron Holstein during the last weeks of my administration as Secretary of State were of timely political interest to me. Late in July, 1900, the Ambassador wrote and told his friend that he did not have very good news for him. As he had probably read between the lines of the dispatches from London, Salisbury was creating difficulties concerning the High Command, and it was impossible to guess what attitude he would finally adopt. The Ambassador was now trying to send Lascelles into the thick of it and to interest Chamberlain in the matter. But he must tell him in confidence that the feeling toward us in English Government circles was not favourable. The Foreign Office was out of sorts, because we had not taken up its suggestion concerning a Japanese intervention in China. Hatzfeldt had not been bashful and had emphatically told the Foreign Office that, in view of German public opinion, the German Government's attitude in South Africa as well as in China had been extraordinarily proper and deserving of thanks. As regards the Japanese intervention, no one could have expected us to incur Russia's enmity, simply "*pour les beaux yeux de l'Angleterre*", when we could not even be sure that we could count on England's support. Lascelles had not denied this fact, but he had continually reverted to the statement that our attitude was certainly not considered as consistently friendly in England. The letter closed with the words:

I hope that you will agree with me that it is best, for the present, not to report about the symptoms officially, as this might be very harmful in influential circles. But I do not think that I can keep the truth from you or from the Secretary of State Count Bülow. You must know that, at the moment, we cannot count on friendly feelings here.

On the 20th of August, 1900, Hatzfeldt had written to Holstein:

With regard to our relations with the present English Cabinet, I regretfully uphold the opinion I have expressed to you so often before: that we cannot expect any favours from Salisbury, the present Prime Minister. I think that I know him better than any other foreigner does, and I know that pride is his most important characteristic. His pride has been hurt by certain political and, above all, personal incidents, and nothing that I can say would change his feeling in the matter. Only political necessity would cause him to raise certain issues, just as he raised the question of the High Command *de mauvaise grâce* and because he could not avoid it. We must, therefore, try to make events move so that he must follow our lead, as he did in the case of the High Command, and so that he does not realise that he is doing us a special favour. Personally I believe that we must contend with him for some time to come, for I do not think the rumours that he will resign are true, nor do I believe that new general elections or other circumstances will lift him out of the saddle. In my opinion, furthermore, we must realise that Lord Salisbury is not the only individual in the Government party who is unfriendly towards us. When I tried to influence some of the other Ministers in our favour in the question of the High Command the other day, I found that, politically, they understood the necessity of meeting us halfway, but that, personally, they were not very enthusiastic. The officials in the Foreign Office, as I have written to you before, are not at all friendly towards us, towards Germany and the Germans, even though they do adopt a friendly manner. People in the Foreign Office are naïve enough to think that our interests in all important political questions, if we understand them correctly, must be in harmony with England's interests and that we ought to follow England's lead, without asking any special rewards or advantages for ourselves. Socially, we are not very popular either. I hear from a very good source that, at Cowes, the other day, circles very close to His Majesty (Lord Ormonde, etc.) were not at all disappointed, when the *Meteor* did not win the race. The sum total of all these considerations seems to me to be, that we should make an effort to show these people without animosity, whenever any question arises, that, as in the Yangtse question, they cannot have what they want from us so easily, unless they show us proper consideration. This presupposes, of course, that we do not commit ourselves irrevocably to Russia either. In so far as one can judge the feeling towards us in Russia by the newspapers, such a commitment would not give us much satisfaction either.

The English Prime Minister's personal ill-humour against us was due, as is well known, to repeated friction between him and William II, which the haughty Lord could not forgive the reckless monarch. The Marquis of Salisbury never forgot his personal quarrel with Emperor William, which he had before I became Chancellor when the Kaiser paid his first visit to England; he never forgave the Kaiser for trying (behind the back of his constitutionally appointed German adviser) to discredit him, leading English minister though he was, in the eyes of his grandmother, Her Majesty Queen Victoria. As a matter of fact, Lord Salisbury was not the only distinguished minister of a Great Power who took attempts such as these on the part of a foreign sovereign amiss. The real reason why Prince Bismarck raised the question of the Austrian alliance so quickly and so vehemently in 1879 was, as everyone will remember, his suspicion that Alexander II — either alone or with the coöperation of Field Marshal von Manteuffel — had tried to incite his uncle, the old Emperor William, who was at Alexandrovo, against Bismarck.

To return to Morocco: Holstein wrote to me on August 24th, 1900, at Norderney:

I, too, feel great anxiety that the Moroccan question may become acute. We must figure that Salisbury may have to give up the entire Moroccan territory as far as the Atlantic Ocean, apart from Tangier, to the French in order to win their acquiescence in other questions, for instance, China and the Yangtse Valley, or in the hope that a French advance towards the Atlantic Ocean would cause Germany to proceed against France. As a matter of fact I am not sure whether we could indeed permit such an advance, and whether we should not undertake some prophylactic but grave diplomatic step in Paris to counteract such a possibility. The Sultan of Morocco's second memorandum (an urgent call for help) might be the starting point for this diplomatic step. It would be necessary for Münster to interrupt his leave on this account. The general trend and the manner of our first communication would have to be decided. We must either enquire what France is planning to do, or we must suggest that we should come to terms in Morocco. Considering the peculiarities of the French the second possibility would seem to be rather hopeless. We ought not to wait too long before taking action, for when the French Government has committed itself to a plan, it will be all the more difficult for it to retract, and naturally the answer we receive from the French will depend very much upon the momentary status of French as well as German relations with other powers, particularly England. If German-English relations are strained, France will perhaps begin to think about war, particularly as France can be sure of Russian support, at any rate after the first French defeat, even though the Russians do not come to their aid at once. It is true, on the other hand, that the most hopeful factor making for peace is the fear that a victorious general might be a danger to the present Government of the Republic. At the present time our relations with England are more important than ever, and I would give a great deal if Salisbury were unwilling to continue in office or if he were incapable of doing so. But it looks as though neither of these alternatives were going to happen. Hatzfeldt's last letter sounded very resigned: no wonder, for everybody is being set against us. Jealousy and hatred of our most gracious Sovereign are increasing steadily because of his excessively arrogant manner. The fact that the miserable little Russian is now going to Denmark is again an obvious demonstration against His Majesty.

My attitude toward a German-English alliance, as I should like to repeat in connexion with previous statements, remained unchanged. It was the same attitude I had expressed, in agreement with Chancellor Hohenlohe and Ambassador Hatzfeldt, during the three preceding years, and it was the same attitude which had been expressed before then by Caprivi and Marschall, and above all by Bismarck. In common with them I should have been glad to conclude any agreement which distributed the obligations and the risks equally between the two Great Powers. We could not possibly enter upon a *Societas leonina* in favour of the British lion. For this reason it was our duty to insist that a German-English agreement should not be secret, but that the Parliaments of both countries should approve of it. This was necessary, if for no other reason, because there would otherwise be a danger that, in case of war, England would try to get out of her obligations by a change of Government.

The second premise for our acceptance of an alliance was a guarantee that if we agreed to protect English possessions, — especially if the Russians attacked India, — the English would agree to help us in case the Russians attacked Austria-Hungary, or the French attacked Italy. Otherwise our relations with Austria-Hungary and Italy would be controlled in London and our two Allies would be dependent on England. Emperor William II agreed with this point of view. Shortly before my resignation, in February, 1909, he wrote a marginal note to an article in the " *Berliner Tageblatt* " about the German-English treaty negotiations of 1899 and 1900 :

I remember distinctly that Chamberlain made an offer of an alliance when I was in Homburg vor der Höhe in the spring. Metternich, who had been assigned to the Foreign Service, was with me and we discussed the matter while we were riding up the *Feldberg*. Chamberlain wanted us to take over the part which Japan later played : to keep Russia away from India by armed force. The matter fell through when I demanded that a treaty of alliance, signed by the English Cabinet, was to be submitted to the English Parliament and be unanimously accepted by both houses.

The last remark of this marginal note was an exaggeration. We had, of course, never demanded a unanimous vote in Parliament. We had only asked that the treaty of alliance should be accepted by the English Parliament in agreement with the two great parties.

Prince Henry continued in sensible letters to inform me about events in East Asia. He wrote me with satisfaction that Herr Wiegand, the excellent director of the Bremen North German Lloyd, had been in Tsingtau and that he had been "extremely pleased" by the local situation. Wiegand expressed "great appreciation" for what had been achieved so far. After a visit to Japan the Prince wrote to me :

A phrase in one of your last speeches in the *Reichstag* which included a compliment to Japan reached me here and was very opportune. Compliments of this kind never fail to make an impression on the Japanese, and fall on the very fertile soil of their great vanity. It is astonishing what this country has done in the last twenty years to achieve the position it now undoubtedly holds. Japan wants to be treated and regarded as a great power and I can only add that it has a right to both.   I was told that Japan's trade relations are always favourable with whatever other country treats her best.   The courtesy, politeness, and consideration with which I was treated in this country are beyond praise.   On the Chinese coast Europeans tend to judge the Japanese harshly and unfavourably, and I must admit that until I had gained personal experience I was strongly influenced by their judgment.   Their aversion is probably due to the fact that Japanese business men are not as reliable as the Chinese and that it is no longer possible to live in Japan in the same conditions in which one lived twenty years ago.   This opinion is, however, one-sided and narrow.   A people like the Japanese, who are making every effort to emancipate themselves from the Europeans and to gain their independence, are naturally not very popular among the latter.   But I do not think it right to misjudge a nation for this reason.   England with her wise, well-trained, and far-seeing attitude towards the world did well when she helped Japan to organise her own administration of justice ; and England was wise, furthermore, to have been the leader among those who were trying to establish this independence in Japan. . . .   To-day no unprejudiced observer can help but see that Japan is no longer the harmless country of Geishas, lacquer ware, and so forth, but that, on the contrary, the country consists of a patriotic and very nationalistically minded people who are already the leading and the most respect-inspiring Power in Eastern Asia.   It would be a wise step, politically, to cultivate good relations with this country.

Prince Henry's letter closed with some words that revealed his simplicity and his kindness of heart :

I continue to enjoy my post which offers so much of infinite interest and in this I see some compensation for the long separation from my home and my family.   On the other hand, I recognise that this sacrifice is my duty and as a naval officer I am proud to make it.   Hoping that you will remember me most kindly to the Countess, I remain, my dear Count, your faithful and devoted,

Prince Henry of Prussia

I had made this letter the subject of a long report to the Kaiser. I tried to persuade him, as I had tried several times before and after, to fulfil certain of Japan's requests (to admit Japanese officers into our War Academy as visitors, etc.) and to treat Japanese Princes and diplomats in a more friendly manner. Finally I made particular effort to have the picture which adorned the walls of our Eastern Asiatic steamships removed, for this picture depicted Germany preaching to the European Nations a Holy War against poor Buddha, and was very sinister and insulting to the Japanese. But my efforts were futile because of the Kaiser's stubbornness, which became more pronounced in connection with relatively unimportant matters than it did in vital questions. He continued to talk about the "yellow peril" and to say fantastic things about a "crusade" of the white peoples against the yellow races.

After his return from eastern Asia, Prince Henry wrote to me from his estate at Hemmelmarck near Eckernförde:

It is true that speech is silver, whereas silence is golden, but I find it frightfully difficult in present circumstances to remain entirely silent. Relying on your usual indulgence, therefore, I must let off steam. It seems to me that the Chinese straw fire is burning itself out and that the conquest of Tientsin and the energetic attitude of Germany and the other Powers are taking an effect. Southern China is still undisturbed. Japan is behaving in an exemplary manner and deserves all credit. Russia has her hands full. Therefore we should give unto Russia what is Russia's and unto Japan what is Japan's. We can now make good the harm we did in Liaotung. The Russians should receive their section of Manchuria and a part of Korea and the Japanese should be granted the other part of the Korea peninsula. England would certainly agree to this plan and we shall have peace among the Powers. It is only wise to recognise Japan as a Great Power.

In those quiet times, when, every Thursday, the representatives of thirty-three German Governments met in Frankfort in Prince Thurn and Taxis' handsome Palace in the Eschenheimer Gasse, my father represented the Kingdom of Denmark on behalf of the Duchies of Holstein and Lauenburg. A highly respected Frankfort merchant of old patrician family, who had been ennobled by Austria under the name of Mumm von Schwarzenstein, acted as Danish Consul in Frankfort. Mumm's son was appointed Secretary of the Imperial Legation in Bucharest early in the 'nineties. I was then Chargé d'Affaires in Bucharest and I learned to appreciate his love of duty, his ability, and his knowledge. He knew more about economic and trade problems than did most German diplomats at that time. When Herr von Ketteler was murdered by the Chinese, I sent for Herr von Mumm and asked him whether he would accept the appointment as Ketteler's successor. He accepted at once with obvious delight. When I congratulated him on his fearlessness in succeeding a man who had been murdered, he said with a smile: "I have studied diplomatic history a great deal and I have found that two representatives of one Power have never been murdered in succession. For this reason I shall be safer in Peking than anywhere else." He left for Peking almost at once and he sent me a long letter with his first impressions shortly after I was appointed Chancellor. In common with most of our foreign representatives he began by saying how happy it made him that His Majesty had chosen me as Chancellor. *Donec eris felix, multos numerabis amicos.* Mumm added, and I believe sincerely, that he considered himself fortunate to have for the third time a chief so human, kind, and approachable, and that he still rejoiced because he had been transferred to Bucharest previously and so had come into contact with me. He gave me a dramatic description of the great difficulties he had encountered on his journey from the coast to Peking. He had undertaken this journey in "the saloon car", that is to say, the only decent carriage on the train. There had been an icy north wind and the train had been surrounded by huge clouds of dust. The carriage in which he travelled was bearable, despite the cold and the bullet holes in the roof, because there was a small stove. He said that, compared with sleeping quarters in Chinese houses, a well-kept pig sty in Germany was like a palace. The doorways of the train were covered only by mats and the windows were made of paper, and a temperature of three or four degrees below zero made itself felt in the compartment. He did not know how he had escaped contracting pneumonia. When he left the train, he continued his journey by carriage. The horses were generally very bad. Luckily there was one East Prussian horse among them, and as a Prussian does his duty in all circumstances it was harnessed to the carriage and we arrived in

Tungchow at about six o'clock. The road from there to Peking made a disconsolate impression on the Ambassador. All the towns he passed were deserted and in ruin. The only living creatures in these deserted towns were half-starved dogs, who could find no more corpses for their food. His first impression of Peking had been equally depressing. The huge stone walls seemed to the Ambassador to be like prison walls and the signs of limitless destruction depressed his spirit. Nothing but débris and wreckage. He drove through the Tung-Pien-Men Gate, on which "our proud black-white-and-red flag" was flying, into the Chinese city, and then, through the world-famous Hatamen Gate, into the Tartar section of the city. The street leading out from the Hatamen Gate, in which Mumm's predecessor had been murdered, was called Ketteler Street in his honour. Herr von Mumm wrote as follows about his relations with the Chinese: "It would be impossible to get on with these people at all if the feeling of mutual responsibility were not so strongly developed amongst them. The headboy is responsible to me for everything that happens. His ears are boxed if anything goes wrong and it is his business to see that his underlings do their duty and to pass these scoldings on. A large number of servants and the ingeniousness of the Chinese make life relatively simple. One gives orders and leaves their execution to the subordinates." The Kaiser, to whom I had shown Mumm's letter, made a marginal note about this last sentence: "Bravo! That is what I like to do." I hardly think that any of the Kaiser's marginal notes were more indicative of his fundamental views than this. Herr von Mumm closed his letter by reporting, very reasonably, that, without offending his Russian colleague, Herr von Giers, who was personally not very attractive, he had entered into the most friendly relations with Mr. Satow, the clever Englishman, and that he got on well with Pichon, the Frenchman, who later became Minister of Foreign Affairs. The Kaiser wrote under Mumm's letter: "Cliquot is beginning his job very cleverly." Ambassador Mumm von Schwarzenstein owned extensive vineyards and cellars in the Champagne. While he was Secretary of Embassy in Paris, old Prince Münster, who was then his chief, and whose great age caused him to forget names, once said to him: "My dear Cliquot, why don't you use only your last name Ratzenstein — it sounds so much better." Münster confused Mumm with Cliquot and Schwarzenstein with Ratzenstein.

During the entire course of the trouble in China, French policy, under the administration of Delcassé, made every effort to estrange us from England and to induce us to come to an understanding with France and Russia. The French tried to persuade us to consider the Eastern Asiatic problem from an anti-English point of view. As, however, the Russians left no doubts in our minds that the French would in no circumstances surrender their pretensions to Alsace-Lorraine and that, despite possible special agreements with us, they would continue their agitation against the Peace of Frankfort, we could not permit ourselves to be forced into any differences with England regarding Eastern Asia any more than we could afford such differences regarding South Africa. The Russians' discomfort at this time was, as might be mentioned, easily understandable. The Chinese disorders meant a weakening of Russia's position as a European power, because they intensified the Eastern Asiatic friction between her, on the one hand, and between China, Japan, England, and America on the other. For Germany this situation meant a disencumbrance on her eastern frontiers and consequently on her western frontiers as well. Some time later, Sergei Yulyevitch Witte said to me in this connexion when, in the summer of 1904, I concluded a very favourable trade treaty at Norderney: "If you had not gone to Kiaochow, I would not now be obliged to sign this treaty." I must add that Witte wanted to live in peace and harmony with us. In common with all far-sighted Russians he recognised that a war with Germany would imply not only the danger, but almost the certainty, of an internal upheaval. Until his death, Witte was a believer in peaceful and friendly relations between Germany and Russia as long as we took into account Russia's wishes regarding the Dardanelles as being compatible with Turkey's continued existence and with our economic interests in the Turkish Empire.

CHAPTER XXVIII

The Federal Council (Bundesrat) — *Emperor William II's Love of Peace — The German Crown Prince Comes of Age (May 6, 1900) — The Rights of the Crown and the Parties — Bülow's Relations with the Kaiser — William II as Described in Eulenburg's Letters to Bülow — The Kaiser and Bismarck — The Kaiser and the Socialists — The Empress's Mental State — Eulenburg's Intrigues against Her Majesty — Eulenburg's Spiritualism — William II's Friendship for the Prince of Monaco.*

AFTER studying the foreign situation, as I found it after my appointment as Chancellor in 1900, I turned my gaze within myself and I found that, as I was quite aware, my whole life had detached me considerably from our domestic conditions. This implied a disadvantage: I often lacked knowledge of details. It was an advantage, on the other hand, because I approached home problems without prejudice, without blinkers, and without any preconceived ideas. It was an advantage, furthermore, for, unlike many efficient, honest, and loyal German officials and deputies, I did not sacrifice important issues to matters of detail; I did not, as many of my fellow countrymen were so apt to do, fail to see the whole forest because of the many trees. It was also comforting to remember that Goschen, the banker, had made an excellent Minister of Marine, and that, in Prussia, Christian Rother, who had been a clerk in the Berlin Police Department, became an efficient chief of the Seehandlung, a capable director of the Royal Bank, and later, for twelve years, an excellent Minister of Finance. It must be remembered, however, that Rother's advance to Secretary of State had occurred in the good old days before 1848. Bismarck had said to Lucius, who had once been a ship's doctor and who refused the post of Minister of Finance because he did not feel that he possessed enough expert knowledge: "The Ministry of Finance is the simplest thing in the world; if Bodelschwingh was able to administer it for eight years, anyone could do it." Lucius became Minister of

Agriculture, even though he had refused the Ministry of Finance, and he did splendidly in this post. And had not Maltzahn-Gültz, a country Junker, become an able Secretary of the Treasury, and von Podbielski, a colonel of hussars, an able Minister of Posts? I felt that I could accomplish what other Junkers had accomplished.

It was with satisfaction that I realised I had finally won the approval of the Federal Government. In a meeting of the Federal Council's Committee for Foreign Affairs, held on July 11th, 1900, I gave a summary of the Chinese situation as well as a summary of international affairs in general. When I had finished, the chairman of the Committee, the Royal Bavarian Secretary of State, Freiherr von Crailsheim, declared in the name of the Federal Council as a whole that the Bavarian Government agreed with the general principles of what I had said and that the Bavarian Government would give me its support in carrying out my policy. State Secretary von Metzsch made a similar statement on behalf of the Saxon Government; this Government approved my programme and aims and recognised my policy, which had already proved its worth, as the right one. All the other representatives of the Federal States supported me in a similar manner. The chairman of the committee, Freiherr von Crailsheim, was therefore able to summarise all the statements made by declaring that the policies propounded by the Secretary of State for Foreign Affairs had been unanimously approved by the Federal Council. Before the meeting was closed, the chairman again made a statement and declared that all the Governments represented in the Council were convinced that the administration of our foreign policy was in capable hands. It was possible to look into the future with confidence, "as long as these hands held the tiller." Crailsheim uttered these last words with a raised voice and with a deliberate emphasis. In response to this vote of confidence, I stated that my political work, of which the members of the Federal Council had approved, was based on the political ideas of His Majesty, the Kaiser, whose politics were always forceful but at the same time temperate and thoughtful.

I was always firmly resolved to do my best to become a sagacious advisor to William II, but even during the honeymoon period of my

Chancellorship, when he showered tokens of his friendship and confidence upon me, I more than once thought of those melancholy words which Madame Mère, the great Napoleon's mother, uttered when the Napoleonic Empire reached its culmination: *"Ça va pourvu que ça dure."* I never felt entirely sure of Kaiser William II's confidence and friendship. I never felt the faith in him as a friend that I felt, during my long sojourn in Paris and Berlin, towards other men, such as Prince Chlodwig Hohenlohe, Loë, Prince Henry VII of Reuss, and Prince Otto Stolberg, who had been my chiefs; or towards Rheinbaben and Schorlemer, towards Bosse and Studt, who were my colleagues; or towards Franz Arenberg or Knesebeck, towards August Dönhoff, or Adolph Deines, or Fritz Vitztum, who were my personal friends. It is certain that, as far as his foreign policy was concerned, His Majesty the Kaiser's love of peace existed beyond a doubt. I can assure anyone on my honour that at no time during my Chancellorship did Emperor William II think of a war of aggression. It was a few years before the World War, if I am not greatly mistaken, that William II had a picture painted by a Polish artist. This picture, which was painted in the form of a triptych, represented Frederick the Great, with his crook-handled staff in his hand on the battlefield of Leuthen; William I, welcomed by his victorious troups at Königgrätz; and William II, with sword uplifted, leading his Royal Uhlans during a manoeuvre attack. William II liked to give away this picture as a present, for it expressed better than a long treatise the sincere love of peace which he harboured. This picture showed what he really wanted: a "smart" conduct and a "dashing" manner, but no real danger, no serious test. He never wanted to ride in any attacks but those made in manoeuvres. It was his misfortune that his naïveté as well as his superficiality and, above all, his childish vanity caused him to take appearance for reality and to try to stamp it as reality. As a matter of fact, as far as war and peace were concerned, he was rather timid. His "wicked" uncle, Edward VII, when he was Prince of Wales, said in Paris to the French, who were apparently alarmed by a war-like speech made by the German Crown Prince: *"Chien qui aboie ne mord pas.*" He was frightened by the mere suggestion of any war-like complications, and there was frequently a danger that our adversaries, trusting in the Kaiser's innate and intense fear of serious complications, would go too far in opposing us.

It was probably even further from Emperor William II's mind to attack England with his beloved fleet than it was to attack our neighbours with the German Army. It never even occurred to William II to go to war against England. Tirpitz, until his enthusiasm for his department carried him off his feet, had the right idea; namely, that we must become strong enough at sea, so that any attack on us would imply a real risk for the aggressor. Then peaceful, safe, and mutually confident relations between the English and the German people would be assured and, as these relations would then be based on equality, nothing would stand in their way. What William II most desired and imagined for the future was to see himself, at the head of a glorious German Fleet, starting out on a peaceful visit to England. The English Sovereign, with his fleet, would meet the German Kaiser in Portsmouth. The two fleets would file past each other; the two Monarchs, each wearing the naval uniform of the other's country and wearing the other's decorations, would then stand on the bridges of their flag-ships. Then, after they had embraced in the prescribed manner, a gala dinner with lovely speeches would be held in Cowes.

No German and, above all, no English pacifist was filled with a profounder or more honest love of peace than was William II. It was his own and our misfortune that his words and his gestures never coincided with his real attitude in the matter. When he boasted or even threatened people in words, it was often because he wanted to allay his own timidity. Heinrich Heine, in a malicious poem, speaks of children who begin to sing loudly in the dark to keep up their own courage. An English periodical, the "*Spectator*", reminded its readers, in connexion with the Kaiser's occasional boastful speeches, of the Irish story about the little boy who whistled, as he crossed the grave-yard, to hide his own fears from himself. William II had also a regrettable tendency to boast and bang the big drum. He did not inherit this tendency either from his noble, chivalrous, fearless, and yet modest father, nor from his grandfather William I, whose very simplicity made him a great man, nor from his highly educated mother who was almost shy in her manner, nor from his two grandmothers, the Empress Augusta and Queen Victoria, who were both unsurpassed in their dignity and tact.

William II's boastfulness was expressed in a particularly characteristic manner in the spring of 1900 when on the 6th of May he drank the health of the Crown Prince on the attainment of his majority. He delivered his speech in the presence of Emperor Francis Joseph, who was almost seventy years old, and of princely representatives of all the German and many foreign States. He declared that this was not simply a family celebration, but "a moment of primary importance in the history of the world."

Alas! the truth was that this declaration of the Crown Prince's majority was merely a courtly intermezzo. Even the birth of Emperor Napoleon III's only son and the birth of Emperor Francis Joseph's only son were not really important historical events. And even the birth of the King of Rome was not important as compared with the Reformation, or the great French Revolution, or the union of Germany by Bismarck, or the Italian Risorgimento, or the declaration of independence of the thirteen Colonies of North America. And even so Victor Hugo sang of the King of Rome's birth:

> Et l'on vit se dresser sur le monde
> L'homme prédestiné,
> Et les peuples béants ne purent que se taire,
> Car de ses deux bras il leva sur la terre
> Un enfant nouveau né.

On this 6th of May, after he had praised his own ancestors and his own family enthusiastically, William II raised his glass, wishing his cousins and his uncles the same satisfaction which he himself enjoyed at this moment, namely, that their countries and their subjects would be as grateful to them as his were to him for his work on their behalf. The Kaiser's more elderly uncles and cousins, who sat opposite me at the table in the White Room, looked surprised after this very self-satisfied outburst. The older ones appeared to be slightly hurt, but the younger ones looked at him ironically. But at any rate it was obvious even to people like myself, who knew the Kaiser's good intentions and who appreciated his really kind heart and his exceptional talents, that his manner and his temperament harboured the constant danger of unpleasant incidents and that, finally, his repeated *faux pas* might endanger the German people's great store of loyal monarchist sentiment. I had determined to defend Monarchy and the rights of the Crown against the Parties and in the Reichstag firmly and, if the need arose, ruthlessly, in the same way as I had encountered the enemy when I was a young hussar on the battlefields of Picardy. But I did not, on the other hand, share the Kaiser's and some of his intimates' animosity towards Parliament. I did not want to eliminate the representatives of the people, to harm their prestige, or to relegate them to an unimportant position. Nor did I want to curtail the rights of the people or the freedom of the press. It was just for William II that these restraints seemed to me particularly useful and necessary, especially in view of the fact that he was so easily impressed by flatterers who had made no impression at all on his father or his grandfather, but who found him easy to influence. Bismarck had said that if there were no parliament, the groom of the chamber would rule in its stead. Cavour had said: "*La plus mauvaise chambre vaut mieux que l'antichambre.*" My convictions were, however, far removed from submissiveness or even timidity and from the exaggerated respect of the Parties arising therefrom. I never gave myself entirely to any Party; reasons of State were always above Party politics in my opinion. I agreed with Jacob Grimm, who wrote in 1838, after he had been dismissed from office:

I have never sacrificed my love for my country to any quarrel between political parties. I have noticed that loving hearts become torpid if they are caught by the bonds of such quarrels. Anyone who does not adopt one or another of the colours which a short-sighted policy has adopted, anyone who does not consider the human soul, which God has endowed with so many gifts, as though it were as black and white as a chess board, is hated by these politicians more than their active enemies who need only put on another uniform to be considered their friends.

For this reason I, too, quarrelled and fought with all the Parties, one after another: with the Conservatives during the last winter of my Chancellorship (1908–1909), with the Centre Party in 1906. I occasionally quarrelled with the Radicals, and with the Social Democrats I fought continually. I have always admitted that there is something good in every Party and though I have consistently recognised that it is the duty of a wise administration to see that no Party's egotism and unreasonable demands harm the Government as a whole, I have always recognised as well how important it is to use the abilities and the strength of each Party for the good of the whole.

In the summer of 1899 Philipp Eulenburg wrote to me from the Northern Cruise:

I notice a sort of bitterness permeating the atmosphere. I used to quarrel only occasionally with fault-finders, now everyone is finding fault in a wearied, hopeless manner, and this lends the entire retinue an Oriental, fatalistic aspect — they all seem like peevish frightened subjects of some Sultan. This makes me deeply melancholy. The poor dear Master grows more and more lonely. I should like to say so much to him, and then his habit of behaving like a Calif gets me by the throat when, just a moment before, I thought I saw Harun-al-Raschid walking kindly among his people.

The next day Eulenburg continued:

I walked with the Kaiser in the pouring rain. We went to the North-Fjord. He said to me: "When you see how people are acting at home, you get tired of ruling. The only thing to do is to pay no attention to them at all. The enormous discredit that has fallen in the Parliamentary system, its collapse, has really made public opinion ill, just as Russia, too, is fundamentally ill. There one escapes into foreign politics; with us the disease finds vent in disarray and discontent. This discontent obstructs the Government's aims, stones are thrown in its way whenever possible."

I summoned all my courage and said the following (almost word for word): "I have noticed this discontent for a long time and it begins to strike me as uncanny, because the Parties, otherwise so widely separated, are coming together in a mutual bitterness against Your Majesty." The Kaiser said: "That is no news to me. If I stood a battle that lasted for eight years with Bismarck, nothing can really make me uneasy now. You can use this argument, if people come to you with their troubles." I answered: "The old battle still reëchoes in the present situation. This old battle is reflected most sharply in a deplorable antagonism between the personality of Your Majesty and the entire people. The part of Your Majesty's character, which places you at the head of new institutions, whatever they may be, is most progressive, but this trend in your character is paralysed by the excessively hard energy which you display in public. Your Majesty's speeches and telegrams give the impression that you want to reëstablish an absolute Monarchy. But there is now no Party in the Reich that would accept or understand such a thing. The parliamentary system is now deeply rooted in every German and what you call its collapse is merely a discontent with certain outward forms of this system." The Kaiser answered not without sharpness: "I demand the same right of free speech as any German. I must say what I want to say, so that sensible people will know whom they must follow. If I were to be silent, the bourgeoisie which is (literally) at the end of its tether would not at all know what to do."

I answered: "It is better for a ruler to act than to talk." His Majesty replied: "And they will see my deeds." Then he smiled: "You are afraid that I will take drastic measures against the Parliament." I answered: "No, I am not afraid, because Your Majesty has told me too often that you could only change the Constitution if the people, that is to say, Parliament, expressed the wish that you do so. You are far too modern and too intelligent not to realise that Germany cannot and does not wish to exist without a Parliament." The Kaiser exclaimed: "That means that Germany must have a modified Parliament — not the one now existing." I answered: "This might be discussed, but only through prescribed channels. And this is impossible as long as the majority of the people disagree with their Kaiser." His Majesty said: "If this is really the case, there will be a Revolution, the crash must come in some form or other. Everything points that way and the battle must therefore be accepted." I said: "Internal conflict? Which a coalition of the European Powers expects, so that they can attack us? The Russians are subsidising newspapers, the English are financing strikes in Hamburg, the French are inciting the Slavs, and we rush into the trap." The Kaiser: "Yes, if only people would understand this situation; I am trying to make it clear through my warnings. But the Germans are much too narrow and too short-sighted, they lose themselves in small passions." I exclaimed: "And we are back at the beginning of our conversation. In their agitation people are turning against the absolute Monarchy and anything that can awaken the impression that we have an absolute Monarch must be avoided." The Kaiser said almost ironically: "Me an absolute Monarch!" At that moment Goertz joined us and interrupted the conversation, which I repeat to you almost literally. His Majesty's tendency towards "Force" is apparent despite all the restraints he imposes upon himself. I encounter a fatal misunderstanding of the whole situation and this lack of understanding should instill grave, tormenting fear into us. Will you be able to hold him back from unaccountable actions? Will you be able to get rid of the things that urge him to actions without his realising their far-reaching results? The Kaiser again referred to our conversation and said: "What you have said to me makes me even more aware of old Bismarck's perfidy. He tried to persuade me to strengthen absolutism and to push Prussia solidly into the foreground at the expense of the other States in the Federal Government. I was too clever to agree to this plan, which, so he intended, would embarrass me and thus make me dependent upon him."

Though Philipp Eulenburg assured me to the contrary, he often took occasion to pour poisoned oil on the fire of the Kaiser's rancour against Bismarck. Eulenburg and Holstein, who was at that time his intimate friend, liked to insinuate, among other things, that Bismarck had tried to urge the young Kaiser William II to stage a *coup d'état* and that, at the same time, he tried to persuade him to betray Austria to Russia. William II liked using this statement, particularly during the early years of his reign, to justify Bismarck's dismissal. Both statements are more or less untrue. Following the bad advice of Caprivi, Marschall, and Holstein, and carried away by his youthful impetuosity, his ignorance of affairs, and his lack of judgment, William II made the incredible mistake of cancelling the German-Russia Re-insurance Treaty. The manner in which he did this was tactless and awkward. However, he tried more than once, later on in his reign, to conclude some treaty with Russia. Soon after Bismarck's fall and until the end of his reign, he frequently demanded of his Ministers that they should adopt legal measures against the Social Democrats and, more than once, he wanted forceful action against them. His attitude in 1890 was a different one, but this was because he wanted, above all, to get rid of his troublesome Chancellor, and not because he considered a *coup d'état* in itself objectionable, or because he considered a treaty arrangement with Russia disloyal towards Austria-Hungary. *"Quand on veut noyer son chien, on dit qu'il est galeux"*, says one of the French proverbs I am fond of quoting.

The way in which Philipp Eulenburg exploited a fire, which broke out on his estate in Liebenberg in the summer of 1899, to incite the Kaiser against the Socialist was very dubious. He wrote to His Majesty that it was a case of arson. The prosecuting attorney had had a workman arrested. The man had come to the place a few years before and according to rumour he was a Social Democrat. The fire had been "terrible", conditions all over the manor house, on the estate, and in the village were "almost unbearable." Eulenburg's children, who had helped put out the fire in a really magnificent manner, could not sleep at night, because they were scared by all kinds of imaginary terrors. Even sensible old people saw murderers and criminals and incendiaries everywhere. Liebenberg resembled a town devastated by warfare. The prosecuting attorney was frightened out of his wits. The letter said literally : "I think I can assume that Socialists are at work to create discontent. My farm laborers are all so well paid and housed, they live in such harmony with my household that arson or even the thought of any crime is out of the question as far as they are concerned."

Insinuations of this kind were dangerous, because William II, in accordance with his mentality and his entire nature, simultaneously over- and underestimated the Socialist Movement. On the one hand, when Prince Bismarck was dismissed, he publicly declared the movement to be "a passing phase", which he would be able to overcome. On the other hand, the Socialists appeared to him as a horde of conspirators and criminals who were only waiting for the moment when they could put up ladders against the Royal Palace in Berlin and, holding knives between their teeth and revolvers in their hands, penetrate into their Majesties' bedroom and strangle them and the Royal Princes. William II did not appreciate the tremendous danger the Social Democrats implied for the power and happiness, the welfare and the future of the German Empire, nor did he realise how deeply rooted were their ideas in the hearts of German workmen. He was not familiar, furthermore, with the brilliant rhetoric of the Social Democrats, which impressed even educated people, nor with the germ of ethical truth which, as I had to admit, was to be found in these ideas, even though I fought them, because, in my opinion, they were ruinous and harmful to us. As far as the Liebenberger fire was concerned, it was soon established that the Social Democrats had had nothing to do with it.

The Empress's frame of mind was reflected in all the letters I received from Eulenburg. When, shortly before my appointment as Chancellor, I was ordered to come to Hubertusstock, Philipp came to meet me halfway between the Imperial shooting lodge and Neustadt-Eberswalde. He joined me in the carriage and told me with feverish agitation that the Empress was in such a nervous state that it would be very advisable if she were separated from the Kaiser soon. When I reached Hubertusstock, Lucanus took me aside and told me that he considered it his duty to attract my attention to the intrigues which Philipp Eulenburg was promoting against the Empress. He said that Eulenburg described her as being excitable, hysterical, and almost out of her mind. This was not the case. The Empress, who was a very devoted mother, found it very difficult to be separated from her younger sons, especially from Prince Joachim, who was very frail. When it was first abruptly suggested to her that the children be sent away from home, she was greatly agitated. But many middle-class women would react in the same way, without being sent to an asylum for it. "The Empress is as sane as you or I. But if she is separated for any length of time against her will from her husband and children, no one can tell what effect this will have on her state of mind." I promised Lucanus that I would make every possible effort to protect our revered Empress.

Many years later, during the trial which was eventually to ruin

Philipp Eulenburg, his efforts to have the wife of his best friend, Count Kuno Moltke, and his own sister-in-law, Clara Eulenburg, née von Schaeffer-Voit (she became Countess Alexander Wartensleben later on), certified insane, came to light and I then remembered his strange attitude towards Empress Augusta Victoria. What abysses are hidden in human nature, what black aspects, from which anyone who is physically and psychologically healthy turns away in horror! Lucanus recognised in these efforts to harm His Majesty's wife an attempt on the part of his most intimate friend to get the Kaiser entirely in his control. Lucanus thought it possible, furthermore, that Eulenburg would try to convert the Kaiser to spiritualism. All my life spiritualistic thoughts and beliefs have not only been remote from my mind, but I have had an active antipathy toward them as well. Whenever Eulenburg spoke to me about these things, he tried to persuade me that his spiritualistic experiments had strengthened his belief in God. The spirits had proved to him the certainty of a future existence. He claimed that this was his one support in life, his comfort in adversity, the most precious thing that he had. I always answered by telling him that I did not want to take this comfort from him, because I believed that everyone should be blessed in his own way. But I must ask him to assure me that he would not let the Kaiser catch his spiritualistic bent and that he would not entice the Kaiser to join him in any of his spiritualistic dallying. The Kaiser's temperament would make this too dangerous an experiment. After His Majesty's mother, the Empress Frederick, had asked me urgently to see that Eulenburg did not infect his friend the Kaiser with his spiritualism, for that would "be the end", I had a serious discussion with Philipp Eulenburg on the subject. I demanded and received his word of honour that he would not try to win the Kaiser over to spiritualism or to involve him in spiritualistic thought.

On July 5th, 1900, he wrote to me from Brunsbüttel:

The Prince of Monaco has just been here. In the long talk he had with the Kaiser the latter said that France was no longer mentioned in China or in the East; only Germany and Russia had anything to say at all — everyone else was silent. The personal relation between him and the Tsar was more intimate and close than the relation between the Monarchs of the two countries had been since the time of Alexander II. I would assume that Monaco passed on this information at once to his companion on the *Alice*, who was once French consul in Hamburg.

The Prince of Monaco was one of the foreigners whom the Kaiser trusted in a manner that was humanly touching but politically blind, despite all warnings, — foreigners whom he honoured not only with his friendship, but also by telling them things they ought never to have known.

CHAPTER XXIX

Indiscretions at the Berlin Court — William II and Foreigners — The Pilot of Bari — The Kaiser's Talkativeness and His Harmless Conversations — The Reichstag Meets — The Debate on the Expedition to Eastern Asia — My First Appearance in the Reichstag as Chancellor.

IN the 'sixties the superiority of Prussian policy, especially over that of France, was partly due to the indiscretion which prevailed at the Court of the Tuileries. Here foreign diplomats learned many things from the gentlemen and the ladies in waiting; the Empress Eugénie's Spanish vivacity caused her to say things which should have remained unsaid, and the Emperor Napoleon III's dreamy nature, which was so removed from the realities of life, caused him to be equally indiscreet. At the Court of William I, on the other hand, the strictest discretion prevailed, the King considered such discretion as his duty, and he insisted on his entire entourage and his servants observing this discretion as well.

But now things were the other way round. Indiscretions rarely occurred at the English Court. Queen Victoria rarely honoured foreigners with political conversations. The Prince of Wales was so cautious and clever that he often enticed their secrets out of foreigners, while he himself never said anything that he did not want to say. At the Berlin Court, Empress Augusta Victoria was very discreet, she spoke about politics only with her immediate entourage and even then she was reserved and careful. But the Kaiser talked habitually, and he was particularly fond of talking with foreigners. They amused and interested him more than his own subjects. He hoped also that these talks with foreigners would make the people in other countries think of him as a great ruler.

During William II's entire reign the reports of foreign representatives in Berlin were packed with eccentric and imprudent remarks made by the Monarch. My old friend, Bodo von Knesebeck, who had been my comrade in our regiment and who was now the Empress' Privy Councillor, told me the following incident. Towards the end of my Chancellorship, it was in the spring of 1908 or 1909, the Kaiser had been waiting with his usual impatience for his journey to his beloved and beautiful château, the Achilleion. From Bari the *Hohenzollern* took him to Corfu. During the journey, Knesebeck was spending a quarter of an hour in the "arbours", the small, half-visible, half-hidden cabins on the upper deck, when the Kaiser appeared suddenly and walked up and down the deck with another gentleman. Knesebeck did not like to come out and speak to His Majesty, because this was apt to irritate him. So he remained where he was and became an unwilling listener of the conversation which the Monarch was conducting in a very loud voice. The Kaiser was talking English, French, Italian, and sometimes German, in quick succession and was discussing his foreign and his domestic policies, his personal relations with other sovereigns, his Ministers, *de omni re scibili et de quibusdam aliis.* Knesebeck racked his brain, wondering to whom the German Kaiser could be pouring out his heart so unreservedly and who, in turn, remained so silent. He guessed in quick succession: an English Lord, a French sportsman, an Italian Admiral, a Russian Grand Duke, or a Greek Prince. After the Kaiser and his companion had disappeared, Knesebeck asked a sailor, who was hurrying past, who the gentleman was with whom the Kaiser had been conducting such a long and animated conversation. "That was the pilot," the good sailor replied, "whom we took on board at Bari, so that he can take us to Corfu." Later, when the Kaiser talked eagerly with foreigners before Knesebeck or me, Knesebeck used to say to me: "The pilot of Bari."

The Kaiser's impulse to talk, his need to unload his mind, his *sfogarsi*, as the Italians express it so aptly and picturesquely, was without limits. He actually suffered from the illness which the Italians (who talk too much themselves) call "*parlantina*" — an exaggerated garrulousness. William II was never really aware of the dangers involved in saying rash things, at any rate he was not aware of these dangers before his imprudent conversations at High-cliffe, which brought about the crisis in November, 1908. On one of his morning visits — the Kaiser came to see me almost every morning between nine and ten o'clock and we usually walked in the gardens of the Chancellor's Palace — he brought his brother, Prince Henry, with him. The Prince seemed out of sorts from the start, the Kaiser's manner toward him was harsh and unfriendly. His remarks were particularly ungracious and sharp when he mentioned the Prince's beloved brother-in-law, the Tsar, whom he called a "weakling", a "sorry sight", and other amiable things. When the Prince had finally gone away, his face very red, I asked the Kaiser whether he was quite sure that, despite his unquestionable loyalty, the Prince might not repeat these remarks to his wife. The Kaiser replied that this was more than probable. I continued: "I have the greatest respect for Princess Henry, who is an excellent wife, mother, and human being. But is it not possible that the good Princess might, on occasion, repeat what her husband tells her to her two sisters in Russia, the Empress Alexandra Feodorovna and the Grand Duchess Elisabeth Feodorovna? Or that she might repeat these remarks to her oldest sister in London, Princess Victoria of Battenberg, who is quite Anglicised and not at all friendly to Germany? The Kaiser admitted that this was sure to happen. "But consider," I continued. "You are making such an effort to win the Tsar's friendship, you almost overdo the deputations, presents, letters, visits, attentions of all kinds, and a single remark, like the one you have just made, can counteract all these efforts towards friendship." The Kaiser replied in the quick manner and with the rhetoric so typical of him: "I am the only man on earth who can never let himself go, even before his own brother. You can say anything to your brothers that you want to say. You can curse God and the world. You can call me a fool, and all the Ministers idiots, without committing an indiscretion or having to fear any unpleasantness for yourself. Only *I* am supposed always to walk about as though I had one of Papageno's locks on my mouth, even in the presence of my brother."

I had to tell His Majesty that I was not a Kaiser and the highest honour meant the greatest responsibility. But I was obliged to admit to myself that William II could be very charming as a human being, he was so natural and unaffected. The Prince of Monaco, whom Philipp Eulenburg mentioned in his letter of July 5, 1900, was entirely French by education and sympathies. He was a personal friend of most of the leading French politicians. When the World War broke out, he at once, and ostentatiously, joined the French ranks. He made speeches in which he attacked his old friend and protector William II in a vulgar manner.

Prince Eulenburg's letter of July 5, 1900, went on:

I am constantly afraid that dangerous messages are being sent to the Tsar direct. I read the one that went to-day, because His Majesty showed it to me at dinner after he had written it. This telegram was not dangerous, it merely concerned the supervision of ships in connexion with the import of arms into China.

The Kaiser had *motu proprio* told me often that he would show me all the letters he wrote to foreign sovereigns. He honestly intended to do so. But it often happened, especially when we were apart and he fought shy of sending to ask for my approval, or when he was in a hurry, that he wrote letters of this kind on his own. In the letters from the Kaiser to the Tsar, which were published after the Russian Revolution, it is easy to tell which of these letters were approved or corrected by his constitutional advisers and which letters he wrote entirely on his own. I do not believe, by the way, that the English Ministers controlled all of the letters written by King Edward and particularly by Queen Victoria, nor do I believe that the English Ministers even knew about all the letters that were sent.

On July 14, 1900, Eulenburg wrote to me from Trondhjem:

One can never settle down here; from half past seven in the morning until half past eleven at night the atmosphere is always restless. The horrible gymnastic exercises at eight o'clock in the morning fill me with disgust. I am grateful to say that His Majesty has been more reposeful since we left, except for a few outbreaks. Since that row in Kiel, he has been touchingly friendly and considerate towards me. The return to the Empress will be a critical moment. This whole relationship is a dangerous one, as far as the further development of the Kaiser is concerned. It is a problem which the Empress will not have enough brains and understanding to solve.

The "row" in Kiel, which occurred a few days before they left for the Northern Cruise, had been a nervous strain for poor Phil. When His Majesty had finally realised that Field Marshal Waldersee would not longer be able to win victorious battles, that Peking might be relieved without him, the Kaiser was so beside himself — Eulenburg described this scene to me — that he completely lost control of himself. He spoke about Russia and England, who had "betrayed" him, in the bitterest terms; he said things against his own advisers; and he finally demanded that Eulenburg write a telegram to the Foreign Office, saying that a Defensive and Offensive Alliance be concluded at once with Japan, a country which he had scorned heretofore. It was only with difficulty that Eulenburg dissuaded him from this plan.

On July 15, 1900, Philipp Eulenburg wrote to me:

Yesterday I wrote and told you that things are a bit quieter. To-day I must tell you about a violent outbreak, which occurred last night, and which worries me very much. I was walking on deck with His Majesty and George Hülsen. We were telling each other harmless stories about the theatre. The Kaiser began to talk about the theatre "public" and then began to discuss Berlin society and then the Conservatives, the Agrarians, etc. His violence in conversation was terrifying, and I am again filled with the fear I have expressed to you before, namely, that he might break with the old Prussian traditions, turn actively against the Conservatives, and throw himself into the arms of the Liberals, so as to smash the Conservatives. I must admit that I saw an abyss of hate and bitterness within him, which nothing can change I have the feeling that any new opposition on the part of the Agrarian-Conservatives would cause the cup to overflow. His Majesty cannot control himself any more when he is filled with anger. Yesterday he did not even notice that there were sailors near by, he simply raved on, so that they could hear every word he said. Hülsen was so terrified that he was taken ill. . . . I consider our present situation a very dangerous one; I see no way out nor does Leuthold know what is to be done about it. He thinks that this condition reflects a certain weakness of the nervous system, but he emphatically denies any possibility of mental disorder. I feel as though I were sitting on a barrel of gun-powder and I am very careful. Curtail your political reports as much as possible and don't ask for any decisions if they can be postponed.

Leuthold, who for many years acted as William I's personal physician, became William II's physician when he ascended the throne. He was a quiet and absolutely loyal man, and worthy of the greatest respect. Late in the evening of that same 15th of July, Eulenburg wrote again, saying that there had been so much excitement at the dinner table about trivial things, that it was impossible to tell what things were coming to. Leuthold had told him that he simply did not know what to do. His Majesty refused vehemently to accept any of his suggestions concerning a change of his habits of life. The letter from His Majesty's best friend to me continued :

Leuthold tells me that life on the yacht is no relaxation. On the contrary it is a strain, but he does not know anything better to suggest. I don't see that there is anything to do, but to await events and to pray to God that His Majesty will not be obliged to confront any complicated problems, for repeated scenes, like the one I witnessed in Kiel, would surely lead to a nervous crisis the character of which cannot be foretold. Good night. It is one o'clock, and I am very tired. These things affect me very much. I had such faith in the Kaiser's ability, — and in the good that time would do, — but now I am losing faith in both and I see a human being whom I love deeply suffering so much, without being able to help.

On September 20th, 1900, four weeks before my appointment as Chancellor, Eulenburg had sent me a letter from Rominten, telling me about a "lively" discussion he had had with His Majesty about the agrarian movement :

I found the Kaiser completely changed: he looked well and fresh; his manner was simple, he was in a natural mood and without any exaltation. The manoeuvres — which, by the way, are said to have been awful because of his leadership, for he cared only about spectacular effects — rested him and took his mind off many things which had made him so nervous. So I found him much better than my sad experiences in July had led me to expect. I am profoundly grateful that such an improvement is still possible, *pourvu que cela dure!* Towards evening we arrived at Cadine, which is a very pretty place. The conversation during and after dinner turned on the fire at my place in Liebenberg. The Kaiser contended that it must have been started by Social Democrats, who wanted to do me harm because I am a friend of his.

On the 21st of September Eulenburg continued:

Their Majesties go out for a ride with their attendants at seven o'clock in the morning. I, of course, go on sleeping in the meantime. After breakfast the Kaiser sends for me to come out on the terrace overlooking the garden. He is reading his dispatches. I begin a conversation, in which I say approximately the following: " The Chinese Question is terribly difficult; there is great danger that the English and the Russians might unite to humiliate him, but the danger of a military coalition against us is not so great. It is imperative for him to exercise great caution. If he made a mistake that could no longer be covered by his officials, those quarters in Germany which are hostile to him might join forces and a domestic coalition against him might be more difficult to deal with than a foreign one." The Kaiser then began to discuss the Agrarian question and grew very vivacious. At the end he said: "If, for any reason, the dogs dare to oppose me in an open, dangerous, and systematic way, a good many heads will roll in the sand, as sure as I stand here, for that would be high treason." I thought it best to change the subject. I wonder how the good man thinks it possible to behead people in the year 1900? . . . Later on, the Kaiser made a number of remarks about the Empress' attitude in the education of the Princes August William and Oscar: She declared in Berlin and in Stettin that she would absolutely refuse to have them sent to Plön. His Majesty is nervous lest there be a big scene. At ten o'clock the Kaiser rides out with me to see some new potato-digging machines. . . . The Empress is offended, because she is not allowed to join us and she made a remark to me at luncheon that she, of course, may not go with him, because I am here. At four o'clock a drive over to the new tile works which His Majesty wants to show me is arranged. The Empress, who says that she is suffering from a cold in the head and a headache, turns up and joins us. Before dinner, when everyone is assembled, the groom of the chamber comes in to say that the Empress is not coming down for dinner. His Majesty is a bit distracted; immediately after dinner he walks up and down the dark garden with me. There has been a terrible scene. Endless discussions, in which the Kaiser remains firm, because he is convinced that a separation is not only good for the Princes, but for the Empress' nerves as well. She does not understand him at all and he is filled with anxiety and worry.

On September 22, Eulenburg continued :

After breakfast I went to the former owner's vault so as to enjoy the lovely view and I noticed someone dashing into the park in a great hurry. . . . I walked towards the path and saw the Empress rushing after the Kaiser like a hunted deer (I won't say like a hunted cow). I was honestly surprised that she did not have a stroke. . . . The poor dear Empress really seems to be in a bad nervous state. In the afternoon we drove to Braunsberg and Tilsit. The Kaiser asked me at once to come into his compartment in the train and poured out his heart to me in the most wretched and painful manner. I shall mention the things which I consider most important, for these things will, unfortunately, be very important in the Kaiser's private life in the near future. Possibly, also, because of their effect on his nerves, they will be important as far as politics are concerned. All night long the Empress made scenes with her weeping and screaming. . . . A regular paroxysm.

In connexion with these things Eulenburg described the helplessness of the Kaiser, who was simply "knocked out" by crises and scenes of this kind. He could not stand it any more. The Empress, he said, was made ill because the daily programme was an impossible one. She could not be a "middle-class" mother, a devoted wife, and a reigning Empress at the same time. Eulenburg declared that the Kaiser had said to him : "Tell me, for God's sake, what I can do about it ; the thought that the poor Empress may end in a hydropathic institute is terrible." Eulenburg answered that, sad as it was, one must assume that the Empress was suffering from a temporary nervous disease of some sort. The only problem was to find a proper medical cure. The political situation, the domestic as well as the foreign situation, was so terribly difficult that the Kaiser must remain extremely cool and quiet. If he lost his peace at home through disturbed nights and scenes of all kinds, the State as well as he himself would suffer from his increased nervousness. There must be a change. His intimate associates would surely interpret any measures which might be taken merely as a protection for His Majesty and not as an affront to Her Majesty. Eulenburg then recommended that the Empress be separated from her sons Prince Oscar and Prince August William and that she keep the youngest, Prince Joachim, and the Princess with her and that she spend a long time somewhere in the country where the air was good and where it was quiet. The Kaiser could then go to see her at stated intervals, but he must, if his sojourn was to last longer than a fortnight, leave after the first scene she made. The danger of losing him must bring the Empress to her senses. In a subsequent letter, Eulenburg emphasised that the Empress was making even "greater scenes." Her nerves needed some cure, this was evident from her wrinkled face, which had aged so young, and from her grey hair. The Kaiser had said to Eulenburg: "She must take a cure for my sake as well, for I must have some rest. . . . It is my duty to see that I have some peace." Eulenburg reiterated again and again that the family happiness must be "saved" by some radical cure, which might be painful for the poor Empress at first. Eulenburg added that great caution was necessary, or the Empress might become seriously ill and attempt some real act of desperation.

On September 25th, Phil wrote that he had slept very badly, because he had been tormented by visions of burning houses just as he had been tormented at Liebenberg. The Kaiser had a bad cold in the head — "caught from the Empress." In the evening they had talked about thought transference, the Kaiser had mentioned the possibility of communication between the living and the dead. "Everyone assumed a rather passive attitude on the subject, but they tended to agree with him. Admiral Hollmann showed himself to be a frank adherent of spiritualism." Obviously with the intention of easing my mind, Eulenburg added that, to end the talk about ghosts and spirits, he had then told a story about a ghost which carried about a dish of stewed fruit. "Whereupon the conversation again touched reality which the Kaiser had lost sight of completely. I have the impression that this quiet circle of decent people won't gossip about this conversation in the provinces."

According to his own reports, Philipp Eulenburg had tried again and again to have the Princes sent away. He had advised His

Majesty to surround the Empress with "educated ladies." He was proud that he had been courageous enough to advise the Kaiser to leave the room if the Empress made scenes at night. He had advised him to go into his own room, to lie down, and to lock the door. The Kaiser had nodded and had said " very thoughtfully " : "The plan could be tried, it 's not a bad idea." Eulenburg added : "The naïveté with which he agreed to so simple and to so obvious a plan showed me clearly what a cult the Imperial nuptial bed had become through the efforts of the Empress and the Empress Frederick." Naturally Philipp Eulenburg did not want the Empress to hear about these talks with the Kaiser. "I hope," he wrote, "that, to preserve his own dignity, the Kaiser won't tell the Empress about these conversations. For, as he admitted, the Empress is very jealous of me, and she admits how much she dislikes to have long visits from his friends, so that it would be very unfortunate if she heard about these talks."

In a letter dated October 1, also from Rominten, Eulenburg seemed very uneasy about a visit I had paid shortly before in Friedrichsruh to Herbert Bismarck. I kept up my old friendly relations with him, even though he was in great disfavour with His Majesty. "Humanly speaking, you will have found very little companionship in Friedrichsruh. The peaceful rustling of the old beech trees contrast sharply with Herbert's worldly, misplaced ambition. The old man was better suited to this place, he was like a strange monster who heard all kinds of daemonic noises in this rustling." Phil comforted me as follows for my cares and efforts in the Foreign Office : "You can be sure that all your work and worries are good for your soul, which you have kept pure and noble — despite all the poison round about, which evil spirits try to inject into it, the spirits of those who were unsuccessful in this world."

On September 28th Eulenburg wrote to me from Rominten about the Kaiser's political frame of mind :

You know Tirpitz' attitude towards England, that is to say, his fear of England. His Majesty said some sharp things against England, and his hatred, particularly of Salisbury, flashed up like a streak of lightning. Tirpitz was afraid to show his fear. His remarks about the impending danger were very carefully worded. At the moment the All-Highest's attitude is very unfriendly towards England as it is towards Russia, and this implies a certain amount of quietude here: *otium cum veneno*. In a long talk I had with Tirpitz on the journey, he told me that he considered Waldersee's mission extremely dangerous. He said that it was undoubtedly a fact that all the other Great Powers were simply waiting to humiliate us.

I have quoted these letters written to me by Eulenburg before I became Chancellor, because they illustrate, better than any remarks of my own could do, how complicated was the situation which prevailed at the Imperial Court. I was quite clear from the very beginning how tragic and far-reaching this situation was. William II's nature was full of contradictions. Prince Guido Henckel-Donnersmarck used to say that the Kaiser reminded him of a dice box in which the dice knock against each other. His character was not unified, harmonious, or self-contained; his various qualities did not interfuse as stubborn substances and elements do during the process of amalgamation. All of his Ministers, and not the least myself, had to suffer because of His Majesty's indiscretions. At other times, however, the Kaiser could be as silent as the grave. He had, for instance, not told Eulenburg, his most intimate friend, who was in Hubertusstock when I was summoned there and did not say a word about his intention of offering me the succession to Prince Hohenlohe.

Eulenburg, who had returned to Vienna in the meantime, was, therefore, greatly surprised to hear that I had been appointed as Chancellor. As was his habit in such circumstances, he saved himself at once by retiring to bed. He did not write to me until twenty-four hours after he had received the news of my appointment:

Dear, beloved Bernhard,
    I am in bed with a cold, but this does not prevent me from doing my work — or thinking about you a great deal. I was not able to write to you yesterday or the day before; I felt too miserable. When I was young and paying attention to Elisabeth Hatzfeldt, who was then so beautiful, she wrote in my album: " Do not dream your experiences — experience your dreams." Well, I have, in many ways, experienced far

more than I have dreamt, but on the whole I have experienced things quite different from my dreams — and dreadful things, too. You, on the other hand, have experienced just what you dreamt — and, what is more, you have progressed with rare constancy, for which you can thank God. You have not been whirled round and round in terrifying curves as I have been, only to find a Prince's cap hanging over your left ear instead of your dreams of laurel wreath twined round the harp. One of the best tasks for which God selected me was to contribute towards the shaping of your life. I have always felt this task as a mission. I know perfectly well what to think of certain strange and fine sentiments which have occasionally beset me. Do you remember our long talk on the green Semmering meadow, where we made our plans: you were to remain State Secretary for some time, so that you would grow familiar with the situation in Berlin and learn to know domestic politics thoroughly. Then you were to become Chancellor at a moment when no crisis was imminent. Curiously enough this is what has actually happened, though I admit that your time as State Secretary seemed to me too long. The fact that this change has come so quickly, that a week ago in Berlin you could tell me you thought nothing could prevent Hohenlohe from remaining Chancellor, shows that we live in an age of surprises. I confess that I myself did not believe that Hohenlohe would again appear before the Reichstag. A very old man can offer the world a great deal, he is like a child in this, and it takes a long time for public opinion to grow "restive", but in this case things had gone far beyond the possible and Lucanus probably realised as much. I dreamed recently — there are, you see, strange dreams — that Hohenlohe was cutting my toe nails. I refused emphatically to let him do so and did not understand what it was all about. "Don't you realise," he said, "that this crooked position is now the most comfortable one for me?" This nonsense might do for the *Simplicissimus*. When we meet again, you must tell me how this change was brought about at Homburg, the change that made you the most important man in the German Empire. The solution suggested in the talk between the Kaiser and Hohenlohe seems to have been somewhat "unintentional." Life is sometimes like that. A cousin of mine called upon a lady with the intention of telling her that he could not marry her daughter. When he began to stammer about the subject, the mother embraced him and quickly fetched her daughter. Suddenly, therefore, everything turned out differently from what he had expected. I realise the difficulties you will encounter, my beloved Bernhard, from the remarks in the press which quite openly call you the "strong man" who must curb the poor dear master. To satisfy Germany and yet not offend the Kaiser — that is what you will have to do. May God hold the balancing rod as you walk across the tight rope — that is my prayer and my hope for you. To have served Europe with your agreement with England as an entrée, as you have done, is a tactical master stroke, quite apart from the fact that the agreement is an incomparable thing in itself.

Your faithful old Philipp

It is true that after Eulenburg had firmly established himself in the Kaiser's favour, he tried earnestly to attract the Kaiser's attention to me. He was convinced that I would be able to perform valuable services to the Kaiser and the country. He wanted, furthermore, to have a friend of his own in an influential position. And besides, as I am convinced to this day, he felt real friendship for me ever since I grew more intimate with him and his family in Paris. He and Holstein, who was then his intimate friend, and who later became his bitterest enemy, did everything in their power to secure my appointment as Ambassador in Rome. Later on he made every effort — and this was not entirely a pleasure for me — to have me recalled to Berlin as Secretary of State. He neither expected nor really desired my appointment as Chancellor. Not that he felt any mean jealousy of me. Prince Hermann von Hohenlohe-Langenburg had been his candidate as Chancellor — so Lucanus told me — and that was when he wanted to replace him as Governor of Strassburg. This post remained the dream of his own ambition until the end of his career. He feared, finally, that, as Chancellor, I might have more to do with the Kaiser than he had and that he himself might cease to be indispensable. I do not say that Eulenburg hoped the Kaiser and I would quarrel, but he was convinced, in view of the Kaiser's temperament, that my Chancellorship would end in a quarrel. So he observed my activities as Chancellor with the same sentiments that inspired the Englishman to follow the animal-tamer Beatty all over the Continent, hoping that he would be present at the thrilling moment when the lion would at last attack and devour Beatty.

The chief reason why the Reichstag did not meet in the summer

Heckling

of 1900 to discuss the troubled situation in China was that neither the Kaiser nor I wanted to expose the Chancellor Hohenlohe, who was in poor health and in need of care, to what promised to be a stormy session. After my appointment as Chancellor, I told the Kaiser that the Reichstag should now be convened as soon as possible. The Kaiser, who as a rule preferred not to have the Reichstag in session, finally agreed that it should be convened on the 14th of November. The debate on the Chinese question, which lasted for four days, began on November 19th. The interpellation about the Twelve-Thousand-Mark Affair occurred on the 24th. The discussion of the Boer question and of the refusal to receive President Kruger was held in the middle of December.

I had often spoken in the Reichstag as Secretary of State for Foreign Affairs, but this was the first time I was confronted with long and important debates which would be attacked from all sides. As I write these memoirs, a newspaper report of a stormy session in the Reichstag lies before me. In this report, the newspaper, which is friendly toward the present Chancellor, describes with solemnity and with a certain amount of sentiment how conscientiously the first official of the Empire read his speech. "The Chancellor," this report said, "rises and hurries to the speakers' table. He opens his rather bulky manuscript. Everything he is to say has been prescribed word for word. There is not room for rhetorical variations. The Chancellor has no real need for rhetoric, for there is hardly any heckling and whenever members do interrupt him, their remarks are unimportant and need no answer."

Fifteen or twenty years ago it would have been out of the question for a Chancellor to read his speech, just as it is impossible to-day in other countries. A French, Italian, or English Minister, who stuck to his manuscript like a helpless student of theology who cannot finish his sermon without holding up a large sheet of white paper, would be compelled to stop speaking amid ironical laughter. But even in those days, early in the century, when the German language and the art of speaking were more seriously cultivated, I noticed how inadequately our people's representatives were equipped for debate. They hardly ever knew how to deal with ironical heckling. According to an old French joke which I think was originated by Alphonse Karr, a German visitor in Paris suddenly began to laugh one afternoon between three and four o'clock without any apparent reason. When French friends asked him why he suddenly felt so merry, he said he had only now understood a joke he had heard at the theatre the evening before. In our parliament sarcasm in debate is hardly understood. Not until it has been pointed out and emphasised by the press is it properly understood and accepted as a good joke, or repudiated as a silly remark, according to the Party point of view,

The Opposition, especially the Radicals, claimed that, in their opinion, the Reichstag had been convened too late. During the discussion on this point, a Deputy whom I did not know (I heard later on that he was a Socialist) placed a press cutting on the table before me so that no one in the House or in the galleries could see him do so. I took up the cutting and noticed that it was an article from a summer number of "*Freisinnige Zeitung*", the Deputy Richter's journal, stating that the summer was too early a time for the Reichstag to meet. The wording was somewhat involved but this was what the article implied. I used this occasion at once, to the great amusement of the House, to show the leader of the Radicals how he was contradicting himself. The next day a fellow member of Richter's Party told me that Eugen Richter had written this article himself. But the reason why this soft-hearted Democrat, who assumed such a bearish manner, had opposed an earlier meeting of the Reichstag, did him honour. His brother was ill with an agonising incurable disease and his wish to be with his brother during the last weeks of his life and to be present at the death bed had caused him to be inconsistent with regard to the meeting of the Reichstag. I sent a message to Herr Richter at once, telling him that if I had known all this I should never have attacked him nor exposed him to laughter in the House. Herr Richter thanked me personally when I met him a few days later in the lobby of the Reichstag.

I have often thought how different things would have been if Prince Bismarck had sometimes treated his adversaries as human beings, instead of always thinking of them as bitter political adversaries. I am convinced that a really great man, such as he was, could have had a more human relationship with Richter and Lasker, or Windthorst and Rickert. Their political differences would have been just as great, but they would not have been so charged with hatred and poison, as these differences often were. Contrary to so many other Left-wing politicians, August Bebel had a sense of humour, but this was not apparent in most of his speeches, for he was too full of feeling and too fanatical. When I repudiated his accusations that the German soldiers in China had been very cruel, with a statement to the contrary from the Chinese Ambassador in Berlin, and told Bebel in this connection that the Ambassador was a born Chinaman, while he himself was only a Chinaman by choice, a Chinaman "by elective affinity", Bebel was highly amused. My defence of the honour and the prestige of our good soldiers in China was, by the way, applauded by the majority of the Reichstag. Only in Germany would it have been possible for the Socialist newspapers to show up their own soldiers as cruel barbarians by publishing alleged soldiers' letters. The fact that the Socialist newspapers could call these undoubtedly unauthentic letters "letters from Huns" was only possible because of the Kaiser's regrettable speech at Bremerhaven on July 27, 1900. But a fouling of one's own nest, such as the Socialist Press undertook in those days, would not have been tolerated by public opinion in any other country.

CHAPTER XXX

COUNT POSADOWSKY, the Home Secretary, was the first of my colleagues on whom I called in Berlin after my appointment. I was particularly and most sincerely friendly towards him, just because I knew that he had hoped to become Chancellor and that my appointment meant a disappointment to him. But despite all the kindness I showed him I was unable to dispel his wintry mood. A few days later, between eleven and twelve o'clock at night, Count Posadowsky was announced at my house. He had come to tell me in a very excited manner that the Socialists' "*Leipziger Volkszeitung*" had published a statement, signed by Deputy Bueck, from the headquarters of the German Federation of Industries. This document which had been addressed to a number of leading industrialists was very embarrassing to him as Secretary of State. The document stated that the Home Office had informed the Directors of the Federation that it would like the industries to contribute 12,000 marks, which would be spent on propaganda for a bill to protect industrial and trade relations. The Executive Committee had submitted this request to its vice-chairman, Geheimer Finanzrat Jencke, who for "comprehensible reasons" had considered it proper not to reject "this somewhat strange proposal." Jencke had contributed 5000 marks on behalf of the firm of Krupp. Herr Bueck had corrected the article in the "*Leipziger Volkszeitung*" in so far as he stated that this occurred in 1899 and not in 1898, but he had not denied the truth of it.

Count Posadowsky, who had apparently lost his nerve completely, was afraid that the Kaiser would drop him and that, furthermore, he would be violently attacked by the Socialists and repudiated by the Radicals and particularly by the Centre Party because he had been so compromised. I assured him that I would never let such a worthy and distinguished civil servant down on account of an incident which may have been inconsidered, but which was in no way disloyal or dishonourable. I could assure him that the whole matter would be properly judged by His Majesty the Kaiser. In the Reichstag, so I promised him, I would support him myself. Count Posadowsky, who was obviously relieved, then told that it was really Dr. von Woedtke, a high official in the Home Office, and not himself, who had been responsible for the request to Dr. Bueck to place the sum of 12,000 marks at his disposal. When I remember, now more than twenty years have passed, that the storm which followed was caused by only 12,000 marks, I realize in what a state of heavenly innocence we lived in the old Germany. The Erzberger case concerned quite other scandals and far greater sums, and a not inconsiderable number of men high up and mighty in the Republic have been accused of greater sins than the admission that 12,000 marks for purpose of publicity would be acceptable to the Government. But in those days we lived in an authoritarian state and our leading men did not have the thick rhinoceros hides which the leaders of the "Peoples' State" had. Our leaders in those days were, in fact, very punctilious in matters of honour and integrity.

Before he left me and after he had thanked me for my friendly assistance, Count Posadowsky asked me for permission to have the matter dealt with "objectively" in the press. This was done in an article that appeared in the official "Berlin Correspondence": "At the suggestion of Director Dr. Woedtke of the Home Office," so the article ran, "who acted as an intermediary in the affair, General Secretary Bueck released a sum of 12,000 marks. This sum was used to pay the expenses incurred in the printing and distribution of official matter. The above-mentioned official possesses documentary evidence relating to the way in which that sum was spent in distributing the above-mentioned official matter which has already been deposited amongst the official publications of the Reichstag.

SECRETARY OF STATE COUNT POSADOWSKY-WEHNER

On the 24th of November, the interpellation concerning this affair was made in the Reichstag by the Socialists. Auer, the Social Democratic Deputy, introduced the subject in a dignified and temperate manner. Ignatius Auer was one of the most agreeable members of the Social Democratic Party. He was the son of a poor peasant girl from the Palatinate, but his innate ability and his ceaseless industry had enabled him to acquire a good education and he always tried to fill the gaps in his knowledge. Herr von Huhn, the Berlin correspondent of the "*Kölnische Zeitung*", told me that he expressed his surprise once when he and Herr Auer were dining together, at the fact that Auer was familiar not only with our own legislation but with the whole of home politics as well. Smiling sadly, Auer had answered, half seriously and half jestingly : "I would give all my knowledge to know whether fish and asparagus are eaten only with a fork or with a knife as well." I have always felt sympathy towards men of Auer's type, I have respected them and understood their ideals. It was, incidentally, Herr von Huhn who first attracted my attention to Eduard Bernstein, who later became a Deputy. At that time he was living in London as a refugee, since a previous conviction made his return to Germany impossible. I arranged the matter so that Eduard Bernstein could return to Germany, where he became very prominent in the Reichstag as a member of the Social Democratic Party. Bernstein was not always in agreement with August Bebel, who was a fanatic but unquestionably honest and sincerely convinced of the doctrines he preached. All the Parties had agreed that the scandal caused by the Twelve-Thousand-Mark Affair could not be readjusted if Count Posadowsky spoke in the Reichstag himself. Count Posadowsky, therefore, sat next to me, but he did not take part in the debate. In my speech I emphasized how ridiculous it was to speak of a "Panama" or a "Mafia" in connexion with this affair. The French Panama Scandal had really been quite different and the Sicilian "*Mafiosi*" did not look at all like Berlin bureaucrats. I particularly emphasised my faith in Count Posadowsky's great ability, his experience, his knowledge, and his character, and this, despite all the attacks against him. He and I both agreed, however, that in future such things should not occur.   As chief Minister of the Empire, I told the Government Department in question of my opinion in the matter.   Nor did I hesitate (while conceding the good faith of the officials involved and the sincerity of their belief that they were serving the Federal Government by their actions, to add that the course they had chosen had been the wrong one. Other measures did not seem necessary, for I would not bend before intrigues and before an attack launched from some ambuscade, I refused to be frightened by dark and questionable tactics on the part of my adversaries.   I would not acknowledge that machinations and intrigues such as these could have the slightest influence on my official decisions.   And in any case, the Socialists could rest assured that I should never again let them get hold of propagandist matter of the kind supplied by this affair.

My declaration had prolonged my colleague Posadowsky's term of office in the Ministry by seven years.   About a week later von Woedtke asked me for an interview.   When he came, I saw before me a completely broken man.   When he said that he felt the need to talk to me, he spoke not so much with symptoms of agitation as of deep grief.   He said he wanted to justify himself in the eyes of his most authoritative chief and not to ask for any favours.   When the *" Leipziger Volkszeitung "* published Herr Bueck's statement, Count Posadowsky had sent for him at once and said to him : "If this accusation in the Socialist newspapers were to remain as a stigma on himself, the Minister concerned, then his official future would be ruined.   He, Woedtke, should shoulder the responsibility. The whole affair did indeed concern his Department, and besides, as he was not such an important official, the affair could not really harm his career.   He, Woedtke, had therefore agreed to be named as the initiator and go-between for the grant of 12,000 Marks in the article that was published in the 'Berlin Correspondence.' "   Now that he had publicly become the scapegoat in this affair, Count Posadowsky had turned away from him and had gone so far as to forbid him to appear in the Reichstag or in any of the Reichstag Committee meetings.   I have rarely felt so much pity for anyone. Woedtke, who had been a conscientious civil servant for many years, was undoubtedly a very honourable man. Herr von Woedtke died a few weeks later. He did not commit suicide, as rumours reported, but he did die after a complete collapse. When Count Posadowsky's colleagues were discussing whether the Count was to attend the funeral, it was decided that it would be better for him not to be seen there. Otherwise the same thing might happen to him that happened to Hagen when he approached Siegfried's corpse and it began to bleed again.

> *Das ist ein grosses Wunder, wie es noch oft geschieht,*
> *Wenn man den Mordbefleckten bei dem Toten sieht,*
> *So bluten ihm die Wunden,*[1]

as it is written in the *Niebelungenlied*.

Count Arthur Posadowsky was a man of many great merits. I have rarely, even in Germany, known anyone who could work as hard as he could. He was an astonishingly good master of every detail that was handled by his large Department. He was rightly credited with being the only man in Germany familiar not only with all trade regulations but with the entire body of insurance legislation as well. His knowledge and his ability would have secured him a distinguished post in any country in the world. But this man, who had so many good points, was entirely without a heart, without love, without human kindness. He was very severe towards his wife, who had an original mind and was very kind-hearted and clever, though not worldly wise. He was equally hard in his dealings with the other people whom Fate brought across his path. Perhaps it was the long struggle for existence that had thus armour-plated his heart. His youth had been very onerous, he had been forced to make his way without a fortune and without connexions. He could have appealed to Tacitus' dictum: "*Eo immitior, quia toleraverat.*"

The oratorical helplessness of most of the Deputies made it relatively easy for me when required to readjust the Kaiser's *faux pas* in the Reichstag, but it was not so easy to deal with Europe as a whole. I was able to save Count Posadowsky, but the Boer ques-

[1] It is a great miracle that often happens still: when he who is murder-stained stands by the corpse, then its wounds bleed.

tion was far more complicated and difficult to deal with. On October 19th President Kruger sailed for Europe from Lorenço Marquez. On December 2nd he arrived in Cologne en route for Berlin. The population of Cologne received him enthusiastically. When the Kaiser read of this reception in the morning papers, he asked me to come over to the New Palace at once and said to me in considerable excitement : that together with the news of President Kruger's arrival in Germany, he had received a telegram from his grandmother, Queen Victoria, in which she urged him not to receive the President, for it was in the interest of friendly relations between the German and the English people, which meant a great deal to her, that he should not do so. I replied that even my great respect for the wise Queen, who was so friendly to Germany, and who was, after all, His Majesty's grandmother, would not influence me in my political decisions or advice. But, leaving the telegram from Her Britannic Majesty out of the discussion (I asked His Majesty not to mention this message to any outsiders), I did think that, in the interest of friendly relations between Germany and England, and therefore in the interests of Germany, it might be advisable for the Kaiser not to receive President Kruger. I would, I said, support this point of view unhesitatingly and emphatically in the Reichstag. The Kaiser was delighted. He did not, at the moment, want to offend his English relatives over whom he was enthusiastic one moment, and whom, at another moment, when he happened to be irritated, he called "the damned family." I returned to Berlin and told the Imperial Minister to Luxemburg, Herr von Tschirschky, to go to Cologne and to tell President Kruger in the most polite and friendly manner that the Kaiser would be unable to receive him. As a result of this message Kruger left Cologne two days later for the Hague.

It has always been a mistake of the German people to get agitated on behalf of foreign interests and to judge events emotionally which occur outside our own boundaries, instead of considering them dispassionately in the light of German interests. During the Polish Insurrection of 1830, the German people were enthusiastic about the "noble" Poles, and German poets, led by that genius,

August Platen, dedicated emotional and enthusiastic verses to the Poles. In 1848, a large part of the German National Assembly, in St. Paul's Church at Frankfort, declared for the aspirations of the Poles, who, in the meantime, were shooting at Germans in West Prussia and Posen. During the second half of the eighties, the Germans in general were enthusiastic over Prince Alexander of Battenberg in Bulgaria, despite the fact that he had never lifted a finger to promote German interests and that our relations with Russia and her Emperor, Alexander III, were far more important to us than our unstable and changeable relations with Bulgaria. It was often stated in defence of our pro-Boer enthusiasm that the Boers, being Dutchmen, were really Germans. True, the Dutch are an excellent people with a glorious history. But they separated themselves voluntarily from the German Empire centuries ago and they have always opposed any economic, political, and particularly any military union with Germany, for which, from their own point of view, they cannot be blamed in the least. The Boers in particular were not at all friendly towards us Germans. Germans who settled in their country were not particularly well received, and, during the World War, the majority of the Boers fought on the English side and joined the English when they invaded our Colonies. But all calm and reasonable considerations did not prevent the majority of Germans from being enthusiastic about the Boers because of the way the English treated them, and from feeling nothing but indignation, enmity, and hatred towards the English. I read in a pro-Boer newspaper, that no human being, not even a German, not even William I or Bismarck, had ever in any German city had a reception like the one "Uncle Kruger" got in Cologne. It was the only time during my long period of office when I was ever warned by the police that an attempt on my life might be made, because I was known to be anti-Boer. Naturally these warnings did not impress me. Had I been assassinated by a friend of the Boers, I would have died doing my duty for the welfare of the German people. It would have been a decent and a beautiful death. Some of the newspapers at the time called me "Lord Bülow" and "Viscount Bülow" alternately. This was supposed to be cruel, devastating irony. Some of the papers which attacked me in this way later reproached me for not having cultivated German-English relations more assiduously. Before I began my speech on December 10th, 1900, Count Ballestrem, a sensible man, who was the President of the Reichstag, urged me not to irritate the House, for the majority of the members disapproved of my policy, which they considered far too friendly towards England. I did not allow him to dissuade me from making my point of view absolutely clear.

My position was made more difficult, because of the telegram which the Kaiser had sent to Kruger (before I took over the conduct of our Foreign Affairs) when Jameson raided the South African Republic. Who was responsible for this telegram? Marschall repeatedly assured me that he had only given his consent because otherwise the Kaiser "would have committed even worse follies." It had, he said, been the Kaiser's wish and intention to "localise" the conflict between the Boer Republic and the English Cape Colony. In 1896 His Majesty had harboured the fantastic idea of concluding a Defensive and Offensive Alliance with the Boers and to fight on their side against the English in Africa. In Europe, on the other hand, he wanted to preserve peace with England. According to Marschall, the Kaiser had been so enthusiastically pro-Boer at this time because he attributed the Jameson Raid to his uncle, the Prince of Wales, and to the latter's two capitalist friends, Beit and Sir Ernest Cassel, both of whom, it might be mentioned incidentally, were German Israelites. Marschall assured me again and again that he had only let the telegram to Kruger pass so that worse things might be avoided. William II, on the other hand, told me, after the events of November, 1908, when he complained how unjust the German people were towards himself, that Marschall, Hohenlohe, and Kayser, who was then the Director of the Colonial Office, had "forced" him to send the telegram. He said that he had refused for a long time to sign the telegram, but that, finally, though unwillingly, he had submitted to his responsible advisers. I must in all impartiality say that this version of the affair is probably not quite true. If it had been, the Kaiser would surely have told me about it sooner, at the time of the Boer debate in 1900.

All those involved were responsible for the Kruger Telegram. One of William II's moods, to which he was subject in those days, made him want to "deal a blow" to the English and his Uncle Edward. Marschall hoped to become popular in the Reichstag because of this telegram, which he emphatically supported in the House, for he suffered under the unpopularity that arose from some sort of personal enmity harboured against him by the Bismarck family. The old Chancellor Hohenlohe was a tired man, who simply let things take their course. And Kayser, the Director of the Colonial Office, was, as Bismarck had said, a sound lawyer and a clever man, but he wrote "with his right or with his left hand" just as his superiors wished.

In my speech on December 10th,[1] I first pointed out that, in the spring of 1899, when I passed through the Hague, I joined the Dutch Government in urging Kruger to be moderate and careful. As early as June, 1899, I had suggested to him that he resort to mediation. But he answered that he did not think the time for mediation had come. In August, 1899, I urged him confidentially for the last time not to refuse the English proposals without due consideration, for I was convinced that any steps the Boers undertook at this critical time as far as a certain Great Power was concerned would lead to nothing and would be very dangerous for the African Republics. We were not, therefore, as I pointed out, in any way responsible for the outbreak of the war. We could not have done any more to prevent it, for we should only have crushed our own fingers in the door. We should not have helped the Boers this way, and we should only have harmed ourselves. At a critical time the policies of a country cannot be decided by emotions, they must be determined after the interests of the country have been quietly and objectively considered. Any attempt on the part of Germany to mediate would have resulted in an intervention, which, in turn, would have resulted in a diplomatic defeat or open warfare. In a war of this kind we should have experienced the fate of the idealistic youth whom Schiller describes in one of his beautiful poems:

[1] Prince Bülow's "Speeches" (large edition), I. 161; (small edition), I. 181.

Doch ach, schon auf des Weges Mitte
Verliessen die Begleiter mich,
Sie wandten seitwärts ihre Schritte,
Und einer nach dem andern wich.[1]

When I emphasised the fact that I had neither the wish nor the right to lead the German people into a situation of this kind, the House, which had not been very friendly at the beginning of my speech, broke out in lively applause.   I then declared that if the Kaiser had received President Kruger, it would have done neither him nor the Boers any good.   The House approved of my statement that I would not let myself be forced into playing the part of Don Quixote as far as England was concerned and that I would not fight English windmills all over the world.   It would be politically stupid to incur England's permanent enmity, and I would not take the responsibility for doing so.

My speech of December 10th was really an answer to the relatively moderate criticism of our attitude in the Boer War which had been made by the Conservative Count von Limburg-Stirum and by Dr. Sattler, a National-Liberal.   Dr. Hasse, a National-Liberal and Chairman of the Pan-German League, was really the chief instigator and leader of the agitation in favour of the Boers.   When, on the 10th of December, I was returning from the Reichstag to the Chancellor's Palace on foot, I met Dr. Hasse in the Tiergarten.   He was accompanied by two ladies, one was young and the other was somewhat older; they were apparently his wife and his daughter.   He bowed to me in a somewhat irritated and embarrassed manner and I noticed that his face was red with anger.   Herr Hasse was as honest as the day.   He had been a Saxon officer, but he had quarrelled with one of his comrades, a Hannoverian, who spoke unkindly about the solution of 1866 and about Prussia.   He had been dismissed from the Army because of this quarrel, for the Saxon Court, which was anything but friendly to Prussia after 1866, supported the Guelphs in the service of Saxony.   Herr Hasse became the Director of the Leipzig Statistical Bureau and later he

---

[1] But alas, even midway my companions left me.   They turned their steps aside, and one vanished after another.

was a professor at the University of Leipzig. No one could have been more honest, and at the same time more naïve, than he was politically. I disregarded his unfriendly attitude, went up to him, held out my hand, and said: "Dear Herr Hasse, I do not doubt your warm and profound patriotism. I know that you mean well, but if you and your friends go on this way, I shall be quite unable to establish friendly relations with England. The English will say that, with the best intentions in the world, the German Government cannot accomplish anything, if German public opinion takes it this way." Herr Dr. Ernst Hasse answered not without dignity: "As a representative of the people it is my right and my duty to express the real sentiments of the German people. It is Your Excellency's duty, because you are the Minister, to see that our foreign relations do not suffer as a result." I must admit that this answer saddened me, for I never felt more keenly how non-political the Germans really are. The whole pitiableness of the Germans was clear to me when Hasse spoke as he did; the ladies, meanwhile, were looking at him with admiration. When, the next day, I replied to his violent attacks in the Reichstag, I said: "A politician is not a judge of moral values. His chief duty is to protect the rights and interests of his own country. I cannot conduct foreign affairs from the standpoint either of pure moral philosophy or of an ale-house bench." The phrase "ale-house bench" was greatly resented, as I realised from a number of letters (they were almost all anonymous) which I received. I threw them all into the waste paper basket. But a wise and experienced friend also wrote to me, saying that German "ale-house" politicians, that is to say, the greater part of the German people, would not forgive me for having used the words "ale-house bench."

As soon as I was able to arrange my affairs, I left on a circular tour of the larger German Courts. As Secretary of State I had purposely avoided visits of this kind. Later Secretaries of State were not so modest. A South German "decoration tour" became the first thing new chiefs of Departments undertook. Before I became Chancellor, I made an exception only of the Baden Court, for Grand Duke Frederick, who was very friendly towards me, had previously sent me an invitation. Now, like the shepherd Damoetas in the Eclogues, I said: *Ab Jove principium!* and went first to visit the Munich Court.

The Prince Regent, who was then nearly eighty years old, received me most graciously and returned my call at once in person. I stayed at the *Bayrischer Hof* Hotel. He climbed the two flights of stairs with vigour and reached my rooms. Then he handed me the Order of St. Hubert with the words: "These are my thanks for the firm way you have defended my *circa sacra jura* in the Reichstag."

At first I did not understand in what way I was supposed to have served Bavaria and the Wittelsbach family in the Reichstag session of the 5th of December. During this session a member of the Centre Party submitted a motion according to which every citizen of the Empire living within its boundaries was to have complete confessional liberty as well as the right to take part in domestic or public services according to the faith of his choice. The purpose of this motion was to counteract the differential treatment of the Catholics (I greatly objected to it myself), particularly in Brunswick and in the Kingdom of Saxony. In my reply [1] I said that I fully appreciated and understood the motion put forward by the Centre Party, but that I could not agree to any motion which would limit the constitutional independence of the Federal States regarding a matter which was subject to the legislations of the individual Federal States themselves. I had no idea how much I was in harmony with the old tradition of the Bavarian dynasty. The Wittelsbach Dynasty claimed a sort of Protectorate over the Catholic Church. The claim was based on the idea of the *jura circa sacra* derived from the Gallican Articles. The attitude of the Wittelsbach Dynasty towards the Episcopate was somewhat like the lord of a manor towards the clergy with a living in his diocese. The House of Wittelsbach kept a jealous watch over this position against which the Church itself fought gently but assiduously. The Prince Regent, who was a devout Catholic, would have considered it a violation of his duties as Regent and a sin against his heritage, if his

[1] Prince Bülow's " Speeches " (large edition), I. 159.

Government had not firmly opposed this motion submitted by the
Centre Party. Prince Bismarck is supposed to have said that a
Bavarian is the transition from the Austrian to the human being.
I remember dining with Count Louis Arco in Bismarck's home a
few years before Bismarck's dismissal. Arco was very witty and
he amused Bismarck. His humorous remarks were enhanced by his
serious face and his solemn tone of voice. While we were dining, and
at a moment when everyone was silent, Arco asked the Chancellor
if he would elucidate one of his most significant utterances. When
the Prince nodded assent, Arco asked: "Did Your Highness say
that the Bavarian is the transition from an Austrian to a human
being, or did you mean that the Austrian is really the transition
from a human being to a Bavarian? The second version would be
far more flattering for us Bavarians." Bismarck laughed heartily.
Then he answered in his fine soft voice, and with great gravity: "I
cannot imagine that any Minister in a responsible position could
ever have made a remark of this kind." As a matter of fact this
utterance was made during Bismarck's Frankfort days, when he was
very bitter against the Austrians and, contrary to his later attitude,
he was then not very friendly towards Bavaria either. It is true
that there were many points of contact, many similarities, between
Bavaria and Austria, between Munich and Vienna and between the
Courts at Munich and at Vienna. Life at the Munich Court, like
life in Vienna, was both natural and dignified, pompous and yet
simple. The Court at Munich, like the Court at Vienna, dined in
the afternoon and the dignified Prince Regent sat next to his sister,
the Duchess Adelgunde of Modena, whom the inhabitants of
Munich called Modelgunde. She had been the last sovereign ruler
of Modena. In front of the Palace in which she lived there is still
a statue of Ciro Menotti. He had been hanged by the previous
Duke of Modena in the same square where the monument to the
martyr and apostle of liberty now stands. Times long past came
back to my memory, when I saw this dignified couple sitting side
by side in Munich. Duchess Adelgunde was the sister-in-law of
Count de Chambord, the last descendant of the senior line of the
House of Bourbon and the last representative of the Legitimacy in

France. The Prince Regent, who was wearing the Order of the Black Eagle in my honour, wore this, the highest Prussian decoration, in a setting almost unknown nowadays. As a brother of the future Queen of Prussia, he had received this Order when he was quite a young man from Frederick William III.

I have rarely met a man of his advanced age who seemed so entirely healthy as Prince Regent Luitpold. He knew that he was healthy and liked to be told that he was physically vigorous and alert. During the summer, when he was at Berchtesgaden, his entourage was fond of inviting mountaineers who were the same age as he was, so that he could enjoy seeing how healthy others of his own generation were. Once, when he asked one of these old men how he felt he answered in the naïve manner of the Alpine people: "Physically I 'm all right, but mentally we are all growing old and feeble." "I don't think so at all," the Prince Regent answered somewhat irritated. "I don't notice it in myself either," the honest Berchtesgadener answered, "but other people do. You may be sure I 'm right." The man was not asked to call on His Royal Highness again.

The evening after my reception by the Prince Regent, I had accepted an invitation to a soirée at the home of Count Crailsheim. Freiherr von Hertling, a Representative in the Reichstag, whom I knew slightly, but with whom I had never talked at length, came right up to me. Hertling had been a friend of Secretary of State Marschall. Marschall had even tried to overcome William II's prejudices against people's representatives in general and members of the Centre Party in particular by asking to have Hertling introduced to the Kaiser. To attain this purpose, Baron Marschall, accompanied by von Hertling and the Bavarian Minister, Count Hugo Lerchenfeld, had once approached His Majesty during a Court Ball in the "White Room." When His Majesty saw Marschall, with Lerchenfeld on his right and a man wearing glasses and looking like a scholar on his left, he knew what was in the wind. With his habitual agility the Kaiser dashed away from the gentlemen to the other end of the hall. When they reached him at last, all they got was a brief and rather frosty reception. The excellent Florentine historian, Francesco Guicciardini, is right when he advises those in power always to treat adversaries, when they cannot be destroyed completely, as though they might be a friend some day; and, on the other hand, he urges the mighty never to forget that times may change and that the best friends may become foes. When William II's sun began to set, he appealed to this same Hertling, whom, eighteen years before, he had treated so superciliously, and who, in the meantime, had become physically and mentally senile. George von Hertling, who was then a Freiherr and later became a Count, belonged to the bureaucratic nobility of the Grandduchy of Hesse. He belonged to a strict Catholic circle in Darmstadt, to which the Biegelebens, the Guaitas, the Hertlings, the Brentanos, the Schlossers *e tutti quanti* belonged as well. When Hertling was still at school, he had made a speech at a meeting of the Catholic Youth Movement and distinguished himself both by unusual eloquence and by his strict adherence to Catholic doctrine. As a student he belonged to a Catholic Students' association. He was for Austria and for Greater Germany [1] with all his heart and soul. Nevertheless he accepted a post as tutor at the University of Bonn, where, during the Kultur Kampf, he was foolishly and unjustly never appointed Professor because he was a Catholic. He was returned to the Reichstag, but showed no bitterness because of the treatment he had received — on the contrary, he associated himself with those members of the Centre Party who were very willing to come to terms with the Government. Hertling's spiritual adviser and father-confessor, both before and during his Chancellorship, was Father Blum, a Jesuit. Hertling did not have much respect for the Mendicant Orders. It was his misfortune that, towards the end of his life, he was appointed Chancellor in a period of infinite difficulty when he was no longer capable of dealing with the task before him.

When I met him in Munich he was only fifty-seven years old. My personal relations with Hertling were never spoiled even by subsequent political disagreements and misunderstandings. He was the only member of the Centre Party in the Reichstag who left

[1] *I.e.* for a united Austro-German Empire.

his visiting card at my home after the dissolution on the 13th of December, 1906, while the other deputies of the clerical party followed the bad German habit of making a personal out of a political issue. This is a bad German habit, which educated people in England and France, in Italy, in all other civilised countries, in fact, cannot understand. Count Hertling was an Aristides, of a severe, I might say defiant, integrity. He was in every way a puritan, and though he was a devout Catholic, he reminded me of English, Genevan, or Dutch Calvinists. Prince Chlodwig Hohenlohe, who did not like Hertling, and who was a very different type of man, used to say that Hertling never had a good glass of wine, never kissed a pretty girl, never had a well-fitting pair of trousers. Hertling was of a cold nature. I do not know whether he ever felt any real friendship. He was just, but not kind. He was entirely free from any pushfulness or any snobbishness. He had great inward nobility. When Prince Heinrich Carolath, the National-Liberal Deputy, welcomed him as Chancellor in the Reichstag and reminded him that Hertling had shown him kindness when they met forty years before in Bonn, the new Chancellor responded: "But, my dear Prince, the situation in Bonn was just the reverse. Your Highness was a kindly benefactor to me, the humble tutor." Hertling was, however, not free from intellectual conceit. He had a certain contempt for uneducated and unscholarly people. He felt an even greater contempt for the half-educated, — amongst whom he included headmasters and county magistrates, who were strongly represented in his Party both in Munich and in Berlin. During the best period of his life, Hertling would have made an excellent Prussian or Bavarian Minister. He worshipped authority. In 1900 he was on close and friendly terms with the Premier Crailsheim, whom he respected very much. He did not think as much of Crailsheim's successor Podewil, who was clever and capable, but too elegant, worldly, and not serious enough to suit Hertling.

I used my stay in Munich to have my portrait painted by Lenbach, and decided at the time that the portrait was to be given to the Reichstag. I had had no idea that I would one day be hung next to Fehrenbach, Joseph Wirth, and Gustav Bauer. I need hardly mention that as soon as I had left Munich, Count Anton Monts, who was the Royal Ambassador in Munich, sent me a report telling me that, in his opinion, my visit had made a tremendous impression. He reported officially:

To-day's "*Münchener Neuste Nachrichten*" gives prominence to a report of Your Excellency's visit which is obviously inspired by the Private Chancellery of His Royal Highness the Regent. This report describes the favourable impression you made on the leading personalities in Munich. Adjutant General von Wiedemann tells me in complete agreement with this account that the Regent was simply charmed by you. Wiedemann, who has the honour of having belonged to His Royal Highness' immediate entourage for many years, says that he has never known His Highness, who is usually very reserved, to express so much satisfaction about any personal meeting. His Royal Highness Prince Ludwig's Lord Chamberlain also assured me that his gracious master expressed his great appreciation of the talk he had with Your Excellency. Freiherr von Crailsheim, with whom I spoke after Your Excellency had left, at once said how impressed His Royal Highness the Regent had been. As a rule the Regent only has his cards left at the residence of the visitor, but the fact that he paid Your Excellency such a long personal call at your hotel shows how highly he approves of you. He, the Minister, hopes that this graciousness on the part of the Regent towards you will promote friendly relations between Munich and Berlin. Your Excellency's remarks to the Minister and his colleagues showed your complete confidence in them and this deepened their respect for the Reich's highest official. Your assurance that you will maintain Bismarck's policy of upholding the Federal basis of the Empire, as far as domestic affairs are concerned, was a great satisfaction to the Bavarian Government. Yesterday evening the minister of the Interior also congratulated me heartily upon the very successful visit you paid here. Other personalities as well, including Count Berchem, Professor von Hertling, the two mayors, etc., expressed their satisfaction to me. In conclusion I take the liberty of enclosing the report I mentioned as well as a further article in the "*Münchener Neuste Nachrichten*" which justly describes the attitude of the general public in Munich towards your visit. This morning's "*Allgemeine Zeitung*" gives Your Excellency special praise for meeting not only princes, statesmen, and diplomats, but also for paying your respects to the efficient and enterprising Munich bourgeoisie.

The Ambassador's love and respect for me was expressed not only in this official report. The very same day Count Monts wrote to my wife as well:

Dear Countess:

I presume that after your visit to poor Empress Frederick, you will return to Berlin before your husband. I want, therefore, to tell you about Bernhard's great success here. He made the most favourable impression on the high and on the lowly and when he left, the general public cheered him spontaneously. The old Regent, who is difficult to charm and who thinks exclusively of his own exalted person, was delighted with him and said so himself to a number of people; the Ministers, etc., were equally delighted, and so was Berchem, who, as you know, used not to be enthusiastic about B. I believe that Bernhard made many friends here. His reception was, of course, prepared by his achievements and his speeches; naturally he is not without enemies, but we shall work all the harder to retain the new supporters he has won here for him. I was very pleased to see Bernhard in such good health and in such a splendid frame of mind. For the Chinese and the Kruger questions were not exactly simple and he is fully conscious of his great responsibilities. I hope Lenbach's portrait of him will be good. Lenbach is not as good as he was, because he paints only for money in a factory-like manner. It is obvious that his wife urges him to do this because she would like to see him make a great deal of money before death takes the brush out of the always tired Master's hand. Lenbach is very irritable, he often reveals his peasant origin by his rough manner. Other artists, whom he had oppressed, are agitating against him; they would like to take his presidency away from him. Perhaps L. will make one last effort in connexion with Bernhard's portrait, it sometimes does happen that ageing artists paint really remarkable pictures. But I must stop now, you are probably very busy getting ready for Christmas and fitting up the Palace, which will undoubtedly be a miracle of good taste and beauty. Donna Laura's advice and help will be more valuable than the help from any of the craftsmen in Berlin. I hope you will have a merry Christmas. Please give my profound respects to Donna Laura and give my regards to dear old Lichnowsky. In unchanging devotion and gratitude, I am your faithful,

Monts

Count Monts' attack on Lenbach was unjust. Lenbach was a great artist and a noble character. His genius will be respected long after Monts has been forgotten. As Holstein used to say, Monts made a mess not only of one post, as many do, but he did so of three: Budapest, Munich, and Rome. Thus spoke Holstein, although Monts was almost as enthusiastic about him, when he was the most influential man at the Foreign Office, as he was about me.

From Munich I went to Stuttgart. In the good old days before the November Revolution, the same Prussian Minister represented Prussia at the Courts of Weimar, Meinigen, and Coburg-Gotha. Once, when he told Grand Duke Karl Alexander that he was leaving Weimar for a few days to present his credentials in Meinigen, the Grand Duke replied with his usual mixture of dignity and kindness: "You will learn to know life on a very small scale there." The Bavarian leaders did not talk about Stuttgart in this way when I left Munich. But it is undoubtedly true that every Bavarian Minister and high official felt that, as compared with other South German States, Bavaria was a Great Power. Considering what Bavarian and German history had been, this point of view was not entirely unjustified. I always considered it my duty to take Bavaria's special position in the Empire into due consideration. I rarely, if ever, forced the Federal Council to accept any decision, which was consciously and decidedly opposed by Bavaria. I always made it my business to retain the confidence of the Bavarian ruling house: of Prince Regent Luitpold, of Prince Ludwig, of Prince Rupprecht. The last named was undoubtedly the most gifted of the three. He was frank, open-minded, and shrewd and, at the same time, a highly gifted general, as was shown during the World War. Prince Leopold, Prince Regent Luitpold's second son, too, was an able soldier. I often met him during the manoeuvres while I was Chancellor, and I was greatly pleased by his military bearing, his frank open-minded judgments, and his manly personality. The favouritism towards Bavaria, which I always harboured in my own mind, did not prevent me from showing the other Federal German States every consideration. I took their peculiarities and their special wishes into consideration insofar as I could do so without harming the unity of the Reich.

> *Eins nach aussen, schwertgewaltig,*
> *Um ein hoch Panier geschart!*
> *Innen reich und vielgestaltig,*
> *Jeder Stamm nach seiner Art!*[1]

These beautiful verses by Geibel, it seems to me, contain the last word in wisdom with regard to the treatment of the various Federal States. The Swabians, by the way, were the last to admit Bavaria's political superiority. My predecessor, Prince Chlodwig Hohenlohe, told me that, when he was Bavarian Premier between 1867 and 1870, he often, in agreement with Bismarck, who was then Chancellor of the North German Confederation, tried to bring the South German States closer together under Bavaria's leadership. This idea of a South German Confederation was welcomed in Stuttgart, but the suggestion that Bavaria should be the leader in such a Confederation or that there should be a Bavarian presidency was emphatically rejected and it was often pointed out in this connexion that Germany owed some of her greatest men to Württemberg: Schiller and Hegel, Hölderlin, Uhland and Mörike, Schelling and Friedrich List, whereas Bavaria, on the other hand, was practically not represented at all on our Parnassus of poets and thinkers. Karlsruhe, in turn, assured Premier Hohenlohe that the "model little country", which was always the advance guard in Germany's political progress, and which could serve as a political model to Germany as a whole, would never bow before Bavaria or Württemberg. In Darmstadt the demands of Baden and the self-assurance of the Badeners were considered out of place. All this goes to show that when Bismarck created the Reich, he acted like Columbus who, according to the well-known tale, stood the egg on end, for in the Empire the "*unitas in necessariis*" was happily combined with "*libertas in dudiis.*"

---

[1] Showing the enemy a united front, rallied round a raised shield! Abundant and multiform, every stock according to its own nature.

King William of Württemberg, who had invited me to stay at the Palace, was a simple man with a heart of gold, a good Swabian but a loyal German patriot. All his life he was deeply attached to the *corps* to which he had belonged in Göttingen when he was a student and he was equally loyal to the Potsdam Hussar Regiment of Body Guards in which he had served as a Captain. In the same way he was unshakably loyal to the Kaiser and to the Reich. He was very democratic and simple, but he was always somewhat aloof from parliamentary life in Württemberg and the Empire. He was surprised when I spoke highly of Gröber, the deputy of the Württembergian Centre Party, for he had apparently never heard his name before. I presume that the rôle which was later played by Mathias Erzberger from Buttenhausen must have surprised King William even more. In Stuttgart as well as in Munich, and in Karlsruhe, Darmstadt, and Dresden, where I went later, I spent most of my time discussing the final draft of the parliamentary bill relating to the tariff question as well as its treatment before Parliament with the leading Ministers. These discussions were very long, often lasting right through the night. All the Ministers agreed with my formula: increased protection for agriculture while leaving the possibility of concluding trade agreements open. The task of carrying out this formula of course remained. Among the Ministers in the central German States, I was greatly impressed by the ability of the Bavarian Minister of Finance, Freiherr von Riedel, and the Baden Minister of Finance, Dr. Buchenberger.

CHAPTER XXXI

Continuation of the Circular Tour: Karlsruhe, Darmstadt, Dresden —
Bestowal of the Order of the Black Eagle (December 23, 1900) — Congratula-
tions from Prince Hohenlohe — Prince Max of Baden, Prince Alexander von
Hohenlohe — Schillingsfürst — Hereditary Prince Erni von Hohenlohe —
Langenburg — Changes in Diplomatic Posts: Prince Radolin Goes to Paris,
Count Alvensleben to St. Petersburg — Anxious Letters from Eulenburg —
Freiherr von Mirbach and Dr. Hugo Preuss.

THE Grand Duke of Baden had invited me to call upon him in
his Palace at Baden-Baden.   Hans Thoma, the great artist, painted
a portrait which is very characteristic of Grand Duke Frederick:
he combined an idealistic philosophy with a realisation of the
demands of practical life.   He had great kindness and yet he could
be firm; he had real nobility combined with spirituality and he
was always guided by spiritual motives.   The Grand Duchess
Louise, who profoundly understood her husband's greatness, sup-
plemented his character in the happiest manner.   I do not think
that even patriarchal Germany produced a ruling Princess who did
her duty as the mother of her people in a more exemplary manner
than Grand Duchess Louise.   Perhaps she overdid it.   *"Elle*
créerait des malheurs pour pouvoir les soulager", a malicious French
diplomat once said about her.   He was unjust, for the tears which
she dried, the wounds which she healed, and the good that she
did will never be forgotten.

The Grand Duke received me in his study, from the corner window of which there was a lovely view of Baden-Baden.   One could
see the ancient Civitas Aurelia Aquensis, the wooded slopes that
flank the Black Forest and the level Rhine valley.   He was a man
of mediation and conciliation.   He fully agreed with my plan
to help agriculture without harming trade and industry.   He
considered it necessary to increase the navy without coming to
blows with England, but he opposed any dependence upon England.

He also considered it important that we avoid any differences with Russia on account of England. His chief worry was the Kaiser, whom he regarded not only as the key-stone of German unity, but whom he loved as a human being and as a nephew. He repeatedly declared that it was my duty to place the Kaiser's good intentions and his good will at the service of the country and to see that the Kaiser's dangerous characteristics did not endanger the future and the existence of the Empire. While the Grand Duke talked to me at length about this subject, his hand rested on the Bible which was lying before him. He gazed at the charming Oos valley before us. "If only we maintain peace, the peace of law and order within, and peace with the world outside, a peace with honour, then I am not afraid for our future. Look at the fruitful, flowery country spread out before you! Even if other regions of Germany are not quite as beautiful as our Baden, Germany is now better off than she has ever been before, she is better off than are most other countries. All we need is order and peace. God help us maintain both."

From Karlsruhe I went to Darmstadt and I realised that German unity had been promoted more effectively by our system of transportation than by anything else. Railways and telegraphs were the greatest enemies of all particularism. If one could travel comfortably from the Baden to the Hessian capital in two hours, no serious differences between these two "States" were really possible. In Darmstadt, too, I was invited by the Grand Duke to stay at the Palace. Everywhere in Darmstadt one was reminded of Russia. The Darmstadters, particularly the ruling House, were proud that two Russian Tsars had married Hessian Princesses and that Alexander II and Nicholas II had ascended the throne with Hessian wives. There were pictures of the Tsars on the walls of the rooms in which I lived. Replicas of the Kremlin, of Peter the Great's beautiful statue in St. Petersburg, and the fine monument to Nicholas I stood resplendently on the tables and on the cupboards. Grand Duke Ernst Ludwig was not very much like his worthy father, Grand Duke Ludwig IV, who had been wounded as a brave divisional leader in the campaign against France. He was more like his brilliant mother, Grand Duchess Alice, who was highly cultured, and whose liberal views on politics and religion had rather astonished the inhabitants of Darmstadt. Grand Duke Ernst Ludwig was interested in the arts, particularly architecture. He was also interested in philosophy though at times in a rather incoherent manner.

At dinner I noticed how stiff and unfriendly the relationship between the Grand Duke and the Grand Duchess seemed to be. Grand Duchess Victoria was the second daughter of Duke Alfred of Coburg and Grand Duchess Maria of Russia, who was the only daughter of Alexander II of Russia. She was very beautiful. A prettier picture could not be imagined than Grand Duchess Victoria side by side with her blonde sister Marie, who later became Queen of Roumania. It is well known that the latter influenced King Ferdinand of Roumania, a Hohenzollern, who had the honour of serving in the 1st Guards Regiment, to take sides with our enemies. Princess Victoria was later on content to turn her back on Darmstadt and to marry Grand Duke Cyril Vladimirovitch of Russia after she was divorced from her first husband. The melodramatic way in which she finally left Darmstadt which had respected her as its ruler for seven years did not reveal very good taste. The Grand Duke's only daughter had died in St. Petersburg after a short illness. The girl's mother came to Darmstadt for the funeral and she was received with all honour. This did not prevent her, after the service, from placing her Hessian order on her daughter's coffin to show that she had made a final break with her old home.

The Detmold inheritance case showed the pettiness and the arrogance so prevalent in small German principalities. Darmstadt, on the other hand, was the scene of a marital comedy, which showed up the helplessness of these small German rulers in a crisis. After the death of his wife, Grand Duchess Alice, who was his intellectual superior, Grand Duke Ludwig IV, who was very lonely, met the wife of a secretary of the Russian Legation at Darmstadt, a Madame Kolemine. She was by birth a Pole, a Countess Czapska; she was pretty, interesting, and full of initiative. After consulting his eldest daughter, Princess Victoria of Hesse, he decided to marry this lady after she had divorced her first husband in Russia. In the

meantime Princess Victoria became engaged to Prince Louis of
Battenberg, who was in the English service. She was to be married
with great ceremony on the 30th of April, 1884, in the presence of
the then Crown Prince and his wife. Many German princes and
Queen Victoria of England were to be present as well. The Grand
Duke and his daughter decided that he should marry Madame
Kolemine quietly in a small chapel on the same day. Frieherr von
Stark, the leading Hessian Minister, had said that he would act as
his Royal Master's best man. Immediately after the ceremony,
however, the worthy Minister suffered pangs of conscience. He
rushed to the Prussian Ambassador, Baron Ferdinand Stumm, who
was subsequently appointed Ambassador to Madrid, and confessed
everything to him. Stumm did his duty and reported the incident
to the Crown Prince and the Government in Berlin. No one knew
what to do, until Queen Victoria took a hand in the matter. As
Queen of Great Britain and Ireland, she was a very constitutional
Monarch. As a mother, grandmother, and particularly as a mother-
in-law, she was very autocratic. She simply declared that her
former son-in-law's marriage with Madame Kolemine was not to be
consummated, she took him by the ear, and left for Balmoral in
Scotland with him that same evening. In Scotland he had time to
ponder over his dream of connubial happiness. In the meantime
his marriage with Madame Kolemine was annulled. She was
given a considerable sum of money and the title of Countess of
Romrod by way of compensation. She subsequently married a
Russian diplomat, Herr von Bacheracht. The marriage was a
happy one. She and her husband lived in Bern, where he was
Russian Ambassador, and during the World War she worked zealously for the Entente. Had Jacques Offenbach still been alive, he
might have made a charming light opera out of this incident. The
only sad thing about it was the way in which this incident reflected
the helplessness and the lack of independence of the Regents of
the Central German States during any crisis. Many German
rulers showed the same lack of decision, presence of mind, and
composure during the Revolution. In 1884 the Hessian people
did not desert their ruler but surrounded him with sympathy after

the short-lived and so imperfect happiness of his second marriage. The Minister Stark who had to resign was obliged to pay the bill.

I remained in Darmstadt only for a short while, but I had time to discuss the tariff question with the leading Hessian Ministers. From there I went to the capital of Saxony. Stuttgart was not politically as important as Munich; Darmstadt was not as important as Karlsruhe and Stuttgart. Dresden, on the other hand, was permeated with the atmosphere of a larger state. In Dresden, above all, I had the honour of meeting King Albert of Saxony again. He was one of the most distinguished figures of the new German Empire. It is well known that Field Marshal Moltke said of him that he was the only German general who made no mistake during the Franco-Prussian War. During the War of 1866 Crown Prince Albert distinguished himself as the leader of the Saxon Army at Münchengrätz, Gitschin and Königgrätz, where he fought on the Austrian side. It was because of him that the Austrian Army was not completely demolished after the Battle of Königgrätz, for the Saxon Army under Crown Prince Albert fought brilliantly. Everyone knew the great part he played in the Victory of Sedan, the greatest victory in German history, as Commander of the Meuse Army. The characteristics which distinguished Albert of Saxony as a soldier, his quiet manner, his firmness, his clear-headedness, and his presence of mind, made of him a distinguished statesman. Bismarck, who was a great friend of the King of Saxony for many years, fully appreciated these qualities in him. King Albert told me many interesting things about Bismarck. I remember his account of the "conciliation banquet", which was held in the autumn of 1866 between Prussia and Saxony in the Royal Palace in Berlin. Old King William and old King Johann sat at the end of the table. They were related and belonged to the same generation. They had been bound by undisturbed friendship for many years. Then, in 1866, they were rudely separated by politics and by Bismarck's genius. Now they were reunited: the King of Prussia as a victorious and the King of Saxony as a defeated monarch. With his usual kindness and his unique tact, King William tried to make the transition easier for King Johann.

He wanted to clear the atmosphere of all bitterness and to show his guest that his, King William's, friendship had not changed. The Prussian Premier, Count Bismarck, and the Saxon Premier, Frei-herr von Friesen, sat at the other end of the table. After looking thoughtfully at the two monarchs, Bismarck said to his colleague : "Your life is easy. You are associated with a highly educated, scholarly chief, who has translated Dante into verse, who has adopted the name of Philaletes, who upholds the arts and sciences. But just look at the old infantry Colonel with whom I have to work." King Albert told me this incident several years after Bis-marck's dismissal. He gravely concluded his remarks with the words : "And yet Bismarck was the greatest servant the Hohen-zollern family ever had. He was one of the greatest statesmen who ever advised a sovereign. And William I was a great, a really great ruler, because he appreciated Bismarck's greatness, because he never allowed himself to be influenced against Bismarck, despite the latter's ill humour, his stubbornness, and his lack of considera-tion. William I overlooked the very, very difficult character of the first Chancellor, because he thought first and foremost of reasons of State, of the State itself, of Prussia, and of the Empire. History will appreciate our old Kaiser as a great ruler. And the relation-ship between him and Bismarck is just as beautiful and just as unique as the friendship between Goethe and Schiller."

When I visited King Albert in 1900, he had already fallen seri-ously ill. He suffered from a very painful kidney disease to which he succumbed hardly eighteen months later. He received me lying on the divan. His facial expression showed that he was in pain, but his mind overcame physical suffering. He described the domes-tic and the foreign situation to me clearly as he saw it. We could not afford to let Austria down, not only because this would be dis-loyal, but because it would not be in Germany's interest to do so. We ought to avoid a war with Russia as long as possible, for we could gain nothing by such a war and we might lose a great deal. "*Le jeu ne vaut pas la chandelle.*" The King was convinced that our naval programme was right and necessary. A war with England seemed to him even more unwise than a conflict with Russia, and, politically speaking, more unnecessary. We must, so he said, increase our sea power to a proper defensive strength without letting the English destroy our trade and our shipping while they could still do so without undue risk to themselves. "Our path in this connexion is narrow and slippery. But for a keen eye, a firm foot, and a brave heart everything is possible — but only if the necessary caution and adroitness are practised as well." King Albert was particularly anxious about the Social Democratic movement, for his country was chiefly industrial and the population was particularly exposed to the influences of socialist propaganda. But he was too wise and too full of sensitive understanding to believe that salvation lay in the use of force. Quite apart from the question as to whether William II was the right man to carry out a *coup d'état*, his chief concern in this connection was: *Et après?* In domestic as well as in foreign affairs, salvation, in his opinion, would come from cool determination and quiet firmness. "If you could gradually make our good Kaiser see this point of view, you would be doing a really great service." King Albert agreed with most German rulers, with Bismarck, with almost all of our older statesmen that the Chancellor's chief function was to deal properly with the Kaiser. "You must exploit the Kaiser's brilliant gifts for the good of the Empire, but you must prevent him from making the terrible mistakes which his weakness and the doubtful side of his character might lead him into, for these mistakes might destroy us." King Albert's divan, on which he was lying as he spoke, stood next to a pretty table made of Meissner porcelain. He used this table to sign the documents which were brought to him from time to time by a secretary. After her husband's death, King Albert's wife, Queen Carola of Saxony, gave me this table, which now stands in my room in Flottbeck and reminds me of one of the finest and most distinguished rulers Germany ever had.

I returned to Berlin and the Kaiser called on me two days before Christmas, on the 23d of December, 1900. He handed me the Order of the Black Eagle with the words: "This is a token of my gratitude for the way you got me out of the awkward situation in the Reichstag." I thanked him heartily, but urged him not to give me cause for any more knight-errantry of this kind. I would be glad to intervene before the Reichstag on behalf of the Kaiser at any time, but I told him that his carelessness, his indiscretion, and his lack of self-control would only harm himself. Nothing could have been more friendly than the way the Kaiser pressed my hand and assured me that he would never again make it necessary for me to intervene on his behalf. Only two decades have passed since this day on which I received the highest Prussian decoration. When I received it I was the youngest Knight of the Order; now I am the oldest. *Eheu fugaces, Postume, Postume, labuntur anni.*

I was greatly pleased to have a letter from my predecessor in office shortly after I received the Order of the Black Eagle. I quote this letter to show to what an extent Prince Chlodwig Hohenlohe combined nobility of character with kindness of heart :

As the oldest knight of the Order of the Black Eagle, I wish to congratulate Your Excellency upon the well-earned distinction which you have received and to wish you and the Countess a very happy New Year. I hope the New Year will bring you happiness and continued success. With the assurance of my friendship and devotion,

Ch. Hohenlohe

A few days later my predecessor's second son, Prince Alexander Hohenlohe, who was the District President in Colmar, wrote to my wife :

This year you will probably have so many New Year greetings that you will not have time to read them all. Nevertheless you must allow me to add my good wishes, with the hope that you will include mine amongst those that are truly and sincerely meant. I need not add that the Chancellor is included in my good wishes, for I do not want to take up his valuable time by sending him any direct messages. Most human beings, who have reached the heights which you have attained this New Year, are easily tempted to believe that no more good wishes are needed. But I believe that there is indeed something which everyone might wish for, something that is really worth more than all honours and successes. That something, as Schopenhauer has said, is good health. And I wish you, and particularly the Chancellor, good health. I hope that he will retain his health despite his very strenuous work, so that he may remain in his post for a long time, for there is no one who can accomplish as much that is useful in this post as he can. You have probably heard so many flattering remarks recently that anything I might say would only sound trite. But I must tell you that I considered his speeches in the Reichstag masterly, both as to content and as to form. What surprised and pleased me most was to see that, in these speeches, he showed himself to be not only an extremely able politician and statesman, but that he showed his independent character in all directions as well. That is just what we need so badly and what has increased the high opinion I have always had of him. I am very curious to see the Magic Palace into which you have converted the old Chancellor's Palace. I have good news from my father in Meran.

Alexander Hohenlohe, together with the Hereditary Prince Ernst von Hohenlohe-Langenburg and Prince Max von Baden, belonged to a group of South German aristocrats who, each in his own way, played a part in our political life. Alexander Hohenlohe was the most gifted of the three. He was an able administrator; he would have made a good Minister or ambassador. He combined a noble character with an open mind. My wish to use him in the diplomatic service was not realised because the Kaiser, who had never liked him, opposed this plan. Later, when Alexander Hohenlohe did not prevent the publication of his father's memoirs, the Kaiser opposed him very violently. Prince Max von Baden aroused all kinds of hopes, but he disappointed everyone when he was finally put to the test. When William II conceived the unhappy idea of appointing this charming amateur as Chancellor in an infinitely difficult period, a terrible fiasco was inevitable. Max von Baden was not a "traitor" or "scoundrel", as the Kaiser, who loved to use strong language, called him after the sad days in November, 1918, but he was a man who, when weighed in a critical hour, was found too light. Prince Ernst von Hohenlohe-Langenburg was politically the least able of the three. He could hold his own as Regent of Saxe-Coburg-Gotha, from 1900–1905, when he only performed the social duties of his Regency (which he did with charm and dignity) and left the work of ruling to his Ministers.

Bismarck liked to tell the story about an Elector of Hesse, who was grieved to hear that a brother-in-law of his, the Duke of Anhalt, had suffered a stroke. He sent his personal physician to examine his brother-in-law and to report to him fully. When the physician returned, the Elector asked him: "Can my brother-in-law still hear anything?" The answer was in the negative. "Can he still see?" Again the answer was No. "Can he speak?" No. "That is terrible," the Elector exclaimed, "for my brother-in-law will now have to abdicate." The physician replied soothingly: "Oh, no, he has enough vitality left to be able to rule quite well." When, in 1905, "Erni" Hohenlohe was appointed Director of the Colonial Department as a result of intrigues and because the Kaiser wished it, he made a mess of things. Later, as Vice-President of the Reichstag, he did not do much better.

Prince Chlodwig Hohenlohe continued to take an interest in politics even after his retirement. At the turn of the century he wrote from Schillingsfürst to Holstein, who had been a friend of his since the time when he had been at the Paris Embassy:

Dear Friend,

Many thanks for your kind, detailed letter about the Kruger affair. I am now fully at rest. Sensible people in South Germany realise that this is a serious matter and that we are faced with the alternative of either making war on England — in which case Russia and France would, of course, let us down — or to leave the Boers to their fate. Only people who want noise and trouble are interested in Kruger. People of this kind want to create difficulties for the Government. Then there are fools, like my brother-in-law Salm, who are keen about Kruger. He is influencing my sister to make silly demonstrations in favour of Kruger. It is regrettable that our police in Cologne are so clumsy, for the Government is blamed for their mistakes. On Monday I am going to Munich to see the Prince Regent, and I shall then proceed to Meran. It's beginning to be uncomfortable here. I can feel the storm that is brewing, even in my bed. I was very much amused about the notice of Miquel's game of blind man's buff. In friendly devotion,

                                                    Ch. Hohenlohe

Until his death, Hohenlohe was hostile to Miquel. In the end both old men died about the same time: Chlodwig Hohenlohe, at the age of eighty-two, on July 6th, and Johannes Miquel, at the age of seventy-three, on September 8th, 1901. *Omnes eodem cogimur.*

After my appointment as Chancellor, I had not given up the hope that Count August Eulenburg's unusual talents might be made use of in our diplomatic service. I made an attempt in this direction, but the Kaiser's opposition had not decreased. After His Majesty's decision had finally been made known, Count August Eulenburg wrote to me not without mournful irony that His Majesty was a great Sovereign and, no doubt, justified in considering his own comfort before considering the interests and the wishes of his servants and his subjects. At the moment the Kaiser wanted to forget — or had really forgotten — that there was twenty years' difference between his age and Eulenburg's. This fact would, in time, only increase Eulenburg's disadvantage. In ten years, if he lived that long, he would be an old man, while His Majesty would still be in the best of health. The separation, he went on to say, would have to come sometime: this disagreeable event was only postponed. The form this separation would take would probably be more unpleasant for His Majesty's servant than for His Majesty himself.

This prediction made by Eulenburg, who was usually so shrewd, was not fulfilled. Who could have predicted that August Eulenburg, many years later, after the Kaiser's fall, would serve the Kaiser with his quiet manner, his presence of mind, his dignity, and his tact and that he would one day be one of the few among William II's intimates who would not lose his head? August Eulenburg closed his letter with this friendly remark: "I must say that it would have been a pleasure and a cause for pride to have worked under you. But even under present conditions you must rest assured that you can always count on my loyalty and grateful devotion." This excellent and noble man, who stood every test in life, kept this promise and remained my faithful friend until his death in 1921.

I was not able to use Count August Eulenburg's talents for the good of the country either in St. Petersburg or in London and I gave way to Holstein's urgent requests to transfer Prince Radolin, who had been in St. Petersburg, to Paris, where Prince Münster, who was now eighty years old, could hardly perform his duties any longer. Not that the venerable Ambassador was convinced of this fact himself. He considered himself entirely efficient and he did not believe that anyone else could have represented the German Empire in Paris better than he did. He was very angry with me when he was retired, although he had been recalled in the most tactful way in the world, and he never made a secret of his aversion towards me. It is true that Münster suited the French particularly well. He was too Anglophile, being partly English, to have been a suitable ambassador to London. He assumed that English customs good and bad, that English institutions and attitudes, were unquestionably superior to those of other countries. He was better suited to Paris, for he was so thick-skinned that nothing could move him, and he had humour and common sense. There were several objections to sending Radolin to Paris. Princess Radolin, née Countess Oppersdorf, had a French mother, a Talleyrand, and she was related to a large section of the Faubourg Saint-Germain, especially with politically active members of the Castellane family. And this connection was dangerous in view of the republican régime in France. Old Marquis de Noailles, who was then French Ambassador in Berlin, allayed my doubts in this respect when he said: "*Nos ministres actuels savent à peine qui fut Talleyrand. Quand aux Castellane, ils ne se doutent pas même de leur existence.*" Holstein urged me so incessantly that I finally gave way. There was a sentimental side to this strange man's nature: he was almost extravagantly attached to Radolin, with whom he had been a fellow student at Bonn. Fritz von Holstein, whose health was poor, and who, under the care of his mother and his aunt, was kept as aloof from the other students as from the Royal Hussars, was attracted by the young Pole, who returned his affection. "I have never asked you for a favour," Holstein said to me, "to-day I want to ask you a really great favour. I have one really great friend, and that is Radolin. Do get him appointed to Paris, if not for his sake, then for mine. I was already a *Geheimer Rat* when you were still a young attaché. Now you are Imperial Chancellor, and I am still *Geheimer Rat.* For myself I crave neither promotions nor decorations nor any honours such as most men desire, but at least do something for my friend." Nine years later, when Holstein died in Berlin, Radolin, who was still ambassador in Paris, probably intended to come to the funeral. He took a train in Paris and travelled as far as Cologne. There, he remembered what his wife's great-uncle, Prince Talleyrand, had said: *qu'il faut se méfier du premier mouvement, car il est le bon.* He remembered that Holstein had not been in favour with His Majesty and returned to Paris. Holstein, whose suspicious moods had caused him to quarrel with so many of his friends during his lifetime, was after his death deserted by the one man whom he had considered his real friend. The fact that I submitted to his wishes and sent Radolin to Paris was one of the not few mistakes I made *in personalibus.* Radolin was so accustomed to being impressed by Holstein, who was more able than he was, and to being led and inspired by Holstein, that in Paris, where steadiness and calm were especially needed, he obeyed Holstein's usually hasty, and often wholly wrong and inconsidered suggestions *stante pede* and *verbo tenus.* Radolin often saw situations only from Holstein's point of view. As early as the Bismarckian era, Holstein had a right to correspond with those ambassadors who were his friends in a secret code, which he used particularly when writing to his spiritual lackey, Radolin. For this reason my political orders to Paris, especially in the Morocco question, were often delayed, evaded, or wrongly executed.

Radolin was replaced in St. Petersburg by Count Alvensleben, who had been my chief when I made my début as a young secretary of Embassy twenty-five years before. He was not a genius, but he was a faithful and conscientious civil servant, who knew St. Petersburg, where, in the seventies, he had acted as Councillor of Embassy under Prince Henry VII of Reuss. He understood the Russians. His political usefulness was, however, greatly curtailed when, later, old bachelor that he was, he accepted Hymen's bondage. Bismarck, who coined the brilliant remark concerning the mortgage of vanity that must be deducted from the value of every human being, once said that the usefulness of all diplomats was decreased by their wives. I have in this connexion heard him suggest that it might be advisable to have diplomats, like Catholic priests, remain celibate.

The great man loved witty paradoxes. When the Representatives of the People irritated him, he would, with apparent gravity, discuss whether it might not be advisable to remove the Reichstag to Kassel. "Then off we go to Kassel!" he would then repeat, laughing. He even claimed that, many years ago, he had made this suggestion to the Kaiser, but that he had unfortunately failed to get the plan accepted. Of course, Prince Bismarck did not carry out all of his ideas; he was, in part, dissuaded from them by his old Master and, besides, after careful consideration, he often gave them up himself. And yet he often carried out ideas which no one considered possible. Once, in 1874, when I was a young attaché, I spent the evening at Princess Bismarck's. Her huge husband came into the drawing room and announced that he would have Count Harry Arnim, who had formerly been an Ambassador, arrested and put in jail on the following day. When I was going down the stairs with Josef Radowitz, who was then a Minister and later became an Ambassador (the Bismarcks were living in the old Foreign Office since the present Chancellor's Palace was still the Radziwill's residence), Radowitz said to me : "Sometimes the great Otto makes remarks which he can't really think people will believe. For example, his remark about Harry Arnim. He will beware of taking any action against Arnim." The next noon Harry Arnim, formerly Ambassador in Paris, was arrested on his estate at Nassenheide. It was Holstein who caused the ruin of this talented but vain and unreliable man. One of the most dramatic scenes in "Richard III" is the one in which Shakespeare had the ghosts of the people he has killed file past the wicked English King. The pale features of King Henry IV, poor Clarence, Lord Hastings, the two young Princes who had been strangled in the Tower, arose before him. I do not know whether this was so, but if Holstein had similar visions before his death, he would have seen a great many faces of men whom he killed, not bodily, but in their work and their careers. Harry Arnim would have opened the procession; Keudell, Kusserow, Radowitz, Schlözer, Ferdinand Stumm, the Under-Secretary of State and subsequent Ambassador Dr. Busch, would have followed. Philipp Eulenburg's melancholy figure would have been the last to pass by. And the mighty Prince, who had received the young attaché Holstein so kindly in St. Petersburg many years before and whom the old bureaucrat stabbed in the back thirty years later, would not have been missing.

When I was appointed as Chancellor, Philipp Eulenburg and Holstein were the best of friends. Just at that time Eulenburg sent his friend Holstein a copy of his uncle Count Fritz Eulenburg's letters. From 1859–1862 Count Fritz Eulenburg conducted the Prussian Expedition to East Asia as special Ambassador; he concluded commercial treaties with Japan, China, and Siam, and later, 1862–1878, he was Minister of the Interior under Bismarck. Philipp Eulenburg sent a copy of these letters to Holstein with the following note:

Dear Friend:

To-morrow the publisher will send you a copy of the letters of my uncle Fritz Eulenberg about the East Asian Expedition, which I have edited. I think these letters will amuse you and I would be happy to think that I could provide you with a little diversion on Christmas Eve. It has been an eternity since we wrote to each other and since we last met. I was very sorry that I could not see you in the autumn. As I look back on past years — and the turn of the century is a cause for much retrospection — and remember all my work and all my battles and unhappiness, I always see your face before my mind's eye, I see you fighting and suffering at my side. I feel that I belong to you always, and even if, temporarily, we should disagree on any issue, this can never really separate us. I feel the impulse to tell you all this with great affection. I am faithful and unchangeably attached to all my old friends — especially to you. With all good wishes for Christmas, I am your old and faithful

Philipp Eulenberg

I could never understand why this long political and personal friendship between Phillip Eulenburg and Holstein, who both, each in his own way, helped to bring about the breach between the Kaiser and Bismarck, could have changed to bitter enmity. Holstein was so moody and wayward and Phil so mollusc-like in his vagueness and his changeability that it was difficult to fathom the reasons for the breach.

Eulenburg's letters to me increasingly reflected his anxiety lest the Kaiser might take my successes in the Reichstag amiss. "Just a line," he wrote, "to congratulate you upon your speeches, which are making a great impression in Vienna. You have moved into the leading position among the politicians of the world. That is my impression. But I tremble when I think of the impression your ever harsher attitude towards His Majesty will make. The Reichstag would be only too happy to join you against His Majesty. All the utterances made in the Reichstag go to show that this is so." At the same time he told me that my "faithful admirer", Monts, wrote to him that in Munich, people did not think the Kaiser would put up with me for long. I telegraphed to Eulenburg:

When the Agrarians were angry with me because of America, you were afraid of the danger from the Right; now you seem to be more afraid of the Left. Storms of this kind must be expected in political life. I am not so easily frightened; there are worse things than political attacks and I am well and in good form. Tell Monts that he had better try to calm down his Munich friends rather than compete with Jeremiah.

Eulenburg wrote and told me soon after that he believed the Kaiser would be paying a short visit to Kiel, where his pulse would beat faster at the sight of the ever-growing Fleet. He would then make a personal statement on the unjust criticisms of the eccentric speech he made during the Chinese summer of 1900. Thereupon I telegraphed to Eulenburg: I had the impression that I had, by my attitude, readjusted a very complicated and difficult situation in the Reichstag, just as I had done before in the Federal Council. Eulenburg himself had always pointed out the dangers of a coalition between the German Princes and the German Reichstag against His Majesty. I urged him to use his great influence on the Kaiser to calm him down and to see that, as long as the Reichstag was in session, the Kaiser did not make fiery speeches in Kiel or anywhere else.

My predecessor, Prince Chlodwig Hohenlohe, judged both the foreign and the home situation with his usual tact. He was a sincere admirer of Empress Augusta Victoria. But when her Court Marshal, Freiherr von Mirbach, apparently by Royal Command, sent a letter to the Berlin City Council, a letter that by reason of its manner and its contents might have been fit for an afternoon sermon, but was a grave *faux pas* as a political document, Prince Hohenlohe wrote to me:

If the letter to the Berlin City Council was drafted by Royal Command, I have nothing more to say. If this is the case, please place my letter in the waste-paper basket and consider that it was never sent. If, however, Freiherr von Mirbach is responsible for the letter, it is a very serious matter. If this is so, I would suggest notifying His Majesty. We cannot allow Her Majesty's highest court official to expose her in this way. The letter makes the worst possible impression, which is all the more regrettable as Her Majesty is so popular.

Freiherr von Mirbach's letter stated that Her Majesty hoped that, in time, the good and loyal members of the City Council would with gentle conciliatory hand alleviate all the many and deep inward defects in the nation's Capital, besides promoting the outward efflorescence of the city. Her Majesty had been saddened to learn that a member of the City Council had disrespectfully used sacred words from the Bible without having been called to order. The disrespectful use of these words must come as a deep shock to all good Christian feelings. Dr. Preuss, who eighteen years later gave birth to that abortion called the Weimar Constitution, was the member who had exposed himself to this stern reprimand. Prince Chlodwig Hohenlohe was certainly right when he said that whatever one might think of Dr. Preuss' inopportune remarks, it was not proper to drag the Empress into political issues of this kind. The good Mirbach did not try this again as long as I was Chancellor. Instead he assiduously promoted the building of churches in Berlin, until his activities even in this direction were no longer desired.

Mirbach did not have much judgment as to what was politically possible, but I found a loyal friend among the Empress' entourage in Bodo Knesebeck, who was then an adviser in her Cabinet and who later became Vice-Chief-Master of the Ceremonies. Knesebeck was not only a loyal friend, but a political support as well. We had been together in the attack on Hallue on December 23, 1870. In remembrance of this event he sent me a beautiful medallion of Prince Bismarck standing on an artistic pedestal and wrote:

Thirty years ago to-day we performed the little escapade which you will remember. The course of events has raised you to that eminence from which the Iron Chancellor once officiated, inspiring the world with awe. It is my privilege to have witnessed your successes. I am sending you a bronze image of your mighty predecessor for your writing desk. May the sight of him remind you of the greatest period in our history and may this anniversary awaken in you the old ardour for the Kaiser and the country. Now, as then, your faithful friend, Bodo Knesebeck.

CHAPTER XXXII

Queen Victoria's Illness — William II Goes to England — Empress Augusta Victoria's Letters to Bülow — Kaiser William Stays for the Funeral (January 21, 1901) — Count Metternich on the Royal Visit — Report to William II in Homburg (February 8, 1901) — Preparations for King Edward's Visit to His Sister, Empress Frederick — Memorandum of State Secretary Freiherr von Richthofen on February 3, 1901 — Our Relations with England — Important Discussions on Anglo-German Negotiations Transferred to Berlin — Prince Lichnowsky's Memorandum.

ON January 19th, 1901, I was summoned by the Kaiser to the Berlin Schloss. When I entered the Imperial study, I found His Majesty talking eagerly with his uncle, the Duke of Connaught. The Kaiser, who was obviously agitated, told me that he had just been informed that his grandmother, Queen Victoria, was seriously ill. He said that he would go to her at once. When I remarked that it might be a good plan to wait and see how she was, the Kaiser answered, not without impatience, that, where the life of his dear grandmother, whom he must see again, was concerned, no other considerations could be taken into account. He had, he said, already reserved cabins on the Flushing-Dover boat.

When the Kaiser left the room for a few moments to give some orders concerning his journey to England, his uncle discussed His Majesty's latest idea with great calm and objectivity. Apart from Queen Victoria, the Duke was probably the only member of the English Royal Family who felt sincere friendship for the Kaiser. Although he was completely English in character, he was convinced, as his mother was convinced, that peaceful and friendly relations between the two great Germanic peoples were desirable for their own sake as well as that of the world at large. He admitted quite frankly that though the Kaiser's visit might be an expression of his kindness of heart, he was not sure how the English Royal Family would receive so sudden a visit from him. The Kaiser would be an "embarrassing" factor at the Queen's deathbed. The Royal

Family would not know quite what to do with him. The English people, and public opinion in England generally, would probably appreciate this generous decision of the Kaiser, and this visit to the deathbed would probably make the Kaiser very popular in England, just as his visit during the Boer War had made him popular there. But he, the Duke, was afraid that in Germany, on the contrary, this visit would turn public opinion even more against England. "And," the Duke concluded, "the most important thing at present, so it seems to me, is not to irritate German public opinion, to quieten people down, and not to annoy them in Germany. No sensible person in England harbours any doubts whatsoever that you and the Kaiser, as well as the German Government and the German ruling Princes, are sincerely and actively desirous of maintaining friendly relations with England. But even in Germany, where conditions are still rather patriarchal, the Kaiser and the Government cannot afford to pursue the policies they choose without consideration for public opinion. I have mentioned this fact to several people in England. I therefore tell you, too, that it would be better if the Kaiser did not undertake this journey."

While we were still talking in the most friendly manner, the Kaiser returned and said that he had made all preparations for his departure. He said that he would be gone only a short time, but that this visit to his beloved grandmother's bed of sickness, perhaps of death, was an impulse that came from the heart. The Duke, who realised that there was nothing more to be done in the matter, excused himself to call on some relatives in Berlin. As he left he pressed my hands and shrugged his shoulders. Kaiser William, since his childhood, had felt not only respect for his grandmother in England, "our English Grandmamma", as all Empress Frederick's children called her, he felt real affection for her as well. She had always been kind to him. She was associated in his mind with his earliest memories. The loveliest days of his youth had been spent with his English grandmother when he visited her in overwhelmingly wonderful Windsor, in Osborne with the view of the sea where he saw the mighty English men-o'-war passing by, or made excursions to the world city of London. Even though

William II probably did not harbour the same mixture of respect and tenderness for any other human being as for Queen Victoria, he rushed to her deathbed like a young man who is going abroad for the first time.   For, especially during the first half of his reign, it was difficult for Kaiser William to bear the even routine of his days.   He always wanted something to happen, he craved for new impressions, new scenes.   It was a particularly hard blow of Fate that this impressionable, unstable, and mercurial man, who was *cupidus novarum rerum* like any Gaul of Caesar's time, should have been condemned, after his fall, to lead the most quiet, monotonous, and narrow life which any man of his age could possibly have lived.

During the Kaiser's crossing to England, I received a number of telegrams, which described the ships on the sea, the picturesque chalk cliffs of England in a joyous tone and a happy frame of mind. The Kaiser reached his grandmother before her death.   She died on January 21st, 1901.   She was one of the greatest figures of English history ; she was one of the most successful, most honoured, and most beloved sovereigns in the history of the world.   The Kaiser told me, deeply moved, of the small services he had been able to render his grandmother before her death ; he said that she had died, "so to speak", in his arms.   Though Empress Augusta Victoria had felt great respect for the grandmother, she was not in favour of this journey to her deathbed.   But her husband had tempestuously disregarded her objections.   Now she urged him to leave England before the funeral, which was not to take place until a fortnight after the Queen's death.   On January 23rd she wrote to me from Homburg, where she had gone to visit her mother-in-law, Empress Frederick, who was seriously ill :

I hope that you will be able to dissuade the Kaiser from staying for the funeral and that you will persuade him to be satisfied with sending the Crown Prince, and, perhaps, Prince Henry, who is burning to go.   Or, if this really cannot be done, that the Kaiser will come here to see his mother between now and the time fixed for the funeral.   Even Empress Frederick does not think he ought to wait for the funeral.   She is personally very anxious to see the Kaiser.   The great lady is in a terrible state.   Her spirit is wonderful.   I do not think her condition will be worse as a result of her mother's death; she has already calmed down sufficiently.

The next day Her Majesty again wrote to me from Homburg:

You will soon learn to detest my handwriting, but I must send you the enclosed telegram. It arrived late last night. It made me anxious for several reasons: (1) I see by the telegram that the Kaiser is again very tired and exhausted. But that occurs easily, as you know, and it is only natural that it should, for he is so entirely absorbed by anything he does. (2) But I think it is particularly dangerous the way everyone — especially the ladies — is trying to besiege his warm, friendly nature and turn his head (they all, of course, want to win him over for their own ends), for the Kaiser will get the impression that his presence is essential there. I think you should try to urge him to return to his mother after he has rested a bit and to let the Crown Prince and Prince Henry attend the funeral. But who knows whether he will agree? I suppose if he really insists on attending the funeral, it would hardly be worth while, or would tire him too much, to come back in the meantime. In a letter of the 21st, which I received to-day, the Kaiser writes that Eckardstein told him that "when it became known in London in the evening that I was coming to be with grandmamma, the people wept for joy, and Eckardstein often told me that my action would never be forgotten by the English people."

The telegram, which the Empress sent me, was dated January 23rd. It referred to the Empress' request that he should come to see his mother, who was so dangerously ill. The Empress had added that she had made this suggestion in the hope that he would give up his intention of staying for the funeral. The Kaiser had answered:

I am so exhausted by my journey, by waiting about day and night and by the flood of telegrams which arrive incessantly, that I am at the moment quite incapable of standing a trip to Homburg. Besides, my aunts here are quite alone and I must help them with many things, I must give them my advice, whenever advice is necessary. They are so kind to me, they treat me like a brother and a friend instead of like a nephew. As soon as things have quieted down a little, I'll see whether I can leave before the funeral. It has been a terribly difficult and exciting time.

On January 26, the Empress wrote to me again from Homburg:

This afternoon I called on my poor mother-in-law, who is a very sad spectacle. She is still suffering a great deal. Now, much to my grief, she is very anxious to go to England, but I think that her condition makes this impossible. This makes her restless and miserable. Between times, she can be quite happy. My fears concerning the Kaiser's stay in England have been verified: he will stay until the funeral is over, and the Crown Prince and Prince Henry will join him as well. To crown everything else, the new English King has made the German Emperor an English Field Marshal. If this is not an irony in present circumstances, I do not know what is. It is supposed to be a gracious act, but I consider it tactless. The Kaiser, of course, has got to look pleased. I wrote and told him that I hoped he did not expect me to congratulate him on this occasion, it was supposed to be a gracious act, but opinions could differ regarding it. I think the country will not like it either. Besides, he will be celebrating his birthday abroad. I can only say that I am suffering from a moral " next-morning headache."

The Empress sent me another telegram from Friedrichshof:

Though Empress Frederick was very much moved at first by her mother's death, she pulled herself together very well. But she asked whether the Kaiser was coming back soon. And she seemed very anxious to see the Kaiser at once.

Even Count Paul Metternich, who was very friendly towards England, appreciated the disadvantages of too long a stay there on the Kaiser's part. On January 23rd, Metternich telegraphed to me that this was so. On January 24th, when he wrote to me, he was less agitated:

Scenes change quickly and to-day I am less anxious about a long visit of His Majesty to Osborne than I was when I communicated with you before. The new King of England himself invited the Crown Prince to come over for His Majesty's birthday. Yesterday I had a chance to attract His Majesty's attention to the danger of any indiscreet remarks about Russia and I believe that, in future, His Majesty will take my remarks into consideration.

Philipp Eulenburg, who had a great deal of flair, wrote to me a few days after Queen Victoria's death, from Vienna:

FOUR GENERATIONS AT WINDSOR

*Queen Victoria, the Prince of Wales (Edward VII), the Duke of York
(George V), and Prince Edward of York (Prince of Wales)*

I am anxious when I think of the beloved Master in Osborne; I think of all the things he will say! — he will be like a child amidst these people, who are crude despite their mourning. Amongst them he forgets all his "shrewdness." A sort of trustful embarrassment takes possession of him and any one of them could easily get at the secrets of his soul (and our state secrets). And at the same time he is really in the way. The family scold him behind his back, and his own adjutants wring their hands and wish they could go home. Despite the seriousness of the situation and the real grief which he feels, I must smile when I think of the way in which he is "exploiting" his deceased grandmother, so that he can avoid seeing "mother" as long as possible. I hope the walks in Osborne and the visits to all the warships, whose crews are receiving him with the greatest indifference, will agree with him. The *"New York Herald"* has reported my forthcoming appointment as Governor of Alsace. God knows where this report came from. Though it is the only post I really want, I have not heard that Langenburg has any desire to retire, nor that Adolf Schaumburg has found any other post.

Prince Hohenlohe-Langenburg was Governor of Alsace-Lorraine and Philipp feared Prince Adolf Schaumburg-Lippe, the Kaiser's brother-in-law, as a competitor for the Strassburg post which he wanted himself. When Eulenburg used the word " mother ", he meant the Empress Augusta Victoria, from whose influence he was trying to free the Kaiser.

Adjutant General von Plessen wrote to me on February 1st, from England:

I can tell Your Excellency my impression frankly: His Majesty by his immediate arrival, his loving sympathy, and his fresh, active helpfulness during the first hours of grief has taken every heart by storm. He has charmed the entire Royal Family, including the ladies, who used to like him least, for instance Queen Alexandra, the Duchess of York, Christian Holstein. The entourage of all of them, as well as their Highnesses themselves, have assured me of this fact. When Queen Victoria's death was approaching, I suggested to His Majesty that he leave at once for Homburg to visit his mother and then return here for the funeral. The world would understand an action of this kind, and here, in the meantime, the German Kaiser was not urgently needed. He discarded my suggestion at once. He had not come as a Kaiser but as a grandson. I am convinced that some of the advantages gained by our prompt arrival have now been lost. Everyone asked us when we first came how long we would be staying and when we would be leaving. When the Kaiser's decision at last became known, people made the best of it. "The King has asked me to stay," His Majesty said. Well, in my opinion many of the things said during this fortnight would best have remained unsaid. The English, at any rate, have left nothing undone to bind us to them. The "Field Marshal", the "Order of the Garter with Diamonds" and then this drive round London so that the public can have a chance to thank the Kaiser for his coming. I hope to God that no misfortune will happen !!! I have the impression that the English are unspeakably gratified by our coming and by the Kaiser's expressions of friendship at a time when they are suffering such calamities (South Africa), when there is a change of Government, and when they are so generally hated that they themselves talk about it. At the moment they are feeling so small that it will be a long time before they feel as small as this again. Our Master has given them self-assurance and they will certainly recover their historic insolence! To crown everything, the Duke of York got the measles in the room next to His Majesty's. We could not persuade him to join the Crown Prince at the *Hohenzollern*. All he did was to change to a more distant wing in the palace. I wish we were again safe at home with them both. And when we return we are to stay in Homburg for some time because the little children might catch the disease. Here the danger of infection is taken lightly, but at home it will be exploited to furnish an excuse to stay away from Berlin as long as possible. I think it is terrible, during these weeks when there is such a dreadful amount to do, that His Majesty is not in Berlin. Or would you rather he kept away from affairs? I hope, at any rate, that you will come to Homburg soon. We shall arrive at 8 o'clock in the morning of February 7th.

It was unwise of the Empress Augusta Victoria, of the Kaiser's military entourage, and of the majority of the German people to be so anti-English. But the Kaiser's exaggerated attitude towards England — some days he was wildly and demonstratively enthusiastic about England, while other days he was very anti-English — agitated people in Germany again and again and to no political purpose. When the victor of the Boers, Field Marshal Roberts, was given the Order of the Black Eagle — I had not been consulted — this gesture made very little impression on the proud and independent English, while in Germany it was widely interpreted as a slap in the face for the country's public opinion on the Boer question. As wise Marco Minghetti used to say, the art of politics consists *"de donner à chaque chose sa juste valeur."* This demonstrative honour did not even win the man who received it for any length of time. Later, when, in a regrettable attack of boastfulness, William II falsely claimed that Lord Roberts had vanquished the Boers only with the help of a strategic plan which he (the Kaiser) had sent to Queen Victoria, the Field Marshal, who was a brave and efficient soldier, and who fought all his life all over the world for the glory of the English flag, became a bitter personal enemy of the German Kaiser. This was one of many times when Kaiser William II, with the best intentions in the world and with the firm conviction that he was on the right path, achieved a result that was the exact opposite of the one he had intended. When I knew that the Kaiser had reached Homburg, I went there to join him. I found him completely under the spell of his English impressions. As a rule he could not change his military uniforms often enough, but now he wore civilian clothes as he had done in England. He wore a tie-pin with his deceased grandmother's initial on it. The officers, who were summoned from Frankfort near by to dine with him, were surprised to find their "Supreme War Lord", as they called him, wearing civilian clothes. They did not seem to be much pleased by his constant enthusiastic allusions to England and everything English, that, in his own words, "ranked far above German habits and customs." Before the Kaiser left England, King Edward had announced his intention of visiting Germany. Though I mentioned to the Kaiser that the King was coming primarily to see his sister, Empress Frederick, who was hopelessly ill, and that for this reason he would probably prefer to stay at Friedrichshof Palace rather than in Homburg, the Kaiser insisted that his uncle must visit him and not stay in Friedrichshof. As the Homburg Palace was not built for the winter, iron stoves had to be installed quickly in all the rooms. When these stoves at last began to function, the heat in the Palace was almost unbearable. And when it became necessary to open the windows, the occupants were terribly chilled by the cold February air. The health of General Hahnke, of Lucanus, the Cabinet Chief, and of other venerable old men in the Imperial entourage was put to a severe test. The attempts to heat the Palace were abandoned when King Edward wrote to tell his nephew that he could not accept his kind invitation to stay in Homburg, because he wanted to be as near his ailing sister as possible. His Majesty was so impressionable that this refusal cooled the Imperial sentiments not only towards his uncle but towards his uncle's country as well.

I was chiefly concerned, in the meantime, with effecting a *rapprochement* between the King and the Kaiser and with profiting by the favourable impression made by the Kaiser's visit on the English people, so that we might come to an acceptable treaty understanding with Great Britain. I telegraphed to the Imperial Embassy in London, saying that if Chamberlain talked to Eckardstein on the subject of a closer understanding between Great Britain on the one hand and ourselves and the Central-European peace group on the other, Eckardstein was to suggest the following: Anglo-German coöperation, based on a community of interests, had recently proved itself to be practical. There were no real differences left between us. Peaceful competition in colonial or economic matters on the part of one country was in no way incompatible with the rights and interests of the other country anywhere. The recent personal *rapprochement* between the sovereigns of the two countries had brought the peoples closer together. In these circumstances, it was not impossible that we might consider a closer union if the same were to take on a definite form and be officially proposed. Our mutual aim must be the consolidation of world peace. Neither England nor we ourselves could consider Russia or France alone. Either of these Powers alone would be harmless as far as England or world peace was concerned. But Russia and France united would be all the more formidable to England, as Germany had not, as yet, decided to maintain an unconditional benevolent neutrality towards Great Britain in the event of a conflict involving England, France, and Russia. Germany would be identically placed if the situation were reversed. The idea of a defensive alliance, therefore, seems almost natural and obvious. In case either Russia or France attacked England or Germany, then either country should place its entire forces on land and sea at the disposal of the other. When such an agreement had been signed by the sovereigns and the responsible ministers, it was to be submitted to both Parliaments and should be effective for five years at first. Baron Eckardstein was to emphasise that such a defensive and pacific alliance would have the advantage of not endangering peaceful relations with any foreign power. He might also give a hint that, later on, a further agreement, based on a defensive Peace Treaty, could perhaps be reached with regard to difficult and highly contentious questions, such as the partition of Morocco.

By way of contrast with Holstein, who, despite his great political gifts, his rich experience, and his industry, was often unstable, morbid, and wrong-headed, Secretary of State Freiherr von Richthofen distinguished himself by thoughtfulness and sound judgment. On the 3rd of February he handed me the following memorandum, which was all the more remarkable because, by reason of his education, his experience, and his general attitude, he had far more sympathy for England than for Russia:

A German-English Alliance would be advantageous to us in two directions in the event of war. 1. The chief advantage, namely, that England would not join our adversaries. 2. The secondary advantage, that England is in a position to sweep our enemy's fleets off the high seas and thus ensure the security of our overseas trade and our colonies. Any support we might have from the British Army would not be of much consequence. At present the British Army is in a disorganised state and is engaged in South Africa. The extent to which Russian and French troops would be engaged on the Indian and other frontiers by the British Army is also of little consequence. The second advantage mentioned above is unimportant, furthermore, because even without an Alliance England would probably use a war between the Dual Alliance on the one hand and Germany or the Triple Alliance on the other, to cripple the fleet of the former, so that if we are at least assured of English neutrality, the German Fleet itself will gradually grow strong enough to protect German overseas trade assisted, perhaps, by Italy and Austria and against

France and Russia.   For us, in my opinion, it is therefore important only
to secure the advantage indicated under (1).   From our point of view an
Alliance would not be necessary to achieve this, a "*pactum de non inter
se bellum gerendo*" would be sufficient.   Such a treaty, excluding wars
against each other, must, of course, include an arrangement whereby all
possible disputes can be settled, which would hardly be possible except on
the basis of arbitration.   Such a treaty even if, in the first instance,
it were valid for only ten years, would, I think, be approved of by the
Reichstag and the German people; and, as it would be in accordance
with the general humanitarian ideas of our time, it would probably be
accepted by the British Parliament as well.   It would exclude everything
hostile to third parties, for the Triple Alliance could offer the Dual Alliance
recognition of the territorial *status quo* and the conclusion of a similar
treaty.   It would remain to be seen whether the British Government
would approve of such a pact.   It would have far fewer advantages for
England than an Anglo-German Alliance, but she would have the security
that a hostile German-Russian-French coalition could not come about.
I consider that it would be very dangerous to go beyond a pact of this
kind and to form an alliance: To have any assurance that England will
keep the pact, a parliamentary sanction would be necessary; and if the
pact is sanctioned in London, we shall be able to keep our own Parliament
out of it.   But we should not be able to obtain the consent of the Reichstag to any pact (especially when pro-Boer feelings are so strong) according to which there is even the slightest possibility that we might have to
go to war to protect non-German interests, such as India.   Our people
might be prepared to defend Italian or Austrian interests, because they
are so accustomed to the Triple Alliance, but for a long time they would
not be willing to fight for English interests unless they correspond with our
own.   An unscrupulous and clever English statesman would have a dangerous weapon against us if we concluded such a defensive agreement on
the model of the Triple Alliance.   Such an agreement, which might
provoke Russia and France against England, would give such an English
statesman an excuse to annihilate the fleets of these two aggressor countries.   It would also give him an opportunity to let England's pre-con-
tinental rivals, Russia, Germany, and France, bleed to death in terrible
conflict so that, in the end, England would remain as Europe's only master.
Any alliance with England would expose us to the danger of fighting a
continental war alone, even when such a war might not be absolutely
necessary.   For this reason I think an alliance of this kind is out of the

question. The kind of pact I mentioned at the beginning of this memorandum, on the other hand, seems to me to be possible and useful from our point of view. Certain agreements concerning individual territorial questions could be concluded, even if no such pact is possible or even in addition to such a pact if the last Anglo-German agreement is not a sufficient incentive, seeing that its value to England is diminished by the actual exploitation of Lorenço Marquez as an English station and seeing that its continuance is put in question by the renewed proclamation of the Portuguese Alliance. Incidentally I would also like to mention that every pact that decreases the danger of a war with England would cause the Reichstag to be less willing to grant further increases in the naval estimates. I believe that by a careful and quiet handling from here of what is, after all, only a passing Chinese phase can be terminated without creating any sort of permanent ill will in Russia against Germany.

On the 5th of February, Richthofen wrote to me as follows:

In my opinion none of the recent events should cause us to abandon our principle that England ought to approach us and not we England. There is insufficient reason for a change in our attitude either in the accession of the new monarch or in the gracious prolongation of the Kaiser's visit to England, or in England's attack on us in the question of the Tientsin Settlement (all they want is to bring us up against Russia, and, as soon as they realised that they were unsuccessful, the attack ceased). Developments in England are probably in our favour. The more England is concerned with South Africa (and it looks as though she would be engaged there for some time) the more she will be paralysed in Europe and Asia and the more she will need the good will of other powers (except America), especially of Russia, France, and Germany. Even after the many talks on the subject I had with Geheimrat von Holstein, the Russian Alliance seems to me to be nothing more than a phantom. England would undoubtedly always be the loser in any arrangements with Russia; she would undoubtedly attain securities for only a short armistice and she would always be faced with Russia's insatiable appetite. What, for instance, can England offer Russia? Manchuria? Russia has taken Manchuria without asking England. Or Korea? If England offered Korea to Russia, Japan would be her enemy for ever. If England offers Russia advantages in Persia or India, she could only offer advantages which Russia could simply take without her or others' leave. Such offers would harm England's own prestige and power in Central Southern Asia.

Besides they would only be an opening for Russia to make further demands. And what is Russia to offer England in return? Non-intervention against British influences in the Yangste valley? A promise not to intervene there would put France in a bad humour, and, besides, it would be useless, for Russia surely has no intention of taking any part in the Yangste question, at least not from a southward direction. As far as the Northern districts are concerned, it is obvious that no pact in the world would prevent Russia from intervening there as soon as she is able. Russian and British interests are too widely different to make even a temporary agreement between the two countries probable. Russia's strength lies in the fact that she does not want colonies; what she wants is to extend her own frontiers. She has in a relatively short time extended her frontiers steadily and powerfully. Every improvement in her transportation system on land, as compared with her relatively slow transportation on the sea, brings this aim nearer. If Russia is patient — and, especially under the present Tsar, there is no reason to believe that she will not be patient — it is probable that she will quietly acquire even more territory. It is barely 50 years since the Crimean War. Would it now be possible to conclude any coalition against Russia, if she reached out for Armenia or even the Golden Horn? Manchuria will fall into Russia's lap in any case. If, after a time, she reaches her hand out from Chihli, would there be anyone who would call out "Stop"? Hardly. England's aspirations in Asia have, as far as Russia is concerned, really been narrowed down to India and the coast; in Persia and China England will hardly be able to undertake any forceful action against Russia. An Anglo-French Alliance is in itself unthinkable. Such an alliance would be directed against us, as far as the French are concerned, and against Russia, as far as the English are concerned. And England has no interest in removing us from the picture, if the power of France and Russia is increased at the same time. France, on the other hand, cannot want to weaken both Germany and Russia and to be confronted with England alone as a result. But we must not overlook the danger which such an Alliance would imply for us and it is an added reason why we should be on friendly terms with England. We are and always shall be England's most convenient support. Our power absorbs Russian and French fighting forces to such an extent that Russia and France are prevented from adventurous undertakings against England here or there, and, as a result, England's power is maintained in a *status quo*. We, on the other hand, are not asking for any of England's possessions; all we want is to be left in peace and that when England feeds from the foreign dish of some weak nation, she will let us have our share. The only return that England can ask from us is that we, in turn, leave her in peace and that we will not interfere with her political interests. We could not but desire an agreement along these lines. But any offensive or defensive pact, or under certain suppositions, any alliance that could be called a defensive alliance, but which, *de facto*, could easily be changed into an offensive alliance by one of the contracting parties, would, in my opinion, be very dangerous for us, because, no matter what form such an alliance might assume, it would always be against Russia, and we, not England, would always bear the brunt in any conflict with Russia. At sea Russia is now not so vulnerable, because, under present conditions, blockades are no longer as effective as they were and some third power (America?) might not even recognise a blockade. If our present relations with France remain as they are, we can prevent England from joining our enemies. And if we treat Russia kindly but very firmly, and do not chase after her, I think we shall secure the most advantageous position for ourselves. The last point is the most difficult one. It must be made quite clear in St. Petersburg and here (Osten-Sacken) that we control our policies, and that they are chiefly administered by the sure, calm, and unchanging hand of the Chancellor. In my opinion an English-French-German balance of power against Russia and America would harm our interests, so we have every reason to refrain from drifting into an antagonism with these two Powers (unless we are absolutely compelled to) and from forcing them into a coalition which would be a great danger to all Central and Western Europe. Besides, such a combination would not be reliable, for as soon as France saw any opportunity to open the Alsace-Lorraine question, she would speedily escape from it.

The Secretary of State's remark that it should be made clear to the Russians that the main conduct of German policy lay in the hands of the Chancellor referred, of course, to the Kaiser, who unfortunately, as far as Russia was concerned, vacillated between naïve importunity and abrupt ill manners.

Before I left for Homburg to see the Kaiser, I told both Richthofen and Holstein of my wish that the main conduct of the German-English negotiations should be taken out of the hands of Eckardstein (who was dominated by the English point of view and who was dependent upon English money) and transferred to

Berlin. If the English Government wanted anything from us, their official representative in Berlin could approach us. Negotiations as important as these could not possibly be carried on by a young secretary, whose reports and entire manner showed only too clearly that his character was just as questionable as his financial integrity. Eckardstein's recent telegrams seemed to show rather conspicuously that he was trying to frighten us by asserting that the English might suddenly withdraw from northeastern Asia and so sacrifice all British interests there. Supported by the British Fleet, the Japanese would, at the moment, be very superior to the Russians in eastern Asia. The effort to egg us on against Russia in the interest of England had been very obvious in connection with the Tientsin Affair. When the Manchurian Agreement was concluded, Lansdowne mentioned the Miaotao Islands, whereas in the telegram from Satow — the English Ambassador — no mention whatsoever was made of the group of islands which dominate the entrance to the Bay of Pechili. Prince Lichnowsky, who was then in the English Department of Foreign Affairs and later became Ambassador in London, and who was very Anglophile, concluded a memorandum as follows:

It would be really naïve of the leaders in English politics if they did *not* try to push us forward against Russia without binding engagements on their own part, in view of their situation in South Africa, their present financial difficulties, the dilemma we are in as a result of Count Waldersee's mission, the anti-Russian statements and speeches made by His Majesty in England, and in view of the fact that people in London realise that these speeches of the Kaiser's have created an unfriendly feeling towards us on the Neva.

CHAPTER XXXIII

King Edward's Arrival in Kronberg — His Impressions during the Journey through Germany — Miss Charlotte Knollys to Bülow — The Kaiser's Visit to Bremen (March 5, 1901) — The Kaiser's Eccentric Speech to the Alexander Regiment — Grand Duke Frederick of Baden's Letter about the Speech — The Muddled Canal Bill — Dismissal of the Minister of Finance von Miquel — His Successor Freiherr von Rheinbaben — Tsar Nicholas' Birthday — William II's Speech at Metz — General Bonnal in Metz — Unveiling of Bismarck's Monument in Berlin (June 16, 1901) — Bülow's Memorial Speech — William II — Herbert Bismarck — The Prophet Jeremiah on the Human Heart — An Understanding Is Reached with the Bavarian Minister of Finance, Riedel, on the Tariff — Peter Spahn, Ernst Bassermann, the Farmers' League, Count Limburg-Stirum.

THE Empress Frederick when she was dying wanted very much to see her oldest brother again. Edward VII's impulse to visit his sister on her bed of pain was a purely human one. Politically, the King's journey had an unfavourable effect on his future attitude towards Germany. Indeed, his entire judgment of German conditions was influenced by it. Contrary to the theoretical Germans, who like to derive their judgments from books, or from the depths of some ethical conviction, the English base their judgments directly on what they observe themselves. When, coming from Flushing, the King entered Germany and travelled by train up the Rhine, he could certainly not have avoided gaining the impression that the anti-English and pro-Boer enthusiasm on the part of the Germans was a real paroxysm. It was difficult for the police, at stations where the Royal train stopped, to guard the King's carriage well enough to save him from being insulted. No political cordon could prevent King Edward from hearing rough abuse against England and her King. About the same time all the newspapers reported that a number of harmless German corps students who were playing football in Heidelberg were taken for Englishmen and were beaten up by workmen.

When the King, who had arrived at Friedrichshof on February 25, 1901, came over to Homburg to see the Kaiser, he was in a very serious frame of mind. He said to me: "Your situation is a difficult one. People in this country are mad. I appreciate all the more your attitude towards England which you have defended even in the Reichstag. Won't the Germans quiet down? They are cracked, they are mad." The next day I had an interview with Miss Charlotte Knollys, who had been Queen Alexandra's Lady-in-Waiting for many years and who was an old friend of mine. In the practical spirit of her people, she said: "What's the good of all this new tenderness between the nephew and the uncle, what's the good of all the efforts made by Ministers, if the people themselves hate each other like cats and dogs? The Kaiser always says that his attitude is all that matters in Germany, that everyone must bend to his will. But I think that even though the people have not as great influence here as they have in England, one must take them into account, nevertheless. Your people are far more anti-English than they are anti-French or anti-Russian. Behind the Kaiser's declarations of love and your sincere efforts to create friendly relations with England, I see, as a real factor, a nation of fifty million people, who are the worst enemy we have in the world. And as far as the Kaiser is concerned, you know that I like him, that I like him very much indeed. He is so amusing, so lively and natural; he is a really good fellow, a very good fellow all round. But, between you and me, is he reliable? Let us be frank with each other, just as we used to be when you were a young Secretary of Legation and not a Chancellor. During the Boer War, your good Kaiser, God bless him, took our poor Ambassador in Berlin, Sir Frank Lascelles, who went to bed late and who liked to sleep until ten, by surprise as early as eight o'clock in the morning. He sat down at the side of Lascelles' bed and did not leave him in peace until Lascelles had written out a telegram which contained a plan of campaign against the Boers drafted by the Kaiser, and which, so he claimed, contained the sure clue to the destruction of this people. The truth, between ourselves, is that this campaign was pure nonsense. Lascelles was forced to send off the telegram at once. This telegram was meant as an emendation to a letter on the same subject sent by your Kaiser to our Queen. Afterwards it was his duty to accompany the Kaiser to his carriage in the Wilhelm-Strasse in the rain, even though he was wearing only pajamas and slippers. Some time later the Kaiser wrote to his uncle that when the Glasgow Football Club has defeated the Birmingham Football Club, the latter do not plan revenge, but shake hands. That is what the English should do after their reverses in South Africa. The King wrote and told his nephew that a war conducted by a Great Power was not a football match. 'I will willingly admit that you and your Government would like to see friendly relations with England, but your Kaiser is unaccountable, and your people, a people of fifty million souls, hates us.'"

The Kaiser announced that he would visit Bremen on March 5th. In view of his special interest in trade and shipping, he felt particularly at home in the Hanseatic cities. Since the good old days, and in true German fashion, Hamburg and Bremen had been jealous of each other. During the first years of his reign, William II favoured the city on the river Weser, and in his original way he based this preference on the fact that the Bremen girls preferred to marry naval officers, whereas the girls in Hamburg preferred rich merchants or landowners or, now and then, handsome cavalry officers. Soon, however, magnificent and mighty Hamburg captured the Kaiser's heart and, during the last few years of his reign, it was his favourite city. But he did not forget Bremen, a city which, above all others, had carried German culture into the East, whose citizens had founded Riga, and whose ships, in the Middle Ages, sailed the Mediterranean Sea. Bremen citizens founded the German Order near Accon towards the end of the 12th century. Max von Schenkendorf deservedly praised Bremen in his beautiful song about the cities of Germany:

> *Den Weg hast du bereitet*
> *Dem höchsten Christengott,*
> *Hast deutsche Art verbreitet*
> *Bis Riga, Novgorod.*

Aus mildem Bürgerstande,
Aus stillem Bürgerfleiss
Erblüht in heil'gen Lande
Der Ritterorden Preis.[1]

When the Kaiser was on his way back to the railway station from the Bremen Ratskeller, which William Hauff's "Phantasies" have glorified poetically, and where a dinner had been arranged in his honour, a workman threw a piece of iron at the Imperial carriage. The Kaiser received a considerable wound on his right cheek. He might easily have lost his right eye. Bleeding profusely, the Kaiser arrived at Bremen station, having retained complete self-control. During the night I received a calmly worded telegram from him. When I called for him early in the morning at the Lehrter Bahnhof, he showed no excitement whatsoever and he mentioned the incident only with amiable equanimity. I accompanied him to the Palace, and, as soon as we were in his study, he asked me to telegraph to the Mayor of Bremen to say that he did not attribute any importance to the incident and that his love and affection for the inhabitants of Bremen would be in no way affected by it. His attitude was really beyond all praise, it was truly regal.

About two weeks later, when he had completely recovered, the Kaiser received the Executive Committee of the Prussian Diet. The Speaker of the House at that time was Jordan von Kröcher. He had all the faults attributed, often unjustly, to the Junkers, but not the great qualities which they really possess. He was coarse but without any real humour, he had a peasant's shrewdness but no real insight, he was assiduously interested in the welfare of his Party and his class, but he was without due consideration for the State as a whole. His haughty and insolent treatment of the few Socialists who had succeeded, despite the very limited Prussian suffrage, in being elected to the Second Chamber caused him to irritate the workmen without making any real impression on them. Herr von Kröcher took the opportunity during his reception by the

---

[1] Thou hast prepared the way for the highest Christian God, thou hast spread German customs as far as Riga and Novgorod. In the Holy Land praise of the Knightly Orders blossoms from amongst the mild, industrious citizens.

Kaiser of pointing out that the attempt to assassinate Emperor William I in 1878 was comparable to the Bremen incident, though it had been proved in the meantime that the man who made the attempt on the Kaiser's life in Bremen was an epileptic and half or wholly mad. Kröcher's comparison implied that now was the time to pass special legislation against the Socialist movement, just as it had been opportune twenty-three years before. This, in the first place, led to an unpleasant discussion in the Prussian Diet between Eugen Richter and von Kröcher, but, more than this, the whole affair stimulated and excited the Kaiser, who was always impressionable. He made a very eccentric speech in the new barracks of the Emperor Alexander Regiment. The First Emperor Alexander Grenadier Guards had a proud past. The regiment had done its duty against the insurgents in March, 1848; it had particularly distinguished itself in 1870 during the attack on Sainte-Marie-aux-Chênes in the battle of Saint-Privat. The regimental flag was the oldest flag in the army. During the battle of Saint-Privat it was carried by Lieutenant von Dewitz, who came of an old Pomeranian family and was the youngest officer in the regiment. He fell with the flag on top of him. It was the Kaiser's right, and even his duty, to remind the regiment of its glorious past. But he added that if Berlin should ever again rise against its King in impudent rebellion, the Alexander Regiment would put down such arrogance and disobedience with all speed. He closed with a declaration that he had an old and powerful ally, the good God in heaven, who, since the days of the Great Elector and the Great King, had been on our side. The impression made by this speech at home and abroad was deplorable. The strictly Conservative orthodox *"Reichsbote"* pointed out that the greatest enemy of authority was an overstraining of this authority. William I's authority was based on the fact that he maintained his self-control towards his advisers and that he applied reason and wise reserve to anything he did. Rulers who lacked this modesty were apt to ruin themselves when they faced the realities of life and, in the end, they looked back upon an unhappy reign. What hard and, alas, prophetic words! The *"Times,"* in a grave article, expressed anxiety as to whether the Bremen incident had not affected the Kaiser's reason, if he was now able to talk such "nonsense." Other English and American newspapers spoke of "moral insanity." The French press published ironical and satirical articles. I first showed the Kaiser the article published in the leading English newspaper, because I knew that English press opinions made a greater impression on him than German ones. I did not spare him the American and French articles either.

A few days later I received a letter from Grand Duke Frederick of Baden, in which he wrote that he was compelled to admit that our situation, as far as public affairs were concerned, had reached the height of danger and that we were obliged to prepare protective measures for the future. The Kaiser's speeches were a danger he considered menacing. All the speeches ought to be submitted to the Chancellor before they were delivered, so that the changes that might be necessary could be made. Otherwise it was to be feared that the authority of the Crown would be decreased, that the prestige of the monarchical form of Government would be gradually shaken throughout the Empire, and that Germany would make an unfavourable impression abroad, which would decrease the confidence in Germany's power. The Kaiser's speeches to the troops ought never to be published. The address to the Alexander Regiment had caused displeasure among large numbers of people, especially among the upper and more experienced classes. Just because he, the Grand Duke, respected the Kaiser's ability, he did not want the Head of the State to be discussed in such a derogatory way. After the Grand Duke had seen the Kaiser, when he passed through Karlsruhe, he wrote to me on May 18, 1901, that he thanked me in the first place for my confidential letter, which he had received meantime, and which gave him an insight into the course I intended to pursue. To his relief he had gathered from the Kaiser's remarks that the latter intended, henceforth, to follow my advice and my suggestions more conscientiously. "This can only result in an improvement of the situation and it will diminish the public discussion." Concerning foreign affairs, the experienced and wise Grand Duke wrote to say that the Kaiser had been particularly annoyed about Russia and that he had spoken disparagingly about the Tsar. He, the Grand Duke, was convinced that as close a coöperation as possible with England was opportune, but that we ought to avoid becoming dependent upon England. We ought not to increase our fleet at the expense of the army. Friendly relations with the Tsar were greatly to be desired, for they increased our chances of promoting our own interests. For this reason, the liberal Grand Duke pointed out, he regretted the Kaiser's excessive sharpness against the Tsar and against Russia, for political wisdom could not overlook the fact that England, more than any other power, strove to promote only her own political interests. The Grand Duke, who had been bitterly hurt at the unfriendly and ungracious manner in which the Kaiser had refused to appoint his son, the excellent and efficient Hereditary Grand Duke, as the Commanding General of the 14th Army Corps, a post which had recently become vacant, closed his letter with the following words :

My son, in the meantime, has been taken seriously ill, so that he has not been told of this disappointment. The end of my life is filled with difficult work and the fulfilment of my duty involves many sacrifices. But I must work hard, none the less, and, as long as God permits, I shall serve Him faithfully and dedicate myself to the welfare of my country. I thank you again for the confidence you so graciously show me and which encourages me again and again to live up to the faith you have in me. I do so all the more willingly, because I appreciate your own heavy burdens of work. Continue to have confidence in me and rest assured of my good intentions. Your most grateful and devoted,

Frederick, Grand Duke of Baden

The Canal Bill had been the pivotal point of Prussian home politics for many a year and day. When the Canal Crisis of 1899 was discussed, I pointed out how muddled this affair had become. Everyone concerned was right and wrong at the same time and, on the other hand, no one was entirely right or entirely wrong. The Kaiser and the other promoters of the scheme were right when they wanted to increase our canal system for the economic benefit of the country. The adversaries of the plan were right when they objected to the autocratic manner in which William II tried to put his scheme through. The Kaiser was wrong when he tried to promote the plan in the manner of Frederick William I, partly because he was not by any means a Frederick William I and partly because times had changed considerably since the latter's reign. The adversaries of the canal plan were very much in the wrong when they showed an exaggerated fear of the import of foreign grain and when they opposed the canal plan because they were filled with the Agrarians' jealousy of industry and when, as East Elbians, they were, to a certain extent, afraid of the competition of the wealthy West and therefore tried to prevent the building of canals. When on January 9th, 1901, I introduced myself to the Prussian Diet as the Prussian Premier, I warned all Parties alike against shortsightedness and selfishness.[1] I had urged the Western regions with their old culture, their highly developed industry, their energy, and their resources to unite with the Eastern regions which were the cradle of the Prussian Monarchy, and had given our civil service and our Army their high standards to act in unison. When I said that my one aim was to promote the welfare of our economic system as a whole and of the entire Monarchy, I was greeted with more than usually tempestuous applause. But when deeds, and not cheering and clapping, were needed, their enthusiasm diminished. The Commission made no progress, the bickering knew no end. There was nothing left to do but to place the whole discussion on a new basis. I called a meeting of the Cabinet and declared that the inhuman game over the Canal Question must be terminated. Even if the Upper Chamber were forced to redraft the Bill which had been mutilated in the Diet (and it was not even certain that the Upper Chamber would do this), we could only be sure that a part of the Central German Canal would be accepted by the Diet. In such circumstances I would have requested and received His Majesty's consent to dissolve the Diet. His Majesty had asked me particularly to express his appreciation of the way in which all the Ministers, especially Vice President Miquel, had promoted the Canal Bill to the best of their ability.

My unexpected announcement impressed my colleagues in

[1] Prince Bülow's "Speeches", (large edition), I. p. 176; (small edition), I. p. 234.

different ways. The Minister of Agriculture, von Hammerstein, and the Minister of Commerce, Brefeld, who had evil forebodings, looked depressed. Poor Miquel looked as though he had suffered a stroke. Count Posadowsky, who saw in Miquel a competitor for the Chancellorship and hated him as a result, was enthusiastic. Tirpitz, too, was much pleased. He did not like Miquel and claimed that he was like men who, after they have experienced all the pleasures of the flesh, go in for perversions when they are very old men. Miquel, he said, had in this way enjoyed the pleasures of all political parties, from Marxian Communism to extreme Conservatism. The next day (it was my birthday), on May 3rd, 1901, I dissolved the Diet, saying that His Majesty's Government regarded the Canal Bill as a whole from which separate clauses could not be excluded. At the same time I asked Herr von Wilmowski, the chief of the Chancellor's Office, to give Miquel a gentle hint that he could offer his resignation. He was replaced by Freiherr von Rheinbaben, a young, fresh, and unusual man, who had been Minister of the Interior.

Rheinbaben was an indefatigable worker, who would sit at his desk for hours, a huge cigar in his mouth, and go through his files. He was an excellent speaker, few could equal him in repartee, and he was a frank, fearless, and noble character. He was very conservative, more from sentiment than from reason, and this somewhat diminished his political chances as far as I was concerned. But no one who knew Georg von Rheinbaben could help loving him. As compared with some of his selfish colleagues, he seemed to me, during the nine years in which he was a member of the Cabinet, as the only feeling heart amongst a lot of larvae. He was the son of an officer who had fallen on the field of honour in 1866; he was the son-in-law of Freiherr Rochus von Liliencron, the universally honoured Nestor of Germanic philology. Freiherr von Hammerstein, who had been Governor of Metz, a Hannoverian, who came from a family of Guelph tendencies, succeeded Rheinbaben as Minister of the Interior. Hammerstein was to develop into an excellent servant of the Prussian State. I never think of him without recalling an incident which is so characteristic of the sad weakness of our national sentiments. A few years later, in the Reichstag, a Guelph attacked Minister von Hammerstein violently and accused him of being the son of an intransigent Guelph, and whose family had been unfaithful to the Guelph tradition. In a way which moved me very deeply, Hammerstein replied that the impression made on him by the events of 1870 (until which time he had been an adherent of the Guelph point of view) had caused him to find the way to Prussia and to Germany. He had fought in the War and had chosen for ever to fight for the black-white-and-red flag, and this War had been his Damascus. In the Italian Parliament a speech of this kind by an Italian who, in his youth, had been a Particularist, would have been welcomed by stormy applause. In our Parliament the speech was interrupted by scornful laughter from the Socialists, the Centre Party, and the Liberals, while the Conservatives observed an embarrassed silence and only the National Liberals applauded timidly.

The Secretary of State for Posts, General von Podbielski, was appointed as Minister of Agriculture. Under the mask of a jovial man about town, Podbielski hid a certain amount of cunning, but he had a great deal of common sense. Above all, he was a practical farmer, who had had a great deal of experience and he understood the real needs of agriculture. In his manner he was like a jovial retired cavalry officer who had been the pride and joy of every mess to which he belonged and who was able to hold his own, as far as drinking was concerned, with any ensign. Theophil von Podbielski was the grandson of a Polish officer born in Warsaw, who, after 1806, remained faithful to Prussia. Podbielski was a very good organiser, whether he organised the paper chases of the riding school in Hannover, or the horse races at Karlshorst, or the post office system, or the Ministry of Agriculture and Forestry. I suggested a National Liberal member, *Kommerzienrat* Möller, as Minister of Trade. Not only did I want to appoint a capable man for this post; I also wanted to accustom the Kaiser and the Parties to intrust the Ministries to the personalities who were equal to their task.

I made a point of parting from Miguel in the most courteous manner. At the farewell dinner which I arranged in his honour,

I said a few words about his unusual intellectual gifts and I expressed my appreciation of his valuable services as Prussian Minister as well as of his valuable services during the formation of the Reich, when he was a member of the National Convention. His melancholy reply indicated how deeply he regretted his retirement. It was a fault in our old system of Government that retired Ministers were rarely, if ever, reappointed. Many retiring Ministers, therefore, considered their dismissal as almost a *"Capitis diminutio"*, as a kind of political death sentence. Miquel had a gifted son, whom I appointed in the diplomatic service when he was still very young and, as was his due (for he was very talented), I promoted him particularly soon after his father's resignation. Unfortunately he died very young. The retirement of Finance Minister and Vice President Miquel was applauded — as he applauded all the fine things I did as well as those that were not so fine — by my "true vassal" Count Monts. He wrote at once to my wife:

I want to congratulate you and B. with my whole heart that this dangerous man has been removed in such a mild and elegant manner. *C'était un coup de maître.* This muddled and dangerous canal affair has been handled by B. in a masterly manner. I now look into the future with great hopefulness. I believe in Bernhard's star. . . . On Bernhard's birthday, modesty alone prevented me from sending him a telegram, but I thought of him constantly. With a respectful kiss on your little hand, I want to congratulate you again before closing. Please give my greetings to Bernhard and to the little group of faithful friends among whom I have the honour to be included. Your devoted servant Monts.

The phrases "modesty" and "little hand" and "devoted servant" would have done honour to a courtier in the XVIIth, the *grand siècle*. A postscript to the letter was even more like the seventeenth century. In this postscript he said that the Semmering, which had hoped to become a historic spot, was now very sad. This flattery referred to the fact that as Ambassador and as Secretary of State I used to spend a part of every summer on the Semmering, whereas now, as Chancellor, I spent my holidays in Norderney, which was nearer Berlin.

In accordance with an old tradition, the Russian Tsar's birthday was observed in Berlin by a dinner at the Prussian Court to which the Russian Ambassador was invited. On May 18th, 1901, this dinner was given at Metz, where the Kaiser happened to be staying. The fact that the Russian Ambassador, Count Osten-Sacken, had accepted an invitation to come to Metz, made a deep impression in Paris. The French Nationalist press saw a proof in his prompt acceptance that the Russian Government had given up all thought of supporting the French plans for revenge. Instead of letting impressions of this kind mature and take deeper roots, William II again and again made futile, if not harmful, efforts to approach the prudish *Marianne.* On May 29th, 1901, he invited the French General Bonnal, who happened to be in town, to attend a luncheon given by the Second Foot Guards Regiment, which the Kaiser was himself attending. After the Kaiser had read out loud a flattering telegram which he had just received from Tsar Nicholas, and which was flattering for Count Waldersee as well as for himself, he mentioned the "quite special honour" done the Brigade by the presence of two French officers. In China, German and French troops had, for the first time, fought side by side "in good comradeship and as brothers in arms" against a common enemy. "Cheers for the two officers and their entire Army, hurrah, hurrah, hurrah!" Some people in France considered this toast as a symptom of Germany's weakness, others thought it was a trap. Only a few people understood the toast at all and no one appreciated it. The Kaiser and General Bonnal corresponded with each other after this luncheon. In his letters the Kaiser said nothing that was out of place, but this correspondence only helped to strengthen his tendency to mistake trivial amenities and meaningless phrases for objective successes and political values. If I am not mistaken, General Bonnal and another high French officer, General Lacroix, with whom the Kaiser had become friendly while the former was in Germany attending a manoeuvre, felt it their duty, when war was declared, to say particularly hateful things about the Kaiser. I think it was General Bonnal who wrote that it would be the greatest good luck for France if the Kaiser would take over the High Command of the German Army himself.

The unveiling of the Bismarck Monument in Berlin had been fixed for June 16, 1901. It is difficult to describe, in a few words, William II's relationship with the greatest German Minister who ever lived. The Kaiser hated Bismarck, but he was forced to admit that he was a great man. He wanted to equal him, and, if possible, to be even greater than Bismarck was, but he gradually realised that this was not so simple and, as a result, William II was very much embittered. He never understood that one cannot imitate genius. He wanted to substitute genius by "Divine Right", but the latter cannot be acquired by force, even if the ruler, who craves divine grace, proclaims himself again and again to be an instrument of heaven and a keeper of God's household. There were times when William II, as the son of his rationalist mother, believed that considerable innate talents, activity, and English common sense played a greater rôle in the world than genius. If necessary, he would attain his ends by force, by the police and the army. Kaiser William II's megalomania was encouraged by flattering courtiers and, regrettable as it is, by unscrupulous scholars, such as Theodor Schiemann or Adolf Harnack as well, just as the megalomania of other rulers, such as blind King George of Hannover, as the Stuarts in England, and the Bourbons in France, was encouraged by their entourage.

During the long years in which I was a Minister, I had an opportunity every year, in the University, the Academy, or the Royal Library, of hearing the speeches made by Professor von Harnack (he had been raised to the hereditary nobility by the Kaiser at his own request). His speeches, for sheer Byzantinism, exceeded everything our officials or our soldiers ever accomplished in that respect. "Give all-highest thanks to our most gracious protector, our King and Master," so Professor Harnack addressed Kaiser William II on May 20th, 1901, at the bi-centenary celebration of the Academy. (Observe the new flower in the bouquet of Rosiflora Bysantinissima Linn — "all-highest thanks.") "The Kaiser has royally honoured our Academy by his all-highest presence. But we, as good Prussians, should show ourselves worthy of this great honour. We work under his protection, he is familiar with the sciences also. We will and shall do our duty. God Save the King."

In a speech made in the Hall of the University on the occasion of the Kaiser's birthday on January 27, 1907, the following was said: "In the heart of every German there is a clear image of the Kaiser and this image is the fruit and the consummation of our whole history. We promise our Kaiser, who looks into the future with strength and courage, eternal loyalty. Reverently do we embody our wishes in one sentence: God protect and God save our Kaiser." Professor Harnack maintained this attitude firmly until November 9, 1918. I was unfortunately not able to hear the speech he made five years after I had resigned when the Royal Library was opened on old Kaiser William's birthday. But I read in the newspapers that Professor Harnack had ecstatically called out to the Kaiser: "I hope that in politics as well as in human insight we may become more and more closely knit together around Your Majesty, our Highest, whom we revere as our master, as the generous scientist, as the beloved father of our country." Then came the World War, and Professor Harnack remained enthusiastically loyal to the Kaiser's flags as long as they were fortunate. On September 29, 1915, he honoured "our glorious army and its great chief, the Kaiser" in a public speech. As late as August 1, 1916, he urged all Germans "to rally round their Supreme War Lord, Kaiser William II, in eternal gratitude, reverence, and loyalty." I regret that in writing my memoirs I shall not be able to omit the fact that Adolf von Harnack, who had proclaimed his undying loyalty to Kaiser William II and to the Hohenzollern in flaming words, as late as October, 1918, reversed his attitude less than two weeks later and changed from an ardent monarchist into an equally ardent Republican. He was one of the men who, as Robert Prutz expressed it, was always willing to change his shirt and his skin if necessary. Kaiser William II made many mistakes, he erred all too often. But if he himself sinned much, it must never be forgotten that bootlickers, flatterers, and incense-bearing crawlers sinned equally against him.

I had begun to discuss the Kaiser's attitude towards Bismarck. His attitude, a mixture of over-assurance and fear, of a bad conscience and a desire for revenge, jealousy, and stubbornness, was indeed a complicated one. During William II's entire reign he was confronted by Bismarck's gigantic figure. The Kaiser would have preferred to kill him by silence. He wanted Bismarck to be mentioned as rarely as possible. But he himself was almost hypnotised by him. There were many things he did not want to do, just because Bismarck had wanted them to be done. And again, he wanted to accomplish certain things so that he would be Bismarck's equal. He tried to justify Bismarck's ungracious dismissal, to make it seem useful, necessary, and right that Bismarck was retired. Thus he somewhat resembled the student Raskolnikoff in Dostojevski's famous novel, who always involuntarily returned to the scene of his crime. He tried to make people think that Bismarck had left him an "impossible inheritance" and that it was his, the Kaiser's mission to reëstablish the connexions which Bismarck had severed and to reëstablish Germany's position. That was why, so William II was fond of saying, he travelled so much, he paid so many visits, and made so many speeches. I should imagine that even to-day in his melancholy château at Doorn, after his fall and his flight, he is really convinced that he was just about to solve the great problem which heaven had given him to solve, when his enemies attacked him and all his efforts came to nothing.

When the day approached on which Bismarck's Monument was to be unveiled in Berlin, William II sent me a message through Lucanus to say that he would not attend this ceremony in any circumstances, as he considered it beneath his dignity to do so. August Eulenburg, the Lord Chamberlain, who realised as keenly as I did that it would make a very bad impression, if His Majesty stayed away so ostentatiously, arranged for me a short meeting with the Kaiser at the Potsdammer Station. The discussion lasted less than ten minutes, but it was very lively. The Kaiser dismissed me as follows: "If you insist, I shall come, but only in a modest uniform." He called to me from the window of the royal coach that he would not make a speech himself, that I was to make a speech he could approve of beforehand. The Kaiser actually did appear at the ceremony on June 16, 1901, in "modest uniform." He was accompanied by the Empress, who had never liked Bismarck, and who looked bad-tempered. I stood opposite the Kaiser, about twenty paces away from him. I spoke[1] very slowly and distinctly, so that he could understand all I said, and, emphasising every word, I declared that the Iron Chancellor would never be forgotten, that his sun would never set, that as long as there were German hearts they would never cease to be grateful to him and to be filled with admiration for him, that he would be remembered as long as German lips could speak, as long as German fists could be clenched. "To-day Germany is even more conscious of his greatness than she was when he was with us; this consciousness is stronger, more vital, and vivid than ever. His gigantic shadow will grow as the German people grow and mature and as national judgment ripens. Bismarck carried out and perfected the longings of our people and the desires our noblest thinkers have been harbouring for centuries; he accomplished what the Ottos, the Salians, and the Hohenstaufens strove for in vain; he attained what the fighters of 1813 hoped vaguely to achieve; he attained the end for which a long array of martyrs for the German idea fought and suffered. He was both the initiator and the pioneer of a new era for the German people. In every way we stand on his shoulders." I closed by saying: "There before us is the '*Siegesallee.*'[2] If this street proudly traces our history from the Nuremberg burgraves to the great German Kaiser, we owe this chiefly to the genius of the man whose iron statue now stands before us; we owe it to his heroic courage and to his work for the dynasty. May the great man's name march before our people like a pillar of flame, may his spirit be with us forever."

My wife was present at the ceremony. Usually I did not wish to have her attend sessions of the Reichstag when there was a chance that I would be speaking, partly because I did not want people to gather from her presence in the House and in the Press Gallery that I was about to speak, and partly, as I used to tell her in jest, I did not like to make a fool of myself in her presence, nor did I like to lose the halo she had placed about my head by having her hear my adversaries' attacks on me. But, accompanied by the chief of the

[1] Prince Bülow's "Speeches", (large edition), I. p. 222; (small edition), I. p. 246.
[2] Victory Avenue.

Chancellor's Office, Wilmowski, she wanted to attend the Bismarck memorial celebration. When I was finishing my speech, Wilmowski said to my wife that I had spoken famously, but that she had best pack her trunks, for the Kaiser would hardly swallow this speech. When I finished, the Kaiser came over to me with a kinder expression on his face than any I had seen for a long time. He pressed my hand and said: "Your words affected me profoundly." How unaccountable William II was! Even at moments when those who knew him best expected him to be in a bad mood, the essentially noble part of his nature would suddenly assert itself. Then he took me by the arm and led me over to Herbert Bismarck, pressed his hand as well and asked him whether I had not made an excellent speech. "The heart is a stubborn and a despairing thing, who can fathom it?" so Jeremiah, the son of Hiskias, from amongst the priests of Anathoth, in the land of Benjamin, lamented.

Not long before the unveiling of the Bismarck monument, I received a cordial letter from Herbert Bismarck which closed with the words: "It is regrettable that China spoiled your holiday. A number of regrettable things might happen to us, if your brakes were ever to become ineffective. In old loyalty, your Bismarck." Herbert knew that I had always been loyal to his father. He had heartily approved my appointment as Secretary of State and even more heartily my appointment as Chancellor. We had been great friends for years. Now he replied to the Kaiser with a somewhat sour countenance: "I think that Levetzow particularly spoke very well." Herr Albert von Levetzow, of Gussow in the Neumark, a member of the Prussian Upper Chamber and of the Council-of-State, a former High Sheriff of the Province of Brandenburg, had been unpopular, and almost hated, at Friedrichsruh since Bismarck's fall because, in 1890, when he was Speaker of the Reichstag he had not been courageous enough to acknowledge publicly the first Chancellor's great achievements in the Reichstag. When the Monument was unveiled, on June 16, 1901, before I spoke, he made a trivial, colourless speech, in which he mentioned only His Majesty and the Hohenzollerns. When Herbert Bismarck mentioned his speech and not mine, the Kaiser gave me a long signifi-

cant look.   Then he invited me for luncheon in the Palace, to
which Field Marshal Loë had also been invited and where, in the
latter's presence, the Kaiser again expressed his satisfaction with
my speech.   Grand Duke Frederick of Baden, who had often had
heated and even irritable controversies with Bismarck (controversies
in which the great Bismarck was not always in the right), thanked
me in a cordial telegram for my "exquisite" speech which he called a
valuable gift to the nation, whose thoughts and feelings it would
serve to guide and stimulate.   I showed, so he said, that to will a
thing is to know it first.   Herbert Bismarck, on the other hand,
in a Conservative meeting in Stendal, the cradle of the Bismarck
family, spoke angrily and bitingly against me, because I had said
in front of his immortal father's monument: that we stood on his
shoulders in every way, but not in the sense that it was our patriotic
duty to approve of everything that Bismarck had said and done, for
only fools and fanatics would claim that Bismarck had never made
a mistake.   We did not revere Bismarck as though he had established maxims which were to be adopted blindly in all circumstances
and in every situation.   There were no rigid dogmas either in
political or in economic life and Bismarck himself was never a
believer in this doctrine.   Thus disciples are often more intolerant
than their master.   Richard Wagner once said to my wife:
"Meyerbeer composed a few very pleasant things.   But you must
not tell this to the Wagnerites, they would scratch your eyes out."

A few weeks before my Bismarck speech, I had presided over
a secret meeting that included the higher Government officials
concerned and representatives of the more important Federal
States on the tariff question.   Prussia was represented by Posadowsky, Wermuth, Thielmann, Richthofen, Mühlberg, Körner,
Rheinbaben, Podbielski, Kapp, Möller.   The following Ministers
from the Federal States were present: Riedel, Feilitzsch, Metzsch,
Rüger, Buchenberger, and Rothe.   Before the discussion began, the
Bavarian Minister of Finance, Riedel, and I decided the following
main points of the general discussion in a private conversation which
we held in a window-niche of the Federal Council Chamber: (1) The
tariff must take a form that will not make the conclusion of com-

mercial treaties impossible. (2) Alternative tariffs must be accepted only for a few commodities. (3) The tariffs for bread grain could be increased by about five or six marks without endangering the people's food supply. (4) It would be desirable to differentiate between the rye and the wheat tariffs, so that we might conclude a commercial treaty with Russia and thus break through the wall which would otherwise close round us. (5) The tariff on barley could not be increased to any extent which would increase the price of beer. (6) The tariffs on live stock and meat could not possibly be raised to an extent which might increase the cost of living in the cities. The question of meat tariffs was a particularly difficult and dangerous one.

The customs tariffs, which were to be introduced in December of the same year, were based on these points. I realised clearly from the very beginning that if agriculture was to be granted the necessary protection, while the possibility of new commercial treaties was not to be curtailed, the new customs tariff must be based on an understanding between the Centre Party, the National-Liberals, and the Conservatives. Only the Centre could constitute the backbone of a coalition of this kind, for the Centre Party was in its whole structure a microcosm of Germany's economic state. The Centre Party included farmers, industrialists, and trade union officials. The Centre Party was by its very nature committed to a diagonal policy, such as I myself pursued, and which represented the interests of the country.

The fact that I was so unfailingly supported by the Centre Party during the long and embittered fights over the tariffs, was due in part to the insight and wisdom with which the Party was led in the Reichstag by the Deputy Spahn. Peter Spahn was not exactly a charmer. He was not a convincing speaker, he spoke dryly and his voice could hardly be heard. And he had no charm when one met him personally. But he was an absolutely honourable man, he was extremely conscientious, and an excellent lawyer. He had belonged to Windthorst's circle far too long not to realise that politics are the art of the possible and that the means used to reach the desired aim cannot be employed successfully without a certain amount of opportunism. The Centre Party, obviously, included a number of simple, undistinguished members, but the Party as such had felt the breath of the spirit which, for centuries, has made strength and success of the Holy See. The National Liberals showed the two souls which, as Eugen Richter jestingly said, lived in their breasts, when it came to the tariff question. The majority of their members agreed with the iron and steel industries that tariffs should be increased as much as possible, while the minority tended to accept the Suburban-Liberalism of the Liberal Party. Deputy Bassermann deserved great credit for the way he kept the Party on the right track, except for a few vacillations in which the Party lost two or three votes.

Most of the Conservatives, including Count Hans Kanitz and Count von Schwerin-Löwitz, two men of patriotism and insight, supported me faithfully. The Farmers' League, on the other hand, was like children who cry for more plums, even though they know they will be sick. The President of the League, Freiherr Konrad von Wangenheim, a man with a noble and upright character, was the most sensible among them. Dr. Gustav Roesicke's point of view was influenced by Party politics in a most dubious manner. The brother of this Agrarian leader was a member of the Reichstag as well, but he had joined the Liberal People's Party. Both were pugnacious natures. Dietrich Hahn, who, since he had been appointed as the itinerant speaker of the League, had changed from a free trader to an exaggerated Agrarian, was even more pugnacious.

Lord Beaconsfield once said that a statesman cannot have great successes without occasional intrigues. Bismarck once expressed the same idea when he said "that only stupid men don't know how it 's done." I was particularly anxious to prevent the extreme Agrarians from thwarting my good intentions for agriculture through their lack of understanding. For this reason it was necessary to force them into a defensive position, that is to say, they had to be forced to defend themselves against the reproach that they were asking too much. They could not be allowed to remain in a position in which they would be believed when they accused the Government of a lack of interest in agriculture. To attain this end I slipped a notice into a democratic South German newspaper saying that everyone who had expected moderate tariffs would be greatly disappointed. According to reports about the future tariffs there was grave anxiety concerning the general increase in the cost of living as well as the probable harm to all our trade relations. Then there followed some *ad hoc* statements about the "regrettably exorbitant" tariffs proposed by the Government. Shortly afterwards I published a statement in the "*Norddeutsche Allgemeine Zeitung*", in which I declared that as, through an indiscretion, a part of the Tariff Bill had become known, I had obtained the Federal Government's permission to publish the Bill in full. I then did so. Then the entire Left-wing press began to complain bitterly. The Democratic papers were wild about the legal fixing of minimum tariffs, the Socialist press threatened to obstruct the Bill. "*Vorwärts*" declared that the tariff was worse than even the Chancellor Bülow's most pessimistic judges had feared it would be. And the "*Tante Voss*", a paper which was much milder, saw the end of commercial treaties and the economic isolation of Germany. The chief organ of the Agrarians, the "*Deutsche Tageszeitung*", tried to meet these blows by declaring that the tariffs proposed by the Government would not satisfy even the most modest farmers. But this declaration was neither believed nor approved of. Public opinion had turned against them, the situation was postponed. The extreme Agrarians were no longer considered as men who had some right to complain, they were now generally considered as greedy people who could never be satisfied. This was just what I had intended. It therefore became easier for Count Stirum, the leader of the Conservative Party, to keep the Party together and to save its members from a suicidal opposition to the Tariff Bill, which would have been quite as disastrous for the Conservative as for agriculture. Count Stirum's leadership was inspired by the national interest and his aims were statesmanlike. Eight years later, under the leadership of Herr von Heydebrand, who was so concerned with Party politics that he forgot the State, the Conservative Party was forced to adopt a line of action which inflicted serious injuries on Prussia, on the Empire, and finally on the Party itself.

CHAPTER XXXIV

Kaiser William at Empress Frederick's Deathbed — Her Death (August 5, 1901) — Count Götz von Seckendorff — Character Sketch of Empress Frederick — Count Waldersee's Return from China — William II's Meeting with Nicholas II at Hela — Insufficient Decorations for the Russian Foreign Minister — William II in Rominten — Eulenburg's Description of the Visit There — Prince Henry Visits the Tsar in Spala — Prince Max of Baden Becomes Engaged to Grand Duchess Helen Vladimirovna — Unveiling of a Monument in the Siegesallee *— William II and the Arts — Death of the Idealist Malvida von Meysenbug and of King Albert of Saxony.*

BEFORE Kaiser William II left for his Northern cruise, he asked Professor Renvers, the great physician who was looking after the Empress Frederick, to notify him in time when his mother was approaching her death. Professor Renvers had diagnosed cancer and, with the help of his eminent medical knowledge and his great kindness of heart, he was trying to make the poor woman feel as comfortable as possible. As soon as the Kaiser received a telegram from Renvers he left Norway for Germany. I travelled to Kiel to meet him. The Kaiser was sadly moved, and, above all, he was very much excited. He showered reproaches on his poor wife, who had come to Kiel with me to meet him, because she was not staying with her mother-in-law, who, as a matter of fact, had not wanted her to stay. Duchess Caroline Mathilde of Glücksburg, the Kaiserin's elder sister, finally succeeded in calming him down. Duchess Caroline, like the Empress, was a good and sensible woman. The Kaiser and I went to the Homburg Palace, and from there he went to Friedrichshof, where he remained until the death of his mother, who suffered terribly. She died supported by Renvers, who never left her for an instant, and by her son. This was on August 5, 1901. The next morning the Kaiser and I took a long walk in the Palace gardens at Homburg. He told me that his mother had decided that her body should be wrapped unclothed in the English flag, and be thus laid in the coffin. She had also ordered her coffin

THE EMPRESS FREDERICK

(*Portrait by Heinrich von Angeli, 1894*)

to be sent to England, for she wanted to be buried there. I agreed with the Kaiser when he said that he did not think these wishes of his mother could be carried out, because they might offend the sensibilities of the German people and the dignity of our country. She was buried a few days later in the Friedenskirche in Potsdam.

I know hardly one fate more tragic than the Empress Frederick's. She was brought up as Princess Royal of Great Britain and Ireland, she was Queen Victoria's eldest daughter, she was accustomed to all the luxury of the English Court. She was surrounded not only by the affection and the tenderness of her parents, brothers, and sisters, but by the affection of the English people as well. Her youth had been most happy. She was Prince Albert's favourite daughter. He early impressed her with his ideas of the world and his ideas of politics, which were of the moderate Liberalism of the fifties but of course with a strong English tendency. Though Prince Albert of Coburg was not really very popular in England, his German ability to adjust himself to new surroundings made him consider himself as an Englishman and he felt himself to be above his German relatives and compatriots. When, after her marriage, his daughter was leaving for Germany, he impressed upon her never to forget that she was Queen Victoria's eldest daughter and Princess Royal of Great Britain and Ireland. The fact that she had become Crown Princess of Prussia was to be a matter of secondary consideration. It is possible that Prince Albert would have altered his opinions about Prussian and German conditions if he had lived longer. As it was, his daughter retained the point of view which her beloved father, who died in 1861, less than three years after her marriage, had impressed upon her. Everything in Berlin and particularly in Potsdam seemed to her poor and small as compared with Windsor and Osborne. There was hardly even a bath room in the Prussian Palace at that time. Twice a week King William I's bath was brought over to his Palace in a covered tub from the Hôtel de Rome. When the young English Princess asked for an egg cup at the breakfast table, the servant replied, somewhat embarrassed, that their Highnesses usually used a wine glass for this purpose. And even the W. C.'s left much to be desired. Self-assured and stubborn as she was, Princess Frederick William of Prussia did not know how to get on with her parents-in-law. She was all the more successful, however, in acquiring a powerful influence over her noble, kind, brave, and yet mild husband in a very short time. Von Schweinitz, who was then Prince Frederick William's adjutant (later he became an Ambassador) and who attended the Prince's wedding, told me that, after the bride had said good-bye to her English family, she took her new husband energetically by the arm and led him to the railway carriage. "She led him all through life in the same way," Schweinitz had added. It would be unjust not to mention that the Princess was her husband's intellectual superior, that she saw things from a broad point of view, that she had fewer inhibitions than he had, that she grasped things more quickly and that her mind was more agile than his. But though she loved her husband tenderly, she never appreciated his magnificent characteristics, his great integrity, his purity, his chivalry, his complete lack of fear, his touching kindness of heart, and his conscientiousness, as she should have done.

I would not like to state that all the gossip about the Crown Princess' affection for her Chamberlain, Count Götz Seckendorff, is silly and completely untrue. Count Seckendorff's position in the Crown Prince's Court was only partly based on the fact that he knew a great deal about managing the household, arranging the house, and buying antiques, and that he helped the Crown Princess with her hobbies, such as painting in water colours, gardening, etc. The secret of his influence was chiefly founded on the inconsiderate and unembarrassed way in which he contradicted his high-born employer, for this frankness was interpreted by her as sincerity and true loyalty. Queen Victoria's attitude toward her beloved husband's chief huntsman, the Scotchman Brown, was similar. The rough frankness which this worthy countryman of Sir Walter Scott displayed on all occasions assured Her Majesty that he was entirely reliable. The Queen's private physician, whom she had sent to Roumania to deliver Queen Marie, told me, when I met him at Sinaja, where we took many walks together, that he had been present one day when the Queen, who had called upon her daughter-in-law, the Duchess of Connaught, got into her carriage. John Brown sat on the box behind the carriage. The Queen asked for her shawl. John Brown told her that she was sitting on it, and added, grumblingly, that she was so absent-minded that she would mislay her head some day. The Queen replied in a gentle voice, "You are quite right. I am a poor widow who has lost her dear beloved husband and who feels very helpless." The allegation that Empress Frederick married Count Seckendorff secretly after her husband's death is one of the silliest lies ever invented. The Chamberlain, Count Götz von Seckendorff, belonged to an old Franconian family, a branch of which had migrated to Prussia by way of Ansbach and Bayreuth in the eighteenth century. The most famous member of the family was a Field Marshal and Imperial Count, Friedrich Heinrich von Seckendorff, who, as Austrian Ambassador to Berlin, succeeded in charming Frederick William I to such an extent that the latter concluded the treaty of December 23, 1728, by which Prussia became virtually dependent upon Austria, just as Prussia became dependent upon Austria almost two hundred years later when Bethmann-Hollweg, in 1914, tied Prussia and Germany to the Austrian diplomats' Ship of Fools. The Chamberlain, Count Götz von Seckendorff, was a courtier but not in the sense described by Baltasar Gracian, the Rector of the Jesuit College at Tarragona, in his "*El discreto*", or in his "*Oraculo manual*", which Schopenhauer has translated for us. Nor was he a worldly and polished courtier of the kind Labruyère describes in his "*Caractères.*" Seckendorff was a courtier in the sense that he judged all situations and events from the point of view of the courts and the ruling families. Though he had been an officer in the First Guards Regiment he lacked firm Prussian and German patriotism. He was entirely influenced by the moods and the desires of the English Court, according to which he adjusted his actions just as a compass needle follows the meridian. His great ambition was to become German Ambassador in London, a post for which he was in no way suited. When I could not and would not grant this request, his friendship for me cooled, and, as he kindly expressed it, his admiration for me diminished as well. He died before the beginning of the

World War without having attained his aim of becoming Ambassador in London. The fact that a man who was not really a good Prussian or a good German spent so many years in Empress Frederick's entourage certainly contributed to the circumstance that she unfortunately never became a good Prussian herself.

She was only German in so far as her feeling for Germany was confined to the modest old Germany of the *Biedermeier* period. She never loved the mighty Bismarckian Germany. The fact that she was never able to get on well with Bismarck was the misfortune of her life. The great statesman made an effort, particularly in the period of his conflict with the Kaiser, to reach some sort of understanding with her, but all his efforts failed because of her stubbornness, for she was even more stubborn than her mother, which is saying a great deal. The daughter lacked her mother's practical experience. She had not, like her mother, become accustomed to the fact that the royal will cannot prevail over the institutions of a country, and that iron limits are put upon it by tradition and by reasons of state. Empress Frederick had a great deal of charm, and her eldest son largely inherited his charm from her. It was a pleasure to discuss things with her even when one knew from the very beginning that one would never succeed in making her change her mind. She painted quite nicely, but, naturally, she was an amateur. She painted several portraits of my wife. Two of these portraits are now in the Villa Malta, one of them is in Flottbeck, but none of them, of course, equal the glorious portraits by Makart and Lenbach. Empress Frederick once asked me how I liked the portraits of my wife which she had painted. I told Her Majesty that a great Monarch, Louis XIV, *le Grand Roi*, had once read one of his sonnets to the Duc de Saint-Simon, asking him what he thought about it. The Duke answered: "*Sire, rien n'est impossible à Votre Majesté. Vous avez voulu faire un mauvais sonnet, vous avez pleinement réussi.*" I concluded: "Your Majesty wanted to paint a poor likeness of my wife and Your Majesty has succeeded." The Empress laughed. She was far from being hurt by my answer; on the contrary she thought the Duc de Saint-Simon's remark very charming. Under all circumstances and no matter into which walk

of life she had been born, Empress Frederick would have been a remarkable woman. Her life made her one of the unhappiest women
who ever lived. She experienced one disappointment after another.
She could never carry out any of her plans. Before her husband
finally ascended the throne, she saw the years pass without being
able to play a part in history. In a talk with me after his death she
compared herself with a human being who stands on the banks
of a river that flows with complete, unfeeling indifference. Empress
Frederick never forgave her eldest son for his heartless behaviour
towards his father before the latter's death in San Remo. She
never forgot, furthermore, how brutally her son treated her in Potsdam after his father's death. The terrible rancour which thereafter she harboured against her first-born child was unfortunately
transferred to her brother, King Edward, who, since his childhood,
had been tenderly devoted to his eldest sister, in whom he had perfect confidence. Politically, Empress Frederick was liberal-minded ;
she also harboured very free views regarding the Church. Would
she have had the strength, as Empress, to carry out liberal reforms?
I hardly think she would, for I believe that a Chancellor, who knew
her feminine, impressionable, and fearsome nature, would easily
have influenced her to confine her activities to the arts and sciences.
William II inherited his respect for science from her. He also
inherited her tendency to air her scientific knowledge, though she
never did so to the same extent as her son. She never boasted in
any way. She was modest in her manner, which was almost embarrassed. She was more dignified than her eldest son, but in a
certain sense he was more of a *bon enfant*, more *gemütlich* in a
German sense, than she was herself. The mother was more profoundly cultured than the son and she had better manners. In justice it should be added that the intellectual horizons of both the
mother and the son were broader than those of the leaders of the
German Republic, such as Scheidemann and Wirth, Preuss and
Erzberger.

Empress Frederick's views about art were very middle-class.
She preferred Handel to Wagner, she did not appreciate Beethoven,
and she considered Schiller's "Hymn to Joy", "terribly exaggerated,

almost as though a drunken man had written it." Tennyson, the
Poet Laureate of the Victorian age, was her ideal. She was very
much interested in arts and crafts, about which she knew a great
deal, and she made an effort, not without success, to civilise not
only the furniture, but also Berlin life and manners as a whole, in
accordance with her views. She was much more interested in her
relatives than was her son, whose love of himself pushed everything else into the background. Empress Frederick was a most
affectionate mother to her daughters; she loved them more than
they loved her. This may have been because her enormous activity
wearied her daughters and made them dislike spending long periods
with her. She was infinitely devoted to all her English relatives
and to the relatives of these relatives, especially the Leiningens,
the Hohenlohes, the Battenbergs, the Augustenburgs, the Coburgs,
and down to the family of Mensdorff-Pouilly.

Empress Augusta Victoria's father was a Holstein, but her mother
was a Hohenlohe-Langenburg, and it was because of this fact that
the Crown Princess Victoria, as she then was, conceived and ma-
tured the plan of choosing the unknown daughter of a half-forgotten
claimant, who had been neglected by history, as the future Queen
and Empress. At that time she and Prince William were still playing
in their nurseries. Later, when they were married, young Princess
Holstein (the wise Minister of Justice Friedberg had predicted that
it would so happen) took her husband's side in all the differences
which arose between him and his mother. She was devoted to him
not only from a sense of duty but with all the warmth of her spirit.
The relationship between Augusta Victoria and her mother-in-law,
therefore, was even less friendly than the relationship between
Victoria and her mother-in-law had been years before. Prince Bismarck was never as fundamentally bitter against Empress Frederick
as he had been against Empress Augusta during the whole time he
was in office. But he neither understood nor appreciated her. Once,
in the 'eighties, when Bismarck had been granted an interview with
the Crown Princess after everyone had pressed this interview on him,
he said to his son Herbert when he returned to his home: "The poor
woman is a stupid goose. She talked the whole time about her

Aunt Feodora of Holstein or Hohenlohe, or God knows who, whose wishes seem to interest her exclusively." This was an unfair judgment on the part of a genius whose own great plans interested him exclusively. If she had been born under a luckier star, Empress Frederick would have had a happier life either in Germany or in England and her activity would have been generally admired and respected. She was ground down between the hard mill-stones of Bismarck's politics and Prussian tradition. I received the following answer to a telegram of condolence which I sent to Empress Frederick's brother, King Edward, after her death: "I thank you with all my heart for your sympathy. The beloved Empress always thought so much of you and your wife."

After Empress Frederick had been buried in the Friedenskirche in Potsdam, where she was laid to rest, after all her suffering, her disappointments, and her unhappiness, next to her royal husband in a beautiful marble coffin designed by Reinhold Begas, the Kaiser prepared to meet with Tsar Nicholas of Russia, who had accepted an invitation to the German naval manoeuvres which were to take place during the first half of September on the Hela Wharf in the Bay of Danzig. William II received Count Waldersee, who had returned from China, in Homburg beforehand. His head high in the air, the Field Marshal approached his ruler. His face showed a tense expectancy, for he wondered what extraordinary honour would be conferred upon him on his return from China, for his departure had been celebrated in an unprecedented manner. Now it chanced that, the day before, William II had received a letter from one of his English aunts, in which she told him that Waldersee had declared in China that he must hurry back to Germany to accept the Chancellorship, as Bülow was played out. When, at the station in Homburg, Waldersee approached the Kaiser, the latter called out to him that he ought to thank me for getting him out of the affair so neatly. The last thing the ambitious Marshal expected was that he would be asked to thank me for anything whatever, and he looked surprised and not much pleased. "The true nature of ambition is but the shadow of a dream," says the Chamberlain Guildenstern to Hamlet, Prince of Denmark. I called upon

Waldersee during the day to discuss the Eastern Asiatic situation with him and he described conditions very reasonably and intelligently. He died shortly afterwards from a serious intestinal complaint which the old man, who was seventy years of age, had contracted during the Chinese Campaign. In my presence the Kaiser read the telegram announcing his death with a most indifferent expression on his face and he did not shed a tear, though he had called the deceased his most distinguished and truest friend at the end of the 'eighties during the Waldersee-Bismarck conflict. Despite his faults Waldersee was a brilliant soldier. In China he not only maintained harmony between the nations but he contributed to building up the great and hopeful political and economic position which we held in eastern Asia up to 1914.

The Kaiser looked forward to the meeting in Hela with tense expectancy and he was even more impatient than usual. I was to accompany His Majesty, seeing that Tsar Nicholas had notified the German Kaiser that he would be accompanied by Count Lambsdorff, the Russian Minister for Foreign Affairs. When I boarded the *Hohenzollern* in Kiel, I was received by Ambassador von Tschirschky, who was staying with His Majesty as the representative of the Foreign Office. Tschirschky told me in great excitement that the Kaiser refused to confer the Order of the Black Eagle on Lambsdorff. Tschirschky assured me that he had exhausted himself in his efforts to persuade the Kaiser what a political mistake it would be to offend the Russian Foreign Minister who heretofore had been amicably disposed towards us. But he had been unable to persuade the Kaiser to change his mind. Just then the Kaiser approached us. Tschirschky left and I discussed the question of this decoration at once. I reminded him that Napoleon had said that decorations play the same part in politics as children's toys do in the nursery: "*Les hommes sont comme les enfants; il leur faut des hochets.*" Decorations were a means of winning people. This case was a special one because it was a tradition to confer the Order of the Black Eagle on Russian Foreign Ministers of Affairs. If we neglected the tradition in Lambsdorff's case, this sensitive man, who was now friendly towards us, would never forgive it. The Tsar was greatly influenced by his advisers and there was no reason why we should insult Lambsdorff. The Kaiser responded with a violence unusual towards me, saying that he could not "throw away" his highest decoration. When I mentioned that this high order had been conferred upon individuals who were less worthy than the Foreign Minister of a Great Power, His Majesty replied that I was always completely dominated by purely political motives and that I had no understanding for his deepest, most sacred sentiments. Tschirschky, he said, understood him better, for he had assured him only an hour ago that he would be quite right not to confer the high Order of the Black Eagle on Lambsdorff. At this moment Tschirschky appeared again very close to us. I motioned to him to come nearer and asked him, looking him sharply in the eye, if he tried to dissuade the Kaiser from conferring the Order of the Black Eagle. Tschirschky grew red in the face, but he did not answer. His Majesty and I continued to talk for some time and he ended by saying that he would ask his cousin, colleague, and friend Nicky, which Prussian Order he wanted Lambsdorff to receive. Later, when I asked old Lucanus how it was possible that the Kaiser could continue to have any confidence in Tschirschky who had lied to him so blatantly, the experienced old man replied: "Tschirschky will simply tell the Kaiser that it was still his conviction that His Majesty was quite right in refusing the decoration and that the Chancellor was ambitious and vindictive and that's why he had to play the part he did."

I was surprised to find Prince Max Fürstenberg, with whom I was then on very friendly terms, in the Imperial entourage. He courted my favour in every way. When, in the spring of 1901, I was stopping in Titisee in the Black Forest, he invited my wife and me to his castle in Donaueschingen, where he showered us with attentions. It was, of course, a political error to include this Austrian grand seigneur in a meeting with the Russian Tsar. A Russian adjutant, who had been a friend of mine for a number of years, said to me, half in jest and half seriously: "What would you have said if we had brought a prominent Frenchman with us?" Like all courtiers Max Fürstenberg made the greatest effort to amuse Kaiser William II. Every morning he had the latest Stock Exchange joke sent him by wire so that he could tell it to the Kaiser at breakfast. He also kissed His Majesty's hand on every occasion. How many catastrophes courtiers have caused in monarchistic states! The jokes which William II's favourite told him to pass the time often did political harm. Phillipp Eulenburg and Kuno Moltke provided the foundation for the unfavourable and ironical judgement which the Kaiser passed on Crown Prince Victor Emanuel of Italy and his wife, who later became Queen Elena, for, during a northern cruise, on which our Kaiser met the Italian Crown Prince and his wife, they made silly jokes about the "little" Prince and the Princess who came from the "wild" mountains of Cernagora.

During the Hela meeting Max Fürstenberg directed his mockery against Lambsdorff. The Russian Minister could not stand the sea and he looked very pale as he approached the *Hohenzollern* in a small boat in a rough sea. He was awkward and frail and the way in which he stepped from the small boat on to the gangway was not exactly a masterpiece of gymnastics. He did not wear the smart yachting uniform which all the gentlemen in His Majesty's entourage were wearing. Instead, he wore the ugly uniform of the Russian Civil Service, which made him resemble an elderly Customs Officer. His cap was very high, it had a long peak, and a high cockade. As he was very small he wore shoes with very high heels, a trick which *Le Grand Roi* Louis XIV also used to make himself appear taller. Fürstenberg attracted the Kaiser's attention to the high heels, the huge cap, and the pale face of Count Lambsdorff and the Kaiser then allowed himself to make some rather unfortunate jokes which obviously embarrassed the Minister. After I had observed this turn of affairs I considered it all the more my duty to insist once again and energetically that the Order of the Black Eagle be conferred upon Lambsdorff. Without being announced, I knocked at His Majesty's cabin door and remained in his cabin while he was changing for dinner. At first he refused, but finally he said that if I would not change my mind he would probably be obliged to give way.

The dinner was a big success and the Tsar talked to me for a long time after we had left the table. He said quite spontaneously that unless Russia and Germany remained friendly and at peace, *en paix et en amitié*, they would destroy each other. The revolution and the Poles would benefit by any conflict between Prussia-Germany and Russia, whereas the two countries and the dynasties themselves would be the losers. He then conferred the Order of St. Andrew upon me and said: *"Comme preuve de mon amitié pour vous et de ma confiance en vous."* While the Tsar was talking with me, Kaiser William distributed the Prussian decorations among the Russian guests. I noticed that Lambsdorff, who had retained a cheerful face despite the Kaiser's jokes about his lack of nautical talent, now wore a discontented, venomous expression. Only once before, in very different circumstances, had I seen the leading minister with such an expression on his face and that was Prince Gortschakov when Bismarck in 1878 at the end of the Berlin Congress paid attention only to Peter Schuvaloff, Beaconsfield, and Andrássy and ostentatiously ignored the Russian Chancellor. Lambsdorff finally came up to me and told me politely but with poorly disguised anger that my most gracious sovereign had not given him the Order of the Black Eagle which had heretofore been granted Russian Foreign Ministers as the only possible decoration, but had given him instead a decoration of which he had never heard before. So as to have his own wish (it was really a whim), Kaiser William had given the Russian Minister the Kaiser William Order, a decoration which he had founded himself sometime before and which even Germans did not want to possess, particularly as it was usually conferred on ministers, generals, and admirals who were being retired and who were not considered worthy of the Order of the Black Eagle. When I asked the Kaiser the next day why he had done this, he claimed that Tsar Nicholas had said that he would be "particularly grateful" if the Order which his true friend and cousin Willy had created and which had been designed by that same exalted Majesty's own hand were conferred upon his Foreign Minister. I was not sure whether this was the truth, but I was sure that Lambsdorff, the former intimate of von Giers, the official who had drawn the final wording of the Re-insurance Treaty, had become our enemy. Philosophers will be justified if they find it regrettable that political relations between great peoples can be influenced and injured by the circumstance that Ministers increase the large number of their decorations by some new decoration or other. Experience unfortunately teaches us that personal vanity, sensitiveness, and vindictiveness can do harm in political as well as in private life. Politics do not always develop as they do in Scribe's comedy, in which a glass of water decides between war and peace and the fate of England and France. But it is equally true that political evolution does not proceed the way unworldly doctrinaires, who sit at their desks and discover "scientific laws", think it must proceed. On the contrary, political events are influenced by human moods and passions.

No one could care less for outward decorations than I do. Quite apart from my philosophy I am indifferent to them because I possess all these decorations: the High Order of the Black Eagle with Diamonds and the Spanish Golden Fleece, the Russian Order of St. Andrew with Diamonds, the Austrian Order of St. Stephen with Diamonds, the Italian Order of the Sacred Annunciation, the Order of the Annunciation and the Very Noble Portuguese Order of the Tower and the Sword, the Danish Order of the Elephant and the Swedish Seraphine Order, the Bavarian Order of St. Hubert and the Saxon Order of the Diamond, Turkish and Japanese, Chinese and Siamese orders — I have all of them, all of them! After my first youth I cared as little about decorations, stars, and chains as a pastry cook cares about sweets and candy. Unless courtesy towards a foreign guest made it necessary for me to wear a foreign decoration, I never wore anything but the Order of the Black Eagle. But now as an old and experienced man who knows the world and the weaknesses, mistakes, and impulses of human beings, I must say that if the Weimar Constitution forbids orders and uniforms, it is another proof that Dr. Hugo Preuss, the father of our Republican constitution, knows as little about human beings as he knows about the world. He sacrificed the possibility of winning and pleasing important foreigners. This sad German Solon is also responsible for the fact that German representatives abroad, since the collapse in November, 1918, stand about in their dress suits without decorations and look like Cinderella amid her festively clothed playmates. The French Republic was careful not to make a serious mistake of this kind and neither abolished uniforms nor decorations. The hope that one may receive the little red ribbon or even the rosette of the Legion of Honour stimulates the patriotism and the ambition of the average Frenchman. The award of the Legion of Honour is a successful means of French propaganda as far as foreigners are concerned. The Legion of Honour awakens sympathy for France all over the world and rewards French sentiment. I herewith close this parenthesis which I have written in connexion with the unfavourable political results called forth by the unwise treatment of the Russian Minister of Foreign Affairs when the monarchs met at Hela. I would again like to emphasise that I understand the aversion which a poet dear to all German hearts felt when he thought of the advisers and chamberlains of kings who with a cold star on their cold breasts do not believe in spirit voices. But a statesman must take the weakness and pettiness of human beings into consideration; they, too, must be exploited for the good of the country. *"Il faut faire flèche de tout bois,"* Prince Bismarck once said to Emperor Frederick, the noble idealist, when he complained that sometimes politics exploit the less desirable qualities of human beings. After a cordial farewell from Tsar Nicholas II at Hela, William II went for his regular hunting expedition to Rominten, where Philipp Eulenburg was waiting for him. The latter wrote to me on September 23, 1901 :

His Majesty accepted my congratulations on his success in Danzig very heartily and told me many details; of course the Tsar's visit to France was a great failure, and the Kaiser let contemptuous, almost hostile, remarks hail down on England. William Proteus. His Majesty spoke of you in the warmest and most appreciative manner. He said you had charmed Tsar Nicholas and that this was the most important thing in the whole visit.

Philipp Eulenburg, who was unusually good at telling a story, then gave me a delicious description of the royal visit to Wyschty-

ten, a small Russian town on the German-Russian frontier, a few
kilometers from Rominten. The small town had been practically
destroyed by fire a few weeks before. Philipp Eulenburg wrote
to me:

Yesterday evening we had barely arrived at Rominten, when a report
about the fire was demanded and this report was given by Saint-Paul,
the forester, who was very sleepy. Then we dined, whereupon it was
announced that to-morrow — that is to say, this afternoon — His
Majesty would don the uniform of a Russian General and dash to
Wyschtyten, where he would distribute 5000 roubles among the unhappy population at the request of the Tsar. One hundred fifty houses
were burned to the ground, all belonging to Jews. It certainly may be
a grand moment when he does this! Holy Jeremiah will bless the hour
and he will rejoice particularly over the new Russian Dragoon uniform.

The next day Eulenburg wrote to me about this "apocalyptical
ride."

His Majesty mounted a horse and galloped across the frontier accompanied by two adjutants, Richard Dohna and Saint-Paul, the forester.
August Eulenburg, Admiral Hollmann, and I followed in a carriage.
What a strange undertaking! Scolding and beating them, the Chief
Police Constable drove the poor Jews into the market place, where His
Majesty had stationed himself to make a speech. The Jews, who were
celebrating their "long night", came out of the synagogue in a dirty state
and against their will. Finally about 200 people stood in the market
place and the Kaiser delivered a winged speech which no one understood.
Then some of the Jews came over to me and asked who the Russian
officer was. They would not believe that it was the German Kaiser,
"who would not come to Wyschtyten anyway, and even if he did, he
would wear a German uniform." In short, no one really understood
what it was all about. His chief desire was probably to see Wyschtyten,
to wear a Russian uniform, and, also, he did really want to help. This
morning, after two unsuccessful pursuits, the Kaiser brought down two
eighteeners. He is in a golden mood.

The next day Philipp Eulenburg telegraphed to me officially, saying that the Kaiser wanted his Wyschtyten speech distributed by
Wolff's Telegraph Agency. The speech read:

His Majesty, Tsar Nicholas, your mighty ruler and my beloved friend, has heard about your great misfortune. He wishes me to tell you how much this news has saddened him and he wishes me to express his heartfelt sympathy. And more than this, through me, he sends you, as a token of his love for his people, 5000 roubles. By this you may know how the eyes of the exalted and loving father of your country sees even the farthest frontier towns of his Empire and how warmly his kind heart is beating even for his remotest populations. You will now express your love for your Kaiser and father by shouting: Ssa sdarvye jevo veliichestvo Gossudarya Imperatora Nicola. Urrah!

If none of his entourage, not even Philipp Eulenburg, his most intimate friend, could see the purpose of this excursion to a small Russian frontier town, I, for my part, cannot understand it psychologically even to-day, — how a man like William II, who in many ways was highly gifted, a man who had many serious interests, who was then forty-two years old and had been a ruler for twelve years, could have enjoyed such childish things and could have staged anything so like a light opera.

Not long after this strange expedition, Prince Henry, who was on the best of terms with his brother-in-law, the Tsar, spent some time with him in his hunting lodge Spala in the Russian-Polish Government of Petrikoff. After his return Prince Henry told me of his impressions: Tsar Nicholas had received him like a member of the family, had urged him to stay longer, had assured him again and again that it was a pleasure to see his Prussian brother-in-law. As a matter of fact these were not, as it happened, mere phrases. The last (for the time being) Russian Tsar felt sincere friendship for Prince Henry. Prince Henry described his brother-in-law as a very well-bred and very gracious man; he said that he was kindly as a whole and even humane, but that he wanted to maintain the autocratic form of Government. Unlike his father, the Tsar was very liberal in religious matters. But publicly he would never oppose the Orthodox Church. He was interested in the army and the navy, he knew quite a good deal about military affairs, and, as a young man, he had been an able company commander. But he was pacifically inclined. Kaiser William impressed the Tsar, but occasionally the Kaiser got on his nerves. Our Kaiser ought not to overdo it as far as the Tsar was concerned. Most Russians, as well as the Tsar, looked upon the ride to Wyschtyten as a strange and somewhat undignified method the Kaiser had found of ingratiating himself. "Try to influence my brother, the Kaiser, to be nice and friendly towards the Tsar, but not to make him suspicious and, above all, to leave him alone. That is the right formula for the way the Tsar should be treated." The Tsar's Chief Aide and Minister of the Household, Fredericksz, exerted the greatest influence on the Tsar; the former was decidedly friendly towards Germany and very reliable. Prince Henry, who was very English, and whose political views were influenced more by his heart than by his reason, "regretted" that the Tsar was not very friendly towards England. The Tsar, he said, distrusted English politics and was contemptuous of the English Army and the constitutional, parliamentary form of Government. In this he was a Muscovite. Nor did he have much respect for his uncle, King Edward. But he had no intention of attacking England any more than he wanted to attack any other country in Europe. If he ever waged war, it would only be because he thought he was being attacked by some other great European Power. The Tsar did not even want Manchuria, but he did not want any one else to have it either. The same was true about Korea. The Tsar told his brother-in-law, Prince Henry, that the presence of the Japanese in Korea would be of such significance that a new Bosphorus Question would arise in Asia. If the Japanese were to try to establish themselves in Korea, this would, indeed, be a *casus belli* for Russia. The Tsar told Prince Henry in confidence that, sooner or later, there would be a conflict between Russia and Japan, but that it would not happen for at least four years, by which time Russia would have gained the naval supremacy in the Pacific. When this had been attained, the Japanese would take care not to begin any trouble. In five or six years, furthermore, the Siberian Railway would be completed, which he, the Tsar, considered as his life work. To build this railway he needed French money, but, politically, he would guard against the French and he would not let them exploit him. Germany and Russia must remain at peace and so preserve the peace of the world.

The reports which I received from our Ambassador Alvensleben, at St. Petersburg, and, now and again, from General von Werder, who was still a personal friend of the Russian family, coincided as a whole with Prince Henry's reports. Werder had written to me in the spring of 1901 that the Dowager Empress, who had been incensed by the Wilhelmshaven speech of the Kaiser ("we don't give quarter"), was convinced that the Chancellor, at least, was making a sincere effort to maintain and strengthen friendly relations with Russia. Werder wrote to me that, on the whole, the Tsar liked the Kaiser, though there were some things about him he did not like. He could understand why Germany desired economic advantages in Turkey, but Kaiser William's enthusiasm for the Sublime Porte, the Koran, and the Sultan irritated the Tsar. He said in Werder's presence: "*Je n'aime pas le Sultan, je le cède à l'Empereur d'Allemagne.*"

For some time Ambassador Alvensleben had been trying assiduously to arrange a marriage between Grand Duchess Helen, the pretty daughter of Grand Duke Vladimir, and some German Prince. Prince Frederick Heinrich of Prussia, who later disgraced his name and his uniform in such a sad way, did not feel inclined to marry, and young Grand Duke William Ernest of Saxe-Weimar was not popular in St. Petersburg. In the latter's case, also, Alvensleben feared a loosening of the Federal Unity through the dynastic connection with Russia. The dangers of a marriage with Prince Louis Napoleon, who was handsome, a good soldier, and probably well able to please a young Princess who needed love, were even more apparent to Alvensleben. A marriage with the Count of Turin would have had its disadvantages as well. In the end the young Princess became engaged to Prince Max of Baden. He resembled his great-grandfather, Nicholas I, only in his outward appearance. He was influenced by his mother, a Russian Leuchtenburg, who ardently desired the match, to get engaged to the young Grand Duchess Helen. But when he thought the matter over, he decided that a marriage with the young and pretty Princess, whom Alvensleben described as temperamental and in need of love, would not be to his liking, and he broke off the engagement. Grand Duke Vladimir accepted this broken engagement in his usual phlegmatic way and comforted his weeping daughter by saying: "*Ne pleures pas, ma chérie, Karlsruhe aurait été pour toi un enterrement sans pompe.*" Grand Duchess Vladimir, on the other hand, was furious, and her devotion to her German home was abated by the incident. The charming Grand Duchess Helen Vladimirovna later married a Greek Prince, who seemed to have had the characteristics which Prince Max of Baden lacked.

Shortly before the end of the year 1901, the last monument in the *Siegesallee* was unveiled. In my opinion the *Siegesallee* is not as bad as its reputation. Donna Laura Minghetti, who combined an innate sense of beauty with the experience gained by her acquaintance with many artists including Morelli, Lenbach, Makart, Barnabei, Baracco, Nieuwekerke, Carpeaux, Ary Scheffer, and others, did not think that the monuments in the *Siegesallee* should have been made of marble, which was not effective in the North. She believed that, to be effective, marble needed a Greek or Italian sun. She also thought that the statues as a whole were somewhat monotonous, seeing that the Hohenzollerns they represented all struck an attitude of excessive self-assurance. Otherwise she did not think the *Siegesallee* so bad. But even the most friendly observers smiled when the Kaiser, in a speech which I did not hear, compared modern schools of German sculptors favourably with the classical age of Greeks, Romans, and the Italian Renaissance. He did not compare himself with Pericles, but he did compare himself with Lorenzo de' Medici and he expressed the hope that his grandchildren and great-grandchildren would also be surrounded by masters as great as those who had helped him build the *Siegesallee*. "The *Siegesallee* makes an overwhelming impression on strangers. An immense respect for German sculpture is noticeable everywhere." In this speech he did not fail to make a violent attack on modern art, which he called an "art that descends into the gutter." The effect of this speech tended to separate the Kaiser, who in some ways was modern and progressive, even more widely from German

intellectuals. I was so busy trying to keep the Kaiser on the
straight and narrow path politically, that I had no time to discuss
aesthetic problems with him. Besides, such discussions would probably have been useless, for Kaiser William was a complete dilettante, and, as is well known, a dilettante's chief characteristic is
his ignorance of the difficulty and the seriousness of art. Once
when Kaiser William II announced that he would dine with us in
our home, I arranged to have him sit next to Cosima Wagner who
happened to be in Berlin. They had a long and interesting conversation. Later, when I asked Frau Wagner, one of the most
distinguished women I ever met in my life, how she had got on
with the Kaiser, she said: "As a human being he is very charming, but it would take me three years on a lonely island to teach
him even the fundamentals of art."

I learned from Frau Cosima Wagner that our dear old friend
Malwida von Meysenbug was not very well. I wrote to her at
once and tried to comfort her, saying: "I hope deeply that you will
soon be better. Why should you not grow as old as the Sybil
of Cumae, who had seen 700 years when Aeneas found her, and
who lived three centuries thereafter? I think of you often. We
are separated by outward appearances, but we are united by
eternal values." She answered with a longish letter which, because
of her illness, it took her five or six days to write. I quote this
answer, because it reflects the marvellous spirit of this wonderful
woman:

No, dear friend, I would not like to live 700 years like the Sybil of
Cumae, for if you take a bird's eye view of history, as I do now, ideals
seem to pass by and only in great, pure, and rare souls are they ever
realised. There is, however, judging by my state this winter, not much
chance of my living even 300 years. And now, in conclusion, a little
story of my innermost experience. No one else but you will know it, for
to tell it would be to desecrate it. But it is the answer to your dear
words: that we are united by eternal values. At the same time this
little story is my friendship's legacy to you which will remind you
of me when, in a short while, I shall have left the world of outward
events. During recent sleepless nights, when my illness was at its

worst, my mind was completely clear and free and I pondered over the highest problems of life. One night, when my mind seemed particularly clear, I felt completely removed from the temporal world, I felt as though I were enjoying the highest ecstacy of fundamental being. Nothing was clearly outlined, I saw no distinct picture, the last veil had not yet been removed, but I felt the presence of the Perfect. And I asked: What is it? Is it love? Great, pure, and liberating love? No, it is something even higher, was the answer, it is the Eternal, the only Truth, the ever Creative, the all embracing. And I floated as though on waves of unspeakable delight and suddenly a voice called from the depths of the Soul, my real Self called, the Self which so rarely speaks in the turmoil of everyday life: "I adore."

This was the last letter I ever received from this "idealist."

Late in 1901 I received a telegram from King Albert of Saxony, in which he expressed the wish that the New Year might give me health and strength for the good of the Empire. A few months later this noble and distinguished King died.

CHAPTER XXXV

Chamberlain's Speech in Edinburgh (October 25, 1901) — Insult to German Army — Conference with the British Ambassador — Instructions to the German Embassy in London — The Honour of Our Army Defended in the Reichstag — The Kaiser's Birthday (January 27, 1902) — Bülow's Conference with the Prince of Wales, Subsequently George V — Incident in Venezuela — President Castro — Rudyard Kipling — Politics and the Eastern Marches — Speeches in the Reichstag and Prussian Diet on the Eastern Marches — William II's Speech at Marienburg.

ON October 25th, Chamberlain, the Colonial Minister, whose quick vacillations Count Hatzfeldt and Count Metternich had often mentioned in their despatches, made a speech in Edinburgh, in which he said that even if England were to assume the severest measures against the Boers in South Africa, who were still offering resistance, no such measures could possibly be as cruel and as barbarous as those adopted by other nations, in Poland, in the Caucasus, in Bosnia, in Tongking, and during the War of 1870. I foresaw that this provocation would stir up considerable excitement in Germany, and I at once asked for a confidential interview with the British Ambassador to Germany, Sir Frank Lascelles, who was politically friendly towards us and whom I had known personally for a quarter of a century. In this interview I asked Lascelles sub rosa, and so as not to offend his pride in any way, whether he could not do something to urge Chamberlain to counteract the impression his speech had made in Germany. Chamberlain need only say that it had not been his intention to offend either the German people or the German Army. Even a simple statement about the manliness and the virile discipline of the German Army would have sufficed. Another member of the English Cabinet might make a statement of this kind, or Chamberlain might hand Count Metternich a letter which I could read aloud in the Reichstag, so I could repel any attack that would be made against him

in the expected debate. I told the English Ambassador that I would
otherwise, and much to my regret, be obliged to defend the honour of
the German people and the German Army in public. The Russian's
savage battles against Shamyl, the battles of the French with the
"Black Flags" in Tongking, the Austrian punitive expeditions
against the Bosnian insurgents, and the Russian's often brutal
repression of Polish revolts could not be mentioned in the same
breath as the defensive war we had waged against France. Chamberlain should, instead, have referred to Napoleon I and the shooting
of Palm, of Andreas Hofer, and of Schill's officers. On the contrary,
we could remind the world of the declaration which Emperor
William I made in 1870, at the beginning of the Franco-Prussian
War: "We are not waging war against peaceful inhabitants."
Sir Frank understood my point of view fully. He said to me on
his own initiative that Chamberlain's statement had been all the
more regrettable because, during the entire Boer War, I had bravely
opposed anti-English feeling in Germany and also because I was
so consistently friendly towards England.

But Lascelles did not succeed in persuading Chamberlain to
make any sort of statement. Our Embassy in London was also
unable to achieve anything of this kind. A Liberal Member in the
House asked Chamberlain why he had offended German public
opinion without any reason at all. Chamberlain replied haughtily:
that no sensible German could have been offended by what he
had said and that the indignation in Germany must have been
artificially created. This, of course, only poured oil into the fire.
I am convinced now, as I was then, that the British Colonial
Minister's haughty manner made it my duty, when his insults
were discussed in the Reichstag during the budget debate of 1902,
not only to defend the heroic character and the ethical foundations
of our struggles for unity but also to repudiate the English Minister's "crooked judgment." It is understandable, I pointed out,
that a people which is so closely and intimately knit with its army
as we Germans are, will rise up even against the mere shadow of an
insult to the people and the army. I assumed, I said, that Mr.
Chamberlain had not intentionally offended us. But even mis-

understandings should be avoided as far as a country like Germany was concerned, for we had always made an effort to maintain good, friendly, and untroubled relations with England. Our army was too exalted, its shield was too bright even to be touched by unjust attacks. An utterance of Frederick the Great's suited this occasion: "Let the man alone and don't be excited; for he is biting granite." When, in the course of the debate, Liebermann von Sonnenberg, one of the extreme Pan-German and anti-Semitic Members, who always liked to break window panes in foreign countries, used a strong expression against the British Colonial Minister, I at once spoke again and expressed my satisfaction because of the fact that the speaker of the Reichstag had censured Herr von Liebermann. I declared, furthermore, that I was convinced that the great majority of the Reichstag was on my side when I expressed the hope that it would not become a custom in the German Reichstag to insult foreign Ministers. This would not be in accord with the habits of the German people, who were an orderly people, nor would such a custom promote our political interests. At the same time I expressed my deep regret at the manner in which the Deputy, Liebermann, had referred to the army of a nation with which we were living in peace and friendship. If we were sensitive to insults to our army, we must not offend foreign armies, for these, too, included men who knew how to die. This reproof was cheered all over the House. I also met with approval when in the further course of the debate I declared that I refused to let myself be forced into an unfriendly attitude towards the English people who had never been our enemies and to whom we were bound by many important mutual interests. I refused to have my foreign policy prescribed by speeches, resolutions, and mass meetings. Our foreign policy was chiefly determined by the country's real interests, and it was in accordance with these interests that we maintained peaceful and friendly relations with England, while upholding our independence, our dignity, and our honour. The attitude of our press and our public opinion towards this incident was, as is unfortunately so often the case in Germany, not uniform or self-confident. A number of German papers, on the one hand, could not emphasise the danger of a war with England emphatically and vividly enough. This was, of course, not to the liking of our own patriots, it encouraged all our adversaries abroad and made the English even more self-conscious and assured than they were already. Military associations and societies, on the other hand, began to make a great noise, and to make such exaggerated statements about Mr. Chamberlain and the English, that quiet observers, such as my friend, August Stein, of the "*Frankfurter Zeitung*", were justified in thinking that they were in a lunatic asylum. I communicated with the Ministry of War and the Ministry of Education, urging them to dissuade the military associations from activities of this kind. The agitation soon subsided. But the whole incident had again shown how excessively anti-English sentiment in Germany was and how unchangeably self-assured and haughty the English were. Two decades have passed since this incident. A completely objective, calm, and purely historical view of the case confirms me in my opinion that I owed it not only to the dignity of our country to make a stand against Chamberlain's insult, but that, politically speaking, it was in the interest of our country for me to do so. Bismarck used to say: "He who is green will be eaten by the goats." If thoughtless and provocative statements made abroad are not repudiated, and if the inexcusable slights of foreign ministers are tolerated, then future attacks will only be provoked and, in the end, general ill-treatment will have been invited. Many years later, after my resignation, when Lloyd George offended the German Empire in connexion with the *Panther's* cruise to Agadir, Bethmann-Hollweg was silent and accepted this insult without a word. Eight weeks later, one of the wisest of Italian diplomats, who had been in London and Rome, said to me: "I, who have been optimistic about the European situation, am beginning to be uneasy about it. The fact that the German Chancellor quietly accepted Lloyd George's insults makes people in England think that Germany is no longer sure of herself. What is even more serious is that the French have become very arrogant since then." The "*esprit nouveau*" was born in France at the moment when Lloyd George's insult was tamely accepted in Berlin.

The Prince of Wales came to Berlin for the Kaiser's birthday on January 27, 1902, at the special wish of his father, Edward VII, who wanted to prove by his son's presence that German-English relations were as friendly and peaceful as ever. After the gala banquet in the *Weisse Saal*, a *Bierabend* was held in the *Heinrich Saal*. William II was fond of informal talks after formal occasions. We had hardly found our seats, when the Prince of Wales came over to me, shook hands, and asked me whether he might hope for a chance to have a frank talk with me. Before and after the banquet I had avoided approaching His Royal Highness myself but rather let him come to me. When the Prince spoke to me so kindly and so frankly, I of course replied at once that I would be very grateful if I could have a frank talk with His Highness. I asked for permission to be as frank as he was himself. The Prince, who made a very clear-headed, sensible, and manly impression, began by mentioning Mr. Chamberlain's great services to England. "We owe it to him that a loyal British spirit now reigns in the Colonies. He originated the idea of a great British Empire. My father, Edward VII, must take this fact into account. Mr. Chamberlain, by the way, assured me before my departure that he had never had any intention of offending the German Army and the German people." I answered that His Majesty the King of England was the only one competent to judge an English Minister's services to England. "But I too," I added, "am far from underestimating the English Colonial Minister's great gifts and achievements; indeed, I admire them very much. I do not doubt that Mr. Chamberlain had no intention of offending Germany. But he made a mistake in not putting the English army and English customs of war and the German army and German customs of war on an equal footing. If he had done this we could not have been offended. Instead, he declared that occurrences in connexion with the war England was conducting in South Africa fell far short of certain things that had occurred in the War of 1870–71. And so, bearing in mind the justified resentment of the German people as well as of the Army, whose uniform I had worn for thirty years, I was forced to make a solemn repudiation of this statement." The

Prince said that I must not forget that Mr. Chamberlain, as Colonial Minister, had spoken to English merchants who understood only colonial affairs, and that his Edinburgh speech had been made from their point of view. I replied that I, too, was obliged to adjust my manner of speaking to my audience. "If I had the honour of making a speech before Your Highness and before all the other Royal guests now assembled in the *Heinrich Saal*, the speech would differ from a speech held before an assembly of German agriculturists, lawyers, and professors. But on the whole it is my opinion that Ministers, whether it be Mr. Chamberlain or myself, should not talk too often, particularly about foreign affairs." The Prince agreed heartily and smiled. Then when he expressed his great satisfaction at the most gracious way he had been received in Berlin, I replied that I had never doubted that the heir to the British throne could be received any other way. "I admit," I said, "that it is not quite easy to explain the present feeling in Germany against England. Because of various incidents, both recent and more remote, people in Germany feel that they are being badly treated by England." Then I gave His Royal Highness a brief summary of Anglo-German relations from the time of the Crimean War and the solution of the Schleswig-Holstein question to the time of the Samoa question and the seizure of our postal boats. Besides, as I pointed out, sympathy was felt for the Boers throughout Europe and all over the world. "But no sensible German has any wish to weaken England politically. Apart from this, Kaiser William II would never pursue an anti-English policy as long as England makes it possible for him to maintain friendly relations. The outcry and scolding on the part of the press here and in England is silly, but it does not endanger peace as long as the Governments themselves remain calm. The German and the English Government are quite capable of maintaining peaceful and friendly relations between the two countries and of assuring an even closer coöperation in the future." The Prince followed my politico-historical remarks with interest, expressed cordial agreement with my conclusions, and then said literally: "My father asks me to tell you that he considers you as his friend now as before. He is convinced that you are just as concerned about maintaining friendly relations with England as he is concerned about maintaining friendly relations with Germany. He only asks you to avoid future recriminations regarding the past and to see that the family letters written in connexion with my visit here for the Kaiser's, my cousin's, birthday celebrations, are not made public. We must forget the past and strive only to be friends in the future." When I, of course, promised him complete discretion and assured him of my political good will, the Prince took leave of me after pressing my hand several times and after assuring me what a relief and pleasure it had been to him to talk to me frankly.

As after a heavy storm, when Poseidon is no longer stirring up the winds, but when, for some time, the movement of the sea is still reflected in the swell, so the aversion and dislike of Germany in England, which had become acute during the Boer War, made itself felt. It was very marked during the Venezuela affair, when, late in November, 1902, the German and the English Governments were making a joint effort to collect the sums owing to German and English subjects by the Venezuelan Government and which this Government stubbornly refused to pay. When the Venezuelan Government continued to refuse to meet its obligations, the German and the English diplomatic representatives were recalled, and the Venezuelan "fleet" of four small boats was seized at La Guaira, and a German and an English vessel destroyed a fort at Puerto Cabello. When, a few days later, England and Germany began the blockade of La Guaira, the President of Venezuela, Mr. Castro, a particularly objectionable individual, accepted my suggestion that the case be submitted to arbitration at the Hague Court. The German and the English Governments coöperated with complete understanding, with loyalty, and with great tact during this incident. Some English newspapers, however, made a sharp and savage outcry against any coöperation with Germany. The *"Times"* declared that any coöperation of this kind was impossible, because the German people, if not the German Government, had been so anti-English during the Boer War. The English poet, Rudyard Kipling, a very gifted man, about whose picturesque descriptions of Indian nature and life Kaiser William was enthusiastic but who was very much of a demagogue and whose chief aim was to please "the man in the street", published sharply pointed and very perfidious verses against any coöperation between Germany and England, even though this coöperation was only in Venezuela.

Our new Ambassador in London, Count Metternich, who succeeded the late Count Paul Hatzfeldt (who died November 22, 1901), wrote to me about Kipling's verses:

The Venezuela affair shows that the anti-German feeling created here during the Boer War is still stronger than common sense or the self-interest of the English. The delusion which seized our own public opinion during the Boer War has now moved across the Channel. The English Government, which has become somewhat unpopular because of its coöperation with Germany in connexion with the Venezuela affair, has acted well. In to-day's "*Times*", Lord Lansdowne objected strongly to Rudyard Kipling's poem. In critical periods, however, it is difficult, particularly in England, to exert any influence on the great newspapers. They are not easily influenced even by the Government. The English press was never as hostile towards us as it was last year when Eckardstein, who only retired recently, was still in charge of our press department. I am far from wanting to reproach him for having left anything undone. No one could have done better, save only if the two Governments had been less hostile to one another than they have been during the last few years. But there was reason enough for the friction that has resulted in the present attitude towards Germany. Personally I consider that this sentiment has been caught from Germany. We ourselves are recovering, but here the crisis of the fever and therefore the delirium have only just been reached.

Paul Metternich did not have the streak of genius which his predecessor, Paul Hatzfeldt, had, but he possessed a great deal of common sense and an unshakable reserve, and these are surely characteristics that are very much needed by a diplomat in critical days.

My birthday on May 3, 1902, was made all the more beautiful for me because Field Marshal von Loë, who happened to be in Berlin, did us the honour of saying that he would come for dinner.

He wore the uniform of our old Regiment and drank my health. Several days later he sent me a copy of his speech. I quote it herewith:

My very much honoured benefactress:

I received your invitation to be present among your intimate friends to-day with the greatest possible joy. You increased my joy by granting my request that I might make a speech and to express my respect and admiration for your husband on this occasion. I do not deny that I hesitated before making this request. For I am not sure whether I shall succeed in finding a form worthy of the general enthusiasm for him. I hesitate to speak before listeners who are accustomed to admire the Chancellor not only as a great statesman, but as a masterly speaker as well. But now that I have begun to speak, I no longer feel hesitant. I am encouraged by the knowledge that I am the Chancellor's oldest friend amongst those gathered here, and that, as such, I have followed his career from the beginning with shining eyes and a warm heart. I shall therefore speak straight from the heart and then I know that you will be satisfied with me. Not long ago, in Rome, I was asked what was the most beautiful memory of my whole long and happy career. I answered: to have commanded a Regiment during a victorious War, to have commanded a Regiment which was ahead of the whole army in the number of distinguished men it produced. I need not mention that among these men, and there are many of them, I thought primarily of the Chancellor. I received the opportunity of watching his development from his father, my close friend, the Secretary of State von Bülow. When the War with France broke out, he himself chose the King's Hussar Regiment for his promising eldest son. It was early in November, 1870, immediately after the fall of Metz and before the beginning of the Northern Campaign, that I inspected the reserve squadron in Bonn. The young Hussar, von Bülow, came to me at this time with a letter from his father. Having joined the 1st squadron, he took part in all the battles of the Northern Campaign. Mindful of his name that was renowned throughout the army the young Hussar distinguished himself so brilliantly in splendid rivalry with his comrades, especially as a patrol, that I was soon able to recommend him for promotion. On January 19, the victorious day of Saint Quentin, he was promoted to the rank of ensign and shortly after he was made an officer. Soon after peace was declared, he again resumed the career he had originally chosen, but his participation in the victorious campaign, his period of active service, considerably enhanced his inborn love of the army. The conviction, indispensable for every Prussian Statesman, namely, that the army is the *"rocher de bronze"* of the Prussian State, was his, unshakably. His ideals in this respect and our mutual memories of the campaign were the bond between this courageous young man and his Commander-in-Chief. This bond, between the Chancellor at the height of his power and the old General, who looks back cheerfully upon his past, has remained unaltered. Our friendship, which has lasted for thirty years, and which began on the battlefields of France, is one of the most valuable achievements of my career. Our own friendship and our family ties caused me to follow this young officer's career attentively after he was no longer in the service. I noticed the gravity with which the young man always kept his aim in view. I observed the iron industry with which he studied the history, the language, and the laws of the foreign country in which he was stationed. This arduously acquired ability to understand foreign situations and people helped him in the gigantic difficulties of the very responsible position he now holds. I am referring to the objectivity of his judgment, his charming manner which is so apparent in his oral and written word, in his diplomatic and political activities, and the urbanity of his ways, all things that have made it possible for him, even when he is vehemently attacked by his bitterest enemies, to carry out his watchword: *"Suaviter in modo, fortiter in re."* *Fortiter in re* — the very essence of his politics is to be found in this part of the watchword, which is the foundation of his character. The *suaviter in modo* is the precious frame. Such a character is not fully formed when a man is young. On the contrary, a character of this kind is hardened and consolidated in a man's fighting life. The prerequisite for such an evolution is a belief in life's ideals that are visioned by the youth and are unshakably held by the man in all life's circumstances. The Chancellor's idealism is the soil in which his personality has so firmly taken root. I watched this plant unfolding and growing and I was fortunate enough to tend it in its youth. And what are the ideal aims the Chancellor follows: stars that shine ahead of him on his difficult path? They are, above all, his faith in the historical mission of the Hohenzollern and in the Army which they created. This faith is the foundation of his loyalty to his King and the corner stone of his politics. His ideal aims are also his conscientious love of duty and justice and his respect for the rights of others from which this love springs — this great, human, and statesmanlike virtue which assures him at home of the confidence of all citizens alike, no matter what their religion, class, or party, and which assures him of the confidence of all leading persons in all foreign countries regardless of their nationality. If he shares our realisation that the general confidence in him is the chief source of his strength, then he is all the more aware that His Majesty's confidence is, above all, the rock on which he stands. I have tried to express in a few words the sentiments which fill us all to-day. But I would not have performed my duty well, if I did not include amongst the ideals of our birthday child the one which is nearest to his heart. I have said that his life is made up of work and effort and that as a reward he has won the confidence of the Kaiser and of the Nation. But the happiness without which every man walks the path of duty in loneliness — the most intimate happiness of life is given him by this gracious lady, into whose eyes he is now gazing. Her tender love is not only the ornament of his life; more than that she helps him to maintain his enthusiasm for his profession. She helps him in the moments of disappointment which are spared no one. It is her heartfelt understanding for the man who is so necessary to the country which preserves the Chancellor for the Kaiser and for Germany. That is her great service which will not be forgotten by history. Now, I think you will agree when I ask you to join me in the heartfelt words: Count and Countess Bülow *sie leben hoch*.

None of the praise I received throughout my whole life pleased me more than this speech by my old Commander in Chief.

From the beginning of my term of office as German Chancellor and Prussian Premier, I had been particularly interested in the problems of our Eastern Marches. I wrote during the World War, 1916, in the special edition of my book about "German Politics", at the end of the chapter dealing with the Eastern Marches, that I considered this one of our most important problems, but I had realised this fact fifteen years before when I was studying conditions in these regions and when I was supplementing my own knowledge by talks with men who knew Posen, West Prussia, and Upper Silesia from personal experience. These men included first of all *Geheimrat* Conrad, who was then the Chief of the Chancellery and who was born in West Prussia; Staudy, who was Chief of Police in Posen for many years, Minister of Education Studt, who had been stationed in the Eastern Provinces for many years, *Regierungspräsident* von Tiedemann of Bromberg and many others. History proves that Germany's attempts to win the Poles by meeting them half way have never been successful; they show on the contrary that these attempts have only harmed German interests. After Posen and West Prussia had been reacquired, Frederick William III treated his Polish subjects with the greatest kindness. Far-reaching consideration was shown for their special characteristics, Polish agriculture was particularly promoted, Polish higher local officials [1] could be elected and were elected, the Prussian Governor was assisted by a Polish *Stadtholder*. The result was the Insurrection of 1830. One advantage, at least, was derived from this Insurrection, namely, that the leadership of new men in the Eastern provinces and the names of General von Grolman and Governor von Flottwell will always be honourably mentioned in German history. But they had only ten years in which to carry out German policy in the East. Frederick William IV, who was a romantic, and appreciated reasons of State far less than his sober-minded father, really found "the rascally State", as he called it, very unsympathetic. By way of penalty he transferred the excellent Governor von Flottwell from Posen to Magdeburg. Frederick William IV reintroduced the unsuccessful policies in vogue between 1815 and 1830; he undertook a so-called "national reorganisation" of Posen and West Prussia, which resulted in a complete political fiasco, even before the events of 1848 gave the Polish agitators an opportunity to show their real aims and sentiments.

A change and a turn for the better did not come until Bismarck, who in this, as well as in so many things, followed up the Great King's [2] traditions, through the Settlers' Law of 1886, began the struggle for the land in these provinces on a big scale. This settlement scheme became the basis of Prussian policy in the Eastern provinces, for it meant that Germans were established in these regions. After Bismarck's dismissal, conditions again deteriorated. Count Caprivi had a marvellous chance when he began his term of office to promote German civilisation in the Eastern provinces. The agricultural depression caused the price

[1] *Landräte.*   [2] Frederick the Great.

of estates to fall rapidly. It would have been simple at that time to purchase land from Polish estate owners and on this land Germans could have been settled later on. But Caprivi thought it was once more time to change the policy regarding the Eastern provinces. That he met the Poles half way in matters of school and church was tolerable. I always believed that it was neither necessary nor politically wise to vex the Poles in this respect. But Caprivi went so far as to subsidise the Polish *Landbank* and so to assist the Polish estate owners from whom the Settlement Commission should really have bought up land. It has been claimed that Caprivi, who saw things from a purely military point of view and who was of a very stubborn nature, believed that a war with Russia was inevitable and that for this reason he thought it advisable to reëstablish an independent Polish State. I think that this is an unjust claim. Caprivi harboured too great a sentiment for Prussia, he was too devoted to the State to have been ensnared by ideas of this kind. He probably looked upon the Poles like a Frederickan General, who might have been quite willing to have the Croats and Slovenes organise their own regiments, but who would never have permitted these regiments to endanger the Prussian Monarchy. The thought of establishing an independent Polish State on our Eastern frontiers could have occurred only to a Bethmann-Hollweg, who had no understanding for the traditions handed down to us by our Great King and our greatest statesman, and who, applauded by Hans Delbrück, Riezler (Rüdorffer), and other fools, and perhaps encouraged and influenced by Austria, made this terrible mistake and put the axe to the roots of the Prussian State.

I was convinced from the beginning that we must, above all, have a stable policy in the East. Nothing had harmed us more than our vacillations and the constant return to old mistakes. I was forced to admit on the other hand — as Count Posadowsky, who had been in the Province of Posen for a long time once pointed out with a sad face during a meeting of the Prussian Cabinet — that the Eastern Marches were not only a problem as far as the Poles in Germany were concerned, but a problem that concerned as well the Germans living among the Poles. I realised that by reason of our good, and also of some of our less admirable qualities, we Germans did not have the desired resistance in any struggle between nationalities and that, in this struggle, there was often a danger that the Germans would lose their national characteristics if the Government did not support and help them. The fact that the national sentiment of the Germans is weak was one of the chief dangers involved in the question of the Eastern Marches. But this weakness proved to me most emphatically that we must pursue a strong and stable policy in these regions. We simply did not possess the qualities, which made it possible for the French to assimilate at least the upper classes in Alsace-Lorraine or to Gallicise Nice or Corsica. Austria shows what happens to the Germans if the State does not hold a protecting hand over them. I knew that the German national sentiment was hemmed in and reduced in Bohemia, Moravia, Carinthia, and in southern Styria as soon as it was not supported by Vienna. I also realised that German national sentiment in Galicia and Hungary was ousted and assimilated when it could no longer cling to Vienna. I was free from any sentimental feelings towards the Poles. I had not forgotten the attitude of the Polish intelligentsia in 1830 or 1848, nor had I forgotten the massacre of Thorn or the first Battle of Tannenberg, the worst defeat we had suffered for centuries. Nor had I forgotten how the Poles themselves treated the Ruthenes in Galicia. The Ruthenes living near the Carpathian Mountains and near the Pruth complained more bitterly, and with greater justification, about the Poles than the Poles living on the Warthe and the Vistula complained about us. I never doubted the fact that if the Poles ever succeeded in subjecting the Germans, they would govern these unfortunates with the greatest harshness and outrageous arrogance.

Weighty considerations of foreign policy also influenced me in my attitude towards the question of the Eastern Marches. One of the most important provisos for the maintenance of friendly relations with Russia (we ourselves, through our errors, had cut ourselves off from Russia and made the Franco-Russian Alliance possible) was a firm policy as far as Poland was concerned. Every time we gave way to the agitation instigated by the Pan-Polish Movement, we awakened suspicion in St. Petersburg, where, since the days of Caprivi, we were suspected of trying to secure Polish coöperation in case of a war against Russia. I always believed that it was in our own interests to avoid a war with Russia. I was convinced that such a conflict could be avoided in all honour and dignity. I believed, above all, that no greater disaster could happen to us than the reëstablishment of an independent Polish state. I was not converted to this opinion *post festum*, after the experiment of Bethmann-Hollweg and his friends proved to be such a terrible fiasco. From the day on which I became Chancellor I was convinced of the danger to us of an independent Polish State and of the necessity of preserving and protecting German national sentiment in the Eastern Marches as consistently and energetically as possible. For many years I kept Treitschke's magnificent essay on Prussia, the land of the Teutonic Order, on my desk. This was why I had declared in the Reichstag in my speech of December 10, 1901, that reasons of State and my duty towards German national sentiment were the only factors which would determine my policy regarding the Eastern Marches. I said that I would always remember my duty. In view of the serious danger which, in my opinion, confronted the Germans in the East, I would do my duty so that the Germans in the East would not go under.[1]

At that time a trivial incident in a board school in the small town of Wreschen led to anti-German demonstrations in front of the German Consulates at Warsaw and Lemberg. In Warsaw the Russian police suppressed these demonstrations energetically. In Lemberg the attitude of the Austrian Imperial and Royal officials was weak and ambiguous: I pointed this out in my speech in the Reichstag, which made the Austrian representative in Berlin, my old friend Szögyényi, very unhappy, but it was a useful *avis au lecteur* for the Ballplatz in Vienna. In a speech in the Prussian Diet, on January 13, 1902, which lasted two hours,[2] I explained my

[1] Prince Bülow's "Speeches", (large edition), I. 227; (small edition), II. 22.
[2] Prince Bülow's "Speeches", (large edition), I. 256; (small edition), II. 93.

attitude regarding the question of the Eastern Marches thoroughly and in detail. I particularly repudiated the reproach that I intended to infringe the rights of the Catholic Church in the East or to wound the feelings of the Catholic inhabitants. I said that everywhere and at all times I intended to respect the religious feelings of these inhabitants. I would never organise the country according to religions. My policy would be no more Protestant than Catholic, nor would it be any more Liberal than Conservative, in a party sense. As far as I was concerned there was neither a Protestant nor a Catholic, neither a Conservative nor a Liberal Germany : before my eyes there was always the one and indivisible Nation, indivisible materially and spiritually. A statement of this kind was needed because in Germany, unfortunately, people saw things not only in the light of their own particular religious views, but also of their own party interests and prejudices. Wretched party quarrels and, last but not least, separatist tendencies were stronger than national considerations or reasons of state. In other great countries such a declaration would not have been necessary. I explained that I was liberal in thought in many ways but that in national questions I would stand no pleasantries. We were not living in Cloud-Cuckoo-Land but on this hard earth, where one must either be the hammer or the anvil. After discussing the administrative regulations which the Government was planning for the Eastern Marches, I said that I agreed with Deputy Hobrecht, Bismarck's Minister of Finance, who had spoken before me, when he declared that he considered the Eastern Marches not only one of the most important of our political problems but also one on which the immediate future of our Fatherland absolutely depended. I quoted the words of our greatest poet in this connexion : "*Was du ererbt von deinen Vätern hast, erwirb es, um es zu besitzen.*" [1]

Our wretched Party politics made it difficult for me to carry out my Eastern policy to which I clung until the last day of my Chancellorship. My dear friend, Prince Franz Arenberg, a Member of the Centre Party, told me from the beginning that many

---

[1] What thou hast inherited from thy ancestors, achieve it, so as to possess it.

members of the Party realised the necessity of taking some action against the insolent Polish agitation and of protecting the Germans in the East, but a consideration of parliamentary tactics prevented them from making a stand against the Polish Party. My honoured friend and benefactor, Cardinal Kopp, a sharp opponent of the Poles, who in Upper Silesia resisted their influence with a firmness beyond all praise, said to me: "I will support you wherever I can. But the Germans, being what they are, the catchword of the bond between the German and the Polish Catholics, will always impress German Catholics. It would never impress the Poles in the slightest, and besides, I do not believe that a Polonisation of our Eastern Marches would be at all in the interests of the Catholic Church." The shrewd Cardinal had realised very early how dangerous the fanatically anti-German agitator Korfanty would be to the Prussian State and to Germany as a whole. During my Chancellorship the Cardinal was already taking steps against this evil creature. The time was to come when Korfanty would enjoy the favour of the Prussian Government. Count Hutten-Czapski, a Pole, who never denied his Polish nationality, but who did his duty as a Prussian officer during the World War and later became Commandant of the Palace in Posen and a member of the Prussian Upper Chamber, told me that in the summer of 1914 he had to his surprise ascertained that Korfanty, who was being watched suspiciously and not without reason by our military authorities, was treated with respect and confidence in the Chancellery by his Excellency Wahnschaffe and, one story higher up, by the Chancellor Bethmann-Hollweg.

The day after my big speech on the Polish question, Herr von Tiedemann-Seeheim, the Chairman of the Ostmarkenverein, wrote to Conrad, the chief of the Chancellery:

I have joyfully observed how the Chancellor has succeeded in winning the sympathy of the Prussian and the German people in ever-growing measure. I meet so many different classes of people that I know I am right when I make this statement. It is my innermost conviction that yesterday the Chancellor succeeded in winning the unreserved confidence of the soul of Germany. The results of Bülow's success cannot as yet be estimated: he has shown the world that he is capable of riding the difficult horse of domestic politics wisely and well. A leading statesman can achieve great things only if he is sure of the eager support of the good and loyal elements in his country. The Chancellor can now be sure of this support. I need not mention to you, who were born in the Eastern Marches, that the path he points out is the right one and that it will lead to victory in the problem of the Eastern Marches.

On the same day the Prussian Minister in Munich reported:

Count Crailsheim assured me to-day how joyfully he welcomed the impressive firmness with which your Excellency replied to the Wrescher Interpellation. The Poles are incorrigible and the firmer the stand which the Prussian Government takes against their efforts to Polonise the Eastern Marches, the greater will be its services to Germany. He, the Minister, did not fail to observe the difference in tone in which Your Excellency referred to our two neighbours. Flabby Austria, if it is still possible to speak of an Imperial and Royal Government in Galicia, could not have complained even if you had used stronger language. All nationally-minded people here are as pleased about your speech as the Minister is. The liberal Press continues commendably to destroy the fairy tales spread by the Poles. At the same time the renewed maltreatment of the non-Polish majority in Galicia by the *Slachta* is being pointed out and Radziwill and his companions are being told to get their own dirty houses in order first. All comments here close with the hope that the Prussian Government will stand firm and that there may never again be cause to complain about weak relapses.

The Kaiser, who loved festivities, particularly such as had a historical background (his enthusiasm for historical grandeur was quite genuine), decided to hold a Chapter meeting of the Order of St. John in the magnificent Marienburg on June 5, 1902. He particularly wished me to attend this meeting and expressed the wish that I should wear the same magnificent uniform as he. Anyone who did not know William II personally will find it difficult to imagine how very charming he was; his charm was all the more bewitching as it was so natural and sincere. The Kaiser's simplicity of mind in the best sense of the word, which made him so attractive to his friends and his servants, became a political danger when he was confronted with strangers and adver-

saries.   Before the solemn church service began in the St. Mary's
Chapel of the Castle, the Kaiser came to my room to see with his
own eyes that my uniform was absolutely correct.   When he asked
my Italian valet, whom he knew well because he accompanied us
on all our journeys, how he liked me as a Knight of St. John, the
valet replied : *"Il cancelliere é magnifico, somiglia a un antico
romano del Trastevere."*   My worthy valet, who had been born
in the Sabine hills, considered an old Roman, especially if he came
from the popular quarter on the other side of the Tiber, as the
essence of all that was magnificent.

In the morning the Kaiser received the Governor General of
Warsaw, who had been sent to welcome him.   General Tchertkoff,
a typical general of the old school, made such an impression on the
Kaiser that he improvised a speech in his honour.   What he said
was roughly as follows : his relations with Russia were so intimate
that he had decided to give up Posen as a fortress, for he needed no
military protection against a friend like the Tsar.   The old Russian,
who, like many of his kind, possessed a certain amount of shrewdness, said to me later (I had met him before in St. Petersburg) :
*" Sa Majesté l'Empereur a parlé comme Cicéron, mais, entre nous,
ce qu'il m'a dit sur Posen ne tient pas debout.   Posen ne vaut plus
rien comme forteresse et vous construisez d'autres forteresses qui rem-
placement Posen avantageusement."*

I took a walk around the Marienburg with my old friend and
regimental comrade, Count August von Dönhoff-Friedrichstein.
On one of the towers we discovered a flag with the old Dönhoff
coat of arms, a black wild boar's head with bristles that stood up
in the air.   This flag had been brought here in the sad days when
those German families which had come to the Eastern Marches with
the German Order had joined the Poles.   We were united in the
wish that the Marienburg would never again see such times of German decline and German helplessness.   We did not even guess
that the unfortunate man who fourteen years later was to reëstablish Poland as an independent State, and so to inflict the most
terrible wound on German civilisation in the Eastern Marches,
was a high official in Potsdam even then.

At the gala dinner in the Marienburg on the evening of June 5, 1902, William II made a speech with a fire and an enthusiasm that astonished even Lucanus and myself. The Kaiser reminded his honourable Brethren of the Order of St. John, that the hand of Divine Providence had been more visible in the history of this Order than of any other. When the Order had given up its un-fruitful and hopeless mission in the Holy Land (this was a piece of courtesy meant for the Sultan and the Islam), the Knights, wearing their white coats with the black cross, had come to the Vistula. And then the Kaiser appealed to the Knights of the Order in glow-ing terms to support him in his fight against the Poles. The same Monarch, who often expressed doubts and hesitation concerning my Eastern policy, and who, during the World War, under Beth-mann-Hollweg's influence, reëstablished the Polish State, now, on June 5, 1902, asked the assembled Knights of the Order, who were mostly old and rather stout, to hold their swords in their strong hands and to fight against the Sarmatians, to punish their insolence, and to destroy them. As so often happened before and after this occasion, I forbade the correspondent of the Wolff Telegraph Agency to report this speech literally. On the back of my menu I quickly wrote a new, firm, but dignified and quiet speech which was free from eccentricities. Quick action was needed, because the Kaiser wanted to return to Potsdam half an hour after the banquet. I went over to him with my draft speech. Lucanus followed me. When he read my version, the Kaiser was furious. He particularly insisted on the phrase "punishment of the Sarmatians", though I told him that this would insult the Russians, as they might think it referred to them. We quarreled for a while about the ancient Sarmatians, and whether they had lived on the Vistula or on the Don. The Kaiser referred to Herodotus, I referred to Strabo. Finally His Majesty said: "My speech was worthy of the old Masters of the Order, such as Hermann von Balk or Hermann von Salza. But you make my speech sound as though I were a teacher of history at a school for young ladies." But Lucanus and I in-sisted there was little time and the Kaiser finally gave in after he had given orders to the Chief of his Civil Cabinet to file the original text of the speech in his private archive. "For," the Kaiser said, "I want my successors to know some day how vigorous I was." After the Kaiser had left, the Russian Ambassador, Count Osten-Sacken, who had shuddered when he heard the Kaiser's speech, and who had noticed my discussion with him after dinner, said to me: "*Sa Majesté l'Empereur est charmant, tout ce qu'il y a de séduisant comme homme. Mais comme souverain, il est bien dangereux et cela sans vouloir, au fond, faire du mal à personne. Voilà, il est incohérent! Dieu vous garde auprès de lui.*" At the same time a French writer named Nauzanne wrote in a study of William II: "*Il fallait à l'Allemagne un chef grave, silencieux et mesuré. Le destin lui donné un maître agréable et primesautier, mais faible et énervé. Militaire, il ne l'est que pour ses diplomates, diplomate il ne l'est que pour ses militaires. Aucun chef d'État couronné n'a fait plus de mal à la monarchie et trahi plus complètement et plus inconsciemment la confiance du meilleur de son peuple. On ne peut que le plaindre, tout en rendant hommage à ses qualités de coeur et d'esprit dont une vanité maladive annule tous les bons effets.*"

I have often noticed that even men who are far more gifted than the average human being like to pretend that they have just those qualities which they lack. William II did not really deny that he lacked the *mens aequa*, the *mens solida*, and the *tenacitas propositi* which Quintus Horatius Flaccus demanded of a man. Just for this reason the Kaiser tried to persuade himself and others, by using strong words and making loud speeches, that he was not fundamentally unsure of himself and full of fears. I am told that this tendency increased even more after my retirement, when he had been told that the French called him "William the Timid." During the critical days in July, 1914, I no longer had the honour of being near His Majesty, but I have been told by men who were in his immediate entourage that the very excited and seemingly warlike marginal notes which he made at the time arose from his desire, before and after the unfortunate ultimatum to Serbia, to remove all doubts as to his bravery. And yet the truth is, as I would now like to state by way of anticipation, the Kaiser wanted War as little in 1914 as he did at any time during his reign.

When, forty-eight hours after the festival in the Marienburg, at the session of the Prussian Diet of June 7th, 1902, the Polish Member von Glembocki attacked the Imperial speech held in the Marienburg, I replied: "Everything was right and proper," and when the Poles interrupted me noisily, I repeated once more: "Gentlemen, it was indeed right and proper that His Majesty the Kaiser said these words in the Marienburg of all places. For just as the Minster of Strassburg is a warning signal in the West, the Marienburg is a warning signal in the East, bidding us protect the frontiers of the German realm and German civilisation." [1]

[1] Prince Bülow's "Speeches", (large edition), I. 339; (small edition), II. 86.

CHAPTER XXXVI

The Bagdad Railway — Our Relations with the United States — William II and Roosevelt — Prince Henry's American Trip — Jubilee of the King's Hussars in Bonn; Regimental Parade — Appointed as Colonel à la suite with the Uniform of the King's Hussars — Renewal of the Triple Alliance (June 28, 1902) — Meeting of William II and Nicholas II at Reval — The Swinemünde Telegram; Agitation in Bavaria — Death of Alfred Krupp.

I HAVE already related how the project of the Bagdad Railway was born of a conversation between George von Siemens and myself during the Imperial visit to Constantinople on a trip from Constantinople to Haidar-Pasha as a canoe was carrying us, swift as an arrow, over the blue waters once swum by Leander, eager to clasp his Hero in his arms. At the beginning of January, 1902, the Imperial edict was published proclaiming the railway concession. The Bagdad Railway with its branch lines was to have a length of 2500 kilometres. It was to begin in Konia and pass through Bagdad. The point at which it was to end, on the Persian Gulf, would be settled later by mutual agreement with the Porte. I worked to bring about this last stipulation because I wished to come to an understanding with England in regard to the terminus of the Bagdad Railway and to avoid everything that might arouse opposition or suspicion in the breasts of India's masters. Herr Arthur von Gwinner, the clever successor of George von Siemens, who died regrettably young, shared my view that the splendid project of the Bagdad Railway could only be carried out if England agreed to it. On account of his manifold connexions with that country Herr von Gwinner, after years of working towards this end, had managed to bring about an Anglo-German understanding with regard to the Bagdad enterprise when the Austro-German ultimatum to Serbia put an end to all such hopes and endeavours.

The more difficult our relations with England grew for reasons already laid down, the more assiduously did I further our friendly connexions with the United States. Kaiser William II was not difficult to win over to my standpoint and my efforts to promote it. The active, enterprising, daring, and unwearied American was a type who by reason of his very individuality was bound to appeal to His Majesty the Kaiser. The American multi-millionaire, who was then beginning to come over to Europe more often, pleased the German Emperor in a very high degree. In this respect William II was like his uncle, King Edward, who was also impressed by large sums of money. Theodore Roosevelt, the President of the United States, exercised a quite particular fascination over the Kaiser. "That's my man!" he used to say, as soon as the name of Roosevelt was mentioned. He read in dispatches from our ambassador that Roosevelt performed feats of riding equal to those of a cowboy, that, like Buffalo Bill, he could hit the bull's-eye with deadly marksmanship at a prodigious distance, that his spirit was unquenchable, fearless, and ready for anything. But, as was generally the case with William II, the danger of exaggeration marred ideas that were correct enough in their inception. He soon began corresponding with Roosevelt very much in the way he did with the Tsar. When he showed me his letters, written in excellent English, before sending them off and permitted me to eliminate one or two dangerous turns of speech, what remained could only have a good effect by reason of its spontaneity and forcefulness. But some kind of prophylactic control of this sort was certainly needed. His Majesty's fatal prejudice against the Land of the Rising Sun was also visible in his correspondence with Roosevelt. The Kaiser was everlastingly warning Roosevelt against the scheming plans of the Japanese. He was convinced that war between Japan and the United States was unavoidable and imminent. From the first day I took up office to the last, he clung to this chimerical idea although by reason of my good relations with both Japanese diplomats and Americans I was constantly assuring him of the contrary. I remember that once he told me that during one of his absences from Berlin he had written a "first class" letter to his friend Roosevelt which really would wake him up. As he and I had been separated by distance at the time, he had not been able to show me this letter, but he did not wish to withhold it from me any longer. Besides very strong language against the "Japs", the letter in question contained rather fantastic news of their preparations for war against America and a vigorously worded hint that Roosevelt might be more on his guard than before against the "Yellow Peril." I told the Kaiser that this communication must never reach Roosevelt: on the one hand I thought the contents incorrect in substance, on the other, the Kaiser must never permit such a weapon against himself to fall into Roosevelt's hands. "But," cried the Kaiser, "Roosevelt is my friend!" When I replied that "friends" in this sense did not exist in the world of politics, he looked at me very suspiciously. In the end I managed to hold up the dispatch box that carried the Imperial missive over the Atlantic, just as it was landed in New York, where it was handed out to our representative and sent back unopened to Berlin. I imagine that when the Great War broke out and Roosevelt, like Monaco, Lonsdale, Lacroix and Bonnal and many other "friends" of His Majesty abroad, turned against him, the Kaiser was pleased that at least the rash letter that was to set Roosevelt against Japan was not in the possession of the admired Theodore who was not ashamed in the summer of 1914 of offering a high price to whoever would bring him the Emperor William alive so that he could have him tied up to a post.

After my resignation, I must add in parenthesis, Roosevelt, who had retired from office in the meantime, was received in Berlin on a circular tour through Europe with almost royal honours. The Kaiser originally wanted his friend to stay at the Palace. This did not happen because the Kaiser's uncle, King Edward, had died a few days before. But in spite of deep family mourning, the Kaiser was present at the lecture given by Roosevelt at Berlin University. This lecture was certainly a disappointment to His Majesty. Roosevelt began, as some of those present assured me, in a particularly loud and incisive voice, fixing the Kaiser with a direct gaze and showing all his teeth, with a panegyric on the subject of the "*Mayflower*", the ship that had brought the first English immigrants to America. "The ship was small," so explained Roosevelt, "and had but a small crew. But as freight she bore a load of principles which were to transform the world : the idea of religious freedom, the fundamental rule that a human being should determine his own relationship to his God without allowing the influence of any hierarchic authority as mediator. And she bore as well the great axiom that men themselves may, and should, determine their own earthly rulers, under certain definite assumptions and conditions, since they do not need a rule of absolutism imposed upon them by the unfathomable decrees of Heaven." While Roosevelt was laying down his religious doctrines the Kaiser was merely astonished. At the direct attack upon the Divine Right of Kings he pulled a long face. I again repeat that when all extravagances and exuberances were deducted, the pursuit of the best possible relationship with America on the Kaiser's part was perfectly clear. The antipathy against America which was prevalent in Conservative circles in Germany was foolish. The annoyance felt by our court and society during the Kiel Week festivities at an alleged favouring of Messrs. Vanderbilt, Armour, Pierpont Morgan, and Carnegie was absurd, and the attacks in the press upon these American gentlemen when they visited by royal permission and invitation the Potsdam palaces, the Marienburg or Cadinen, were narrow-minded and petty.

On February 15th, 1902, Prince Henry embarked at Bremerhaven on board the Lloyd boat, *Kronprinz Wilhelm*, for New York. Before his departure I had sent him a long communication in which among other matters I explained that no political activity was expected from the Prince in America. He himself was not expected to bring back either a political treaty or a commercial agreement, or any form of concession either economic, political, or territorial. The aim of his journey was, in the main, to please the Americans and win their sympathies, to convince them of the sentiments felt by the Kaiser and the German nation for the great and powerful American people as well as of the advantage of good connexions between the German and the American nations. America and Germany were not separated by any political differences, but on the contrary bound together by countless and deeply important interests, by old traditions that stretched back to the days of the great Frederick and the great Washington. They were bound by ties of blood as well. The Prince was not to touch upon the Boer War on his own initiative. Should this subject be approached from another quarter it was his business to be as silent as possible. Too lively sympathy with the Boers would not be in keeping with the attitude of neutrality, loyalty, and (within the scope of these sentiments) friendliness we had displayed toward England during the South African War. On the other hand, there was no need for us to act on behalf of England in America. *Chacun pour soi et Dieu pour tout le monde.* Nor was the Prince to speak on his own initiative of conditions in Central and South America, and on no account to let any German aspirations in regard to these countries come to light. If the Americans displayed uneasiness on the subject of German plans to gain a foothold in these regions, the Prince could assuage all such fears by pointing to the peacefulness of our policy and the many other urgent tasks that demanded our attention elsewhere in the world, while dismissing thoughts of military conquest as quite absurd. This would be done better in an ironical manner than by pompous declarations. Throughout the whole western hemisphere, Germany desired peace and friendship with the United States. It would be better to avoid mentioning the Philippine question and events at Manila in 1898. *C'était un incident clos.* I advised the Prince, should he not be able to avoid making speeches in America, where speeches are frequent, to write down his phrases beforehand and so counteract any subsequent false interpretation or wilful falsifying of his words. The American was justifiably proud of the speed and extent of his country's development, which was indeed without precedent in the world's history. He was ambitious, eager for fame, and wanted to hear his country praised. Every criticism of American conditions from a stranger offended Americans. But the honour of a Princely visit was thought more of in this country in the pristine freshness of its own history than in Europe, and Americans would gladly listen to all the Prince had to tell about Germany, the Kaiser, our army, our science, and our art. The Prince would find in our Ambassador von Holleben a conscientious and sincere man, well acquainted with American ways of thinking and living, by reason of his long residence in that country.

I concluded with the words: "For many years past no journey undertaken by any royal Prince was of such significance to the Fatherland as this one of yours to the great Republic which Columbus drew out of the ocean." At the time and for all eventualities I gave the Prince a memorandum on the subject of the Spanish-American War so as to meet, in case of need, the perfidious hints and suspicions of the English press which accused Germany of having displayed unfriendliness to America four years before.

The Prince's trip passed off without untoward incident. His simple, natural, and sincere manner pleased the Americans. When necessary he spoke, and spoke freely, but he was never tactless. The speech, at once humorous and tactful, he made at the dinner given him by the American Press met with particular approval. That he spoke English like a native was of course a great aid to the Prince. He accomplished his task most satisfactorily, and it was bad taste on the part of the Socialist member of the Reichstag, Dr. Gradnauer, to attack "this kind of political travelling." Would to God that we had had a Prince Henry to send to America to work on behalf of our welfare in those black days that followed our collapse in November, 1918, days when we needed a friendly attitude on the part of America so badly. Herr Gradnauer, now advanced to the post of Saxon ambassador in Berlin, would probably realise this himself to-day. In happy possession of this sinecure he will doubtless no longer in "flaming indignation" take as target for his criticism the "drones in the state."

In the middle of June, 1902, the Golden Wedding between the city of Bonn and the King's Hussars regiment was celebrated. The regiment had been garrisoned in the beautiful Rhenish city for fifty years. I did not want to miss this great day in the history of my regiment, which I held in greatest affection. I accepted the invitation of Field Marshal von Loë and stayed with him. He had bought himself a little house in the city which had become his home and in which his widow still lived in 1922 at the age of nearly ninety. She was a sister of Prince Hermann Hatzfeldt, for many years *Oberpräsident* of Silesia, and of handsome Princess Elizabeth Carolath. Early on the seventeenth, their Majesties, accompanied

by myself, arrived in Bonn. The regiment paraded on the Hof-
gartenwiese, facing the Rhine, with the trumpeter corps at the rear
facing the University. Facing the regiment were the troops of
former King's Hussars. At 11 o'clock the Kaiser appeared on a
beautiful bay horse, followed by the Crown Prince. He inspected
the regiment and made a good speech to the Hussars. During
the march past in squad formation, Field Marshal von Loë and the
Kaiser's brother-in-law, Prince Adolf of Schaumburg-Lippe, rode
ahead. While the regiment was forming into squadrons for the
march past, the Kaiser, in whose train I was, rode up to me and
said that he appointed me colonel *à la suite*, with the uniform of my
old regiment. I had appeared on parade as cavalry captain of the
reserve. At the same time His Majesty invited me to ride in front
in the second march past. Then the Kaiser took his place with von
Loë and myself at the head of the standard-bearing squadrons and
led the regiment to the barracks where just thirty-one years ago I
had received my army clothes and had groomed my horse. At
lunch in the casino, where I had so often drunk my glass of Moselle
as a young lieutenant, the Kaiser replied to the toast of the commander, Lieutenant Colonel von Hertzberg, saying that there were
few regiments led by three officers who wore the Order of the Black
Eagle. The King's Hussars was not only one of the best training
grounds in the army for distinguished officers and generals but for
great statesmen as well and he was glad that the Chancellor of the
Empire had served in this fine regiment.

In the afternoon I took a long walk with old comrades of war along
the banks of the calmly flowing Rhine and reflected on days gone
by. It was one of the most enjoyable days of my life. Before us
stretched "the Rhine Paradise", the Seven Mountains. The rock
where Siegfried slew the dragon rose out of the water. Opposite lay
the ruins of Rolandseck, where Roland sorrowed for the fair Hildegarde. Between Rolandseck and the Drachenfels lay the isle of
Nonnenwerth, peacefully shrouded by elms, willows, and poplars.
Here stood the convent whither Hildegarde had withdrawn from
the world to live for Heaven alone. The mightily pulsating wings
of German legend embrace this river, reviving memories of Roland

and Siegfried, of Ernst Moritz Arndt as well, of Baron von Stein, and of old Blücher, who crossed the Rhine on the hallowed New Year's night of 1814.   The river on whose banks the destiny of the German people is determined again and again, the national river where French arrogance now stands and swells, the river for which savages black and white yelled like hoarse and greedy ravens until they forced their yoke upon it.   To break this yoke is the first and last thought of every German worthy of the name!

The renewal of the Triple Alliance was due when summer was at its height in 1902.   Both in Vienna and Rome a tendency was displayed to modify the Treaty at this juncture.   Vienna wished Germany to bind herself more closely and with more precision of detail than formerly to the Hapsburg monarchy in the event of Austrian differences either with Russia or with the Balkan states. In Italy, on the other hand, there was a desire to qualify the obligations imposed by the Triple Alliance.   I wished it to be renewed in exactly the same form, not only on account of the impression to be made on the world but as a brake on our Allies as well.   I had seen for some time past that Viennese policy would gladly have banked on more German support and showed less control than hitherto in the Balkan peninsula; that there was a tendency among the Austrian General Staff to open an attack at every suitable opportunity whether against the Italy of traditional hatred or against the Serbs and Roumanians who were partly despised and partly suspected, particularly by the Hungarians.   I knew just as well that on the other side the Italians desired as great a freedom of personal decision as possible, that they sought their own security in all eventualities, and that they were traditionally determined to have as many irons in the fire as possible.   Whoever reads the dispatches of the Venetian ambassadors and the instructions of the papal Cancellaria during the fifteenth and sixteenth centuries is filled with admiration for the political intelligence displayed therein. At the same time he is left in no doubt that Italian politicians, long before Prince Bismarck proclaimed publicly that Governments and Ministers can only keep to their treaties of alliance as long as the safety of their own countries is not menaced by them, were accustomed to adjust their political actions to this axiom. During a short stay I made in Venice in the spring of 1902 the Italian Foreign Secretary Signor Prinetti came to see me and was very insistent on the subject of certain alterations in the Triple Alliance Treaty. I took up the standpoint maintained by the Jesuit general of the eighteenth century when a reform of the Order was demanded of him : *"Sint ut sunt aut non sint."*

In the same speech in which I was obliged to refute the Edinburgh pronouncements of Mr. Chamberlain, I said publicly that the Triple Alliance was a useful bond between three states forced to be good neighbours by reason of their geographical position and historical tradition, but that, on the other hand, all aggressive and warlike intentions were remote from its scope, that it coincided with the sentiments and the memories of the German people but was not an absolute necessity for Germany. This phrase disquieted the venerable Emperor Francis Joseph, and annoyed the Viennese chiefs of staff and the Hungarian Jingoes. Poor Phil Eulenburg, who lost his nerve, at once sent me a lachrymose letter in which he said that Goluchowski was "beside himself", the Emperor "deeply vexed", and the whole of Austria "very annoyed." But the effect of the speech was that Vienna hastened to declare an unaltered renewal of the Triple Alliance acceptable. Old Austria was one of those horses which has to feel the bit occasionally if the rider wishes not to be thrown. In dealing with Italy I used the often-quoted phrase : "In a happy marriage the husband must not get violent if his wife ventures to dance an innocent extra turn with another. The main thing is that she does not run away from him and that she will not do so as long as she is better off with him than with any other." I was well aware that Italian diplomacy wished to uphold the Alliance but at the same time to obtain securities against the eventuality of French opposition if Italy ever stretched out a hand for Tripoli. I also knew that Italy, like many pretty women, would remain faithful the more readily if everything was avoided which looked like brute force or even like too binding a connexion. I was always of the opinion in politics that the spirit is of more importance than the letter and that not this or that individual point but the main object is the goal. On June 28th, 1902, the Triple Alliance was renewed, in a completely unchanged form, in the summer parlour of the Chancellor's Palace, signed by the ambassadors Szögyényi, Lanza, and myself.

After the interview at Hela I had explained to the Kaiser several times how greatly he jeopardised the friendship he so very much and almost too openly desired with the Tsar, through his unfriendly treatment of the Russian Foreign Secretary. Such "mental massage", as I used to call this influencing of William II, was at that date still successful. At the new meeting which took place between the Tsar and the Kaiser in my presence at Reval, in the beginning of August, William II greeted the Russian Foreign Secretary with quiet friendliness as though nothing untoward had ever happened between them. He shook his hand and personally presented the high Order of the Black Eagle. He also refrained from jesting comments when the noise of the guns during the naval manoeuvres appeared to upset the nerves of Count Lambsdorff very considerably. The old *Geheimrat* Lucanus used to say that William II unhappily often made mistakes, but generally readjusted them if he had the right adviser at his side. That was the most encouraging thing about him.

I recall the moment in the long conversation I had with the Tsar when I reminded him of what I had mentioned once before, namely, Bismarck's opinion that although nobody could foretell the military result of a war between the three Empires, most probably all the three monarchs would have to pay the penalty. Tsar Nicholas seized my hand, looked long at me with his melancholy eyes, and said: *"J'en suis aussi convaincu que vous!"* To my surprise, I observed during our stay at Reval that the Russian naval attaché in Berlin, Paulis, whose intimacy with Senden I had remarked with annoyance, appeared extremely often on board the *Hohenzollern*, where he conferred with the chief of the Naval Cabinet. I taxed Senden with this, and with the obstinate simplicity peculiar to him he declared that the naval captain von Paulis was an admirer of the Kaiser, a friend of Germany, and an enemy of England. "What more do you want? He can be trusted!" I informed the

Kaiser, who always disliked saying anything disagreeable to his aide-de-camps both because he was good-tempered and because he objected to anything but pleasant expressions on the faces around him. King Edward's latent enmity towards his Imperial nephew and the suspicions already present in wide English circles against Germany's politics were constantly fanned by careless words dropped by the Kaiser and his entourage in talks with Russians, Frenchmen, or Americans. It was on the occasion of this meeting at Reval that William II uttered the jesting words as he approached me arm in arm with the Tsar: "Do you know how we have decided to style ourselves in future? Tsar Nicholas is from now onward Admiral of the Pacific, and I am Admiral of the Atlantic!" Tsar Nicholas looked very embarrassed at this. To help him I remarked that I was not surprised that a monarch, who in spite of his great power appreciates the welfare wrought by peace as well as the Tsar does, had decided upon this title of "pacific." The ruler of all the Russians agreed very emphatically. But when we were alone I urged the Kaiser to refer no more to his horrible joke. His Majesty with the obstinacy of an *enfant terrible* brought up the matter again at table, to the obvious discomfort of the Tsar. At last the hour of parting arrived. The two Emperors embraced and kissed; the Russian yacht steamed for Kronstadt when Kaiser William signalled the Russian Emperor by way of farewell: "The Admiral of the Atlantic bids farewell to the Admiral of the Pacific." After a few minutes came the cool reply: "Goodbye!" The commander of the *Hohenzollern* with great tact at once forbade officers and men to let anything about this signal leak out. The Russians were obviously less discreet. A few weeks later the whole story was in a big English newspaper and gave the English and French press the opportunity of suspecting the Kaiser — who in reality had never indulged in any Napoleonic dreams — of desiring to wrest the trident of Neptune from Old England who rules the waves; and of course, the Cologne trident speech of June, 1897, was dug up once again.

In the conferences between the two emperors the possibility of friction between Russia and Japan played a considerable part. Tsar Nicholas was convinced that the little "Jap" would not let matters come to a head once great Russia took a firm stand towards him. The Tsar was seriously preoccupied by the constant attacks of the Russian revolutionaries. In April the Minister of the Interior, Szipyagin, had been assassinated by a dismissed university student. The murderer was hanged at once. But not long after this, the governor of Vilna, General Wahl, was wounded by revolver bullets. Szipyagin was a distinguished, elegant, and rather mild aristocrat; Wahl one of those harshly active Baltic types whom Tsar Nicholas made use of by preference, believing them to be harder and more reliable than the native Russian with his *"schirokaya natura"*, his expansive, kindly ways. While we were in Reval the governor of Kharkov was wounded by a would-be assassin. In a confidential dispatch from Kiev I read even as far back as those days that a respected Israelite citizen of the Dnieper City had said: We 'll manage it! We 'll do it! We 've got the organisation and we 've got the money. In spite of all pogroms we shall be masters of Russia." In any case it was clear that below the surface Russia was in a state of ferment.

On the return journey from Reval, August 10th, 1902, a Sunday, the *Hohenzollern* reached Swinemünde again. I was present at the service held by the Kaiser. The widespread belief that the Kaiser used to preach extemporaneously on the inspiration of the moment in these services on board ship is false. On such occasions he read a sermon written by one of the court preachers, Pastor Keller, I believe. He did not attempt to conceal the fact that it was somebody else's sermon he was reading. On English ships the Captain holds a service with the crew on Sunday. It really could not be taken amiss that the Kaiser introduced this custom in our country. I was present at the Imperial luncheon and returned to Berlin immediately the meal was over.

When I got there, I was not a little astonished to read in the papers a telegram which William II had sent from Swinemunde to the Prince Regent of Bavaria immediately after my departure. In Munich the clerical Centre majority of the Second Chamber had curtailed the budget of the Bavarian Ministry of Education to annoy the Crailsheim Cabinet, which had refused to fulfil this party's own

selfish desires.   The move was obviously directed against the Prince
Regent as it made purchases for the State picture galleries, to which
the old gentleman had already committed himself, an impossibility.
In his telegram to the Prince Regent the Kaiser expressed his deepest "indignation" over the refusal of the Bavarian Government to
vote these sums for the furthering of art.   He gave vent to his
"anger" over this "miserable ingratitude" and offered the Prince
Regent the sum his clericals had struck off, so that he would be
able to attain the object he pursued in the realm of art "to the fullest extent."   In a polite but cool telegram drawn up by Crailsheim,
the Prince Regent thanked the Kaiser for the warm interest he
took in his artistic aspirations.   He was pleased to be able to
inform the Kaiser that, owing to the generosity of one of his privy
councillors, the Bavarian Government was in a position to go on
cultivating the arts in accordance with the traditions of the
Wittelsbachs.   It was, indeed, only the comparatively small sum of
100,000 marks that was involved.   The donor was the wealthy
Count Ernest Moy, who was among the guests at a shooting party
given by the Regent when the Imperial telegram burst like a bomb-
shell into the idyllic peace of the royal camp in Linderhof.   When
I asked why the Kaiser's telegram had been published by Wolff's
Agency without consulting me first, I was told that this was done
by direct orders of the Kaiser to Tschirschky, which the latter had
carried out without protest.   Tschirschky either did not consider
that it was necessary to consult me, although I was available at any
time between Berlin and Swinemünde, or he did not dare to hold up
the despatch of the telegram and its publication until my arrival
in Berlin.

The impression made by this episode was deplorable, not only
in Bavaria but in the whole Empire.   It was not only the newspapers of the Centre party that were loud in their protests.   Liberal
papers also declared that Imperial interference in the domestic
affairs of a Federal State, and in this case the second largest State,
was dangerous and deplorable.   Unpleasant debates, inimical to the
idea of Imperial unity, were predicted in the Reichstag.   The position of Crailsheim, an excellent minister, deeply loyal to the Empire,

was badly shaken. I demanded of Tschirschky how he, as responsible representative of the Foreign Office with the Kaiser, could have allowed this telegram to be sent off without insisting upon consulting me beforehand, which would have been quite an easy thing to do. The ambassador replied, with mingled embarrassment and obstinacy, that he had no wish to offend the Kaiser. "Once you are in the Kaiser's bad books no Chancellor can be of any help." He was referring to a remark of the Dutch naval hero, Cornelius Tromp, whom the Kaiser often quoted, to the effect that in Tromp's opinion the honourable thing to do was to carry out every order at once without giving it any further thought. A discussion began, carried on politely but acridly on my part, in which, to my great regret, I learned from Tschirschky, who was now at bay, that I had (and this was his excuse) invited him very rarely, that I had but seldom conferred with him personally on any subject, and that I had, in general, done so little for him that he really saw no reason why he should particularly uphold any standpoint of mine. It was a sad sign of the times and for me a disquieting symptom that Tschirschky, the son of a good Saxon official, took so slovenly, so egotistical, and opportunist a view of his duties.

With the Kaiser I had the most serious argument I had had since his ominous speech at Bremerhaven. In the end he quite melted. But I thought it my duty to go on stressing the point firmly, that the security and the future of the Empire depended upon the impregnability of its federal basis. Bavaria in particular must be treated with care and tact. When I returned again and again to this point, the worthy Empress, who was much too sensible not to regret the Swinemünde telegram but could not bear to see her husband suffer (so tenderly did she feel for him), burst out : "For goodness sake, do stop! The Kaiser isn't sleeping as well as he used to!" I had succeeded to this extent at least when chance brought a well-known South German professor to the Imperial dining table. This good man had no sooner taken his seat than, turning to the Kaiser, he thanked him "with his whole heart" for the "splendid" Swinemünde telegram which had enchanted all South Germany. "That's very interesting!" cried the Kaiser, with lively pleasure. "And my Chancellor keeps scolding me for sending it!" If William II often sinned politically, he was more sinned against by sycophants and toadies. *"Du sublime au ridicule il n'y a qu'un pas,"* said Napoleon over and over again to his ambassador, Abbé de Pradt, in Warsaw when he came to him during the retreat from Moscow. Once during the crisis brought about by the Swinemünde telegram, when the Bavarian Premier, Count Crailsheim, sat at dinner in the Prussian embassy at Munich next to the wife of the Prussian ambassador, Countess Gisela Pourtalès, this pretty and charming but politically untutored lady asked him whether it were really true that he had bought a villa at Swinemünde in which to end his days, as she had heard? The always dignified but stiff Count Crailsheim, who believed at first that the Prussian ambassadress was mocking him, was upset by this remark until the honest surprise and sincere regret of the charming ambassadress left him in no doubt that she had taken the malicious joke of one of his enemies seriously.

On November 22nd, 1902, Alfred Krupp, the son of the masterful founder of the greatest steel works in the world, died suddenly. Besides the iron foundry at Essen the firm of Krupp owned the Gruson machine works and foundry at Buckau, which it had purchased, the Germania Wharf at Kiel, the steelworks at Annen, the Sayner foundry, three coal mines, four blast furnace plants, and over five hundred iron mines. Krupp's concern had long ago surpassed the Schneider iron and machine works at Creusot, which were the pride of France. Krupp had spread Germany's reputation and the renown of German work and industry over the whole world, which now envied us this mighty concern. Perhaps still more to our honour was the magnificent manner, hardly equalled anywhere else in the world, in which the firm had cared for its employees by building hospitals, coöperative stores, household and industrial schools, homes and houses for its staff, both clerical and manual. This was social policy! This was practical Christianity! In contrast to his father, the powerful, strong-willed, harsh, and four-square founder of the gigantic firm — a man born to rule — Alfred Krupp was a delicate man, sensitive, nervous, tender-hearted. Krupp's works had for some time been a thorn in the flesh of Germany's Socialists because of the content displayed by both wage and salary earners.   Ferdinand Lassalle coined the notorious words : "Damned contentment."   It was said of Miquel that when he was a student and, in youthful wrong-headedness, leaning toward Communism, he broke in on a friend who was about to give a beggar a few small coins with the words : "Don't delay the social revolution !"   What annoyed the Socialist leaders in those days was that the great majority of Krupp's men particularly did not vote for the Socialist candidate at the elections.

A few weeks before the death of Alfred Krupp, "*Vorwärts*" published an article in which it was stated that Krupp, during a stay in Capri, had offended against paragraph 175 of the penal code and had therefore been deported from Italy.   The Italian Government denied this assertion at once spontaneously and Krupp sued the "*Vorwärts*" for libel.   He died soon afterwards, hardly forty-eight years old.   The rumour that Krupp took his own life is unfounded. What is certain is that the somewhat melancholy, excessively high-strung man, suffering from grave heart disease, had two strokes in quick succession as a result of the excitement caused by the libellous attacks launched at him.   At the same time it was discovered that these libels emanated from a south Italian gang of blackmailers who hoped to wrest a few millions from the German nabob in this way. It was clear the "*Vorwärts*" was perfectly aware of the falsehood of its attacks.   If the "*Vorwärts*" action displayed a crudeness and coarseness of mind inexcusable even in the most violent political fight, the hypocrisy with which the leading Socialist paper strove to defend this action was still more disgusting.   It claimed that its only aim was to prove the necessity of abolishing paragraph 175. The Kaiser had, as a young man, frequented the hospitable home of the Krupps and he was intensely interested in the firm's mighty concern.   He attended the funeral of the deceased and on this occasion he made a speech which did honour to his friendship, and to his warm and noble heart, but which, for a monarch, was too violent and extreme.   His grandfather would never have spoken so, even in his youth.   Besides, the Kaiser did not reserve his indignation, which, I repeat, was justifiable, for this occasion, but at Breslau

BÜLOW WITH THE EMPRESS' CHIEF MASTER OF
CEREMONIES, BARON VON MIRBACH

a week later addressed a delegation of workmen, who had been sent to him on this account, in still more passionate phrases.   In spite of this I would readily and gladly have defended His Majesty's speech in the Reichstag against the Socialists.   The Kaiser in this case did not act differently from the good Samaritan in the Bible, who pitied the man fallen among thieves, and anointed his wounds while priests and Levites passed coldly by.   Unfortunately the President of the Reichstag, Ballestrem, would not even permit the subject to be raised, giving as the reason that a discussion as to the manner of an unblemished man of honour's death could not even be tolerated. In this way an opportunity was lost of showing the country how brutally and hypocritically Socialism, which is founded on alleged ideals, could act, while the impulsive and warm-hearted action of the Kaiser was taken amiss by many as sign of yet another lapse from self-control.

CHAPTER XXXVII

*Confessional Conciliation — The Trèves Incident and Bishop Korum —
Crown Princess Louise of Saxony — Second Reading of the Tariff Bill —
Longest Session of the Reichstag (December 13, 1902) — Bülow Refuses the
Princely Title — The Swinemünde Telegram in the Reichstag (January 19,
1903) — Dean Schädler — First Criticism of the Kaiser's Speeches —
Resignation of Count Crailsheim — Conference with the Socialist Leader
von Vollmar — Leaders of the Conservatives — Centre and National Lib-
erals Appeal to the Chancellor on the Subject of Continuous Imperial
Tactlessness — Bülow's Letter to William II.*

IN the Polish debate I had emphatically stated that I regarded it
as one of my most important tasks to maintain peace between the
two great Christian religions. I understand the attitude of those
who regret that the German nation in the sixteenth century did not
embrace the new faith in its entirety. No less a personage than
Napoleon I said that the Emperor Charles V committed one of the
greatest errors in history by not placing himself at the head of the
Reformation. I can also put myself in the place of those who, on
the other hand, deplore the split within the Church and wish that
Germany, like so many other countries, Italy, Spain, Belgium, and
France, too, for the most part, had remained within the fold of the
ancient religion. But politics must reckon with things as they are.
The confessional schism is a reality which cannot be gainsaid.
It has in the past caused so much misery in Germany that it would
be criminal not to work for conciliation in every way between the
two faiths, for their *"unitas in necessariis."* This is not easy,
considering the quarrelsome and stubborn qualities of Germans.
During the War a great festival was held in the Trocadero in Paris
at which the Catholic archbishop of Paris, a minister of the Lutheran
church and of the Reformed Church respectively, a Rabbi, and an
Imam made patriotic speeches. When the audience applauded
at the end, all five appeared simultaneously. The archbishop,
in the centre, held the hand of the Lutheran on his right and

of the Calvinist on his left. The latter held that of the Rabbi, and the Lutheran that of the Moslem. The audience rose and began to sing the " *Marseillase*," the battle song of the revolution. The men of religion on the platform joined in. In the past, German religious differences outweighed national and patriotic standpoints only too often. When the Great War was at its height, a Bavarian monk of my acquaintance, a worthy man otherwise, told me he had been requested to address the Bavarian troops together with a Protestant chaplain, on the occasion of a Bavarian prince's visit to the Front, but that he had indignantly refused. A member of a Catholic Order could not place himself on a footing with a Protestant in the presence of a Wittelsbach. The padre was quite proud of this refusal. At the same time a good third of Bavaria's population is Protestant. I am very pleased to say that since the War differences of faith have retreated more and more to the background.

I believe that without undue conceit I may claim to have done something towards bridging these differences during my term of office. In any case I always worked so as never to make a difference between Protestants and Catholics nor to injure the feelings and rights of Catholics. I was therefore all the more unpleasantly surprised when this peace was suddenly broken by an ill-considered action of Bishop Korum of Trèves, who had a statement read from the pulpit threatening with ecclesiastical penalties Catholic parents who permitted their daughters to attend the State Schools. The National Liberal Party moved an inquiry in the Reichstag, which was put forward with much temperament by the Deputy Hackenberg, a Protestant pastor from the Rhineland. In my reply to this interrogation,[1] I expressed deep regret at the Bishop's action, but urged both parties to reach a conciliatory settlement. The difference in faith which separates our people imposes upon both Catholics and Protestants, I declared, the duty of adaptation and accommodation. Principles, I said, are irreconcilable, but in spiritual matters differences of principle must be settled by spiritual weapons. In practical life, I said, we had to keep the peace. I expressed the hope that the Holy See would help me in preventing the unfortu-

[1] Prince Bülow's "Speeches", (large edition), I. 426; (small edition), II. 281.

nate incident from having further disturbing effects on the relations existing between Church and State and on the public at large. The Centre Party's point of view was maintained with tact and moderation by the Catholic member, Dietrich. Not long afterwards it was announced from the pulpits in Trèves that the Bishop, in agreement with the Holy Father, and in view of altered circumstances, ordered his former edict to be regarded as never having been issued.

Bishop Korum was an Alsatian and quite French in culture, but a man of fine intelligence and great gravity. As a young priest in the 'seventies he had aroused the interest of the *Stadtholder*, Manteuffel, who recommended him to Prince Bismarck. He was invited to Varzin and pleased the Prince, who insisted upon his nomination as Bishop of Trèves in 1881, although there were misgivings on this account in Germany and even the cautious Leo XIII warned the Chancellor quietly through Rampolla against Korum, whom he designated as "*troppo zelante.*" As a matter of fact, the great man was right again. With the sole exception of the *faux pas* just mentioned, Korum was a complete success as Bishop of Trèves. His piety was above suspicion. He not only exhibited the Sacred Cloak of Trèves but also wrote a book on the miracles it wrought. He proved himself on every occasion to be a good German patriot as well, particularly during the Great War. He was intimate with my own friend, the excellent Baron Klemens von Schorlemer-Lieser, Minister of Agriculture and, later on, *Oberpräsident* of the Rhine Province. In smoothing over the Trèves episode, Herr Spahn as well as Cardinal Kopp did useful work. Before it occurred, Cardinal Kopp wrote to me from Rome on the occasion of an attack launched against me by a Clerical paper : "You may depend on the Pope as well as on the Cardinal Secretary of State and the leading Vatican circles. Confidence in you here is unshakable and neither the Poles nor the Jesuits will succeed in making the Holy See put obstacles in your path. The bishops of Prussia look upon Your Excellency with complete confidence, as the stronghold of all that makes for parity in the administration." At the same time Leo XIII said to a Catholic official of the Foreign Office, Secretary of Embassy Baron von Schauenburg, who was received in private audience by the Pope on the occasion of his honeymoon: *"Et n'oubliez pas de saluer mon ami, le chancelier* Bülow.*"*

A few days after the Trèves debate I sat opposite Crown Princess Louise of Saxony at a dinner in the Berlin palace. She pleased me not only because of her charming appearance but by her delightful manners and animated conversation as well. A sad contrast to his pretty wife was her husband, Crown Prince Friedrich August, who was rendered so comic not only by his marked Saxon accent but by the clumsiness of his ways and his silly questions and observations, that it was difficult to remain as serious as was fitting for a Chancellor in dealings with the Prince of a Federal State. A week later the Saxon ambassador, Count Wilhelm Hohenthal, called on me to inform me with the utmost agitation that Crown Princess Louise had eloped with her children's tutor, a Belgian named Giron. The Crown Prince, Friedrich August, so the ambassador continued, who loved his wife as dearly as before, would have forgiven her very gladly. But she had already permitted herself to be photographed with Giron, in déshabille, in their mutual bedroom at Geneva for a Parisian illustrated paper. After the Crown Princess had demonstrated her marital lapse so publicly the Crown Prince no longer believed possible the reunion he so desired. This episode reacted over a long period and gravely affected the Saxon dynasty. The people in Dresden and in the whole of Saxony took the part of the Princess, "our Louise", as she was called with great warmth. She was beloved in Saxony as she was less proud and stiff than her father-in-law, King George, and her very unpopular sister-in-law, Princess Mathilde, who (unjustly by the way) was nicknamed "Schnapps Mathilde." Princess Louise's popularity was increased by the fact that she was not accounted ultramontane. Whereas the wise King Albert, like his father King John, was always careful to spare the feelings of his preponderantly Protestant people, his brother and successor George was considered clerical, and the worthy Friedrich August and his brother Johann Georg (who was hated because of his pride) also had this reputation. The worst offender in this respect was the sister of Friedrich August, Princess Maria

Josefa, wife of the libertine Archduke Otto (whose excesses in the end took on pathological forms) and mother of the not only simple-minded but also traitorous Emperor Charles. Through her narrow anti-German sentiments during the Great War she did a great deal of harm at Vienna. The sons of Friedrich August and his so sadly backsliding consort inherited the vivacity and amiability of their mother, but proclaimed their Catholic feelings more demonstratively than was exactly wise and tactful in Saxony. The marriage tangle of Crown Princess Louise and its consequences had much to do with the fact that Saxony became more and more of a Socialist stronghold and developed into the "red kingdom." Kaiser William II acted as the true friend of the Dresden court during this sore trial. At the request of King George, when excitement in Saxony had reached its height, he paid him a visit to show the world that in his eyes the Saxon dynasty had suffered no loss of prestige and dignity. King George himself so far lost his self-command that in his proclamation to his people he referred to his daughter-in-law as "a woman who had long ago fallen from the path of virtue in secret", which of course aroused the suspicion that M. Giron was not the first man with whom she had deceived her husband. It was widely supposed that the King wished, by this opprobrious description, to hint that the Crown Prince was not the real father of the royal children.

In October, 1902, the second reading of the tariff duties began. I introduced it with a long speech, in which I justified the necessity of strengthening our commercial armaments by the rise in tariffs which other countries were planning. The more definite specification of our new tariffs was, more particularly, to provide an effective weapon in the forthcoming treaty negotiations. It was only at the urgent desire of the Agrarians that a maximum and minimum duty had been imposed upon the four chief cereals : rye, wheat, barley, and oats. I believed I had calculated the amount of these cereal duties correctly, so as to preserve agriculture in its present extent and intensity on the one hand, and, on the other hand, to make it still possible to conclude long-term commercial treaties. The Left reëchoed the word "still!" with ironical shouts. This shout at once led me to develop the reasons which made it our duty in the interest of the whole nation to remain independent of foreign foodstuffs and fodder. But at the same time I stated that the duty of 5 marks and 5.50 marks would be the highest which could be obtained in raising the duties on cereals. I declared, with great emphasis in a raised voice, that any rise or extension of the minimum duties would render the conclusion of commercial treaties an impossibility. I asked the Left in the Reichstag not to delay or protract the negotiations by artificial means. Amid a great noise on the part of the Social Democrats, I insisted that every obstruction would injure the prestige, the importance, and the general influence of Parliament and of parliamentary institutions. Next day the Conservative and Clerical newspapers unanimously declared that it was impossible to accept the tariff duties. The Radical member, Gothein, said that with this tariff and this Chancellor we might have destructive but never protective trade treaties. I never heard that Gothein ever acknowledged or repented his error when later on I succeeded in negotiating trade treaties with the help of which trade and industry entered upon a period of brilliant prosperity. On the other hand, the leader of the Farmers' League told me emphatically when the tariffs were accepted that we were standing on the brink of the ruin of agriculture. This did not prevent the farmers from maintaining in the election campaign ten years later that the statement that they were dissatisfied with the tariffs of 1902 was a perfidious lie of the Manchester group. "*Tutto il mondo è paese*," says the Italian proverb. This, amplified, means: our political parties have little cause for mutual reproach, for there is little to choose between their methods of fighting, their egotism, and their untruthfulness.

During the following weeks the Socialists were busily engaged in delaying the progress of the negotiations by means of constant divisions. I felt it necessary to intervene, and went to Count Ballestrem, the speaker of the Reichstag, for this purpose. Count Franz Ballestrem was a splendid fellow. His ancestor emigrated from Piedmont to Prussia, under Frederick the Great; he joined the great king's army as a captain of cavalry and came into large

estates by his marriage with a Fräulein von Stechow. Our speaker
was a fine Prussian and at the same time a practising Catholic.
He had been in the Breslau Lifeguards for many years. This was a
sturdy regiment to whose officers old King William had said after
the victorious campaign of 1866, "You are the gentlemen I depend
upon." Ballestrem was proud of wearing the uniform of a regiment in which he had distinguished himself in 1866 and 1870. He
had a witty tongue. After a regimental dinner and in the regimental casino, a brother officer somewhat the worse for drink
asked him tactlessly what he, as a Catholic, thought about duelling.
Ballestrem replied that, like his Church, he repudiated duelling.
"What would you do then," demanded the questioner, "if I insulted
you?" Ballestrem answered quietly with an appropriate gesture
of his hand, "Try it and see!" I discovered this excellent man,
when I called at his home to see him on behalf of the Parliamentary
situation, at half past twelve noon in front of a big bottle of
champagne. When I looked at him in some surprise he said:
"Before I go to preside over the Reichstag I always drink a bottle
of champagne, — it puts me into the right mood."

He entirely agreed, as Herr von Kardorff and other Conservatives
had suggested, that the procedure of voting should be curtailed in
accordance with a motion submitted by a member of the Centre
Party. On November 13th the Reichstag passed the suggested
alteration by a majority. Former divisions had lasted half an
hour, sometimes three-quarters of an hour. After the new method
was introduced they took 20 minutes at first but were then reduced
to only nine or ten minutes. November 12th, 1902, when a stormy
debate took place, was a great day for Eugen Richter. In contrast
to many of his friends in the party, and particularly to the Radical
People's Party, twin sister of the Radical Association, he opposed
Socialists, to their lively annoyance and amid the enthusiastic
applause of the Right. He saw further than Theodor Barth, the
"crazy fanatic", as Rudolf von Bennigsen called him in a letter to
his party colleague Hammacher on August 22nd, 1901. Richter
understood that a victory of the Socialist party would not only be a
grave danger to the Fatherland but also to the principles upheld

by the Radical party and by all the Radical citizens, and thus for the whole future and structure of the People's Party. Under the energetic presidency of Count Ballestrem and after an understanding had been reached on the chief points of the tariff duties between the majority parties and myself, the Kardorff bill was passed by a large majority. I had agreed to the reduction of a number of industrial duties as well as to the suggested normalising of meat duties and of the veterinary police. The way was open for an acceptance of the tariffs. It was now only necessary to overcome the expected obstruction of the Socialists and to ignore the protesting shouts of the Farmers' League, whose mouthpiece, the *Deutsche Tageszeitung*, called the day on which an agreement on the Kardorff bill was reached a *"dies ater"* for agriculture.

On December 2nd, 1902, the Kardorff bill was passed by 200 votes to only 44. During the standing-orders debate which followed this division, the Socialists endeavoured to drown the speeches of the majority's members by shouting "Rhubarb! Rhubarb!" in rhythmical unison. They had learnt this cry of "Rhubarb!" from the actors of Meiningen, who had gained great applause in the famous second scene of "Julius Caesar's" third act, where Antony works up the people after Caesar's assassination. When the Socialists came into power after the collapse of the authoritarian state, many a meeting of orthodox majority Socialists was disturbed by Independent Socialists and Communists who used the same rhubarb recipe. During the fight for the tariffs the National-Liberal member Sattler hit the nail on the head when he described the Kardorff bill as a defensive measure because the Socialists used the standing orders only to hinder the course of proceedings. On December 13th there began at ten o'clock in the morning the longest Reichstag session I ever took part in, one of nineteen hours. I had to speak three times to lay down the Government's standpoint on the subject of the second reading of the bill for improved conditions for working-class families who lost their breadwinner, and also for the subsequent introduction of widows' and orphans' insurance; on the subject of the minimum duties on imported horses, cattle, and meat; and, finally, in connexion with the much-questioned minimum duty of 4 marks on barley malt, provided all other duties on barley were dropped. I asked the Reichstag to assure the consummation of the great work of tariff reform for the benefit of the Fatherland. When the Socialists interrupted me noisily at the words "benefit of the Fatherland", I repeated my last words in a raised voice. The Deputy Barth had stated in one of his party newspapers some days before that only a Chancellor so ignorant and narrow-minded as Count Bülow could believe the tariff bill would ever become law. During the third reading he declared with much impudence that these duties would make commercial treaties impossible. I replied that I was a careful man, but I would like to say that the prophecies of the Deputy Barth regarding both duties and treaties would not be fulfilled. Among the Socialist speakers obstructing the bill the Deputy Antrick distinguished himself by thundering against the tariff from half past four to half past twelve — eight hours in all. When he had finished, Bebel patted his shoulder with paternal benevolence. Not long afterwards August Bebel, who, as one can gather from "Memoirs of a Socialist" by Lily Braun, held strict views upon morality, excluded Herr Antrick from the Socialist party because he had sinned with the wife of a fellow Deputy *"al tempo de' dolci sospiri"*, which Paolo and Francesca paid for in Dante's Inferno. The session ended at five o'clock in the morning. I had not left the Reichstag once during the whole time.

Next day I received a telegram from His Majesty thanking me "from the bottom of his heart", praising my "statesmanlike vision", my "patience" and "skill", and informing me that he had raised me to princely rank. Although considerably tired, for I had slept scarcely two hours, I went to Potsdam, where the Kaiser was staying, and urged him to refrain from doing me this honour. For one thing, it was painful for me to accept an important distinction for a victory fought on an internal party issue. Besides I felt no desire for a rise in rank. These were not merely phrases; the words expressed my true feelings. I was, and am, proud of my ancient name. I do not see why I should not be pleased that the family, whose name I bear, entered history 800 years ago. I am still proud to-day that my family live up to the motto of its old coat of arms, *"Alle Bülowen ehrlich"*,[1] and that it has given Germany many excellent men in various walks of life. When I was still a schoolboy at the college in Halle, I wrote on the first page of Varnhagen von Ense's biography of General Bülow von Dennewitz the words from " Iphigenia : "

> *Wohl dem, der seiner Väter gern gedenkt,*
> *Der roh von ihren Taten, ihrer Grösse*
> *Den Hörer unterhält und still sich freuend*
> *Ans Ende dieser schönen Reihe sich*
> *Geschlossen sieht!* [2]

As Herr von Bülow I felt just as satisfied and just as good as Count or Prince. The Kaiser did not relinquish his plan willingly, and told me he had already telegraphed to my mother-in-law in Rome that her daughter was a Principessa once more. I stood by my refusal. I also succeeded in stopping the telegram to Donna Laura Minghetti on the way. I print it here because it is a proof of William II's great kindness of heart, friendliness, and spontaneity :

Bernado Bülow grande vittorie tarifale in Parlamento perciò creato Principe di Bülow e la vostra figlia Principessa.   Guglielmo I. R.

The distinguished teacher of jurisprudence at Berlin University, Professor Heinrich Dernburg, author of a classical work on the Pandects, telegraphed me :

My congratulations on the victory won by fair means and a good faith over chicanery and sedition.

Dr. E. Schwetschke gladdened me with the following rhyme :

> *Es lebe hoch der Zolltarif*
> *Und Er, der g'rade macht, was schief!*
> *Ich sag' es unverhohlen,*
> *Doch höher soll Er leben noch.*
> *Macht er uns autonom vom Joch*
> *Des Erzefeinds erst — der Polen.* [3]

---

[1] All Bülows are honest.

[2] Happy is he who remembers his fathers with gladness
Relating their prowess with pride, rejoicing in silence
That he himself stands at the end of their glorious line.

[3] Long live the tariff, and he who makes the crooked straight! And longer may he live (I say it without hesitation) who frees us from the yoke of the arch-enemy, the Pole.

My dear friend, the poet Adolf Wilbrandt, wrote to my wife from Rostock: "May your husband be as successful in everything his German heart suggests to him." The *Stadtholder* of Alsace-Lorraine, Prince Hermann Hohenlohe-Langenburg, not always free from jealousy of me in former times, expressed his conviction that the Fatherland would owe me the recrudescence of its prosperity. The Bavarian Premier Crailsheim wrote me that the great economic project, now brought by skilful and energetic management to a satisfactory conclusion, would be a boon to the nation and a blessing to the Fatherland. He has not been disappointed. Looking back on those tempestuous days, I recall with pleasure the excellent support I received in drafting the tariff and in getting it through parliament from my assistants, especially Count Posadowsky, Baron von Richthofen, and His Excellency Körner.

Unfortunately my task was not completed with the achievement of a reasonable tariff system which should at one and the same time protect the farmers and make the conclusion of trade agreements possible. I still had the even more difficult and unpleasing duty of defending the last, well-meant but explosive utterances of the Kaiser, particularly his lapse at Swinemünde, against critics in the Reichstag and in the country. The Swinemünde telegram had been mentioned by the Deputy Schädler in the first reading of the budget on January 19th, 1903.

There were men in the Centre Party who were distinguished as much by their political acumen as by their integrity of mind and character. I may mention, besides Count Franz Ballestrem, my old and dear friend Prince Franz Arenberg, Spahn, Herold, Gröber, Count Praschma, Huene, Count Galen, Hertling, Porsch, Müller-Fulda, Buol, Count Preysing. The democratic wing of the Centre was at that time led by Ernst Lieber. The aristocrats of the Centre, who together with the Bishops gave the casting votes in those days (to the good of the party), did not like him. But despite many little weaknesses he was a man both noble-minded and gifted. As in every flock, there were black sheep in the Centre too. The chaplain Dasbach was not even popular in his own party. Arenberg told me once that when Dasbach quarrelled with a brother Bavarian at one of the Centre's convivial evenings, the latter said to him with native frankness: "I'd like to slap your face but I'd be sorry to soil my hands." More cultured but just as unpleasant was the deacon Schädler from Bamberg. It was his great wish to become Archbishop of Bamberg. Unfortunately his reputation for being too attracted by the female employees in the public houses he frequented there stood in the way of promotion. Now Horace, as is well-known, sang as follows:

> *Ne sit ancillae tibi amor pudori*
> *Xanthia Phoceu.*

But what was fitting for this gay libertine was not suited to a prelate. But Schädler did not abandon hope of mounting the episcopal throne in the city where St. Henry and the pious Kunigunde sleep. To this end he paid assiduous court to Chancellor Hohenlohe, who, as an old friend and contemporary of Luitpold the Prince Regent, had some influence over him. When the wife of Prince Chlodwig Hohenlohe, Princess Marie, died, the cathedral deacon Schädler offered to preach her funeral sermon. The sermon was fine and impassioned. Schädler called the device of the house of Hohenlohe, "*Ex flammis orior*", to mind. Like the phoenix from the flames Princess Marie would rise from her tomb, but her exalted spouse must remember that he too must overcome this, his sorest trial, for the sake of the German nation whose hope and stay he was, — for the sake of all those who placed their confidence in him. When, four years later, the aged Prince followed his wife to her grave, the family, who deeply loved their parents and who had been much gratified by Dean Schädler's first funeral oration, asked him to preach at their father's grave-side. Schädler complied with their request, but the result was less a funeral sermon than a reprimand. He had nothing more to expect from Prince Chlodwig Hohenlohe, and so he forgot none of his sins, in particular the sin of which the old Prince had been guilty thirty-two years ago when he questioned the dogma of infallibility. Not Paradise, but Purgatory, was the prospect held out to him. In the end Schädler died without becoming Archbishop of Bamberg. When, on January 19th, 1903, he planted himself, arrogant and bumptious, on the Reichstag tribune, the Bavarian ambassador, Count Lerchenfeld, remarked to me with the bluntness of his vigorous race: "That 's what we call a pig of a priest in Bavaria."

In my reply to Schädler's attacks, that were weakened because they were so palpably inspired by a pretended indignation, I outlined my attitude in regard to the speeches, utterances, and actions of the Kaiser for the first time. I pointed out that the Chancellor's responsibility, as testified by his signature, did not, according to our constitution, extend to personal manifestations of the monarch. The right to a free expression of opinion was as much the Kaiser's as any citizen's. But I did not refrain from telling the country that a Chancellor conscious of his moral responsibility could not remain in office if, according to his conscientious judgment, he could not prevent occurrences calculated gravely and permanently to injure the welfare of the Empire. I was well aware that I was responsible to the Federal Council as well as to the Reichstag for managing affairs in a way guaranteed to keep the peace both at home and abroad. In replying to Herr Schädler I emphasised the fact that the Imperial idea was not a mere figure of speech for our nation, but that it typified the dearest memories of the German people, our prestige abroad, our future in the world. When next day the upholder of moderate views in the Socialist camp, the Deputy von Vollmar, reproached Kaiser and monarchy with anti-social tendencies, it was easy for me to repudiate this absolutely unfounded criticism by pointing to the Imperial manifesto of November 17th, 1881, and our social laws, in particular those relating to workmen's insurance. The German monarchy has indeed done very much more for the workers than the French Republic. On this occasion I mentioned what our ambassador in Paris, Prince Radolin, had lately reported of Millerand: "Millerand was earnestly pursuing the advancement of the lower classes, to which the bourgeoisie is not much inclined." When I read out this passage from the Paris dispatch, the Socialists called out: "Same here!" I took the bull by the horns and at once replied: "This remark is striking! I 'm greatly struck by the remark. What you have just said is

exactly what our Kaiser has written on the margin of this Paris
dispatch!" The Socialists pulled long faces. I read some more
of the Radolin dispatch: "M. Millerand is far from trying to
undermine the constitution!" Turning to the Socialists I added:
"Gentlemen, I wish you had a Millerand!" At the close of my
speech I reëmphasised the fact that a Chancellor deserving of the
name, a Chancellor who was a man and not an old woman,
would support nothing he could not reconcile with his own conscience. A Chancellor was not a mere executive, an instrument.
That would be compatible neither with the wishes of the Kaiser nor
the interests of the German people.

The Socialists, who after our collapse could not find words enough
to condemn the policy pursued by the former government towards
England, and who were prone to boast of their "power of binding
the nations together", agitated against England both during and
after the Boer War. Even Vollmar, who was so sensible in other
ways, reproached me with the fact that my policy during the South
African War was not in accordance with "national feeling." I had
to remind him, and the anti-Semite Liebermann von Sonnenberg
still more emphatically, that foreign politics were made not with the
heart but with the head, and defended our refusal to receive the
Boer generals who had arrived in Berlin shortly before. Sentiment
in Berlin was still so anti-English that the hotel where General de
Wet and his two comrades stayed was surrounded the whole day by
crowds that sang *"Die Wacht am Rhein"*, Luther's song of the
Firm Stronghold, and *"Deutschland über alles."* If I am not
mistaken, the Boer general, who was so fêted by Berliners at the
time, fought against us on the English side in the Great War. I told
the Pan-Germans on this occasion, and not only them but a great
number of other Germans as well, that rudeness was not dignity and
offensiveness not firmness. I told them how every business man
knows that bad manners are not necessary in commercial dealings,
Jingoism and love of country were not identical, a constant grumbling and threatening and scolding of foreign countries are not proof
of national consciousness. If the art of being Foreign Secretary consisted chiefly in thumping the table every once in a while, then many

were fit to be Foreign Secretaries. We ought not to act the part of braggarts and bombasts, but follow the good German tradition of the strong, silent man who without heroic verbiage defends himself and his family. The Pan-Germans, I may add to-day, have done us much harm by their exaggerations, their tactlessness, and their absolute lack of political judgment. I own that they sinned less from malice than from naïve simplicity which German politicians display only too often.

The regrettable consequence of the Swinemünde telegram was that it led to the resignation of Count Crailsheim. who was a statesman. I heard of it on the day when the resignation was made known by none other than the Centre member and future Bavarian Premier and German Chancellor Hertling. The immediate cause of the Count's overthrow was Schädler, who in a speech at a popular assembly in Munich talked with absurd exaggeration of the "boiling Bavarian national soul." This worthy national soul had quite different reason to "boil" during the Eisner era. My mention of the imperial comment on the margin of the Millerand despatch led to a meeting between myself and the Socialist member Vollmar. The latter, who led the moderate wing of the Socialists, the so-called Revisionists, asked me for an interview which I accorded him gladly. I got the impression not only of a clever but of a sincere and strong-principled man, with whom, regardless of the difference in our views, a practical understanding was quite possible. But it would have been necessary to begin by drawing Ministers from amongst various parties and to this the Kaiser would never agree, even after my election victory of January, 1907, through his fear of having his personal liberty curtailed, his speeches, his journeys, his abrupt decisions, and extempore addresses controlled and limited to narrow confines. Of course I did not mention my interview with Herr von Vollmar. But Bebel seemed somehow to have got wind of it, for on one of the following days he declared in one of his longest speeches, with a grim glance in Vollmar's direction, that he would never permit a Socialist to take over a Minister's portfolio without definite guarantees and under quite definite conditions.

After the temporary conclusion of these Kaiser debates, which were not only disagreeable but in many ways dangerous, the delegates of the three parties who had brought about the tariff reform, Count Hompesch for the Centre, Count Limburg-Stirum for the Conservatives, and Ernst Bassermann for the National-Liberals, all three men whose loyalty to the throne was above suspicion, came to see me. They handed me a memorandum in which it was stated that the thoughtlessness displayed by William II in his speeches and behaviour boded a grave danger for the Monarchy. They did not doubt the Kaiser's good will nor that his intentions were of the best. But through his overweening pride and his *faux pas* he was undermining the prestige and the future of the Monarchy. I, so they said in their memorandum, should see that the Kaiser displayed greater self-control and care in future. I told the gentlemen that with all respect for their loyal and patriotic sentiments and intentions I could not accept this memorandum. It would not be in keeping with my own royalist feelings nor with the traditional position of the monarchy in Germany and the spirit of our constitution. But I would nevertheless have a serious talk with His Majesty on the subject of their representations. The gentlemen assured me spontaneously that nothing of their present step would be made known outside. As I knew that my written protests made a more lasting impression on the Kaiser than my spoken words, I addressed a very detailed and earnest letter to him next day in which I said things much to this effect: I knew very well that any serious thought of a *coup d'état* and a breach of the Constitution was far from his thoughts, not only from motives of conscience, but also because he was too clever not to realise that if so radical a step were taken, the opportunity had offered itself in 1890 but had been missed. Besides we were united in believing that only the creator of the Empire and author of its Constitution, Prince Bismarck, could have carried out such a life-and-death operation. If an attempt were made on the part of revolutionaries to overthrow order, disrupt the Constitution, and bring about an upheaval, any such efforts would be parried with firmness not only by myself but by any Chancellor worthy of the name. But the Kaiser would certainly share my conviction that we desired neither to wage a prophylactic war outside, nor bring about a prophylactic overthrow at home. But just because the Kaiser had so often expressed himself to this effect in earnest conversation, so must he be careful not to give both Germany and the world at large a false picture of his intentions by means of his speeches and his gestures. If he did not exert greater reserve on this head and use more self-control, a catastrophe might occur sooner or later. It is a fine proof of the noble core of the Kaiser's character that he did not take this communication amiss at the time, nor bear any grudge against me for it afterwards. He replied that he knew perfectly that I meant well with him and believed I was doing my duty towards the Crown. But he could not change his character and must remain his old self. Everything else we must leave to God, who had always held His protective hand over the house of Hohenzollern and would not desert him either. William II was not of a dæmonic nature. Still less was he a son of Tantalus. But the god had forged a bronze fetter around his brows as well. And what Goethe's Iphigenia said to King Thoas about the regrettable consequences that overtake princes when they lose sight of "patience, wisdom, moderation, and counsel" was true as well of William II.

CHAPTER XXXVIII

William II's Trip to Rome — Diplomatic Shuffle Preceding It — Philipp Eulenburg Resigns, Karl Wedel Succeeds Him in Vienna, Monts Transferred to Rome — The Kaiser's Suite — His Personal Relationship with Victor Emanuel III — Bülow's Interviews with the King of Italy and Giolitti — William II Visits Leo XIII — His Written Account of This Meeting — The Pope's Costly Gift to Bülow — His Holiness' Reception of the Imperial Suite — Confidential Dispatch of Philipp Eulenburg as to His Majesty's Mood, Her Majesty, and Life on Board the Hohenzollern.

FOR some time past the Kaiser had been planning a trip to Rome. William II was to return the visit paid by King Victor Emanuel to Berlin and Potsdam in August, 1902. After considerable negotiating between the two courts the journey was fixed for May, 1903.

The Kaiser always went to Italy gladly. Like his parents, he was attracted by the beauties of its landscape and the treasures of its art galleries. He was also eager to see Leo XIII again. The Pope's fine intellect had great attractions for him.

An important change of office had preceded this Rome journey. Prince Philipp Eulenburg, ambassador in Vienna, had temporarily retired. I was sorry to see him leave Vienna, where he had a satisfactory position, was liked by the old emperor Francis Joseph, and had gained great influence in widespread circles by means of the great talent he showed in dealing with people. I have never been quite certain of the reasons for his resignation. When the unhappy man broke down six or seven years later, it was maintained that he had succumbed to blackmail levied on him in Vienna. There were no proofs. I incline rather to the opinion that Eulenberg had so far lost himself in the labyrinth of personal intrigues that he saw no way out save his resignation, which he himself regarded as only temporary. He was more than ever intent upon retaining the goodwill and friendship of the Kaiser.

To make this situation intelligible, I shall have to throw some light on a very disagreeable set of circumstances with which I had endeavoured to avoid contact because I was fully taken up with affairs of state. The intricacies and the whole inside truth of the events only became clear to me later on. In his letters Eulenburg had for years called my attention to the growing influence of the brothers Hülsen upon His Majesty. This had not made any particular impression upon me, for being fully taken up with more serious matters, I took little notice of goings-on at court. When the elder of the two brothers, Count Dietrich Hülsen, who later became chief of the military cabinet, came to Vienna as military attaché, he was accorded the friendliest reception by the ambassador, Eulenburg. That unfortunately did not prevent Eulenburg from making fun of Hülsen and his excellent wife in his letters to the Kaiser. This was done partly to amuse His Majesty and partly perhaps to discredit a possible rival before it should be too late. The couple with their pronounced Berlin manners did not, it is true, altogether suit Viennese society. The Kaiser read the letters, laughed over them, and then marked them with the usual sign "M. K.," that is to say, "Military Cabinet." They were added to the personal archives of General Count Hülsen-Haesller. When in 1901 Hülsen was nominated chief of the Military Cabinet, he took all personal documents including those relating to himself. There he found the sarcastic remarks made by Eulenburg, whom he had thought his friend, about himself and his wife. Ever since then he was a bitter enemy of the ambassador in Vienna. Eulenburg, who noticed this, tried to win back Dietrich Hülsen and hoped to do so by appointing his brother, George Hülsen, director of the Court Theatre at Wiesbaden, as manager of the Court Theatre at Berlin. This post had been in the hands of Count Bolko Hochberg, who until that day was a friend of Eulenburg, at whose silver wedding he had made a speech toasting him before a large circle of people in sincere and heartfelt language. This friendship was now turned to enmity, which was not good for Eulenburg, seeing the general esteem in which Hochburg was held. Still more grave was the fact that it also brought about a complete rupture as well with the friend of Count Hochburg, Prince Richard Dohna, who at the time had introduced Philipp Eulenburg to the Kaiser's circle but who now declared that he was weary of his

continual intrigues and wished to break off acquaintance. Prince
Dohna later on did much to bring about the fall and ruin of Philipp
Eulenburg. When I look back upon those intrigues, so often petty,
still more often spiteful and low, I understand everything said by
great poets from Sophocles to Shakespeare, and deep thinkers from
La Rochefoucauld and Montaigne to Schopenhauer, about the low
instincts of mankind and the worthlessness of the world. Though
here I must not forget to add that I believe things to be no better in
other countries, other strata of society, and under other constitutional forms. The reason for such occurrences lies as little in the
form of government as in the climate or in the race; it is to be
found in the baseness of human nature itself.

To overthrow Hochberg, Eulenburg had blackened the reputation
of his factotum in the management of the Royal Theatre, *Geheimrat* Pierson, in various influential places and in particular in the
eyes of His Majesty. Pierson heard of this and threatened Eulenburg with a libel action, as he had also accused him of tampering
with the receipts. Very frightened at this unforeseen turn taken by
the suspicions he himself had launched, Eulenburg begged the chief
of the Civil Cabinet, His Excellency Lucanus, in a long and agitated
communication, to prevail upon Pierson to withdraw his action, for
if so grave a case were brought before the courts, it would not only
damage him but the Kaiser indirectly as well. Eulenburg declared
that, owing to his state of health, he had been thinking of retiring for
some time past, but urged him not to let him fall from grace over
a public scandal. He was ready to give Pierson every satisfaction
required. At the same time Eulenburg wrote to me:

I feel terribly about causing you nothing but trouble all the time! For
this reason it is better that I should go. The stupid affair, Hochberg-
Pierson, is taking on an aspect which is not only grave for me but for His
Majesty as well. The libel action of Pierson, who, I may tell you in confidence, is a most dangerous man, must be avoided, that is to say, it must
be withdrawn. I do not think this will be difficult, as Pierson is a civil servant and we have him in our hands. Be so kind as to talk to Lucanus
immediately. You can imagine what the effect of a case would be in
which I would be accused of libel. I am so absolutely done up that you

must seriously consider my resignation. I really am taking this step for reasons of health, but want to do it in peace, and think of settling for the first years in my house on Lake Starnberg or in Munich — far away from all the turmoil which I can no longer stand. I implore you now: put this dreadful thing to rights. It is causing me the most terrible agitation because I cannot bear the disappointment caused me by old friends I believed faithful. Forgive your tenderly loving and grateful,

Philipp Eulenburg

A few days later Eulenburg wrote me:

It worries me unspeakably to think that I am again the one to cause you embarrassments and worry! This must come to an end. The least I can do for you out of the deep gratitude I feel towards you is to give you a little more peace on my account. I don't want your loyalty and your friendship for me and mine to be made a constant burden through the shadows that pass over my own life. There are only a very few people who love you as I do. I hope indeed that the present threatening question will be settled. But this must be the final one. It is now only the question of settling the most favourable moment for my resignation. The reason is my health. Certain people must be told too that this health can only be restored in the south, far from Berlin and all social life, and that I shall go to the Bavarian Highlands. My state of health is agonising, that is the plain truth, I can now find no other word to describe it. Ten years of uphill work with our dear Master have completely exhausted me. My brother's fate was the last straw. If I want to live at all, I must think of retiring. Besides there is the duty I owe you as a friend. I shall permit nothing to alter my resolve. With regard to the unfortunate affair with Pierson, which affects me deeply because I have been disappointed to a positively dreadful degree, it would perhaps be as well if you asked Prince Dohna to come and see you. Envy has made the old playmate of my childhood my enemy. He is, deep down, both egotistical and false, but he is extremely ambitious and vain and you can twist him round your finger like a ribbon. He will come round when you tell him that I was always useful to H. M. and never lied to H. M.!! Tell him he would do a good thing if he managed to settle the Pierson-Hochberg affair. I would then in memory of the friendship of our early days and our ties of relationship be willing to draw the veil of affection over the bitter insults I have suffered. Always your eternally grateful,

Philipp Eulenburg

The situation became more complicated because Eulenburg called a Frau Bach as witness on behalf of everything he had spread abroad regarding the alleged defalcations of Pierson and in particular all that he told His Majesty on the subject. Now, when the Kaiser was told by a Bavarian prince that Eulenburg practised spiritualism with a Frau Bach, he — Eulenburg — gave his word of honour that he did not know a woman of this name. The unfortunate Eulenburg had caught himself in his own net, a thing that does occasionally happen to skilful people. His fears and sorrows were very quickly ended. Death stepped in as *Deus ex machina*, to cut yet another Gordian knot. *Geheimrat* Pierson, first provoked and then feared, was called from this world at a day's notice. Eulenburg, who found the death of this Mortimer very convenient, wrote to me :

The libel action has found a queer ending in Pierson's death. Whether Pierson has gone to Heaven or to Hell only the God who has summoned him knows. I thank you for your help with my whole heart! But how can I ever thank you, my good Bernhard? God will reward you one of these days, seeing that I myself can offer you only so feeble a reward.

Phil was like a tumbler, he got up as quickly as he fell down. He remained obstinately firm to his resolve to give up the Vienna post. But his relationship with His Majesty remained the old one. On his silver wedding the Kaiser telegraphed to him :

The Lord preserve you for our Fatherland, my faithful friend for me, and your splendid wife and dear and excellent children for you.

The ambassador in Rome, Count (later on Prince) Karl Wedel, who had been military attaché in Vienna in Prince Bismarck's day, appeared to me the suitable successor for Eulenburg. The Kaiser accepted this suggestion. Karl Wedel was one of the most efficient, honest, and, in the best sense of the word, distinguished men I have ever met. A typical native of East Frisia in his love of truth and his sincere and chivalrous spirit. He came from the Hannoverian army, in whose ranks he had fought at Langensalza. Holstein, who did not like him, used this fact for occasional insinuations. "A man

with the Langensalza Medal is impossible as Prussian Ambassador."
Naturally I did not permit such machinations to influence me. I
thought of the fine words which, in truly regal manner, William I
addressed to an officer of pure Hannoverian family, who, on the eve of
the Battle of Gravelotte, presented himself with a small detachment
as night guard of the royal tent. When the old King noticed the
Langensalza Medal on the officer's breast, he said to him: "I see
that you are a Hannoverian and have done your duty as a Hannoverian officer. I am doubly glad to place myself under your protection."

Wedel had gained much respect and many friends in Rome
through his open disposition. I chose as his successor Count
Monts. That was a sad mistake. I certainly did not make this
choice on account of the flattery Monts had bestowed upon me for
many years past with untiring zeal. His fulsome adulation was
unpleasant because it was exaggerated. I chose Monts because
I believed that his vivacious wit and his rather democratic political
attitude would lighten his task in Rome. When I told the Italian
ambassador, Lanza, of my intention of sending Monts to Rome,
he urged me to refrain from doing so, as Monts was notorious in
the whole diplomatic world of Europe for his tactlessness and bad
manners. Next day Count Lanza mentioned the matter again.
He showed me a telegram from the Italian ambassador in Munich,
whose opinion he had asked, and who informed him that Monts
had made himself impossible in every Munich circle, at court, in
society, and in artistic coteries as well. He was also an arch enemy
of Catholicism, which would arouse as little pleasure in Rome as it
had done in Munich. But I refused to listen to this. I stubbornly
insisted on my choice, and the unfortunate nomination took place.
I scarcely need add that the gratitude of Count Monts, who had
never dreamed of getting as far as an Embassy, was at first boundless. He wrote to my wife that he well knew that the great advancement was only due to myself. In his joy he underlined the word
"only" three times. "And you," he added, "were the good fairy
who protected me and furthered my candidacy." The last was not
even true, for my wife never mixed in personal politics. To give

his gratitude outward expression the "most devoted and thankful" Monts had a nail, which he declared he had found when walking with my wife, mounted on a silver ashtray as a symbol of good luck, and sent it to her. *Eheu!* Nail and ashtray must still be in some cupboard or other at Flottbeck or in the Villa Malta with other old souvenirs. After my resignation I heard no more from Count Monts.

Early in May the Kaiser began his trip to Rome. I noticed that at the station at Berlin he was surrounded only by very tall officers: Hellmuth Moltke, Dietrich Hülsen, Plessen, and others. After they had started, the even taller Kleist joined us and then General Jacoby, one of the tallest officers in the army, and last of all the very, very tallest, Colonel von Plüskow, who was called in Paris "*Plusquehaut*" once when he was there on a special mission. The Kaiser wished to impress Rome with these giants, which was in itself a wrong idea; there are many very tall men in Italy, especially in the north, and the Guardia Regia, the Italian Royal Guard, consists of positive giants. The very idea was scarcely tactful, for as King Victor Emanuel III is short of stature, it was not a happy notion to confront him with this gigantic array. I particularly urged the Kaiser to be amiable towards the King, who, accustomed himself to behaving modestly, did not like what the Italian calls "*prepotenza*" in others. And so this time matters went smoothly between King and Kaiser. Toward Queen Elena, the Kaiser had not yet developed that inexplicable antipathy into which he was driven later by the tactless dispatches of Count Monts.

It was after my resignation that the Kaiser let himself go more and more in his treatment of the Italian royalties. Ultimately the fault was Herr von Bethmann's. It was his own as well as our misfortune that after his nomination as Chancellor, he selected *Geheimrat* von Flotow to instruct him in the Arcana Imperii. Flotow made a point of explaining to the new Chancellor that it was because of my fondness for playing tutor to His Majesty that he had grown tired of me long before the events of November, 1908. As Bethmann was filled with a burning desire to stay in office — no Minister clung to office as he did — he yielded to the Kaiser in everything from the very beginning. One of the many consequences of this weakness was the ever-increasing tension between the German Kaiser and the Italian sovereign.

In 1903 the relationship was still fairly good. King Victor Emanuel told me in the long interview he honoured me with on our arrival at the Quirinal that he was mainly interested in Albania, where he could permit no other power, least of all Austria-Hungary, to gain a footing. Italy could not allow any extension of Austria in the Balkan peninsula, particularly on the Adriatic coast. This was a vital issue for the Italian dynasty. I emphatically told the King that Austria desired neither extension of territory in Albania nor Macedonia. She possessed ancient rights guaranteed by the Treaty of Berlin and various special agreements with Russia in Bosnia and Herzegovina. Albania and Macedonia would never be touched and we should not permit any hot-blooded Magyars or restless members of the general staff to display military sentiments toward Servia and Roumania. "*L'Allemagne veut la paix.*" The Magyars were, by the way, against an enlargement of the Hapsburg monarchy because this would affect their hegemony. I found full understanding of my explanations on the part of the Chancellor Zanardelli and the Foreign Secretary Admiral Morin. The King was less amenable. He was openly distrustful of Austria. He told me with the candour I had always found in him that it was a disgrace that the Viennese visit of King Humbert had not yet been returned in Rome.

That, he said, was a "slap in the face", aimed not only at his dead father but at himself, his dynasty, and his country.

The Marquis Visconti-Venosta, with whom I dined *à trois* at my mother-in-law's house, insisted upon what I had so often heard from Italians: that relations between Italy and Austria could not, like those between Italy and England, or Austria-Hungary and France, be a shade better or a shade worse without risk. Italy and Austria-Hungary must be either sincere friends or conscious enemies by reason of the past and of irredentism. Any serious cooling of Italian-Austrian relations would soon lead to direct enmity. He, Visconti, did not demand of me that I act as perpetual mediator between Austria-Hungary and Italy, but I must keep a sharp eye on both and prevent either from careless acts. *"L'Autriche-Hongrie et l'Italie sont deux chevaux très enclins à se mordre; c'est au cocher, c'est-à-dire à l'Allemagne, de les faire marcher ensemble. En somme, tout dépend de l'Allemagne, de l'habileté de sa politique, du doigté de son chancelier."*

The King spoke to me of the Minister of the Interior, Giolitti, with the greatest warmth and esteem, because he understood how to treat the masses. The constitutional question had to be relegated to the background, behind the economic question, and a reconciliation had to be brought about between the dynasty and the masses. It was undeniable, he said, that in Italy, particularly in the South, there was still everything to be done as far as social reform was concerned. Giolitti was personally devoted to him and too clever to believe that an Italian Republic could be permanently maintained. He had good nerves, no fear, and was a born Minister of the Interior. Giovanni Giolitti pleased me personally by his quiet and businesslike manner. The friendly relations I maintained for many years with this distinguished Italian statesman were begun during that Imperial visit to Rome in 1903. In those days there was much grumbling over Giolitti as well as over the royal couple in the drawing-rooms of Roman society, because the democratic views of both were displeasing to the aristocratic classes. But both were on the right path under the circumstances as they were then. Giolitti was a supporter of the Triple Alliance and instrumental in preserving its unaltered form when it was renewed.

As for relations with France, the King told me they were very good, which was, indeed, to Italy's interest. All the Italian politicians with whom I spoke expressed the wish to remain friendly with France, on the one hand, so that Italy might obtain the necessary loan for building railways and not injure its commercial interests, yet, on the other hand, I encountered the general conviction that not only the Italian monarchy but Italian unity would be endangered if Italy were solely dependent upon France. Concerning Barrère the King said in English at the time to the Kaiser: "I don't like him. He is a liar and a nasty man." Great mistakes

must have been made in Vienna and Berlin to drive the King into
the arms of Barrère.

On May 3rd we drove to the Vatican. The Kaiser had had his
gala carriage and the magnificent Trakehn chargers sent to Rome
as well as two squadrons of the Gardes-du-Corps regiment which rode
in front and behind. It was a singular spectacle to see Pope and
Kaiser together in one of the ceremonial halls of the Vatican. The
Kaiser just forty-four, and in his prime, outwardly even younger than
his years, full of enthusiasm and warmth, impressionable and imaginative to a high degree; so may Kaiser Otto III have faced Pope
Sylvester II. Leo XIII, ninety-three years old but upright and
unbent, his finely cut Italian features marble in a pallor that was
heightened by his white vestments; everything about him had a
spiritual aspect. He was very amiable, but, in accordance with
Italian *gentilezza*, without too much emphasis or officiousness. His
poise was perfect, particularly in the sense that no impression from
without could shake his equilibrium, let alone endanger it. Shortly
before he had said, smiling, to a lady who, at the close of her audience,
told him she prayed to God that he might live to be a hundred:
"Pourquoi mettre des limites à la bonté divine?" At the same
time he treated his body so austerely that he would not allow himself to be chloroformed during a painful operation at this great age.
He had wonderfully fine eyes in which shone the unassailable faith
of the earthly representative of Christ convinced of his sacred
mission, and at the same time something of that impalpable scepticism peculiar to many Italian statesmen of the Holy See, in the
council chambers of Venice and Genoa, on the princely thrones of
Florence and Ferrara. This shade of scepticism was not missing
either in those men who constructed the united and national Italian
state under tremendous difficulties, in Massimo d'Azeglio nor
Ricasoli, Minghetti nor Visconti-Venosta, Ratazzi nor Depretis.
Nor was it absent from the greatest of them all, Cavour. It did not
exclude glowing patriotism and firm faith in the *Stella d'Italia*, but
it prevented many foolish actions which were committed elsewhere.

Immediately after the audience with the Pope a *déjeuner dîna-
toire* was given by the Prussian ambassador at the Vatican, Baron

Rotenhan, in the Kaiser's honour, to which several Cardinals and Prince Baldassare Odescalchi were invited. After lunch Odescalchi, who, by the way, was an old Garibaldian and once drove through the streets of Rome in a red shirt at the hero's side, engaged in lively conversation with Cardinal Gotti, who was considered a Papabile. As I came up the Prince was just asking the Cardinal jestingly: "What is going to happen later on when Church and State are reconciled? Must all Cardinals become Princes or all Princes become Cardinals?" Pleasantly, but in all seriousness, Gotti replied: "The joke is delicate and between ourselves as Italians we can say everything. We always understand one another in the long run." With a glance in my direction the dignified prince of the church added in a low voice: "We must be careful when foreigners are present."

The guests had barely withdrawn when the Kaiser dictated his whole interview with Leo XIII to Rotenhan. I append this because it not only throws an interesting side-light on the Kaiser's character but is a valuable historical document as well.

The Pope was pleased to welcome me for the third time: God gave him so long a life that he was able to celebrate this extraordinary jubilee. I had taken notice of this by means of a special mission and had sent General von Loë to him, a man who particularly gratified him, for which he was quite specially grateful to me. Myself: I hoped that Providence may grant that he may live to celebrate his jubilee when he is a hundred.

The Pope: That lay in God's hand. He was glad to call my attention to the fact that his room was ornamented with gifts I had sent him. (A reference to porcelain vases.) He was always surrounded by them.

Myself: They were tokens of my devotion and respect for his venerable person which, so I hoped, might long be preserved for the well-being of Christendom.

The Pope: He was glad to have this opportunity of thanking me in particular for the fact that I was constant in my care for the welfare of my Catholic subjects. He had heard this from so many sides that he laid stress on telling me in person how grateful for my care he and these subjects were. He could assure me that in good times and evil, my Catholic subjects would stand by me in absolute loyalty. "*Ils resteront absolument et infailliblement fidèles.*"

Myself : I consider it my duty as a Christian sovereign to look after all my subjects to the best of my endeavours without distinction of religious faith and the practice of their duties towards the head of their Church. This was one of the maxims guiding my life and I would never depart from it.

The Pope : He could only confirm the principles with which I governed, and accord them the fullest recognition. He had followed my reign with the greatest interest and observed with great pleasure that I had built up my rule on the basis of an absolute Christianity and was guided by such exalted religious principles that he could do no more than implore the blessing of Heaven for myself, the dynasty, and the German Empire, and bestow it upon me.

Myself : I thanked him for the kindly dispensation of his blessing with the remark that it would certainly be a benefit to me in my future life and one of which I should always be proud.

The Pope : By meeting one another half-way we had settled the little matter in Strassburg to our mutual satisfaction. There were some small difficulties to be overcome which had been easily settled. The Strassburg clericals had certainly shown opposition, but as we had been so obliging he had put the affair in order and hoped I would be satisfied.

Myself : I was deeply grateful and believed the clericals would derive great benefit from it, so that they would soon recognise the advantage of the agreement.

The Pope : Monsieur Hertling had taken great pains and "*ce très cher* Cardinal Kopp" as well. He was a man we could both rely on, for he was candid and sincere and always presented things as they really were. He was always pleased to see him and I could have full confidence in him as a loyal subject.

Myself : The Cardinal enjoyed my fullest esteem ; he always helped in smoothing over difficult points and bridging differences. I thought very highly of him. I would soon have an opportunity of seeing him. The portal of Metz Cathedral, the reconstruction of which His Holiness had doubtless heard of, would be unveiled in a solemn manner after my return. If His Holiness agreed, Cardinal Kopp and the Archbishop of Cologne would be invited as *Testes Solemnes* to the ceremony which the excellent Bishop Benzler would conduct in person.

The Pope : He had heard of it, was looking forward very much to the photograph, and was glad that Bishop Benzler had done so well in Metz.

Myself : I thank His Holiness heartily for this man whom he had nominated. He was the right man in the right place, enjoyed great popularity and had considerably enhanced the prestige of the episcopacy all the more so as the long vacancy that followed Sprengel had begun to make itself felt disadvantageously, and, in the interests of my Catholic subjects, I thought such vacancies bad from the religious standpoint as the religious needs of the parishes suffered under them.

The Pope: This also showed him that I was constantly caring for the maintenance of religion among the people.

Myself: I suggested to His Holiness, as a particular honour for the diocese of Metz, that he should permit himself to be represented personally by Cardinal Kopp. It would not only honour Metz but the whole province.

The Pope: He was extremely flattered, thought the idea an excellent one, and would have it carried out immediately. He wished to know the date the consecration was to take place.

Myself: I thank His Holiness heartily for the great pleasure he was affording my Catholic subjects in Alsace-Lorraine.

The Pope: Above everything he wished me to know what an indelible impression my speech in Aix-la-Chapelle had made upon him : it had given him enormous pleasure. At a time when most of the European sovereigns were weak, timid, or indifferent to religion, it had particularly rejoiced his heart that the German Kaiser had placed himself, his dynasty, and the whole great Empire under the protection of the Cross, regardless of what the rest of the world in its avoidance of the Cross might say. That was the way in which the monarch of a great country ought to speak, and those were principles which he could not but recommend to all my royal colleagues. He wished to add, and this not in a spirit of flattery, that there was only one sovereign who had thought and acted in the same manner, and that was Charlemagne. He was the great ruler who at God's command had subjected the whole civilised world of that day to the Cross and to whom this mission had been entrusted by Pope Leo III. As he pondered over my speech a dream came into his mind and that was the idea of the German Kaiser of to-day receiving from him, Pope Leo XIII, the same mission, to fight socialist and atheistic ideas, and bring Europe back again to Christianity. He knew very well that Europe was divided into nations and countries that could not politically be united under one sceptre, but in a spiritual sense the Kaiser of the German Empire could by influence and exhortation prevail upon these countries to incline towards Christianity and the Church once more.

Myself: I would gladly undertake the mission the Pope had, so to speak, set before me and by word and deed and with unimpaired energy work towards the end that princes and peoples would at last be convinced that all power, all progress, and all glory availed nought unless founded upon the Person of our Saviour and the Cross. That a Pope ninety-three years old could utter such exalted words to so young a monarch as myself would fill me with pride for my whole life and I hoped that he would not find me an intractable pupil, and that God might give him life and health to support me in my endeavours and favour the success of the mutual coöperation of Kaiser and Pope.

The Pope: Wickedness was very rife in the world, unhappily many personal attacks were still be ng made, as for instance on King Humbert ("*Il a été tué, cruellement tué*"). But it was possible to fight evil with spiritual weapons and religion must be defended and strengthened against it. He knew that I occupied much of my time with religious questions, particularly in what concerned Biblical research; it would interest me to know that he had convened a commission for renewed research into the scriptures. The library and all archives were open to the research workers, and as proof of how highly he esteemed the German spirit of investigation he mentioned that eleven Germans had been summoned to join the commission. Altogether he had had much to do with Germans of late. He had had the pleasure of receiving several trains of German pilgrims, among them 2000 from Cologne, and had rejoiced at their devout and meditative spirit. A number of German bishops had been present, he had ordered them to present themselves to me. In short, he was surrounded by Germans and of late had become almost half German himself ("*Je suis devenu presque un demi-Allemand*").

Myself: I was pleased that the piety of my subjects and fellow countrymen had met with his approval, and could assure him that the German Catholics were certainly the most religious sons of the Church, and, in their German loyalty, his most devoted subjects.

The Pope: He would compare me not only with Charlemagne. I seemed to follow in the path of my great ancestor Frederick II also. When he was younger, he had studied Frederick's life zealously and felt great admiration for the soaring flight of his spirit as well as for his views on the religious communities: he had always looked after the interests of his Catholic subjects, for when he conquered Silesia there were fears for the welfare of the Catholic population. But these fears were groundless. The king guaranteed the Catholics the safe practice of their religion and cared for them well. I was doing the same thing and that was why he made the comparison. But he felt obliged to add that Frederick the Great was not particularly firm in his own religious convictions ("*Il était peu croyant*"). Therefore it was all the more to be esteemed that the King had done so much to promote religion, including the faith of the Catholic Church; he hoped I would follow this good example.

Myself: His Holiness was too flattering, and all this praise embarrassed me, but I would certainly follow his good advice. If I might once more refer to his comparison with Charlemagne and his mission, I would like to remark that the Great World Empire of Romans which the Emperor, at the behest of Leo III, had endeavoured to found as the heritage of the Roman Caesars, was, according to my conviction, now incorporated and perpetuated more grandiosely in a spiritual sense than ever before, in the person of the Pontifex seated in front of me. Millions in all corners of the world venerated him as their leader. For that reason he, Leo XIII, was to be regarded as the Imperator (Imperii Romani) and the heir of the Roman Caesars. The Pope sat up straight in his chair, looked at me for a while with an astonished mien, and said, after a short pause, gratitude shining in his eyes: "*Eh bien, ce n'est pas mal cela, et peut-être vous avez raison.*" Wilhelm I. R.

So much for the Imperial report of this memorable and remarkable conversation between the chief of the German Empire and the Pontifex Maximus. The Kaiser had added a postscript in his own writing: "The Pope also asked His Majesty how German naval construction stood and how much he hoped that he would get a strong and powerful navy to safeguard peace and German cultural interests."

As a souvenir of the Kaiser's visit, Leo XIII sent me the twenty-five gold medallions made by the Papal mint which was renowned for its fine workmanship. These had been minted at intervals from the beginning of his term of office to the year of his jubilee and commemorated, according to the tradition of the Holy See, any particularly memorable sacerdotal or political act of the Pope: a very valuable gift from the artistic point of view and one very precious to me. The Pope's favours were also extended to the Kaiser's personal servants and his suite, a fine proof of the human sentiments of the Pontifex. The subordinate officials of the three Imperial cabinets, the body servants of His Majesty, the body guards, the clerks of the Chancellery and personal staff, sixty people in all, were received by His Holiness in a special audience. Leo XIII, who received them under a red canopy, asked whether they understood Italian. Nobody replied, but my old Italian valet, Augusto, approached him with Italian bravado and declared that he had been born in Valmontone in the Sabine hills and wished to act as interpreter. The Pope asked in a low voice whether those present were Catholics or Protestants. Augusto replied: "*Santo Padre, sono tutti heretici, ma non cattivi, anzi bravissima gente.*" Whereupon the Pope gave everybody present his hand. His particular interest was aroused by two subalterns of the Gardes-du-Corps, whose appearance, typically German, in their magnificent uniforms caused him to exclaim: "*Questi sono davvero Germani!*" Finally the Holy Father made the following speech in French: "You serve the German Kaiser who has given me great pleasure by his visit. You can be proud of serving such an Emperor and I exhort you always to be loyal to him. In expectation of this I give my blessing to you and your families." When the Imperial party left Rome on May 5th, a long train full of German pilgrims had just arrived. They greeted the Kaiser with indescribable enthusiasm, singing the national anthem and the "*Wacht am Rhein.*" It was a grand moment.

Philipp Eulenburg, who accompanied the Kaiser on his northern trips after his resignation just as before, kept me informed from there and Rominten about His Majesty's state of mind and his actions. Early in August, 1903, he wrote me from Odde on the Hardanger Fjord, from the spot whence William II, eleven years later, was to return to the Great War:

You will not find H. M. altered in the slightest: he is lively and in good humour, pleased to see you again and confide his political troubles to you, perhaps a shade less grave than they are now made to appear. He has a mixture of respect tempered with fear with regard to yourself, for he occasionally has a dim, and sometimes a clear feeling, that without you he cannot get any further. . . . I do not think a crisis with regard to his health imminent. It could only occur if any difficult or very serious political events broke in upon the Kaiser's overwrought nerves. Nor would this crisis — as so many think, or hope — take the form of a mental disturbance; it would manifest itself in a nervous breakdown. The Kaiser's nature, if he collapses entirely, will become a prey to dreadful convulsions, the effect of which on the business of government and on his association with the highest officers of the Empire cannot be foreseen. The crisis will take on abnormal forms without being abnormal and through its indefinite character place all the responsible parties in terrible difficulties. If H. M. is not forced either by his own decision or the will of his doctors into a temporary state of rest, both mental and physical, the slightest thing might upset his equilibrium. Leuthold is not the man to fight for this period of rest, he is yielding and timid, and H. M. is too accustomed to him.

Eulenburg told me further that outwardly things on board the *Hohenzollern* were much as "in the most frivolous lieutenant's casino." Those who were forced to deal with official matters, Moltke, Scholl, Usedom, Tschirschky, Lyncker, were "completely done up." A few days ago an article written by the historian, Oncken, "The Flight of the Prince of Prussia to England 1848", was read aloud in the evening and put the Kaiser into a state of "pathological violence." He described the coming revolution and its overthrow. He desired to take Revenge!! for 1848. Then he went on, nothing but contradictions, complete vagueness, incredible exclamations: "Every human being is a beast that can only be controlled and directed by very definite orders." As the generals of 1848 were the subject of conversation this remark was meant to be applied to generals in particular. The Kaiser then walked about for hours with a disturbed countenance. Then he, Eulenburg, approached him and talked of all sorts of unimportant matters so as to calm him. "But he listened to me absentmindedly. Then he began to tell — yes, I had better say it straight out — the most frightful lies. All about ancient private affairs concerning himself. He must have known that I knew all about them, but appeared to have forgotten. I listened in complete silence. But there was no end to it. He made a terrible impression on me — pale, glancing about him uneasily, orating, and piling lie upon lie.

Not healthy — this is probably the mildest verdict that can be given. Kessel told me that even during the short period of his command as general in Berlin, H. M. told him twice in open telegrams on quite insignificant occasions to open fire on the people. Kessel said the discretion of the post-office appeared to him worthy of all admiration. As he did not obey instructions he expected some kind of remark — but nothing at all happened."

Eulenburg also wrote that the Kaiser was under the influence of the agitation set up by the feeling that his efforts to woo England and Russia had been in vain. He also had the feeling that he no longer dared risk the startling coups his great vanity longed for. Besides this, there was the ridiculously unhealthy life led during the northern trip "on board this floating theatre." From Rominten, Eulenburg complained of the Empress in his customary manner.

Her love for H. M. is like the passion of a cook for her sweetheart who shows signs of cooling off. This method of forcing oneself upon him is certainly not the way to keep the beloved's affections.

With his acute sensibilities Eulenburg already felt that certain differences were developing between the Kaiser and his eldest son, who was very different from him. The Kaiser had given the Crown Prince a very strong-willed aide-de-camp because His Imperial and Royal Highness displayed a certain tendency to indulge in nonchalant modern manners, and this must be driven out of him. "There are strange contrasts developing here. On the one hand the Kaiser wants to make a modern monarch of the Crown Prince, on the other, to uphold old traditions. The modernity expresses itself as much in the artistic and fashionable tendencies as in the promotion of the great movements of world trade and traffic. The Crown Prince will never become a hybrid mixture of feudal feelings and commercial passions."

CHAPTER XXXIX

Death of Leo XIII (July 20, 1903) — Secret Report of Cardinal Kopp on the Conclave — Autumn Manoeuvres — Journey to Vienna, Archduke Francis Ferdinand and His Wife — William II after Some Demur Visits Princess von Hohenberg — Bülow's Interview with Goluchowski — Audience with the Emperor Francis Joseph — The Italian Ambassador Count Nigra — Tsar Nicholas in Hesse, William II in Wolfsgarten (February 4, 1903) — The Possibility of a Russo-Japanese Clash Becomes More Imminent — Conversations with Count Lambsdorff and Tsar Nicholas — Conversations of the Two Emperors — Operation on William II's Vocal Cords, His Courageous Behaviour.

In the course of the summer, Leo XIII sent my wife a handsome medallion and his blessing through Cardinal Kopp, and a message saying that he wished her to have a souvenir of him after his death — an event in all probability not far ahead. On July 20th this great Pope died. He is buried in the Lateran, appropriately next to Innocent III, *omnium ecclesiarum urbis et orbis mater et caput*. Many legends have circulated in regard to his successor. It is quite untrue that I abetted the Austrian veto on Rampolla. On the contrary, at my last meeting with Cardinal Kopp before the new Pope was elected, I expressly said that we had to remain as neutral as possible. Besides, according to a famous Italian proverb, many enter the conclave black who come out white, and sometimes it is the other way round.

On the day of the election Cardinal Kopp wrote me a letter giving me all details of proceedings in conclave which, owing to its documentary interest, I append here:

After the death of Leo XIII, the Papal legate in Munich sent the two German Cardinals an invitation to repair to Rome as soon as was possible. The other foreign Cardinals received this invitation as well, and nearly all arrived soon enough to participate in some of the ten general conferences held every day since the Pope's death to settle pressing episcopal matters. Among these was the particularly important question at which spot the new Pope should show himself to the people for the first time to bestow his first blessing. Before 1870 this took place of course from the foremost balcony overlooking St. Peter's square. But Leo XIII had by his Cardinals' advice performed this ceremony from the inner balcony leading to St. Peter's, so as to demonstrate by this act his attitude toward the new political order in Rome. It did not seem advisable to the Cardinals now for Leo XIII's successor to do otherwise, so as not to arouse vain hopes on the one side and suspicion on the other. Meanwhile, the Italian Cardinals had had time to come to an understanding on the election of Leo XIII's successor. Various groups had been formed, of which the strongest favoured Cardinal Rampolla. Other candidates were Serafino Vannutelli, de Pietro, and Gotti. There was nothing to be done except for the foreign Cardinals to try and form their own groups and make them as strong as possible. Therefore the German and Austrian Cardinals joined together (5 and 2) and tried to gain an influence on the other foreign Cardinals. This was successful in the case of the North American Cardinal, Gibbons, who did not openly join the group but voted with it; in the beginning, too, Cardinal Goossens, Archbishop of Malines, appeared to incline towards the Austro-German group, but seemed later on to join the French. It was not possible to get into touch with the French group; their leader was Cardinal Langénieux, but their real leader was the French Cardinal Matthieu. They had received from Delcassé the order to vote in a body for Rampolla and if his candidacy was hopeless, to vote for Serafino Vannutelli. The Spanish Cardinals had had orders from their Government to join with the Austrians, but the change of cabinet in Madrid made them uncertain, and under the leadership of the Spanish Cardinal Vives y Tuto, they all five joined the French. Any definite attitude on the part of the Portuguese Cardinal Netto and the Irishman Logue was not visible. With these groups the conclave opened on the evening of July 31st. The Austro-German Cardinals had determined at the beginning to vote for Cardinal Serafino Vannutelli, as they had been informed by the Austro-Hungarian ambassador, or by Cardinal Puscyna, that both the candidacy of Cardinal Rampolla and that of Cardinal Gotti was undesirable since it had been proved that they had both acted inimically to Austrian interests and only lately Cardinal Gotti had shown himself to be either inimical or incompetent in an Albanian affair. But at the last council of Austro-German bishops before the conclave so many misgivings had been uttered against Cardinal

Serafino Vannutelli, by Cardinal Fischer (Cologne), that the majority supported Gotti. During the discussion of Rampolla's candidacy many unjust and reckless charges and verdicts against the ecclesiastical administration and the policy of Leo XIII were made which, in spite of being refuted vigorously, had sullied the memory of the great Pope. The first counting of votes took place on the morning of August 1st. Rampolla received 24, Gotti 17, Sarto 5, Serafino Vannutelli 4, di Pietro 2, Oreglia 2, Agliardi and the others one each. At the second voting at five in the afternoon, Rampolla received 29, Gotti 16, Sarto 10 votes, the others were split up. After this ballot Cardinal Agliardi came to the undersigned, and said the situation was very serious. He said among other things that Rampolla was holding fast to the tiara although he well knew that he would only be Pope by Loubet's and Combes' favour. He was a deadly enemy of Austria and certainly no sincere friend of Germany, for which he felt no less fear than hatred. Gotti was also not to be recommended, and was compromised by the banking house of Pacelli. I supported the candidacy of Sarto, who deserved confidence in every respect. I informed Cardinal Fischer of this immediately and we then conferred with the Austrian Cardinals on the situation. After long consideration we came to the conclusion that the Gotti candidacy must be dropped, as it was hopeless, and that we must give our votes to Sarto. Only Cardinal Vaszari refused to join; he had been making himself conspicuous by his peculiarities the whole time. Cardinal Puscyna was given to understand that he could carry out his order of handing in the Imperial objections against Rampolla. Puscyna was still doubtful on this evening. Meanwhile the Austrian ambassador at the Holy See had informed Oreglia at the beginning of the conclave, on my advice, that he had an order of his Imperial master to execute at the conclave and therefore begged an audience. As he would not receive any more I advised him at the same time to inform the Camerlengo in writing that Cardinal Puscyna had an order from the Emperor Francis Joseph to submit reasons against the election of Cardinal Rampolla. Oreglia had not yet informed the Cardinals' Council of this. On the morning of August 2nd Cardinal Puscyna informed me that he had sent his order to Cardinal Oreglia in writing, but that the latter refused to inform the Council. When on the morning of August 2nd we assembled for the third ballot in the Sistine chapel, Cardinal Puscyna came to me and asked in a low voice: "What are we to do — and what am I to do?" I answered: "Sarto; proceed at once." This aroused no comment.

When the session had opened, Cardinal Puscyna asked the Camerlengo for the first speech and informed the council what he had given the Camerlengo. The latter was now obliged to mention the special order sent by the Austrian Crown concerning Cardinal Rampolla and had the Puscyna communication read aloud. I had the impression that this caused far less agitation among the Cardinals than I had feared. There had been a danger that the greater part of the Cardinals in their objection to interference in the Papal ballot would take the side of Rampolla and his election. But nobody rose to protest against the Austrian order save Rampolla himself. He protested with passionate indignation against this procedure as a new *Ictus contra libertatem Ecclesiae*. He made no impression, for in the third ballot he received 29 votes, while Sarto had 20 and Gotti was reduced to 9. In the fourth ballot on the afternoon of August 2nd Rampolla had only one more vote, bringing the number up to 30, while Sarto had 24 and Gotti 3. In the fifth ballot the morning of August 3rd Rampolla had only 24 votes, while Sarto already had 27 and Gotti again 6. In the sixth ballot in the afternoon Sarto rose to 35, while Rampolla fell to 16 and Gotti received 7. In the meantime Sarto had begged us, gravely and much moved, to refrain from electing him. Everybody was touched by his humility and anxiety, but nobody took any notice of his refusal. His friends even urged him to recant. In the seventh ballot the decision was made (August 4th at 10 o'clock in the morning) Sarto received 50 votes, Rampolla 10, and Gotti 2. Sarto was therefore elected. To the question of the Camerlengo as to whether he accepted the decision he replied with trembling voice that he must perforce acquiesce in God's will if the cup would not pass him by. He then took the name of Pius X. The outward appearance of the new Pope is not particularly impressive; he is humble and modest, amiable and kindly; he is accounted a zealous bishop, who administrated his dioceses of Mantua and Venice in exemplary manner. Born under Austrian rule in 1834 in the neighbourhood of Treviso, he was still kindly disposed towards Austria, and had some recollection of the German language. He had maintained good relations with the Italian government. The Queen Dowager Margherita respects him highly. He was once presented to His Majesty the German Emperor in Venice. He bestowed the first Papal blessing from the inner balcony for reasons mentioned above. I must add further that for seven years past I have prophesied to Cardinal Rampolla and again this winter, at the negotiations on the Samasses affair, what would threaten him from the Austrian

side. On the day of my arrival, July 23rd, I told him plainly what was
before him; he said that all he wanted was perfect peace. Yet he apparently hoped for his election and believed this to be so certain that he did
not believe my words. I took no part in the agitation against him.

Card. Kopp

Many complaints and much serious criticism reached me, particularly from the higher military circles, with regard to the autumn
manoeuvres of 1903. From the beginning of his reign, the Kaiser
had reserved the function of chief umpire at the big manoeuvres for
himself. It is only fair to recognize that he was particularly fitted
for this task. King Albert of Saxony told me that he knew few
generals who were such good critics at manoeuvres as William II
was. In this respect his peculiar gifts were a help to him; his
quick grasp and capacity for assimilation, his unquenchable flood
of eloquence. "If he is accompanied by one or two staff officers
who whisper what must be done at a manoeuvre, he will criticise
it afterwards in a manner which makes his listeners sit up." The
King added laughing: "For all that, he cannot lead three men
safely across a gutter." The King here expressed fears which he
shared with many others, that the Kaiser, in case of war, would
seize the supreme military command, a position he was by no means
equal to. I was able to reassure King Albert completely in this
respect. I always had the conviction that if matters grew serious,
the Kaiser would not take upon himself such responsibility, and
subsequent events proved I was right. At manoeuvres it was different. The Kaiser did not only want to criticise, he wanted to
command. But as commander he wanted to win every time.
This led to great bother, sometimes to scenes which were almost
comic. I remember manoeuvres when the Kaiser was commanding
the Blue Army. When the Red Army was receiving orders for
action the next day on the eve of an expected battle, the Red Chief
of Staff observed a royal aide-de-camp in the background. Asked
what he was doing there the intruder replied: "His Majesty's
orders!" It was clear that the Kaiser always remained victor if
he gained knowledge of his adversary's plans beforehand in this
way. Another weakness of His Majesty was for stupendous cavalry

attacks such as would never have been possible in warfare in face of the enemy's machine guns and artillery. These attacks were specially prepared for His Majesty. The ground was chosen months beforehand and put in order. The royal horses were taken over it till they knew it perfectly. As far as human calculation could foresee everything would go well. For the year 1903 at the manoeuvres of the fourth army corps the Kaiser had arranged that the most brilliant attack should take place on that historic battlefield where General von Seydlitz — "Herr Seydlitz on the Roan", as Theodor Fontane calls him in his great poem — with the cry of "Forward!" threw his pipe in the air in front of his line of cavalry as signal for one of the most brilliant cavalry attacks of history and one of the finest Prussian victories. From this battlefield the Kaiser telegraphed me on September 9th, 1903, concerning his attack: "The attack ended at Rossbach! I had sixty squadrons behind me whereas Seydlitz won his victory with only thirty-five squadrons! I hear that the impression made was a very deep one." The last sentence was intended to reassure me. The Kaiser knew that I never interfered in military matters on principle, but that I did not like his military games and in particular disliked this kind of nonsense at the manoeuvres. I did not conceal this from the Chief of Staff, the brilliant Count Alfred Schlieffen. He regarded the matter as I and all other sensible people did, but upheld the opinion that if the Kaiser left him a free hand in everything else, particularly in artillery matters, this "manoeuvre nonsense" was of no great importance. The troops were too well controlled by their commanders and the commanders too well trained for such false ideas of fighting to do harm.

A visit to Vienna concluded the manoeuvres. I awaited the Kaiser at Vienna-Neustadt. He had been staying at the Hungarian estate of the Archduke Frederick, where he had made dreadful havoc among the stags which had been carefully preserved for him. Archduke Frederick was married to a Princess Croy, who came from a mediatised, that is to say, royal, but not reigning house. She was all the more eager for her daughters to make wonderful matches. She had in the first place naturally cast an eye upon the heir presumptive, Archduke Francis Ferdinand, and was no little pleased when the latter paid frequent visits to her house. She was convinced that the visits were made because of her pretty daughters. All the greater was the shock when she suddenly noticed a gold bracelet with the Prince's portrait in miniature on the wrist of her maid of honour, Countess Sophie Chotek. There was a scene, at the end of which the maid of honour was brusquely dismissed. It is well known that the Archduke, in a manner which does him credit, kept faith with the girl he loved, and after surmounting great difficulties, married her. After that relations between Sophie Chotek, who was made Duchess of Hohenberg, and the Archduchess Frederick were very strained. The Archduchess made use of the Kaiser's hunt to influence that very impressionable monarch against morganatic marriages in general and the marriage of the Archduke Ferdinand in particular. The Kaiser received me at Vienna-Neustadt with the words: "Of course I shall take no notice of Francis Ferdinand's wife." Then he repaired with the ambassador Karl Wedel and myself to his saloon carriage. Wedel combated the unfriendly intentions of His Majesty concerning the wife of the heir to the Austrian throne with arguments both thorough and verbose, but only aroused a more and more irritable contradiction on His Majesty's part. The Kaiser burst out at length: "If I give way here I shall find my own sons one day marrying maids of honour or perhaps even chamber-maids!" The last case, thank goodness, did not happen, but the first came to pass, for the fifth son of the Kaiser, Prince Oscar, ten years later, married the charming Countess Ina Bassewitz, who was raised to the rank of Princess of Prussia and is an excellent wife to her wise and sensible husband. William II gave his consent unwillingly. When the lunch celebrating the engagement at last took place in the Imperial palace, the Kaiser received the bride's father, the Mecklenburg Premier, Count Bassewitz-Levetzow, with the ungracious words: "This marriage is not very welcome to me." With the phlegm of the typical Mecklenburger, the father replied dryly and with dignity, "Nor to me either." But we had not then got as far as this. As I knew that the Kaiser would not give way in the presence of a third person I suggested in a low voice to Wedel that he should leave the carriage with some excuse or other. Meanwhile we passed through Baden. I told the Kaiser that I would be the last person to bind our future entirely to that of Austria. But we had no reason to make the future Emperor of Austria our enemy for purely personal and theoretical reasons. While the Kaiser was still violently protesting we passed Mödling. "Your Majesty," I said, growing more insistent, "you are not there to preserve people of rank from marrying beneath them all over the world in general and in Austria in particular, you only have to consider German interests. These would be gravely injured if you offended the heir to the Austrian throne." The Kaiser still protested. The train entered the Viennese terminus. We saw from the windows the green Austrian plumes, we already heard the strains of "*Heil Dir im Siegerkranz*" when I made a last appeal to the Kaiser. "You have the choice now of making the future Austrian Emperor our friend or our enemy for ever." The Kaiser gave me a glance that was half angry and half laughing. The train stopped. After the Kaiser, *more solito*, had embraced the old Emperor of Austria and kissed him on both cheeks he went to the Crown Prince with the friendliest air and said to him, "When may I have the honour of paying my respects to your wife?" The Archduke went red with pleasure, then bowed and kissed the Kaiser's hand. The same afternoon the Kaiser visited the Princess, future Duchess of Hohenberg. The Archduke awaited the Kaiser on the threshold of his house and led him to his wife. The meeting came off in the best possible manner and laid the basis of a sincere friendship between Kaiser and Archduke until the crime of Serajevo put an end to it.

The Austro-Hungarian Minister for Foreign Affairs, Count Agenor Goluchowski, a friend of long-standing, told me, when I saw him, everything concerning the internal and foreign affairs of the Hapsburg monarchy with the candour which harmonised with our intimacy. As long as Russian politics kept within peaceful limits Austria must and would suit her own policy to Russia's ability to coöperate in it. He upheld two standpoints: firstly, to do everything to avoid conflicts between Turkey and the Balkan States;

secondly, to localise such conflicts in the event of their breaking out. Goluchowski added that the last would be more difficult than the first, therefore the one feasible course of action was to exert a calming influence on Turkey as on all other Balkan states. This was a sensible view, shared by myself, whereas, unfortunately, after my resignation Bethmann, under the influence of Kiderlen and Wangenheim and to a certain degree that of Field Marshal Colmar von der Goltz and with full consent of the Kaiser, did not regard a conflict between Turkey and the Balkan States at all unwillingly. This was in the belief that Turkey would win a smashing victory over "the sheep thieves of the lower Danube", as Kiderlen used to call them, an expectation which we know was not fulfilled. Goluchowski praised Lambsdorff, whose carefulness pleased him. That Lambsdorff was not enthusiastic about the Kaiser since the bad treatment he had received in Hela did not seem a misfortune for the country, even if he did not say so to me. Goluchowski said decisively that Austria-Hungary could not permit either a partitioning of the Balkan peninsula between Russia and herself, as Prince Bismarck had often suggested, nor the formation of a Great-Servia, nor could she allow the Russians to settle in Constantinople. The minister agreed with me when I said that the Dardanelles question was a European question; Austria had no reason to display a particularly zealous opposition to Russia but had better let the western powers take the initiative. The sensible motto of Count Goluchowski was that we should try and keep up the *status quo* in the Balkan peninsula as long as possible and solve the Oriental question slowly and by degrees. Turkish rule must be superseded gradually by an autonomous form of government, a Greece as large as possible, a large Bulgaria, a strong Roumania, a weak Serbia, a modest, because small, Montenegro, an independent Albania.

Like all Austrian aristocrats and military men, Goluchowski spoke irritably about relations between Austria and Italy, about Italian irredentism and Italian propaganda in Albania. I replied that years ago on a visit to Lugano I had seen on the market square there an obelisk which commemorated the union of the canton with

Switzerland. It bore the inscription: *"Sempre liberi, sempre Svizzeri"!* If an obelisk of this kind could be erected in Trieste, there would be no more irredentism. The ideal of Count Goluchowski would have been to replace the Triple Alliance by a Three Emperors Alliance — a state of affairs which Prince Bismarck would have preferred above everything, but which, since the termination of our re-insurance treaty with Russia, lay outside the realm of practical possibility. Looking back it seems to me strange that Goluchowski, who had spent a large part of his life in Paris, who was married to a Frenchwoman and possessed numberless ties with France, told me in 1903 that a real and lasting *rapprochement* between France and England was impossible. There were too many conflicting interests and disturbing memories between them.

Emperor Francis Joseph, who received me with his usual graciousness, spoke at the same time with sympathy of Lambsdorff, but with more irritation than his Minister, of Italy. As a gallant old grand seigneur he praised Queen Elena, who was a beautiful and charming woman, but he thought her husband too ambitious and active. It had been easier to keep friends with King Humbert. While Goluchowski, true to his temperament, regarded the situation in the manner of *"Jean qui rit"*, more or less optimistically, the old Emperor, although he seemed physically very well, made a melancholy impression, — *"Jean qui pleure."*

Whereas most of the foreign ambassadors in Vienna had nothing of importance to say, the most intelligent of them, the Italian ambassador, Count Nigra, explained to me in a long dissertation that a clash between Austria and Italy was undesirable from an Italian standpoint as well. Austrian policy towards Italy was often very clumsy. There were in Austria a number of die-hard anti-Italian elements which needed close watching. From the viewpoint of far-seeing Italian policy, the old and crumbling Austria-Hungary, which had not de-nationalised any Italian for ninety years past, was an easier neighbour than one or other of the larger Slav states which could pursue an anti-Italian policy and in doing so find support, more or less open, from France, and fight the Italian nationality to the knife within its own frontiers as well. Count Constantino Nigra, already seventy-six years old, was one of the finest diplomats I have ever met. He united the chief quality a diplomat must possess, imperturbable calm, with a deep and penetrating intelligence, great insight and flair, flexibility, and when necessary, iron energy. In his youth he had been a volunteer in the battle of Novara in 1849. Then Cavour had nominated him, a secretary of barely thirty-three, of no fortune, no great name, and no connexions, as ambassador in Paris, to the Italian Foreign Office, which office he filled from 1860 to 1876. He understood how to win the full confidence of the Emperor Napoleon III whose dreamy nature was impressed by the clear and acute intelligence of the Piedmontese. He won the heart of the Empress Eugénie by his delightful manners and his graceful poems, he dominated the hot-tempered and tempestuous Prince Jerome Napoleon by his iron composure. It was due in great measure to him that Napoleon III permitted the unification of Italy as far as Rome in spite of the strong opposition his pro-Italian policy met with in France, of the attacks nearly all the elder French statesmen, Thiers at the head of them, levelled against it, of the clericalism and the private anti-Italian sentiments of the Empress Eugénie, although, at the outset, he would gladly have set up his brother Prince Jerome as King of Etruria at Florence, and made his cousin Murat King of Naples. The reports of Count Nigra during this period need not fear comparison with the finest dispatches of the Venetian ambassadors and Papal nuncios. When the Empire collapsed, the situation of Nigra was no easy one in the conflict between his Bonapartist sympathies and affections and the necessary consideration for the new Republican régime. He naturally was obliged to adapt himself to the international policy of his country, modified now by the French defeats. He surmounted these difficulties with skill and tact. When he took leave after a long conference with the then President of the French Republic, Thiers, who did not like either Nigra or Italy, his coat tails caught in the door. Smiling, Thiers came to help him and remarked: "*Voyez comme vous êtes attaché à la France.*" Nigra replied with composure: "*Il vous fallait pour me détacher.*" In St. Petersburg, just as afterwards in London and Vienna, Nigra understood how to make a great position for himself under the most·diverse circumstances, most of all perhaps in the Austrian capital which he had fought for many years with arms and intellect. Nigra retired at the age of seventy-seven and died at the age of eighty at Rapallo within sight of the sea that Odysseus and Aeneas sailed, and Homer and Virgil sang, the blue Mediterranean he loved so well.

I have already mentioned the affection the Tsarina Alexandra Feodorovna felt for Darmstadt and Hesse. Under her influence Tsar Nicholas visited Hesse in October, 1903. The Russian royalties stayed at the little castle of Wolfsgarten near Darmstadt, where the autocratic Tsar who ruled over so many millions of apparently devoted subjects led an idyllic life — in the morning a little trip to Frankfort or Mainz, in the evenings a visit to the court theatre at Darmstadt, in between walks in the park or perhaps a game of lawn tennis.

Before I started out to greet the Russian royalties with the Kaiser in Wiesbaden and Darmstadt, the Japanese ambassador came to me and left me in no doubt that a war between Japan and Russia lay within the realm of possibility. His utterances showed that he feared we were bound by secret agreements to come to Russia's aid in the event of a war with Japan. I had no hesitation in explaining to the representative of the Land of the Rising Sun that there was neither a general nor a partial agreement between ourselves and Russia and, in particular, no agreement concerning Eastern Asia. So long as Russia was the ally of France she would never guarantee us our present possessions, which must be the first consideration and the inevitable condition of every German alliance. We should, therefore, in the event of any Russo-Japanese conflict, remain neutral. As regards the treatment of the present issues at stake between Russia and Japan, I could give the Japanese no advice because of the heavy responsibility attached to such advice, but, in consonance with our own neutral and loyal attitude and free from all commitments I would not, I said to him, hesitate to tell them the plain truth. The truth was that in my opinion we had no need to undermine the self-confidence and initiative of the militant Japanese, for a war in the Far East removed the latent war danger for us in Europe. We had just as little reason to offend the Japanese or to make them suspicious. And even if the Russians, which was not very probable, were to hear of this conversation, it appeared to me, convinced even as I was of the usefulness of good relations between Germany and Russia, only desirable to make the gentlemen at St. Petersburg, inclined as they were to self-esteem, realise that a closer relationship between Germany and Russia must be based on mutual concessions. At the end of our talk I told M. Inouyé that our further behaviour would depend on the attitude of the other Powers towards us. This flexible phrase preserved us our freedom with regard to later decisions.

The Kaiser could of course barely wait to see his friend and cousin Nicky again. The latter appeared, after many invitations, with his brother-in-law, the Grand Duke of Hesse, for a few hours in Wiesbaden, where the Kaiser was waiting for him. The meeting was short and therefore did not upset the Russian autocrat's comfort and temper. On November 4th the Kaiser returned the visit in Wolfsgarten. In the afternoon I was to meet the Russian Foreign Secretary in the castle at Darmstadt. In the evening a dinner had been arranged with the Russian monarchs at the castle of Wolfsgarten. Before I went to Darmstadt the Russian ambassador, Count Osten-Sacken, came to me and said, not without embarrassment, that Count Lambsdorff felt himself in an uncomfortable position. Tsar Nicholas had placed everything to do with Russia-Japanese relations, and in particular, everything connected with Far Eastern affairs, under a special committee, of which His Majesty was president. This meant that Lambsdorff was actually debarred from discussions on the eastern Asiatic questions, particularly the differences between Russia and Japan. This was a slight in *optima forma*. The Russian ambassador did not disguise from me the anxiety this move inspired in him. The ukase appointing a special committee for these questions arose from the intrigues of grand dukes and courtiers who wished to exploit coal fields and forests in Korea. The whole affair bore a fatal resemblance to the beginning of the Mexican expedition which had once done Napoleon III so much harm. The French Emperor had been led by greedy speculators into an adventure he had paid for dearly. The ambassador was worried because the Russian generals already began to rattle their sabres so as to intimidate the Japanese. The Russian governor Alexejeff had held a big parade in Port Arthur. Another general had occupied Mukden. All this did not please the old and experienced ambassador at all. "God grant," he said, "that we do not founder on the Japanese reef." Finally Count Osten-Sacken told me, with some hesitation, that his chief, Count Lambsdorff, wished me not to mention Far Eastern questions to him. It would be too painful for a Russian Minister to say that by command of the All-Highest these matters had been taken out of his sphere of influence. "*Ce pauvre Lambsdorff est comme un petit garçon qu'on a mis au coin.*" I took this hint, of course, and confined myself in my talk with Count Lambsdorff to those matters on which it was permitted him to utter an opinion. The Russian Minister praised Count Goluchowski, with whom he got on well in spite of the latter's Polish extraction. He and Goluchowski desired peace on the Balkan pensinsula above everything. "*Quieta non movere*" was the formula they had agreed upon. Russia had been bent on active conquest in the Orient under Catharine II, Alexander I, Nicholas I, and Alexander II. Contrary to these, Nicholas II wished to keep the *status quo* as far as possible in the Balkans and in Turkey. This altered standpoint of Russian policy was not, as Lambsdorff explained smiling, due to pure nobility, but to the definite desire to avoid a big war. Tsar Nicholas, moreover, agreed with him, Lambsdorff, that any change in the Balkan *status quo* would not be to the present interests of Russia. The Empire must avoid everything likely to further revolutionary interests in Europe. The last Turkish war had resulted in the assassination of Tsar Alexander II. For that reason alone, no encouragement must be given to movements of unrest on the part of the Balkan races. The conditions of a conservative and peaceful Russian-Eastern policy were, of course, that Austria maintain its present contact with Russia and that Turkey accept the programme laid down by Russia and Austria at Mürzsteg. It would be a suicidal move on Turkey's part not to carry out this Russo-Austrian programme, for that plan of reform did not even go far enough for England and France.

After we had conversed in this sensible fashion for some time and discovered a far-reaching agreement between our views, Lambsdorff owned to me that he felt very worn and tired. Would I take it amiss if he made *un petit somme,* — took a little nap? I replied that, on the contrary, I would be pleased if he reserved his strength for important occasions. I was no Macbeth and would not murder sleep

> that knits up the ravelled sleeve of care,
> The death of each day's life, sore labour's bath,
> Balm of hurt minds, great nature's second course,
> Chief nourisher in life's feast.

And so he slept an hour in the armchair under my eyes. I noticed how pale and weary he looked in his sleep. Lambsdorff died barely three years later, after a long illness in San Remo. He was not the man to steer the Russian ship of state through the storm of the Japanese war. Alas, fifteen years later, Germany was to see just such another tired and sick man in Chancellor Hertling in a still more serious and onerous position at the helm of her storm-tossed ship.

In his conversation with me, Tsar Nicholas expressed himself in the same terms as his ministers. He declared with the same emphasis as in Peterhof, Hela, and Reval, that between our two peoples there were no conflicting interests. A skirmish between us would only bring advantages to our bitterest enemies. *"Ce serait faire le jeu de la révolution."* Fear of the revolution obsessed the Tsar so much that he outlined to me as one of the most important tasks of the conservative powers, the necessity of supporting the monarchy in Italy and easing its position. With regard to the Italo-French *rapprochement,* Tsar Nicholas said that according to news which had reached St. Petersburg it was not so far advanced as the French press stated.

As I always did, before meetings with foreign monarchs, I impressed upon Kaiser William discretion, reserve, and the need for biding his time in the interview at Wolfsgarten. I reminded him of the excellent advice of our dear Dr. Martin Luther, which I even wrote down for him:

> *Es gibt auf Erden kein grössere List,*
> *Als wer seiner Zunge Meister ist.*
> *Viel denken, wenig sagen,*
> *Nicht antworten auf alle Fragen.*[1]

From what the Kaiser told me on his return from Wolfsgarten it appeared that he had only followed this sound advice up to a certain point. He boasted of having convinced the Tsar of the godlessness of the French Republic, the unreliability of French Ministers, and the double-dealing of the English. The Tsar had smiled in agreement when the Kaiser said to him, "France is a sinking nation with a decided downward tendency; the blood of its murdered King and nobility is on the nation which is being destroyed by atheism." As in his letters to the Tsar when they were not submitted to me before being sent off, the Kaiser could not in conversation with the Tsar refrain from working him up against the French Republic, although I more than once reminded him of Tasso's words to the Princess, in Goethe's play:

> *Wenn Sie auch*
> *Die Absicht hat, den Freunden wohlzutun,*
> *So fühlt man Absicht, und man ist verstimmt.*[2]

The Kaiser shared an impression I gained from this conversation, namely, that the Tsar desired neither the conquest nor the collapse of Turkey and that he did not desire a war with Japan but was preparing for one. A favourite idea of William II's, which he often outlined in talking with Russians, was the neutralisation of Denmark and Danish waters. Contrary to this, I upheld the conviction that in view of our relations with England we could enter into no agreement concerning the Baltic or take on any obligations to defend the Russian Baltic front unless Russia guaranteed us our

---

[1] There is on earth no greater art than to control the tongue, to think much, say little, and not answer all questions.

[2] Though you indeed desire to please your friends, they feel the intentions and are sad.

own possessions beforehand. With regard to the Russo-Japanese relations I asked the Kaiser before we went to Darmstadt to undertake no obligations without adequate return while assuring Russia of our traditional friendship which ensured our benevolent neutrality. At dinner, which took place in the evening at Wolfsgarten, the Tsarina, Alexandra Feodorovna, appeared in a very handsome toilette. She wore a rope of pearls reaching to her feet, of which each individual pearl was as big as a hazel nut.

This beautiful woman, who appeared to be made for life's choicest gifts of fame and fortune, who shared the mightiest throne in the world, and whose husband worshipped her, was to be butchered fourteen years later by brutal and dirty Communist hands, far away in the Urals, very far indeed from her native Odenwald — Odin's Forest, over which the storm of the tempestuous hordes thunders, where the spring flows at which Siegfried fell, where the tree stands of which the German folk-song sadly tells.

A few days after the meeting in Wiesbaden and Wolfsgarten, Kaiser William underwent an operation on the vocal cords. The Kaiser had already noticed a slight hoarseness in Wiesbaden. An examination of his throat showed that a polypus had formed. I visited him on the same day. His attitude was admirable. I appeal to every just-minded critic: where is the human being who, aware that both parents died of cancer, that his father perished of a dreadfully painful cancer of the throat, would not be very deeply affected by the knowledge that there was a growth in his own throat? The behaviour of the Kaiser during this moment of trial was beyond all praise. When I entered, he waved me a melancholy but warm greeting; he had been forbidden to speak. He gave his orders in writing, on little slips, which aroused sad memories of the last weeks of Emperor Frederick. William II, in spite of the protests of the Empress and his doctors, gave orders that authentic bulletins of his health should be issued. Nothing must be withheld; the people had a right to know everything. It was decided that an excellent specialist, Professor Schmidt, should be summoned from Frankfort to operate on the polypus. Until this operation had been carried out and the small growth carefully inspected, everything appeared uncertain. Anxiety was only assuaged when the growth was proved to be of harmless nature. I thought, and still think, that the Empress was right when she wrote to me, deeply moved, that the Kaiser had behaved like a hero. As Schiller says in a fine poem:

Zwei sind der Wege, auf welchen der Mensch zur Tugend emporstrebt
Schliesst sich der eine dir zu, tut sich der andere dir auf,
Handelnd erringt der Glückliche sie, der Leidende duldend.
Wohl ihm, de sein Geschick liebend auf beide geführt.

Two are the ways in which mankind aspires to virtue
As one path closes, another path opens before you.
The fortunate achieve it by action, the suffering by patience.
Happy is he whom destiny has led along both paths.

May the strength to suffer patiently be granted to William II in exile and misfortune as well!

INDEX

INDEX

MEMOIRS OF PRINCE VON BÜLOW
From Secretary of State to Imperial Chancellor
1897–1903

BERNHARD, PRINCE VON BÜLOW